ON THE ROAD

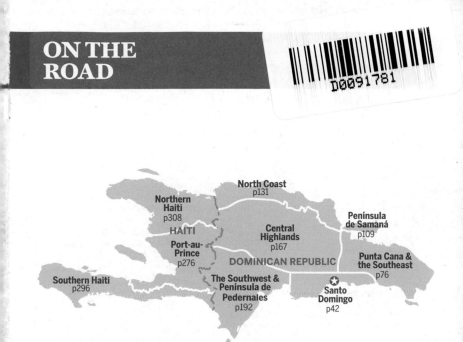

North Coast
p131

Northern
Haiti
p308

HAITI

Port-au-
Prince
p276

Southern Haiti
p296

Península
de Samaná
p109

Central
Highlands
p167

DOMINICAN REPUBLIC

Punta Cana &
the Southeast
p76

The Southwest &
Península de
Pedernales
p192

Santo
Domingo
p42

SURVIVAL GUIDE

VITAL PRACTICAL INFORMATION TO
HELP YOU HAVE A SMOOTH TRIP

THIS EDITION WRITTEN AND RESEARCHED BY

Paul Clammer, Michael Grosberg, Kevin Raub

3-29-13

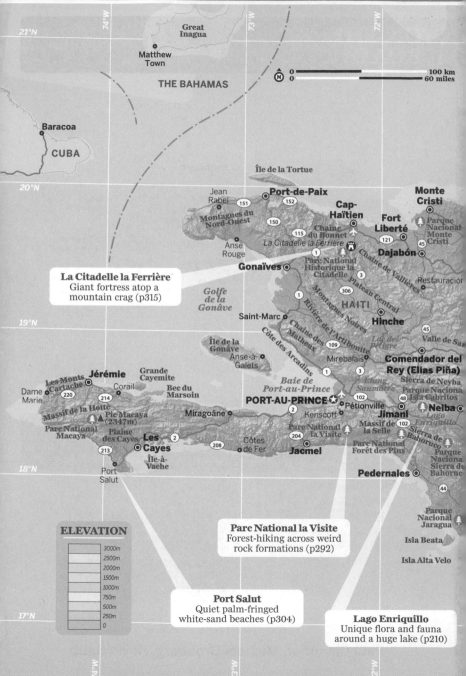

La Citadelle la Ferrière
Giant fortress atop a
mountain crag (p315)

Parc National la Visite
Forest-hiking across weird
rock formations (p292)

Port Salut
Quiet palm-fringed
white-sand beaches (p304)

Lago Enriquillo
Unique flora and fauna
around a huge lake (p210)

ELEVATION

3000m
2500m
2000m
1500m
1000m
750m
500m
250m
0

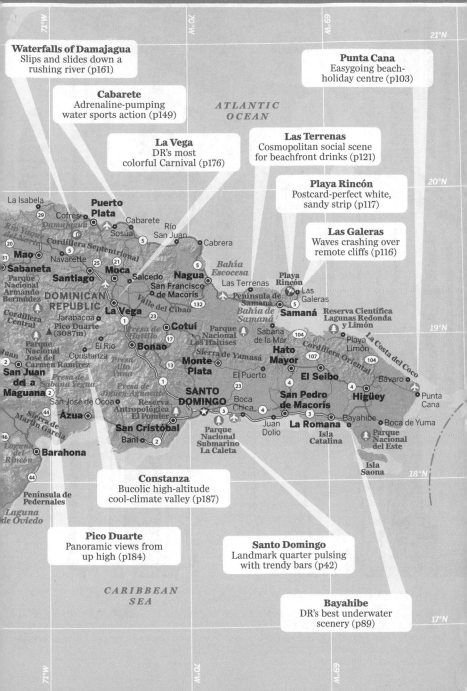

Waterfalls of Damajagua
Slips and slides down a
rushing river (p161)

Punta Cana
Easygoing beach-
holiday centre (p103)

Cabarete
Adrenaline-pumping
water sports action (p149)

*ATLANTIC
OCEAN*

Las Terrenas
Cosmopolitan social scene
for beachfront drinks (p121)

La Vega
DR's most
colorful Carnival (p176)

Playa Rincón
Postcard-perfect white,
sandy strip (p117)

Las Galeras
Waves crashing over
remote cliffs (p116)

Constanza
Bucolic high-altitude
cool-climate valley (p187)

Pico Duarte
Panoramic views from
up high (p184)

Santo Domingo
Landmark quarter pulsing
with trendy bars (p42)

Bayahibe
DR's best underwater
scenery (p89)

*CARIBBEAN
SEA*

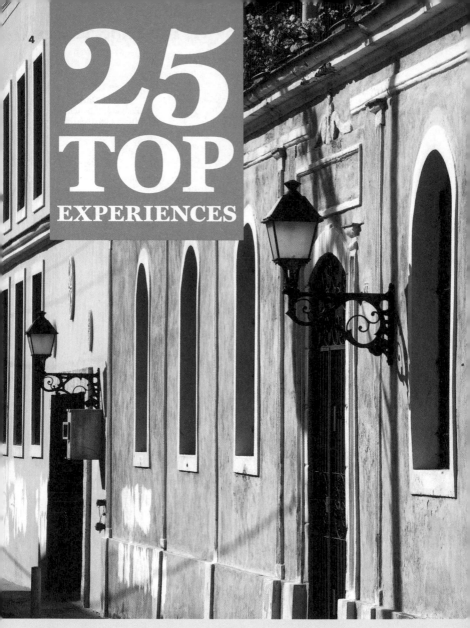

25 TOP EXPERIENCES

Santo Domingo's Zona Colonial, DR

1 Take a walk through history in the oldest city in the New World. With its cobblestone streets and beautifully restored mansions, it's easy to imagine Santo Domingo's landmark quarter as the seat of Spain's 16th-century empire. But the past and present coexist rather gracefully here; follow in the footsteps of pirates and conquistadors one moment, the next pop into a shop selling CDs from the latest Dominican merengue star.

Sun, Sea & Sand at Playa Rincón, DR

2 Consistently rated one of the top beaches in the Caribbean by those in the know – people who courageously brave heatstroke and sunburn in a quest for the ideal – Rincón is large enough for every day-tripper to claim their own piece of real estate without nosy neighbors peeking over the seaweed and driftwood. A thick palm forest provides the backdrop and fresh seafood can be served upon request.

La Citadelle la Ferrière, Haiti

3 If ever a country settled on making a statement of intent on winning its independence, Haiti found it in the mighty Citadelle la Ferrière. A giant battleship of a fortress sitting atop a mountain crag, with a Versailles-like ruined palace at its base, it commands its landscape as a proud symbol of the world's first black republic. Epic in concept and execution and largely hidden from the world's gaze, it easily holds its own against the best historical sites the Americas can offer.

Leisurely Las Galeras, DR

4 This sleepy fishing village at the far eastern end of the Península de Samaná is an escape from your getaway. Fewer tourists and therefore less development means that the area around Las Galeras includes some of the more scenic locales in all the DR. Swaying palm trees back beaches ready-made for a movie set, and waves crash over hard-to-get-to cliffs. For at least one sunset, venture out to Restaurant El Cabito, where you might glimpse migrating whales and a dolphin or two.

Bahía de Las Águilas, DR

5 The remoteness and loneliness add savor and spice to the adventure of getting to Bahía de Las Águilas, a stunning 10km-long stretch of yellow sand. That you have to take a boat to get there – and that there won't be any tourists there except for you – transform it into one of the most beautiful beaches in the country.

Santo Domingo Nightlife & Dancing, DR

6 Get dressed to the nines, do some stretching and get your dance moves on. Nightclubs in the seaside resort hotels host some of the best merengue and salsa bands this side of Havana. No museum showcase, even the Zona Colonial is chockablock with bars, from trendy hangouts for the fashionable set to loud and sweaty corner stores for locals.

Whale-Watching, DR

7 North Americans and Europeans aren't the only ones who migrate south to the Caribbean in the winter. Every year, thousands of humpback whales congregate off the Península de Samaná to mate and give birth, watched (from a respectful distance) by boatloads of their human fans. For an even more intimate experience, week-long live-aboard excursions to the Silver Bank north of Puerto Plata offer the extremely rare opportunity to snorkel alongside these massive mammals.

DOMINICAN REPUBLIC MINISTRY OF TOURISM/WWW.GODOMINICANREPUBLIC.COM

Descending the 27 Waterfalls of Damajagua, DR

8 A short drive from Puerto Plata, a hard-won slosh to the far side of the river and a trek through the lush forest lead to these falls. Experiencing this spectacular series of cascades involves wading through clear pools, swimming through narrow, smooth-walled canyons, hiking through forest, and climbing rocks, ropes and ladders through the roaring falls themselves. And yet the real fun is on the return trip, when you can leap and slide back down the falls, some jumps as high as 10m.

White-Water Rafting, DR

9 The Caribbean's only raftable river, the Río Yaque del Norte in the central highlands of the DR, is tailor-made for those looking to recharge their batteries after too much sun and sand. Short but intense series of rapids will get the adrenaline going, as will a spill in the cold roiling river; fortunately, however, there are as many stretches of flat water where you can loosen your grip on the paddle and gaze at the mountain scenery in the distance.

DOMINICAN REPUBLIC MINISTRY OF TOURISM/WWW.GODOMINICANREPUBLIC.COM

Winter Baseball, DR

10 Dominicans don't just worship at Sunday Mass: baseball makes a solid claim for the country's other religion. Hometown fanatics cheer their team on with a passion and enthusiasm equal to bleacher creatures in Yankee Stadium or Fenway Park. The Dominican league's six teams go *cabeza a cabeza* several nights a week – Estadio Quisqueya in Santo Domingo is home field for two longtime rivals – culminating in a championship series at the end of January.

WILMAR TOPSHOTS/ALAMY

Kitesurfing in Cabarete, DR

11 Do your part for the environment: use wind-powered transportation. Year-round strong offshore breezes make Cabarete on the DR's north coast one of the undisputed capitals for the burgeoning sport of kitesurfing. Harnessing the wind's power to propel you over the choppy surface of the Atlantic isn't like another day at the beach. It takes training and muscles, not to mention faith, before you can attempt the moves of the pros from around the world who ply their trade here.

CHRIS CAMERON/ALAMY

GREG JOHNSTON/LONELY PLANET IMAGES ©

Resort Relaxing in Punta Cana, DR

12 The crown jewel of Dominican tourism, scores of all-inclusive resorts claim the choicest beachfront property in the southeast of the country. Synonymous with all-you-can-eat buffets and Club Med–like group activities, resorts here are justly famous for delivering care-free indulgent holidays. But there are as many classy acts as those geared toward pool parties and as many people on family vacations as there are singles imbibing vast quantities of rum-based cocktails.

Lago Enriquillo, DR

13 Toward the border with Haiti you'll find Lago Enriquillo, an inland sea and remnant of the strait that once bisected the island from Barahona to Port-au-Prince. Several hundred crocodiles call the lake home, and everywhere you'll see rocks of fossilized coral. In the middle of the lake is Isla Cabritos, a national park where iguanas and cacti, as well as other endemic flora and fauna thrive.

JÁNOS CSERNOCH/ALAMY

Aquatic Bayahibe, DR

14 Underwater visibility and consistent ocean conditions make this coastal village, near La Romana in the southeast, the country's best scuba-diving destination bar none. You'll find boat services to the islands of Saona and Catalina, and the island's best wreck dive, the *St George*, is out here, too. Snorkelers will find themselves equally well catered to, and there's the unique opportunity to spend a few hours cruising the shoreline in a traditional fishing vessel.

Las Terrenas Cafe Culture, DR

15 Mellow out in this cosmopolitan beachfront town where European accents are as common as Dominican. International camaraderie is contagious when every day begins and ends with a drink at a beachfront open-air restaurant, overlooking the ocean. But the town's relaxed vibe is a marriage between water-sports adventurers swapping tips and tales after an exhausting day and the more sedentary set content to admire their exploits from afar.

Santiago Scenes, DR

16 Emblematic of the country's complexity, the most prominent landmark in the DR's second city is an enormous monument built by and for Trujillo, since renamed in honor of others. Santiago's laid-back charm is best appreciated from a bench in the Parque Central, by strolling along downtown blocks lined with pastel-colored homes, or with a late night at one of the dozen or more bars, restaurants and dance clubs that surround the monument where the city's disparate elements come together to party into the wee hours on weekend nights.

Hiking Pico Duarte, DR

17 Hispaniola has some surprisingly rugged terrain in the Central Cordillera, including Pico Duarte, the Caribbean's highest mountain (3087m). You'll need good shoes and several days, but if you summit when the clouds have dispersed, the views out to both the Atlantic and the Caribbean are more than worth the blisters.

M. TIMOTHY O'KEEFE/ALAMY

Mountain Vistas in Constanza, DR

18 The scenery found in the central highlands of the DR is a surprise to most visitors. Cloud-covered peaks whose slopes are a patchwork of well-tended agricultural plots and galloping forest growth rising from the valley floor are vistas not often associated with Caribbean islands. A stay on the outskirts of Constanza, truly a world away from the developing coastline, provides a front-row seat to often spectacular sunsets – it's also this time of day when the temperature begins to dip and the chilly air calls for sweaters and blankets.

La Vega Carnival, DR

19 Look out for the whips when dancing with costumed devils in La Vega's raucous Carnival. Garish, colorful, baroque and elaborately and painstakingly made outfits – capes, demonic masks with bulging eyes and pointed teeth – are worn by marauding groups of revelers. The entire city turns out for the parade and every corner and park is transformed into a combination impromptu concert and dance party.

Beachside Meals at Playa Grande, DR

20 After an afternoon spent sun worshipping and body boarding in this beach's warm waters, nothing hits home like a made-to-order seafood meal served up on your towel. A feast of whole grilled fish, rice and beans, accompanied by mixed cocktails, is good value.

Mountain Biking the Dominican Alps, DR

21 Hardcore cyclists rave about the rough trails of the DR's central highlands, where they feel like pioneers. Free styling their way on rocky descents, through alpine meadows and through coursing streams, is an adventurer's dream. Less strenuous rides abound, too: pedal along dirt roads through farming communities and sugar-cane fields, and smiles and friendly invitations to stop and grab a Presidente or two will greet you along the way.

Hiking in Parc National la Visite, Haiti

22 Haiti is such a mountainous country that it would be a shame to only experience them while whizzing by in traffic. The perfect hike is through Parc National la Visite, from Furcy, high above Port-au-Prince, down to Seguin. The park still has plenty of Haiti's original pine forest, weird broken rock formations, and as the scenery opens up, great views out to the Caribbean Sea. A long day's walk on a path shared with local farmers, it's the perfect leg-stretching antidote to the buzz of the big city.

Port Salut, Haiti

23 Haiti is a rare Caribbean country in that it isn't really thought of as a beach destination, but that doesn't mean its beaches should be ignored. While the north coast has dramatic cliffs and crashing Atlantic breakers, the south coast – particularly at Port Salut – has great stretches of beautiful white sand fringed with palm trees. The water is warm. There's grilled fish and rum. Oh, and remember that line about no tourists in Haiti? You get the beaches almost entirely to yourself.

Carnival at Jacmel, Haiti

24 You want shiny sequins and sanitized carnival bling? Plenty of places will serve that up for you. Jacmel's street theater is another game altogether, close to the surreal, where individuals and troupes parade and act in homemade costumes and papier-mâché masks from local artisans. Vodou, sex, death and revolution all play their part, mixed with street music and wild antics, in a parade where both crowd and performers mix as participants. And where else will you see a donkey dressed in sneakers and hat, talking on a cell phone?

Vodou Ceremony, Haiti

25 If you're thinking zombies and dolls with pins in them, you need to disconnect from Hollywood. Vodou is the wellspring of the Haitian character, a spiritual religion borne of the country's African roots but which took adopted practices from both the island's original Indian inhabitants and French colonial masters. Attending a Vodou ceremony, with its drums and sung prayers, bright imagery and often-healing nature is the best way to plug yourself in to Haiti's subconscious.

Dominican Republic

Dominican Republic

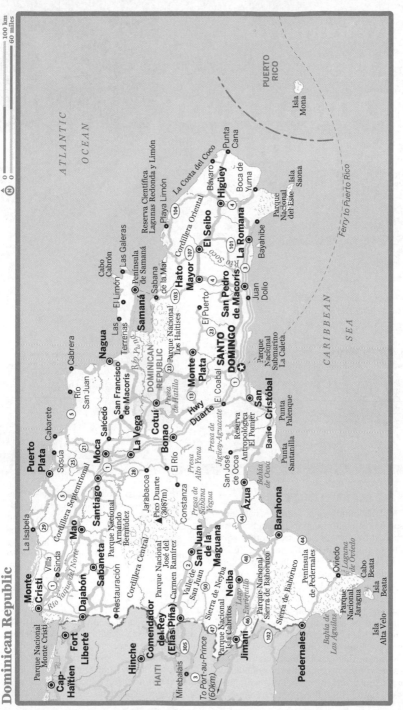

100 km
60 miles

N

ATLANTIC OCEAN

CARIBBEAN SEA

PUERTO RICO

Isla Mona

Ferry to Puerto Rico

Punta Cana
Bávaro
Boca de Yuma
Isla Saona
Higüey
La Romana
Bayahibe
Parque Nacional del Este
El Seibo
San Pedro de Macorís
Juan Dolio
Hato Mayor
Sabana de la Mar
El Puerto
Parque Nacional Submarino La Caleta
SANTO DOMINGO
Monte Plata
El Coabal
San Cristóbal
Punta Palenque
Baní
Punta Santanilla

Parque Nacional Los Haitises
Cordillera Oriental
La Costa del Coco
Reserva Científica Lagunas Redonda y Limón
Playa Limón
El Limón
Las Galeras
Cabo Cabrón
Península de Samaná
Samaná
Las Terrenas
Cabrera
Nagua
San Francisco de Macorís
Salcedo
Moca
La Vega
Cotuí
Bonao
El Río
Presa de Hatillo
Reserva Antropológica El Pomier
Río Yuna
DOMINICAN REPUBLIC
Hwy Duarte

Puerto Plata
Cabarete
Sosúa
Santiago
Jarabacoa
Pico Duarte (3087m)
Parque Nacional Armando Bermúdez
Constanza
Parque Nacional José del Carmen Ramírez
Cordillera Central
Cordillera Septentrional
La Isabela
Villa Sinda
Monte Cristi
Parque Nacional Monte Cristi
Río Yaque del Norte
Sabaneta
Mao
Dajabón
Presa de Sabana Yegua
Presa de Alto Yuna
San José de Ocoa
Azua
Bahía de Ocoa
Barahona
Bahía de Neyba

HAITI
Cap-Haïtien
Fort Liberté
Hinche
Mirebalais
To Port-au-Prince (60km)
Comendador del Rey (Elías Piña)
Restauración
San Juan de la Maguana
Valle de San Juan
Sierra de Neyba
Neiba
Lago Enriquillo
Parque Nacional Isla Cabritos
Jimaní
Parque Nacional Sierra de Bahoruco
Sierra de Bahoruco
Pedernales
Península de Pedernales
Oviedo
Laguna de Oviedo
Parque Nacional Jaragua
Cabo Beata
Isla Beata
Isla Alta Velo
Bahía de Las Águilas

Ríos: Río Chavón, Río Soco, Presa de Tavera, Higüey-Aguacate

Road numbers: 104, 107, 4, 101, 3, 23, 1, 13, 103, 5, 21, 25, 28, 29, 2, 44, 48, 50, 46, 47, 102, 305

welcome to
the Dominican Republic

Coastal Culture

The DR's hundreds of miles of coastline – some of it picturesque white-sand beaches shaded by rows of palm trees, other parts lined dramatically with rocky cliffs or backed by wind-swept dunes or serene mangrove lagoons – define the country. Whether it's fishing villages where the shoreline is used for mooring boats, indulgent tourist playgrounds with aquamarine waters, small towns where the social glue is all-night merengue blasting from modest corner stores, or cities like Santo Domingo, the Caribbean's largest, the sea is the common denominator, symbolizing both limits and escapes. Even with their glory days behind them, former engines of industry like crumbling San Pedro de Macoris or Puerto Plata still see waves crash over their Malecóns. Some of the bays and coves where pirates once roamed are the temporary home of thousands of migrating humpback whales, and part of an extensive network of parks and preserves safeguarding the country's natural patrimony.

Peaks & Valleys

Beyond the capital, much of the DR is distinctly rural: driving in the vast fertile interior, you'll see cows and horses grazing alongside the roads, tractors ploughing large fields, and trucks and burros loaded down with produce. Further inland you'll encounter vistas reminiscent of the

Much more than beach resorts, this is one of the Caribbean's most geographically diverse countries, from stunning mountain scenery to desert scrublands, not to mention an evocative colonial architecture and warm welcoming people

(below) The old town hall and clock tower, Santo Domingo
(left) Tropical beaches and aquamarine seas, Isla Saona

European Alps, rivers carving their way through lush jungle and stunning waterfalls, small towns where life revolves around the Parque Central, and villages ruled by the sun's rhythms. Four of the five highest peaks in the Caribbean rise above the fertile lowlands surrounding Santiago and remote deserts extend through the southwest, giving the DR a physical and cultural complexity not found on other islands.

Past Present

The country's roller-coaster past, a history of migrations of various peoples, is writ large in the diversity of ethnicities, not to mention the physical design of its towns and cities. Santo Domingo's Zona Colonial exudes romance with white-washed and pastel-colored buildings, flowers blooming through wrought-iron filigree, beautifully restored monasteries and cobblestone streets where conquistadors once roamed. The crumbling gingerbread homes of Puerto Plata and Santiago remain from more prosperous eras, and scars from decades of misrule are marked by monuments where today people gather to celebrate. New communities have arisen only a few kilometers from the ruins where Christopher Columbus strode and where the indigenous Taíno people left physical traces of their presence carved onto rock walls.

need to know

Currency
» Dominican peso (RD$)

Language
» Spanish

When to Go

Puerto Plata
GO Oct-Dec

Santo Domingo
GO Oct-Jan

Punta Cana
GO Jan-Mar

Dry climate
Tropical climate, wet-dry season
Tropical climate, rain year-round

High Season
(mid-Dec–Feb)

» July to August and the week before Easter are also high season.

» Expect significantly higher hotel prices and beaches.

» Most water sports are prohibited throughout the DR during the week before Easter.

Shoulder
(Mar–Jul)

» You may see short but strong daily rains in Santo Domingo (through October).

» March is generally one of the drier months in Samaná.

Low Season
(Aug–early Dec)

» Hurricane season (typically impacting the eastern part of DR), but if there are no storms it's still an excellent time to travel.

» Temperatures don't vary much (mountains are an exception).

» Room rates are deeply discounted.

Your Daily Budget

Budget less than
US$60

» Budget room RD$1140 (US$30)

» Take *motoconchos* (motorcycle taxis) and *gua-guas* (small buses) to get around

Midrange
US$90

» Internet deal on all-inclusive accommodations RD$3040 (US$80)

» First-class bus tickets between major destinations RD$300 (US$10)

» Join group tours for activities like snorkeling, hiking etc

High End over
US$200

» Beachfront resort RD$8580 (US$225)

» Eat out at top restaurants in urban areas

» Rent a car for the entire trip or at least for special excursions; gas prices will eat into expenses

Money
» ATMs widely available. Credit cards accepted in some hotels and restaurants.

Visas
» Generally not required for stays of up to 30 days. Can pay extra fee upon departure up to 90 days.

Cell Phones
» Local SIM cards can be used or phones can be set for roaming.

Driving
» Drive on the right; steering wheel is on the left side of the car.

Websites

» **www.debbies dominicantravel.com** Reviews of sites and accommodations.

» **www.dr1.com** Busy online forum.

» **www.godominican republic.com** Official tourism site.

» **www.lonelyplanet .com/dominican -republic** For up-to-date travelers' reports.

Exchange Rates

Australia	A$1	RD$41
Canada	C$1	RD$40
Europe	€1	RD$56
Haiti	HTG1	RD$1
Japan	¥100	RD$46
New Zealand	NZ$1	RD$30
UK	UK£1	RD$63
US	US$1	RD$38

For current exchange rates see www.xe.com.

Important Numbers

Remember that you must dial 📞1 + 809 or 829 for all calls within the DR, even local ones. There are no regional codes.

Country code	📞1 + 809
Emergency	📞1 + 911
Information	📞1 + 1411

Arriving in the Dominican Republic

» **Aeropuerto Internacional Las Américas (Santo Domingo)**
Taxis – US$30 to US$35 (22km) p74

» **Aeropuerto Internacional Punta Cana**
Taxis – US$30 to US$40 (30km) p104

» **Aeropuerto Internacional Gregorío Luperón (Puerto Plata)**
Taxis – US$25 (18km) p139

Big Digs

Several new highways were recently completed and others were under construction at the time of research – these have the potential to alter not only tourist patterns but the country's development as well. The most important of the finished projects is the Santo Domingo–Samaná highway, which has cut driving time nearly in half. There's a major new road being built in the Punta Cana area to alleviate heavy traffic and the long commute between the airport and resort areas. Another notable road-building project is the one between the mountain towns of Jarabacoa and Constanza; when this is completed, even compact cars should be able to make the trip in around 40 minutes.

if you like...

White-Sand Beaches

Full of breathtaking beaches, from oases of calm to party central, the country's coastline can satisfy every taste. It is blessed with year-round warm temps and waters, so bring a boatload of lotion to soothe your sunburned skin.

Playa Rincón The prototypical tropical paradise (p117)

Bahía de Las Águilas This far-flung hard-to-get-to beach is definitely worth the struggle (p208)

Playa Bávaro Long strand of sand and epicenter of all-inclusive resorts (p98)

Playa Grande Half-moon cove with good surf waves (p158)

Nightlife & Dancing

Things get jumping when the sun goes down. Whether it's an impromptu neighborhood block party gathering around the local *colmado* or swanky hotel nightclub, Dominicans love to drink, socialize and get down. Not that they need any excuse, but with a calendar filled with local, regional and national fiestas, there's no shortage of opportunity.

Santo Domingo *Capitaleños* know how to let loose and the city has more bars and nightclubs than anywhere else in the country (p67)

Santiago Rub elbows and booties at one of the dozen-plus bars and clubs in the city's center (p174)

Cabarete More than just an action-sports destination, the beach here is lined with restaurants and bars (p148)

Parque Central Wherever you are in the country, every town's central square is usually the nighttime gathering place

Romantic Getaways

Couples, both those on silver wedding anniversaries and those whose relationships are only a few hours old, will find plenty of places in the DR to make their hearts pound. From secluded hideaways to candle-lit restaurants, there is no shortage of options.

Casa Bonita Out-of-the-way hillside retreat to the south of Barahona (p204)

Peninsula House Exclusive French chateau mansion overlooking the beach (p129)

Plaza España Come here for an intimate dinner on the balcony of one of this plaza's many atmospheric restaurants (p63)

Sunset horseback ride It may sound like a cliché but the color of the sky, ocean waves lapping at your horse's feet and holding your partner's hand are the ingredients for romance (p152)

GREG JOHNSTON/LONELY PLANET IMAGES©

» Flamingos at Laguna Oviedo (p207)

Architecture

In addition to an enduring economic and social legacy, the Spanish colonizers left a physical one in the form of early-16th-century churches and buildings. Homes built by beneficiaries of several industrial boom-bust cycles have also had a lasting impact on urban design.

Zona Colonial Compact neighborhood steeped in history and colonial-era buildings (p44)

Puerto Plata Pastel gingerbread Victorian homes around Parque Central (p133)

San Pedro de Macoris Fine homes, survivors from the late-19th- and early-20th-century sugar-boom days (p84)

Churches From colonial-era gothic to contemporary postindustrial, Catholic cathedrals are often a town's most striking building

Wildlife

A large national park system and an increasing number of scientific preserves ranging from semi-deserts to lush valleys protect the country's biological diversity and a surprising number of endemic species.

Parque Nacional Jaragua Flora and fauna galore at Laguna Oviedo (p207)

Whale-watching These massive mammals take their winter break in Bahía de Samaná (p112)

Parque Nacional Los Haitises Birdwatching from a boat cruising through mangrove forest (p108)

Lago Enriquillo & Isla Cabritos Crocodiles and iguanas in a remote saltwater lake and desert island (p210)

Diving & Snorkeling

With hundreds of miles of coastline it's no surprise that the DR's subaquatic adventures are the priority for many visitors. Warm waters and consistently good year-round conditions mean every region has something to offer.

Bayahibe Experienced divers consider this the best destination in the country (p91)

Playa Frontón Boat out to the reefs here, some of the best on the Península de Samaná (p116)

Sosúa The base for North Coast underwater adventures as far afield as Luperón and Monte Cristi (p145)

Boca Chica Two small wrecks and shallow reefs a short drive from Santo Domingo (p80)

If you like... coffee
Organic farms in the highlands of the DR can show you all the steps it takes to turn out a cup of joe (p182)

Relaxing at a Resort

One can only imagine what the DR coastline looked like 30 years ago. These days, many of the best beaches are colonized by all-inclusive resorts, the quintessential Caribbean beach break. Certainly, they come in all shapes and sizes, though sprawling city-states seem to be the norm.

Punta Cana Top-end accommodations and relative privacy (p103)

Playa Dorada Good deals in the geographic center of the North Coast (p141)

Las Terrenas Easy access to adventure in this charming town (p121)

Juan Dolio Shallow, calm water and close proximity to Santo Domingo (p82)

Out-of-the-Way Spots

Not what comes first to mind to those contemplating a vacation in the DR, these hard-to-get-to places are nevertheless good reasons themselves for travel here. Their beauty is only highlighted by the effort it takes to reach them and the relative scarcity of others sharing the experience.

Los Patos White-stone beach and Edenic pool for swimming (p204)

El Cabito Good food but even more amazing views of sunsets, whales and crashing waves (p120)

Cachóte Off-road it to these cabins in a cloud forest (p205)

Playa Limón Rural mountain scenery, a beach backed by rows of palm trees and a little-visited lagoon (p105)

Outdoor Adventures

Blessed with a varied geography, both inland and coastal, the DR is an extreme-sport mecca. Ditch the car and try one of these alternative methods of transportation.

White-water rafting The only river in the Caribbean for this adrenaline-pumping experience (p178)

Kitesurfing Skim across the waves at high speeds powered by strong year-round winds (p150)

Hiking Overnight it to Pico Duarte, the highest peak in the Caribbean (p184)

Mountain biking Explore the network of little-used trails through striking landscapes (p35)

month by month

1 **Whale-watching**, mid-January–mid-March

2 **Carnaval**, February

3 **Santo Domingo Merengue Festival**, July

4 **Festival of the Bulls**, August

5 **Winter baseball**, end of October–end of January

January

The North American winter coincides with whale-watching season in the Bahía de Samaná, making this a popular time of year to visit. Winds on the north coast around Cabarete are generally strongest this time of year.

Whale-watching
This seasonal display of thousands of humpback whales doing their best impersonation of gymnasts takes place in the Bahía de Samaná and Silver Bank area.

Virgen de Altagracia
One of the most important religious days of the year falls on January 21, when thousands of pilgrims flock to the basilica in Higüey.

Day of Duarte
Public fiestas are held in all the major towns on January 26, celebrating the Father of the Country.

February

This is a month of intense partying throughout the DR, hotel prices rise and popular tours can be booked solid. February to March are generally the driest months in Samaná.

Carnaval
Celebrated with great fervor throughout the DR every Sunday in February, culminating in a huge blowout in Santo Domingo on the last weekend of the month or the first weekend of March. Masks and costumes figure prominently in all – Santiago even hosts an international *caleta* (Carnival mask) competition. The largest and most traditional Carnivals outside of Santo Domingo are celebrated in Santiago, Cabral, Monte Cristi and La Vega.

Master of the Ocean
Called a 'triathlon of the waves', this thrilling competition in the last week in February sees the world's best windsurfers, kitesurfers and surfers go board to board on Playa Encuentro outside Cabarete (www.masteroftheocean).

Independence Day
February 27, 1844, is the day that the DR regained independence from Haiti; the holiday is marked by street celebrations and military parades.

March

Semana Santa (Holy Week), the week before Easter, is when the DR takes a vacation; businesses close, Dominicans flock to beaches and reservations are vital. Water sports are mostly prohibited. North American college students arrive for Spring Break.

Sailing Regatta
On the Saturday of Semana Santa, the seaside village of Bayahibe turns out to watch a race of traditionally handcrafted fishing boats.

April

Dominicans travel domestically during the end of April around Good Friday. This is also a good time to visit

Laguna Oviedo and the southwest; from March to June cactus flowers bloom in the desert.

Nighttime Turtle-watching

Hawksbill and leatherback turtles lay and hatch their eggs on the beaches of Parque Nacional Jaragua.

June

From May to November Santo Domingo can experience strong daily rains, though usually only for short periods, while from June to September the north coast experiences generally sunny skies.

Puerto Plata Cultural Festival

This weeklong festival brings merengue, blues, jazz and folk concerts to the Puerto Plata's Fuerte San Felipe at the end of the Malecón.

San Pedro Apóstal

A raucous festival on June 29 in San Pedro celebrating *cocolo* culture. Roving bands of *guloyas* perform this traditional dance routine on the streets.

July

The beginning of the holiday season for Dominicans and Europeans. Scorching temperatures are recorded in the southwest around Lago Enriquillo.

Santo Domingo Merengue Festival

Santo Domingo hosts the country's largest and most raucous merengue festival. For two weeks at the end of July and the beginning of August, the world's top merengue bands play for the world's best merengue dancers all over the city.

August

The beginning of hurricane season, which can last all the way to December, means you should keep an eye out for developing strong storms. Of course sunny days prevail and you can find good deals on accommodations.

Festival of the Bulls

Higüey's *fiesta patronal* (patronage festival dedicated to the town's saint) sees horseback-borne cowboys and herds of cattle mosey down the city's streets.

Restoration Day

August 16, the day the DR declared its independence from Spain, is marked by general partying and traditional folk dancing and street parades.

October

Rain showers a few days a week are common throughout the country, especially inland around Santiago. Tropical storms are a threat, however, expect mild temperatures, fewer visitors and reduced accommodations costs.

Puerto Plata Merengue Festival

During the first week in October the entire length of Puerto Plata's Malecón is closed to vehicular traffic, food stalls are set up and famous merengue singers perform on a stage erected for the event. Also includes a harvest festival and an arts-and-crafts fair.

Latin Music Festival

This huge, annual three-day event – held at the Olympic Stadium in Santo Domingo – attracts the top names in Latin music, including jazz, salsa, merengue and *bachata* (popular guitar music based on bolero rhythms) players.

Master de la Cordillera

An endurance event that resembles an iron man crossed with a X-games contest, this newly inaugurated race involving mountain biking, hiking, rafting, rappelling and tubing is held in Jarabacoa the last weekend in October.

November

Winter baseball

The boys of winter get into full swing in November. Six teams in five cities (Santo Domingo has two) play several games a week.

Cabarete & Santiago Jazz Festival

Top Dominican and international musicians play on alternating days in Santiago and on the beach in Cabarete the last week in November.

December

Hotel and flight prices rise as Americans and Canadians begin their yearly migration to the beaches of the Caribbean, including the DR. Surfers head to the north coast where the waves are best from December through March.

Christmas

Decorations are ubiquitous, as early as October, and extended families gather to celebrate the holiday. Specialties like *cerdo a la pulla* (roasted pork, marinated with sour orange, oregano, garlic and sazon completo) are part of traditional family meals and holiday songs are played nonstop on the radio.

itineraries

Whether you've got six days or 60, these itineraries provide a starting point for the trip of a lifetime. Want more inspiration? Head online to lonelyplanet .com/thorntree to chat with other travelers.

Two Weeks
Dominican Circuit

Start with a couple of days exploring **Santo Domingo**, hitting the Zona Colonial and the essential Dominican experiences of baseball and dancing to merengue. On day three head to **Jarabacoa**. Visit the waterfalls in the afternoon, with white-water rafting or canyoning the next day. Head north to **Cabarete**, which has world-class water sports and mountain biking. There's great diving and beaches in nearby **Sosúa** and **Río San Juan** – enough to keep you happy for several days. Next you're off to **Península de Samaná**. If it's mid-January to mid-March, go whale-watching. Otherwise take a boat trip to **Parque Nacional Los Haitises** to see the mangroves and cave paintings, or visit the waterfall near **El Limón**. Spend another two days hiking or boating to the beaches around **Las Galeras**. For more nightlife, base yourself in **Las Terrenas**. Allow for some relaxing beach time. The southeast is perfect – go for either deserted **Playa Limón** or perennially popular **Bávaro** and **Punta Cana**. Return to Santo Domingo. To the southwest it's a spectacular drive to **Barahona**, and crocodiles in **Lago Enriquillo**. Spend a night or two before returning to Santo Domingo.

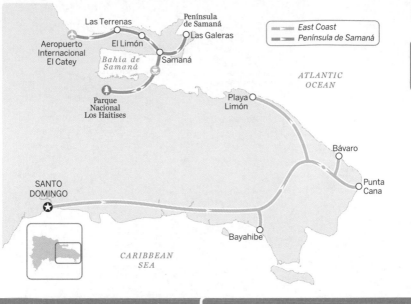

| | East Coast |
| | Península de Samaná |

One Week
East Coast

Whether you fly into Santo Domingo or directly to the airport outside Punta Cana, allow a full day to explore the old colonial center of **Santo Domingo**.

Base yourself in the southeast at the deservedly popular beaches of **Bávaro** and **Punta Cana**, the hub of Dominican tourism. All-inclusive resorts are tailor-made for families; if all you want to do is splash about in the water, you could do worse than book at the resorts here. Many are particularly child-friendly, and activities include go-karts, bowling, sailing trips and parasailing. Resorts also offer tours to local sights; for more independence, rent a car and head out on your own.

Singles, couples and those seeking nightlife can certainly find their own Shangri-La here as well.

Not far south of here is **Bayahibe**, a tiny town on the edge of a national park with the best scuba diving in the DR and a number of excursions including catamaran tours to an island beach and snorkeling trips. For more privacy head to deserted **Playa Limón** further up the coast.

Five Days
Península de Samaná

If you can, fly directly into Aeropuerto Internacional El Catey, the closest airport to the peninsula. Otherwise, get in a puddle jumper from another DR airport or consider taking a bus from Santo Domingo – the new highway makes it a painless transfer.

If possible, plan your trip for mid-January to mid-March, when humpback whales migrate to the Bahía de Samaná and boat-based **whale-watching** tours are in full steam.

Otherwise, base yourself either in **Las Terrenas** or **Las Galeras**. The former has a cosmopolitan mix and a relatively sophisticated European vibe. Kitesurfing and other water sports are deservedly popular here and you can choose from day-trips like horseback riding to the waterfall near **El Limón** or a boat trip to **Parque Nacional Los Haitises** to see the mangroves and cave paintings.

Las Galeras, the other option, is a small laid-back town at the far eastern tip of the peninsula. The beaches around here rival any in the DR and there are chances to really get to the proverbial end of the road.

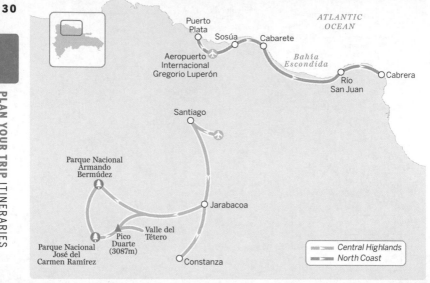

One Week
North Coast

Fly into the Aeropuerto Internacional Gregorio Luperón, basically the geographic center of the north coast. From here, choose your base for the week, but allow yourself at least an afternoon in **Puerto Plata** either at the beginning or end of your trip. Wander the city's downtown streets lined with dilapidated 19th-century homes, educate yourself at one of the city's amber museums and settle in for a drink at a seafront restaurant.

Active types will assuredly want to stay in or around the water-sports mecca of **Cabarete**, east of Puerto Plata; it also has a happening bar and restaurant scene. Carve out several hours or days learning the ropes from the best of kitesurfing, windsurfing or just plain surfing. Of course, the beaches are equally alluring for doing absolutely nothing but sipping cocktails and making headway in a good book.

Scuba divers and those looking for a more raucous nightlife should look into staying in **Sosúa**.

Further east near the quiet town of **Río San Juan** are several terrific beaches and snorkeling and diving opportunities nearby. If you have a big group, renting a villa around **Cabrera** is a good choice.

One Week
Central Highlands

Fly into the airport outside **Santiago** and spend a day exploring downtown and taking in Dominican painting at the Centro Leon. Don't miss a bar crawl around the monument, the center of the city's nightlife, and a baseball game at the stadium just north of downtown if you're here during the winter season.

On the following day, head to **Jarabacoa**, gateway to **Parques Nacionales Armando Bermúdez** and **José del Carmen Ramírez**. The two parks cover much of the DR's central mountain range, including **Pico Duarte**, the highest peak (3087m) in the Caribbean. Visit the waterfalls in the afternoon, with white-water rafting, or canyoning and mountain biking the next day or two. Or arrange your trip around climbing Pico Duarte. The standard trip is three days, but consider arranging a side trip to beautiful **Valle del Tétero**, which adds two days.

Unwind in the mountain town of **Constanza**, now only a short drive from Jarabacoa, where you'll find cooler temperatures and stunning views. Rent a 4WD and off-road it through mountain passes to remote valleys and waterfalls.

Dominican Republic Outdoors

Best Mountain Biking

From **Jamao** near Moca to the isolated **Magante Beach** near Rio San Juan **Country roads** in Central Highlands **Septentrional range** around Cabarete

Best Month to Go

February for migratory birds in the southwest, whale-watching in Samaná, and wind sports in Cabarete.

Best Adventures to Try for the First Time

Kitesurfing
Canyoning
Paragliding
White-water rafting

Best Base for Active Adventures

Jarabacoa in Central Highlands
Cabarete on the North Coast
Las Terrenas in Península de Samaná
Bayahibe in the southeast

Best Places for More Leisurely Exploration

Parque Nacional Los Haitises
Parque Nacional Jaragua
San José de las Matas
Parque Nacional del Este

Water Sports

If it involves standing on a board, the Dominican Republic's got it in spades – you'll find world-class kitesurfing, windsurfing, surfing and wakeboarding. The undisputed water-sports capital of the DR is Cabarete on the north coast, and Las Terrenas on the Península de Samaná is the runner-up, but the adventurous can find a few other more isolated spots as well.

Kitesurfing

Kitesurfing (also known as kiteboarding) is the sport *du jour,* and involves strapping a board to your feet and a powerful kite to your torso, which propels you through the waves at sometimes breakneck speeds.

The learning curve to get good enough to enjoy kitesurfing – not to mention learning the lingo for tricks like 'kitelooping' and 'back-side handle passes' – is steep. On average, it takes a week's worth of lessons to go out solo, and months of practice to get competent. It's also expensive – to make this a regular hobby, you'll end up spending a few thousand dollars on lessons and gear. No wonder, then, around 90% of wannabes who try it out don't generally advance to become regular kitesurfers.

That said, if you've got the time and the money, and you relish a challenge, the DR is one of the world's leading kitesurfing destinations – so much so that the **International**

Kiteboarding Organization (www.ikointl. com) has its headquarters in Cabarete.

Unlike surfing or windsurfing, where risk increases with ability – you have to be good to get out to the reef line – kitesurfing is risky from the very beginning. The kite leads, pulled taut by the wind, are diving, swooping knife blades, and it's important you learn from qualified instructors, for your safety and for that of others.

Plenty of kitesurfing schools offer instruction in Cabarete. Most people need a minimum of four days of lessons at a cost of around US$350 to US$450. Schools and instructors vary considerably in personality, so spend some time finding one where you feel comfortable.

There's also a few good kitesurfing spots in Las Terrenas in Samaná, although the wind is lighter and the water shallower.

Windsurfing

Cabarete's bay seems almost custom-made for windsurfing, and it's here that the sport is most popular – although you'll also find a small windsurfing school in Las Terrenas. The best time to come is generally in winter, when the wind is strongest – in general, windsurfing requires stronger winds than kitesurfing does.

The beach at Cabarete is lined with outfits small and large, renting windsurfing equipment and offering lessons for beginners. Renting a board and sail will cost about US$35/65/300 per hour/day/week. Lessons range from just one hour (US$50) to a complete four-session course (US$200).

In general, windsurfing is much easier to learn than kitesurfing, meaning you can be out on the water enjoying yourself within a few days' time. Lessons and equipment rentals are also significantly cheaper.

Surfing

Cabarete is also the top spot in the country for surfing, although the intrepid surfer traveling with board bag in tow could easily explore many of the lesser-visited beaches along both the north and south coasts. The bestseason to surf is December through March, when the region can get waves up to 4m high.

Playa Encuentro, 4km west of Cabarete, has the best waves on the island, where awesome tubes often pound into shore. Other popular places for surfing are Playa Grande and Playa Preciosa, both near Río San Juan, and Playa Bonita outside Las Terrenas on the Península de Samaná.

There are a number of surf shops in Cabarete and on Playa Encuentro itself where you can rent boards or take surfing lessons. Rentals cost US$25 to US$30 for half a day; courses vary from three-hour introductory sessions (US$45 to US$50) to a full-blown five-day surf camp (US$200 to US$225 per person). You can also rent surfboards at Playa Grande.

Wakeboarding

Water skiing has gone the way of corduroy bellbottoms, and in its place is this new sport – the principle is the same but instead of 'water skis' you use a 'water board,' or 'wakeboard.' The sport has a small but passionate community of enthusiasts, and kiteboarders swear it's a great way to develop your board skills.

There's only one wakeboarding school in the DR, at La Boca just outside Cabarete, where there's more than 2km of flat, straight river water to play with. The spot attracts devoted wakeboarders from around the world, and on windless days they are joined by displaced kiteboarders.

Diving & Snorkeling

Compared to other Caribbean islands, the DR is not known as a diving destination. That being said, it has some great places for underwater exploring – the offshore area around Bayahibe on the southeast coast is generally considered the best. The warm Caribbean waters on the southern coast have pretty fields of coral and myriad tropical fish that make for fun easy dives. Two national parks east of Santo Domingo – Parque Nacional Submarino La Caleta and Parque Nacional del Este – can be reached through dive shops in Boca Chica and Bayahibe, respectively.

La Caleta is an underwater preserve covering just 10 sq km but is one of the country's most popular dive destinations. The main attraction is the *Hickory*, a 39m salvage ship with an interesting past (see p225) that was intentionally sunk in 1994. Parque Nacional del Este has a number of interesting dives, too, including another wreck – a massive 89m cargo ship – and a site ominously called Shark Point.

RESPONSIBLE DIVING

Please consider the following tips when diving and help preserve the ecology and beauty of reefs:

» Never use anchors on the reef, and take care not to ground boats on coral.

» Avoid touching or standing on living marine organisms or dragging equipment across the reef. Polyps can be damaged by even the gentlest contact. If you must hold on to the reef, only touch exposed rock or dead coral.

» Be conscious of your fins. Even without contact, the surge from fin strokes near the reef can damage delicate organisms. Take care not to kick up clouds of sand, which can smother organisms.

» Practise and maintain proper buoyancy control. Major damage can be done by divers descending too fast and colliding with the reef.

» Take great care in underwater caves. Spend as little time within them as possible as your air bubbles may be caught within the roof and thereby leave organisms high and dry. Take turns to inspect the interior of a small cave.

» Resist the temptation to collect or buy corals or shells or to loot marine archaeological sites (mainly shipwrecks).

» Ensure that you take home all your rubbish and any litter you may find as well. Plastics in particular are a serious threat to marine life.

» Do not feed fish.

» Minimise your disturbance of marine animals. *Never* ride on the backs of turtles.

The DR's north coast provides a very different diving experience. Facing the Atlantic, the water there is cooler and somewhat less transparent, but the underwater terrain is much more varied, making for challenging dives and unique profiles.

Sosúa is the dive capital here, and from where excursions can be organized to all points along the coast. Divers exploring the waters near the Península de Samaná can sometimes hear humpback whales singing; Las Terrenas and Las Galeras have a few small dive shops.

Other off-the-beaten-track options are two diveable freshwater caves – Dudu Cave, near Río San Juan, and Padre Nuestro, near Bayahibe. Dudu, with two openings, three different tunnels and a spacious stalactite-filled chamber, is one of the most memorable cave dives in the Caribbean (although dive shops will want to see an Advanced Diver certificate, or at least 20 logged dives in order to take you out here). Located within the Parque Nacional del Este, Padre Nuestro is a challenging 290m tunnel that should be attempted only by trained cave divers. With the exception of the cave dives, most of the sites mentioned here also make for excellent snorkeling.

Dive prices vary from place to place, but average US$30 to US$40 for one tank, plus US$5 to US$10 for equipment rental (if you need it). Most people buy multidive packages, which can bring the per-dive price down to around US$25. You must have an Open Water certificate to dive with any of the shops recommended in this book; if you're new to the sport, all the dive shops also offer the Discover Scuba and Open Water certification courses. For snorkeling, trips cost around US$25 to US$40 per person.

White-Water Rafting

The Dominican Republic has the only navigable white-water river in the Caribbean, the Río Yaque del Norte. It's mostly a Class II and III river, with a couple of serious rapids, and the rest consists of fun little holes and rolls. The river winds through bucolic hilly countryside and makes for a fun half-day tour. Be aware that the water can be cold – you'll be issued a wetsuit along with your life vest and helmet. While you can make this a day trip from the north coast or Santo Domingo, it's a long journey in a bus – you'll enjoy yourself a great deal more if you spend a couple of nights in Jarabacoa. Trips cost around US$50 per person.

BEHOLD LEVIATHAN

Between mid-January and mid-March more than 80% of the reproductively active humpback whales in the North Atlantic – some 10,000 to 12,000 in all – migrate to the waters around the Península de Samaná to mate. The Bahía de Samaná is a favorite haunt of the whales, and one of the best places in the world to observe these massive, curious creatures. Most tours depart from the town of Samaná, and you are all but guaranteed to see numerous whales surfacing for air, lifting their fins or tail, jostling each other in competition, and even breaching – impressive jumps followed by an equally impressive splash. Whale-watching season coincides with Carnival (every weekend in February) and Independence Day (February 27) – major holidays here – so you should make reservations well in advance.

Fishing

Like most places in the Caribbean, there is good sport fishing to be had for those so inclined. Blue marlin peaks in the summer months, there's white marlin in springtime, and mahi-mahi, wahoo and sailfish in wintertime.

The best places to go deep-sea fishing are the north-coast region and Punta Cana. Expect to pay around US$70 to US$100 per person (US$60 to US$70 for watchers) for a group half-day excursion. Most captains will also gladly charter their boats for private use; expect to pay upwards of US$700/900 for a half/full day.

Land Sports

Cascading & Canyoning

Cascading – climbing up through a series of waterfalls, and then jumping and sliding down into the pools of water below – is hugely popular at the 27 waterfalls of Damajagua, on the north coast. For many travelers it's their favorite experience in the DR. You'll be issued a life jacket and safety helmet, and guides will lead up, sometimes pulling you up bodily through the force of the water. Some of the jumps down are as much as 8m high. You can visit the waterfalls by yourself – foreigners pay only RD$420 per person, and while a guide is mandatory, there's no minimum group size. Alternatively, you can come with a tour group, but all the package 'jeep safari' tours go only to the 7th waterfall – disappointing. Only a very few tour agencies offer the trip to the very top (see p152).

Canyoning – often referred to as 'canyoneering' in the US – is cascading's technical, older brother and is even more

of an adrenaline rush, involving jumping, rappelling and sliding down a slippery river gorge with a cold mountain river raging around you. You'll be issued a safety helmet and usually a shorts-length wetsuit. It's becoming more popular in the DR, but there are really only two reliable and experienced companies: Iguana Mama in Cabarete on the north coast and Rancho Baiguate in Jarabacoa in the mountains. We highly recommend it.

Hiking
Pico Duarte

The most famous hike in the DR is the ascent of Pico Duarte (3087m), the tallest peak in the Caribbean. First climbed in 1944 as part of the 100th anniversary celebration of the Dominican Republic's independence from Haiti, it's a tough multi-day hike, but involves no technical climbing, and most people hire mules to carry their supplies and equipment up the mountain.

DIY KAYAKING

The DR holds great potential for both sea and river kayaking, a potential that is largely unfulfilled. While a few scattered shops and hotels around the country can rent you a sea kayak for a paddle along the beach, the activity remains unpopular.

Gung-ho river kayakers looking for some crazy rapids (and who don't mind traveling with a kayak in their luggage) should head to Jarabacoa, where Class III, IV and V rapids surge past on the Río Yaque del Norte, which flows nearby.

BEST GOLF COURSES

» **La Cana Golf Course** (p100) Best in the area; designed by Pete Dye.

» **Cap Cana** (p101) Three Jack Nicklaus Signature courses.

» **Teeth of the Dog** (p87) One of four Pete Dye–designed courses in Casa de Campo.

» **Playa Grande** (p159) Last course designed by Robert Trent Jones Sr.

» **Playa Dorada** (p141) Robert Trent Jones Sr course.

About 3000 hikers make it to the top yearly. There are two main routes to the summit (see p186) and several side trips you can take along the way, including hikes through two beautiful alpine valleys and up the Caribbean's second-highest peak, La Pelona, just 100m lower than Pico Duarte.

While the destination – the peak itself and the views – is stunning, the well-traveled walker may be disappointed by the journey required to get there. You pass quickly through the ferns and moss-bound rainforest of the lower elevations, and once you hit 2200m all you see are burnt-out forests of Caribbean Pine, spaced at regular intervals, with no animals and only cawing crows for company. Still, if it's clear at the top when you get there – and you have time to linger at the summit – then the hard work to get there may be worth it. You'll also enjoy the trip more if you spend part of it on the back of a mule.

Shorter Hikes

The DR is not a world-class hiking destination. Still, there are a number of waterfalls and quite a few challenging trails around Jarabacoa. The Península de Samaná has some beautiful hikes near Las Galeras, with picturesque deserted beaches as your reward at the end. In the southwest, there's some decent half-day and full-day hikes just outside Paraíso, although they are best visited as part of a tour.

Lesser-known trails are slowly being developed for organized hikes in the mountains outside Puerto Plata. Contact Tubagua Village (see p141) for customized itineraries.

No matter what hike you choose to take, it's a good idea to have sturdy shoes. For Pico Duarte they are absolutely essential – boots would be even better – while some of the coastal hikes can be managed in good sandals with heel straps.

Mountain Biking

The Jarabacoa area is the best and most popular area for mountain-bike riding. Tucked into the mountains, there are a number of dirt roads and single-track trails offering challenging climbs and thrilling descents. The crisp air and cool climate make for ideal cycling, and thick forests and a number of waterfalls are within easy reach.

Cabarete also has a number of good rides and is home to the DR's best cycling tour operator, Iguana Mama, and one of it's more passionate advocates/guides, Maximo Martinez. It offers mountain-bike tours ranging from half-day downhill rides to 12-day cross-country excursions. It can also customize a trip to fit your interests, available time and experience level.

Tour prices vary widely depending on the length of the ride, but begin at around US$45 per person for half-day trips.

Paragliding

Head out to Jarabacoa for the thrill of soaring on a thermal with a bird's-eye view of the spectacular mountains surrounding this valley town, with its unusual sights of pine trees and Swiss-type A-frame houses – right in the middle of the Caribbean. There's a great local group of pilots living here year-round (see p181).

Horseback Riding

Those equestrian-inclined will find good riding on beaches and in the mountains. You may be somewhat disappointed in the horses, however – Dominicans themselves tend to use mules, and the few horses on the island are principally for tourists and rich Dominicans. Don't expect to ride a thoroughbred.

A number of stables offer their services through the many tour agencies and resorts listed in this book. Expect to pay roughly US$50 to US$70 per person for a half-day ride. You can also ride a mule to the top of Pico Duarte.

The most popular trip is to the waterfalls around Limón on the Península de Samaná.

HANDY WEBSITES

» **www.drpure.com** – An overview of outdoor adventure activities; good place to start.

» **www.cabaretekiteboarding.com** – Listing of schools, rental and retail outfits and more.

» **www.cabaretewindsurfing.com** – Ditto above but for windsurfing.

» **www.activecabarete.com** – Features listings, information and reviews about sporting activities in and around Cabarete.

» **www.godominicanrepublic.com** – Information on outdoor activities, golfing and beach activities.

» **www.medioambiente.gob.do** (in Spanish) – The home page of the federal Department of the Environment, has information on national parks.

Birdwatching

The DR is a popular destination for gung-ho birders looking for the island's endemic bird species – 31 in all (depending on who you ask and how you count). The very best place to go birding is the southwest, especially the north slope of the Sierra de Bahoruco, where you can spot nearly all the endemics, including the high-altitude habitat-loss-threatened La Selle's thrush, western chat-tanager, white-winged warbler, rufous-throated solitaire and Hispaniolan trogon.

The Jardín Botánico Nacional in Santo Domingo are, surprisingly, also a good spot to look for birds, especially the palm chat, black-crowned palm tanagers, Hispaniolan woodpeckers, vervain hummingbirds and Antillean mangoes.

Parque Nacional Los Haitises is the only place you're likely to see the highly endangered Ridgway's hawk.

While numerous overseas birding groups bring enthusiasts here, there's only one tour company devoted to birdwatching based in the DR (see p201).

regions at a glance

Santo Domingo

History ✓✓✓
Nightlife ✓✓✓
Food ✓✓✓

Zona Colonial
Cobblestone lanes give way to courtly looking plazas surrounded by exquisitely restored 16th-century buildings in the capital's Zona Colonial. The heart of the Spanish empire's original seat in the New World is chockablock with museums and sights – some of which are European firsts in the western hemisphere – to transport you back in time. However, this is no sanitized artificial neighborhood – ordinary life continues apace amid a picturesque backdrop.

p42

Nightlife
Inhabitants of the Caribbean's largest city take pride in their ability to let loose. Whether it's a modest *colmado* (corner store) or posh nightclubs that wouldn't be out of place in any major world capital, Santo Domingo is the place to party. Merengue, *bachata* and salsa reverberate on the streets, gritty and posh alike. National holidays and religious celebrations are when the city takes it to a whole new level.

Food
Restaurants in the country's culinary capital display a sophistication and range not found elsewhere – from Middle Eastern to French to Japanese, this is truly a cosmopolitan dining scene. There's little reason to settle for the *plato del día* when you can feast alfresco on the balcony of a colonial-era building on locally caught seafood with a *haute cuisine* twist. Meanwhile, vendors hawk tasty fried quick eats and refreshing frozen desserts from streetside carts.

Punta Cana & the Southeast

Beaches ✓✓✓
Resorts ✓✓✓
Water Sports ✓✓✓

Beaches
Planeloads of tourists make a beeline for the postcard-perfect stretches of white sand around Baváro and Punta Cana. But there are less-developed patches to the north for the more adventurous.

All-Inclusives
Much of the country's reputation as a sybaritic holiday land is based on this region. Every stereotype is true; regardless, there's something very intoxicating about having everything indulgently close at hand.

Aquatic Adventures
Beneath the ocean's surface, there are more surprises. Bayahibe, a fishing village near La Romana, is the center of what's widely regarded as the country's best scuba diving. Snorkelers have offshore reefs to choose from as well.

p76

Península de Samaná

Landscapes ✓✓✓
Water Sports ✓✓
Social Scene ✓✓

Landscapes
Rolling mountains with hard-to-get-to waterfalls, a sea of hillocks pushing their way to a long coastline of protected beaches and picturesque coves; a touch of the exotic is added by cliffs and hidden lagoons, once refuges for pirates.

Water Sports
Be it surfing, kitesurfing, snorkeling or scuba diving, active travelers will find it all here, as well as a community of experienced pros to show beginners how it's done.

Social Scene
A motley crew of mainly European and North Americans have brought a cosmopolitan flavor to the peninsula: Las Terrenas is the center of cafe culture and nightlife, while Las Galeras' sophistication is under the radar.

p109

North Coast

Beaches ✓✓✓
Water Sports ✓✓✓
Nightlife ✓✓

Beaches
Rivaling the southeast in terms of the beauty of its shoreline, the long ocean corridor stretching from Monte Cristi to Cabrera offers seclusion or development, whatever your fancy.

Water Sports
Generally considered the mecca of water-based sports in the DR, the north coast offers virtually every means of propelling yourself across or through liquid. From kitesurfing to wakeboarding to canyoning, the conditions are close to ideal.

Nightlife
Indulge in *la dolce vita* sipping tropical cocktails on Cabarete's beachfront or a leisurely sundowner on Puerto Plata's Malecón. More rowdy Sosúa or resort discos round out your options.

p131

Central Highlands

Adventures ✓✓✓
Scenery ✓✓✓
Tranquility ✓✓

Outdoor Adventures
Blessed with a roaring river and four of the five highest peaks in the Caribbean, the Cordillera Central is becoming an adventure-sport destination. Get up high while paragliding or scramble on your hands and knees down a rocky canyon.

Mountain Vistas
The pretty pastoral panoramas of this region's forested slopes are the stuff of escapist fantasies. More evocative of the European Alps than a Caribbean island, a drive along one of the winding, switchback roads passes from cloud-shrouded jungle to sun-dappled plateaus.

Tranquility
Because it can be relatively challenging to access, time spent in the highlands is generally a break from the coastal hordes. Tourism is less developed and you're more likely to slow down and rise and shine to the rhythms of the sun.

p167

The Southwest & Península de Pedernales

Landscapes ✓✓
Nature ✓✓✓
Escape ✓✓✓

Landscapes

Millennia-old tectonic movements have given the Península de Pedernales its unique geographic features: unspoiled sanctuaries, characterized by the beautiful beach along the Bahía de las Águilas and cactus-covered deserts.

Wildlife

Very slowly emerging as an ecotourism destination, this is the best place on the island to go birdwatching: nearly all of the island's endemics are found here. That's to say nothing of the crocodiles, lizards, turtles and marine life.

Tranquility

Get away from the coastal crowds, where any stranger is sure to turn heads. And yet despite this thinly populated region's remoteness there are still a few luxurious hideaway retreats.

p192

Look out for these icons:

 TOP Our author's
CHOICE recommendation

 A green or
sustainable option

 No payment
required

On the Road

Santo Domingo

POPULATION: 2.9 MILLION

Best Places to Eat

» Pat'e Palo (p63)
» La Taberna Vasca (p63)
» Vesuvio Malecón (p65)
» Mitre Restaurant (p65)

Best Places to Stay

» Sofitel Nicolás de Ovando (p60)
» El Beaterío Guest House (p60)
» Coco Boutique Hotel (p60)
» Casa Naemie Hotel (p61)

Why Go?

Santo Domingo, or 'La Capital' as it's typically called, is a collage of cultures and neighborhoods. It's where the sounds of life – domino pieces slapped on tables; backfiring mufflers and horns from chaotic traffic; merengue and *bachata* (Dominican music) blasting from corner *colmados* – are most intense. At the heart of the city is the Zona Colonial, where you'll find one of the oldest churches and the oldest surviving European fortress among other New World firsts. Amid the cobblestone streets, it would be easy to forget Santo Domingo is in the Caribbean. But this is an intensely urban city, home not only to colonial-era architecture, but also to hot clubs, vibrant cultural institutions and elegant restaurants. Santo Domingo somehow manages to embody the contradictions central to the Dominican experience: a living museum, a metropolis crossed with a seaside resort, and a business, political and media center with a laid-back, casual spirit.

When to Go

The city hosts a blowout merengue festival in July and three-day Latin music event in October. Baseball is played almost five nights a week at Quisqueya Stadium from the end of October to the end of January. Carnaval, at the end of February and beginning of March, is a big deal in the capital. Hurricane season, from August through December, means strong rains and developing storms can be a threat, though sun usually prevails. September on average sees the most precipitation and February the least.

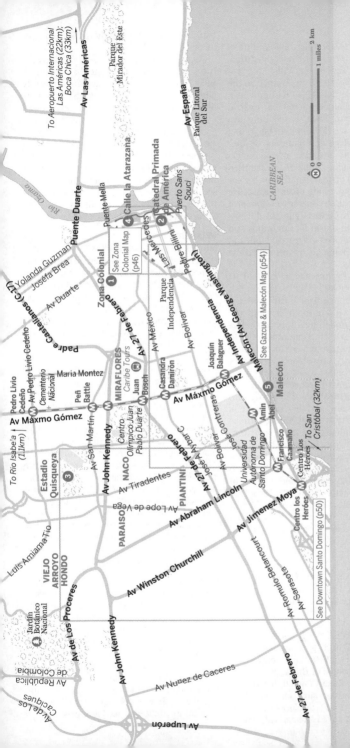

Santo Domingo Highlights

1 Wandering the 500-year-old cobblestone backstreets of the **Zona Colonial** (p44)

2 Entering the **Catedral Primada de América** (p45) – the first church in the New World – and imagining how 16th-century worshippers felt

3 Rooting for the home team at raucous **Estadio Quisqueya** (p68), one of the premier places to watch a baseball game in the Dominican Republic

4 Letting the night slip away after a late dinner along romantic **Calle la Atarazana** (p63) off Plaza España

5 Dancing to **merengue**, **bachata** or **salsa music** (p67) or just plain-old grinding down at one of the capital's vibrant nightclubs in Malecón

To Aeropuerto Internacional Las Américas (22km); Boca Chica (33km)

Parque Mirador del Este

Av Las Américas

Av España

Parque Litoral del Sur

Catedral Primada de América

Calle la Atarazana

Puerto Sans Souci

CARIBBEAN SEA

Puente Mella

Puente Duarte

Río Ozama

Pedro Mella

Yolanda Guzman

Josefa Brea

Av Duarte

Zona Colonial

See Zona Colonial Map (p46)

Las Mercedes

Padre Billini

See Gazcue & Malecón Map (p54)

Malecón (Av George Washington)

Av 27 de Febrero

Padre Castellanos (C-17)

Av/Pedro Livio Cedeño

Cementerio Nacional

Peñ Battle

María Montez

MIRAFLORES

Caribe Tours

Juan Bosch

Casandra Damirón

Parque Independencia

Av México

Av Bolívar

Joaquín Balaguer

Av Independencia (Av George Washington)

Av Máxmo Gómez

Amín Abel

Francisco Caamaño

Centro Los Héroes

To San Cristóbal (32km)

Av Máxmo Gómez

Av San Martín

Av John Kennedy

Centro Olímpico Juan Pablo Duarte

NACO

PARAISO

Av Tiradentes

PIANTINI

Av 27 de Febrero

José A Aybar C

José Contreras

Universidad Autónoma de Santo Domingo

Centro Los Héroes

See Downtown Santo Domingo (p50)

To Río Isabela (1.1km)

Estadio Quisqueya

Av Lope de Vega

Av Abraham Lincoln

Av Jimenez Moya

Av Rómulo Betancourt

Av Sarasota

Av Winston Churchill

Luis Amiama Tío

VIEJO ARROYO HONDO

Jardín Botánico Nacional

Av de Colombia

Av República

Av de Los Próceres

Av John Kennedy

Av Núñez de Caceres

Av 27 de Febrero

Av Lupéron

Av de Los Caciques

N

0   1 miles
0   2 km

History

In a way it can be said that the founding of Santo Domingo was an act of desperation. Columbus' first settlement, Villa La Navidad in present-day Haiti, was burned to the ground and all settlers killed within a year. His second settlement, La Isabela, west of present-day Puerto Plata, lasted only five years and was beset from the beginning by disease and disaster. Columbus' brother Bartholomew, left in charge of La Isabela and facing rebellion from its disgruntled residents, pulled up stakes and moved clear around to the other side of the island. He then founded Nueva Isabela on the east bank of the Río Ozama. The third time, evidently, was the charm for Columbus and this city, though moved to the west bank and renamed Santo Domingo, has remained the capital to this day.

That's not to say the city hasn't had its fair share of troubles. In 1586 the English buccaneer Sir Francis Drake captured the city and collected a ransom for its return to Spanish control. And in 1655 an English fleet commanded by William Penn attempted to take Santo Domingo but retreated after encountering heavy resistance. A century and a half later a brazen ex-slave and Haitian leader by the name of François Dominique Toussaint Louverture marched into Santo Domingo. Toussaint and his troops took control of the city without any resistance at all; the city's inhabitants knew they were no match for the army of former slaves and wisely didn't try to resist. During the occupation many of the city's residents fled to Venezuela or neighboring islands. It was in Santo Domingo on February 27, 1844 that Juan Pablo Duarte – considered the father of the Dominican Republic – declared Dominican independence from Haiti, a day still celebrated today.

◉ Sights

The highest concentration of sights are conveniently located within walking distance of one another in the Zona Colonial.

ZONA COLONIAL

For those fascinated by the origin of the so-called New World – a dramatic and complicated story of the first encounter between native people of the Americas and Europeans – the Zona Colonial, listed as a Unesco World Heritage site, is a great place to explore. It is 11 square blocks, a mix of cobblestoned and paved streets, on the west bank of the Río Ozama, where the deep river meets the Caribbean Sea.

As might be expected, many of the structures in the Zona Colonial that still have their 16th-century walls have more recently altered facades and structural additions like new floors and roofs. The western end of Arzobispo Portes is especially attractive, a quiet leafy avenue with colonial homes, stone churches and pleasant parks. Keep your eyes open for the little nooks and crannies – the small pedestrian alleys, men playing dominos at an aluminum folding table set on the street. These scenes, as much as the historical sites and buildings, make the Zona Colonial unique.

Museums

Museo de las Casas Reales   MUSEUM
(Museum of the Royal Houses; Map p46; Las Damas; admission RD$50; ☺9am-5pm Tue-Sun) Built in the Renaissance style during the 16th century, this building was the long-time seat of Spanish authority for the entire Caribbean region, housing the Governor's office and the powerful Audiencia Real (Royal Court), among others. It showcases colonial-period objects, including treasures recovered from Spanish galleons that foundered in nearby waters. Several walls are covered with excellent maps of various voyages of European explorers and conquistadors. Each room has been restored according to its original style, and displays range from Taíno artifacts to dozens of hand-blown wine bottles and period furnishings. Also on display is an impressive antique weaponry collection acquired by dictator/president Trujillo from a Mexican general (ironically, during a 1955 world peace event); you'll see samurai swords, medieval armor, ivory-inlaid crossbows and even a pistol/sword combo. One of the more interesting museums, partly because of its history and the high quality of its exhibits.

Museo Alcázar de Colón   MUSEUM
(Museum Citadel of Columbus; Map p46; Plaza España; admission RD$60; ☺9am-5pm Tue-Sat, to 4pm Sun) Designed in the Gothic-Mudéjar transitional style, this was once the residence of Columbus' son, Diego, and his wife, Doña María de Toledo, during the early 16th century. Recalled to Spain in 1523, the couple left the home to relatives who occupied the handsome building for the next hundred years. It was subsequently allowed to deteriorate, then was used as a prison and a

WANT MORE?

Head to **Lonely Planet** (www.lonely planet.com/dominican-republic/santo -domingo) for planning advice, author recommendations, traveler reviews and insider tips.

warehouse, before it was finally abandoned. By 1775 it was a vandalized shell of its former self and served as the unofficial city dump. Less than a hundred years later, only two of its walls remained at right angles.

The magnificent building we see today is the result of three restorations: one in 1957, another in 1971 and a third in 1992. Great pains were taken to adhere to the historical authenticity during its reconstruction and decor. Today it houses many household pieces said to have belonged to the Columbus family. The building itself – if not the objects inside – is definitely worth a look.

FREE **Museo Mundo de Ambar**   MUSEUM
(World of Amber Museum; Map p46; www.amber worldmuseum.com; 2nd fl, Arzobispo Meriño 452; ⊙9am-6pm Mon-Sat, to 2pm Sun) An impressive collection of amber samples from around the world, and excellent exhibits explaining in Spanish and English its prehistoric origins, its use throughout the ages, Dominican mining processes, and its present-day value to the science and art worlds. The collection includes fine amber jewelry and various samples containing a wide array of critters and bugs. The 1st-floor shop sells jewelry made from amber, larimar and more ordinary stones.

FREE **Museo del Ambar**   MUSEUM
(Map p46; Calle El Conde 107, Parque Colón; ⊙9am-6pm Mon-Fri, to 4pm Sat) Not nearly as impressive as its competitor, it has a few decent exhibits and high-quality samples, plus an exhibit on larimar, a beautiful blue stone only found in the Dominican Republic (the only larimar mine in the world is located near Bahoruco in the southwest).

FREE **Larimar Museum**   MUSEUM
(Map p46; www.larimarmuseum.com; 2nd fl, Isabel la Católica 54; ⊙8am-6pm Mon-Sat, to 2pm Sun) This museum is a better place to learn about larimar, the equal to the Museo Mundo de Ambar in terms of the thoroughness of its

exhibits. Signage is in Spanish and English. Of course, the museum is meant to inspire you to make a purchase from the strategically located jewelry store on the 1st floor.

Museo de la Familia Dominicana   MUSEUM
(Museum of the Dominican Family; Map p46; cnr Padre Billini & Arzobispo Meriño; admission RD$40; ⊙9am-4pm Mon-Sat) Located in the Casa de Tostado – the beautifully restored 16th-century home of writer Francisco Tostado – the museum is as interesting as much for its architectural features (it has a double Gothic window over the front door – the only one of its kind in the Americas) as for its exhibits displaying well-restored 19th-century furnishings and household objects. Ask to go up the spiral mahogany staircase for a rooftop view of the Zona Colonial. Tours in Spanish only.

FREE **Museo del Ron y la Caña**   MUSEUM
(Map p46; Isabel la Católica 261; ⊙9am-5pm Mon-Sat) This new museum, housed in a restored 16th-century building, is a celebration of rum and sugar cane, two of the country's most important exports. Displays and photographs explain the history of their production and importance to the DR's economy. Of course, you can sample the wares at the small bar or buy some to go.

Museo del Duarte   MUSEUM
(Map p46; cnr Isabel la Católica & Emiliano Tejera; admission RD$10; ⊙9am-5pm Tue-Fri, to noon Sat) The birthplace of Juan Pablo Duarte has been converted into a modest museum. Three rooms display documents, artifacts and photos from his life and La Trinitaria, the underground independence organization he founded.

FREE **Quinta Dominica**   MUSEUM
(Map p46; cnr Padre Billini & 19 de Marzo; ⊙9am-6pm Mon-Sat, to 2pm Sun) This small art gallery, in a renovated 16th-century home, features ever-changing exhibits of colonial and contemporary art. A shady courtyard at the back with tables and chairs provides a great place to just sit and relax. BYO snacks and drinks.

Churches
Catedral Primada de América   CHURCH
(Primate Cathedral of America; Map p46; Parque Colón; ⊙9am-4pm) Diego Columbus, son of the great explorer, set the first stone in 1514, but construction didn't begin in earnest

Zona Colonial

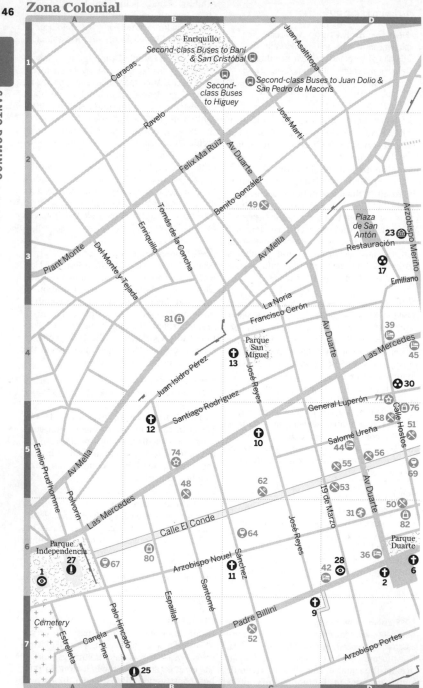

Enriquillo
Second-class Buses to Baní & San Cristóbal

Second-class Buses to Higuey

Second-class Buses to Juan Dolio & San Pedro de Macoris

Caracas

Ravelo

José Marti

Juan Asaltitopa

Felix Ma Ruíz

Av Duarte

Benito González

49

Tomás de la Concha

Enriquillo

Plant Monte

Del Monte y Tejada

Av Mella

Plaza de San Antón
Restauración

23

17

Emiliano

Arzobispo Meriño

La Noria
Francisco Cerón

81

Av Duarte

39

Las Mercedes

45

Parque San Miguel
13

José Reyes

30

Juan Isidro Pérez

Santiago Rodríguez

General Luperón

71

Calle Hostos

58

76

12

10

Salomé Ureña

44

51

74

55

56

69

Emilio Prudhomme

Av Mella

Polvorin

48

62

53

19 de Marzo

Av Duarte

31

50

82

Las Mercedes

Calle El Conde

64

Parque Duarte

Parque Independencia
27
1

67

80

Arzobispo Nouel

Sánchez

José Reyes

28

36

2
6

11

42

Santomé

Espaillat

9

Cemetery

Estrelleta

Canela

Palo Hincado

Pina

Padre Billini
52

Arzobispo Portes

25

until the arrival of the first bishop, Alejandro Geraldini, in 1521. From then until 1540, numerous architects worked on the church and adjoining buildings, which is why the vault is Gothic, the arches Romanesque and the ornamentation baroque. It's anyone's guess what the planned bell tower would have looked like: a shortage of funds curtailed construction, and the steeple, which undoubtedly would have offered a commanding view of the city, was never built.

Although Santo Domingo residents like to say their cathedral was the first in the Western hemisphere, in fact one was built in Mexico City between 1524 and 1532; it stood for four decades, until it was knocked down in 1573 and replaced by the imposing Catedral Metropolitano. It *can* be said that Santo Domingo's cathedral is the oldest cathedral in operation, which is something for sure, but its current interior is a far cry from the original – thanks to Drake and his crew of pirates, who used the basilica as their headquarters during their 1586 assault on the city. While there, they stole everything of value that could be carried away and extensively vandalized the church before departing.

Among the cathedral's more impressive features are its awesome vaulted ceiling and its 14 interior chapels. Signs in English and Spanish beside each chapel and other features describe their rich histories. Shorts and tank tops are strictly prohibited.

Convento de la Orden de los Predicadores
CHURCH

(Convent of the Order of Preachers; Map opposite; cnr Av Duarte & Padre Billini; ⊙varies) Built in 1510 by Charles V, this is the first convent of the Dominican order founded in the Americas. It also is where Father Bartolomé de las Casas – the famous chronicler of Spanish atrocities committed against indigenous peoples – did most of his writing. Be sure to take a look at the vault of the chapel; it is remarkable for its stone zodiac wheel, which is carved with mythological and astrological representations. On the walls are various paintings of religious figures, including Pope Saint Pius V.

Capilla de Nuestra Señora de los Remedios
CHURCH

(Chapel of Our Lady of Remedies; Map opposite; cnr Las Damas & Las Mercedes; ⊙varies) The Gothic-style chapel was built during the 16th century by alderman Francisco de Avila and was

Zona Colonial

intended to be a private chapel and family mausoleum. Early residents of the city are said to have attended Mass here under its barrel-vaulted ceiling. It was restored in 1884.

Iglesia de Nuestra Señora de las Mercedes
CHURCH
(Church of Our Lady of Mercy; Map p46; cnr Las Mercedes & José Reyes; ☉varies) Constructed during the first half of the 16th century, the church was sacked by Drake and his men and reconstructed on numerous occasions following earthquakes and hurricanes. The church is remarkable for its pulpit, which is sustained by a support in the shape of a serpent demon. The intricate baroque altarpiece is carved from tropical hardwood. Of the group of buildings that pay homage to the Virgin Mary, only the cloister adjacent to the church is in original condition.

Iglesia de Santa Clara
CHURCH
(Map p46; cnr Padre Billini & Isabel la Católica; ☉morning Sun) Home to the first nunnery

in the New World built in 1552. Years after being sacked by Drake and his men (who apparently hated all things Catholic), it was rebuilt with funds from the Spanish Crown. This simple, discreet church has a severe Renaissance-style portal with a gable containing a bust of St Claire.

Iglesia de Santa Bárbara
CHURCH
(Map p46; cnr Gabino Puello & Isabel la Católica; ☉varies) This baroque church was built in 1574 to honor the patron saint of the military. After being done over by Drake, however, the church was rebuilt with three arches – two of these are windowless and the third frames a remarkably sturdy door. These additions have proved invaluable in protecting the building against pirates and hurricanes alike.

Iglesia de la Regina Angelorum
CHURCH
(Map p46; cnr Padre Billini & José Reyes; ☉varies) Paid for by a woman who donated her entire fortune to construct this monument for

the cloistered Dominican Sisters, this church was built toward the end of the 16th century. In addition to its imposing facade, the church is known for its elaborate 18th-century baroque altar, which is crowned with the king's coat of arms.

HAVE YOUR SAY

Found a fantastic restaurant that you're longing to share with the world? Disagree with our recommendations? Or just want to talk about your most recent trip?

Whatever your reason, head to lonelyplanet.com, where you can post a review, ask or answer a question on the Thorntree forum, comment on a blog, or share your photos and tips on Groups. Or you can simply spend time chatting with like-minded travelers. So go on, have your say.

Iglesia de San Lázaro   CHURCH
(Map p46; cnr Santomé & Juan Isidro Pérez; ⊙varies) Completed in 1650, but altered several times since, this church was erected beside a hospital that treated people with infectious diseases. The church was constructed to give the patients hope – a commodity that no doubt was in short supply for patients with tuberculosis, leprosy and other common diseases of colonial times.

Iglesia de Nuestra Señora del Carmen   CHURCH
(Map p46; cnr Sánchez & Arzobispo Nouel; ⊙varies) Since 1596 this church has served as a hospital, a jail and an inn, but is now famous for its carved-mahogany figure of Jesus, which is worshipped every Holy Wednesday during Easter Week. The small church, originally made of stone, was set aflame by Drake in 1586 and was rebuilt using bricks. During colonial times its small square was used to stage comedies.

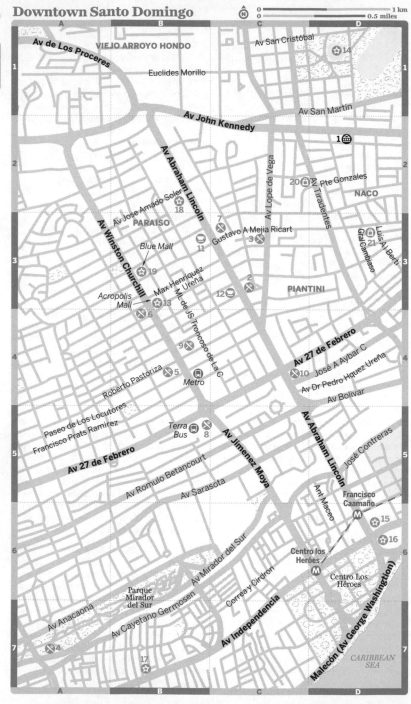

N

0 _____ 1 km
0 _____ 0.5 miles

SANTO DOMINGO

Av de Los Proceres

VIEJO ARROYO HONDO

Av San Cristóbal

14

Euclides Morillo

Av San Martín

Av John Kennedy

1

Av Lope de Vega

20 Pte Gonzales

NACO

Av Abraham Lincoln

Av Jose Amado Soler

18

Luis A Berti
Gral Cambiaso

21

PARAISO

7

Gustavo A Mejia Ricart

Av Winston Churchill

Blue Mall

11

3

19

Max Henríquez
Ureña

2

PIANTINI

Acropolis
Mall

13

12

6

ML de JS Troncoso de La C

Av 27 de Febrero

9

José A Aybar C

10

Av Dr Pedro Hquez Ureña

Roberto Pastoriza

5

Av Bolivar

Metro

Paseo de Los Locutores

Terra
Bus

8

Av Jimenez Moya

Francisco Prats Ramirez

Av Abraham Lincoln

José Contreras

Av 27 de Febrero

Av Romulo Betancourt

Av Sarasota

Ant Maceo

Francisco
Caamaño

15

M

16

Av Mirador del Sur

Centro los
Héroes

M

Parque
Mirador
del Sur

Av Cayetano Germosen

Correa y Cidron

Centro Los
Héroes

Av Anacaona

4

17

Av Independencia

Malecón (Av George Washington)

CARIBBEAN
SEA

Iglesia de San Miguel   CHURCH
(Church of Michael the Archangel; Map p46; cnr José Reyes & Juan Isidro Pérez; ⊙varies) In 1784 Spain ordered that the Iglesia de San Miguel be turned into a hospital for slaves. The decree, however, was never followed. Note the appealing juxtaposition of its rectangular stone doorway with the curved shape of the structure's exterior.

Capilla de la Tercera Orden Dominica   CHURCH
(Chapel of the Third Dominican Order; Map p46; cnr Av Duarte & Padre Billini) Built in 1729 and the only colonial structure in Santo Domingo that remains fully intact. These days the building is used by the office of the archbishop of Santo Domingo. It's not open to the general public, but the graceful baroque facade is worth a look.

Historical Sites
Being the first colonial city in the New World, the Zona Colonial boasts several historical 'firsts,' including the first church, first paved road and first hospital.

Parque Colón   PARK
(Map p46; cnr Calle El Conde & Isabel la Católica) Beside the Catedral Primada de América, this historic park contains several shade trees and a large statue of Admiral Columbus himself. It's the meeting place for local residents and is alive with tourists, townsfolk, hawkers, guides, taxi drivers, shoeshine boys, tourist police and thousands of pigeons all day long. El Conde Restaurant, at the corner of Calle El Conde and Arzobispo Meriño, has seating inside and out and is

the premier people-watching corner in the Zona Colonial.

Plaza España   PLAZA
(Map p46) The area in front of the Alcázar de Colón has been made over many times, most recently during the early 1990s in honor of the 500th anniversary of Christopher Columbus' 'discovery' of the New World. The plaza is a large, open area that makes for a lovely stroll on a warm afternoon. Running along its northwest side is Calle la Atarazana, fronted by numerous restaurants in buildings that served as warehouses through most of the 16th and 17th centuries. This is a popular place for a meal or a drink in an outdoor table around sunset.

Fortaleza Ozama   HISTORICAL SITE
(Map p46; ☑809-686-0222; Las Damas; admission RD$70; ⊙9am-6:30pm Mon-Sat, to 4pm Sun) This is the oldest colonial military edifice in the New World. The site of the fort – at the meeting of the Río Ozama and the Caribbean – was selected by Fray Nicolás de Ovando. Construction of the fortification began in 1502 under the direction of master builder Gómez García Varela and continued in various stages for the next two centuries. Over the course of its history the fort has flown the flag of Spain, England, France, Haiti, Gran Columbia, the US and the DR. Until the 1970s, when it was opened to the public, it served as a military garrison and prison.

As soon as you walk into the site, you'll see the oldest of the buildings here – the impressive **Torre del Homenaje** (Tower of Homage). Its 2m-thick walls contain dozens of riflemen's embrasures and its roof-top lookout offers 360-degree views of the city. To its right, solid and windowless, stands **El Polvorín** – the Powder House – which was added in the mid-1700s; look for the statue of St Barbara over the door, the patron saint of the artillery.

Running along the riverside wall are two rows of cannons: the first dates from 1570, the second was added in the mid-1600s. Both served as the first line of defense for the city's port. The living quarters, now almost completely destroyed, were added along the city-side wall in the late 1700s. On the esplanade is a bronze statue of Gonzalo Fernández de Oviedo, perhaps the best-known military chronicler of the New World.

Near the door you'll find several guides, whose knowledge of the fort generally is quite impressive. Although the fee for a 20-minute tour is around US$3.50 per person, be sure to agree on a fee before you use their services. Tours are offered in Spanish, English and French, and there is occasionally a guide who speaks German, Italian or even Japanese.

Las Damas   STREET
(Map p46; Calle de las Damas, the Ladies' Street) Heading north and south in front of the fortress is the first paved street in the Americas. Laid in 1502, the street acquired its name from the wife of Diego Columbus and her lady friends, who made a habit of strolling the road every afternoon, weather permitting.

Panteón Nacional   MONUMENT
(National Pantheon; Map p46; Las Damas; ☺9am-5pm Tue-Sun) Originally constructed in 1747 as a Jesuit church, this was also a tobacco warehouse and a theater before dictator Trujillo restored the building in 1958 for its current usage. Today many of the country's most illustrious persons are honored here, their remains sealed behind two marble walls. The entire building, including its neoclassical facade, is built of large limestone blocks. As befits such a place, an armed soldier is ever present at the mausoleum's entrance – along with a powerful fan since it does get hot. Shorts and tank tops are discouraged.

Plaza de María de Toledo   STREET
(Map p46) Named in honor of Diego Columbus' wife, this plaza connecting Las Damas and Isabel la Católica is remarkable for two arches that were once part of the Jesuits' residence in the 17th century. Note the

buttresses that support the Panteón Nacional: they are original, dating back to the construction of the Jesuit church in 1747, and a likely reason the building has survived the many earthquakes and hurricanes since.

Reloj del Sol   MONUMENT
(Map p46) Across from the Museo de las Casas Reales, this sundial was built by Governor Francisco Rubio y Peñaranda in 1753 and positioned so that officials in the Royal Houses could see the time with only a glance from their eastern windows.

Monasterio de San Francisco HISTORICAL SITE
(Map p46; Calle Hostos) The first monastery in the New World belonged to the first order of Franciscan friars who arrived to evangelize the island. Dating from 1508, the monastery originally consisted of three connecting chapels. It was set ablaze by Drake in 1586, rebuilt, devastated by an earthquake in 1673, rebuilt, ruined by another earthquake in 1751 and rebuilt again. From 1881 until the 1930s it was used as a mental asylum until a powerful hurricane shut it down – portions of chains used to secure inmates can still be seen. The buildings were never repaired. Today the monastery is a dramatic set of ruins that is occasionally used to stage concerts and artistic performances.

**Ruinas del Hospital San
Nicolás de Barí**   HISTORICAL SITE
(Map p46; Calle Hostos) Standing next to a bright, white Iglesia de la Altagracia are the ruins of the New World's first hospital. They remain in place as a monument to Governor Nicolás de Ovando, who ordered the hospital built in 1503. So sturdy was the edifice that it survived Drake's invasion and centuries of earthquakes and hurricanes. It remained virtually intact until 1911, when after being devastated by a hurricane, public-works officials ordered much of it knocked down so that it wouldn't pose a threat to pedestrians. Even today visitors can still see several of its high walls and Moorish arches. Note that the hospital's floor plan follows the form of a Latin cross.

Puerta del Conde   MONUMENT
(Gate of the Count; Map p46; Calle El Conde) This gate is named for the Count of Peñalba, Bernardo de Meneses y Bracamonte, who led the successful defense of Santo Domingo against an invading force of 13,000 British troops in 1655. It's the supreme symbol of Dominican patriotism because right

beside it, in February 1844, a handful of brave Dominicans executed a bloodless coup against occupying Haitian forces; their actions resulted in the creation of a wholly independent Dominican Republic. It also was atop this gate that the very first Dominican flag was raised. Just west of the gate inside **Parque Independencia** look for the **Altar de la Patria**, a mausoleum that holds the remains of three national heroes: Juan Pablo Duarte, Francisco del Rosario Sánchez and Ramón Matías Mella. The park itself has a few benches but little shade.

Puerta de San Diego   MONUMENT
(Map p46; Av del Puerto) For a time, this imposing gate built in 1571 downhill from the Alcázar de Colón was the main entrance into the city. Beside it you can still see some of the original wall, which was erected to protect the city from assaults launched from the river's edge.

Puerta de la Misericordia   MONUMENT
(Map p46; Gate of Mercy; Arzobispo Portes) This gate was erected during the 16th century, and for many decades served as the main western entrance to the city. It obtained its name after a major earthquake in 1842, when a large tent was erected beside it to provide temporary shelter for the homeless.

Casa del Cordón   NOTABLE BUILDING
(House of the Cord; Map p46; cnr Isabel la Católica & Emiliano Tejera; ⊙8:15am-4pm) Said to be not only one of the first European residences in the Americas, but also one of the first residences in the Western hemisphere with two floors briefly occupied by Diego Columbus and his wife before they moved into their stately home down the street. Named after its impressive stone facade, which is adorned with the chiseled sash-and-cord symbol of the Franciscan order, it is also believed to be the site where Santo Domingo's women lined up to hand over their jewels to Drake during the month he and his men held the city hostage. Today the structure is home to Banco Popular, and while you can go in to exchange money, visiting the house beyond the main lobby is not permitted.

Casa de Francia   NOTABLE BUILDING
(French House; Map p46; Las Damas 42) This was the originally the residence of Hernán Cortés, conqueror of the Aztecs in what is today central Mexico. It was in this building that Cortés is believed to have organized

his triumphant – and brutal – expedition. Built in the early 16th century and sharing many elements with the Museo de las Casas Reales, experts theorize that these buildings were designed by the same master; both have a flat facade and a double bay window in the upper and lower stories, repeating patterns of doors and windows on both floors, and top-notch stone rubblework masonry around the windows, doors and corner shorings.

Although the Casa de Francia served as a residence for nearly three centuries, it has had several incarnations since the beginning of the 19th century: a set of government offices, the Banco Nacional de Santo Domingo, a civil courthouse and the headquarters of the Dominican IRS. Today it houses the French embassy. While visitors are not permitted past the lobby, this marvel of masonry is worth a walk by, if only to check out its facade.

Hostal Nicolás de Ovando   NOTABLE BUILDING
(Map p46; Las Damas) A handsome building with a Gothic facade built in 1509, this was originally the residence of Governor Nicolás de Ovando, who is famous for ordering Santo Domingo rebuilt on the west bank of the Río Ozama following a hurricane that leveled most of the colony. Today it houses the posh Sofitel hotel.

Fuerte de Santa Bárbara   HISTORICAL SITE
(Map p46; cnr Juan Parra & Av Mella) Built during the 1570s, this fort served as one of the city's main points of defense. It proved no match for Drake, however, who along with his fleet of 23 pirate-packed ships captured the fort in 1586. Today the fort lies in ruins at the end of a lonely street. There isn't much to see here anymore, mostly rooftops and occasionally a cruise ship in the distance.

GAZCUE
Plaza de la Cultura   PARK
(Map p54; Av Maxímo Gómez) Located near the city center is this large park area with three museums, the national theater and the national library. The land was once owned by the dictator Trujillo, and was 'donated' to the public after his assassination in 1961. At least two of the museums are worth visiting, though the plaza itself is mostly a sun-baked expanse and fairly unkempt; the theater and library will appeal to travelers with specific interests.

Gazcue & Malecón

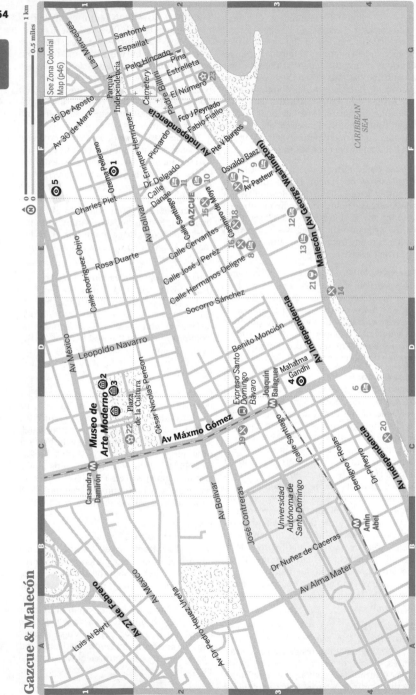

See Zona Colonial Map (p46)

1 km
0.5 miles

CARIBBEAN SEA

Santomé
Espaillat
Palo Hincado
Piña
Estrellieta
Parque Independencia
Cemetery
Padre Billini
El Número
16 De Agosto
Av 30 de Marzo
Fco J Peynado
Fabio Fiallo
Las Mercedes
Calle Enrique Henríquez
Pichardo
Av Independencia
Pte V Burgos
Ozema Pellerano
Dr Delgado
Osvaldo Baez
Charles Piet
Calle Danae
Calle Santiago
GAZCUE
Av Bolívar
Calle Moya
Av Pasteur
Rosa Duarte
Calle Cervantes
Calle José J Peréz
Calle Hermanos Deligne
Socorro Sánchez
Av México
Calle Rodríguez Objío
Leopoldo Navarro
Benito Monción
Museo de
Arte Moderno
Plaza
de la Cultura
César Nicolás Penson
Expreso Santo
Domingo
Bávaro
Mahatma
Gandhi
Joaquín
Balaguer
Av Máximo Gómez
Casandra
Damirón
Av Bolívar
Calle Santiago
José Contreras
Universidad
Autónoma de
Santo Domingo
Benigno F Rojas
Dr Piñeyro
Av Independencia
Dr Núñez de Cáceras
Amín
Abel
Av Alma Mater
Av 27 de Febrero
Av México
Luis Al Bertí
Av Dr Pedro Habizz Ureña
Malecón (Av George Washington)
Av Independencia

Gazcue & Malecón

Museo de Arte Moderno

(admission RD$50; ☺10am-6pm Tue-Sun) The museum's permanent collection includes paintings and a few sculptures by the DR's best-known modern artists, including Luís Desangles, Adriana Billini, Celeste Woss y Gil, José Vela Zanetti, Dario Suro and Martín Santos. The temporary exhibits tend to be fresher and more inventive – more installation and multimedia pieces. Note that the entrance is on the 2nd floor – don't miss the artwork on the bottom level, accessed by a set of stairs just past the ticket counter.

Museo del Hombre Dominicano

(Museum of the Dominican Man; ☑809-687-3622; admission RD$75; ☺10am-5pm Tue-Sun). The most extensive of the museums highlights are the impressive collection of Taíno artifacts, including stone axes and intriguing urns and carvings, and the small but interesting section on Carnival, with the masks and costumes used in various cities around the country. Other sections focus on slavery and the colonial period, African influences in the DR (including a small section on Vodou) and contemporary rural Dominican life. Unfortunately, the explanations are all in Spanish and the displays very old-fashioned. English-speaking guides can be requested at the entry – the service is free, but small tips are customary.

Museo Nacional de Historia y Geografíca

(☑809-686-6668; admission RD$50; ☺10am-5pm Tue-Sun) This museum's exhibits include ones on the battles between Haitians and Dominicans; General Ulises Heureaux, the country's most prominent dictator during the 19th century; and Trujillo, the country's most prominent dictator during the 20th century – displays include his personal effects such as combs, razor, wallet etc.

Palacio Nacional   NOTABLE BUILDING
(Map opposite; ☑809-695-8000; cnr Av México & Av 30 de Marzo) The Dominican seat of government was designed by Italian architect Guido D'Alessandro and inaugurated in 1947. The palace is built of Samaná roseate marble in a neoclassical design and is outfitted in grand style with mahogany furniture, paintings from prominent Dominican artists, magnificent mirrors inlaid with gold, and a proportionate amount of imported crystal. Of special note is the **Room of the Caryatids**, in which 44 sculpted draped women rise like columns in a hall lined with French mirrors and Baccarat chandeliers.

The Palacio Nacional sits on most of a city block and is primarily used as an executive and administrative office building. It has never been used as the residence of a Dominican president, who is expected to live in a private home. Unfortunately, the palace is not regularly open to the public, but you may be able to wrangle a VIP tour; they are offered free of charge and by appointment only on Monday, Wednesday and Friday. Dress appropriately – no flip-flops, shorts or T-shirts – if you are granted a tour.

Palacio de Bellas Artes NOTABLE BUILDING
(Palace of Fine Arts; Map p54; ☎809-687-9131; Av Máximo Gómez) This huge recently renovated neoclassical building was used infrequently in the past for exhibitions and performances. Check the weekend edition of local papers for events.

OUTLYING NEIGHBORHOODS

Some of these sights are worthwhile as much for the taxi ride there and back, catching a glimpse of the Santo Domingo where ordinary people live and work. The shantytowns that ring much of the city are known as Zona Apache – an allusion to the forbidden territory of the Old West in the US.

Faro a Colón MONUMENT
(Columbus Lighthouse; ☎809-592-1492, ext 251; Parque Mirador del Este; admission RD$65; ⊙9am-5:15pm Tue-Sun) Resembling a cross between a Soviet-era apartment block and a Las Vegas version of an ancient Mayan ruin, this massive monument is worth visiting for its controversial and complicated history. Located on the east side of the Río Ozama, the Faro's massive cement flanks stretch nearly a block and stand some 10 stories high forming the shape of a cross. High-power lights on the roof can project a blinding white cross in the sky, but are rarely turned on because doing so causes blackouts in surrounding neighborhoods.

At the intersection of the cross' arms is a tomb, guarded by stern white-uniformed soldiers, that purportedly contains Columbus' remains. Spain and Italy dispute that claim, however, both saying *they* have the Admiral's bones. Inside the monument a long series of exhibition halls display documents (mostly reproductions) related to Columbus' voyages and the exploration and conquest of the Americas. The most interesting (though deeply ironic) displays are those sent by numerous Latin American countries containing photos and artifacts from their respective indigenous communities.

Jardín Botánico Nacional GARDEN
(National Botanic Garden; Map p43; ☎809-385-2611; www.jbn-sdq.org; Av República de Colombia; adult/child RD$50/40; ⊙9am-6pm, ticket booth 9am-5pm; 🚶) The lush grounds span 2 sq km and include vast areas devoted to aquatic plants, orchids, bromeliads, ferns, endemic plants, palm trees, a Japanese garden and much more. Great care is taken to keep the grounds spotless and the plants well tended,

and it's easy to forget you're in the middle of a city of over two million people. In fact, birders can contact Tody Tours (p72) for an expert eye on the many species found here. The garden hosts a variety of events, including an orchid exhibition and competition in March and a bonsai exhibition in April. The on-site **Ecological Museum** (⊙9am-4pm, ticket booth 9am-5pm) exhibits and explains the major ecosystems found in the DR, including mangroves and cloud forests, plus a special display on Parque Nacional Los Haitises. Once inside you can stay until 6pm. An **open-air trolley** (⊙every 30min until 4:30pm) takes passengers on a pleasant half-hour turn about the park and is especially enjoyable for children. A taxi from the Zona Colonial costs around RD$200.

FREE **Museo Bellapart** MUSEUM
(Map p50; ☎809-541-7721; Av JF Kennedy & Dr Peguero; ⊙9am-6pm Mon-Fri, to 12:30pm Sat) Incongruously located on the 5th floor of the Honda building, which looks like a parking garage, is this significant private collection of Dominican painting and sculpture from the late 19th century to the 1960s.

Los Tres Ojos NATURAL SITE
(The Three Eyes; Parque Mirador del Este; admission RD$50; ⊙8am-5pm) Consisting of three very humid caverns with still, dark lagoons inside and connected by stalactite-filled passages, this is a mildly interesting site frequented by organized tours. The caves are limestone sinkholes, carved by water erosion over thousands of years. The entrance is a long stairway down a narrow tunnel in the rock; once at the bottom, cement paths lead you through the caves or you can visit them by boat for another RD$20. Unfortunately, the tranquility of the setting is usually upset by guides aplenty (which are unnecessary) and vendors aggressively hawking their services and wares, like postcards and jewelry, to tourists at the entrance.

Parque Mirador Del Sur PARK
(Southern Lookout Park; Map p43; Av Mirador del Sur) A long tree-filled corridor atop an enormous limestone ridge, this park is riddled with caves, some as big as airplane hangars. One of the caves has been converted into a restaurant (p66), another into a dance club (p67). The park's seemingly endless paths are a popular jogging spot for 30-something professionals, many of whom live in the middle- and upper-class

Though former president Joaquin Balaguer gets the lion's share of credit, the idea of commemorating Columbus' landing with a lighthouse wasn't Balaguer's: the **Faro a Colón** was suggested as early as the middle of the 18th century and later revived at the Fifth International American conference in Santiago, Chile, in 1923. The site of the memorial was always Santo Domingo. An international design competition was launched in 1929 and after sorting through hundreds of submissions from dozens of countries, the reward of US$10,000 eventually went to JL Gleave, a young British architect. Trujillo finally broke ground for the project in 1948, though one that incorporated his own design plans, but financial pledges from other Latin American governments never materialized and the project was scrapped.

Balaguer took up the issue again in 1986, appointing Nicolas Lopez Rodriguez, archbishop of Santo Domingo and a friend, as head of a commission for the celebration of the centenary of the 'discovery and evangelization of America' (he had also recently provided a blessing for the inaugural test run of the Santo Domingo metro). More than 50,000 shantytown dwellers were moved from their homes and tens of millions of dollars were spent on the project (some estimate the final cost to be around US$100 million) so that the beacon could project light visible 320km to the east in Puerto Rico – this in a city and country that at the time was often without power because of a poorly maintained electrical grid and high gas prices. The joke, not without some basis in fact, was that when the lighthouse was switched on the rest of the country went black.

Balaguer pulled the switch for the first time on October 12, 1992, with Pope John Paul II and King Juan Carlos and Queen Sofia of Spain in attendance – contemporary representatives of the dual powers that initiated the historic journey over 500 years ago. When responding to critics, supporters of the project – government officials at the time and some Dominicans – compared the lighthouse to the Eiffel Tower, explaining that both are in essence function-free white elephants.

neighborhoods north of the park. Av Mirador del Sur is closed to traffic from 6am to 9am and 4pm to 8pm daily, when it fills with men and women jogging, rollerblading and bicycling up and down the broad avenue, and mobile juice bars and snack stands for anyone who's hungry.

Parque Zoológico Nacional ZOO
(☎809-378-2149; www.zoodom.gov.do; Av La Vega Real; adult/child RD$100/60; ⊙9am-5pm Tue-Sun) Some recent remodeling and renovations have improved the experience somewhat for the animals here, one of the larger zoos in all Latin America. The collection of animals is extensive: rhinos and chimps, flamingos and the endangered solenodon, an extremely rare, rat-like creature endemic to the island. Located in a neighborhood in the northwest corner of the city (the makeshift homes of the slum perched just above the zoo appear as if they're likely to collapse onto the property at any moment), it's a bit hard to find. A taxi here from the Zona Colonial costs around RD$250; be sure to arrange a return trip with the driver, as you won't find many taxis out here.

🎓 Courses

Instituto Intercultural del Caribe SPANISH LANGUAGE
(☎809-571-3185; www.edase.com; Aristides Fiallo Cabral 456, Zona Universitaria) The Spanish Department of Edase, a German-Dominican Language and Culture Institute, was founded in 1994. It offers Spanish courses of 20 and 30 hours per week in small classroom settings. There are more than a dozen price combinations, depending on the length and intensity of instruction and whether or not accommodations are included. Call for current course listings and prices. It also offers merengue dance lessons (eight hours of private lessons US$55) and maintains a language school in Sosúa.

Entrena SPANISH LANGUAGE
(☎809-567-8990; www.entrenadr.com; Calle Virgilio Diaz Ordoñez 42, Ensanche Julieta) Providing Spanish-language instruction since 1982 for everyone from Peace Corps volunteers to professional baseball players. Its base program is a four-week intensive Spanish and Dominican Culture course,

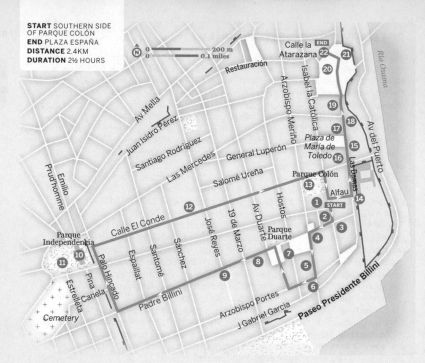

Walking Tour
Zona Colonial

❯ Start at ① **Catedral Primada de América**, the oldest working church in the New World. Then turn south on Isabel la Católica – you'll see the ② **Larimar Museum** and the simple ③ **Iglesia de Santa Clara**. Turn west on Padre Billini and walk to the ④ **Museo de la Familia Dominica**, with its famous Gothic window. Turn south onto Arzobispo Meriño and you'll pass ⑤ **Casa de Teatro** – see an art exhibit or ask about upcoming performances. Continue south to the corner of Arzobispo Portes to the ⑥ **Centro Cultural Español** with its exhibits and full calendar of events. Head west on Arzobispo Portes, one of the Zona Colonial's prettiest streets. Turn right onto Av Duarte, which opens onto a plaza with two churches on either side – the spectacular ⑦ **Convento de la Orden de los Predicadores** and the baroque ⑧ **Capilla de la Tercera Orden Dominicana**. In front is Parque Duarte, a popular spot for locals.

Turn west onto Padre Billini and continue to José Reyes, where you'll see the ⑨ **Iglesia de la Regina Angelorum**, with its ornate facade and baroque-style altar. Continue west

on Padre Billini for four long blocks until Palo Hincado. Turn right and walk a block to the ⑩ **Puerta del Conde**, the supreme symbol of Dominican patriotism. Just inside the gate is Parque Independencia and the ⑪ **Altar de la Patria**, a mausoleum of three national heroes. Backtrack back past the gate; ⑫ **Calle El Conde**, the Zona Colonial's busy commercial walkway, begins in front of the park entrance. Wander down Calle El Conde until you reach leafy ⑬ **Parque Colón**. Grab a drink from one of the cafes on the cobblestone alleyway just east of El Conde.

From the southeastern corner of the park take Alfau, a small pedestrian street, one block to the entrance to ⑭ **Fortaleza Ozama**, the oldest military structure in the New World. Continuing north on Las Damas, check out the lovely facades of the ⑮ **Hostal Nicolás de Ovando** and the ⑯ **Casa de Francia**. Further down Las Damas, you'll pass the ⑰ **Panteón Nacional** and the ⑱ **Capilla de Nuestra Señora de los Remedios**. Next you'll come upon the interesting ⑲ **Museo de las Casas Reales** before reaching ⑳ **Plaza España**, a large plaza overlooking the Río Ozama, with the ㉑ **Museo Alcázar de Colón** on one side. Head to one of the ㉒ **restaurants** lining the northwestern edge of the plaza for a drink or meal.

Santo Domingo isn't particularly kid-friendly. Outside of the Zona Colonial, it doesn't cater for pedestrians, there are no beaches and few parks, or at least ones that are well maintained and shady. **Parque Colón** (p51) and **Parque Duarte** (Map p46; cnr Padre Billini & Av Duarte) in the Zona Colonial are basically flagstone plazas where you can sit on a bench and feed pigeons.

Museo Infantil Trampolín (Map p46 ☎809-685-5551; www.trampolin.org.do, in Spanish; Las Damas; adult/child RD$100/60; ☺9am-5pm Tue-Fri, 10am-6pm Sat & Sun) is a high-tech, hands-on natural history, biology, science, ecology and social museum all wrapped into one. Enthusiastic guides (most are Spanish-speaking) lead kids through the exhibits: the earthquake machines and volcano simulations are big hits, less so the exhibit on children's legal rights.

If the kids won't have a chance to snorkel and see underwater creatures in their natural habitat, the **Acuario Nacional** (National Aquarium; ☎809-766-1709; Av España; adult/child RD$50/20; ☺9am-5:30pm Tue-Sun) can substitute. It's rundown in parts, however. That said, the long, clear underwater walkway where you can watch sea turtles, stingray and huge fish pass on the sides and overhead can be exciting. Signs in Spanish only. Across the street is **Agua Splash Caribe** (☎809-591-5927; adult/child RD$200/150; ☺11am-7pm Tue-Sun), a not very well taken care of water park. It's a lot of concrete and safety probably isn't the best but...

Adrian Tropical (p65) is an especially good place to eat with unruly youngsters. Hotels with pools, all those along the Malecón (p62), are especially recommended and will allow you and the kids to take a break from the sightseeing for several relaxing hours.

which includes six hours of one-on-one instruction, competency-based language training and a homestay (US$1650). Programs can also be coordinated on a per-hour basis (US$8 to US$13), allowing students to take as many or as few classes and hours as they wish.

Hispaniola Academy   SPANISH LANGUAGE
(Map p46; ☎809-688-9192; www.hispaniola .org; Arzobispo Nouel 103) Offering six levels of Spanish-language instruction, this the only language school in the Zona Colonial. A week-long course – the shortest of those offered – consists of 20 lessons per week (ie four 50-minute classes per day) and your choice of accommodations. Prices begin at US$260 (with a homestay) and rise to US$580 (with hotel accommodations). Private classes available. Cooking (private US$48) and dance classes are also offered.

☞ Tours

Interesting and informative walking tours of the Zona Colonial are offered on a daily basis by a number of official guides – look for men dressed in khakis and light-blue dress shirts, but always ask to see their official state tourism license. Tours cover the most important buildings in the zone

and can be tailored to your specific interests. Walks typically last 2½ hours and cost US$20 to US$30 depending on the language that the tour is given in (Spanish and English are less expensive). To find a guide, head to Parque Colón – you'll find a number of them hanging out under the trees. Also be sure to agree upon a fee before setting out.

A more leisurely option is a **horse drawn carriage tour** (with/without guide US$50/30). Look for the carriages pulled to the side of the road near the corner of Las Damas and El Conde.

If you want to hook up with a bus tour that may include outlying sights in addition to the Zona Colonial, try one of the local agencies that provide city tours to guests of all-inclusive resorts. A few popular ones include **Omni Tours** (☎809-565-6591; Roberto Pastoriza 204), **Prieto Tours** (☎809-685-0102; Av Francia 125) and **Turinter** (☎809-226-5342; Plaza Las Bromelias, Av Duarte). This isn't a bad option if you're short on time.

✯ Festivals & Events

Carnival   CARNIVAL
Carnaval (in Spanish) is celebrated throughout the country every Sunday in February, culminating in a huge blowout in Santo Domingo during the last weekend of the month or first weekend of

March. Av George Washington (the Malecón) becomes an enormous party scene all day and night. Central to the celebration are the competitions of floats, and costumes and masks representing traditional Carnival characters.

Merengue Festival MUSIC
The largest in the country, this two-week celebration of the DR's favorite music is held yearly at the end of July and beginning of August. Most of the activity is on the Malecón, but there are related events across the city.

Latin Music Festival MUSIC
Held at the Estadio Olímpico (Olympic Stadium) every October, this huge three-day event attracts the top names in Latin music – jazz, salsa, merengue and *bachata* (popular guitar music based on bolero rhythms). Jennifer Lopez and Marc Anthony have performed in the past.

🛏 Sleeping

The Zona Colonial is the most distinctive part of the city and therefore where most travelers prefer to stay. Sights and restaurants are within walking distance and there's an excellent choice of midrange and top-end hotels to choose from, some in attractive restored colonial-era buildings. Budget travelers have fewer options. Gazcue, a quiet residential area southwest of Parque Independencia, has several hotels in the midrange category, though there are far fewer eating options and you're likely to have to rely on taxis, especially at night. The high-rise hotels on the Malecón are best if you're looking for resort-style amenities like swimming pools, health clubs and tennis courts, and on-site entertainment like nightclubs and casinos.

ZONA COLONIAL

Sofitel Nicolás de Ovando HISTORIC HOTEL $$$
(Map p46; ☎809-685-9955; www.sofitel.com; Las Damas; s US$220-336, d US$238-354; P🅿️❄️🛜🏊) Even heads of state must thrill when they learn they're sleeping in the former home of the first Governor of the Americas. Oozing character, old-world charm and a historic pedigree tough to beat, the Nicolás de Ovando is as far from a chain hotel as you can get. Indisputably one of the nicest hotels in the city, if not the nicest, the 107 rooms are definitely 21st century – flat-screen TVs, recessed Jacuzzi, luxurious boutique-style fixtures and linens. However, all this modernity is offset by beautifully crafted wood and

stone interiors, cobblestone walkways, lushly shaded courtyards and a commanding view of the Río Ozama – the fabulous pool probably didn't exist during the governor's time. An excellent buffet breakfast is included in the rate; La Residence, the hotel's superb and elegant restaurant (mains US$17 to US$35), has a separate entrance down the street and opens for lunch and dinner.

TOP
CHOICE **El Beaterío**
Guest House HISTORIC GUESTHOUSE $$
(Map p46; ☎809-687-8657; www.elbeaterio.com; Av Duarte 8; s/d with fan incl breakfast US$50/60, with air-con incl breakfast US$60/70; ❄️🛜) Take thee to this nunnery – if you're looking for austere elegance. It's easy to imagine the former function of this 16th-century building, the heavy stone facade, the dark and vaulted front room – now a beautiful reading room and dining area – giving way to a lush and sunny inner courtyard, all inspiring peace and tranquility. Each of the 11 large rooms is sparsely furnished, but the wood-beamed ceilings and stone floors are truly special; the bathrooms are modern and well maintained.

Coco Boutique Hotel BOUTIQUE HOTEL $$
(Map p46; ☎809-685-8467; www.cocoboutique hotel.com; Arzobispo Portes 7; s/d US$70/90; ❄️🛜) There's little traffic on this block in the southeastern corner of the Zona Colonial, which makes this hotel, four rooms in a renovated home, a particularly peaceful refuge. It doesn't have the old-world character of some of the other renovated hotels, but the owners have designed each room individually with particular color schemes and themes; the black-vanilla room is probably the nicest. All have beautifully polished wood floors and access to the rooftop lounge with a Balinese-style bed and waterfront vistas. The meticulously maintained Plaza de Castro is right out the front door.

Hotel Atarazana BOUTIQUE HOTEL $$
(Map p46; ☎809-688-3693; www.hotel-atarazana .com; Calle Vicente Celestino Duarte 19; s/d incl breakfast US$80/100; ❄️🛜) A boutique hotel for the design-conscious only a few meters away from Plaza España. Housed in a beautifully renovated building from the 1860s, all six rooms sport custom-made furniture from native materials along with high-concept fixtures and textiles you'd find in a magazine. Each of the light and airy rooms has a balcony and breakfast is served in a

secret garden-like patio shaded by lush vegetation; there's even a small Jacuzzi to relax in. Another option is the rooftop, which has fabulous views of the Zona Colonial and river.

Sofitel Francés   HOTEL $$$

(Map p46; ☎809-685-9331; www.accorhotels .com; cnr Las Mercedes & Arzobispo Meriño; s/d incl breakfast US$150/170; P❉✿) It's hard living up to family expectations. Of course, the Francés suffers by comparison to its sister property, the Nicolás de Ovando, but what hotel wouldn't? Taken on its own merits, the Francés is a charming throwback to the same era. Housed in a colonial mansion only a few blocks away, rooms with high ceilings, stucco walls and tasteful decor surround a handsome stone patio. Some of the rooms are larger and quieter than others, so ask for layout specifics. A nice bar and restaurant are on site and guests can access the pool at the Ovando.

Casa Naemie Hotel   HOTEL $$

(Map p46; ☎809-689-2215; www.casanaemie .com; Isabel la Católica 11; s/d incl breakfast RD$2000/3000; ❉✿) This charming oasis only a few blocks from the oldest cathedral in the Americas feels like a European pension. Surrounding a narrow central courtyard are three floors of cozy, clean rooms with large modern bathrooms. An elegant lobby with a vaulted entranceway and brick flooring does double duty in the morning when the excellent breakfast is served.

Hotel Palacio   HOTEL $$

(Map p46; ☎809-682-4730; www.hotel-palacio .com; Av Duarte 106; s/d incl breakfast from US$70/ 90; P❉✿) Cross colonial with a little touch of medieval and you have the Palacio, a maze-like hotel occupying a 17th-century mansion only a block north of the Calle El Conde pedestrian mall. Service is exceptional and you'll need it to find your way past the charming nooks and crannies, which include reading areas, a gym, a small bar, a lush interior courtyard and stone-walled walkways. First-floor rooms are German conquistador minimalist while the larger 2nd-floor rooms are more modern and generic. Bathrooms throughout are spacious and comfortable. The small rooftop pool is a big plus, as is the gym for the physically fit.

Hotel Conde de Peñalba   HOTEL $$

(Map p46; ☎809-688-7121; www.condepenalba .com; cnr Calle El Conde & Arzobispo Meriño; s/d

US$60/70; ❉@) There's no location more central in Santo Domingo. Rooms in this 20-room hotel overlook the Parque Colón; the downside is that noise can be an issue, especially from the ever-popular hotel restaurant on street level. Rooms have high ceilings and cable TV, but the furnishings have seen better days.

Antiguo Hotel Europa   HOTEL $$

(Map p46; ☎809-285-0005; www.antiguohotel europa.com; cnr Arzobispo Meriño & Emiliano Tejera; r incl breakfast US$65; P❉@) Considering the impressive-looking facade, spacious lobby and uniformed bellboys of this hotel only two blocks west of Plaza España, the rooms are a letdown. Ask for one with a balcony to ensure your room receives light. Continental breakfast is served in a classy rooftop restaurant with a spectacular view of the Zona Colonial.

Hotel Doña Elvira   HOTEL $$

(Map p46; ☎809-221-7415; www.dona-elvira.com; Padre Billini 209; s/d incl breakfast from US$64/89; P❉@✿≋) Housed in a renovated colonial building, Doña Elvira is a friendly place geared toward travelers; you can hang out in the inner courtyard, take a dip in the pool (it's too small for swimming), lounge on the rooftop solarium or read in the lobby/ dining area. For such a pretty building, it's unfortunate the 13 rooms are a somewhat haphazard amalgam of mostly plain styles and furnishings.

Hodelpa Caribe Colonial   HOTEL $$$

(Map p46; ☎809-688-7799; www.hodelpa .com; Isabel la Católica 159; r incl breakfast US$85; P❉@✿) Only a block from Parque Colón, the Hodelpa Caribe is a convenient choice for those seeking modern comforts without the colonial ambience. There are some curiously discordant design touches, but the beds are comfortable and service is attentive. A rooftop solarium has several lounge chairs and good views.

Hostal La Colonia   HOTEL $$

(Map p46; ☎809-221-0084; hostallacolonia @yahoo.com; Isabel la Católica 110-A; s/d US$50/60; ❉) Ideally located around the corner from Parque Colón, La Colonia is a good option if character is not an issue. In addition to shiny, polished floors and large rooms, each of the floors has its own spacious street-side sitting area and balcony. Rooms are mostly shielded from the noise on this lively block.

Hostal Nomadas HOTEL $
(Map p46; ☎809-689-0057; www.hostalnomadas
.com; Hostos 209; s/d incl breakfast US$30/50;
❋☏) Good value for its central location on
a quiet block only a few blocks from Parque
Colón. The eight rooms here are rather
nondescript with small TVs as well as bathrooms but the rooftop terrace and restaurant is a big plus.

**Bettye's Exclusive Guest
House** BUDGET GUESTHOUSE $
(Map p46; ☎809-688-7649; marshallbettye@hot
mail.com; Plaza de María de Toledo, Isabel la Católica
163; dm per person US$22, r US$35; ❋☏) Look
for the nondescript iron doorway opening
onto Plaza de María de Toledo; don't be
discouraged by the messy art gallery space.
There are several dorm rooms (one only has
a fan) with five to six beds, and while the
spaces are hectic, they get good light and
there's access to a common kitchen and
bathroom. For privacy but not quiet, there's a
private room that opens directly onto Isabel
la Católica – the bathroom is extremely
small.

Hotel Freeman BUDGET HOTEL $
(Map p46; ☎809-688-4263; www.hostalfreeman
.com; Isabel la Católica 155; s/d US$30/40; ❋) It's
difficult to spot the entrance to the Freeman,
and once you do you might want to turn
around. The lobby desk does double service
as a small car-rental agency and the stair-
well has all the ambience of a police station.
The six rooms themselves are spare and
clean and have cable TV.

GAZCUE
Just west of the Zona Colonial this residential area of quiet, tree-lined streets has
a number of hotels, restaurants and some
services; it's a short walk to the Malecón.

Hotel La Danae HOTEL $$
(Map p54; ☎809-238-5609; www.ladanaehotel
.com; Calle Danae 18; s/d US$29/40; ❋) Domini-
can-owned La Danae is the best of a number
of similar small hotels located on this quiet
residential street. Choose from the older,
cheaper rooms in the front building and the
more modern ones in the back annex. The
former have higher ceilings, but are subject
to street noise. All have cable TV, and there's
a kitchen area for common use.

Hostal Duque de Wellington HOTEL $$
(Map p54; ☎809-682-4525; www.hotelduque.com;
Av Independencia 304; s/d RD$1500/2000; P❋)

@☏) With such an old-fashioned name, it's
not surprising this hotel isn't fashionably
modern. In fact, it's downright conservative,
with room furnishings and decor that try
terribly to be tasteful but are in the end fairly dowdy. Rooms on the 2nd floor have higher ceilings, and more expensive ones have
balconies that provide more light. There's a
restaurant and travel agency on the 1st floor.

Hostal Riazor HOTEL $$
(Map p54; ☎809-685-5566; hostal_riazor
@hotmail.com; Av Independencia 457; s/d incl
breakfast US$58/65; P❋) Professional
English-speaking front-desk staff and
clean rooms; the breakfast served in the
next-door restaurant is nothing special.

Jecasergian Hotel HOTEL $$
(Map p54; ☎809-476-7960; Calle Danae 31;
r RD$1500; P❋☏) Friendly and secure,
rooms are kept spotless at this small hotel
on a quiet side street between Independencia and Santiago.

MALECÓN
Less appealing than you might otherwise
expect considering its waterfront Caribbean
setting, Santo Domingo's Malecón, a long
expanse of baking concrete, has several
high-rise hotels. The upside is that many
rooms have views, all have pools and health
clubs, and most have casinos and nightclubs. The downside is you'll have to take a
taxi almost everywhere you go – you'll sweat
just walking from the street to the hotel
entrance – and the accommodations are
generally international-chain style, with
nothing particularly Dominican about it.

Hilton Hotel HOTEL $$$
(Map p54; ☎809-685-0000; www.hiltoncaribbean
.com/santodomingo; Av George Washington 500;
r from US$130; P❋@☀) Easily the nicest
of the luxury hotels on the Malecón, the
Hilton is part of a huge complex, includ-
ing a casino, movie theaters and several
restaurants (however, much of it still
remains vacant). The highest of the high-
rises, it's a long elevator ride in the atrium
to the top. Rooms are nicer and newer than
its nearby competitors, and there's a bar and
restaurant with stunning ocean views.

Hotel InterContinental RESORT $$$
(Map p54; ☎809-221-0000; www.intercontinental
.com/santodomingo; Av George Washington 218;
r from US$120; P❋@☀) Other than the Hil-
ton, the InterContinental has the plushest

lobby of the hotels on the Malecón and an even more hip bar-lounge area. Like all the big hotels on the waterfront, the hotel also has a pool, a spa, tennis courts and a casino, popular both with tourists and Dominicans on weekends.

Renaissance Jaragua Hotel RESORT $$$
(Map p54; ☎809-221-2222; www.marriott.com; Av George Washington 367; r from US$90; P❋@☎❄) Las Vegas comes to the Malecón at this hotel boasting the largest casino in the Caribbean. Under the Marriott brand, the spacious rooms in the 10-story tower and low-slung annex have been upgraded, though furnishings are still dated. It's generally good value considering the resort-style facilities; there's a popular nightclub on the premises.

Meliá Santo Domingo Hotel RESORT $$
(Map p54; ☎809-221-6666; www.solmelia.com; Av George Washington 365; r from US$75; P❋@ ☎❄) The curiously designed and cavernous lobby at the Meliá doesn't inspire confidence, but this hotel does have the nicest pool area on the Malecón. Be sure you get one of the renovated rooms, which have plush bedding and marble bathrooms.

✗ Eating

Unsurprisingly, Santo Domingo is the culinary capital of the country. It offers the full range of Dominican cuisine, from *pastelitos* (pastries with meat, vegetable or seafood fillings) sold from the back of street-vendors' carts to extravagantly prepared meals in picturesque colonial-era buildings. The Zona Colonial has some of the best restaurants and is most convenient for the majority of travelers. Gazcue, only a short walk from the Malecón, has a number of good choices; the downtown area north and west of Gazcue, between Av Tiradentes and Av Winston Churchill, is another fine area for dining with a large number of restaurants.

ZONA COLONIAL

TOP CHOICE **Pat'e Palo** SPANISH, MEDITERRANEAN $$$
(Map p46; ☎809-687-8089; Calle la Atarazana 25; mains RD$550; ⏱4:30pm-late Mon-Thu, 1:30pm-late Fri-Sun) Part of Plaza España's restaurant row, Pat'e Palo is for gourmands and anyone tired of the same old bland pasta and chicken. Everything here is special but two personal recommendations are the grilled angus rib eye with rocket and parmesan with potato fricassee, mushrooms and bacon, and the

Chilean sea bass served over Spanish sausage risotto in a creamy beer sauce.

Mesón del Jamón SPANISH $$$
(Map p46; Calle la Atarazana; mains RD$500; ⏱lunch & dinner) Another of Plaza España's eateries, Mesón del Jamón is distinctive for its elegant 2nd-floor balcony. Only four or so tables for two fit out here, but they provide wonderful views of the goings-on below – it's hard to give up the spot even after several hours. Along with grilled sirloin, pasta dishes and fish, Jamón has an extensive menu of hot and cold tapas, like cured ham and mussels in vinaigrette sauce.

La Bricola ITALIAN $$$
(Map p46; ☎809-688-5055; Arzobispo Meriño 152; mains RD$550; ⏱lunch & dinner) From the candlelit open-air patio to the soft melodic piano, La Bricola embodies romance – a meal here is the perfect place to pop the question. Set in a restored colonial-era palace, the ambience can't help but trump the food, which is international- and Italian-inspired mains, including fresh fish specials.

Café Bellini MEDITERRANEAN $$$
(Map p46; ☎809-686-0424; Plazoleta Padre Billini; mains RD$500; ⏱noon-3am Mon-Sat) This fashionable restaurant off Plazoleta Padre Billini (look for the statue of Don Francisco X Bellini) serves haute cuisine – interpretations of Italian meat, seafood and pasta with Dominican flourishes – like you'd find in the toniest restaurants in Paris or New York. A beautiful interior courtyard leads into an elegant and modern dining room that is designed to the hilt.

Mesón D'Bari DOMINICAN $$
(Map p46; cnr Calle Hostos & Salomé Ureña; mains RD$350; ⏱lunch & dinner) A Zona Colonial institution popular with tourists and sophisticated *capitaleños* on weekends, Mesón D'Bari occupies a charmingly decaying colonial home covered with bright, large paintings by local artists. The menu has Dominican and international standards, different versions of grilled meats and fish; the long attractive bar is equally appealing. Live music on some weekend nights.

La Taberna Vasca MEDITERRANEAN $$$
(Map p46; ☎809-221-0079; Emiliano Tejera 101; mains RD$600; ⏱noon-midnight Mon-Sat) Discreetly signed, this charming French bistro feels like a discovery. The intimate dining room, though small, is cheerfully

decorated and the kitchen turns out well-prepared seafood and meat dishes – we recommend the lobster ravioli or scallops Carpaccio. The gratis *amuse-bouche* and liqueur digestif are welcome perks.

El Meson de Luis   DOMINICAN $$
(Map p46; Calle Hostos; mains RD$250; ☺lunch & dinner) This simple and unpretentious restaurant is a downscale version of Mesón D'Bari across the street. Mostly loyal locals line up at the small bar or in the open-air dining room for filling plates of seafood and meat. Even though service isn't with a smile, it's a good choice, especially at dinnertime, when it's not uncommon for a trio of musicians to serenade your table.

Hostal Nomades Hookah
Bar & Restaurant   MIDDLE EASTERN $$
(Map p46; cnr Las Mercedes & Calle Hostos; mains RD$150; ☺lunch & dinner) This surprisingly atmospheric restaurant is located on the rooftop of the hotel of the same name. Lounging in one of the beds, puffing on a hookah with Middle Eastern music playing on the sound system, it's easy to imagine you're only a few blocks from a souk rather than a mercado. It has a small menu; try the delicious *bandederia*, a plate with servings of five different dishes.

El Rey del Falafel   MIDDLE EASTERN $$
(Map p46; cnr Sánchez & Padre Billini; mains RD$250; ☺5pm-late) This restaurant's stunning open-air dining room is the courtyard of a ruined building lit by shimmering candles. It's an unfair mismatch to expect the food, mostly standard fare like falafel and shwarma platters, to live up to it. Warm and attentive service and a good place for a drink as well.

D'Luis Parrillada   DOMINICAN $$
(Av George Washington 25; RD$350; ☺lunch & dinner) Strange but true, only a few restaurants take advantage of the Malecón's setting. This casual open-air restaurant perched over the ocean only a few blocks from the Zona Colonial is one of them. The large menu includes fajitas, grilled and barbeque meats, sandwiches and little-found *pulpofongo* (*mofongo* with Creole-style cuttlefish, RD$330). Wonderful place for a drink as well.

Dajao & Mimosa Restaurant
& Bar   DOMINICAN $$
(Map p46; Arzobispo Nouel 51; mains RD$300; ☺lunch & dinner) These two restaurants, Dajao,

a sleek, modern side resembling a European cafe, and Mimosa, an older, fan-cooled side much like an ordinary *comedor* (eatery), share a kitchen and you can order from either menu regardless of where you sit. The former has mains like rib eye (RD$675) and fish in coconut soup (RD$375), while the latter does a filling *plato del dia* (RD$275).

Todo Tambo   SEAFOOD $$$
(Map p46; Calle la Atarazana; mains RD$450; ☺lunch & dinner) Occupying the western corner, Todo Tambo is Plaza Españas seafood option: ceviche, fish tacos and *casuela de mariscos* (mixed seafood flambéed with whiskey topped with cream and parmesan cheese) are the standouts.

Pasatiempo   ITALIAN $$$
(Map p46; ☎809-689-4823; Isabel la Católica 204; mains RD$550; ☺lunch & dinner Mon-Sat) This small Italian bistro boasts a preservative- and additive-free menu and handmade pastas. The dining room is a little cramped but it's a pleasant and romantic restaurant on a quiet block of the Zona Colonial.

La Cafetera Colonial   DINER $
(Map p46; Calle El Conde; RD$60; ☺breakfast, lunch & dinner) Everyone knows everyone else's name here. That can seem intimidating at first, especially because the narrow entranceway means new customers can't pull up a stool at the long lunch counter unnoticed. It's a classic greasy-spoon menu: eggs and toast, simple sandwiches and strong espresso (RD$30).

El Taquito   FAST FOOD $
(Map p46; Emiliano Tejera 105; mains RD$50; ☺9am-1am Mon-Thu, 9am-3am Fri & Sat, 5pm-1am Sun) Head over to this stamp-sized restaurant, really a stall, for tacos, burgers or sandwiches. It's especially good for a late-night snack.

Restaurant Mariscos   SEAFOOD $
(Map p46; Calle El Conde; mains RD$75; ☺lunch & dinner) Literally a hole-in-the-wall. There's only room for a few cramped tables, but there's no better lunchtime deal around. A plate of rice with your choice of seafood goes for only RD$100. More substantial meals like grilled shrimp are slightly more expensive.

La Despensa   GROCERY $
(Map p46; cnr Calle El Conde & Av Duarte) Largest grocery store in the Zona Colonial, which means lines can be long especially around

closing time. Load up on cheap water, soda, alcohol and juice.

A handful of Chinese restaurants serve fast and inexpensive Cantonese-style meals in the small Chinatown neighborhood just north of Avs Mella and Duarte; typical of the bunch is **Comida China e Internacional** (Map p46; Av Duarte 16; mains RD$200). **Expreso Pekin** (Map p46; mains RD$100) at the corner of Calle El Conde and 19 de Marzo is more convenient for dinner. Grab an empanada (RD$10) for a quick bite to go at the hole-in-the-wall **Cafeteria La Tostada** (Map p46; Santomé).

GAZCUE & MALECÓN

TOP CHOICE **Hermanos Villar**　　　DOMINICAN **$$**
(Map p54; cnr Avs Independencia & Pasteur; mains RD$175; ☺breakfast, lunch & dinner) Occupying almost an entire city block, Hermanos Villar has two parts: the bustling Dominican-style diner serving cafeteria food and hot, grilled deli sandwiches, and a large outdoor garden restaurant that is slightly more upscale in terms of menu. The chicken *mofongo* (mashed yucca or plantains with pork rinds, RD$175) is delicious. Finding an empty table inside during the heavy lunchtime traffic is a challenge, so getting things to go is always an option.

Vesuvio Malecón　　　ITALIAN **$$$**
(Map p54; ☎809-221-1954; Av George Washington 521; mains RD$500; ☺lunch & dinner) A Malecón institution only a few blocks from the Hilton and one of the city's better restaurants since 1954, Vesuvio is elegant without being snooty. Expect refined Neapolitan-style seafood and meat dishes; lobster and shellfish are featured in beautifully plated antipasti. Next door is a more casual pizzeria under the same ownership.

Adrian Tropical　　　DOMINICAN **$$**
(Map p54; Av George Washington; mains RD$200; ☺8am-11pm Mon-Fri, 24hr Sat & Sun; ⚑) This popular family-friendly chain occupies a spectacular location overlooking the Caribbean. Waiters scurry throughout the two floors and outdoor dining area doling out Dominican specialties like yucca or plantain *mofongo* as well as standard meat dishes. An inexpensive buffet (RD$200) is another option and the fruit drinks hit the spot. There are three other outposts in Santo Domingo.

El Conuco　　　DOMINICAN **$$**
(Map p54; Casimiro de Mora 152; mains RD$350; ☺11:30am-midnight) Unashamedly touristy, El Conuco is stereotypically Dominican in the same way the Hard Rock Café is authentically American. Nevertheless, Dominicans as well as tour groups come here to get traditionally prepared dishes while taking in traditional dancers – the real highlight – in a dining room covered with traditional decorations.

Ananda　　　VEGETARIAN **$**
(Map p54; Casimiro de Moya 7; mains RD$50; ☺11am-9pm Mon-Fri, to 4pm Sat & Sun; ✍) Hardcore vegetarians will want to try out this cafeteria-style restaurant-cum–yoga center run by the 'International Society of Divine Realization.' They may not find the offerings enlightening but more the equivalent of a downward facing dog. Dominican dishes like brown rice and roast beans outnumber the Indian offerings.

La Cadena　　　GROCERY **$**
(Map p54; cnr Calle Cervantes & Casimiro de Moya; ☺7:30am-10pm Mon-Sat, 9am-2:30pm Sun) In Gazcue, La Cadena is within walking distance of hotels in the neighborhood and carries produce, meats and everything you should need.

DOWNTOWN

West of Gazcue between Avs Tiradentes and Winston Churchill is a fairly high-end area of businesses, restaurants, apartment buildings and homes.

Mitre Restaurant　　　FUSION **$$$**
(Map p50; ☎809-472-1787; cnr Gustavo Mejía Ricart 1001 & Av Abraham Lincoln 1005; mains RD$600; ☺lunch & dinner) This sleek restaurant, located in a nondescript building in an upscale business and residential district, serves a creative fusion of Asian, Italian and Dominican cuisines. The results are satisfying to both the eye and stomach; an outdoor patio and 2nd-floor wine and cigar bar are more casual than the white-tableclothed stylish dining room.

Fellini Ristorante　　　ITALIAN **$$**
(Map p50; ☎809-335-5464; cnr Roberto Pastoriza 504; mains RD$400; ☺noon-1am) This long-running restaurant named for the Italian filmmaker (with movie posters decorating the walls) has an extensive wine menu and serves up quality pasta and seafood dishes.

El Mesón de la Cava DOMINICAN $$$
(Map p50; ☎809-533-2818; Av Mirador del Sur; mains RD$600; ⊙noon-1am) This is where Batman would take a date – this craggy stalactite-filled limestone cave is home to a unique and romantic restaurant. Formally clad waiters and soft merengue and salsa music add to the atmosphere though the food, primarily grilled meats and fish, isn't especially outstanding.

Aka Sushi JAPANESE $$
(Map p50; ☎809-533-2818; Max Henríquez Ureña 50; mains RD$350; ⊙noon-1am) Tucked inside a small shopping plaza, this Japanese eatery does good sushi for reasonable prices.

Mijas Restaurante SPANISH $$$
(Map p50; ☎809-567-5040; Max Henríquez Ureña 47; mains RD$450; ⊙noon-2am Thu-Sat, to midnight Sun-Wed) Upscale and trendy restaurant serving some of the best tapas in the city.

Restaurante Bella Cristal CHINESE $$
(Map p50; ☎809-540-2923; Calle Roberto Pastoriza 458; mains RD$300; ⊙noon-11:30pm) Authentic Chinese cuisine.

Plaza Lama La Supertienda (cnr Avs Jímenez Moya & 27 de Febrero) and **Supermercado Nacional** (cnr Avs Abraham Lincoln & 27 de Febrero) live up to their names, the latter (an enormous megastore occupying several city blocks) especially so; it's located at one of the busiest intersections in the city. There's another branch in Gazcue (Map p54).

🍷 Drinking

Santo Domingo has a lively bar and club scene, much of it located conveniently in the Zona Colonial. Restaurants and cafes along Plaza España and the eastern end of Calle El Conde are happening spots at night; that being said, most restaurants tend to be good places to linger with a few drinks. Otherwise many of the nicer bars are in strip malls around the city, and whatever neighborhood you're in you can always strap on a few Presidentes at the *colmado*.

Only a 10 minute ride or so from the Zona Colonial on the eastern side of the Río Ozama is Av Venezuela, where more than half a dozen bars and clubs are concentrated in the span of only three or so blocks; a taxi is recommend there and back.

ZONA COLONIAL

[TOP CHOICE] **El Conde Restaurant** CAFE
(Map p46; Hotel Conde de Peñalba, cnr Calle El Conde & Arzobispo Meriño; ⊙8am-midnight) Hands down, the place for an afternoon drink. As much a restaurant as a cafe, El Conde's appeal isn't its varied menu of decent food, but its commanding location at the busiest corner in the Zona Colonial crowded with tourists and locals alike.

Segafredo Zanetti Espresso CAFE, BAR
(Map p46; Calle El Conde 54; ⊙9am-1am Mon-Thu, to 3am Fri & Sat) One of a number of establishments lining this cobblestoned alleyway, Segafredo stands out because of its cool indoor bar, which wouldn't be out of place in a trendy neighborhood of New York or Paris. You can lounge around with a mixed drink (RD$150) on one of the day beds or retreat to a nook in the back. Crepes, paninis and other morsels are also served inside and out.

Grands Café CAFE
(Map p46; cnr Calle El Conde & Palo Hincando; ⊙8am-1am) A down-market version of El Conde, if only because Grands' location as the western bookend of the pedestrian plaza means you have to contend with exhaust fumes and the persistent pleas of shoeshine boys.

Double's Bar BAR, DANCING
(Map p46; Arzobispo Meriño; ⊙6pm-late) Good-looking 20-somethings grind away to loud pop and Latin music at Double's. Others lounge around in groups downing bottles of Presidente, while the classic long wood bar is better for conversation.

Los Tres Mosqueteros BAR, CAFE
(Map p46; Calle El Conde 56; ⊙10am-1am; 🛜) This bar-cafe is one of several lining a cobblestone alleyway a few steps from Parque Colón. In addition to outdoor seating, it has an elegant indoor space with high ceilings and overhead fans. For those looking to make an afternoon of it, there's free wi-fi and a full menu.

Blu Limon Bar & Lounge BAR
(Map p46; cnr Isabel Católica & Arzobispo Portes; ⊙4pm-midnight Tue-Sun) A small sophisticated spot with a table or two on a quiet plaza in the Zona Colonial.

El Patio del Canario COCKTAIL LOUNGE
(Map p46; Calle la Atarazana 1) Owned by a Dominican salsa star, this bar is for

grown-ups; if the music gets too loud step out into the beautiful courtyard.

Onno's Bar
BAR
(Map p46; Hostos btwn Calle El Conde & Arzobispo Nouel; ✆5pm-1am Sun-Thu, to 3am Fri & Sat) There's always something going on at this fashionable hot spot just off El Conde: several flat-screen TVs, lasers, illuminated bar, DJs and smoke machine...

Cacibajagua Bar
LIVE MUSIC
(Map p46; Sánchez 201; ✆8pm-1am Sun-Thu, to 3am Fri & Sat) Also known as 'La Cueva' (the Cave), this popular and welcoming spot favors good ol' rock music like Pink Floyd and Led Zeppelin.

Colmado Omar II
BAR
(Map p46; Isabel la Católica) In the Zona Colonial; it gets loud and crowded on weekend nights.

GAZCUE & MALECÓN

La Parada Cervecera
OUTDOOR BAR
(Map p54; Av George Washington 402; ✆8am-midnight) This classic Dominican joint, a combination carwash-bar, isn't exactly a good advertisement against drinking and driving. It's an open-air place directly on a busy intersection of the Malecón; the loud music barely drains out the backfiring and honking traffic.

DOWNTOWN SANTO DOMINGO

Caribbean Coffee & Tea
CAFE
(Map p50; Gustavo A Mejia Ricart; ✆8.30am-midnight) Tucked into Plaza Andalucia, a small strip mall, this cafe is popular with a young upscale crowd from the surrounding Los Angeles–like neighborhood. While there's nothing to see other than a busy intersection, sitting at one of the outdoor tables sipping a cappuccino (RD$70) or tea (RD$55) is a pleasant way to while away an afternoon. Wraps (RD$300), paninis (RD$250) and salads (RD$200) are also available.

Haagen-Dazs
CAFE
(Map p50; Av Abraham Lincoln; ✆11am-11pm; ✚) We know it's a Haagen-Dazs, but this modern, sleek and most importantly air-conditioned place is an oasis for families and those foolhardy enough to walk along this sun-baked stretch of asphalt. Shakes (RD$175), ice-cream sodas (RD$135), ice coffees (RD$100) and, of course, plain old ice cream are available.

Praia
BAR, LOUNGE
(Map p50; Gustavo A Mejia Ricart 74; ✆10pm-2am) Replete with an upstairs VIP area and transparent wine cellar, this bar and wine lounge has a little bit Soho with a dash of Miami Beach. The drinks are expensive, though maybe not for the well-heeled Dominican clientele, and the music, suitable for the modern minimalist decor, is electronica.

☆ Entertainment

Santo Domingo has the country's best entertainment scene, from glitzy hotel nightclubs and casinos to small bars and dance spots. And lest you scoff, hotel nightclubs are hugely popular, especially among Santo Domingo's rich, young and restless. Merengue and *bachata* are omnipresent, but house, techno, and American and Latin rock are popular as well. A number of clubs in town cater to gays and lesbians, or at least offer a welcoming mixed atmosphere. Newspapers are a good place to find out about upcoming concerts and shows, and if your Spanish is good, radio stations hype the capital's big events.

Live Music & Nightclubs

Nightclubs come and go, and change names and ownership; however, those in hotels on the Malecón tend to have longer life spans. Most of the clubs have live music some nights and DJs others. Some of the venues attract the wealthiest and hippest in Santo Domingo, but wherever you go, expect people to be dressed to the nines, so definitely no T-shirts, runners or sandals. Admission is up to RD$250 when there's a DJ (most nights) and RD$350 when there's a band.

Guácara Taína
NIGHTCLUB
(☎809-533-1051; www.guacarataina.net; Av Mirador del Sur 655; admission RD$300; ✆9pm-3am Thu-Sun) A somewhat legendary nightclub, now maybe at least as popular with cruise-ship passengers as Dominicans, Guácara Taína is still an interesting place to party. Located inside a huge underground cave in the Parque Mirador del Sur, this club hosts everything from raves to live merengue and hip-hop acts.

Jubilee
NIGHTCLUB
(Map p54; ☎809-221-2222; Renaissance Jaragua Hotel, Av George Washington 367; ✆9pm-4am Tue-Sat) A long-standing hot spot, this nightclub in the Jaragua Hotel continues to draw in

good-looking, well-heeled and well-dressed hordes looking to get down to live merengue music; most nights it doesn't get hopping until around midnight. Drink bills can be pretty steep at the end of a long evening.

Mint
NIGHTCLUB

(Map p54; ☑809-687-1131; www.napolitanohotel.com; Av George Washington 51; admission RD$150; ☺10pm-morning, closed Mon) A smaller and less-glamorous version of the Jubilee is the nightclub at this fairly rundown hotel. But because of its proximity to the Zona Colonial and its more reasonable drink prices, it still gets packed on weekends.

Monte Cristo
NIGHTCLUB, LOUNGE

(Map p50; ☑809-542-5000; Av Jose Amado Soler; ☺6pm-5am) This sophisticated club doubles as a cigar lounge with good wine and mixed drinks thrown in as well. There's a dance floor for merengue and salsa and live music on Wednesday. Weekends tend to be a hodge-podge of salsa, merengue, reggaeton and Latin rock.

Jet Set
NIGHTCLUB

(Map p50; ☑809-535-4145; Av Independencia 2253; admission US$7; ☺9pm-late) A trendy, good-looking crowd flocks to this 7th-floor disco. Besides offering great views of the city, there's live music – salsa, merengue – most nights of the week and *bachata* on Mondays. Happy hour from 5pm to 9pm.

Gay & Lesbian Venues

CHA
NIGHTCLUB

(Av George Washington 165; ☺6pm-3am Fri-Sun, 6pm-1am Sun) A fun place with a Miami beach vibe, good music, shows and strippers. A bar in front is open other days of the week.

Esedeku
BAR

(Map p46; Las Mercedes 341; ☺Tue-Sun 8pm-late) Only a block from Calle El Conde, Esedeku is an intimate bar, popular with local professionals with a huge selection of cocktails; not for hustlers.

Jay-Dee's
NIGHTCLUB

(José Reyes 10; admission RD$250; ☺10pm-3am Wed-Sun) Tourists aren't unusual at this raucous club, which gets crowded on weekends when there are drag shows and strippers. Admission buys you a drink as well.

Arena
NIGHTCLUB

(formerly Aire; Calle Mercedes; ☺10pm-late Wed-Sun) Mix of straight and gay, this rave joint is the place to dance, generally to music from the 1970s and '80s.

Amazonia
BAR

(Dr Delgado 71; ☺8pm-late Fri-Sun) A mostly lesbian bar, the oldest in Santo Domingo, located in Gazcue.

Baseball

Estadio Quisqueya
STADIUM

(Map p50; ☑809-540-5772; www.estadioquisqueya.com.do; cnr Avs Tiradentes & San Cristóbal; tickets RD$250-1000; ☺games 5pm Sun, 8pm Tue, Wed, Fri & Sat) One of the better places to see a game and experience the madness is at the home field for two of the DR's six professional teams, Licey (www.licey.com) and Escogido (www.escogido.com). You can get tickets to most games by arriving at the stadium shortly before the first inning; games between the hometown rivals or Licey and the Águilas sell out more quickly. Asking for the best seats available at the box office is likely to cost RD$1000 and put you within meters of either the ballplayers or the between innings dancers. Scalpers also congregate along the road to the stadium and at the entrance (see p231). A taxi back to the Zona Colonial should run around RD$170.

Cinemas

There are no cinemas in the Zona Colonial. Centro Cultural Español periodically showcases alternative films, mostly by Spanish and Dominican filmmakers. The theater is actually a gallery with a big white wall where DVDs are projected – unfortunately the acoustics aren't the best. Stop by for a current schedule.

Palacio del Cine (Map p50; Blue Mall, Av Winston Churchill), Malecón Center Cinemas (Map p54; Av George Washington 500) and Caribbean Cinemas (Map p50; Acropolis Mall, Av Winston Churchill) all screen Hollywood films as well as a smattering of Dominican and other films; tickets range from RD$75 to RD$300. Check www.cine.com.do for current listings.

Cultural Centers

Casa de Italia
CULTURAL CENTER

(Italian House; Map p46; ☑809-688-1497; cnr Calle Hostos & General Luperón; admission free; ☺9:30am-9pm Mon-Thu, to 6pm Sat) Regularly hosts art exhibits in its 1st-floor gallery; also doubles as an Italian-language institute.

Casa de Teatro   CULTURAL CENTER
(Map p46; ☑809-689-3430; www.casadeteatro
.com; Arzobispo Meriño 110; admission varies;
☺9am-6pm & 8pm-3am Mon-Sat) Housed in
a renovated colonial building, this fantastic arts complex features a gallery with
rotating exhibits by Dominican artists, an
open-air bar and performance space where
music and spoken word shows are held every
weekend, and a theater that regularly hosts
dance and stage productions.

Centro Cultural Español   CULTURAL CENTER
(Spanish Cultural Center; Map p46; ☑809-686-
8212; www.ccesd.org, in Spanish; cnr Arzobispo
Meriño & Arzobispo Portes; admission free; ☺10am-
9pm Tue-Sun) A cultural space run by the
Spanish embassy, this institute regularly
hosts art exhibits, film festivals and musical
concerts, all with a Spanish bent. It also
has 15,000 items in its lending library. For a
listing of events, stop by for a brochure.

Theaters

El Teatro Nacional Eduardo Brito   THEATER
(National Theater; Map p54; ☑809-687-3191; Plaza
de la Cultura; tickets RD$150-500) Hosts opera,
ballet and symphonic performances. Tickets for performances at this 1600-seat theater can be purchased in advance at the box
office from 9:30am to 12:30pm and 3:30pm
to 6:30pm daily. For show dates and times,
call or check the weekend editions of local
newspapers.

Casinos

After baseball, cockfighting and playing the
lottery, gambling is one of the DR's favorite
pastimes. Casinos generally open at 4pm
and close at 4am. Bets may be placed in
Dominican pesos or US dollars. Las Vegas
odds and rules generally apply, though
there are some variations; it doesn't hurt
to ask the dealer what differences he or she
is aware of before you start laying down
money. All of the dealers at these casinos
speak Spanish and English. All of the large
hotels on the Malecón have casinos, as does
the **Hotel Santo Domingo** (Map p50; ☑809-
221-1511; cnr Avs Independencia & Abraham Lincoln)
and **Hispaniola Hotel** (Map p50; ☑809-221-
7111; cnr Avs Independencia & Abraham Lincoln).

🔒 Shopping

More than anywhere else in the country,
shopping in Santo Domingo runs the gamut
from cheap tourist kitsch to high-end quality
collectibles. The easiest – and best – neighborhood to shop in is the Zona Colonial,
where you'll find rows of shops offering
locally made products at decent prices.
Large, American-style malls scattered
around the city have good selections of
clothing, music and shoe stores.

Amber & Larimar

If you're considering buying something in
amber or larimar, shop around since these
stones, considered national treasures, are
virtually ubiquitous in Santo Domingo.
Typically they're presented as jewelry, but
occasionally you'll find figurines, rosaries
and other small objects. For help on choosing amber, see p137. Quality and price vary
greatly and fakes aren't uncommon. In Zona
Colonial, the most recommended places are
Museo de Ambar and Larimar Museum.
Flor Ambar Gift Shop (Map p46; Las Damas
44; ☺9am-6pm) is another recommended
shop.

Cigars

Dominican cigars are widely respected by
aficionados around the world, so much so
that the DR is one of the leading exporters.
To try one for yourself, stop in at one of the
many cigar stores around Santo Domingo –
you'll see several just strolling down Calle El
Conde. Typically, prices vary from US$2 to
US$6 per cigar and boxes can run as high
as US$110.

Boutique del Fumador   CIGARS
(Map p46; Calle El Conde 109; ☺9am-7pm Mon-Sat,
10am-3:30pm Sun) A small boutique shop selling Cohibas (a box of hand rolled for as little
as RD$430) as well as other brands; also
organic Dominican chocolate (RD$200),
coffee (RD$160) and rum (RD$140). They
explain the process from start to finish and
you can see *tabacos* being rolled in the upstairs workshop.

La Leyenda del Cigarro   CIGARS
(Map p46; Calle Hostos 402) This small shop several blocks north of Parque Colón has a good
selection of premium cigars, but equally
importantly, the helpful staff are more than
willing to answer the naive questions of
cigar novices.

Handicrafts

Felipe & Co   HANDICRAFTS
(Map p46; Calle El Conde 105; ☺9am-8pm Mon-Sat,
10am-6pm Sun) This shop on Parque Colón is
stocked with charming high-quality handicrafts, like ceramics, jewelry and handbags,
with also a good selection of paintings. Some

of the best finds are stocked way in the back of this deep shop, easily one of the best in the Zona Colonial.

Muñecas Elisa
HANDICRAFTS

(Map p46; Arzobispo Nouel 54; ◷9am-6pm Mon-Sat) Specializing in Dominican faceless dolls, this spacious shop sells high-quality figurines. Dolls are handcrafted in-house and are made of porcelain; all are also dressed in late-18th-century garb. Prices vary widely according to the size and detail of each and run from US$10 to US$550.

Bettye's Galería
HANDICRAFTS

(Map p46; Plaza de María de Toledo, Isabel la Católica 163; ◷9am-6pm Wed-Mon) Browse through this gallery, connected to the guesthouse of the same name, if you like antiques, jewelry, and quirky souvenirs and paintings.

Art

Walking around Santo Domingo you'll see sidewalk displays of simple, colorful canvases of rural life and landscapes. This so-called Haitian or 'primitive art' is so prevalent that it's understandable if you mistake it for the country's de facto wallpaper. Most of what you see on the street is mass-produced, low-quality amateur pieces with little value. For unique and interesting Dominican pieces, there are a number of more formal galleries in Santo Domingo.

Galería de Arte María del Carmen
ART

(Map p46; Arzobispo Meriño 207; ◷9am-7pm Mon-Sat, 10am-1pm Sun) This place has been selling art long enough to attract a wide range of talented Dominican painters.

Galeria de Arte Candido Bido
ART

(Map p54; Calle Dr Baez 5) Displays the intensely colorful and exuberant works reflecting affection for the rural people of this well-known painter's native Cibao region.

De Soto Galería
ART

(Map p46; Calle Hostos 215; ◷9am-5:30pm Mon-Fri, 9am-noon Sat) This is a small gallery specializing in Dominican and Haitian painters. A rambling array of antiques is also for sale.

Outside of the Zona Colonial are dozens of other galleries that feature Haitian and Dominican art. Galería de Arte El Greco (Map p50; Av Tiradentes 16; ◷8am-noon & 2-6pm Mon-Fri) and Galería de Arte El Pincel (Map p50; Gustavo Mejía Ricart 24; ◷8am-noon & 2-6pm Mon-Fri) are good options.

Markets

Mercado Modelo
MARKET

(Map p46; Av Mella; ◷9am-5pm) Housed in an aging two-story building just north of the Zona Colonial near a neighborhood of Chinese restaurants and stores. Bargain hard at this local market, which sells everything from love potions to woodcarvings and jewelry. The more you look like a tourist, the higher the asking price.

Pulga de Antigüedades
MARKET

(Map p46; Plaza de María de Toledo, Calle General Luperón; ◷9am-4pm Sun) Poke around the clothes, shoes, handicrafts and antiques at this open-air flea market, held every Sunday on a small plaza a block north of Parque Colón.

Maps

Located on the 3rd floor of an aging office building, Mapas Gaar (Map p46; 3rd fl, cnr Calle El Conde & Espaillat; ◷8am-5:30pm Mon-Fri, to 2:30pm Sat) has the best variety and the largest number of maps in the Dominican Republic. Maps are designated by city or region (eg Santo Domingo and Environs, North, Central, South) and include a country map, as well as several city maps on the back of each (RD$250). Road atlases are also sold here.

ⓘ Information

Bookstores

Editorial Duarte (cnr Arzobispo Meriño & Mercedes; ◷8am-7pm Mon-Fri, 8am-6pm Sat) This dusty shop in the Zona Colonial has a good selection of Spanish-language fiction books, foreign-language dictionaries and maps.

Librería Cuesta (www.cuestalibros.com; cnr Av 27 de Febrero & Abraham Lincoln; ◷9am-9pm Mon-Sat, 10am-8pm Sun) This modern, two-story Dominican version of Barnes & Noble is easily the nicest and largest bookstore in the city; upstairs cafe with wi-fi. Attached to the Supermercado Nacional.

Libreria La Trinitaria (Av Arzobispo Nouel 160) Best shop for those interested in Dominican poetry.

Librería Pichardo (cnr José Reyes & Calle El Conde; ◷8am-7pm Mon-Thu, to 5:30pm Fri, to 1pm Sun) Some early and antique Spanish-language books, mostly on colonial history and Latin American literature and poetry, plus some curios. Bargain to get a good price.

Thesaurus Musica Libros Cafe (cnr Avs Sarasota & Abraham Lincoln; ◷9am-9pm Mon-Sat, 10am-3pm Sun) Rivals Librería Cuesta for nicest bookstore; upstairs cafe.

Dangers & Annoyances

Pick-pocketing, especially on buses or in clubs, is the main concern for visitors to Santo Domingo. Being alert to the people around you and being careful with your wallet or purse (or even leaving them in the safety deposit box back at the hotel) is the best defense. Muggings are less common, especially of tourists, but they do happen occasionally. The Zona Colonial is generally very safe to walk around, day or night. The Malecón is safe as well, but be extra cautious if you've been drinking or you're leaving a club or casino especially late. Gazcue is a mellow residential area, but street lights are few and far between. If you have a long way to walk or you're unsure of the neighborhood, play it safe and call or hail a taxi.

Emergency

Politur (tourist police; ☑809-682-2151; cnr Calle El Conde & José Reyes; ⊘24hr) Can handle most situations; for general police, ambulance and fire dial ☑911.

Internet Access & Telephone

Most charge around RD$35 per hour.

Abel Brawn's Internet World (2nd fl, Plaza Lomba; ⊘9am-9pm Mon-Sat, 10am-4pm Sat) Fast internet access, as well as international phone service.

Centro de Internet (Av Independencia 201; ⊘8:30am-9pm Mon-Sat, 8:30am-3pm Sun) Internet and call center in Gazcue.

Codetel Centro de Comunicaciones (Calle El Conde 202; ⊘8am-9:30pm) Large call center and has internet access to boot.

Cyber Red (Sánchez 201; ⊘9am-9pm Mon-Sat) Just off Calle El Conde; you can also make international calls here.

Internet/Phone Center (Calle El Conde; ⊘9am-10pm) On last block of Calle El Conde before you reach Parque Independencia.

Internet Resources

Colonial zone (www.dr-colonialzone.com) A detailed site with information and reviews on everything – historical sites, hotels, restaurants, bars – as well as discussions on Dominican history, superstitions and more.

Laundry

Many hotels do laundry, though they typically charge per piece, which adds up real fast. The only other place to go in the Zona Colonial is **Lavandería Colonial** (Padre Billini 205).

Medical Services

Centro de Obstetricia y Ginecología (☑809-221-7322; cnr Av Independencia & José Joaquín Pérez; ⊘24hr) This hospital specializes in gynecology and obstetrics, but is equipped to handle all emergencies.

Clínica Abreu (☑809-687-4922; cnr Av Independencia & Beller; ⊘24hr) Widely regarded as the best hospital in the city, this is where members of many of the embassies go.

Farmacia San Judas (☑809-685-8165; cnr Av Independencia & Pichardo; ⊘24hr) Free delivery.

Farmax (☑809-333-4000; cnr Av Independencia & Dr Delgado; ⊘24hr) Free delivery.

Hospital Padre Billini (☑809-221-8272; Sánchez; ⊘24hr) The closest public hospital to the Zona Colonial, service is free here but expect long waiting lines.

Money

There are several major banks with ATMs in the Zona Colonial. Gazcue also has a number of banks and others are scattered throughout the city, especially around major thoroughfares like Av 27 de Febrero and Av Abraham Lincoln. Large hotels, particularly those on the Malecón, all have at least one ATM.

Banco de Reservas Zona Colonial (cnr Isabel la Católica & Las Mercedes); Gazcue & Malecón (cnr Av Independencia & Máximo Gómez)

Banco Popular (cnr Av Abraham Lincoln & Gustavo A Mejia Ricart)

Banco Progreso (cnr Av Independencia & Socorro Sánchez)

Scotiabank (cnr Isabel la Católica & Las Mercedes)

Post

Federal Express (☑809-565-3636; www.fedex.com; cnr Av de los Próceres & Camino del Oeste, Arroyo Hondo) Recommended for important shipments.

Post office (Map p46; Isabel la Católica; ⊘8am-5pm Mon-Fri, 9am-noon Sat) Facing Parque Colón in the Zona Colonial.

Tourist Information

Tourist office (Map p46; ☑809-686-3868; Isabel la Católica 103; ⊘9am-3pm Mon-Fri) Located beside Parque Colón, this office has a handful of brochures and maps. Some English and French spoken.

Travel Agencies

Colonial Tour & Travel (☑809-688-5285; www.colonialtours.com.do; Arzobispo Meriño 209) A few meters north of the Calle El Conde promenade, this long-running professional outfit is good for booking flights, hotel rooms, and any and all excursions from mountain biking to rafting to whale-watching. English, Italian and French spoken.

Explora Eco Tours (☑809-567-1852; www.exploraecotours.com; Gustavo A Mejia Ricart 43) Specializes in organizing customized tours, from a single day to a week long, of national parks, nature preserves and rural communities. Website announces regularly scheduled trips open to general public.

Giada Tours & Travel (☎809-682-4525; www .giadatours.com; Hostal Duque de Wellington, Av Independencia 304) Friendly professional outfit arranges domestic and international plane tickets, and also conducts area tours.

Tody Tours (☎809-686-0882; www.todytours .com) Former Peace Corps volunteer who specializes in tropical birding tours all over the country and at the National Botanical Gardens in Santo Domingo (three hours per person US$10).

ℹ Getting There & Away

Air

Santo Domingo has two airports: the main one, **Aeropuerto Internacional Las Américas** (SDQ; ☎809-947-2220), is 22km east of the city. The smaller **Aeropuerto Internacional La Isabela Dr Joaquin Balaguer** (JBQ, aka Higuero; ☎809-826-4003), north of the city, handles mostly domestic carriers and air taxi companies.

AeroDomca, Air Century, Caribbean Air Sign, DominicaShuttles, Take Off and Volair connect Santo Domingo, primarily Aeropuerto La Isabela, to Punta Cana (US$99), Las Terrenas (US$80), Santiago and La Romana. See p251 for more information.

Most international flights come into and depart from Las Américas. The major carriers:

Air France Airport (☎809-549-0309); Central Santo Domingo (☎809-686-8432; Plaza El Faro, Av Máximo Gómez 15) The city branch shares its office with KLM.

American Airlines (☎809-542-5151; Bella Vista Mall, Av Sarasota 6)

Continental Airlines (☎809-262-1060; Ste 104, cnr Max Henríquez Ureña & Winston Churchill)

Copa (☎reservations 809-472-2233, airport 809-549-0757)

Delta (☎809-955-1500; Plaza Comercial Acropolis Center, cnr Av Winston Churchill & Andres Julio Aybar)

Iberia Airport (☎809-950-6050); Santo Domingo (☎809-227-0188; Av Lope de Vega 63)

Jet Blue (☎809-947-2220) Located at the airport.

LanChile (☎809-682-8133; Av George Washington 353)

Lufthansa/Condor (☎809-689-9625; Av George Washington 353)

US Airways (☎809-540-0505; Gustavo Mejía Ricart 54)

For more details on international air travel to and from the Santo Domingo area, see p250.

Boat

The DR's only international ferry service, *Caribbean Fantasy*, now run by **America Cruise Ferries** (☎in Santo Domingo 809-688-4400, in Mayagüez, Puerto Rico 787-832-4800, in San Juan, Puerto Rico 787-622-4800) connects Santo Domingo with San Juan and Mayagüez, Puerto Rico. The ticket office and boarding area are in the Puerto Don Diego on Av del Puerto opposite Fortaleza Ozama in the Zona Colonial. The ferry departs Santo Domingo at 7pm on Sunday, 8pm Tuesday and Thursday and returns from San Juan at 7pm Monday and Mayagüez at 8pm on Wednesday and Friday. The trip from Santo Domingo takes 12 hours (eight hours in the other direction; difference is because of prevailing currents) and costs US$189 round-trip.

The other major terminal that handles cruise ships is the **Puerto Sans Souci** (www.sans souci.com.do) on the eastern bank of the Rio Ozama, directly across from the Zona Colonial.

Bus

FIRST-CLASS BUSES The country's two main bus companies – **Caribe Tours** (Map p43; ☎809-221-4422; www.caribetours.com.do; cnr Avs 27 de Febrero & Leopoldo Navarro) and **Metro** (Map p50; ☎809-227-0101; www.metro serviciosturisticos.com; Calle Francisco Prats Ramírez) – have individual depots west of the Zona Colonial. Caribe Tours has the most departures, and covers more of the smaller towns than Metro does. In any case, all but a few destinations are less than four hours from Santo Domingo.

It's a good idea to call ahead to confirm the schedule and always arrive at least 30 minutes before the stated departure time. Both bus lines also publish brochures (available at all terminals) with up-to-date schedules and fares, plus the address and telephone number of their terminals throughout the country – handy if you'll be taking the bus often.

Expreso Bávaro Punta Cana (Map p54; ☎in Santo Domingo 809-682-9670, in Bávaro 809-552-1678; cnr Juan Sánchez Ruiz & Av Máximo Gómez) has a direct service between the capital and Bávaro, with a stop in La Romana. Departure times in both directions are 7am, 10am, 2pm and 4pm (RD$350, four hours). Some drivers are flexible and let passengers off at other stops in the city.

SECOND-CLASS BUSES Four depots surround Parque Enriquillo in the Zona Colonial. All buses make numerous stops en route. Because the buses tend to be small, there can be a scrum for seats, especially for destinations with one to a few departures a day. Since Metro and Caribe service the major destinations, especially those over several hours away, these should be avoided in the interest of comfort and

First-Class

DESTINATION	FARE (RD$)	DURATION (HR)	DISTANCE (KM)	FREQUENCY (PER DAY)
Ázua	180	1¼	120	8
Barahona	260	3½	200	4
Dajabón	350	5	305	4
Jarabacoa	270	3	155	4
La Vega	200	1½	125	every 30min 6am-8pm
Las Matas de Santa Cruz	350	2½	250	4
Monte Cristi	350	4	270	6
Nagua	310	3½	180	11
Puerto Plata	320	4	215	hourly 6am-7pm
Río San Juan	320	4½	215	5
Samaná	310	2½	245	6
San Francisco de Macorís	250	2½	135	every 30-60min 7am-6pm
San Juan de la Maguana	260	2½	163	4
Sánchez	310	4	211	6
Santiago	270	2½	155	every 30min 6am-8pm
Sosúa	320	5	240	hourly 6am-7pm

Second-Class

DESTINATION	FARE (RD$)	DURATION (HR)	FREQUENCY
Baní	100	1½	every 15min 5am-10pm
Boca Chica	caliente/ expreso 40/50	½	caliente every 10min, expreso every 15min 6am-8pm
Higüey	210	2½	every 30min 6am-7pm
Juan Dolio	75	1	every 30min 6am-9:30pm
La Romana	caliente/ expreso 125/160	1½	caliente every 10min, expreso every 20min 5am-9pm
Las Galeras	325	6	daily btwn 11:30am & 12:30pm depending on when bus arrives from Las Galeras
San Cristóbal	50	1	every 15-30min 6am to 10pm
San Pedro de Macorís	80	1	every 30min 6am-9:30pm
Santiago	200	2½	take any Sosúa bus

sanity. *Caliente*, literally 'hot' buses, refer to those generally without air-con; *expreso* buses stop less often.

BUSES TO HAITI Capital Coach Line (Map p43; ☎809-530-8266; www.capitalcoachline .com; Av 27 de Febrero 455) and Caribe Tours offer daily bus services to Port-au-Prince. Capital Coach Line has one 8am departure daily that stops in Tabarre and ends in Petion Ville, neighborhoods in Port-au-Prince, and another at 10am that goes only to Tabarre; Caribe Tours has daily departures at 9am and 11am to Petion Ville. Both companies use comfortable, air-con buses, the trip takes from six to eight hours and both cost around US$68 (includes taxes). If possible, make a reservation at least two days in advance as the buses are frequently full.

Car

Numerous international and domestic car-rental companies have more than one office in Santo Domingo proper and at Las Américas International Airport – the majority have a booth in a small building just across the street from the arrivals exit. All are open daily roughly from 7am to 6pm in Santo Domingo (sometimes later) and from 7am to 11:30pm at the airport. For more information about costs, rental requirements etc, see p254.

Recommended car-rental companies:

Avis Airport (☎809-549-0468); Central Santo Domingo (☎809-535-7191; Av George Washington 517)

Dollar Airport (☎809-549-0738); Central Santo Domingo (☎809-221-7368; Av Independencia 366)

Europcar Airport (☎809-549-0942); Central Santo Domingo (☎809-688-2121; Av Independencia 354)

Hertz Airport (☎809-549-0454); Central Santo Domingo (☎809-221-5333; Av José Ma Heredia 1)

National/Alamo Airport (☎809-549-8303); Central Santo Domingo (☎809-221-0805; Av Independencia at Máximo Gómez)

Thrifty (☎809-549-0930; Las Américas International Airport)

❶ Getting Around

To/From the Airport

There are no buses that connect directly to either of Santo Domingo's airports. From Las Américas, a taxi into the city costs US$30 to US$35, with only a little room for negotiation. The trip is a solid half-hour. If there are any other travelers arriving when you do, try sharing a ride. Taxis are available at the airport 24 hours a day.

---

❶ SANTO DOMINGO–SAMANÁ HWY

Though the recently inaugurated Santo Domingo–Samaná Hwy (aka Juan Pablo II or DR-7) is extremely important to the Península de Samaná's development for good or ill, the turnoff to the two-lane, 102km road is extremely difficult to find. Hopefully, the signage will be improved in the near future, but until then here's some help in finding your way coming from Santo Domingo: drive east on the coastal road and past the toll booth for the airport; make a U-turn and continue slowly in the far right lane until you spot the small sign for Samaná.

Many taxis, including Apolo Taxi, may be willing to take you from the city to the airport for less.

The fare from La Isabela is more reasonable at US$10 to US$15. There's no permanent taxi stand there, but at least one or two taxis meet every flight. If, for whatever reason, there are no taxis around when you arrive, call one of the companies mentioned in the Taxi section.

Car

Driving in Santo Domingo can challenge the nerves and test the skills of even the most battle-hardened driver. Heavy traffic, aggressive drivers, especially taxis and buses, and little attention to or enforcement of rules means a free-for-all. Drive with caution and whenever possible have a passenger help you navigate the streets. Finding parking is not typically a problem, though if you are leaving your car overnight, ask around for a parking lot. Many midrange and top-end hotels have parking with 24-hour guards. In any case, be sure not to leave any valuables inside your car.

Public Transportation

BUS The cost of a bus ride from one end of the city to the other is around RD$10 (6:30am to 9:30pm). Most stops are marked with a sign and the word *parada* (stop). The routes tend to follow major thoroughfares – in the Zona Colonial, Parque Independencia is where Av Bolívar (the main westbound avenue) begins and Av Independencia (the main eastbound avenue) ends. If you're trying to get across town, just look at a map and note the major intersections along the way and plan your transfers accordingly.

METRO Only Line 1 from La Feria (Centro de los Héroes) near the Malecón to the far northern suburb of Villa Mella was in operation at the time of research (6:30am to 11:30pm Monday to Friday, to 10pm Saturday). There are 16 stations over the 14.5km route that primarily runs north–south above and below ground along Av Máximo Gómez. It's worth a trip for travelers primarily to get a sense of Santo Domingo's size and sprawl and for the rather stunning views over the rooftops and scattered palm trees and mountains in the distance. The entrances, stations and subway cars are modern and clean, certainly a world above New York City subways for one. Each ride costs RD$20; however, it's best to purchase a card at one of the ticket booths for RD$50, which can then be refilled when needed. Place the card on top of the turnstile to enter the station. If and when the total six lines are completed (the inauguration target date for the other lines are unclear), it should help to alleviate the terrible city traffic.

PÚBLICOS Even more numerous than buses are the *públicos* – mostly beaten-up minivans

'Centro de Héroes to Mamá Tingó.' Not exactly the same ring as 'Times Square to Broadway,' but functional nevertheless. Caribbean islands and underground metros usually don't appear to go together; but Santo Domingo is joining San Juan, Puerto Rico, as the second city in the region to have a commuter train system. Dominicans are already riding to work on the 14km track from the northern suburbs to downtown (16 stops, 10 underground). Whether this will have any impact on the city's disastrous traffic is another matter. And whether this is a misguided and even cynical project that will only benefit politicians and contractors, a white elephant on par with the Faro a Colón, or whether it's a much needed modernization of Santo Domingo's failing transportation system is up for debate.

Ask any taxi driver in the city what they think of the project and they're likely to respond skeptically. Many will question whether this is a good use of public funds in a country with substandard education and health care. And the big dig certainly isn't doing anything to help traffic in the meantime. Pop culture has weighed in on the debate: 'Now we have a Metro' is the sarcastic refrain for a song about the country's failures by the Dominican rap group La Krema.

The fact that stations are named after well-known Dominicans (and foreigners like John F Kennedy and Abraham Lincoln) rather than streets may be inconvenient, but it may also lead some to brush up on their history. The Santo Domingo metro: convenient and educational.

and private cars that follow the same main routes but stop wherever someone flags them down. They are supposed to have *público* on their license plates, but drivers will beep and wave at you long before you can make out the writing. Any sort of hand waving will get the driver to stop, though the preferred gesture is to hold out your arm and point down at the curb in front of you. The fare is RD$12 – pay when you get in. Be prepared for a tight squeeze – drivers will cram seven or even eight passengers into an ordinary two-door car.

Taxi

Taxis in Santo Domingo don't have meters, so you should always agree on the price before climbing in. The standard fare is around RD$150 from one side of the city to another; rates tend to be higher in the evening. Within the Zona Colonial it should be even cheaper. Taxi drivers don't typically cruise the streets looking for rides; they park at various major points and wait for customers to come to them. In the Zona Colonial, Parque Colón and Parque Duarte are the best spots.

You can also call for a taxi or ask the receptionist at your hotel to do so. Service is usually quick, the fare is the same, and you don't have to lug your bags anywhere. Many of the top hotels have taxis waiting at the ready outside, but expect to pay more for those. Reputable taxi agencies with 24-hour dispatches include **Aero-Taxi** (☎809-685-1212), **Apolo Taxi** (☎809-537-7771), **Super Taxi** (☎809-536-7014) and **Amarillo Taxi** (☎809-620-6363).

Punta Cana & the Southeast

Includes »

Best Places to Eat

» Restaurante Playa Blanca (p103)

» Mama Mia (p94)

» Chez Mon Ami (p103)

» Ristorante El Sueño (p83)

Best Places to Stay

» Paraíso Caño Hondo (p107)

» Casa de Campo (p87)

» Barceló Bávaro Palace Deluxe (p102)

» Hotel Limón (p106)

Why Go?

A Caribbean workhorse of sun and sand, the southeast is synonymous with go-big-or-go-home tourism and carries the weight of the Dominican Republic's most dramatic beaches and cerulean seas on its tanned, well-toned shoulders. Sprawling resort developments, some like city-states unto themselves, line much of the beachfront from Punta Cana to Bávaro, offering families, couples and the young and restless alike a hassle-free Caribbean holiday on some of the most idyllic environs in the region. But there is life beyond Punta Cana. Less-crowded beach towns like Bayahibe and Juan Dolio offer only slightly less dramatic seascapes but sands that go unshared with the masses; and isolated getaways like Playa Limón, beyond the sugar plantations and inland mountains to the north, showcase a different and worthwhile side of the Southeast if you can tear yourself away from the buffets long enough to take the rewarding journeys required to make their acquaintance.

When to Go

If you're looking for a fiesta, North American Spring Breakers descend upon Punta Cana – March sees the most traffic, both petrol-fueled and margarita-fueled. If you're not on Spring Break, this is probably a bad time for that leisurely family vacation. If you can hold off just past the winter holidays, January and February offers the same sun and sand as Christmas and New Year's Eve – but a whole lot less people. And for those pinching pesos, October rides the tranquil fence between hurricane season and the preholiday onslaught. *¡Salud!*

History

Before sugar, it was cattle ranching and the cutting and exporting of hardwoods that drove the region's economy. But Cuban planters, fleeing war in their country, began to arrive in the southeast in the 1870s and established sugar mills with the Dominican government's assistance (this migration also explains baseball's popularity and importance in the region). Rail lines were built and La Romana and San Pedro de Macorís, formerly sleepy backwaters, began to prosper as busy ports almost immediately when world sugar prices soared. Hundreds of families from the interior migrated to the area in search of jobs. In 1920, after peasants were dispossessed of their land during the US occupation, many fought a guerrilla war against the marines in the area around Hato Mayor and El Seibo. Until the 1960s, the economy in the southeast was still strictly driven by sugar despite fluctuations in the world market and agriculture in general. However, when the US company Gulf & Western Industries bought La Romana's sugar mill, invested heavily in the cattle and cement industries and, perhaps most importantly, built the Casa de Campo resort, tourism became the financial engine of the southeast, and remains so today.

ⓘ Getting There & Around

The majority of international visitors to this region fly directly to the airport in Punta Cana (see p104) and then are whisked away in private vehicles to their respective resorts. Otherwise, it's anywhere from a 2½- to four-hour drive, depending on your destination, from Aeropuerto Internacional Las Américas in Santo Domingo. La Romana has an airport as well, though it mostly handles charter flights (see p89).

Traffic between the resort centers can be surprisingly heavy and it's difficult to navigate much of the road system, which is being revamped and expanded. Though the distances aren't great, travel in the region, especially along the coast north of Bávaro all the way to Sabana de la Mar, can be slow and unreliable because of the poor condition of the roads. It's now possible to fly between Punta Cana and the Península de Samaná.

Cross Río Ozama, the eastern border of the Zona Colonial in Santo Domingo, and the claustrophobia fades, the horizon opens and you remember that you're in the Caribbean. The highway hugs the coast for some time with promising views but then retreats inland once again, passing service stations and shops hugging the roadside until the turnoff for the beach resorts of Boca Chica and Juan Dolio a little further on.

Parque Nacional Submarino La Caleta

In the past this underwater park was a park in name only; little was done to protect the 12 sq km of underwater acreage in front of the Aeropuerto Internacional Las Américas. As a result of lax controls and the damage from Hurricane Jean in 2004, the number of coral and fish species here is very low. It is also the resting place of the *Hickory*, a salvage ship that was scuttled in 1984, the year the park was founded and now a popular dive site, depending on which dive operator you choose. If you're interested in diving here, contact one of the dive shops in Boca Chica or any of the resorts in Juan Dolio. Some will tell you they refuse to go there as the site has been over-dived and is destroyed, while others say it's still full of marine life.

Boca Chica

POP 58,200

Boca Chica is a survivor. After enduring development boom-bust cycles and being overshadowed by resorts further east, it staggers on, albeit catering to a weathered crowd and marred by sex tourism. It held a certain amount of cachet when the moneyed class built vacation homes here during Trujillo's regime, and in the 1960s when a few bayside hotels were built, and even again in the early 1990s during another construction boom. These days, however, aside from its proximity to the capital and the airport, there's not a lot to recommend it; after all, it's not much further to nicer resorts to the east.

◉ Sights

The thing about the beach at Boca Chica is that it's in Boca Chica. This means that

Punta Cana & the Southeast Highlights

1 Relaxing on endless soft white beaches and diving into bottomless all-inclusive buffets in **Bávaro** and **Punta Cana** (p98)

2 Plying the mangrove-infested forests of **Parque**

Nacional Los Haitises (p108) on a serene kayak excursion

3 Riding the wind on a local's sailboat along the coast near **Bayahibe** (p89)

4 Plunging into crystal-clear waters on a snorkeling or diving trip in the waters around **Parque Nacional del Este** (p89)

5 Journeying through colorful Caribbean *colonias*

ATLANTIC OCEAN

N

| 0 | | 30 km |
| 0 | | 20 miles |

Reserva Científica
Lagunas Redonda
y Limón

Laguna Redonda
Punta Gorda

5 Playa Limón

104

La Mina
de Miches   El Cedro   Las Lisas

Sabana de Nisibón

Los Tosones   Playa del Muerto

El Eslabón

Oriental

104

El Seibo   Lagunas
de Nisibón   Playa del Macao

Cañada   El Macao
Honda

105   Playa El Cortecito

El Cortecito   Playa Bávaro

El Pintado   Bonao

Otra Banda   **1 Bávaro**

4   Chava de   Playa Cabeza de Toro
Bávaro

Batey Sabana   La Enea   Playa Cabo Engaño
de Chabón

El Guanito   Veron
HIGÜEY   *Aeropuerto
Internacional*   **1 Punta Cana**
Guayamate   Magdelena   Punta Cana   Playa Punta Cana

Guerrero   **La Altagracia**

La Romana

101

**LA
ROMANA**   Juanillo   Playa
Juanillo

4   San Rafael del Yuma

Altos de Chavón

Boca de Chavón   Boca de Yuma

Playa Minitas   **3 Bayahibe**   Playa Blanca

Cueva del Puente   *Bahía
de Yuma*
Playa Dominicus   Cabo
San Rafael

Guaraguao   **4**   Martel
*Parque
Nacional
del Este*

El Peñon   Granchorra

Punta
Algibe
Paseo del   Isla Catalinita
Catuano   Shark Point
Punta Gorda   Punta Roca

Isla Saona

Mano Juan   Punta Cana

and lush mountains to the wild
and deserted **Playa Limón**
(p105)

6 Going deep into the
fascinating illuminated
underworld at **Cueva de las**

Maravillas (p85), an enormous
cavern complex near La Romana

7 Blissing out on the tranquil
sands of **Juan Dolio** (p82),
the best beach near Santo
Domingo

8 Taking in the 7th Inning
stretch at **Estadio Tetelo
Vargas** (p84) in San Pedro
de Macorís, the DR's baseball
capital

despite the powdery white sand and tranquil waters, it's unlikely to be a relaxing experience. Flanked by Av Caracol and Av 24 de Junio, **Playa Boca Chica** is lined with coconut palms and food stands, restaurants and bars. During the day, the beach is filled with locals and foreigners, and vendors selling everything from fruit to cigars to large canvases of Haitian paintings. The view is unfortunately of loading cranes and a sugar refinery in the distance.

🏃 Activities

There are over 25 dive sites in the area; most are located in the Parque Nacional Submarino La Caleta, with its two shipwrecks and myriad coral heads, though views are mixed if any sites within the park are still worth diving. A more recent shipwreck, the *Catuan*, a 33m-long troller sunk in 2006, is reportedly in better shape (if you head to the park, do so in a large dive boat). The water is warm – averaging 25°C – and the visibility ranges between 5m and 28m, depending on the season. Dive trips to a nearby cave are also offered, as are trips to the waters near Bayahibe and Isla Catalina.

There are two reputable dive shops in town – **Treasure Divers** (☑809-523-5320; www.treasuredivers.net; Don Juan Beach Resort; ☺8:30am-5pm), on Playa Boca Chica at Don Juan Beach Resort, and **Caribbean Divers** (☑809-854-3483; www.caribbeandivers.de; enter at Av Duarte 28; ☺8:30am-5pm), also on the beach. Dives average US$40 with equipment rental, but multidive packages bring the prices down a little. PADI courses (open water diver US$425) are also offered.

👉 Tours

Cigua Tours (☑809-877-1689; www.erika-cigua-tours.com; cnr Av Duarte & Calle Domínguez; ☺9am-noon & 4-6pm), a German-run tour company operating out of a clapboard kiosk, also has an office in Juan Dolio. Trips on offer include Santo Domingo (per person US$30), Isla Saona (per person US$60), Isla Catalina (per person US$60) and Los Haitises National Park (per person US$65).

🛏 Sleeping

TOP CHOICE **Rita Neptuno's Refugio** GUESTHOUSE **$$**
(☑809-523-9934; Calle Duarte; www.dominicana.de /hotel-neptuno-english.htm; r from US$50, 1-bedroom apt US$60, with seaview US$65; P ❋ @ ☞ ☎) This friendly hotel is your best bet for comfort

and mainstream traveler atmosphere – a textbook testament to the definition of refuge with chirping birds, friendly cats, lush common areas and Caribbean views. Service is relaxed but efficient and the cozy apartments come with fully equipped kitchens, private balconies and a well-maintained pool area.

Be Live Hamaca HOTEL **$$$**
(☑809-523-4611; www.belivehotels.com; Calle Duarte near Av Caracol; all-incl s/d from US$173/ 252; P ❋ @ ☞ ☎ ♨) Just because it's the prettiest of Boca Chica's upscale resorts, doesn't mean it's the belle of the ball – service and reservation issues abound, along with a curiously dark lobby that will put a depressing spin on your sun-drenched fun. But its location, on a strategic piece of beachfront property on the eastern edge of town, is a winner, as is the new, Mykonos-blue-on-white 'Presidential Suites' annex, featuring sleek, pastel-hued tropical motifs and earthy stone bathrooms.

Hotel Residencial El Candil HOTEL **$$**
(☑809-523-4252; www.hotelcandil.com; cnr Calle Juanico García 2 & Av 20 de Diciembre; r from US$37; P ❋ @ ☎ ☞) Although it's located several blocks from the beachfront, El Candil is nevertheless good value. There are 24 apartments with kitchenettes in several three-story buildings surrounding a small but well-kept pool and garden area.

🍴 Eating & Drinking

Av Duarte is lined with restaurants and bars, many of which spill over with an unwholesome crowd. Where possible, we have chosen restaurants where this is less prevalent.

TOP CHOICE **Neptuno's Club Restaurant** SEAFOOD **$$$**
(☑809-523-9419; Calle Duarte 12; mains RD$440-1100; ☺lunch & dinner) This wind-shaken restaurant-club across the street from Rita Neptuno's Refugio is tops for style and food. The expansive overwater deck gleams with illuminated-shell lighting over lounge-style beds and all-white mini-cabanas. The food excels, with above-average seafood specialties like lobster lasagne (RD$990; more *au gratin* than traditional lasagna), seafood casserole (RD$850) and signature red snapper stuffed with saffron and calamari (RD$825).

Pequeña Suiza SWISS, ITALIAN **$$**
(☑809-523-4619; Av Duarte 56; breakfast RD$160-270, fondue RD$430-620; ☺breakfast, lunch &

dinner; ☎) One of the better places to eat any time of day – English breakfast in the morning and fondue, the house specialty, at night. There's a lengthy list of excellent pastas that bridge the gap (try the spicy *fra diavolo*). Hardly *pequeña* (little), it's a great cafe-bar right on busy Av Duarte with an elegant dining room in the back. Real lemons even make an appearance here!

La Svolta   ITALIAN **$$**
(Calle Pedro Mella near Av Duarte; mains RD$180-580; ☻lunch & dinner; ☎) An excellent Italian-run seafooder offering a breezy dining room under a cozy thatched roof. Well-presented pasta and seafood dishes are the rule, highlighted by the wondrously simple *mero alla criolla*, a revelation with an imported tomato sauce that pops with flavor. There's real Italian espresso and a small bar that opens at 5pm.

Restaurant Buxceda II   SEAFOOD, CARIBBEAN **$$**
(cnr Av Duarte & Calle Hungria; mains RD$200-775; ☻breakfast, lunch & dinner) A solid, unpretentious spot serving a wealth of fresh fish, shrimp, lobster, paella and conch from a hand-painted wall menu. Simple dishes come in a variety of preps with your choice of rice, plantains or fries and arrive on white tablecloths that give the place an air of upscaled dreams it wouldn't otherwise induce.

Restaurant Boca Marina   SEAFOOD **$$$**
(Calle Duarte 12A; mains RD$380-980; ☻breakfast, lunch & dinner) For something more civilized, plop yourself down at this trendy overwater bar and restaurant on the eastern edge of town – the sunset scene on the gorgeous, rice-white patio evoke painstakingly more hip locales than the DR, and, candlelit at night, it's quite romantic as well. The pricy seafood menu is average – a sundowner is the way to go (cocktails RD$90 to RD$270).

❶ Information
Dangers & Annoyances
Boca Chica is home to a brazenly aggressive sex tourism industry, which has only flourished further since the Port-au-Prince earthquake in 2010, when destitute Haitian women – many of whom are underage – flooded the DR. Tourism police do occasional sweeps of Av Duarte and its surroundings, but are little match for the world's oldest profession. If you've just come for an airport-adjacent overnight, you're in for a shock.

Emergency
Politur (☎523-5120; Av Duarte) Tourist police.

Internet Access & Telephone
Codetel Centro de Comunicaciones (Av San Rafael near Av Caracol; ☻9am-6pm Mon-Sat, 9-12am Sun) International telephone service; the main entrance is on Av Duarte.

Internet Flash (Av Duarte; ☻9am-8pm; per hr US$1.60) Just west of Parque Central.

Punto.com (La Plaza, Av Duarte; ☻8am-7pm; per hr US$1.90) Small internet cafe just past the Italian deli in La Plaza shopping center.

Medical Services
Farmacia Boca Chica (Av Duarte near Av Juan Bautista Vicini; ☻8am-9pm Mon-Sat, 9am-7pm Sun)

Money
Banco Popular (cnr Av Duarte & Av Juan Bautista Vicini; ☻8am-3pm Mon-Fri, 9am-1pm Sun) Opposite the southwest corner of Parque Central.

BanReservas (cnr Av San Rafael & Calle Juanico García; ☻8am-5pm Mon-Fri, 9am-1pm Sat)

Post
Post office (Av Duarte near Av Juan Bautista Vicini)

❶ Getting There & Away
Boca Chica comprises a 10-by-15-block area between Hwy 3 and Bahía de Andrés. From the highway there are three main avenues – 24 de Junio, Juan Bautista Vicini and Caracol – that lead downhill to the oceanfront streets of Av San Rafael and Av Duarte. It's only 8km to Aeropuerto Internacional Las Américas and 33km to Santo Domingo, both to the west.

Gua-guas service Boca Chica to Santo Domingo (*caliente/expreso* RD$40/50, 30 minutes, *caliente* every 10 minutes, *expreso* every 15 minutes, from 6:30am to 10:45pm), departing on the north side of Parque Central and along Av San Rafael.

If you're heading east, *caliente gua-guas* stop at the intersection of the highway and Av Caracol. Destinations include Juan Dolio (RD$30, 15 minutes, every 30 minutes from 6am to 10pm), San Pedro de Macorís (RD$50, 40 minutes, every 40 minutes from 6:30am to 10pm), La Romana (RD$125, 1½ hours, every two hours from 5:30am to 10pm) and Higüey (RD$200, 2½ hours, every two to three hours from 6am to 7pm). *Expreso* services leave from Santo Domingo only.

If you prefer taxis, you can often find one near the intersection of Av San Rafael and Av Caracol. Alternatively, you can get door-to-door service by calling the **Taxi Turístico Boca Chica** (☎809-523-4946). One-way fares include Aeropuerto Internacional Las Américas (US$25), Santo Domingo (US$40), Juan Dolio (US$30), San Pedro de Macorís (US$45), La Romana (US$100) and Higüey (US$130).

ⓘ Getting Around

Boca Chica is small and easily covered on foot. Despite this, you'll likely by asked if you need a ride by every passing *motoconcho* (motorcycle taxi). When not cruising the streets, they can be found congregating near the Parque Central. Rides around town cost RD$50. Use only those with orange vests.

Juan Dolio

The recession hasn't been kind to parts of Juan Dolio, a tranquil beach town about 20km east of rambunctious Boca Chica. Once tipped as the Caribbean's next hot spot, real estate speculation and investors flocked here since development began in earnest in the late 1980s, but these days, you'll see more 'For Sale' signs and half-finished condos on the west side than smiles and sunshine. Of course, the news isn't all bad: Juan Dolio is one of the few beach towns in the area that caters somewhat to independent budget travelers and the laidback feel around town makes losing a few days here far from difficult.

The public beach itself on the west side of town is fairly small and cramped, but the area in front of the resorts to the more prosperous east side of town is wider and softer than in nearby Boca Chica. Most tourists stay at one of the several all-inclusive resorts on the east side, however there's enough of a trickle of guests, independent travelers, loyal expats (mainly retired Germans and Italians) and Dominicans to keep a handful of bars and restaurants on the more free-spirited west side of town in business.

🛏 Sleeping

The intersection of Entrada a los Conucos and Carretera Local is the main area in town, with a number of restaurants, bars, shops and services clustered nearby. Most of the hotels, including all of the resorts, are east of there, and not within walking distance if you're carrying baggage.

Hotel Fior di Loto　　　GUESTHOUSE **$**
(☎809-526-1146; www.fiordilotohotel.com; Carretera Vieja; dm US$5; d US$15-25, d with kitchen

US$30, apt with kitchen US$45; ℗@🛜) A little ashram on the Caribbean, this small idiosyncratic place about 500m west of the main intersection in Juan Dolio is for the traveler looking to mellow out in a backpacker-style hotel. That's not to say the rooms aren't comfortable; they're the equivalent of any midrange place nearby and have clean, tiled floors, fans and some with cable TV. There's meditation and yoga classes on offer – and some of the proceeds from the hotel go to supporting a girl's foundation in India. Guests can also take advantage of an airport taxi that's half the street rate.

Barceló Capella Beach Resort　RESORT **$$$**
(☎809-526-1080; www.barcelo.com; Carretera Nueva; all-incl s/d from RD$2930/4380; ℗❄@🛜🏊) One of Juan Dolio's more glamorous choices, the rooms at the Capella are spread out around lush grounds with reflecting pools and the occasional flamingo and peacock. Inevitably for a resort this size, room quality is a bit uneven – the best are in the 4000 block just steps from the shady-palmed beach. The pool area is a little small considering the number of guests, but it's generally less of a party scene than the Coral Costa Caribe.

Coral Costa Caribe Resort　　RESORT **$$$**
(☎809-526-2244; www.coralcostacaribe.com; Carretera Local; all-incl s/d/tr US$155/250/350; ℗❄@🛜🏊) Certainly every day isn't Spring Break but this all-inclusive place does have a party scene. Loud music is pumped from giant speakers around the pool area – the center of the action amongst a variety of sizes and professions – and though the beach here is nice, it's small for a 432-room resort. This high-rise property has fairly good motel-style rooms and several restaurants to choose from. Five bars and a disco round out a lively atmosphere. If you're staying further west and want to imbibe here, a day pass is RD$1500.

Habitaciones Don Pedro　　GUESTHOUSE **$**
(☎809-526-2147; Carretera Local; arqjuandolio@hotmail.com; r with fan/air-con RD$1000/1200; ℗❄🛜) The matriarch of the Don Pedro family is a bit standoffish, so look for her considerably nicer son, Antonio, across the street at the strategic beach bar owned by the same family. Otherwise, the 22 rooms here are simple and uninspired (you're better off at Fior di Loto), but are directly across the street from the town beach, 200m east of the main intersection.

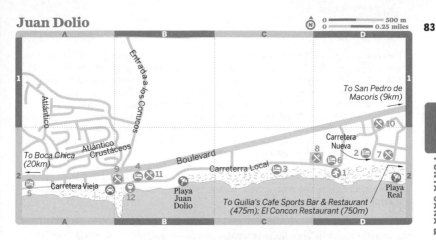

Talanquera Beach Resort RESORT **$$**
(☎809-526-1510; www.talanqueraresort.com; Carretera Local; all-incl s/d per person US$123/190; P❋🛜🏊) In a major state of flux when we came through. The Talanquera was in the middle of slowly transforming itself from the party pick of the inebriated college set to something a little more attractive to more mild-mannered European tourists. Newly renovated rooms reflect this change with more adult-oriented furnishings. Once it's complete, it should be good value.

🍴 Eating & Drinking

Don't worry if you're staying at an all-inclusive with less-than-stellar buffet food – Juan Dolio has several decent restaurants, both in town near the main intersection and strung out along Carretera Nueva east of the main resort area.

TOP CHOICE **Ristorante El Sueño** ITALIAN **$$**
(Carretera Local; meals RD$230-630; ⊗lunch & dinner Tue-Sun) The Italian owners and their Azurri cohorts sit around this casual open-air eatery *Godfather*-style, giving it a nod of authenticity it doesn't need – the pizzas are the real deal and do the job on their own. The lobster fettuccine also stands out, a favorite of local expats, as pretty much does any pasta you choose. Fish and meat round out Juan Dolio's most consistently great menu and it's a good spot for a drink, too.

El Mesón SPANISH, ITALIAN **$$**
(Carretera Nueva, across from Club Hemmingway; mains RD$250-490; ⊗lunch & dinner) If the waft

Juan Dolio

🎯 Activities, Courses & Tours
1 Cigua Tours D2

🛏 Sleeping
2 Barceló Capella Beach Resort D2
3 Coral Costa Caribe Resort..................C2
4 Habitaciones Don Pedro B2
5 Hotel Fior di Loto A2
6 Talanquera Beach Resort..................D2

🍴 Eating
7 El Mesón..D2
8 Fredy's Snack.......................................D2
9 Naito Gift Shop Mini Mart B2
10 Paladart D1
11 Ristorante El Sueño............................B2

🍷 Drinking
12 Bar Cacique B2
    Chocolate Bar..............................(see 8)

of fresh-off-the-grill whole lobster doesn't suck you in, go for the spot-on *paella* at this perennially popular Spanish restaurant. You'll also find smoked chorizo, lamb, *morcilla* (blood sausage) and heaps of the usual suspects, all excellently prepared with little regard for your waistline. There's live music on Friday evenings.

Paladart CAFE, DELI **$$**
(Plaza los; items RD$150-550; ⊗lunch & dinner, closed Mon) Armed with Illy espresso, cheesecake, pecan pie, a good selection of more sophisticated tapas and seafood dishes and sandwiches, this smart deli fulfills a niche –

PLAY BALL!

Baseball is king is the Dominican Republic, so it would be a travesty not to take in the national pastime live if you're visiting during the winter baseball season from mid-November to February. A great spot to do so is in San Pedro de Macorís, located 70km east from Santo Domingo between Juan Dolio and La Romana. The city's most prominent building, Estadio Tetelo Vargas on the north side of Hwy 3, is home to the **Estrellas Orientales** (www.estrellasorientales.com.do) or the Eastern Stars.

Despite being ridiculed as the Chicago Cubs of the six-team Dominican Winter Baseball League due to their prolonged drought without a championship (their last was 1968), San Pedro is a baseball prodigy factory, a centerpiece of a country that has given birth to more Major League Baseball players than any other country outside the US (perhaps explaining their sad track record – all the great players bolt for the Big Leagues).

To attend a game, pre-order tickets from the **ticket hotline** (📞809-529-3618; RD$450-400) or at the box office before the game.

the everything-but-Italian niche. The patio is one of the town's most pleasant.

Guilia's Café Sports Bar
& Restaurant
BAR, BURGERS $$

(Carretera Nueva; meals RD$100-460; ⊙lunch & dinner Wed-Mon) Juan Dolio's interpretation of a sports bar, Guilia's offers a flatscreen TV and pool table and serves up homemade burgers (RD$130) and freshly cut fries. It's popular with foreigners.

El Concon Restaurant
SEAFOOD, ITALIAN $$

(Carretera Nueva; mains RD$210-760; ⊙lunch & dinner) Mostly locals make the long-haul (relatively speaking) to this thatched-roof favorite at the end of Carretera Nueva. There's nothing unique about the menu, but the tropical atmosphere feels more Dominican than others.

Fredy's Snack
BAKERY

(Plaza Chocolate, Carretera Local; ⊙from 10am Wed-Mon) Fans of fresh *brot* can do no wrong at this small Swiss-German bakery, which also stocks a tiny selection of German imports.

Naito Gift Shop Mini Mart
MARKET

(cnr Carretera Local & Entrada a los Conucos; ⊙8:30am-10pm) This is the largest market in the center of town, with basic groceries and supplies.

Bar Cacique
BAR

(Carretera Local; ⊙midnight Sun-Thu, 2am Fri-Sat) A quintessential dive popular with expats and Dominicans alike. Single men may not feel welcome, however.

Chocolate Bar
BAR

(Plaza Chocolate, Carretera Local; ⊙9am-3am) Convivial outdoor bar catering to all-inclusive escapists near Coral Costa Caribe Resort. DJs spin house on Thursdays at 9pm.

❶ Information

The Shell gas station on the boulevard west of Entrada a los Conucos has a 24-hour Banco León ATM. There are also two ATMs on the property of the Coral Costa Caribe Resort.

Banco Popular (Carretera Nueva) Another ATM, located 200m north of Barceló Capella Beach Resort.

Cigua Tours (📞809-877-1689; www.erika-cigua-tours.com; Playa Real; ⊙9am-11pm) This small travel agency on the beach just east of Talanquera Beach Resort organizes day trips to Santo Domingo (per person US$30), Isla Saona (per person US$60), Isla Catalina (per person US$60), Parque Nacional Los Haïtises (per person US$65) and 4WD safaris to sugar cane plantations and waterfalls (per person US$50). If this beach shack is closed, the main office is in Boca Chica (p80).

Farmacia La Formula (Plaza Colonial Tropical, Carretera Nueva; ⊙8am-7pm) Small pharmacy and sundries.

Galmedical Internacional (⊙809-526-2044; off Carretera Nueva; ⊙24hr) Serious matters should be seen in San Pedro de Macorís, but the good doc here speaks English, German, French and Italian. It's off Carretera Nueva just north of Guilia's.

Ilsa (Plaza de la Luna, Carretera Local; internet per hr RD$60; ⊙8am-11pm Tue-Sun) Internet access and international calls.

Internet Center (Plaza Chocolate, Carretera Local; per hr RD$60; ⊙8am-9pm) Internet access.

Karina Call Center (Carretera Nueva; internet per hr RD$100; ⊙9am-6pm Mon-Sat, 9am-3pm

Sun) Several computers with high-speed access; international call center. Barber shop in front.

Politur (☏809-526-3211; Av Boulevard; ☒24hr) Police station for emergencies; next to the National Police building.

ℹ Getting There & Around

Gua-guas pass through Juan Dolio all day every day, going westward to Boca Chica (RD$30) and Santo Domingo (RD$75), and east to San Pedro de Macorís (RD$30), La Romana (RD$100) and Higüey (RD$190). No buses originate here, so there is no fixed schedule, but they pass roughly every 15 minutes from 6am to 7pm – stand on Boulevard at the corner of Entrada a los Conucos and flag down any one that passes.

Taxis can be found in front of any of the resorts in town. One-way fares for one to four people range from US$30 (to Boca Chica), US$50 (Aeropuerto Internacional Las Américas), US$60 (to Santo Domingo) and up to US$140 (to Bávaro). You can also call **Sitraguza Taxi Service** (☏809-526-3507) for door-to-door service.

When driving from Santo Domingo on Hwy 3, take the turnoff marked Playa Guayacanes.

LA ROMANA TO HIGÜEY

La Romana

POP 230,000

This traffic-congested and bustling city is a convenient stop for those traveling between Santo Domingo, 131km to the west, and the beach resorts further east. Surrounded by vast sugar plantations, the industry that bolsters its economy, and the enormous Casa de Campo resort a few kilometers to the east, La Romana feels slightly more prosperous than neighboring cities. There isn't much beyond Casa de Campo other than some great restaurants to refuel on cuisines and dishes you don't see on every other menu between here and Santo Domingo – nearly worth a stop alone.

◉ Sights & Activities

Altos de Chavón   LANDMARK
While a trip to a faux 15th-century southern Italian–Spanish village created by a Paramount movie set designer won't exactly give you a window onto Dominican culture, Altos de Chavón has some redeeming qualities, especially the excellent views of the Río Chavón (a scene from the film *Apocalypse Now* was filmed here). A visit to this little slice of the Old World created in the 1970s is de rigueur for many tourists, who arrive by the busload packing the cobblestone streets, restaurants, galleries and shops – it's more Times Square than a Roman piazza. There's a handsome church, a small but well-done pre-Columbian museum and a 5000-seat amphitheater, which attracts big-name performers – Frank Sinatra did the inaugural gig here.

Part of the Casa de Campo resort complex (see p87), Altos de Chavón can be visited independently. You'll have to pay a US$5 entrance fee. Most people visit in the morning and early afternoon as part of a group tour from resorts around Bayahibe and Bávaro/Punta Cana.

Motoconchos (motorcycle taxis) are prohibited from entering the area. If you're driving from La Romana, take the main road past the gated entrance to Casa de Campo and continue for 5km until the turnoff on

---

WORTH A TRIP

CUEVA DE LAS MARAVILLAS

More than 500 pictographs and petroglyphs can be seen on a tour of **Cueva de las Maravillas** (Cave of Wonders; adult/child RD$300/50; ☒9am-5:15pm Tue-Sun), an enormous cavern complex discovered in 1926 on the highway some 20km west between San Pedro de Macorís and La Romana. Extending for 840m between Río Cumayasa and Río Soco, this massive underground museum is well marked and beautifully illuminated with motion-sensing lights. As far as caves go, it's pretty stunning. The entrance fee includes a 45-minute guided tour (some English is spoken as well as French, Italian and German) so there's little reason to wander around on your own. A new equestrian center (horseback riding RD$400 per hour) and a small iguana exhibit have recently been added.

Coming from San Pedro de Macorís, look for the easy-to-spot entrance on your left not far past the Playa Nueva Romana resort complex. Best way to get here is to take your own car, though taxis are also an option.

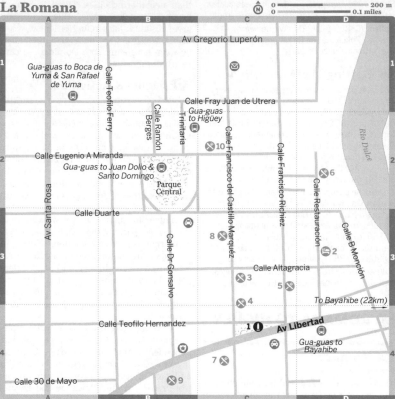

La Romana

your right, marked with a small 'Altos de Chavón' sign. A cab from La Romana costs around RD$400 one way or RD$700 round-trip with an hour's wait. Others arrive at the end of a group tour to Isla Catalina; the 250 steps from the pier to the top of the bluff can be challenging for some.

Isla Catalina   NATURE RESERVE
In the 15th century, pirates including Francis Drake would lurk around Isla Catalina waiting to pounce on Spanish ships on their way to and from Santo Domingo. Today, this island ringed by fine coral reefs teeming with fish in shallow water is a popular destination for groups from nearby Casa de Campo; the resort has frequent shuttles making the 2km trip, as do large cruise ships. Combine this traffic with a bar and restaurant and you won't feel like you've found paradise lost. Most groups spend a couple of hours for snorkeling and lunch, and divers head to a steep drop-off called The Wall. With enough people or cash it's possible to charter a boat (most tour companies in the area, from Bayahibe to Romana to Punta Cana and Bávaro, would probably be open to this

for the right price) to an infrequently visited beach on the far side of the island. In order to camp on the island you must gain permission from the Parque Nacional del Este office in Bayahibe (see p89) – Isla Catalina is officially part of the park protected area.

Golfing
GOLF

Within the grounds of the Casa de Campo (see below) are four Pete Dye–designed golf courses, including 'The Teeth of the Dog' (greens fees are US$267 for nonguests), open since 1971, which has seven seaside holes. 'Dye Fore' (greens fees nonguests US$267) and 'Links' (greens fees nonguests US$180) are also highly recommended. All of the courses are open to guests and non-guests alike, but you should make reservations as far in advance as possible. Tee times can be reserved by email or fax (t.times@ccampo.com.do; ☑809-523-8800) only.

El Obelisco
MONUMENT

(Av Libertad btwn Calles Márquez & Ducoudrey) Modeled after the George Washington monument in Washington, DC, the Obelisk is a much smaller version in central La Romana, painted on all four sides with contemporary and historical depictions of Dominican life.

🛏 Sleeping

TOP CHOICE **Casa de Campo**
RESORT $$$

(☑800-877-3643; www.casadecampo.com.do; Av Libertad; r US$445-950, villas US$975-6000, all-incl supplement per adult/child US$159/89; P❋@☂☀♞) Known as much for its celebrity guests (LeBron James, Beyoncé, Kanye West) and villa owners (Shakira, Vin Diesel, Sammy Sosa) as for its facilities and wealth of activities, this enormous, 28-sq-km complex truly resembles a city-state, albeit one with G8 conference security and disproportionate amount of 'beautiful people' per capita. Casa de Campo is an all-inclusive, super-sized place that remains discerning despite its enormity. Fresh off a modern, US$40 million makeover that has left the 225 or so hotel rooms with masculine hardwood furnishings, wonderful local art, 42-inch LCD televisions, Nespresso machines and a golf cart for all, the complex is home to 16 restaurants, an equestrian center, polo fields, a private beach, a shooting range – the list goes on and on. Catering mostly to celebrities, golf enthusiasts and families, Casa de Campo feels less like a resort than a tropical Beverly Hills, mainly

due to the independent design of the 2000 or so extravagant luxury villas (of which 200 or so are in the rental pool, complete with personal butlers, maids and pools). All-inclusive rates include unlimited horseback riding, tennis, one round of skeet/trap shooting and nonmotorized water sports at the beach. Other available activities include kayak trips down the Río Chavón (per person US$30 to 40) and buggy tours through sugarcane country (per person US$73). Four Pete Dye–designed golf courses (see left) and Altos de Chavón (see p85), a Tuscan-style 'village' and a Mediterranean-style piazza overlooking a massive marina round out the resort's offerings.

Day passes (US$75) are available for nonguests and can be purchased at the information office on the right before the entrance gates. Whether this is good value is debatable: you are allowed to enter the property, access the beach (towel included) and have a meal and one alcoholic drink at the beachside restaurant. A property tour pass (US$25) includes a visit to Altos de Chavón and the marina – no lunch or beach access.

Most guests arrive at the resort by air, either at the private landing strip or the airport that serves La Romana, and are then driven onto the property. If arriving by private vehicle, follow Av Libertad east across the river, and stay in the right lane for 4km until you see the entrance on your right.

All of the resort's restaurants – the best in the region – are open to nonguests. You must email the **concierge** (a.concierge @ccampo.com.do) for a reservation and be prepared to show identification at the security gate.

Hotel River View
HOTEL $$

(☑809-556-1181; hotelriverview@gmail.com; Calle Restauración 17; s/d/tr RD$1200/1350/1500; P❋☂) The only hotel in La Romana proper that has both a pleasant enough location and the right price, this multistory place is perched a block from the Río Dulce and an excellent choice for independent travelers. You can have a coffee in the tiny patio area out back overlooking the parking lot – not exactly taking full advantage of its 'river view'. The rooms are clean and modern and are a pleasant surprise from the exterior, though some feel darker than an Edgar Allen Poe epic.

Eating & Drinking

TOP CHOICE **Trigo de Oro** BAKERY $
(Calle Eugenio A Miranda 9; mains RD$90-260; ☺breakfast, lunch & dinner, closed Sun dinner; 🛜) There's no better oasis from the heat, exhaust fumes and backfiring *motoconchos* than the charming, shaded courtyard of this French cafe and bakery inside an historic mansion – hours can slip away sipping the specialty coffee and teas. The bakery has freshly made pastries like mini-lime tarts and cheesecake, and a good selection of wines. The sandwiches are served on flaky, baguette-sized croissants, a real treat.

Shish Kabab Restaurant MEDITERRANEAN $$
(Calle Francisco del Castillo Marquéz 32; mains RD$300-750; ☺lunch & dinner, closed Mon) The wall beside the bar is covered with photos of famous guests, attesting to the popularity of this local *institución*. The Palestinian owners dish out limited Middle Eastern dishes like hummus, baba ganoush and delectable shish kebabs (one should note), but the menu also includes fish (RD$360 to RD$525), grilled meats (RD$325 to RD$550), pizza (RD$400 to RD$600) and perhaps the DR's coldest Presidentes beer, served here nearly frozen.

ArteCaribe CARIBBEAN $$
(cnr Calles Altagracia 15 & Francisco del Castillo Marquéz; mains RD$100-500; ☺lunch & dinner; 🛜) From cheap and tasty snacks like chicken and beef *empanadas* (RD$45) to *mofongo* (RD$195) and various fish preparations (RD$350 to RD$475) this cute, post-age-stamp-sized cafe is an ideal place to get your bearings when walking through town and a great opportunity to try some *Comida Dominicana*. It also does sandwiches and grilled meats.

Pizzeria al Rio ITALIAN $$
(Calle Restauración 43; pizza RD$110-680; ☺lunch & dinner, closed Tue lunch) New Italian owners put this thatched-roof pizzeria back in favor. The pizza is good (though the Pizzaioli would die if they saw those canned mushrooms), the river views are outstanding. Pies come in three sizes, including a perfect-sized mini for solo diners. As if it's impossible to be *just* a pizzeria – you'll find the menu is filled out with standard fare as well.

El Taquito Mexicano MEXICAN $
(Calle Francisco del Castillo Marquéz 13; mains RD$160-290; ☺from 4pm) The low-scale menu board at this fast-food-style Mexican clashes with the rather upscale (for a *taqueria*) and pleasant outdoor patio. The food is distinctly average (skip the guac, the refried beans are good, burritos are a far cry from a San Francisco Mission burrito). But hey, it's cheap!

Nao's Coffee CAFE $$
(Calle Francisco Richiez 3; items RD$110-550; ☺breakfast, lunch & dinner; 🛜) A sophisticated Italian-run cafe with good specialty coffee, cheap and fresh croissants, house-made gnocchi and ravioli and more sophisticated mains.

Supermercado Jumbo SUPERMARKET
(Av Libertad; ☺8am-10pm Mon-Sat, 9am-8pm Sun) Occupying a full city block, this massive grocery sells everything imaginable; there are several fast-food outlets, four ATMs and an office of American Airlines inside.

Punto Italia MARKET
(Av Libertad; ☺9am-10pm Mon-Sat) Imports gourmet Italian and European brands and stocks fresh meat and cheeses.

ℹ Information

La Romana has a main town square (Parque Central) from which you can easily walk to most hotels, restaurants, internet cafes, post office and more.

Cultural Centers
BoMana (☎809-556-2834; bomana@gmail.com; cnr Calle Altagracia & Calle Teofilo Ferry; ☺8am-8pm; programs RD$50) A cultural center/art gallery/small theater space that hosts music performances, theater and art exhibitions.

Emergency
Politur (tourist police; ☎809-754-2972; Av Libertad 7, 2nd fl; ☺24hr) Inside the Secretary of Tourism office across from Supermarket Jumbo.

Internet Access
Cybernet Café (Calle Eugenio A Miranda; per hr RD$40; ☺8:30am-9pm Mon-Sat, 8:30am-6pm Sun) Also offers international calling.

Medical Services
Clínica Canela (www.clinicacanela.com; cnr Av Libertad 44 & Restauración) A private clinic with 24-hour pharmacy and emergency room.
Farmacia Dinorah (Calle Duarte; ☺8am-9pm Mon-Sat, to 6pm Sun) Free delivery available.

Money
BanReservas (Av Gregorio Luperón)

Banco León (Calle Duarte; ⊘8:30am-5pm Mon-Fri, 9am-1pm Sat) Located at southeast corner of the main park.

Banco Popular (Calle Dr Gonsalvo)

ScotiaBank (cnr Av Gregorio Luperón & Santa Rosa; ⊘8:30am-4:30pm Mon-Fri, 9am-1pm Sat)

Post

Post Office (Calle Francisco del Castillo Marquéz near Av Gregorio Luperón; ⊘9am-3pm Mon-Fri)

❶ Getting There & Away

Air

Aeropuerto La Romana/Casa de Campo is 8km east of town. There are a few regularly scheduled flights, but most of the traffic here is chartered. Carriers include **American Airlines/ American Eagle** (☑809-813-9080), with flights from Miami and Puerto Rico; and year-round charters by **Blue Panorama** (www.blue -panorama.com) from Italy, **Air Berlin** (www .airberlin.com) from Germany and **Thomson Airways** (www.flights.thomson.co.uk) from the UK. There is a surge in charter flights in high season.

Bus

Gua-guas to Bayahibe (RD$100, 20 minutes, every 20 minutes from 6:20am to 7:20pm) depart from a stop on Av Libertad at Restauración. *Gua-guas* for other destinations leave from stops near or on Parque Central.

Boca de Yuma (RD$90, one hour, every 35 minutes from 7am to 7pm)

Higüey (*caliente/expreso* RD$80/90, 1¼ hours, every 30 minutes from 5:30am to 10pm)

Juan Dolio (RD$80, one hour, every 20 minutes from 5am to 9pm)

San Rafael del Yuma (RD$90, 45 minutes, every 20 minutes from 7am to 7pm)

Santo Domingo (*caliente/expreso* RD$125/ 160, 1½ hours, *caliente* every 10 minutes, *expreso* every 20 minutes, from 5am to 9pm)

Getting Around

Motoconchos and taxis are typically found near the southeast corner of Parque Central. *Motoconcho* rides within the city normally cost RD$50; taxis within town are RD$100. You can call **Santa Rosa Taxi** (☑809-556-5313; Calle Duarte) or **Sichotaxi** (☑809-550-2222) for a pickup, or wait for the latter at a stop across the street from El Obelisco on Av Libertad. A taxi to or from the airport costs about RD$400; round trip to Cueva de las Maravillas, including wait time, runs to RD$2000.

To rent a car, try **Avis** (☑809-550-0600; cnr Calles Francisco del Castillo Márquez & Duarte).

Bayahibe & Dominicus Americanus

POP 2000

Bayahibe, 22km east of La Romana, was originally founded by fishermen from Puerto Rico in the 19th century. Today, it's a tranquil beach village caught in a schizophrenic power play. In the morning it's the proverbial tourist gateway, when busloads of tourists from resorts further east hop into boats bound for Isla Saona. Once this morning rush hour is over it turns back into a drowsy village. There's another buzz of activity when the resort tourists return, and then after sunset another transformation. What sets Bayahibe apart is that it manages to maintain its character despite the continued encroachment of big tourism.

A short drive from Bayahibe is Dominicus Americanus, an upscale Potemkin village of resorts, hotels and several shops and services centered on a terrific public beach. Listings for Dominicus Americanus appear along with those for Bayahibe – be sure to double check the address of the listings you're interested in.

◉ Sights & Activities

One advantage of staying in Bayahibe is that virtually every water-related activity is right outside your front door, so you avoid the long commute that most travelers make here daily from resorts further east.

Parque Nacional del Este   NATURE RESERVE
More than simply Isla Saona, which is all that most people see on a group tour, the Parque Nacional del Este includes eight emerged reef terraces, 400 or so caverns, some with pictographs and ceramic remains, and Islas Catalinita and Catalina, in addition to Saona. Designated a national park in 1975, it stretches over 310 sq km of territory, the majority of which is semihumid forest.

The park is also home to 539 species of flora, 55 of which are endemic. There is also a good variety of fauna: 112 species of birds, 250 types of insects and arachnids, and 120 species of fish. There are occasional sightings of West Indian manatees and bottlenose dolphins, and the much rarer Haitian solenodon (p237), a small bony animal with a long snout and tiny eyes.

There's a **park office** (Map p90; ☑809-833-0022; ⊘8am-4pm) in the parking lot in Bayahibe. One entrance is at Guaraguao, a ranger

Bayahibe

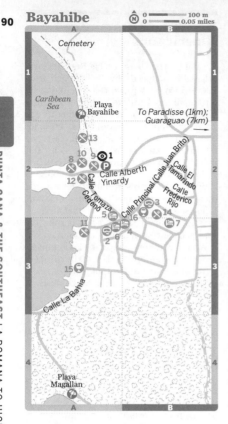

Bayahibe

post 5km past Dominicus Americanus. The other entrance is in the town of Boca de Yuma (p95), on the eastern side of the park. There is a ranger station there but no formal services. A road leads along the coast for several kilometers and has a number of nice vista points.

Isla Saona

There's a reason why boatloads of tourists descend upon this island daily. The powdery, white-sand beach doesn't seem real from afar, and a dip in the aquamarine surf is a gentle restorative, like the waters of the most luxurious spa; palm trees provide a natural awning from the intense sun. All of this would be perfect if it weren't for the fact that ear-splitting dance music is blasted from competing sound systems and vendors wander the beach in search of buyers in need of hair braiding, shells and other knickknacks. There isn't much coral to speak of, much of it damaged by heavy boat

traffic and inexperienced snorkelers. Much of this 12km by 5km island is taken over by various companies and all-inclusive resorts that have set up lounge chairs, small dance floors, bars and buffets. **Mano Juan** (population 500) is the only established community on this island separated from the mainland by the narrow Paseo del Catuano.

The majority of visitors are ferried to Bayahibe early in the morning from resorts further east expecting a booze-cruise-like experience, and they usually aren't disappointed. Most trips include a catamaran ride out to the island and then a speedier motorboat trip back or vice versa. A stop at the **piscina natural**, a shallow sandbank that extends far from the shore and has crystal-clear water, often includes young Dominican men and women wading through the water serving up glasses of rum and soda to tourists in need of a drink. The buffet lunch tends to be large and quite good. Unless you specifically request a trip that avoids the standard stops, don't expect a peaceful paradise, much less a protected national park. The dive shops in Bayahibe tend to offer more-rewarding trips that stop for lunch at Isla Saona, but only after visiting other spots for hiking, snorkeling or both (see p92). Every hotel, restaurant and shop advertises

Saona trips with little variation in quality and price (US$65 to US$80).

Isla Catalinita

This tiny uninhabited island on the eastern edge of the park is a common stop on snorkeling and diving tours. Arriving on the island's western (leeward) side, it's about a half-hour hike to the other side, where a lookout affords dramatic views of the powerful open-ocean waves crashing on shore. There is a coral reef in about 2m of water that makes for great snorkeling, and a good dive site called Shark Point, where sharks are in fact often seen.

Cueva del Puente

The park also has more than 400 caves, many of which contain Taíno pictographs (cave paintings) and petroglyphs (rock carvings). Archaeologists have found several structures and artifacts in and around the caves, including what appears to be the remains of a large Taíno city (perhaps the largest) and the site of a notorious massacre of indigenous people by Spanish soldiers.

Only one of the caves that contain Taíno pictographs, **Cueva del Puente**, can be easily visited. It is partially collapsed, but has a modest number of Taíno pictures, mostly depicting animals and human-like figures that may represent people or deities. The cave also has some impressive stalagmites and stalactites.

To visit Cueva del Puente, you must first drive to the national park entrance at Guaraguao 5km past Dominicus Americanus (turn right 350m down a dirt road after the new Cadaques Caribe Resort). There you will pay the RD$100 entrance fee and the guard will guide you to the cave – it's a little over 3km, about a 40-minute walk; you'll need a flashlight and good shoes. South of here is **Cueva Penon Gordo**, a smaller cave but with more pictographs.

La Punta de Bayahibe   NATURE WALK

This short, pleasant walk (10 minutes) follows a path beginning just past the Bamboo Beach Bar. It passes by the attractive Iglesia de Bayahibe, a small green, wooden structure, and signs in both English and Spanish outline interesting facts about the town's history and flora and fauna.

Snorkeling & Diving

Bayahibe is arguably the best place in the country to dive or snorkel, featuring warm, clear Caribbean water, healthy reefs and plenty of fish and other sea life. The diving tends to be 'easier' (and therefore ideal for beginners) than it is on the DR's north coast, where the underwater terrain is less flat, the water cooler and the visibility somewhat diminished.

There are about 20 open-water dive sites; some favorites include **Catalina Wall** and an impressive 85m ship in 41m to 44m of water, known as **St Georges Wreck** after Hurricane Georges. Deep in the national park, **Padre Nuestro** is a weaving 290m tunnel flooded with freshwater that can be dived, but only by those with advanced cave diving training. See Tours, right, for details. In town you can also snorkel in the waters around La Punta.

Casa Daniel   DIVING

(Map p90; ☎809-833-0050; www.casa-daniel.de; Calle Juan Brito, Bayahibe; ☺8am-6pm) This German-run operator offers one-tank dives with/without equipment rental for US$52/45. Packages of six dives are US$280/235, 10-dive packages are US$429/351. PADI certification courses are available. Ask about accommodations packages.

Scubafun   DIVING

(Map p90; ☎809-833-0003; www.scubafun.info; Calle Juan Brito 28; ☺8am-6pm) In operation for over nine years and located on the main strip in the middle of town, this PADI dive center offers two-tank dives in nearby reefs (US$90) and dive/day trips to Isla Catalina (US$159) and Isla Saona (US$169). Beginner and advanced PADI courses are also offered.

🏊 Beaches

Much of **Playa Bayahibe** (Map p90), the town beach to the right of the parking lot, is occupied by dozens of motorboats waiting to ferry tourists to Isla Saona. There's a relatively small, uninviting and narrow stretch of sand between the last of these and the start of the all-inclusive Sunscape Casa del Mar – the beach here is restricted to guests of the resort.

The advantage of staying in Dominicus Americanus is being able to walk to **Playa Dominicus** (Map p92), a beautiful stretch of thick, nearly-white sand, and good water for swimming. It does tend to get crowded, especially because there's easy public access via a parking lot at the far eastern end of the enclave, which means no cutting through hotels or restaurants to get to the beach. You

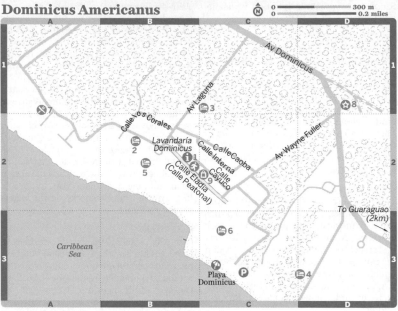

Dominicus Americanus

can rent beach chairs for US$3 or eat at one of various food stands or restaurants.

👉 Tours

Virtually every hotel in Dominicus Americanus offers a wide variety of tours. Most are more expensive than those arranged

through one of the two dive shops in Bayahibe, or from Max Tours. Both of the dive shops listed here have multilingual guides and instructors, with Spanish, English, German, French and Italian spoken, and can accommodate groups of both snorkelers and divers.

One of the more enjoyable ways of spending a few hours exploring the coastline is to take a **sail** on a local's fishing boat. No doubt you wouldn't have to ask many people before finding a taker; one particularly nice man who can read the winds like a soothsayer is **Hector Julio Brito** (☎829-285-4368), who charges US$130 for one to three people for a half-day trip. A longer outing, from 9am to 4pm to the piscina natural, will run around US$200.

Max Tours   DIVING
(Map above; ☎809-399-0225; Calle Eladia, Dominicus Americanus; ⏰8am-noon & 5-10pm) A friendly tour company in Dominicus Americanus affiliated with Casa Daniel. Full-day snorkel and beach trips to Isla Saona are USD$65, including a lobster feast on the more secluded beach in Mano Juan away from the Spring Break mayhem of the hotel tour groups, and all the rum you can drink. Isla Catalina trips with snorkeling, lunch on the beach and a stop at Altos de Chavón are

US$45. Locals can also arrange things for independent travelers.

✨ Festivals & Events

Every year on the Saturday of Semana Santa (late March/early April), Bayahibe hosts a **regatta** of handmade fishing boats. The race runs from the town cove to Catalina Island and back.

🛏 Sleeping

Bayahibe proper has several good budget hotels all within walking distance of one another; locals can point you in the direction of a family willing to take on temporary boarders. A stay here affords you excellent eating options and the chance to experience the rhythms of the town away from the masses. The enclave of Dominicus Americanus has several midrange and top-end options – the advantage here is that it's a short walk to an excellent beach. There is a string of all-inclusive resorts in Dominicus Americanus and along the road between there and Bayahibe; only Dreams La Romana is within walking distance of town.

TOP CHOICE Iberostar Hacienda
Dominicus RESORT **$$$**
(Map opposite; ☎809-688-3600; www.iberostar.com; Playa Dominicus; all-incl r from RD$6950; P❀@🛜🏊🐾) An impeccably maintained resort doused in soothing pastels, the Iberostar Hacienda Dominicus has beautifully landscaped grounds – most of the buildings surround quiet interior courtyards with beautiful historic Spanish tiles and there are duck-strewn ponds and tranquility-inducing fountains throughout. Some big, gaudy art means the whole thing teeters precariously on the fortunate side of Vegas flamboyance but it wins points for restraint in the end. Standard rooms aren't as grandiose as the common areas – they're even cramped – but the awesome pool (with its Jacuzzi island) and huge beach (with a picturesque lighthouse bar) is where you'll be spending your time, anyway.

TOP CHOICE Hotel Bayahibe HOTEL **$$**
(Map p90; ☎809-833-0159; www.hotelbayahibe.net; s/d/tr RD$1300/2000/2500; P❀@🛜) The staff is cute, friendly and useless, but what you get for your money here means the Bayahibe has the best budget rooms in town. This three-story modern building is easily noticeable, since it's the biggest around.

Large, colourful rooms are very comfortable with cable TV, balconies, small bathtubs and some even boast good views. It all surrounds an inner atrium and is on par with far more expensive options on the coast. Breakfast is RD$200 extra.

Villa Iguana GUESTHOUSE **$$**
(Map p90; ☎809-757-1059; www.villaiguana.de; Calle 8, Bayahibe; r with/without air-con US$59/39, 1-bedroom apt US$69, penthouse US$120) If the Hotel Bayahibe is booked, or if you prefer a more homey atmosphere, walk on over to the Villa Iguana. This friendly German-owned hotel has 11 well-kept rooms, though there's little character and no TV in standard rooms. A simple complimentary breakfast is served in a covered-over indoor patio area and is included with all rooms except apartments. The penthouse, with its own small pool, is a little rooftop oasis that beckons longer stays (a common pool is also on the cards).

Hotel Eden HOTEL **$$**
(Map opposite; ☎809-833-0856; www.santodomingovacanze.com; Av La Laguna 10, Dominicus Americanus; s/d/tr/q RD$60/70/90/100; P❀🛜🏊) A good choice for those seeking hotel-style comfort, amenities and service alongside peace and quiet. Because it's located on the access road to the resort area, you might confuse the Eden for a hotel somewhere in Arizona or Florida, just not necessarily on a Caribbean beach. The pool area and grounds are attractive and a good restaurant is attached.

Cabaña Elke HOTEL **$$**
(Map opposite; ☎809-833-0024; www.viwi.it; Av Eladia, Dominicus Americanus; d/apt US$70/US$90; P❀🏊🛜) Sandwiched between the road and a high fence marking the boundary of the Viva Wyndham Dominicus Beach property, Elke's rooms are arranged in two long narrow rows. Rooms are airy, especially the split-level apartments with kitchenettes, but the furnishings are aging. There's a nice pool area with lounge chairs, but unfortunately no view.

Viva Wyndham Dominicus
Beach RESORT **$$$**
(Map opposite; ☎809-686-5658; www.vivaresorts.com; Playa Dominicus; all-incl r from US$191-254; P❀@🛜🏊🐾) This Italian–American resort occupies an excellent beachfront property lined with thick, soft sand. The pricier oceanfront bungalows are actually smaller than the superior rooms, but

command sand right from the doorstep and Caribbean views beyond, making them a smart choice for just US$15 per person above superior prices. The standard rooms, of which there are 181, have been given the *Queer Eye* treatment but are too tight unless you are a couple in a perpetual spoon. Otherwise, it's a typically sprawling property that is too big for its own britches (guest service complaints are not rare). Attached is the sister resort, the Viva Wyndham Dominicus Palace, a step up in room and food quality and overall property maintenance.

Two additional options in Bayahibe, **Cabañas Trip Town** (Map p90; ☑829-879-1120; Calle Juan Brito; cabins with/without air-con RD$1000/800; P✱) and **Cabañas Francisca** (Map p90; ☑829-968-5877; Calle Juan Brito; r with/without air-con RD$1000/800; P✱) are comparable budget choices located across from one another near the center of action in town. Pop your head into both before making a decision. Both have dead basic rooms with old furnishings, small porches and private bathrooms with hot water. Some have cable TV.

✗ Eating

Bayahibe has a surprising number of good restaurants for a town of its size. Most offer relaxing waterfront seating and fresh seafood, with Italians running the show in most cases. Dominicus Americanus has a number of modern tourist-ready restaurants serving a mix of international standards and fish, though none have views.

TOP CHOICE **Mama Mia**   ITALIAN $
(Map p90; Plaza La Punta, Bayahibe; mains RD$80-240; ☺lunch & dinner, closed Mon) It's very hard to eat this well for these prices in the DR, but this spaghetteria specializes in classic pasta recipes like *all'amatriciana* (tomato sauce, bacon and chilli – our fave), carbonara, *all'arrabiata* and *aglio, olio e peperoncino* (garlic, olive oil and chilli powder) in yet another endlessly charming dive near Bayahibe Beach. Dishes are palatably simple – concentrating on flavor nuance rather than huge portions or other gastro-bells and whistles – and priced to please.

Mare Nostrum   ITALIAN $$
(Map p90; cnr Calle Juan Brito & Calle La Bahia, Bayahibe; mains RD$250-900; ☺lunch & dinner, closed Mon) Freezing red wine aside, this is the classiest restaurant in Bayahibe, a

breezy, 2nd-story patio affair overlooking beautiful nighttime views of the darkened sea. Lanterns and tablecloths add a romantic ambience and the food is equally impressive, offering excellent homemade pastas and melt-in-your-mouth risottos, among others. Casual is a word that doesn't quite do the service justice, however – our waiter checked his cell phone while we were ordering! At these prices, that's criminal.

Trocadero   ITALIAN $$$
(Map p92; ☑809-906-3664; Playa Dominicus; mains RD$380-1200; ☺breakfast, lunch & dinner) The top choice in the area for a blowout meal, anniversary celebration or sunset proposal. Inside the exclusive Club Nautico Beach Club, the Italian chef at this romantic and sophisticated restaurant is generous with the wine in his dishes – rosemary oil and green pepper-marinated beef tenderloin in Barolo sauce (RD$700), prawns sautéed in pinot grigio (RD$700) – and there's an alfresco patio and loads of sandside day beds, tables and a few private dining cabanas amid drapes of bougainvillea in which to enjoy them. Beautiful spot. Excellent food.

Cafecito de la Cubana   CAFE $$
(Map p90; Playa Bayahibe; mains RD$110-600; ☺lunch & dinner, closed Tue) One of several little kiosks set up around the parking lot and beach area in town, la Cubana is particularly charming and serves a well-rounded menu that includes authentic Cuban sandwiches (RD$140) and a few wild cards like chicken curry (RD$310) and shrimp enchiladas (RD$570).

Restaurante Leidy   DOMINICAN $$
(Map p90; Playa Bayahibe; mains RD$50-500; ☺breakfast, lunch & dinner, closed Wed) Leidy is popular with locals for its cheapish *comida criolla* on the beach. Set plates of fried chicken (RD$250) and grilled fish (RD$400) highlight the small menu, served on bright-blue tables on the sand. On Thursday night at 10pm, it turns into a moonlit bar, with DJs and all.

The atmospheric **Bamboo Beach Bar** (Map p90; Plaza La Punta, Bayahibe; mains RD$220-700; ☺lunch & dinner, closed Tue) and **La Punta** (Map p90; Plaza La Punta, Bayahibe; mains RD$150-600; ☺lunch & dinner), the town veteran, are excellent duelling open-air eateries near the beach in town, serving succulent grills (a specialty of the former) and freshly caught fish and shellfish (front and center at the latter).

BOCA DE YUMA

The antithesis of big DR tourism, the ramshackle little town of Boca de Yuma plays the role of the end-of-the-road like a seasoned actor in an indie film festival flick that only the critics love. Off the beaten track in terms of mass tourism, the town sits at the southeast end of Hwy 4 and offers rough, unpaved roads and half-finished buildings leading to a quiet seaside promontory where waves crash dramatically into the rocky shore. Like a town forgotten, Boca de Yuma's slow-pace, near-apocalyptic crowdless feel is its appeal, along with cinematic sunrises and a wealth of fresh seafood, and makes for a great little getaway from the grandiose resorts that are encroaching on the town in all directions.

Several kilometers west of town on the way toward the entrance of the national park is **Cueva de Berna** (☺7am-6pm; adult/child RD$100/20), a large cave with scattered Taíno pictographs (and graffiti) and stalactite and stalagmite formations. A caretaker usually sits outside the entrance and will gladly accompany you up the rickety ladder and deep into the cave (a small gratuity is appreciated). To find the cave, follow the paved road that runs along the ocean wall west (away from the mouth of the river) past the cemetery and follow the sign; you need no more than 15 minutes inside.

A few kilometers further west down the same road (4WD only), past several ranches with grazing cows and horses, is the eastern entrance of **Parque Nacional del Este** (admission RD$100). A park ranger sleeps at the small cabin just past the gate, and should be around for much of the day, but there's little formality or information as few people enter here. A long, easy-to-follow road hugs the coast for many kilometers and involves some hiking up a moderately steep slope to make it to the top of the rugged bluffs with beautiful views of the ocean. There is good birdwatching here if you're out early enough.

While **Playa Blanca** is a pretty, mostly deserted beach about 2km east of town on the other side of the river, the hassles of getting here may not make the trip worth it. The easiest and most expensive option is to hire a boat from one of the boatmen congregated at the mouth of the river at the east side of town (round trip RD$1500). One alternative is to have them ferry you to the other side of the river and walk to the beach; however, the path is hard to find and follow and the sharp rocks are a hazard.

Should you stay the night, bed down at **El Viejo Pirata** (☎809-780-3236; hotelelviejo pirata@hotmail.com; Calle Duarte 1; r RD$1200; ❋❀). Both forlorn and inviting at the same time, this Italian-owned hotel with eight clean, modern rooms produces these contradictory feelings. It could stand to be friendlier as well, but its appeal lies in its off-the-beaten-path ethos, just the same as Boca de Yuma itself. Few visitors stay on overnight, hence the sometimes low occupancy rate, but the well-maintained saltwater pool and patio with good ocean views makes it feel like a well-kept secret.

Almost a dozen restaurants are lined up along the road overlooking the ocean. Two of the better ones, both with wonderful views, are **Restaurant La Bahia** (mains RD$225-475), owned and operated by a friendly Dominican family, and the Italian-owned **El Arponero** (mains RD$170-650; ☺lunch & dinner) in the center of town. The latter has pizza (RD$170-350) and pasta (RD$220-550) in addition to grilled fish and seafood.

To stock up on your own rations, **Supermercado La Defensa** (Map p90; off Calle Juan Brito, Bayahibe; ☺7:30am-9pm) is the biggest market in town.

🍷 Drinking & Entertainment

Barco Bar　　　　　　　　　　　BAR
(Map p90; ☺8am-midnight) An old standby and still going strong, right on the water in Bayahibe – it generally gets going in the afternoons, the best time for sunset views from the homemade tree house.

Bubaraba　　　　　　　　　NIGHTCLUB
(Map p92; Diamante Casino, Av Dominicus at Av Wayne Fuller, Dominicus Americanus; ☺9pm-5am, closed Mon; cover RD$500-700) The area's true nightclub, with a medium-sized dance floor and requisite flashing lights. House, merengue and reggaeton rule the decks, the latter two sometimes live. It's inside the out-of-place Diamante Casino.

ℹ️ MONEY

BanReservas in Bayahibe will do cash advances with a credit card and passport without a fee – handy when the area's only ATM, at the Dominicus Americanus branch, goes on the fritz.

Paradisse NIGHTCLUB
(Map p90; ☎809-753-7943; Av Dominicus, Bayahibe; ⏰10pm-late, closed Tue) On the highway between Bayahibe and Dominicus, this seemingly ramshackle outdoor club is nicer than expected, with a large bar and breezy patio. Call ahead for a free ride from nearby resorts.

Super Colmado Bayahibe BAR/MARKET
(Map p90; ⏰7am-noon & 3-9pm) Town square, town bar and town grocery rolled into one, this *colmado* is where locals gather to talk, drink and listen to music all day long.

ℹ️ Information

Banca Agüero (Calle Juan Brito, Bayahibe; ⏰9am-9pm Mon-Sat, 9am-6:30pm Sun) Moneychanger next to the Hotel Llave del Mar. Cash dollars and euros accepted.

Banco Popular (Dominicus Americanus; ⏰24hr) Has an ATM located just outside the Viva Wyndham Dominicus Beach Hotel.

BanReservas Bayahibe (Calle Juan Brito) Dominicus Americanus (Calle Eladia) The only ATM in the area is at the Domincus Americanus branch.

Bayahibe Color Internet Center (Calle Juan Brito 1, Bayahibe; ⏰9am-1pm & 2-9pm; per hr RD$70) Convenient internet in Bayahibe.

Centro Clinico Bayahibe (Calle El Tamarindo 15, Bayahibe; ⏰24hr) English and Italian are spoken at this small home clinic run by friendly Dr Gustavo Brito Morel.

El Mundo (Calle Eladia, Dominicus Americanus; ⏰8am-10pm Mon-Sat, to 8pm Sun) Can arrange day-old editions of world newspapers like the *New York Times, Le Monde and Corriere della Sera* with a day's notice, plus souvenirs, snacks and sundries. It's also a bar, restaurant (mains RD$150-600) and social gathering point.

Farmacia Job (Calle La Bahia; ⏰8am-9pm Mon-Sat, 8am-noon Sun) Pharmacy across from Restaurant La Bahia de Capitan William Kidd.

Lavandaría Dominicus (btwn Calle Eladia & Calle Cayuco, Dominicus Americanus; ⏰9am-6pm Mon-Sat; per piece RD$40-55) One of the few independent laundry facilities.

Politur (☎809-833-0019; Calle Juan Brito, Bayahibe; ⏰24hr) Tourist police; at the entrance to Bayahibe.

Via Mia (Calle Eladia, Dominicus Americanus; ⏰10am-10pm; per hr US$6) Friendly but expensive internet in Dominicus.

Western Union (Calle Juan Brito, Bayahibe; ⏰8am-6pm, to 1pm Sun) Has telephone services; also changes cash dollars and euros.

ℹ️ Getting There & Away

A single road not more than 2km long connects the coastal highway with Bayahibe. The road splits about 1km south: the right fork heads to Bayahibe, the left on to Dominicus Americanus.

Gua-guas are the only means of public transportation to and from Bayahibe. Servicio de Transporte Romana-Bayahibe *gua-guas* leave from a stand of trees across from Super Colmado Bayahibe in the center of town, a block north of the Hotel Bayahibe. Services run to La Romana (RD$50, 25 minutes, every 20 minutes from 7am to 6:45pm) and Higüey (RD$100, 40 minutes, irregular hours). You can also catch a ride over to Dominicus Americanus (RD$20, five minutes, every 15 minutes).

Sichotuhbared (☎809-842-4345) is the local taxi union, with a stop next to the Viva Wyndham Dominicus Beach. One-way rates for one to five people include La Romana airport (US$30), Casa de Campo (US$35), Higüey (US$40), and Bávaro resorts (US$100). Be sure to agree upon a price before you get in the car.

To rent a car, look for the aptly named office for **Rent A Car** (☎809-833-0701) across from the Hotel Eden in Dominicus Americanus.

Higüey

POP 151,000

Higüey is a hectic, working-class hub kept in line by its giant concrete basilica, famous around the country and the lone needle worth visiting in this massive concrete haystack surrounded by sugarcane fields in all directions. The basilica, rising from the center of town like an arched stone rocket set to launch, is both odd and beautiful and well worth a day trip or pit stop while passing through – in fact, you're bound to end up here at some point traveling around the southeast. If not, its prominence on the RD$50 note will have to do.

◉ Sights

Basilica de Nuestra Señora de la Altagracia CHURCH
(⏰7am-7pm) From the outside, this is a strange mixture of the sacred and profane. A

utilitarian concrete facade, not far removed from a military bunker, is topped by an elongated arch reaching high into the sky. But it's one of the most famous cathedrals in the country because of the glass-encased image of the Virgin of Altagracia housed inside. According to the story, a sick child in Higüey was healed when an old man thought to be an Apostle asked for a meal and shelter at the city's original church, the **Iglesia San Dionisio** (cnr Calle Agustín Guerrero & T Reyes; ⊙varies). On departing the following day, he left a small print of Our Lady of Grace in a modest frame. Since that day the 16th-century image has been revered by countless devotees, upon whom the Virgin is said to have bestowed miraculous cures. Originally housed in the handsome Iglesia San Dionisio, the image of the Virgin has been venerated in the basilica since the mid-1950s. Designed by Frenchmen Pierre Dupré and Dovnoyer de Segonzac, and completed in 1956, the long interior walls consist mostly of bare concrete and approach each other as they rise, connecting at a rounded point directly over the center aisle. The entire wall opposite the front door consists of stained glass and is quite beautiful, especially in the late afternoon when the sunshine casts honey-colored shadows across the floor.

✯ Festivals & Events

Thousands of people travel to Basilica de Nuestra Señora de la Altagracia in a moving and intense homage to the Virgin every January 21. Pilgrims, dressed in their finest, file past the Virgin's image, seeking miracles and giving thanks. The church's bells chime loudly throughout the day.

⊨ Sleeping & Eating

Hotel Don Carlos   HOTEL **$**
(☑809-554-2344; cnr Calle Juan Ponce de León at Sánchez; r old/new bldg RD$1160/1392; ⓟ✳️🛜) Only a block west from the basilica, Don Carlos is a maze of rooms. It's friendly and professional, but deserving of only a night when passing through – and that's nothing to do with IKEA catalogs being passed off as magazines in the lobby. Ask to stay in the newer annex, whose rooms are modern and larger; rooms in the older building are cramped and dark. A restaurant (mains RD$100 to RD$500; open for breakfast, lunch and dinner) and small convenience store are attached. Wi-fi is lobby only.

Restaurant Doña Carmela   DOMINICAN **$$**
(Av La Altagracia; mains RD$240-620; ⊙lunch & dinner) Unlike the causal snack shacks and bars lining the median, this open-air restaurant has an elegant thatched ambience, with tablecloths, silverware and uniformed wait staff. Lobster (RD$520), elusive paella for one (RD$620) and a good list of excellent *mofongos* (RD$240 to RD$370) are highlights of a menu that also includes cheaper fish and pasta fare.

Don Silvio Grill   STEAKHOUSE **$$**
(Av La Altagracia; mains RD$240-600; ⊙lunch & dinner) Like Carmela, Don Silvio is a souped-up thatched-roof affair parallel to the median, but here the concentration is on juicy grills – steak, chicken and pork, nicely seasoned and cooked to your liking. Try the *filete de res* (RD$370).

There is also a number of snack shacks and bars with tables on the first several blocks of Av La Altagracia's leafy median, east of the basilica, that get going in the late afternoon, blasting merengue and showing Dominican baseball or the NBA on projection screens. You can get sandwiches, empanadas and other light fare, plus beer, soda or juices. Great place for a drink – **Manny Café** was the liveliest when we came through.

ⓘ Information

All of the internet places listed here operate as call centers as well.

Banco Popular (Calle Santiago at Calle Sanchez) ATM at the Esso gas station, kitty corner from Hotel Don Carlos.

BanReservas (Av La Altagracia) Has an ATM on the western end of the median.

Cyber Station Internet (Av La Altagracia; per hr RD$20; ⊙8am-11pm) Internet access at the beginning of the median.

Scotiabank (Calle Cleto Villavicencio) ATM on the plaza in front of Iglesia San Dionisio.

Tropical Internet Center (Calle Juan XXIII; per hr RD$40; ⊙8:30am-10:30pm Mon-Sat) Internet access. Just off the southwest corner of the basilica.

ⓘ Getting There & Away

Coaches to Santo Domingo (from RD$210, 2½ hours, every 15 minutes from 5am to 7pm) leave from the large Sichoprola terminal on Av Laguna Llana at Colón.

Gua-guas to La Romana (RD$90, one hour, every 15 minutes from 5:30am to 10pm) leave from the small Sitraihr station on Av Altagracia just west of Av Laguna Llana. For Samaná, walk

DON'T MISS

CASA PONCE DE LEÓN

Outside the small town of San Rafael del Yuma, just east of the two-lane highway linking Higüey to Boca de Yuma, is a fine rural Dominican town surrounded by fields in all directions, with dirt roads. Spanish explorer Juan Ponce de León had a second residence built in the countryside near San Rafael del Yuma during the time he governed Higüey for the Spanish crown. Still standing nearly 500 years later, **Casa Ponce de León** (Ponce de León House; admission RD$50; ☑9am-5pm, closed Mon) is now a museum to this notorious character of the Spanish conquest.

Born in 1460, Ponce de León accompanied Christopher Columbus on his second voyage to the New World in 1494. In 1508 he conquered Boriquén (present-day Puerto Rico) and served as governor there from 1510 to 1512. While there, he heard rumors of an island north of Cuba called Bimini, which had a spring whose waters could reverse the aging process – the fabled fountain of youth. Setting off from Puerto Rico, Ponce de León reached the eastern coast of present-day Florida on April 2 1513, Palm Sunday, and named it Pascua Florida (literally 'Flowery Easter'). He tried to sail around the peninsula, believing it to be an island, but after realizing his mistake he returned to Puerto Rico. When he resumed his quest eight years later, landing on Florida's western coast, he and his party were attacked by Indians. Wounded by an arrow, Ponce de León withdrew to Cuba, where he died shortly after landing.

The residence-turned-museum contains many original items belonging to Ponce de León, including his armor and much of his furniture. Also original are the candelabra and his bed; his coat of arms is carved into the headboard. Signs are in Spanish only.

If you have a car and are entering from the north, you'll encounter a fork in the road right past the police station. Bear left and then turn left onto a dirt road just before the cemetery (it's surrounded by a tall white wall and there's a sign). After 1.2km you'll see a long access road on your right with a boxy stone building at the end, which is the museum.

a few meters east and take a *gua-gua* to Hato Mayor (RD$110, 2½ hours, every hour from 4:40am to 8:10pm) or El Seibo (RD$90, one hour, every 20 minutes from 4:30am to 8:10pm) and transfer to the bus for Sabana de la Mar, where there are ferries across the bay. Buses for Hato Mayor and El Seibo use the same stop on Av La Altagracia at Av Laguna Llana. Be sure to tell the driver that you are planning to connect to another bus, as they will often drop you right at the next terminal.

Gua-guas to Bávaro and Punta Cana (RD$110, 1½ hours, every 15 minutes from 4:55am to 10:30pm; express air-con service RD$120, every 30 minutes from 4:50am to 10:30pm) leave from two adjacent terminals on Av de la Libertad past Calle Luperón.

PUNTA CANA TO SABANA DE LA MAR

Bávaro & Punta Cana

It wouldn't be out of line to equate the eastern coast of the Dominican Republic as a sort of sea and sun Disneyland – after all, it is here where the megalomaniacal all-inclusive resorts snatch up broad swaths of cinematic beaches faster than the real estate agents can get the sun-soaked sands on the market. There are over 30,000 hotel rooms from Punta Cana to El Macao, with more on the way, and for good reason: its beaches do rival those anywhere else in the Caribbean, both in terms of their soft, white texture and their warm aquamarine waters. Despite a lack of restraint on development in the area, the resorts and beaches here still manage to offer an idyllic Caribbean seascape for a seemingly endless crowd of sunseekers.

Punta Cana, shorthand for the region as a whole, is actually somewhat of a misnomer. The majority of resorts are scattered around the beaches of Bávaro, really nothing more than a series of small commercial plazas, and El Cortecito, a short strip of shops along a 'town beach'. Punta Cana (Grey-Haired Point), the easternmost tip of the country and where the airport is located, has some of the more luxurious resorts and Caribbean-hugging golf courses.

At the time of research, the expansion of DR-3, known as the Coral Highway, from

San Pedro de Macorís to Punta Cana was in full force, which should dramatically cut driving time from Santo Domingo.

⊙ Sights

🏞 Indigenous Eyes
Ecological Park & Reserve NATURE RESERVE

(☎809-959-9221; www.puntacana.org; ⊙8am-4pm) Though development may eventually cover every inch of the Dominican coastline, for now there are still large areas of pristine coastal plains and mangrove forests. About 500m south of (and part of) the Puntacana Resort and Club, this ecological park covers over 6 sq km of protected coastal and inland habitat and is home to some 100 bird species, 27 of which are indigenous species native only to the DR, 160 insect species and 500 plant species. Visitors can take very worthwhile 90-minute guided tours (adult/child US$15/10) in English, French, German or Spanish through a lush 30-hectare portion of the reserve with 11 freshwater lagoons all fed by an underground river that flows into the ocean. The tour also includes a visit to the park's botanical and fruit gardens, iguana farm (part of a conservation program) and a farm-animal petting zoo.

The visitor center has a great collection of insects that was compiled by entomology students from Harvard, and interesting maps and photos of the area. One- or two-hour horseback riding tours (US$45/65) through the park and along the coast can also be arranged with advance notice. The park is operated by the Puntacana Ecological Foundation, a nonprofit foundation created in 1994 that works to protect the area's ecosystems – including 8km of coral reef along the reserve's shoreline – and to promote sustainable tourism and hotel practices. Nearly 4 hectares of the reserve are dedicated to the Center for Sustainability, a joint project with Cornell and other American universities to survey and study native plants, birds and insects. Unfortunately, there is no hotel pickup service and only invited guests or guests of Puntacana Resort and Club can do self-guided tours; a cab here will cost around US$35 each way from Bávaro or El Cortecito.

🏊 Beaches

Superlatives describing the beaches here are bandied about like free drinks at a pool bar, but they're mostly deserved; keep in mind, however, that the best pieces of property have been claimed by developers and are either already occupied by all-inclusives and condos or will be in the near future. This means you will not be alone. In fact, you will be part of a beach-lounging crowd.

Public access is protected by the law, so you can stroll from less-exclusive parts like Playa El Cortecito, which tends to be crowded with vendors, to nicer spots in front of resorts – but without the proper color wrist bracelet you won't be able to get a towel or chair. Playa El Cortecito is a good place to parasail (12-15min US$40), though, or to find a boat operator to take you fishing or snorkeling.

North of El Cortecito is Playa Arena Gorda, lined with all-inclusive resorts and their guests, many topless, riding around on banana boats, parasailing or just soaking in the sun. A further 9km north of here is Playa del Macao, a gorgeous stretch of beach best reached by car. It's also a stop-off for a slew of ATV (All-Terrain Vehicle) tours that tear up and down the beach every day – there's less noise at the far northern end of the beach.

In the other direction, south of Bávaro and El Cortecito, is Playa Cabo Engaño, an isolated beach that you'll need a car, preferably an SUV, to reach.

WORTH A TRIP

DOWN UNDER IN THE DR

For something down'n'dirty, check out Cueva Fun Fun (☎809-553-2812; www.cuevafunfun.com; Rancho Capote, Calle Duarte 12, Barrio Puerto Rico, Hato Mayor; adult/child US$120/68), which runs spelunking trips to one of the largest cave systems in the entire Caribbean. The day includes a horseback ride, a walk through a lush forest, a 20m abseil and 2km walk through the cave, which involves a good deal of splishing and splashing in the underground river. Breakfast is provided, as is the equipment, including boots, harness, crash helmet and colorful jumper outfits – the overall effect is of a group of disposable extras for a James Bond baddie in a missile silo. Trips are generally booked as groups from hotels in the Bávaro/Punta Cana area, a 2½-hour drive away, but singles or small groups can piggyback on with enough advance notice.

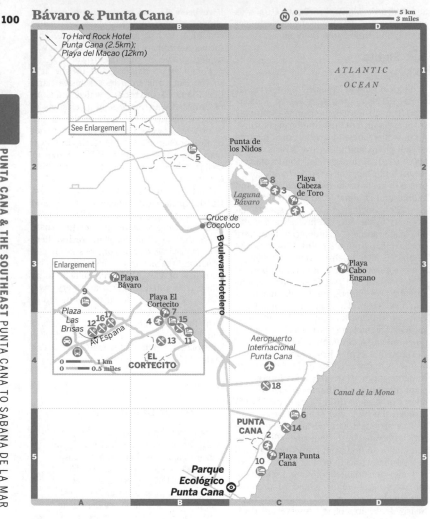

Activities
Water Sports

Virtually every water activity is available but some involve a long commute to the actual site. Every hotel has a tour desk offering snorkeling, diving and boat trips to destinations such as Isla Saona. Parasailing is done from the beach all over Punta Cana and Bávaro. A popular family outing is a snorkeling trip to the **Marinarium** (www.marinarium.com; adult/2-12yr US$89/44.50), a natural offshore pool near Cabeza de Toro, which is arguably more ecofriendly than other excursions. Rays, nurse sharks, tropical fish and patches of coral are all on hand.

Golf

La Cana Golf Course   GOLF COURSE
(☎809-959-4653; www.puntacana.com; Punta Cana Resort & Club, Punta Cana; ☺7:30am-6pm) Punta Cana's top golf course is located at the area's top resort. The 18-hole course, designed by Pete Dye, has several long par fives and stunning ocean views. Green fees are US$135/175 for guests/nonguests for 18 holes or US$80 (guests only) for nine, including a golf cart. Club rental is US$45

Bávaro & Punta Cana

for 18 holes or US$25 for nine, and golf cart costs US$40 per round. Tee times may be booked online. Also part of the Punta Cana Resort is the new Tom Fazio-designed Corales Golf Course, inaugurated in April 2010. It features six oceanfront holes but is limited to Corales residents and Punta Cana and Tortuga Bay hotel guests. A third course called Hacienda, also designed by Pete Dye, was under construction at time of research and was slated to open mid-2011.

Cap Cana　　　　　　　　　GOLF COURSE
(☑809-688-5587; www.capcana.com; Punta Cana) Near La Cana is the site of an enormous development project in the works, which has three Jack Nicklaus Signature golf courses already complete and open for play (non-guest greens fees May to October US$275, November to May US$375).

Catalonia Bávaro Resort　　GOLF COURSE
(☑809-412-0000; Cabeza de Toro; ⊗7am-6:30pm) If you'd like to get in a round but La Cana is too upmarket, the Catalonia Bávaro

Resort has a decent nine-hole par-three course that costs US$90 for one round and US$110 for two (carts included). Club rental is just US$25.

☞ Tours

Every resort has a separate tour desk that can arrange all manner of trips, from snorkeling and deep-sea fishing to the popular Isla Soana trip. A handful of locals set up on El Cortecito beach offer one-hour **snorkel trips** (per person US$20) and two-hour **glass-bottom boat rides** (per person US$35) to a nearby reef and **parasailing** (15min, US$50). Most also offer **deep-sea fishing trips** (min 4 people, 4hr, per person US$60) for marlin, tuna, wahoo and barracuda. There are a few kiosks near the north end of the beach, although the odds are that you'll be approached by touts as soon as you set foot in town and on the beach.

RH Tours & Excursions　　　DAY TOURS
(☑809-552-1425; www.rhtours.com; El Cortecito; ⊗9am-6pm) If you're looking to explore the region, this tour operator offers a number of decent day-trips for tourists. Popular excursions include exploring Parque Nacional Los Haitises (US$115), boat trips to Isla Saona (US$79 to US$97) and tours of Santo Domingo's Zona Colonial (US$69). Most trips include lunch and drinks. English and German are generally spoken.

Bávaro Runners　　　　　　DAY TOURS
(☑809-455-1135; www.bavarorunners.com; adult/child US$90/60) Offers all-day trips taking in a sugarcane plantation, cigar museum, beach and horseback riding (price includes lunch and drinks).

Helidosa　　　　　　HELICOPTER TOURS
(☑809-732-8809; www.helidosa.com; Aeropuerto Internacional La Isabela) For a bird's-eye view of the area, this operator offers sightseeing trips from 10 minutes (per person US$189) to 40 minutes (per person US$319).

🛏 Sleeping

For resorts in the area, walk-in-guests are about as common as snowstorms; if you can convince the suspicious security guards that your intentions are innocent and make it to the front desk, you'll be quoted rates that absolutely nobody staying at the resort is paying. Book all-inclusive vacations online or through a travel agent, as they can offer discounts of up to 50% off rack rates. Bear in mind that most resorts cater to a particular niche, whether it's families, honeymooners, golfers or the Spring Break crowd. For help on your decision, see p243.

BÁVARO

[TOP CHOICE] Hard Rock Hotel Punta Cana
RESORT $$$

(☎809-731-0099; www.hardrockhotelpuntacana.com; Playa Macao; all-incl d from US$492; P✳☀☎) Imagine Las Vegas with a Caribbean sea. The old Moon Palace Resort was transformed into a den of decadence and cool in late 2010, catapulting it to the top of Punta Cana's bold and beautiful resorts. The lobby now feels like a Rock and Roll Hall of Fame, with memorabilia galore, including Madonna's sequined-covered limo. It caters to diverse crowds of hipsters who, with its 18-bars-to-nine-restaurants ratio, aren't here to linger at the buffet. The 13 pools (seven oceanfront) and sprawling grounds are mostly unchanged, with the rooms bridging the gap between old and new – they feature party-size Jacuzzis at the foot of the beds. There's nothing slicker in Punta Cana and the gorgeous casino is the DR's largest.

Barceló Bávaro Palace Deluxe
RESORT $$

(☎809-686-5797; www.barcelobavarobeach.com; Playa Bávaro; all-incl d from US$338; P✳☀@☎✉🍴) Madeover to the tune of US$250 million, this brand new resort – a combination of three former Barceló resorts in a complex that now houses three resorts instead of five – is an over-the-top behemoth that manages to come off as a boutique hotel with its beautiful public spaces and sleek rooms. The highlight: 897 new junior suites, each with an outdoor Jacuzzi patio, motion-sensor lighting and no shortage of Danish-like design touches. The main pool area (there are five) is gorgeous, with in-pool ceramic chaise lounges, spewing showers and fountains and a spacious swim-up, thatched-roof bar. Choose from 16 restaurants, 13 bars and a disco to entertain yourself – leave the kids at the water park. Though the lobby feels like a fashion mall and staff was overwhelmed during the soft opening when we came through, just wait until the kinks are worked out. Did we mention the 18-hole golf course re-designed by Pete Dye?

🌿 Natura Park Eco-Resort & Spa
HOTEL $$$

(☎809-221-2626; www.blau-hotels.com; Cabeza de Toro; d from US$218; P✳☀@☎✉) Natura Park has a narrow beach outside the village of Cabeza de Toro, halfway between Bávaro and Punta Cana. From the Lincoln Logs–style recycled coconut wood lobby furniture to the beautiful free-growing mangroves on property, it's all got a sustainable edge and the resort has won awards for reducing its environmental impact. It's extra popular with Canadians and those who care more about reducing their carbon footprint than hopping in and out of bars and clubs at night. The pool is a bit small, but the beach quite nice. Free-range swans, geese and flamingos and the Laguna Bávaro creeping on its doorstep means nature is never too far away.

Paradisus Punta Cana
RESORT $$$

(☎809-687-9923; www.solmelia.com; Playa Bávaro; all-incl d from US$211; P✳☀@☎✉🍴) Almost jungly and discerningly quiet, this resort feels nothing like most in the area. It attracts singles and families alike and takes appreciated steps to keep them separate where desired. The classic standard rooms feel more urban than Caribbean and the 192 new Reserve rooms feature lush courtyards, modern art, patios and Jacuzzi tubs for two. Both the large and winding main pool and the beach (full of day beds) are gorgeous and the separate Royal Services pool feels like a Roman bath. Kids get batting cages and a climbing wall, adults get topless sunbathing in cordoned off areas. Everybody wins.

Villas Los Corales
HOTEL $$

(☎809-552-1262; www.los-corales-villas.com; Playa Bávaro; r US$115-250; P✳☀✉☎) This small Italian-owned development has none of the grandiose ambitions of the nearby all-inclusives to be all things to all people. For those seeking more modest surroundings and a community feel, Los Corales will do. Of the 50 or so apartments, all have small private patios and balconies, and private kitchenettes; some have oceanfront views. There's an Italian and Asian restaurant, bar, holistic spa and small swimming pool.

El Cortecito Inn
HOTEL $$

(☎809-552-0639; www.hotelcortecitoinn.com; s/d incl breakfast US$45/60; P✳☀✉) One of the few independent, reasonably priced choices in the area. Smileless service, confrontational staff and uninspiring breakfasts are the rule, but the rooms are spacious and the pool and grounds pleasant enough. Expect to leave your ID at reception.

PUNTA CANA

Even though it's commonly used as short-hand for the vacation area of the southeast, Punta Cana actually refers to the area just east and south of the airport. It's much more isolated than Bávaro as there is really only one coastal road, which eventually peters out further south and doesn't connect with the highway to Higüey. There are few services here and no towns in the immediate area.

Puntacana Resort & Club   RESORT $$$
(☎809-959-2262; www.puntacana.com; Punta Cana; d incl breakfast US$120; P✹@🛜🛝) Famous for its part-time residents like Julio Iglesias, Oscar de la Renta and Mikhail Baryshnikov, this discerning and quiet resort is also notable for its environmental efforts, especially the associated ecological park across the street from the entrance to the resort. Three-story buildings with newly modernized rooms line an average beach, which, like Club Med, sees seaweed mucking up the sands but offers miraculous water, and there are six restaurants to choose from within the 60-sq-km complex as well as a Six Senses Spa. Unlike all-inclusives, however, lunch, dinner and drinks aren't included in the rates. It's a low-key resort for people happier to read a book by the pool rather than do aqua-aerobics to loud disco music in the pool, though service is hit-or-miss (it took us 10 minutes to get a towel at an empty pool but guest service is sweet as waffles). The newer Tortuga Bay (designed by de la Renta), an enclave of 15 1-, 2- and 3-bedroom luxury villas, is part of the main resort property and sets the bar for luxury in Punta Cana.

Club Med Punta Cana   RESORT $$$
(☎809-686-5500; www.clubmed.com; Punta Cana; all-incl d per person from US$215; P✹@🛜🛝🏄) You know the drill: Club Med offers young, enthusiastic international staff and activities galore; it's especially good for parents looking to outsource care for their kids and teenagers. This one holds 1700 folks at capacity, so it feels like a small village, but decked out in typical pastel-hued Caribbean plantation architecture, it's pleasantly tranquil. Newly madeover rooms are nice, with separate but small living rooms attached and soothing earthen rust and lime motifs. New oceanview suites, 32 in all, are huge and come with Nespresso machines and desktop computers in addition to an exclusive pool and bar to escape the main

pool chaos. The food is so-so, save the world famous white chocolate bread, and the beach has too much seaweed though the water is a kaleidoscopic maze of turquoise, made all the more spectacular by a visible 25-year-old shipwreck just offshore.

🍴 Eating & Drinking

Most visitors are hardly hungry after gorging themselves at their resort's buffets, but there are enough condos and villas and locals to support numerous independent eateries. Most are in various shopping centers in the area, easily reached by *motoconcho* or taxi.

TOP CHOICE Restaurante Playa Blanca FUSION $$$
(Puntacana Resort, Punta Cana; mains US$11-29; ☉lunch & dinner) Flanked by an army of palms, this atmospheric, open-air restaurant is within the Puntacana Resort complex but open to the public and worth the trip. The beach here (Playa Blanca) is better than Club Med or Puntacana Resort, and you can eat on the sand for lunch. The hip, white-on-white space reeks of cool, but the innovative surf and turf menu, highlighted by some wild cards like spicy Dominican goat (UD$12), *criolla*-style guinea fowl (US$15), an organic salad (US$7) and a seafood rice (Arroz del Chef; US$15) that is a revelation, steals the show. Service could be more precise, but it's otherwise flawless, right down to properly cooled wine, a rarity.

TOP CHOICE Chez Mon Ami   FRENCH $$
(☎809-552-6714; Plaza Nautica, Bávaro; mains RD$350-780; ☉lunch & dinner Mon-Sat) This sexy French bistro, walking distance from El Cortecito, offers a lovely terrace on which to enjoy a mean filet of beef (RD$580), duck confit (RD$650) and the occasional curve-ball like fish carpaccio with spicy coconut sauce (RD$380). The chef and owner are French, so you're getting the real deal. Reservations are a good idea in high season (and so is a date).

El Burrito Taqueria   MEXICAN $$
(Puntacana Village, Punta Cana; mains RD$160-550; ☉lunch & dinner, closed Sun dinner) First sign of a great Mexican place is fresh chips and salsa, and our instincts proved correct at this small and festive *taqueria*. An excellent burrito the size of a shoebox followed (RD$360); and the tacos (RD$160 to 360) and enchiladas (RD$240 to 320) should

quell your cravings when you are tired of ubiquitous fish and pasta choices.

Brot
CAFE $$
(Puntacana Village, Punta Cana; bagels RD$230-300; ⊙breakfast, lunch & dinner, closed Sun dinner; ☎) Slammed at breakfast, this is where Punta Cana comes for its bagel fix. Fab bagelwiches (also available on baguettes) are the call, in such rarely seen flavors in the DR as Hummus Supreme and Montecristo, among others. There's a wealth of salads and wraps, too. Just what the doctor ordered for homesickness!

Solo Pollo
DOMINICAN $$
(Plaza Las Brisas, Bávaro; meals RD$225; ⊙breakfast, lunch & dinner) A legion of locals flock to this simple *comida crolla* restaurant serving – as the name implies – only chicken. Juicy, perfectly-seasoned *pollo horneado* (baked chicken) is the specialty of a menu that is scribbled out on a paper receipt each day. Meals include rice, beans and salad and you can get out of here for under RD$300 even if you tack on a fresh *tamarindo* juice.

Big Burger
CAFE $
(Plaza Las Brisas, Bávaro; burgers RD$130-280; ⊙breakfast, lunch & dinner). For those that sometimes just need a fat, juicy burger, this one's courtesy of the French. Also serves baguettes, panini and curried bratwurst (RD$190).

The new and huge **Super Mercados Nacional** (Puntacana Village, Punta Cana; ⊙8am-8pm Mon-Sat, 8am-3pm Sun) is the best in Punta Cana. In Bávaro, the best options are **Super Mercado Estrella** (Plaza Estrella; ⊙8am-10pm Mon-Sat, 9am-6pm Sun) and **Supermercado Metro** (Plaza La Realeza; ⊙8:30am-midnight). There's also **Super Mercado Alalé** (⊙8am-10pm Mon-Sat, 8am-8pm Sun) in El Cortecito.

ℹ Information
Most of Bávaro's services are located in one of several outdoor plazas (malls) just north of El Cortecito, the small one-road enclave where there's another cluster of shops and tour companies.

Emergency
Politur (tourist police; ☎809-552-0848) There are 24-hour stations next to the bus terminal in Bávaro, in Cabeza de Toro and at the Punta Cana airport.

Internet & Telephone
Cone Xion.com (Plaza Punta Cana, Bávaro; per hr RD$60; ⊙9am-10pm Mon-Sat, 9am-11pm Sun) A small dual internet/call center.

Sea & Surf (El Cortecito; per hr RD$60; ⊙9am-7pm) Along the main beach road in El Cortecito proper.

Laundry
Lavanderia El Tronco (Plaza El Tronco, Bávaro; ⊙8am-8pm Mon-Sat, 8am-noon Sun; per 7 pieces RD$170) Same-day service if you drop off in the morning.

Medical Services
All-inclusive hotels have small on-site clinics and medical staff, who can provide first aid and basic care. Head to one of several good private hospitals in the area for more serious issues.

Centro Médico Caribe Bávaro (www.caribe asistencia.com/cmcb; Plaza las Brisas, Bávaro; ⊙24hr) For emergencies.

Centro Médico Punta Cana (www.rescue -puntacana.com; btwn Plaza Bávaro & the bus terminal, Bávaro) The name notwithstanding, this is the main private hospital in Bávaro, with a multilingual staff, 24-hour emergency room and in-house pharmacy.

Farmacia El Manglar (☎809-552-1533; Plaza Punta Cana, Bávaro; ⊙8am-midnight) Offers free delivery service to local hotels.

Farmacia Estrella (Plaza Estrella, Bávaro; ⊙8am-midnight)

Hospitén Bávaro (www.hospiten.es; btwn airport & turnoff to Bávaro) Best private hospital in Punta Cana, with English-, French- and German-speaking doctors and a 24-hour emergency room. The hospital is located on the road to Punta Cana, 500m from the turnoff to Bávaro.

Pharmacana (Puntacana Village, Punta Cana; ⊙9am-10pm Mon-Sat, 8am-11pm Sun) Punta Cana's main pharmacy.

Money
Almost every major Dominican bank has at least one branch in the Bávaro area. All of the following have ATMs.

Banco León (Plaza Progresso, Bávaro)

BanReservas (Plaza Progresso, Bávaro)

Scotiabank Bávaro (Plaza Las Brisas) Punta Cana (Puntacana Village) ATMs.

ℹ Getting There & Away
From the small village of El Cortecito, the road follows an endless cluster of strip malls to a Texaco gas station, where you'll find the bus station and the route to resorts further north and Higüey to the southwest.

Air
Several massive thatched-roof huts make up the complex of the Aeropuerto Internacional Punta Cana, located on the road to Punta Cana about

9km east of the turnoff to Bávaro. The arrival process, including immigration, purchase of a tourist card (US$10), baggage claim and customs, moves briskly.

Several airlines have offices here, including **American Airlines** (☑809-959-2420), **British Airways** (☑800-247-9297), **Continental** (☑809-959-2039), **Air France** (☑809-959-3002) and **LAN** (☑809-959-0144) but they are tucked away behind the scenes and hard to find. Other airlines serving the Punta Cana airport include US Airways, Air Canada, Air Transat, Alitalia, Condor, Copa, Delta, Gol/Varig, Iberworld, JetBlue, Southwest/AirTran, KLM, United, USA3000 and Westjet. See the Transportation chapter (p250) for airline information.

For domestic air connections, **Dominican Shuttles** (☑in Santo Domingo 809-738-3014; www.dominicanshuttles.com) has direct domestic flights on five- and 19-seat planes between Punta Cana and Santo Domingo's La Isabela airport (one way $99, 9:15am Mon-Fri, 6:15pm Sun-Fri, and 4:30pm Sat) and daily to Samaná/El Portillo (one way $159, 3:30pm). They also serve Puerto Plata (one way $149, Fri 3:30pm & Mon 7am).

There is a Banco Popular ATM located in the arrivals area in Terminal A and an internet facility. Several car agencies have small booths near baggage claim, including **Avis** (☑809-688-1354), **Thrifty** (☑809-333-4000), **Budget** (☑809-480-8153) and **Europcar** (☑809-686-2861).

Resort minivans transport the majority of tourists to nearby resorts, but taxis are plentiful. Fares between the airport and area resorts and hotels range between US$30 and US$80 depending on the destination.

Bus

The bus terminal is located at the main intersection in Bávaro, near the Texaco gas station, almost 2km inland from El Cortecito.

Expreso Santo Domingo Bávaro Bávaro (☑809-552-1678); Santo Domingo (Map p50; ☑809-682-9670; cnr Juan Sánchez Ruiz & Máximo Gómez) has direct 1st-class service between Bávaro and the capital (RD$350, four hours), with a stop in La Romana. Departure times in both directions are 7am, 10am, 2pm and 4pm.

Sitrabapu (☑809-552-0617), more or less the same company, has departures to La Romana at 8:30am and 4:30pm (RD$225) from the same terminal. To all other destinations, take a local bus (marked Sitrabapu) to Higüey and transfer there. (You can also get to/from Santo Domingo this way, but it's much slower than the direct bus.) *Caliente* buses to Higüey leave Bávaro's main terminal (RD$110, 1½ hours, every 30 minutes from 1:30am to 10:30pm), as does the express service (RD$120, 1¼ hours, every 30 minutes from 6am to 7:30pm).

Getting Around

Local buses start at the main bus terminal, passing all the outdoor malls on the way to El Cortecito, then turn down the coastal road past the large hotels to Cruce de Cocoloco, where they turn around and return the same way. Buses have the drivers' union acronym – Sitrabapu – printed in front and cost RD$40. They are supposed to pass every 15 to 30 minutes, but can sometimes take up to an hour.

Daytime traffic is sometimes gridlocked between the resorts clustered just north of Bávaro and El Cortecito. Despite the stop-and-go pace of driving, renting a car for a day or two is recommended if you prefer to see the surrounding area independently. Consider paying more for extra insurance coverage, especially if you'll be driving north toward Playa Limón, Miches and Sabana de la Mar. Some agencies allow you to drop off the car in Santo Domingo, usually for an extra charge, but check in advance. Rental agencies include **Avis** (☑809-535-7191; Plaza Caney, Carr Arena Gorda), **Europcar** (☑809-688-2121; near Plaza Punta Cana, Bávaro) and **National/Alamo** (☑809-466-1082; Carr Bávaro Km 5).

Otherwise, there are numerous taxis in the area – look for stands at El Cortecito, Plaza Bávaro and at the entrance of most all-inclusive places. You can also call a cab – try **Arena Gorda taxi** (☑809-552-0711). Fares vary depending on distance, but are typically from US$6 (pretty much minimum charge on a short trip within Bávaro) to US$30 (to the airport). Water taxis also can be found on El Cortecito beach and cost between US$10 and US$50 per ride. *Motoconchos* congregate around Plaza Punta Cana in Bávaro and along the beach road in El Cortecito, and you can generally find one or two parked in front of the entrance to most resorts. Fares run around RD$70 to RD$100 within the El Cortecito/Bávaro area.

Playa Limón

The drive alone justifies the trip to **Playa Limón**. Hwy 104 passes through rolling mountain scenery, past bucolic ranches, where any unrecognized vehicle is sure to turn the heads of locals. Playa Limón itself, about 20km east of Miches and just outside the hamlet of El Cedro, is a 3km-long, isolated Atlantic beach lined with coconut trees leaning into the ocean – coveted property that you're likely to have to yourself for much of the time. Horseback-riding tours descend upon it a few hours a day, generally from late morning to early afternoon.

The rugged area surrounding Playa Limón has two important wetland areas, including **Laguna Limón**, a serene fresh-water body of water surrounded by grassy wetlands and coastal mangroves. The lagoon feeds into the ocean on the eastern end of Playa Limón and is known for bird-watching; tours are organized by Rancho La Cueva. The other lagoon – **Laguna Redonda** – is just 5km away, but is more commonly visited from Punta El Rey.

Sleeping & Eating

Hotel Limón   HOTEL $$
(☎809-282-1005; www.hotel-limon.com; s/d US$40/45; P@🛜🏊) Both options in Playa Limón are nearly interchangeable, sur-rounded by a lush palm-tree forest and a short walk from an isolated beach, but this hotel has a leg up for its better kept rooms, fresh juices sourced on premises, hot show-ers, pool (and pool table!) and properly trained Swiss chef. There are 14 or so rooms, with hillside bungalows featuring nice views of the area going for the same price as ground-level rooms. It caters mostly to German speakers whereas Rancho La Cueva next door, though Austrian-owned, draws more of a mixed international crowd. It runs whale-watching tours (p112) in the Bahía de Samaná in season and trips to Cayo Levantado (p111) other times of the year.

Rancho La Cueva   HOTEL $
(☎809-470-0876; www.rancholacueva.com; s/d/tr w/fan US$30/40/45; P@🛜) Horses and pigs roam this rural property. It's an end-of-the-road, out-of-the-way destination that feels like a true find. The 10 large spick-and-span rooms are sparsely furnished and what furniture there is tends to be fairly fragile (beds excluded). An open-air restaurant hosts daily tour groups for a seafood buffet, but breakfast and dinner are more simple affairs – guests need to check in advance to see what's available. The hotel can ar-range a trip that includes a visit to a coffee plantation, a ride in the mountains, seafood buffet and a boat ride across the lagoon for US$60 per person (warning: includes brief cockfighting *gallera* stop).

ℹ Getting There & Away

The road to Playa Limón, though severely potholed in parts, is empty and passes through beautiful scenery. From Higüey or other parts south, take Hwy 104 until you reach the very east-ern edge of El Cedro. Head north on a rough dirt road (a normal car can make it if it's dry; otherwise a 4WD is recommended) – look for the color sign

reading 'Playa Limón'. The hotels are about 3km down this road and the beach only another 500m.

Keep in mind that the only gas station between Otra Banda (the start of Hwy 104) and Miches is in the town of Lagunas de Nisibón. From Playa Limón it's only 27km to Miches, about a 35-minute drive in your own vehicle.

Gua-guas running between Higüey (RD$125, two hours) and Miches (RD$70, 30 minutes) can be flagged down from the main road during daylight hours – just make sure you are on the right side of the street for where you want to go. If arriving, be sure to let the driver know that you want to get off in El Cedro; it's easy to miss. Then catch a *moto-concho* for the remaining 3km or so (RD$150).

Miches
POP 9200

From the surrounding hills, Miches, on the southern shore of the Bahía de Samaná, is fairly picturesque. A slim 50m-high radio tower marks the geographic center of what appear to be well-ordered streets, and Playa Miches, just east of the town proper, looks inviting. Upon closer inspection, however, it's a fairly tumbledown place and the beach, though long and wide, is not very attractive. The water isn't good for swimming, mainly because the Rió Yaguada empties into the ocean here. Miches sometimes makes na-tional headlines as the launching point for Dominicans hoping to enter the USA ille-gally, via the Mona Passage to Puerto Rico.

Sleeping & Eating

TOP CHOICE Hotel La Loma   HOTEL $$
(☎809-553-5562; hotellaloma@codetel.net.do; Miches; s/d/tr RD$1300/1600/1900; P❄✖🛜) Perched atop a hill at the end of a rather steep driveway, rooms at Hotel La Loma have commanding views of the city and bay to the north and sweeping mountaintops to the south. It's a comfortable place to stop for the night on your way to Sabana de la Mar, and it's certainly the best place to stay in town. Rooms are sparse but large and clean and have equally spectacular views – the real draw here. Open for breakfast, lunch and dinner, the restaurant (mains RD$140 to RD$420) serves good food and huge portions. Ask about Andrea's lovely horse-back riding tours along the wild Costa Esmeralda nearby (US$50).

ℹ Information

BanReservas (cnr Calle Fernando Deligne & Gral Santana) is at the western end of town, one block south of Calle Mella; there's an ATM accessible 24 hours. **Banco Agricola** (⊙8:30am-4pm), a fairly primitive affair, is two blocks north of Calle Mella and can change cash and traveler's checks in a pinch.

Check email at the extremely unfriendly **Cyber Café PYP** (opposite La Bomba; ⊙7am-11pm; per hr RD$30).

ℹ Getting There & Away

Gua-guas to Higüey (RD$150, three hours, every 30 minutes from 5:20am to 5:20pm) leave from a terminal at the Isla gas station at the east end of town just before the bridge. *Gua-guas* going to and from Sabana de la Mar (RD$100, 1½ hours, every 25 minutes from 7am to 6pm) leave from the corner of Calle Mella and Calle 16 de Agosto.

If you are simply passing through town, whether from Sabana de la Mar to Higüey or vice versa, let the driver know you want to catch an onward bus and he will most likely drop you at the next terminal, saving you a *motoconcho* or taxi ride between the two.

Sabana de la Mar

POP 14,800

The literal and figurative end of the road, this small, ramshackle and largely forgotten town is the gateway to Parque Nacional Los Haitises. However, until the roadways in the area are improved, especially Hwy 104 east to Miches, Sabana will continue to miss out on sharing a slice of the economic pie from the growing number of tourists visiting the bay for whale-watching and Los Haitises tours. Sabana is the departure point for the passenger ferry across the bay to Samaná, as well as for the dangerous Mona Passage crossing to Puerto Rico, the first stop for many Dominicans hoping to make their way to the USA.

☞ Tours

The **Paraíso Caño Hondo** (☎809-248-5995; www.paraisocanohondo.com) is a highly recommended hotel 9km west of town and 1km past the park entrance, and offers good tours inside Parque Los Haitises as well. Boat excursions range between US$50 and US$85 for groups of two to four depending on the extent of the tour, and **hiking trips** (US$18 per guide) through the park's *bosque humedo* (humid forest) also can be arranged. During the humpback season, Paraíso organizes whale-watching tours (US$56 per person) in the waters near Samaná.

The **local guide association** has set up shop near the pier, offering whale-watching tours in season (per person US$70), trips to Los Haitises (per person US$50) and Cayo Levantado (per person US$60). The best English speaker of the bunch is **Robert Jackson** (☎809-974-1753), whose English isn't has good as his name implies, but it'll do.

At the entrance to Los Haitises, town **boatmen** also offer to take visitors on tours of the park (RD$500 per person for groups of less than 10, RD$400 for 10 to 25). While the excursions are similar to those offered by the tour operators, background information on the sights is often less detailed.

🛏 Sleeping & Eating

The turnoff to Caño Hondo and Parque Nacional Los Haitises is a short distance north of the Miches intersection – look for a Brugal rum sign saying 'Caño Hondo'. There's a gas station 2km south of town on the road to Hato Mayor.

TOP CHOICE **Paraíso Caño Hondo**   HOTEL **$$**
(☎809-248-5995; www.paraisocanohondo.com; s/d/tr incl breakfast RD$2000/3150/4350; 🕸🅿☒) Nothing good comes easy and this quirky and rustic retreat, one of the more special places to stay anywhere in the DR and the antithesis of the all-inclusives for which the country is famous, won't persuade you otherwise. Coming upon Paraíso Caño Hondo so far out of the way after a long and rough road feels like an epiphany. The Río Jivales, which runs through the property, has been channeled into 10 magical waterfall-fed pools, perfect for a soak any time of the day. Rooms are large and rustic, made mostly of wood, though extremely comfortable. Bathroom ceilings are made of aged dried palm fronds and energy-saving light fixtures are used throughout, giving the whole place a sustainable edge. The

PARQUE NACIONAL LOS HAITISES

Eight kilometers west of Sabana de la Mar, **Parque Nacional Los Haitises** (admission RD$100; ☻7am-8pm) is certainly the best reason to visit this small bayside town. Its name meaning 'land of the mountains', this 1375-sq-km park at the southwestern end of the Bahía de Samaná contains scores of lush hills jutting some 30m to 50m from the water and coastal wetlands. The knolls were formed one to two million years ago, when tectonic drift buckled the thick limestone shelf that had formed underwater. The turnoff to the park is near the crossroads of Hwys 104 and 103, at the south end of town (near the bus stop). The road is passable in a normal car but pretty rough. The western side of the park is accessed via the new DR-7 highway to Samaná, about 75km north of Santo Domingo.

The area receives a tremendous amount of rainfall, creating perfect conditions for subtropical humid forest plants such as bamboo, ferns and bromeliads. In fact, Los Haitises contains over 700 species of flora, including four types of mangrove, making it one of the most highly biodiverse regions in the Caribbean.

Los Haitises is also home to 110 species of birds, 13 of which are endemic to the island. Those seen most frequently include the brown pelican, the American frigate bird, the blue heron, the roseate tern and the northern jacana. If you're lucky, you may even spot the rare Hispaniolan parakeet, notable for its light-green and red feathers.

The park also contains a series of limestone caves, some of which contain intriguing Taíno pictographs. Drawn by the native inhabitants of Hispaniola using mangrove shoots, the pictures depict faces, hunting scenes, whales and other animals. Several petroglyphs can also be seen at the entrance of some caves and are thought to represent divine guardians. **Las Cuevas de la Arena**, **La Cueva del Templo** and **La Cueva de San Gabriel** are three of the more interesting caves and shouldn't be missed.

criolla restaurant here is the best place to eat in the area any time of day (the hotel offers all-inclusive packages but it's cheaper to order from the menu á la carte). Don't let the ominous black crow here scare you – it's all vaguely eerie and Edgar Allen Poe-esque, but it's harmless save its brazen attempts to steal your breakfast (and our shift key!). To find it, follow the Brugal rum sign toward 'Caño Hondo' one block south of the intersection of Hwys 103 and 104 in town for around 9km down a nasty road.

Hotel Riverside   HOTEL $
(☎809-556-7465; r with/without air-con RD$400/700; ❄) A block south of the *gua-gua* station is this place where you can lay your head for the night; a family rents out 14 or so large rooms next door to their home.

❶ Information

Sabana de la Mar is a small town with relatively few services. **BanReservas** (Calle Duarte; ☻8am-5pm Mon-Fri, 9am-1pm Sat) is three blocks south of the ferry pier and has an ATM.

❶ Getting There & Away

Hwy 103 from Hato Mayor descends from the hills straight into Sabana de la Mar, turning into Calle Duarte, the main street, and eventually bumping right into the pier where the Samaná ferry leaves and arrives. The road from Miches intersects with the Higüey highway just outside (south) of town. *Gua-guas* to Miches, Hato Mayor, El Seibo, Higüey and Santo Domingo all congregate at or near that intersection.

Gua-guas are the only means of public transportation out of town. They leave from the entrance of town, at the crossroads of Hwy 104 and Hwy 103. *Gua-guas* headed to Santo Domingo (RD$200, 3½ hours, every 35 minutes from 4:15am to 4:40pm) stop along the way in Hato Mayor (RD$80, 1 hour) and San Pedro de Macorís (RD$130, 2 hours). *Gua-guas* also provide service to Miches (RD$100, 2 hours, every 25 minutes from 6:45am to 6pm).

Passenger ferries across the Bahía de Samaná to Samaná depart from the town pier (RD$200, 1¼ hours, 9am, 11am, 3pm and 5pm). From there you can catch *gua-guas* to Las Galeras, Las Terrenas or puddle-jump to other destinations on the north coast. Bad weather means rough seas and frequent cancellations, and some of the boats are rickety, making even a voyage under sunny skies a potentially seasickening experience for those with sensitive stomachs. Buy your ticket on the boat.

Península de Samaná

Best Places to Eat

» Restaurant El Cabito
(p120)

» La Terrasse (p126)

» El Rancho Du' Vagabond'
(p115)

» Restaurant Rubi (p120)

» Big Dan's Café Americano
(p126)

Best Places to Stay

» Peninsula House (p129)

» Hotel Bahía las Ballenas
(p130)

» Lomita Maravilla (p125)

» El Rincón de Abi (p125)

» Casa Por Qué No? (p118)

Why Go?

This small slither of land is the antithesis of the Dominican-Caribbean dream in the southeast, where resorts rule and patches of sand come at a first-class premium. Far more laid-back and, in a certain sense, more cosmopolitan, Samaná offers a European vibe as strong as *espresso*; it's where escape – both from the workaday, urban milieu of New York or Paris and from Santiago or Santo Domingo – is the operative word; and where French and Italian are at least as useful as Spanish. Of course, the majority come to gasp at the North Atlantic humpback whales doing their migratory song and dance from mid-January to mid-March, but the peninsula is no one-trick pony. Sophisticated Las Terrenas is the place to base yourself if you crave a lively social scene, and sleepy Las Galeras boasts several of the best beaches in the DR, their beauty enhanced by the effort it takes to get there.

When to Go

Over 10,000 North American humpback whales put on a show of monstrous proportions in the Bahía de Samaná – February is the best month to see them. Or bypass the crowds of whale-watching season and have the peninsula to yourself in April. In December, keep dry as winter sets in – and beat the holiday crowds.

History

Because of Bahía de Samaná's fortuitous geography – its deep channel, eastward orientation and easy-to-defend mouth, perfect for a naval installation – the Península de Samaná has been coveted, fought over and bought several times over. At least six different countries, including Haiti, France, Spain, the US and Germany, have either occupied the Samaná area or sought to do so.

Founded as a Spanish outpost in 1756, Samaná was first settled by émigrés from the Canary Islands, but the political turmoil of Hispaniola – the sale of the island to the French, a Haitian revolution and two British invasions – kept Samaná town's population growing and changing. It was deemed a prize even as early as 1807 during the brief French possession of Hispaniola. France's commander in Santo Domingo, an ambitious leader no doubt, proposed building a city named Port Napoleon in Samaná, but France was dispossessed of the island before the plan could move forward.

After its independence from Spain, the DR was taken over by Haiti, which controlled Hispaniola from 1822 to 1844. During this period Haiti invited more than 5000 freed and escaped slaves from the US to settle on the island. About half moved to the Samaná area. Today, a community of their descendents still speaks a form of English.

During Haitian rule, France pressured its former colony to cede the Península de Samaná in return for a reduction in the debt Haiti owed it. Incredibly, Haiti had been forced to pay restitution to France for land taken from French colonists in order to gain international recognition. Of course, France

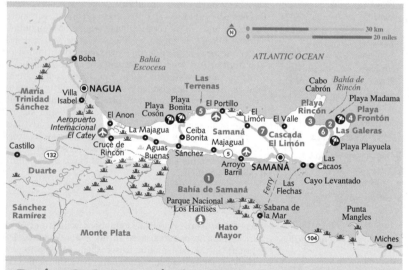

Península de Samaná Highlights

❶ Scouring the Bahía de Samaná in search of majestic 30-ton humpbacks breaching and diving on a **whale-watching trip** (p112)

❷ Dining precariously above crashing waves, quite literally on the edge of the Dominican Republic, at **Restaurant El Cabito** (p120) in Las Galeras

❸ Taking a long, *long* walk on the gorgeous sand of **Playa Rincón** (p117)

❹ Swimming with the fishes on a snorkeling trip through the best reefs the peninsula has to offer at **Playa Frontón** (p116)

❺ Wining and dining amid sophisticated European flare in cosmopolitan **Las Terrenas** (p121)

❻ Losing a few days at the end of the road in **Las Galeras** (p116), one of the few independent-traveler-friendly locales in the DR

❼ Taking in the rugged mountain scenery of Samaná's interior on a trip to 52m-high **Cascada El Limón** (p123)

never paid restitution to former slaves for their ordeal.

After Dominican independence from Haiti in 1844, the new Dominican government feared Haiti would reinvade, so sought foreign assistance from France, England and Spain. The DR eventually resubmitted to Spanish rule in 1861, and Spain immediately sent a contingent of settlers to the Samaná area and reinforced the military installations on Cayo Levantado, a large island (and site of a luxury all-inclusive resort today) near the mouth of the bay.

Even after independence in 1864, the Península de Samaná remained a tempting prize for other countries. Beginning in 1868, the US, under President Ulysses S Grant, sought to purchase the peninsula from the DR in order to build a naval base there. Dominican president and strongman Buenaventura Báez agreed to the sale in order to obtain the money and weapons he needed to stay in power. However, the US Senate, under pressure from Dominican exile groups and strong opposition from France and the UK, rejected the proposal in 1871. A year later, Báez arranged to lease the area to the US-based Samaná Bay Company for 99 years. To the relief of most Dominicans, the company fell behind on its payments and Baez's successor, Ignacio María González, rescinded the contract in 1874. The US revisited the idea of annexing Samaná in 1897 as the Spanish-American war loomed, but decided to build its Caribbean base in Guantánamo Bay, Cuba after it quickly defeated Spain.

German intentions toward the Península de Samaná are less clear, but US documents from the 1870s suggest that Germany was also seeking to establish a military base in the Caribbean. In 1916, during WWI, the US occupied the DR in part because it feared that Germany was seeking to establish itself here.

❶ Getting There & Around

Península de Samaná is accessible by air at Aeropuerto Internacional El Catey, on the highway between Nagua and Sánchez. It receives international flights from Canada (Air Canada and Westjet) and various cities in Europe through charter flights.

Two other airports – 'international' by name only – serve the peninsula. Several small domestic airlines have regularly scheduled flights to Aeropuerto Internacional El Portillo, several kilometers west of Las Terrenas, and during the height of whale-watching season less frequently to the otherwise charter-only Aeropuerto Internacional Arroyo Barril near Samaná.

Other than arriving by cruise ship, the only sea option is the regular ferry service between Samaná and Sabana de la Mar in the southeast. Cars are not allowed and the schedule is subject to the weather.

The new DR-7, the country's newest highway, opened in 2009 and cut travel time from Santo Domingo to Samaná to less than two hours. The 102km or so stretch of highway begins at Autopista Las Américas DR-3 (30km east of Santo Domingo near the international airport) and ends at the Cruce Rincón de Molinillos, 18km west of Sanchez. The toll road – practically an autobahn compared to other roads in the country – costs RD$347 for the entire journey.

For more information, see p251.

EASTERN PENÍNSULA DE SAMANÁ

Samaná

POP 12,500

Samaná is another far-flung Dominican town swimming hard against the currents of the global recession: come here outside whale season and it feels like a ghost town, with as many daily closures of local business as glorious sunrises over the bay. Without the pristine coastlines and international expat flare of nearby Las Terrenas and Las Galeras, Samaná just barely clings to the slow daily rhythms of an ordinary Dominican life: fishermen's days are lived on the water; the ferry from Sabana de la Mar comes and goes; and the Malecón (main street; literally 'sea wall') takes on a somnolent air. That all changes from mid-January to mid-March, of course, when scores of tourists descend upon Samaná to catch glimpses of the great North Atlantic humpback whales without whom Samaná would scarcely warrant more than a glimpse in the rearview mirror.

In fact, Samaná was little more than that until 1985, when the first whale-watching expedition from this isolated fishing village set out. Because North Atlantic humpbacks find the bay water particularly suitable for their annual version of speed dating, Samaná is transformed by tens of thousands of tourists who flock here to go on a whale-watching tour, a natural spectacle with few equals.

◉ Sights

Cayo Levantado ISLAND

Only the western third of this lush island 7km from Samaná is open to the public;

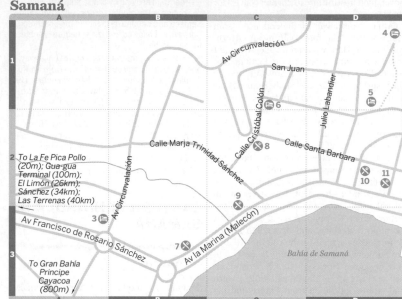

the eastern two-thirds is now occupied by a five-star hotel. The public beach here is gorgeous – all white sand and turquoise waters – but the idyll is somewhat marred by the Disneyfication of the experience. Large cruise ships dock here regularly, and the facilities, including a few restaurants and bars and 2000 lounge chairs, don't offer much peace and quiet. Touts wander the beach looking for tourists who want to have their photographs taken with exotic animals, some endangered and on leashes, such as parrots, boa constrictors, monkeys and even sea lions – not a practice to be encouraged. If you choose to visit, try going in mid- to late afternoon, when most of the activity is winding down. Boatmen at the pier make the trip for RD$250 per person round-trip; if you have a group of up to 15 people you can negotiate the boat round-trip for RD$1300. Another option is to travel to Carenero, a village 6km east of Samaná, where there are several boats with permits, or wait at Gran Bahía Principe Cayo Levantado's mainland wharf, where guests are ferried to and from the resort, only 1km further on, and join a group for around RD$200 per person.

If you arrive and no boats are around, try **Julian** or **Hormiga** (📞809-376-4271), two boatmen reachable on the same cell phone.

FREE Shipwreck Museum   MUSEUM
(Av La Marina 1; ⊙10am-6pm Tue-Sun) A small but interesting museum, especially for shipwreck buffs. It contains recovered artefacts from *La Scipion*, a 74-gun French war ship that was sunk while on the run from British war ships in 1782. The museum also houses a few items from various other sunken vessels and offers narration in English. The attached Spanish-owned restaurant is quite atmospheric, serving excellent but pricy tapas.

Playa las Flechas   BEACH
This small beach several kilometers east of Samaná is thought by many historians to be the site of a small and short battle between Columbus' crew and the Ciguayos, a Taíno *cacique* (chiefdom), in which the Spaniards were driven back to their ship. A week later, somehow their differences were reconciled and they formed an alliance against the rival *caciques*.

🏃 Activities
Whale-Watching
For sheer awe-inspiring, 'the natural world is an amazing thing' impact, a whale-watching trip is hard to beat. Samaná is considered to be one of the top 10 destinations in the world

Scale: 0 — 200 m / 0 — 0.1 miles

To Playa Las Flechas (5km); Las Galeras (28km)

To Cayo Levantado (7km); Sabaná de la Mar (15km); Parque Nacional Los Haitises (18km)

PENÍNSULA DE SAMANÁ SAMANÁ

for whale-watching. Around 45,000 people travel here every year between January 15 and March 20 to see the majestic acrobatics of these massive creatures. February is peak season for humpback whales, but try to avoid the weekend of February 27: the Independence Day holiday 'Carnaval' for Dominicans makes it the busiest weekend of the winter and Samaná is packed.

Most of the whale-watching companies have a morning and afternoon trip. There's little difference in terms of your likelihood of seeing whales, and although the water may be slightly rougher in the afternoon, it also tends to be quieter, with fewer boats out. There are 43 vessels with legal permits: eight companies, two of which are foreign-owned (Canadian and Spanish) and the rest owned by Dominicans from Samaná, and around 12 independent operators. A co-management and self-regulation agreement was established in 1994 between the boat owners and various departments of the Dominican government, including the Ministry of Tourism and the Ministry of the Environment. A manual of rules and responsible behavior was created and every year all the stakeholders sign it to renew their commitment. One of the more important objectives is ensuring a minimum boat size of 8.7m: in big seas small boats are low to the water and sometimes aren't aware of the whales until they're too close.

Private vessels are strictly prohibited from whale-watching; this applies to yachts and boats of any size. They can only transit into or out of the bay. Additionally, do your part by not frequenting illegal operators. Your vessel should have a registration number and a yellow flag issued by the Ministry of Environment.

🏄 Whale Samaná
WHALE-WATCHING

(☎809-538-2494; www.whalesamana.com; cnr Calle Mella & Av Malecón; adult/under 5yr/5-10yr US$55/free/30; ⊙office 9am-1pm & 3-6pm) Samaná's most recommended whale-watching outfit. It's owned and operated by Canadian marine mammal specialist Kim Beddall, who was the first person to recognize the scientific and economic importance of Samaná's whales, back in 1985. Whale Samaná tours use a large two-deck boat with capacity for 60 people (though most tours have around 40). The skilled captains religiously observe the local boat-to-whale distance and other regulations – most of which Beddall helped create – while on-board guides offer interesting facts and information in five languages over the boat's sound system. Sodas and water are provided free of charge. Tours leave at 9am and last three to four hours. There is also a 1:30pm trip when demand is high, and tours can include a stop at Cayo Levantado on the way back. The price above does not include admission fees to the marine sanctuary, which have traditionally been RD$100 but were being raised to between RD$200 to RD$400 for the 2011 season. As an added bonus, Whale Samaná will allow you to reuse your ticket for a second trip if you don't see any whales – there is no expiration date for this offer. Off-season, this is the only outfitter taking kayaks into Parque Nacional Los Haitises – a definite highlight.

☞ Tours

In addition to Whale Samaná, several other agencies also offer whale-watching excursions, as well as trips to Cascada el Limón and Parque Nacional Los Haitises, both for about US$50 per person. Most of these will generally have a tour guide as part of a larger group who can often answer questions, though there are no permanent naturalists associated with these operators.

Luna Tours/Samaná
Runners   ADVENTURE TOUR
(✆809-538-3109; www.bavarorunners.com; Av Circunvalación 41; ⊙8:30am-6:30pm) Next to Hotel Bahía View.

Moto Marina   ECOTOUR
(✆809-538-2304; motomarina@yahoo.com; Av la Marina 3; ⊙8am-noon & 2-6pm Mon-Sat, 8am-noon & 4-7pm Sun)

🛏 Sleeping

There's little reason to stay in Samaná proper and most people booking whale-watching or Los Haitises trips do so from Las Terrenas, Las Galeras or further afield. Hotels here don't generally include breakfast, but do toss in coffee or tea.

TOP CHOICE ❯ **Gran Bahía Principe Cayo Levantado**   HOTEL $$$
(✆809-538-3232; www.bahia-principe.com; Cayo Levantado; all-incl r from US$208; ❋@🐾🏊) This romantic five-star hotel has a lot going for it, namely its 'private' beach on privileged real estate on the supremely idyllic sands of Cayo Levantado. The hotel itself sits on extra-lush grounds and offers classic luxury á la Ritz-Carlton (ie slightly stuffy), though the excellent rooms, with hardwood floors and some with patio ocean views and vaulted ceilings, suffer from that less so than the lobby. There are two excellent pools, the best of which is accessed via an outdoor elevator. The downside is you're on an island and need to take a boat (provided by the hotel) to get there... Well, that's the upside, too.

Hotel Bahía View   HOTEL $
(✆809-251-4000; wendydlsr@hotmail.com; Av Circunvalación 31; r with/without air-con RD$1600/1200; ❋🐾) A longstanding hotel popular with independent travelers, the Bahía View unfortunately doesn't have great views of Bahía. Definitely ask for a room with a balcony anyway. Each of the 10 rooms is arranged differently, with multiple beds, but all have high ceilings and clean, modern bathrooms. The new manager is a refreshing change from the norm – her friendliness is contagious – and there's a good Dominican restaurant (mains RD$90 to RD$425, serving breakfast, lunch and dinner).

Hotel Chino   HOTEL $$
(✆809-538-2215; Calle San Juan 1; d/tr RD$1800/2700; P❋🐾) Located above a Chinese restaurant on top of a hill, Hotel Chino's rooms have balconies with fantastic views of town and the waterfront. But while the rooms are shiny and clean, with cable TV and air-con, there's only a small patio lounge and no other amenities. The restaurant is popular for its outstanding views.

Gran Bahía Principe Cayacoa   HOTEL $$$
(✆809-538-3131; www.bahiaprincipe.com; all-incl d per person US$280; P❋@🐾🏊) Samaná town's fanciest hotel is perched on a cliff above the city with spectacular views of the bay (and maybe even of humpbacks during whale season). Food and rooms, however, are less attractive than their sister property on Cayo Levantado. If the beach here, accessed via an outdoor elevator, isn't to your liking, there are free daily shuttles from this resort to Cayo's private beach.

Samaná Spring Hotel   HOTEL $$
(✆809-538-2946; samanaspring@hotmail.com; Calle Cristobal Colón; s/d RD$1400/2000; ❋) Extra-friendly and new; rooms are basic but still in new condition with cable TV, including HBO, and hot water.

Hotel Docia   HOTEL $
(✆809-538-2041; www.hoteldocia.blogspot.com; cnr Teodoro Chasereaux & Duarte; d with/without air-con RD$1200/1000; ❋) The rooms at this concrete hotel on a hill are certainly no-frills, but for budget travelers that might be enough. The pleasant 2nd-floor patio overlooking the bay is a nice consolation.

✗ Eating & Drinking

The majority of restaurants are located along Av Malecón.

TOP CHOICE El Rancho Du' Vagabond' ITALIAN $$
(Calle Cristobal Colón 4A; pasta RD$275-375, pizzas RD$265-395; ☺lunch & dinner Wed-Mon) In a region wrought with Italians but unfortunately not the fabulous pizza that usually follows, this pizzeria stands out as the real deal. You'll be pleasantly surprised as you walk past the nondescript entrance to the charming back dining room, where you'll find no views whatsoever – this spot is all about the food. There's an extensive list of fresh pasta with a concentration on specialty gnocchi and an even better pizza menu; the namesake pie (Serrano ham, fresh tomatoes, freshly grated Grano parmesan and truffle oil) won't soon be forgotten.

L'Hacienda Restaurant STEAKHOUSE, SEAFOOD $$
(Calle Santa Barbara; mains RD$390-680; ☺dinner Thu-Tue) A friendly French chef-owner with a Spanish name (José) has been running this intimate spot since 1996. It's a small and simple menu highlighted by big meat (RD$580) and seafood (RD$680) grills. The dining room is equally cozy.

Restaurant Mate Rosada CARIBBEAN, SEAFOOD $$
(Av Malecón; mains RD$230-750; ☺lunch & dinner, closed Wed dinner) Another reliable Malecón mainstay, Mate Rosada has a more extensive menu of seafood and grills than others in its price range. The classy front patio is the town's most formal, but that doesn't mean it's immune to *motoconcho* exhaust. The small bar is one of the better in town.

Bahía Snack CAFE $
(Av Malecón; mains RD$125-350; ☺lunch & dinner; ☺) Part of the brightly painted fake village that stretches along the western part of Av Malecón, this place is a snack bar dressed up as an elegant restaurant. The outdoor patio is the town's most pleasant, especially at night when the air cools and a breeze blows in from the bay, and it fills up quickly with tourists munching on mediocre pizza, pasta and simple sandwiches, washed down with cocktails in leaning glasses.

La Fe Pica Pollo DOMINICAN $
(Av Francisco de Rosario Sánchez; meals RD$90-180; ☺breakfast, lunch & dinner) A small hole in the wall close to the *gua-gua* terminal serving tasty fried chicken plus a few other Dominican dishes.

Bambú Restaurant CARIBBEAN, SEAFOOD $$
(Av Malecón; mains RD$220-530; ☺lunch & dinner) Probably more popular for Malecón prominence than premiere cuisine, it nevertheless has a breezy patio that seems to draw in crowds.

You can also get cheap eats at a series of food stands that line Av Malecón near Calle Maria Trinidad Sánchez. Beginning around 6pm and lasting until the early hours of the morning, fried chicken is served up with Presidente beers for Dominican and foreign customers alike.

There is an expensive **mini-market** (Av Malecón; ☺10am-1pm & 2-7pm) in the faux Caribbean village for basic sundries, wine, cigars and other kitschy souvenirs.

ℹ Information

Banco Popular (Av Malecón; ☺8:15am-4pm Mon-Fri, 9am-1pm Sat) Located on the Malecón across from the ferry dock.

BanReservas (Calle Santa Barbara; ☺8am-5pm Mon-Fri, 9am-1pm Sat) One block north of the Malecón.

Clinic Assist (☺809-538 2426; Av Francisco de Rosario Sánchez) Doctors on call 24 hours. Located in the pastel faux village.

Farmacia Giselle (cnr Calles Santa Barbara & Julio Labandier; ☺8am-9pm Mon-Sat, to 1pm Sun) Good selection of meds and toiletries.

Farmacia Maritere (Av Francisco Rosario de Sánchez; ☺8am-9pm) On the second traffic circle up from the Malecón, on the road to Sánchez.

Hospital Municipal (Calle Trinidad Sanchez; ☺24hr) A very basic hospital near the Palacio de Justicia.

Internet Café & Snack Bar (Av Circunvalación; per hr RD$20; ☺8am-11pm) The cheapest and best internet in town, with private cabins.

Politur (tourist police; ☺809-754-3256; Av Francisco de Rosario Sánchez; ☺24hr) On the traffic circle near Av Circunvalación.

Post office (cnr Calles Santa Barbara & 27 de Febrero; ☺8:30am-5pm Mon-Fri)

Scotiabank (Av Francisco Rosario de Sánchez; ☺8am-4pm Mon-Fri, 9am-1pm Sat) Closest ATM to the *gua-gua* terminal and the municipal market.

ℹ Getting There & Away

Arriving in town from the direction of El Limón or Sánchez, it's about 1km downhill past the municipal market where the *gua-gua* (small bus) station is, around several traffic circles and along a newly built faux Caribbean village to the main street – Av Malecón or Av la Marina. Most of the restaurants, banks and bus stations are located here.

Air

The nearest airport in regular operation is **Aeropuerto Internacional El Portillo** (EPS), just outside of Las Terrenas, but it only serves sporadic domestic flights. The newer **Aeropuerto Internacional El Catey** (AZS; 809-338-0094), 40km west of Samaná, receives international flights. The closest airstrip to Samaná, Aeropuerto Internacional Arroyo Barril, receives mostly charter flights only. For details of domestic and international airlines servicing the DR, see p250.

Bus

Facing the pier, **Caribe Tours** (809-538-2229; Av Malecón) offers services to Santo Domingo at 8am, 10am, 2pm and 4pm (RD$310, 2½ hours, daily). The same bus stops along the way at Sánchez (RD$60, 30 minutes).

For direct service to Puerto Plata 210km to the west, there are two options. **El Canario** (809-291-5594) buses leaves at 11am beside the Banco Popular. **Papagayo** (809-802-3534, ask for Salvador) has a service at 1:30pm from under the mango tree on the eastern side of the little park next to Banco Popular on the Malecón. If you miss him there, he waits at the municipal market until 2pm. Both charge RD$250 and the trip takes about 3½ to four hours. Call ahead to double-check the day's departure. Locals say the latter is a safer though slightly slower ride. Arrive 30 to 45 minutes early to reserve a seat.

For service to towns nearby, head to the **gua-gua terminal** (Av Malecón) at the *mercado municipal*, 200m west of the Politur station, near Angel Mesina. From here, trucks and minivans head to Las Galeras (RD$80, 45 minutes to one hour, every 15 minutes from 6:40am to 6pm), El Limón (RD$60, 30 minutes, every 15 minutes from 6:30am to 6:30pm), Las Terrenas (RD$100, 1¼ hours, hourly from 6:30am to 4:45pm) and Sánchez (RD$70, 45 minutes, every 15 minutes from 6:30am to 8pm). Destinations further afield also leave from the same block: Santo Domingo (RD$275, three hours, every 30 minutes from 4am to 4:30pm) and Santiago (RD$275, four hours, hourly from 4:30pm to 2:30pm).

Ferry

Transporte Maritimo provides the only ferry service – passengers only, no vehicles – across the Bahía de Samaná to Sabana de la Mar (RD$200, one hour plus, daily at 7am, 9am, 11am and 3pm). Buy tickets on board. From there, it's possible to catch *gua-guas* to several destinations in the southeast and then on to Santo Domingo, though the road network in this part of the country is rough and public transportation is not so comfortable.

ℹ Getting Around

Samaná is walkable, but if you're carrying luggage, catch a *motoconcho* (motorcycle taxi) – they're everywhere. 4WD vehicles are your only option in terms of car rental – roads on the peninsula are bad enough to warrant the extra expense. Rates average around RD$2500 per day (tax and insurance included) and discounts are typically given for rentals of a week or longer. Try **Xamaná Rent Motors** (809-435-6828; Av Malecón; ☻8am-6pm Mon-Sat, to noon Sun).

Las Galeras

The road to this small fishing community 28km northeast of Samaná ends at a fish shack on the beach. So does everything else, metaphorically speaking. One of the great pleasures of a stay here is losing all perspective on the great big world beyond; even a trip to one of the beautiful and isolated outlying beaches seems far away. But Las Galeras, as much as anywhere else on the peninsula, offers terrestrial and subaquatic adventures for those with a will strong enough to ignore the pull of inertia and overcome the temptation to do nothing more than lie around your bungalow or while away the day at a restaurant watching others do the same.

Las Galeras has not only been discovered by the French and Italians, but Bulgarians, Canadians, Americans, Belgians, Spaniards and Germans, making it a more eclectic global village than other more touristy spots on the peninsula; and it's one of the few independent-traveler-minded locales in the DR – there's barely an all-inclusive resort in sight.

◉ Sights

Las Galeras has a number of natural attractions that can be visited by boat, foot, car or horseback. All can be reached on your own, provided you're in decent shape or have a sturdy vehicle.

Playas Madama & Frontón   BEACH

Preferred by some locals over Playa Rincón, Playa Frontón boasts some of the area's best snorkeling. Apparently it's also popular with drug smugglers, Dominicans braving the Mona Passage on their way to Puerto Rico, and reality show contestants – in 2002 *Expedición Robinson*, Colombia's version of the reality show *Survivor*, was filmed here. Playas Madama is a small beach framed by high bluffs; keep in mind there's not much sunlight here in the afternoon.

DON'T MISS

PLAYA RINCÓN

For those who are connoisseurs of such things, Playa Rincón is a pitch-perfect beach. Stretching uninterrupted for almost 3km of nearly white, soft sand and multihued water good for swimming, there's even a small stream at the far western end, great for a quick freshwater dip at the end of a long, sunny day. A thick palm forest provides the backdrop. Some historians claim that it's here, not Playa las Flechas, where Columbus and his crew landed. One downside: an awful lot of flotsam and jetsam lay uncollected along the pristine sands.

Several small restaurants serve mostly seafood dishes and rent beach chairs, making this a great place to spend the entire day. Most people arrive by boat; the standard option is to leave Las Galeras around 9am and be picked up at 4pm – it's around 20 minutes each way. It costs about RD$500 to RD$1000 per person round-trip but with a group of seven or more, it's better to negotiate for the boat itself (boatmen will start at RD$5000) and split the fare. They start high but won't let you walk away.

A rumor hovers about town – surely perpetuated by the boatmen – that you cannot drive to Rincón. You can, but it requires patience and will – the last 2km or so are especially rough for small or midsize cars, especially after a hard rain. The turnoff to Playa Rincón is 7km south of Las Galeras on the road to Samaná. A round-trip taxi to Rincón, including wait time (9am to 5pm), is RD$1800.

The trail to both begins at the far eastern end of the Grand Paradise Samaná beach, about 200m past the resort's entrance, near a private house that most people know as 'La Casa de los Ingleses' (House of the English) after its original owners. Coming from town, the house and the trail will be on your right. In the first kilometer you'll pass La Hacienda before reaching the first of two cut-offs to Playa Madama. If you turn left there (or at the next cut-off a kilometer later) you'll walk another 2km until you reach Madama. If you continue on the main trail, you'll pass a second cut-off to Playa Madama (not indicated) and a few kilometers later the cut-off to Playa Frontón (easily missed) and from here it's another four winding kilometers to Frontón itself. Truth be told, heading out on your own is not recommended – people often get lost and dehydrated. If you insist, pick up a trail map from La Rancheta and leave early (though your author and five Italians still couldn't find it, even with help from locals along the way). Bring plenty of water. It's much simpler to take a boat to either of these beaches, for around RD$500 to RD$1000 per person round-trip depending on your bargaining skills, with a pickup in the afternoon or whenever you wish; or, a much cheaper option is hiring a local guide to simply show you the way. Contact Karin at La Hacienda (p119).

Playita   BEACH
Better than the beach in town, Playita (Little Beach) is easy to get to on foot or by *motoconcho*. It's a swath of tannish sand, with mellow surf and backed by tall, dramatically leaning palm trees. There is a decent outdoor restaurant (owned by a local resort) and a simpler Dominican affair, where you can get grilled fish or chicken, plus water, soda and beer. On the main road just south of Las Galeras, look for signs for Hotel La Playita pointing down a dirt road headed west. Or if you're OK with clambering, follow the road that goes west at the main intersection, past Villa Serena until you reach a gated development; let yourself in and follow the path until you reach the remains of a barbed wire fence. It's easy enough to get over and the beach is just on the other side. Beach chairs rent for RD$100 for the day.

Boca del Diablo   LANDMARK
'Mouth of the Devil' is an impressive vent or blowhole, where waves rush up a natural channel and blast out of a hole in the rocks. Car or motorcycle is the best way to get here – look for an unmarked dirt road 7km south of town and about 100m beyond the well-marked turnoff to Playa Rincón. Follow the road eastward for about 8km, then walk the last 100m or so.

🏊 Activities
Water Sports
For experienced divers, **Cabo Cabrón** (Bastard Point) is one of the North Coast's best dive sites. After an easy boat ride from Las Galeras, you're dropped into a churning

channel with a giant coral formation that you can swim around; you may see dolphins here. Other popular sites include **Piedra Bonita**, a 50m stone tower good for spotting jacks, barracudas and sea turtles; **Cathedral**, an enormous underwater cave opening to sunlight; and a sunken 55m container ship haunted by big morays. Several large, shallow coral patches, including **Los Carriles**, a series of underwater hills, are good for beginner divers.

Las Galeras Divers (☑809-538-0220; www.las-galeras-divers.com; Plaza Lusitania; ◷8:30am-7pm) is a well-respected, French-run dive shop at the main intersection. One-/two-tank dives including all equipment cost US$50/85 (US$10 less if you have your own). A 10-dive package brings the rate down to US$44 per dive, including gear. Various PADI certification courses can also be arranged.

Scuba Libre Diving Center (☑829-877-7462; www.lacompagniadeicaraibi.com; Grand Paradise Samaná resort; ◷8:30am-5pm) is located at the far end of Grand Paradise Samaná's beach. In addition to diving, it also offers snorkeling trips (US$15) and windsurf and catamaran rental and instruction (US$15 to US$20 per hour), all available to guests and nonguests alike. It's easy enough to walk to the dive shop here by following the path along the beach from town; resort security will let you through.

Hiking

The spectacular El Punto lookout is a 5km walk from La Rancheta. To get there, simply continue past the turnoffs to Playas Madam and Frontón and keep climbing up, up and up. Allow at least an hour to get to the top.

Horseback Riding

The Belgian owner of La Hacienda leads well-recommended horseback riding tours to various spots around Las Galeras, including El Punto lookout, Playas Madama, Frontón and Rincón, as well as the surrounding hills. Her trips cater to all skill levels and range from two-hour excursions (US$35 per person) to full-day (US$70) and overnight (US$200) trips.

Tours

While you can visit many of the beaches and sights on your own – or hire a *motoconcho* driver to act as your chauffeur and guide – organized tour operators include **R-azor Tours** (☑809-538-0218; www.azortour.eu; Calle Principal), **Dario Perez Excursions** (☑809-809-924-6081; Plaza Lusitania) and **Scuba Libre Diving Center** (☑829-877-7462; www.lacompagniadeicaraibi.com; Grand Paradise Samaná resort; ◷8:30am-5pm). Day-trips include whale-watching in Bahía de Samaná (US$60 to US$72 per person with lunch), land and boat excursions through Parque Nacional Los Haitises (US$72 per person) and boat tours to the area's isolated beaches (US$30 to US$40 per person).

Sleeping

With the exception of a few, all of the hotels and bungalows in Las Galeras are within walking distance of the main intersection. The unimpressive Grand Paradise Samaná is the only resort in town.

TOP CHOICE Casa Por Qué No? B&B $$
(☑809-712-5631; s/d incl breakfast US$50/60; closed May-Oct; P❄) Pierre and Monick, the charming French-Canadian owners of this B&B, are consummate hosts and rent out two rooms on either side of their cozy home – each room has a separate entrance and hammock. Only 25m or so north of the main intersection on your right as you're walking toward the beach, the house is fronted by a long, well-groomed garden where great breakfasts (deliciously crunchy homemade bread!) are served (RD$300 for nonguests). When you tire of DR's ubiquitous restaurant offerings, Monick can whip up a Thai dinner for you. It's definitely not the fanciest spot in town, but it offers the warmest hospitality.

TOP CHOICE Todo Blanco BOUTIQUE HOTEL $$
(☑809-538-0201; www.hoteltodoblanco.com; r US$86; P❄@☎) Whitewashed in colonial sophistication, this well-established inn run by a cheerful Dominican-Italian couple sits atop a small hillock a short walk from the end of the main drag in Las Galeras. The multilevel grounds are nicely appointed with gardens and a gazebo, all with views of the ocean below. The rooms are large and airy, with high ceilings, private terraces overlooking the sea and pastel headboards, which help prevent snow blindness here. Rooms aren't fancy – in fact, rather sparse

save the mosquito nets – but a homey living room area has a TV and DVD player and owner Maurizio is a fun Italian to sip an *espresso* with. One downside is the extra US$8 breakfast – almost nobody else charges guests for breakfast.

Casa Dorado
B&B **$$**
(📞829-933-8678; www.casadoradodr.com; r US$70-85; P🌐📶) This beautiful house, a kilometer from both the main intersection and Playita, is in the *'barrio'* and was decked out in Mexican-style interiors by the American-Dominican owners. Four rooms are available; the largest and most expensive comes with a Jacuzzi. There are ample hang spaces, from expansive hammock-strung terraces to cozy living rooms – if the weather turns sour, this is where you want to be. Breakfast in the gorgeously tiled kitchen is the real deal and guests from other hotels often find their way here, happy to fork over US$8 for the privilege. The owners run sport-fishing trips (up to four people from US$280 to US$550) and snorkeling excursions to Rincón and Frontón.

Sol Azul
BUNGALOWS **$$**
(📞829-882-8790; www.elsolazul.com; bungalows incl breakfast US$50-70; P🌐📶🏊) A fun Swiss couple run these four earthy, natural-hued and spacious bungalows, all set around a pristinely manicured garden and pleasant pool area just 50m from the main intersection. Two of the bungalows feature mezzanine levels – good for children – and the breakfast buffet gets high marks from travelers. If Casa Por Qué No? is full, it's the best alternative in this price range.

La Rancheta
BUNGALOWS **$**
(📞829-889-4727; www.larancheta.com; r/bungalow US$35/60; P) Buried in the lush jungle, 2.5km from the main intersection, is this hotel with a number of funky and simple two-storied bungalows that can accommodate between four and six people comfortably. Semi-outdoor rustic kitchens lend an eclectic cabin-in-the-woods feel to this traveler favorite. Ronald is Belgian and brings his beer over – a Godsend after too many intimate evenings with Presidente. The restaurant is quite good as well and serves a huge breakfast for RD$250.

La Hacienda
GUESTHOUSE **$**
(📞829-939-8285; www.larancheta.com; s/d US$27/35; P🌐📶) One kilometer further on from La Rancheta (on the trail/road to Playa Madama/Frontón), another Belgian, Karin, runs

a one-woman show with five rustic rooms, a communal kitchen and a pleasant open-air porch with sea and mountain views. Guests can help themselves to the fruit and vegetable garden; and pluck fresh eggs for RD$10. Those who don't want to cook for themselves often take meals down at La Rancheta. The big reason to stay here is to take advantage of Karin, an expert tour guide, who leads fabulous day and overnight hiking and horseback riding trips to out-of-the-way beaches and mountaintops, but keep in mind, this is nature – expect cold showers and don't be surprised if you find a frog in your toilet.

El Cabito
CAMPGROUND, GUESTHOUSE **$**
(📞829-697-9506; www.elcabito.net; campsites & hammocks per person RD$250, treehouses RD$750, cabins RD$1400) For those looking to rough it, this property in lush farmland 4km east of the main intersection in town has one of the few campgrounds in the entire DR. If you like the out-of-the-way location but want a little more comfort, there's a treehouse and two cabins. Stunning views are to be had all around, including from the dramatic restaurant perched over crashing waves below – the real coup here. It's also a short walk to Playa Madama. Pickup from Las Galeras is available if arranged in advance.

Casa Calliope
VILLA **$$**
(📞829-929-8506; www.caacalliope.com; d/q US$70/80; P@) Located near El Cabito, around 4km east of town, this two-bedroom hilltop Mexican-style villa offers funky luxury in beautiful surroundings. Each of the two large bedrooms has a full bathroom and terrace, and there's also a fully equipped kitchen for guests' use – vegetarian and healthy meals can be ordered up as well. The owners, a friendly couple from Boston, are a great source of information on the area. Two-night minimum stay generally required.

Villa Serena
BOUTIQUE HOTEL **$$$**
(📞809-538-0000; www.villaserena.com; r with/without air-con incl breakfast US$174/164; P❄@📶🏊) A cross between a Victorian England manor home and a Caribbean villa, this hotel, 300m east of the main intersection, has gorgeous ocean views and is probably the nicest place in Las Galeras. That being said, the room furnishings are a little worn and kitschy, and while every one of the 21 rooms is different, it's mostly in terms of the color schemes, bedspreads and shower curtains. Each has a balcony, some face the ocean directly and others open on to the meticulously

DON'T MISS

RESTAURANT EL CABITO

Clinging spectacularly on the edge of the Dominican Republic, this rustic, postcard-perfect **restaurant** (☏829-697-9506; mains RD$180-750; ☺breakfast, lunch & dinner) will floor you. Not only are the cliff-hugging views insane, you get several nearby blowholes (along with crashing waves) providing the soundtrack; and a gastro-centric humpback-whale viewing platform in whale season. The best time is sunset, when a kaleidoscopic flurry of hues melts into the sea as you sip on Belgian beers, which the Dutch-German owners pilfer from La Rancheta. But wait, there's food, too. Go for the excellent grilled calamari (RD$550) or dorado (RD$650) but really, who cares what you're eating? Reservations are essential and it offers a pick-up/drop-off service to anywhere in Las Galeras. Paradise found!

landscaped garden and swimming pool area. Off the main lobby is a peaceful terrace with rocking chairs. There's an excellent snorkeling spot just offshore and the hotel provides bikes and kayaks for guests.

Plaza Lusitania Hotel HOTEL **$$**
(☏809-538-0093; www.plazalusitania.com; Plaza Lusitania, Calle Principal; r incl breakfast from US$50; ▣✿@☎) Situated on the main intersection on the 2nd floor of a tiny mall complete with a good Italian restaurant and Haitian art gallery. Rooms are large and extremely comfortable; but steer clear if you don't like cats.

Paradiso Bungalows BUNGALOWS **$$**
(☏829-787-1276; oaradisobungalowslasgaleras @hotmail.fr; bungalows with/without air-con RD$1200/1000; ▣✿☎) You can't get more dead center than these simple budget bungalows tucked behind Le Taínos restaurant. Of the seven bungalows in jungle surrounds, two have kitchenettes and one offers air-con.

✖ Eating

For a town of its size, Las Galeras has an abundance of fantastic food and many restaurants are located at the single intersection on the main street. Several of the hotels also offer meals when ordered in advance.

TOP CHOICE Restaurant Rubi CARIBBEAN, SEAFOOD **$$**
(Playa Rincón; mains RD$300-700; ☺lunch) This dressed-up beach shack perhaps justifies the trip to Playa Rincón regardless of the long and beautiful beach on whose eastern end it sits. Picnic-table-style seating is juiced up with bright tablecloths and a single chalkboard relays the offerings: Fresh fish, *langosta* (lobster), grilled chicken etc, all done up on a massive, open-air grill. The whole fish

in coco sauce melts off the bone and again in your mouth; and don't forget to douse your coconut rice in the excellent salsa. Not only is it a perfect meal on a dreamy beach, but also it's a great place to give some of your money to actual Dominicans.

TOP CHOICE Le Taínos FUSION **$$**
(Calle Principal; mains RD$270-410; ☺dinner) The focal point of the center of town, this atmospheric eatery is the town's most cosmopolitan, with a small but exciting menu of all sorts of scrumptious dishes you don't see elsewhere, beautifully presented on massive plates fit for a king. The honey-oregano pork mignon (RD$330) is a real treat, as is the key lime chicken (RD$270) and seafood taboule (RD$170), all served in a candlelit alfresco space with a designer thatched-roof. The bar is the most sociable around, too, and the cocktails are huge, adding a level of value uncommon on the peninsula.

Boulangerie La Marseillaise BAKERY, BAR **$**
(Calle Principal; items RD$45-210; ☺7:30am-2:30pm & 3:30-7pm) Locals carry hip-hugging bags of car-length baguettes from this French bakery, the real deal serving wonderful crusty panini with ham and brie (RD$190), quiche lorraine (RD$90) and of course fresh croissants and *pain au chocolate*. It's also a small bar. Across from Supermercado No 1.

Plaza Lusitania Italian Restaurant ITALIAN, SEAFOOD **$**
(Plaza Lusitania, Calle Principal; mains RD$180-520; ☺breakfast, lunch & dinner) This long-time staple serves a varied menu of Italian dishes, including homemade pasta (tagliatelle with gorgonzola or fresh tomatoes?), large pizzas (RD$200 to RD$470), meat and fish dishes and an extensive list of Italian and

American desserts and artisanal ice cream (coconut gets a round of applause). Despite the fact that the ambiance is anchored by what basically amounts to lawn chairs, it's still one of the town's most popular.

El Pescador
SPANISH, SEAFOOD $$$
(Calle Principal; mains RD$200-600; ☺from 3pm Tue-Sun) Located across from BanReservas on the main road, this is a good seafood option, notably for its *paella* for two (the owner is Spanish) and anything in his *salsa verde* (white wine, garlic and parsley) sauce. Locals give the pizza (RD$220 to RD$400) high marks and the coconut flan is a nice little treat before calling it a night.

Chez Denise
FRENCH $$
(Calle Principal; mains RD$90-390; ☺lunch & dinner Mon-Sat) One of the first restaurants in town and still going strong. Locals favor the beef bourguignon and there's crêpes for the more budget conscious (RD$90 to RD$170).

There's a **mini-market** (☺8am-10pm) at the Grand Paradise Samaná resort. The rather uninspired **Europa Center** (Calle Principal) has some European imports and a small selection of fresh bread, meats and cheeses. The largest grocery store is **Supermercado No 1** (Calle Principal; ☺7:30am-9:30pm).

☆ Entertainment
Much of the nightlife involves drinks at one of the restaurants in town – the bar at Le Taínos is the best for connoisseurs of the cocktail. Further up on the road is **L'Aventura** (Calle Principal), which also has a healthy bar scene. On the way out of town is **La Indiana** (Calle Principal), an open-air bar–disco popular with locals that also has a big-screen TV that shows sports, music videos and movies.

❶ Information
The paved road coming from Samaná winds along the coast and through lovely, often-forested countryside before reaching the outskirts of Las Galeras. There's one main intersection in town (about 50m before the highway dead-ends at the beach) and most hotels, restaurants and services are within walking distance from there.

BanReservas (Calle Principal) The most convenient ATM. There is another at Grand Paradise Samaná Resort.

Especialidades Medicas Samaná (Calle Principle; ☺24hr) A small clinic run by a team of Cuban doctors.

Farmacia Las Galeras (Calle Principal; ☺8am-9pm Mon-Sat, 9am-5pm Sun) Basic meds and supplies near the main intersection.

Grand Paradise Samaná (☺24hr) Has a small clinic that nonguests can use in emergencies.

Las Galeras Tourist Service (Calle Principal at main intersection; internet per hr RD$180; ☺9am-1pm & 2:30-7pm Mon-Sat) Internet and money exchange. Wi-fi is free if you have a laptop.

RP Rent-A-Car (☑809-538-0249; Calle Principal; ☺8am-7pm Mon-Sat, to 1pm Sun) Exchanges cash dollars and euros; also rents cars.

❶ Getting There & Around
Gua-guas head to Samaná (RD$80, 45 minutes, every 15 minutes from 6:40am to 6:45pm) from the beach end of Calle Principal, but also cruise slowly out of town picking up passengers. There are also three daily buses to Santo Domingo (RD$325, three hours, 5:30am, 1pm & 3:05pm).

You can pretty much walk everywhere in Las Galeras proper. **Taxis** (☑829-559-8217) are available at a stand just in front of the main town beach. Some sample one-way fares are Aeropuerto Catey (RD$1500), Las Terrenas (RD$1800), Samaná (RD$700) and Santo Domingo (RD$7000). You may be able to negotiate cheaper fares, especially to Samaná.

Renting a car is an excellent way to explore the peninsula on your own. Prices are generally around US$65 to US$85 per day.

Caribe Fun Rentals (☑809-912-2440; ☺9am-1pm & 3-6:30pm Mon-Sat) Located 50m west of the intersection. Offers quads (US$50 per day) and motorcycles (US$33) as well.

RP Rent-A-Car (☑809-538-0249; Calle Principal; ☺8am-7pm Mon-Sat, to 1pm Sun) On the way out of town.

WESTERN PENÍNSULA DE SAMANÁ

Las Terrenas
POP 8400
No longer a rustic fishing village, today Las Terrenas is a cosmopolitan town and seems as much French (approaching a colony) and Italian as Dominican. Fashionable-looking European women in designer sunglasses ride their personal ATVs with a bag of baguettes in tow, battling on roads with way too many *motos*. It's a balancing act between locals and expats – one that has

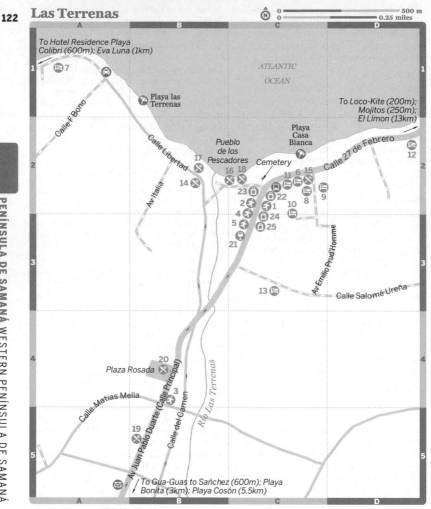

produced a lively mix of styles and a social scene more vibrant than anywhere else on the peninsula. Either way you walk along the beach road leads you to a beachfront scattered with hotels, high palm trees and calm aquamarine waters.

Like Las Galeras, Las Terrenes is independent-traveler-friendly and a good place to hook up with fellow nomads.

◉ Sights

Parque Nacional Los Haitises NATURE RESERVE
Since so few independent travelers make it to Sabana de la Mar, the closest entrance to

Parque Nacional Los Haitises across the bay on the mainland, Las Terrenas has become a popular place to book tours to the park. **Flora Tours** (☏809-360-2793; www.flora-tours.net; Calle Principal) offers tours of Los Haitises by motorboat. For kayak tours, see p124. Virtually every tour operator in town offers trips to Los Haitises (US$60), though only twice a week unless you're part of a group of six or more, in which case you can arrange things at your own convenience. There should be at least one company with a tour on offer five days a week, but schedules change, so it's best to book as soon as you arrive in town.

Cascada El Limón WATERFALL

Tucked away in surprisingly rough landscape, surrounded by peaks covered in lush greenery, is the 52m-high El Limón waterfall. A beautiful swimming hole is at the bottom, though it's often too deep, cold and rough for a dip; other times it's an absolutely perfect place to wash off the sweat and mud from the trip there. The departure point is the small town of El Limón, only a half-hour from Las Terrenas.

Just about everyone who visits does so on horseback, and almost a dozen *paradas* (horseback-riding operations) in town and on the highway toward Samaná offer tours (though it is not recommended to hire someone off the street, as there's little saving and the service is consistently substandard). All outfits offer essentially the same thing: a 30- to 60-minute ride up the hill to the waterfalls, 30 to 60 minutes to take a dip and enjoy the scene, and a 30- to 60-minute return trip, with lunch at the end. Your guide – who you should tip, by the way – will be walking, not riding, which can feel a little weird but is the custom. Walking on or horseback, you will get wet as there are several river crossings along the way – rubber sandals are a good idea.

Otherwise, it's a minimum 40-minute walk (from the main intersection in El Limón its roughly 5.6km), sometimes up a very steep trail over rough terrain and even a river or two to ford. It's not difficult to follow the path once you find it, though, especially if there are groups out on the trail. If you set out on your own, you will need to pay the entrance fee (RD$50).

Spanish-owned **Santí** ([809-342-9776; www.cascadalimonsamana.com; rides per person with/without lunch RD$900/650; 8am-6pm), at the main intersection in El Limón, is a good choice but also the most expensive. The lunch is excellent and the guides and staff (all adults) are better paid than elsewhere (though that doesn't make them any more professional). If you book with a tour company in Las Terrenas, transportation to/from El Limón is often not included (*guagua* US$50). Typically the tour (horse, guide and lunch) costs per person from US$35 to US$50. Most other operators charge around RD$750/375 with/without lunch; try **Parada la Manzana** ([829-931-6964; 8am-5pm), 5km east of El Limón toward Samaná, which has the added advantage – depending on your perspective – of being much closer to the falls. A *motoconcho* to either costs RD$100.

Tours may also be booked from Las Terrenas, some of which include transportation

ⓘ TOUTS

If you are driving yourself to El Limón, beware of *motoconcho* touts who will pull up alongside your vehicle and try to persuade you to a *parada* that pays them a commission, or suggest they show you the way to the ones mentioned here. Keep driving.

to El Limón by quad bikes, followed by the standard horseback ride and lunch (US$50); try Casa de las Terrenas.

🏃 Activities

Diving & Snorkeling

Las Terrenas has reasonably good diving and snorkeling and at least three shops in town to take you out. Favorite dive spots include a wreck in 28m of water and Isla Las Ballenas, visible from shore, with a large underwater cave. Most shops also offer special trips to Cabo Cabrón near Las Galeras and Dudu Cave near Río San Juan. Standard one-tank dives average US$55 with or without equipment. Four-, 10- and 12-dive packages don't save you more than about US$5 US$15 per dive. Two-tank diving day-trips to Cabo Cabrón are US$165, including gear, lunch and transportation; and one-tank day-trips to Dudu Caves are US$105, also including gear, lunch and transportation. Open Water courses average around US$430 all in.

A popular full-day snorkel trip is to Playa Jackson, several kilometers west of town, reached by boat (US$120 per person including a lobster lunch).

Recommended operators:

Las Terrenas Divers (☎809-889-2422; www.lt-divers.com; Hotel Bahía las Ballenas, Playa Bonita; ⊙9am-noon & 3-5pm) Well-respected German-run operation.

Turtle Dive Center (☎809-903-0659; www.turtledivecenter.com; El Paseo shopping center; ⊙8am-12:30pm & 2-7pm) Upstart SSI-affiliated shop, run by a safety-first Frenchman.

Kitesurfing & Windsurfing

Second only to Cabarete, Las Terrenas is a good place to try out a wind sport in the DR. The beach at Punta Popy, only 1km or so east of the main intersection, is a popular place for kitesurfers and windsurfers. No outfits offer windsurfing but a recommended

kitesurfing school is **Loco-Kite** (☎809-801-5671; www.lasterrenas-kitesurf.com; Calle 27 de Febrero), run by a friendly Frenchman who speaks Spanish, Italian and English. It rents surfboards and kitesurfing equipment (wakeboarding on the way) and provides lessons for all these activities. Six hours of kitesurfing lessons (really the minimum needed to have a sporting chance of making it work) cost US$300; a two-hour surfing lesson is US$40.

🎓 Courses

To hold your own on the dance floor, or at the very least to avoid embarrassment, **Escuela Salsa Caribe** (☎829-946-6223; www.salsacaribegroup.com; Calle Principal; ⊙8am-noon & 2-8pm Mon-Sat) offers merengue, salsa and *bachata* classes, both in groups (RD$190 to RD$250; 6pm to 8pm daily) and privately (RD$450 to RD$980 per hour).

👉 Tours

Along with booking airline tickets, hotels and car rentals, the full-service travel agency **Bahia Tours** (☎809-240-6088; www.bahia-tours.com; Calle Principal 237; ⊙8am-7pm Mon-Fri, 9:30am-1pm & 4:30-6:30pm Sat) organizes many area tours. Popular day-trips include whale-watching in Bahía de Samaná (from US$55 per person), excursions to Parque Nacional Los Haitises (US$65 per person), visits to Playa El Rincón (US$90 per person) and horseback riding to Cascada El Limón (from US$30 per person). Overnight trips include rafting, canyoning and trekking in Jarabacoa as well as climbing Pico Duarte, the highest peak (3087m) in the Caribbean. English, French, Italian and Spanish are spoken.

Aerodomca (☎809-240-6571; www.aerodomca.com; Plaza Kalinda; ⊙9am-noon & 2-6pm) offers sightseeing flights of the peninsula leaving from El Portillo airport (US$300 per hour, three-passenger maximum). **Fun Rental** (☎809-240-6784; www.funrental.fr; Plaza Creole, Calle Principal) rents quad bikes (US$55 per day) and scooters (US$25).

There are several other recommended tour companies in town:

Flora Tours ECOTOURS
(☎809-360-2793; www.flora-tours.net; Calle Principal 262) Specializes in Los Haitises, hard-to-access beaches and trekking.

Casa de las Terrenas ADVENTURE TOURS
(☎809-240-6251; www.lasterrenas-excursions.com; Calle Principal 280) Small, friendly, French-run operation run out of a little kiosk in front of Plaza Taína.

Indrinatour QUAD TOURS
(☎829-348-7245; www.quad-lasterrenas.com;
Calle Principal) Does a variety of quad excursions in the area (US$150 to US$200).

🛏 Sleeping

The majority of accommodations options in Las Terrenas are located along the beachfront roads to the east and west of the main intersection in town. Those to the east are across from the beach on the paved highway, while the newly cobblestoned road to the west means the area is somewhat quieter and feels more secluded. Prices drop dramatically in the low season, but at any time of the year discounts are negotiable for long-term stays.

TOP CHOICE **Lomita Maravilla** BOUTIQUE HOTEL $$$
(☎809-240-6345; www.lomitamaravilla.com; Calle Salome Ureña; villas US$120, with private Jacuzzi US$210; P☀⊛🌐☒) A short walk down a dirt road – often muddy – off Av Duarte, you'll find one of the gems of Las Terrenas. This European-inspired, Swiss-run boutique hotel consists entirely of thatched-roof private bungalows set along palmed paths and a center swimming pool. Rooms are like boutique apartments, with TVs, DVD players and fully loaded kitchens. Enjoying your morning cup of Joe at your own private coffee bar on your porch might make you forget that you're a 10- or 15-minute walk from the sea, the only downside to this hotel.

TOP CHOICE **El Rincon de Abi** HOTEL $
(☎809-240-6639; www.el-rincon-de-abi.com; Av Emilio Prud'Homme; d/tr incl breakfast RD$1500/1800; P🌐☒) This French-owned hotel is well maintained and full of cute colors and character. Even better, there's a somewhat established independent traveler scene here, a welcome respite from the norm. There's a nice communal outdoor kitchen, a Jacuzzi that holds three (they are French, remember?) and a small pool. Rooms come in the whitewashed two-story building topped with a thatched roof (a tad sterile, but high-pressure showers) and roomy bungalows, the latter with more vibrant colors, wicker furniture and a nouveau-hippie vibe – for the same price.

Casa Robinson HOTEL $
(☎809-240-6496; www.casarobinson.it; Av Emilio Prud'Homme; r/studio RD$1100/1400, apt RD$1500-1600; P🌐) Set in leafy grounds down a side street a block from the beach,

this hotel offers privacy on the cheap. Fan-cooled rooms in the all-wood buildings are simple and clean and the little balconies have rocking chairs. Bathrooms, however, are more modern and some rooms have kitchenettes. Service doesn't always happen in a flash but it's friendly when it does finally arrive. It's a family-run place where debauchery is not appreciated.

Eva Luna VILLAS $$$
(☎809-978-5611; www.villa-evaluna.com; Calle Marico, Playa Las Ballenas; villas for 2/4 people US$100/210; P☀🌐) A paragon of understated luxury, Eva Luna is a collection of five Mexican-style villas west of town and 300m from Playa Las Ballenas. The beautiful villas come with fully equipped kitchens, living rooms and terraces where a delicious gourmet breakfast is served. The bedrooms are a bit cramped but the serenity at this seemingly hidden refuge and exquisite decor more than makes up for it. The villas all face a quiet pool and a garden area (could use a spruce up, truth be told).

Hotel Residence Playa Colibrí HOTEL $$$
(☎809-240-6439; www.playacolibri.com; Francisco Cámaño Deño; apt US$87-169; P☀🌐☒) One of the last hotels along this stretch of Playa Las Ballenas, Playa Colibrí is a good option for those seeking peace and quiet. Regardless of the room layout you choose, all are spacious and good value with fully equipped kitchens – though they won't let you soon forget your destination with the arresting aqua and turquoise color schemes. Split-level apartments are especially good for families. Each has a terrace that overlooks a palm-tree-shaded pool area.

Casa del Mar Neptunia HOTEL $
(☎809-240-6617; www.casas-del-mar-neptunia .com; Av Emilio Prud'Homme; r incl breakfast RD$1500, apt RD$2000; P🌐) An acceptable budget alternative to Abi and Casa Robinson and on the same street, this whitewashed hotel is also homey and quiet with 12 large, airy rooms. You're better off at one of the former at the RD$1500 price point, but the apartments here are artsy and cute with spacious living rooms and kitchens. It lacks privacy, though, and the French owners seem to be off-site often, leaving everything in the hands of an untrained local.

Alisei Hotel HOTEL $$$
(☎809-240-5555; www.aliseihotel.com; Calle Francisco Alberto Cámano; apt incl breakfast from

US$152; P❄🛜🏊) This hotel is a hipper and more luxurious version of Hotel Residence Playa Colibrí and only a short walk away, though it feels more like someone trying too hard to be hip decorated it rather than someone who is actually certified hip. Modern rooms come with fully stocked kitchens and there's an on-site spa, swim-up pool bar and yoga classes. Of the 54 apartments, several are villas that can sleep up to six. The attached restaurant, **Baraonda**, is elegantly designed with a large round open-air dining room supported by gnarled tree trunks.

Albachiara Hotel APARTMENT HOTEL $$$
(☏809-240-5240; www.albachiarahotel.com.com; Calle 27 de Febrero; apt incl breakfast from US$100; P❄🛜🏊) It suffers from a bit of street noise, but this brand-new, 46-apartment hotel is well located close to the beach and center of Las Terrenas. It offers large apartments with king-sized beds, big kitchens and cozy patios that look out at the grand columns endemic to the architecture of the hotel – feels a bit like the Antebellum South.

La Dolce Vita APARTMENT HOTEL $$$
(☏809-240-5069; www.ladolcevitaresidence.com; Calle 27 de Febrero; r US$90; P❄@🏊) The apartments at this aqua-trimmed Caribbean plantation–style seafront complex are good long-term rentals.

Hotel Guayacan MOTEL $
(☏809-240-6643; hotelelguayacan@live.com; Calle 27 de Febrero; s RD$700, r from RD$1150; P❄🛜) Imminently dismissible were it not for its one single backpacker crashpad for RD$700 and location steps from the beach and in the heart of the action. Small, but a deal for solo travelers.

🍴 Eating

The best restaurants in Las Terrenas are in Pueblo de los Pescadores, a cluster of fishermen's shacks–cum–waterfront restaurants just west of the river on what was the original site of the town. Virtually every restaurant has an entrance facing the road and an open-air dining or bar area out back, overlooking the ocean and narrow beach.

La Terrasse FRENCH $$
(Pueblo de los Pescadores; mains RD$280-680; ⊙lunch & dinner) The Dominican chef at this sophisticated French bistro deserves a few Michelin stars for his steak *au poivre* (RD$480) – you'll be genuflecting at his kitchen's door after it graces your lips – one of the most perfect meals in the entirety of the Dominican Republic. The menu carries on with lovely seafood like calamari Provençale (RD$430) and a French cheese plate (RD$300), and, like Mosquito Art Bar next door, the sea nearly steals back its wares every time a wave comes crashing in. But the best part of all might just be eating this for well under US$15 – a tall order anywhere in the world.

Big Dan's Café Americano CAFE, AMERICAN $
(Calle 27 de Febrero; mains RD$85-325; ⊙breakfast, lunch & dinner Mon-Sat, dinner Sun; 🛜) Big Dan does American specialties like chili, BBQ chicken and a cheeseburger and fries (RD$165) that can go toe-to-toe with any in the Caribbean. Daily lunch specials for RD$100 means it's all extremely affordable as well. He has a second location on Calle Principal doing frozen cocktails, frappucinos and light snacks. It's a bit nauseatingly patriotic but the food stands on its own despite the flag-waving. A don't miss for all, a Godsend for expats.

La Yuca Caliente SPANISH, ITALIAN $$
(Calle Libertad 6; mains RD$290-850, pizzas RD$120-350; ⊙breakfast, lunch & dinner; 🛜) Unlike some of its trendier neighbors, La Yuca Caliente is casual in menu and appearance, but a step above in food and service. Huge portions of Spanish, Italian and fish dishes and excellent pizzas are served by a professional and courteous staff who run circles around most others in town – our server might have even come back *twice* to see how we were getting along. Tables are set out on the beach amid swaying palm trees and the low-key sound system is conversation-friendly; and the massive water goblets make you feel like a guest at the Last Supper.

Atlanticó JAPANESE $$
(Pueblo de los Pescadores; mains RD$250-480; ⊙dinner Wed-Mon) Moody lounge music sets the tone at this hip sushi spot, full of hardwoods and typical Asian-inspired decor. Keep in mind, though, it's Latin sushi, so cream cheese is prevalent in alarming amounts. Try the Crispy California or Hari Maku rolls, the best of the limited menu that basically doesn't aspire beyond tuna and salmon but does a decent enough job with those two. Staff mean well, but are a tad aloof and in over their heads. If you're not into raw fish, there's yakitori and stir-fries as well.

Brasserie Bárrio Latíno CAFE $$
(El Paseo shopping center, Calle Principal; breakfast RD$50-230, mains RD$150-420; 🛜breakfast, lunch & dinner; 🛜) Occupying the busiest corner in town – and milking that for all it's worth – this open-sided tropical *brasserie* has a large menu of international standards like sandwiches, burgers, pastas and meat dishes. It's a popular breakfast spot for fresh pastries and the morning news from Paris. There's a small bar that in addition to beer and alcoholic drinks mixes up smoothies and a delicious *morir soñando* (tasty combination of orange juice, milk, sugar and crushed ice).

Aventura Terrenera DOMINICAN $
(Calle Principal; meals RD$150-300; 🛜lunch Mon-Sat) Dead simple affair but a good choice for cheap Dominican set meals like *sancocho*, fried chicken and *la bandera* (white rice, red beans, stewed meat, salad and fried green plantains). Vela runs the show here, easily adoptable as your Dominican grandmother. With its shaded patio, it's a step up from the average shack, too.

Indigo FRENCH, SEAFOOD $$$
(Pueblo de los Pescadores; mains RD$350-620; 🛜dinner Mon-Sat) The house specialty lobster ravioli is so good it compensates for a few notable shortcomings (skimpy wine pours, allowing peddlers in, a slow kitchen) at this intimate choice.

Boulangerie Française BAKERY $
(Plaza Taína; items RD$25-100; 🛜breakfast & lunch Mon-Sat) Transport yourself to Paris at this pleasant bakery serving fresh *pain au chocolat*, croissants, *beignets* and other traditional French pastries and desserts. The streetside patio practically feels like Montmartre.

La Casa Azul ITALIAN $$
(Calle Libertad; pizzas RD$190-300; 🛜dinner Wed-Mon) Service leaves *mucho* to be desired but the Italian owners turn out decent pizza, with a few tables right on the sand.

Mini-Market Plaza Taína (🛜7:30am-8:30pm Mon-Sat, 8am-1pm Sun) has snacks and basic necessities. **Punto Italia** (Calle Principal; 🛜9am-1pm & 4-8pm Mon-Sat, 9am-1pm Sun), a small Italian-owned chain grocery, is a vital resource for expats who demand high-quality meat, cheese, bread and brand-name European exports. Easily the largest and best supermarket in town, **Supermercado Lindo** (Plaza Rosada, Calle

Principal; 🛜8:30am-1pm & 3-8pm Mon-Sat, 9am-1pm Sun) is the place to go for canned foods, pasta, produce, snacks, nice imported wine and any other supplies.

🍷 Drinking

Most of the restaurants have bars and stay open well after the kitchen has closed. Barhopping could scarcely be easier, as it takes about 45 seconds to walk (or stagger, depending on the time of night) from one end of Pueblo de los Pescadores to the other. There are a few notable spots outside of Pueblo de los Pescadores as well.

El Mosquito Art Bar LOUNGE
(Pueblo de los Pescadores) The waves practically crash into the couches at this sophisticated lounge, strategically located practically *in* the ocean. It's a bit of a potpourri of animal print and second-hand French furniture and draws a sociable crowd as the night wears on. The cocktails (RD$200 to RD$250) are good (but someone please explain caipirinhas do not contain rum), the dramatic sea soundtrack even better.

Mojitos BAR, RESTAURANT
(Calle 27 de Febrero; 🛜9am-9pm) The problem with mojitos is they go down too fast. The ones here – made by Cubans with Cuban rum – go down even faster in both traditional and *chinola* varieties (RD$200). They aren't cheap, but the sunset views at this upscale beach shack at Punta Popy are included. There is great seafood as well – try the vinaigrette octopus (RD$300).

La Cave Au Vin WINE BAR $
(El Paseo shopping center, Calle Principal) When you tire of Presidente and freezing red wine, this small wine shop and deli dishes out (very) French tapas and properly chilled wines by the glass.

☆ Entertainment

Gaia/Pasarela/VIP NIGHTCLUB
(Pueblo de los Pescadores; 🛜10pm-5am; cover RD$500) A Catalonian expat runs this trendy three-in-one disco. Gaia, on the bottom floor, is a small disco that feels like partying inside a bar code – a black-and-white discoball nightmare set to techno and Latin music. Upstairs, Pasarela is better, a windswept outdoor lounge dressed in sexy reds, set to house and other temperamental tunes – a great spot to plop yourself down on a souped-up porch swing and people-watch the night away. We never made it to VIP, the third option!

🔒 Shopping

Calle Principal and around are virtually wallpapered with the typical Haitian art found everywhere in the DR. The three shopping centers a stone's throw away from one another on Calle Principal – **Plaza Taína**, **Casa Linda** and **El Paseo** – have several high-end boutiques, eateries and a few shops selling basic tourist kitsch. All are open from 9am to 8pm Monday to Saturday and from 9am to 3pm Sunday. For more of a selection of paintings, other than the ubiquitous cookie-cutter mass-produced ones, stop by the **Haitian Caraibes Art Gallery** (Calle Principal 159; ☺9am-1pm & 4-8pm Mon-Sat); it also sells interesting crafts, jewelry and typical batiks and sarongs.

Toward the rear of the El Paseo shopping mall, **Prensa International** (El Paseo shopping center, Calle Principal; ☺8:30am-7:30pm) sells a variety of international newspapers and magazines – most are a day or two old and the majority are in French, though the *International Herald Tribune* is sometimes available.

ℹ️ Information

Emergency
Politur (tourist police; ☎809-754-3342; Calle Libertad; ☺24hr)

Internet Access
A&M Communications (Calle del Carmen; per hr RD$60; ☺8am-6pm Mon-Sat, to noon Sun)
Casa de Denis (Plaza Taína, Calle Principal; per hr RD$50; ☺8:30am-8pm)

Laundry
Lavandería Amy (☎809-624-0000; Plaza Aubergine, Calle F Bono 2; ☺8am-10pm Mon-Sat) Do-it-yourself laundry. Wash per load RD$125, dry per cycle RD$150; detergent and fabric softener each RD$30; call for pick-up/drop-off service for just an extra RD$60.
Lavandería Tu Net (Lavandería Pat y Memo; Centro Colonial, Calle del Carmen; ☺8am-6pm Mon-Fri, to 3pm Sat) Wash and dry RD$70 per pound; same-day service not always available.

Medical Services
Centro de Especialidades Medicas (Calle Principal; ☺24hr) Small private hospital.
Hospital Pablo A Paulino (Calle Matias Mella; ☺24hr emergency room)
Super Farmacia del Paseo (El Paseo shopping center, Calle Principal; ☺9am-7pm Mon-Sat) Well-stocked pharmacy.

Money
In addition to those listed here, there are also two ATMs at El Paseo shopping center.
Banco Leon (Calle Principal) Has a 24-hour ATM.
BanReservas (Calle Principal; ☺9am-6pm Mon-Fri, to 1pm Sat) Has a 24-hour ATM.
Fort Knox Money Exchange (El Paseo shopping center, Calle Principal; ☺8am-1pm & 4-8pm Mon-Sat, 9am-noon Sun)

Post
Post office (Calle del Carmen) Stamps may be purchased at Blue Corazon Joyeria in El Paseo shopping center – far more convenient.

Telephone
Claro/Codetel Centro de Comunicaciones (Calle Principal; ☺8am-7pm) International telephone calls.

Travel Agencies
Bahia Tours (☎809-240-6088; www.bahia-tours.com; Calle Principal 237; ☺8am-7pm Mon-Fri, 9:30am-1pm & 4:30-6:30pm Sat) Full-service travel agency that can handle airline, hotel and car-rental reservations. Area excursions are also organized, and English, French, Italian and Spanish are spoken.

ℹ️ Getting There & Away

Air
Domestic airlines service the mostly private **Aeropuerto Internacional El Portillo** (EPS), a one-strip airport located 4km east of Las Terrenas along the coastal road in the hamlet of El Portillo. International flights arrive at **Aeropuerto Internacional El Catey** (AZS), located 8km west of Sánchez and a 35-minute taxi ride (US$70) to Las Terrenas. **Air Canada** (☎888-760-0020) and **Westjet** (☎in Puerto Plata 809-586-0217) offer direct flights from El Catey to Montreal and Toronto, respectively. There are also a handful of charter flights.

DominicanShuttles (☎in Santo Domingo 809-738-3014; www.dominicanshuttles.com) and **Aerodomca** (☎809-240-6571, in Santo Domingo 809-826-4141; www.aerodomca.com) operate propeller planes between El Portillo and Santo Domingo. DominicanShuttles flies daily to El Portillo from Aeropuerto La Isabela in Higuero, north of Santo Domingo (US$99, 30 minutes, 10am and 4pm). Aerodomca has three flights daily from La Isabela to El Portillo (US$80, 30 minutes, 7:30am, 10am and 4pm) and at least two flights back to Santo Domingo's Aeropuerto Internacional Las Américas from El Portillo (US$80, 30 minutes, 2pm and 4:30pm).

Both also offer an air-taxi service – as long as you have enough people or are willing to pay the total amount, flights leave whenever the passengers choose. Regular or air-taxi tickets can be arranged through Bahia Tours.

Bus

Las Terrenas has two *gua-gua* stops at opposite ends of Calle Principal. *Gua-guas* headed to Sánchez (RD$60, 30 minutes, every 20 minutes from 7am to 6pm) take on passengers at a stop 100m north of the Esso gas station on the edge of town. From Sánchez you can connect to an El Caribe bus to Santo Domingo; alternatively, *Gua-guas* direct to Santo Domingo leave from in front of Casa Linda on the corner of Calle Principal and the coastal road five times daily (RD$285, three hours, 5am, 7am, 9am, 2pm and 3pm).

Those going to El Limón, 14km away (RD$50, 20 minutes, every 15 minutes from 7:15am to 7pm), leave from the same stop at Casa Linda; for an onward connection to Samaná, a further 26km, wait at the main intersection in El Limón.

There is one daily *gua-gua* to Puerto Plata (RD$285, 3½ hours, 6:30am) but no designated stop – flag it down as it makes its morning rounds along Calle Principal.

Car

Las Terrenas is easily accessible by road if you're motoring on your own. Once you arrive in Sánchez, continue bearing left until Secondary Road 7 splits off the main Hwy 5 to the north, 100m east of the Texaco gas station and steeply climbs out of town, and descends into Las Terrenas 19km later. It's a beautiful drive, incidentally.

Taxi

The local **taxi consortium** (☑809-240-6339) offers rides for one to six passengers to just about everywhere. Some sample one-way fares are Playa Cosón (US$25), El Limón (US$25), Samaná (US$60), Las Galeras (US$90), Cabarete (US$160), Santo Domingo (US$180) and Punta Cana (US$375).

❶ Getting Around

The two main roads in town, Calle Principal (also known as Av Juan Pablo Duarte or Av Duarte for short) and the parallel Calle del Carmen, form a figure eight of sorts, crisscrossing in the middle.

You can walk to and from most places in Las Terrenas, though getting from one end to the other can take a half-hour or more. Taxis charge US$15 each way to Playa Bonita and El Portillo and US$25 to Playa Cosón and El Limón. *Moto-conchos* are cheaper – RD$100 to Playa Bonita and RD$200 to Playa Cosón – but are less comfortable. There are taxi and *motoconcho* stops in front of El Paseo shopping center and *motoconchos* are plentiful on Calle Principal and around Pueblo de los Pescadores. A bike can be handy for getting around town.

There are several local rental-car agencies but rates are exorbitant (between US$59 and US$130, with unlimited kilometers only with a three-day or more rental). One of the more established and reliable ones is **ADA Rental Car** (☑809-704-3232; Plaza Taína; ⊗9am-1pm & 2:30-7pm Mon-Sat). At Aeropuerto El Catey, **Sixt** (☑809-338-0107) is the lone option.

Playa Bonita

A getaway from a getaway, this appropriately named beach only a few kilometers west of Las Terrenas is a better alternative for those seeking a more peaceful, reclusive vacation. Playa Bonita (Pretty Beach) is not without its imperfections – the half-moon-shaped beach is fairly steep and narrow, and parts are strewn with palm-tree detritus. However, backed by a handful of tastefully landscaped hotels, many with well-manicured lawns that rival the beach in terms of attractiveness, this is an enticing spot.

◉ Sights & Activities

Surfers and bodyboarders hit the waves around the eastern part of Playa Bonita near Calle Van der Horst. Just around the southwestern bend is the secluded, 6km-long Playa Cosón. The sand here is tan, not white, and the water greenish, not blue, but nevertheless it's a good place to pack a lunch and lose the bathing suit for a day. There are two small rivers that run through the thick palm-tree forest and open onto the ocean; the easternmost is said to contain agricultural runoff.

Las Terrenas Divers (☑809-889-2422; www .lt-divers.com; Hotel Bahía las Ballenas; ⊗9am-noon & 3-5pm) offers dive trips and courses (one tank US$50, equipment US$10, open-water certificate US$395) as well as snorkel trips to Isla Las Ballenas (US$15, one hour) and Playa Jackson (minimum three people, US$35 per person). You can also rent kayaks, bodyboards and surfboards by the hour or the day.

🛏 Sleeping & Eating

TOP CHOICE/ **Peninsula House** BOUTIQUE GUESTHOUSE $$$
(☑809-962-7447; www.thepeninsulahouse.com; Playa Cosón; r US$580; P🤖) One of the Caribbean's most exquisite and luxurious hotels, this discerning Victorian B&B perched high on a hill overlooking Playa Cosón is the choice for those seeking the utmost

exclusivity and service. Only six rooms grace this mansion, each different and dressed up French Chateau-style (a Franco-American couple are your hosts). The Argentine chef focuses on simple preparations sourced locally and from their organic vegetable garden (the three-course dinner is US$70). For lunch, guests are served at the Beach Club on Playa Cosón (mains RD$500 to RD$650), which is also open to the public. It's popular with Americans and South Americans and the average stay is five days, but you'll want to move in – it's that gorgeous. If there's a flaw, it's two-fold: the French owner smokes inside the house; and there are four dogs (three belonging to the owners and the chef's Chihuahua) traipsing around on the beautiful hardwood floors.

TOP CHOICE **Hotel Bahía las Ballenas**   HOTEL **$$$**
(☑809-240-6066; www.bahiaballenas.net; Calle José Antonio Martínez; d incl breakfast UD$125-160; P❋❋☎❄) Occupying a large swath of Playa Bonita property, this hotel combines the virtues of a luxurious resort and private retreat. Each one of the 32 huge airy villas scattered over the meticulously manicured lawn and garden is inspired by a Mexico–south of France aesthetic – pastel stucco walls, high thatched ceilings, tile floors and even roofless toilet and shower areas. Large wooden decks look out to an especially nice pool area lined with towering palm trees. An open-air restaurant serves international fusion. There's an on-site dive shop as well.

Hotel Atlantis   HOTEL **$$**
(☑809-240-6111; www.atlantis-hotel.com.do; Calle F Peña Gomez; s/d from $85/95; P❋@☎) This rambling and charming hotel is straight out of a children's fairy tale – all twisting staircases, covered walkways and odd-shaped rooms. The furnishings are comfortable, not luxurious, and each of the 18 rooms is different – some have balconies and fine ocean views. There's a palm-tree-covered patio and a fine French restaurant on the premises.

Hotel Acaya   HOTEL **$$**
(☑809-240-6161; www.acaya-hotel-fr.com; Calle F Peña Gomez; r US$70, with air-con US$95; P❋@☎❄) Evocative of a more genteel era, the Acaya's two-story colonial building sits back from the beach on a finely manicured lawn. This French-owned hotel is understated and tastefully furnished and there's a relaxing lounge-restaurant on the property,

a small spa, a surf school and a half-hearted playground for kids. Rates include breakfast.

Coyamar   HOTEL **$$**
(☑809-240-5130; www.coyamar.com; cnr Calles F Peña Gomez & Van der Horst; s/d/tr US$45/55/70; ❋☎❄) Located at Calle Van der Horst and the beach road, Coyamar is the least luxurious of the Playa Bonita hotels. The vibe is casual and friendly, especially good for families, and the restaurant near the front of the property and the pool are good places to hang out. Batiks and bright colors rule the day here and the fan-cooled rooms are simple and comfortable. There's a pool no bigger than a Jacuzzi.

🛈 Getting There & Away

By car, Playa Bonita is reachable by a single dirt road that turns off from the Sánchez–Las Terrenas highway. In theory it's possible to walk from Playa Bonita to Playa Cacao in Las Terrenas via a coastal dirt/mud trail, but it requires clambering over a steep pitch, and some water wading. A taxi ride here is US$10, a *motoconcho* around US$1.75. There are usually a few *motoconchos* there when you're ready to return but it's best to set out before nightfall.

Sánchez

POP 11,800

Sánchez is a nondescript town that is notable mainly as a transportation hub. *Guaguas* to and from Santo Domingo (RD$280, two hours, 5:30am, 7:30am, 9:30am, 2:30pm and 3:30pm) and Puerto Plata (RD$300, 3½ hours, 7am, 9am, 11:45am and 2:45pm) stop here briefly, and pickups wait at the intersection of Hwy 5 and Secondary Road 7 to take passengers on the gorgeous, winding road over the coastal mountains to La Terrenas (RD$60, every 20 minutes from 7am to 7pm). For Puerto Plata, it's best to wait at the nearby Texaco gas station and flag the bus down when it comes through. *Gua-gua* services to Samaná (RD$70, every 15 minutes from 7am to 6:40pm), from where you can catch the ferry to Sabana de la Mar, leave from the center of town. There's at least one bank with an ATM if you need to pick up cash on the way.

Caribe Tours (☑809-552-7434) has services to Santo Domingo from Sánchez (RD$310, two hours, 8:30am, 10:30am, 2:30pm and 4:30pm). The office is 1.5km west of the turnoff for Las Terrenas.

North Coast

Best Places to Eat

» Otra Cosa (p156)

» Mares Restaurant (p137)

» Castle Club (p156)

» Beach barbecue (p158)

Best Places to Stay

» Casa Colonial Beach & Spa (p141)

» Natura Cabañas (p155)

» Tubagua Plantation Eco-Village (p141)

» Swell Surf Camp (p154)

Why Go?

From east to west on the DR's north coast, you'll find world-class beaches, some of the best water sports in the country and out-of-the-way locales evocative of timeless rural life. This long coastal corridor stretching from Monte Cristi and the Haitian border in the west to Cabrera in the east has enclaves of condo-dwelling expat communities that have endowed some towns with a cosmopolitan air. There's dry desert scrub, forested hills and jungly nature preserves. There are waterfalls to climb, sleepy little Dominican towns where it's possible to escape and mile after mile of sandy beaches. In the middle is Puerto Plata's international airport; nearby is the city itself and where most of the coast's all-inclusive resorts are located. Independent travelers will surely want to explore the area, especially Cabarete, where you can kitesurf, surf or just plain bodysurf.

When to Go

Winds on the north coast pick up during the North American winter months, making this an ideal time to try out surfing and kitesurfing; check out the world's best, who compete in the Master of the Ocean competition the last week in February. Puerto Plata's week-long June Cultural Festival brings the party to this coastal city's streets, while a jazz festival takes over Cabarete's beach the last week in November. The north is generally wetter from October to January and spectacularly sunny from June to September.

North Coast Highlights

1 Jumping and sliding down the thrilling **27 Waterfalls of Damajagua** (p161)

2 Digging your toes into the sand and your fork into some great grub while dining on the beach in **Cabarete** (p149)

3 Finding tranquility in the typical small-town Dominican atmosphere of **Río San Juan** (p158)

4 Worshiping the sun as the waves crash nearby on beautiful **Playa Grande** (p158)

5 Going to school to learn how to **kitesurf** (p150) or **windsurf** (P152) from the pros

6 Exploring the underwater marine life around **Sosúa** (p144)

ATLANTIC OCEAN

0   30 km
0   20 miles

ⓘ Getting There & Around

Aeropuerto Internacional Gregorío Luperón is the second-largest airport in the country, and within two hours' driving distance from almost everywhere on the north coast. It's also your best place to rent a car, although you'll probably want an SUV, considering the state of the roads.

Buses and *gua-guas* (small buses) offer frequent service all along this coast – it's as easy as sticking your hand in the air – although you may find the cost of the fare to be inversely proportional to your Spanish language ability. Keep in mind the relatively small size of the country – Puerto Plata is only 215km from Santo Domingo.

Puerto Plata

POP 147,000

Squeezed between a towering mountain and the ocean is this working port town, the oldest city on the north coast. Puerto Plata's natural features notwithstanding, wandering the Malecón or the downtown streets surrounding the Parque Central there's a palpable feeling of neglect. Intermingled with run-of-the-mill shops are the fading, once-opulent homes built by wealthy German tobacco merchants in the 1870s. Several restaurants are worth a visit, as are a few interesting museums, and the cable car ride to the nearby bluff, if not clouded over, offers panoramic views.

History

As Columbus approached the bay in 1493, the sunlight reflected off the water so brilliantly it resembled a sea of sparkling silver coins and so he named it Puerto Plata (Silver Port). He also named the mountain that looms over the city Pico Isabel de Torres (799m), in honor of the Spanish queen who sponsored his voyages. In 1496 his brother Bartolomé Colon founded the city.

An important port for the fertile north coast, Puerto Plata – and, indeed, the entire north coast – was plagued by pirates. It eventually became more lucrative for colonists to trade with the pirates (who were supported by Spain's enemies, England and France) rather than risk losing their goods on Spanish galleons. Such trade was forbidden and enraged the Spanish crown. In 1605 the crown ordered the evacuation of Puerto Plata – as well as the trading centers of Monte Cristi, La Yaguana and Bayajá –

rather than have its subjects trading with the enemy.

The north coast remained virtually abandoned for more than a century, until the Spanish crown decided to repopulate the area to prevent settlers from other countries – namely the French from present-day Haiti – from moving in. Puerto Plata slowly regained importance, suffering during the Trujillo period, but eventually reinvented itself as a tourist destination. The early 1990s were golden years for the city, and for the first time tourism revenues surpassed those of its three main industries – sugar, tobacco and cattle hides – combined.

◉ Sights

Teleférico   CABLE CAR
(Camino a los Dominguez; round trip RD$300; ⊙8am-5pm) A cable car takes visitors to the top of the enormous flat-topped Pico Isabel de Torres. On clear days there are spectacular views of the city and coastline – go early, before the mountain clouds up. The botanical gardens at the top are good for an hour's stroll. There's also a large statue of Christ the Redeemer (similar to but smaller than its counterpart in Rio de Janeiro), an overpriced restaurant and aggressive knick-knack sellers.

Board the *teleférico* at its base at the southern end of Camino a los Dominguez, 800m uphill from Av José Ginebra. A *moto-concho* (motorcycle taxi) here costs RD$50, a taxi US$7. The ride is notorious for opening late or closing early, so cross your fingers before heading up there. Officially licensed guides will no doubt try to coax any independent travelers to use their services, though they really aren't necessary.

In theory, you can also walk up (or down) the mountain, paying only a one-way fare to return (the trail begins under the cable car). However, this can't really be recommended, in part because it's a strenuous two- to three-hour walk (we estimate about 7km) and certainly impossible to do without a guide. On weekends, local guides sometimes hang out at the ticket office (US$10) – only go with an experienced one. Alternatively, Iguana Mama (p152) offers this tour.

Galería de Ambar   MUSEUM, SHOP
(www.ambercollection.itgo.com; Calle 12 de Julio; admission RD$25; ⊙8:30am-6pm Mon-Fri, 9am-1pm Sat) Despite its unfortunate location, housed in a rundown office-like building, there are museum-quality exhibits on the

NORTH COAST

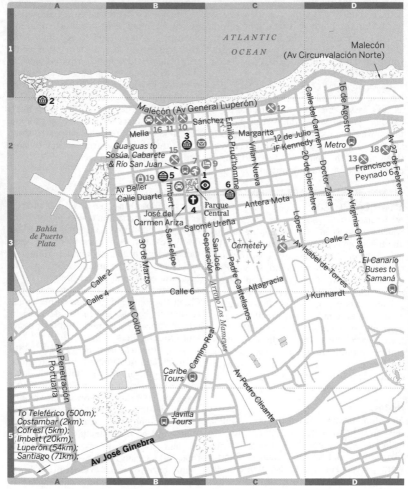

history of amber mining in the DR as well as on rum, sugar, tobacco and coffee. Multilingual guides walk visitors through the displays answering any questions. Of course, the *raison d'etre* of the tour is the soft-sell pitch guides give to buy the gallery's very own proprietary cigar brand, as well as jewelry and other gifts in the shop on the ground floor (the *mamajuana* is a particularly good buy here).

Museo del Ambar Dominicano MUSEUM, SHOP
(www.ambermuseum.com; Calle Duarte 61; admission RD$50; ⊙9am-5pm Mon-Sat) The colonial-era building housing this similar collection

of exhibits on amber is certainly a step up compared to its competition. Exhibits include valuable pieces with such rare inclusions as a small lizard and a 30cm-long feather (the longest one found to date). Tours are offered in English and Spanish. A gift shop on the ground floor has a large selection of jewelry, rum, cigars, handicrafts and souvenirs.

Fuerte de San Felipe HISTORICAL SITE
(San Felipe Fort; admission RD$100; ⊙9am-5pm Sun-Fri) Located right on the bay, at the western end of the Malecón, the fort is the

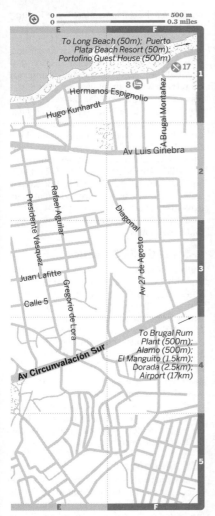

To Long Beach (50m); Puerto Plata Beach Resort (50m); Portofino Guest House (500m)

Hermanos Espignolio
Hugo Kunhardt
A Brugal Montañez
Av Luis Ginebra
Rafael Aguilar
Presidente Vásquez
Diagonal
Av 27 de Agosto
Juan Lafitte
Gregorio de Lora
Calle 5
Av Circunvalación Sur

To Brugal Rum Plant (500m); Alamo (500m); El Manguito (1.5km); Dorada (2.5km); Airport (17km)

0 ———— 500 m
0 ———— 0.3 miles

⊙ Sights
1 Casa de la Cultura	B2
2 Fuerte de San Felipe	A2
3 Galería de Ambar	B2
4 Iglesia San Felipe	B3
5 Museo de Arte Taíno	B2
6 Museo del Ambar Dominicano	C2

⊘ Activities, Courses & Tours
7 Cafemba Tours	B2

⊜ Sleeping
8 Aparta-Hotel Lomar	F1
9 Hotel Kevin	C2

⊗ Eating
10 Aguaceros Bar & Grill	B2
11 Barco's	B2
12 Jamvi's	C2
13 Mares Restaurant & Pool Lounge	D2
14 Mercado Municipal	C3
Restaurant Entre Amigos	(see 16)
15 Sam's Bar & Grill	B2
16 Tam Tam Café	B2
17 Terraza Las Almendras	F1
18 Tropical Supermarket	D2

⊜ Shopping
19 La Canoa	B2

of cannonballs. The views of the bay are impressive, though, and a large grassy area in front of the fort makes for a restful stop.

Also at the fort is Puerto Plata's **lighthouse**, which first lit up on September 9, 1879, and was restored in 2000. The white-and-yellow tower – 24.4m tall, 6.2m in diameter – is a melding of neoclassical style with industrial construction.

Iglesia San Felipe CHURCH
(Parque Central, Calle Duarte; ⊘8am-noon & 2-4pm Mon-Sat, 7am-8pm Sun) The twin-steepled church has been completely renovated since Hurricane George devastated the town in 1988. The principal attractions here are the small but beautiful Italian stained-glass windows donated by local families during the renovation. It's on the southern side of the refurbished Parque Central, which is distinguished by a large gazebo in the center.

Malecón STREET
The Malecón (also known as Av General Luperón and Av Circunvalación Norte) runs

only remnant of Puerto Plata's early colonial days. Built in the mid-16th century to prevent pirates from seizing one of the only protected bays on the entire north coast, San Felipe never saw any action. For much of its life its massive walls and interior moat were used as a prison. Included in the price of admission is an audio tour (English, French, German and Spanish); however, it's disappointingly thin in terms of historical breadth and depth. There are extremely short explanations of the objects displayed in the small museum – a few rusty handcuffs, a handful of bayonets and a stack

NORTH COAST PUERTO PLATA

along the shore. It has been completely re-paved and the informal food stalls on the beach side removed. There are a handful of recommended restaurants, as well as a new development – several beachside shacks selling drinks and food are on Long Beach, the main city beach around 2km east of downtown. A few experienced Dominican and Czech kitesurfers launch themselves into the waves here on windy days.

Casa de la Cultura CULTURAL CENTER
(Parque Central, Calle Duarte; admission free; ☺9am-noon & 3-5pm Mon-Fri) In addition to dance and music workshops, the center often showcases work by Dominican artists in its 1st-floor gallery.

Brugal Rum Plant FACTORY TOURS
(☎809-586-2531; Carretera a Playa Dorada; admission free; ☺8am-4pm Mon-Fri) The local joke has it that everyone wants to be the quality-assurance tester here at this rum distillery and bottling facility. Some package tours come through here, but it's an underwhelming 15-minute tour from a 2nd-floor gangway. There are complimentary rum-based cocktails at the end.

🏃 Activities

All the nearby all-inclusive resorts listed in this book organize tours for their guests. For independent travelers, Mark Fernandez, owner of several interlocking tour companies under the banner of **Caribbean Ocean Adventures** (☎809-586-1239; www.caribbean oceanadventures.com) is the man to go to. For big-game fishing trips contact **Gone Fishing** (☎809-586-1239; www.caribbeanoceanadventures .com); you'll pay around US$100 (US$70 for watchers) per half-day trip in larger groups, or you can charter a boat for US$700/900 per half-/full day. **Freestyle catamaran boat trips** with snorkeling stops near Sosúa leave from Playa Dorada; these are a fun way to spend a half-day, especially because of the crew's comedic shtick and all-you-can-drink bar. And finally, scuba divers looking to explore the north coast's reefs can contact **Sea Pro Divers** (www.seaprodivers.com).

Yasikia Adventures (☎809-650-2323; www .yasikaadventures.com; ☺8am-5pm Mon-Sat), a well-run zip-line park, is around a half-hour drive from Puerto Plata; the US$84 admission includes transportation from Puerto Plata area hotels.

✦ Festivals & Events

Cultural Festival CULTURAL
The third week in June sees merengue, blues, jazz and folk concerts at Fuerte de San Felipe. Troupes from Santo Domingo perform traditional dances that range from African spirituals to sexy salsa tunes. At the same time, the town hosts an arts-and-crafts fair for local artisans at nearby Parque Central.

Merengue Festival MERENGUE
In early November the entire length of the Malecón is closed to vehicular traffic, food stalls are set up on both sides of the oceanside boulevard and a stage is erected for merengue performances.

🛌 Sleeping

Unless you're after budget accommodations there's no real reason to spend more than a night in Puerto Plata, considering that there are better options elsewhere nearby. When we stopped by, the Puerto Plata Beach Club was under construction across the street from Long Beach, east of the city center. With its prime location, newly built pastel-colored buildings and outdoor pool, it looks to be one of the choicest accommodations in the city.

Hotel Kevin HOTEL $
(☎829-603-9173; hotel_kevin1@hotmail.com; Calle Juan Bosch 41; s/d with fan RD$750/850, with air-con RD$1100/1200; ❋☞) Only a block from the Parque Central and housed in a building with Victorian-era facade and bones, this is a good-value choice. The basic rooms

ℹ WATCHING IT

Most foreigners in Puerto Plata fall into two categories: grizzled expat or day-tripper from a nearby all-inclusive. And in part because tourism hasn't particularly benefited Puerto Plata itself, visitors who look obviously well heeled might receive more attention than preferable, including extremely persistent shoe-shine boys and those few who might try to take advantage of other's naïveté. One way to not call attention to yourself is to dress like you're visiting a city and not the pool bar, and another is to wear your watch over your all-inclusive bracelet, the universal signifier for easy mark.

Dominican amber is widely regarded as the finest in the world. It not only exhibits the largest range of colors – from clear (youngest) and pale lemon to warm oranges, gold, brown and even green, blue and black (oldest) – but it contains the greatest number of 'inclusions': insects, tiny reptiles and plant matter that became trapped in the resin before it fossilized. Such inclusions add character to a piece of amber and increase its value.

Fake amber (made of plastic) is occasionally sold in the DR, especially by street and beachside vendors. You're advised to buy only from a reputable shop, which will always permit you the following tests to satisfy yourself that it is genuine:

» Examine the amber under a fluorescent lamp. If the glow changes, it's amber; if it doesn't, it's plastic.

» Rub the piece against cotton and bring it close to your hair. If the hair moves, it's real. Amber acquires static electricity; plastic doesn't.

» Place unadorned amber in a glass of salt water. If it floats, it's amber. If it sinks, it's plastic. Remember: this won't work if the piece is in a setting.

» Ask the salesperson to hold a match to the amber. Heated amber gives off a natural resin, plastic smells like a chemical.

Be aware also that a significant amount of the amber sold in the DR is actually imported from Europe, especially Poland. This amber is often good value, and will satisfy all of the above tests. While only experts can tell for sure where a particular piece comes from, one thing to look for is 'spangles' – flashes of light embedded inside the amber. This is typical of Polish amber and normally absent from the Dominican gem.

Finally, blue amber is mined exclusively in the DR (there are five amber mines in total). It is the most spectacular and most expensive form of amber, and if it passes the above tests you can be sure it is, in fact, Dominican.

are clean and relatively well furnished with cable TV and comfortable bathrooms. Wi-fi is accessible from the sunny front lobby.

Portofino Guest House HOTEL $
(✆809-586-2858; Av Hermanas Mirabal 12; r RD$1000; P❀🛜🏊) A long way from the center but a short walk to Long Beach, this no-frills guesthouse has 20 clean rooms – all have hot water, air-con and cable TV. The small swimming pool in a concrete inner courtyard is far from alluring but will do for a quick dip on a hot afternoon. An excellent pizzeria by the same name is next door.

Aparta-Hotel Lomar HOTEL $
(✆809-320-8555; Malecón 8; r RD$1100; P❀🛜) This hotel does little to take advantage of its location, though some of the 2nd- and 3rd-floor rooms do have balconies with ocean views. The furnishings, old and mismatched, look like they've come from a rummage sale from a Trujillo-era public school. Wi-fi is available in the small sitting area adjoining the parking lot.

🍴 Eating & Drinking

All the restaurants listed here are also good places for a drink, with or without a meal. The Malecón has a handful of eateries, some informal, that at least afford a beach atmosphere.

TOP
CHOICE **Mares Restaurant & Pool Lounge** DOMINICAN $$$
(✆829-451-6075; Francisco Peynado 6; mains RD$600; ☉dinner Wed-Sat) Distinguished chef Rafael Vasquez-Heinsen has converted his elegant home into a destination for foodies. *Top Chef* and food channel fans won't be disappointed. The kitchen turns out what elsewhere might be defined as haute fusion cuisine – dishes that creatively combine Dominican ingredients with other culinary traditions: try Dominican goat marinated with sour orange, oregano and garlic, served with pigeon peas, yucca fritters and chipotle sauce (RD$475). Reservations recommended.

RAFAEL VASQUEZ-HEINSEN – CHEF

Renowned Chef Rafael Vasquez-Heinsen is the owner-chef of Mares Restaurant & Pool Lounge, Sushito and Tostacos, all in Puerto Plata. Vasquez pursued professional culinary training in Switzerland, France and the US and has worked in Thailand, Mexico and Europe, as well as in other Caribbean countries, but credits his grandmother for his skill and passion.

What does Dominican food say about the country?

The Spanish, African and other dishes with foreign origins reveal that the DR has been dominated by many cultures, but they're integrated with our island's own flavors. Dominican food is for the soul – we're an open and welcoming culture and this is clear in our desire to share our passion for food.

What's your ideal meal in the DR?

A traditional Dominican meal of *tostones* (fried plantain), fish and a salad enjoyed on a plastic table right on the beach, where your feet might just get wet from the waves.

What are some Dominican specialties you suggest trying?

A full Dominican breakfast of eggs, mashed *mangu* (plantains) or boiled yucca (cassava), fried white farm cheese and Dominican salami, accompanied with *cafe con leche*, or hot chocolate with cinnamon. For an afternoon snack, *kipe* (bulger stuffed with ground meat and fresh mint) and fried (from the Lebanese influences) or an *empanada*, which are turnovers filled with conch, chicken or ground beef, accompanied with a fresh juice or our world-famous Presidente beer, well-chilled.

El Manguito Restaurant & Liquor Store
SEAFOOD $$
(mains RD$350; ⊙lunch & dinner) Nestled at the side of the highway just east of the Costa Dorada complex (and just west of Playa Dorada) is this good-value seafood joint, a short walk from your resort. Beers here are only US$2, and the lobster (US$14) is great value. Service is excellent, and there's also a variety of desserts.

Jamvi's
PIZZERIA $$
(☏809-320-7265; cnr Malecón & Calle López; pizzas RD$275; ⊙10am-late) This gargantuan open-air pizza joint sits above street level on the Malecón, offering a pleasant sea breeze and great views. Good for a pizza and wine fix (there's a decent wine list); from 10pm onward it pumps the merengue and reggaeton till late. Also delivers.

Sam's Bar & Grill
PUB FOOD $
(José del Carmen Ariza 34; mains RD$150; ⊙8am-9pm Mon-Sat, 9am-5pm Sun; @☎) Occupying a historic building with ragged flags flying over a clapboard facade, Sam's is the favored watering hole of heavy-drinking resident gringos. The food here is great value, especially the *plato del día* (RD$100) and house special fish and chips.

In addition there's French toast, chicken Kiev, Mexican scramble, Philly cheese steak and Tijuana-style chili.

Restaurant Pizzería Portofino
PIZZERIA $$
(Av Hermanas Mirabal 12; mains RD$250; ⊙breakfast, lunch & dinner) Connected to the guesthouse of the same name, Portofino's is a thatch-roofed, open-sided restaurant with a huge menu of Italian and Dominican dishes as well as excellent pizzas (RD$100).

Aguaceros Bar & Grill
TEX-MEX, DOMINICAN $$
(Malecón 32; mains RD$350; ⊙lunch & dinner) This open-sided, thatch-roofed, fan-cooled bar and grill is pleasant for its casual-Caribbean, low-light ambience and its location on the Malecón. Specialties here include fajitas, burritos and a combo plate with nachos, quesadillas, soft tacos, chimichangas, flautas and more for under RD$500.

Kite Bar
BEACH SHACK $
(Malecón 32; mains RD$70; ⊙lunch & dinner) Of the handful of beach shacks that have been allowed to set up shop on the eastern end of the Malecón on Long Beach, this one has become something of a favorite to a group of expat regulars and Dominicans alike. All are

great spots for a morning coffee or sundown Presidente, along with simple meals.

Terraza Las Almendras DOMINICAN **$$**
(cnr Malecón & Calle A Brugal Montañez; mains RD$250; ⊗8am-late) With pleasant outdoor seating under bright umbrellas, this sea-facing restaurant makes a good place for an inexpensive breakfast or a couple of beers. The food consists almost entirely of *pinchos* – if it once roamed the earth (or sea), you can get it here served on a stick.

Barco's, Restaurante Entre Amigos and Tam Tam Café (all open breakfast, lunch and dinner) are relatively interchangeable restaurants next to one another on the northern end of the Malecón. All are primarily hangouts for the longtime expat community; menus include standard Dominican fare (grilled fish RD$350) with other 'international' dishes (pasta RD$200). Wi-fi and street-front seating make these good places to get your bearings or relax for an afternoon drink.

The modern **Tropical Supermarket** (cnr Avs 27 de Febrero & Beller) is the best place in the center for groceries; a **cafe** (⊗breakfast, lunch & dinner) with free wi-fi from 3pm to 11pm is attached.

Mercado Municipal (cnr Calles 2 & López; ⊗7am-3pm Mon-Sat) is housed in what looks like an enormous, crown-shaped, reinforced-concrete gas station from the 1960s. Here you'll find a large variety of meat and vegetables, and pushy salesmen selling tourist knick-knacks.

🛍 Shopping

La Canoa (Av Beller 18; ⊗8am-6pm Mon-Sat, 10am-1pm Sun) is a large, rambling gift shop. There's an enormous amber exhibit – almost a museum – and a good selection of amber and larimar jewelry. It also sells the usual acrylic Haitian paintings, boxes of cigars, and postcards.

ℹ Information

Banco BHD (JF Kennedy)

Banco León (JF Kennedy)

Cafemba Tours (✆809-586-2177; cafemba tours@hotmail.com; Calle Separación 12) Half a block north of Parque Central, Cafemba can arrange plane tickets and package tours.

Centro Médico Dr Bournigal (✆809-586-2342; Antera Mota; ⊗24hr) A highly recommended clinic.

Clínica Brugal (✆809-586-2519; José del Carmen Ariza; ⊗24hr) The heart specialist here is recommended by many.

Codetel (cnr Av Beller & Padre Castellanos; internet per hr RD$36) Doubles as a call center.

Discover Puerto Plata (www.discoverpuerto plata.com) Official tourism website with general information for visitors.

Dot Com (Calle 12 de Julio 69; internet per hr RD$30)

Farmacia Carmen (Calle 12 de Julio)

Post office (cnr Calle 12 de Julio & Separación) Two blocks north of Parque Central.

Puerto Plata Report (www.popreport.com) Regional news and travel information from the north coast of the DR.

ℹ Getting There & Away

Air

Puerto Plata is served by **Aeropuerto Internacional Gregorio Luperón** (POP; ✆809-586-0107; www.puerto-plata-airport.com), 18km east of town along the coastal highway (past Playa Dorada), and just a few kilometers west of Sosúa. Numerous charter airlines, including several Canadian ones, use the airport, mostly in conjunction with the all-inclusive resorts. A taxi to or from the airport costs US$25. You can also walk 500m from the terminal to the main highway, where you can flag down a *gua-gua* to Puerto Plata (RD$55, 45 minutes) or Sosúa (RD$15, 10 minutes).

Some of the airlines with international service here are:

Air Canada (✆809-541-5151; www.aircanada.com)

Air Turks & Caicos (✆in US 954-323-4949, in Turks & Caicos 649-946-4999; www.flyairtc.com) Daily flights to Turks & Caicos and new route to San Juan, Puerto Rico.

American Airlines (✆809-200-5151; www.aa.com)

Continental (✆809-200-1062; www.continental.com)

Delta (✆809-586-0973; www.delta.com)

Jet Blue (✆809-200-9898; www.jetblue.com)

LTU (✆809-586-4075; www.ltu.com)

Lufthansa (✆809-200-1133; www.lufthansa.com)

Martinair (✆809-200-1200; www.martinair.com)

Bus

Caribe Tours (✆809-576-0790; btwn Real and Kunhardt) and **Metro** (✆809-586-6062; Calle 16 de Agosto) serve Puerto Plata.

EASTBOUND GUA-GUA Leave from a stop on the north side of Parque Central, passing

TOURS & BUS SERVICES FROM PUERTO PLATA

DESTINATION	FARE (RD$)	DURATION (HR)	FREQUENCY
La Vega	150	2	Santo Domingo bus
Santiago	110	1¼	Santo Domingo bus
Santo Domingo	300	4	hourly 6am-7pm
Sosúa	50	½	hourly 6am-7pm

by the entrance of Playa Dorada and through Sosúa (RD$30, 30 minutes), Cabarete (RD$50, 45 minutes) and Río San Juan (RD$100, two hours). From Río San Juan you can catch another van to Nagua and then another to Samaná. Alternatively, **Papagayo** (☎809-749-6415) buses leave daily for Samaná (RD$250, 3½ to 4 hours) at 6am from in front of the public hospital. Make two calls the day before – one to reserve a spot and the other to a taxi line to arrange an early-morning pickup.

SOUTH & WESTBOUND GUA-GUA Javilla Tours (☎809-970-2412; cnr Camino Real & Av Colón; ⊙every 15min 5am-7:30pm) serves Santiago (RD$130, 1½ hours) with stops along the way at Imbert (RD$40, 20 minutes) and Navarrete (RD$80, 50 minutes). To get to Monte Cristi, take Javilla's bus to Navarrete and tell the driver to let you off at the junction, where you can change for the Expreso Linieros bus (RD$140, 1½ hours) to Monte Cristi.

Car

Your best bet for renting a car is to pick one up at the airport when you arrive. Discounts are available in low season (May to October) and if you rent for several days or weeks.

All of the following also have offices at the airport, where they are open 7am to 10pm (and are usually on call overnight, but charge extra for late pickup or delivery).

Alamo (☎809-586-1366, airport 809-586-0285; www.alamo.com; ⊙8am-6pm) East of town on the road to Playa Dorada.

Avis (☎809-586-4436, airport 809-586-7007; www.avis.com; ⊙8am-6pm)

Europcar (☎809-586-0215; www.europcar.com)

National (☎809-586-1366, airport 809-586-0285; www.nationalcar.com; Playa Dorada; ⊙8am-5pm) In the Playa Dorada shopping center.

ⓘ Getting Around

The old town and parts of the Malecón are walkable. Otherwise, you're going to have to either get comfortable taking *motoconchos*, rent a car or shell out cash for taxis.

GUA-GUA The main trunk roads in Puerto Plata are serviced by *gua-guas* following lettered

routes, which cost RD$12. Lines C and F will be of most interest to you: they run from as far west as Cofresí, through town and past Playa Dorada in the east. Line C runs direct; line F makes lots of twists and turns as it barrels through town.

MOTOCONCHO Officially licensed drivers wear numbered, colored vests and tend to be more cautious in traffic. The in-town fare was RD$25 when we were there.

TAXI You'll find taxi fares priced almost exclusively for tourists. The in-town fare is around RD$150 to RD$200. Taxis don't generally cruise the streets looking for customers, so try **Taxi Puerto Plata** (☎809-586-5335). There are several taxi stands around the city, including along the central park and across the street from the Caribe Tours office.

Around Puerto Plata

Just outside Puerto Plata proper lies Playa Dorada, a string of all-inclusive resorts. To the west of town, the beach hamlets of Costambar and Cofresí are home to many expat condo-dwellers (principally Canadians escaping their winter heating bills). Both have a good community feel, but regular hotels are in short supply – you'll get better value renting a condo by the week or month.

PLAYA DORADA & COSTA DORADA

These two adjacent beaches a few miles east of Puerto Plata string together more than a dozen all-inclusive resorts and one five-star hotel. Both developments are marked by large archways – Playa Dorada is the much larger one and the first you come to on the highway from the airport. For a complete list of resorts and businesses in the area see www.playadorada.com.do. A recent downturn in tourism to the area has meant some properties are not as well maintained as others and occupancy rates can be low, a concern for those looking for a lively social scene.

TUBAGUA VILLAGE

Ideal for the eco-conscious traveler, this rustic mountaintop retreat is about as far from an all-inclusive as you can get. Set high on a ridge with breathtaking views of the valley below, **Tubagua Plantation Eco-Village** (☎809-696-6932; www.tubagua.com; r incl breakfast US$25; ☎) is the vision of longtime DR resident and Canadian consul Tim Hall. By his own description, accommodations here are 'Robinson Crusoe style' which shouldn't discourage anyone. There are several wooden cabins with palapa roofs and basic bedding – simple but comfortable. A shared bathroom, closed on three sides, is open on the fourth with an empty hanging picture frame highlighting the panoramic scene. The owner's sense of humor and dedication to conservation is revealed in the makeshift outdoor 'gym', essentially a bench press with concrete-filled coffee cans as weights. Tim, an enthusiastic advocate of low-impact sustainable tourism, can arrange day, overnight and week-long itineraries for travel anywhere in the country. A half-day hike to the pools of Charcos los Militares is especially recommended. Tubagua is continually evolving, and one day soon Tim will complete the construction of more upscale cabins on a nearby property. Don't try driving here at night – 20km from Puerto Plata (taxi US$30) and around 40km from Santiago – since the road is rough and there are no lights.

Most of the all-inclusive places on Playa Dorada and Costa Dorada offer both day and night passes (US$45 to US$60), which entitle you to unlimited access to their facilities for either a buffet lunch, drinks and beach/pool access, or buffet dinner and access to their bars and disco (if they have one). The Playa Dorada shopping mall contains dozens of infrequently visited stores as well as a cinema (RD$200), bank with ATM, internet and call center (wi-fi can be very expensive at the resorts), Pizza Hut, several cafes and Budget rent-a-car.

🏃 Activities

Playa Dorada Golf Club (☎809-320-3472; www.playadoradagolf.com; ☉7am-7pm), designed by Robert Trent Jones, is a well-regarded 6218m, par-72 course that is the centerpiece of the massive Playa Dorada hotel complex. The greens fee for nine holes is US$50, for 18 holes, US$75; caddies (US$8/15 for nine/18 holes) are obligatory, golf carts (US$20/25 for nine/18 holes) are not. Some resorts offer discounted rates for their guests – be sure to ask at your hotel before you reserve your tee time.

🛏 Sleeping & Eating

TOP CHOICE Casa Colonial Beach & Spa   LUXURY HOTEL $$$
(☎866-376-7831; www.casacolonialhotel.com; r US$450-1450; P❋@☎☎) This extraordinary hotel is arguably the best in the country. It offers 50 indulgent suites, each with marble floors, sparkling fixtures, canopied beds,

ample balconies, a cedar-lined closet, plus plush bathrobes and slippers. There's even a claw-foot bathtub on some of the balconies, should you want a romantic bubble bath with a view. The grounds are set in a sprawling mansion and boast a tropical garden with orchids growing at seemingly every turn. An infinity pool with four Jacuzzis is located on the roof, providing a spectacular view of the blue ocean beyond. A high-end spa and two elegant restaurants are also on site. Unlike those of its neighbors, the rates at the Casa Colonial are not all-inclusive. Owned and designed by the family-run VH Hotels and Resorts.

Hotel Iberostar Costa Dorada   LUXURY HOTEL $$$
(☎809-320-1000; www.iberostar.com; all-incl s/d US$135/165; P❋@☎☎) One of the better-value all-inclusives in the Puerto Plata region, Iberostar, part of an international chain, receives its fair share of repeat customers. There is a certain Disneyland cheesiness about the place – you'll be greeted at reception by a porter wearing a pith helmet, for instance – but the grounds are enormous and well kept, the pool is immense, and we found the food (always a sticking point) is definitely better than average. The rooms are not luxurious, but for what you're paying, still good value.

VH Gran Ventana Beach Resort RESORT $$$
(☎809-320-2111; www.granventanahotel.com; all-incl s/d US$180/260; P❋@☎☎) Upholding the high standards of the VH Hotels and

Only a day's sail north of Puerto Plata is Silver Bank, part of a protected migratory area that extends all the way from the Bahamas to Banco de la Navidad, and one of two places in the world (the other is Tonga) where you can snorkel with humpback whales, some 60ft long. These 'soft water encounters' are both intimidating and exhilarating. However, because of the trip's relatively costly price tag (US$3000) it remains under the radar to most visitors to the DR. Tom Conlin (☑in US 954-382-0024; www.acquatic adventures.com), an American naturalist who has been running week-long live-aboard trips here for 20 years, is the preeminent guide; the season is from January to April and boats depart from Puerto Plata. Mini-seminars are conducted on board every night in which the ins and outs of the species are explained as well as safety precautions – for the whales' and your benefit.

Resorts chain, the Gran Ventana attracts 30-somethings and families – the nightlife here usually doesn't last past midnight though it's still a good idea to request a room away from any areas where music emanates from. We found the well-trained staff especially friendly and the grounds kept almost obsessively clean. There are 506 tastefully decorated rooms, all with balcony or terrace, and there's direct beach access under a string of almond and beach grape trees.

Be Live Grand Marien Resort RESORT $$$
(☑809-320-1515; www.belivehotels.com; all-incl s/d US$131/169; [P][✳][@][♠][❄][♻]) Next door to the Iberostar in the Costa Dorada complex, this resort has more stylish boutique touches than the average all-inclusive in the area. Despite a change in management (it was formerly the Grand Oasis Marien), it still gets rave reviews for its well-manicured and lovely grounds, friendly staff and better-than-average food. Excellent facilities for children.

Suncamp APARTMENTS $
(☑809-320-1441; www.suncampdr.com; Calle Principal; camp US$10, r US$20; [♠]) Surrounded by lush jungle and set on a river near the village of Muñoz, only 2km from Playa Dorada, rustic Suncamp looks much like a typical Dominican structure – concrete floors and corrugated iron roof. A stay here, long or short, can be worthwhile as long as your standards of comfort are low. Diane, the Canadian owner, is friendly and welcoming and can help you plan trips in the region. There's a variety of rooms, some have private bathroom and their own kitchen but all are simply decorated with what looks like secondhand furniture. Bring a flashlight and mosquito repellent. Can arrange airport transfers (US$30). Attractive for long-term

stays: Suncamp rents rooms by the week and month.

Hemingway's Café AMERICAN $$
(mains RD$450) Key West meets ESPN Zone at this Plaza Dorada spot. Come for the free wi-fi, stay for the slightly overpriced fare and sports on TV.

❶ Getting There & Around
The taxi association of Playa Dorada charges many times the price you'd pay if you hailed a regular taxi on the street.

Taxis can be found at any of the hotel entrances and also in front of Playa Dorada Plaza. A taxi to the airport will cost you US$33, to Sosúa US$35, to Cabarete US$40, and within the hotel complex US$10; to Puerto Plata US$7.

For a taste of local life, walk to the front entrance and hail down a *gua-gua* to Puerto Plata (RD$20) – when you want to get off, just bang on the side of the van.

COSTAMBAR
Less a traveler's destination than an expat hideaway, Costambar is still worth a look – it's got a beautiful, secluded beach (with a view of the ships leaving the harbor to the east) with several informal restaurants. All of Costambar's main services are in the small village just past the gated entrance.

However, this is a private community (see www.costambartoday.com) that consists primarily of time-share units and vacation homes, many occupied for six months of the year by Canadians on the run from winter. If you're after up-to-the-minute eating and sleeping info, log on to www.incostambar.com. Some of the condo associations will rent by the week and occasionally by the night in low season, and you'll find a grocery store here, plus internet access (but no

ATM). A local monthly newsletter (www .costambarmonthly.com) can keep you up to date with the goings-on.

A small time-share, **Club Villas Jazmin** (☎809-970-7010; www.villasjazmin.com; apt up to 4 people US$100; [P][❄][@][✉]) will rent apartments to independent travelers during the low season (roughly April to June and September to December). The units aren't exactly alluring, though they do include full kitchens, cable TV and firm beds. The club, a five- to 10-minute walk from the beach, has a small pool and tennis court.

Yenny's Market (Calle Principal; ⊘8am-9:30pm) is a medium-sized market located just as you enter town. There's also a call center and internet cafe, and a small fast-food eatery that pumps out good hearty eats – fried fish, club sandwiches, tacos and burritos.

A *motoconcho* from Puerto Plata will cost you RD$100, and a taxi US$17. If you're already in Costambar, try the local **taxi association** (☎809-970-7318). *Gua-gua* lines C and F from Puerto Plata pass the front gate (every 15 minutes from 6am to 6pm), although the village is a good kilometer from the highway, and the beach another kilometer past that.

PLAYA COFRESÍ

Five kilometers west of Puerto Plata lies the quiet, condo-dwelling hamlet of Cofresí. At one end of town sprawls an enormous all-inclusive resort and at the other, Ocean World. In the middle, sandwiched between the two on a 500m stretch of beach road, is a tiny community of expats and condo dwellers, and a small, beautiful beach.

Ocean World (☎809-291-1000; www.ocean world.net; adult/child US$55/40; ⊘9am-6pm) is a Dominican version of Sea World. Dolphins, sharks, sea lions and manta rays, the aviary and the tiger pool and show are the main attractions; you can also swim with the dolphins (per person US$155) or the sharks (US$60). There are several restaurants, a disco and a casino on site, and boaters who tie up at the new marina get free entrance to the park as part of their mooring fee. The all-you-can-eat Sunday brunch (US$35) includes prime rib and lobster, and is reportedly excellent.

Three large resorts, all under the Riu banner, line the Bay of Maimon around 5km west of the access road to Cofresí.

Lifestyle Hacienda Resorts   RESORT $$$
(☎809-586-1227; www.hacienda-resorts.com; all-incl r per person US$150; [P][❄][@][✉]) At the heart of this sprawling resort village is a by-the-numbers all-inclusive; as long as you don't expect glitz or panache you won't be disappointed. However, because so many guests say yes to the somewhat annoying time-share rental pitch in exchange for access to the 'VIP' half of the resort – basically roped-off portions of the beach filled with Miami-style day beds instead of beach chairs – the non-VIP parts are less crowded. The rooms are well maintained and the buffet restaurant has enough variety that you'll always leave satisfied; whereas the ambience of the 'specialty' restaurants is undermined by sub-par food. At the moment it is the only resort on a fairly beautiful half-moon bay beach.

Playa Cofresí Villas   RENTALS $$
(www.puerto-plata.com) This enterprise manages around 10 houses in Cofresí, ranging from two-bedroom cottages to seven-bedroom houses. Some have an ocean view and/or swimming pools. A housekeeper is assigned to each house and will help with cooking, cleaning, laundry and even shopping. Prices range from US$600 to US$6000 per week in high season (December 15 to April 30) and drop considerably in low season. With many repeat guests, the houses can get booked up months in advance – email for availability.

✕ Eating & Drinking

Los Charos   MEXICAN $$
(mains RD$200; ⊘11am-late; ☏) If you should tire of your hotel buffet, this warm, airy restaurant – with a motorcycle as decoration in the indoor dining room – has a menu full of Mexican fare like quesadillas, tacos and chili con carne. On the road to Ocean World.

Los Tres Cocos   CONTINENTAL $$
(☎809-993-4503; Las Rocas; mains US$8-20; ⊘dinner Wed-Mon) Located 800m east of Cofresí in the Las Rocas neighborhood is this excellent Austrian-owned restaurant. Hidden away down a side street off the highway, this is a favorite of expats and locals alike – there's gourmet food (like duck breast in orange sauce, RD$525), and Teutonic favorites like liver dumpling soup (RD$275).

Le Papillon   CONTINENTAL $$
(☎809-970-7640; mains RD$300; ⊘dinner Tue-Sun) This German-run restaurant, 100m

east of Cofresí up a small hill, serves excellent meals in a large palapa-roofed dining area with dark-wood tables, a checkerboard floor and seafaring decor, including a tank of sea turtles. Favorites include leg of rabbit, smoked yellowtail or dorado, pepper steaks and vegetable curry. Daily specials are usually a good deal.

Chris & Mady's SEAFOOD, INTERNATIONAL **$$** (mains RD$350; ⊙8am-11pm; 🛜) Under an open-air thatched roof with tile floors and sturdy wooden tables, the restaurant serves good seafood, including fettuccine with shrimp and the grilled catch of the day, at reasonable prices. On Sunday there's a barbecue popular with local residents and expats alike.

❶ Information

Plaza Taína Has an internet cafe (per hour RD$100, 8am-7pm), and sells hats, sunscreen and film. On main beach road.

Tourist Medical Services (⊙24hr) A medical clinic affiliated with the Hacienda resorts. Has multilingual staff and serves guests and nonguests alike; for more serious cases.

❶ Getting There & Away

Take *gua-gua* C or F (RD$12) from Puerto Plata. Going back to town take only the C – the F does lots of twists and turns in the city and takes twice as long to get you to the center. It's a steep downhill walk of about 700m to the main beach area. There's *gua-gua* service until about 7pm. If you're driving, simply follow the main highway west.

There's also a taxi stand located just outside Ocean World. One way to Puerto Plata is US$20 and to the airport US$45.

East of Puerto Plata

Cabarete long ago stole the crown of tourism capital of the north coast – here you can fill your days with surfing and mountain biking but still dig into great seafood at a beachside restaurant. Sosúa, Cabarete's seedier neighbor, has a pretty beach, and a good selection of restaurants and hotels. Further east are several low-key small towns that see few tourists, but are good bases for visiting nearby beaches.

SOSÚA

POP 45,000

Sosúa by day and Sosúa by night are two very different creatures. When the sun is out, the beach and calm bay ideal for swimming attract a broad swath of Dominicans, foreigners and families alike. When evening comes it's no longer a PG destination. The inescapable fact is that Sosúa is known for sex tourism. Bars fill up with sex workers, and men, single and in groups, can expect to be accosted and propositioned. Nevertheless, there are a number of hotels and good restaurants. And despite its more confronting qualities, Sosúa is a good base for exploring the north coast and the base for the area's scuba diving operations. The town's seemingly curious status as the cheese and dairy capital of the DR was established by around 350 families of Jewish refugees who fled Germany and other parts of Europe in 1940. Most left after just a few years, but not before building many fine homes.

◉ Sights

Museo de la Comunidad Judía de Sosúa MUSEUM
(Jewish Community Museum of Sosúa; Calle Dr Alejo Martínez; admission RD$100; ⊙9am-1pm & 2-4pm Mon-Fri) This museum, near Calle Dr Rosen, has exhibits describing the Jewish presence in the DR. At the multinational Evian conference in 1938 the DR was the only country to officially accept Jewish refugees fleeing Nazi repression in Germany. Around 350 families of refugees were settled in and around Sosúa. Most stayed only a few years – few were farmers by trade – but those who remained have been very successful in the dairy business, and Sosúa cheese is well known throughout the country. The museum has signs in Spanish and English, and is worth a stop.

🏖 Beaches

Playa Sosúa is the main beach, and practically a city within a city. Located on a crescent-shaped bay with calm, turquoise waters, this tawny stretch of sand is backed by palm trees and a seemingly endless row of souvenir vendors, restaurants, bars and even manicurists. The crowds of Dominican families and long-term visitors staying in local hotels and condos make this lively beach a great place for people-watching. To get there take the downhill road between the Ruby Lounge and La Roca. Look for Raffelito, about halfway down the beach, to rent snorkel gear (two hours RD$400, includes life jacket, bottle of Coca-Cola for you and bread for the fish).

Playa Alicia, a half-moon of yellow sand lapped by blue water, began to appear spontaneously around 2003. To get there, walk to the Sosúa By the Sea hotel and enter the parking lot. At the end on the left is a door, and a narrow alleyway provides beach access to the public.

🏃 Activities

DIVING & SNORKELING

Sosúa is generally considered the diving capital of the north coast. In addition to the dozen or so dive sites within boating range of Sosúa Bay, dive shops also organize excursions as far afield as Río San Juan (through mangroves and freshwater Dudu Cave) and Cayo Arena. There's a good variety of fish here – 200 different kinds, according to some – plus hard and soft corals, drop-offs and sponges.

Among the popular dive spots nearby are Airport Wall, featuring a wall and tunnels in 12m to 35m of water; Zíngara Wreck, an upright 45m ship sunk in 1993 as an artificial reef in around 35m of water; and Coral Gardens and Coral Wall, both offering excellent coral formations in depths ranging from 14m to 53m.

Prices vary somewhat from shop to shop, but are generally US$80 for two dives with gear, around US$10 to US$20 less if you have your own equipment, and slightly more for dives further afield. Booking a dive package brings the price down considerably – with a 10-dive package, the per-dive price can be as low as US$25 if you have your own gear. All of Sosúa's shops offer certification courses. Snorkeling trips are available at all shops, and cost US$30 to US$45 per person, depending on the length and number of stops; equipment is always included.

One big difference among the shops is that the predominant language among the staff is German, though English and Spanish are spoken by all. Some of Sosúa's most established dive outfits:

BEST DIVES ON THE NORTH COAST

Three Rocks Good for beginners; three giant coral heads; 55ft

Airport Wall Sharp drop-off with small cave; 70ft

Garden Fan coral and tube sponges to 80ft

Pyramids Gulleys, cliffs and swim-throughs; 60ft

TOP CHOICE **Northern Coast Diving**   DIVING
(☎809-571-1028; www.northerncoastdiving.com; Calle Pedro Clisante 8; ☺8am-6pm) This well-respected dive shop is one of the best, and the most willing to create customized excursions to little-visited dive sites (although it'll cost you).

Dolphin Dive Center   DIVING
(☎809-571-3589; www.dolphindivecenter.com; Playa Sosúa; ☺9am-5pm) This operation has its office at the Sosúa Bay Resort.

🎓 Courses

Casa Goethe   SPANISH LANGUAGE
(☎809-571-3185; www.edase.com; La Puntilla 2; ☺9am-5pm Mon-Fri) This German-run outfit has private and group Spanish classes, both on ordinary (four hours per day) and intensive (six hours per day) schedules. Classes are held in the mornings, and the center can organize activities like scuba diving or salsa-dancing classes in the afternoon. Long-term housing can be arranged either at the center itself or in area hotels.

Holiday Spanish School   SPANISH LANGUAGE
(☎809-571-1847; www.holiday-spanish-school .com; Calle Pedro Clisante 141) Spanish classes, for beginners and advanced students alike, are offered at El Colibrí Resort, a small hotel east of the town center. Most are given in two-hour increments; the first hour typically focuses on grammar and vocabulary, the second is centered around speaking. Prices vary according to the length of the course and the number of students. Housing packages are available.

🧭 Tours

There are a lot of cheesy package tours on offer at numerous agencies along the north coast. Many involve spending the majority of your day on a gaudily painted 'safari' bus getting to and from your destination. Be especially wary of any tour that purports to show you 'Dominican culture' – the 'local school' you'll visit will be more a Potemkin village than an authentic place of learning.

Tours that are most worth doing include rafting in Jarabacoa (four hours each way, US$60 to US$80), Cayo Arena for snorkeling (three hours each way, US$55 to US$65), whale-watching in Samaná (from mid-January to mid-March, four hours each way, US$120 to US$140), and anything involving a boat – catamaran tours (US$55 to US$90)

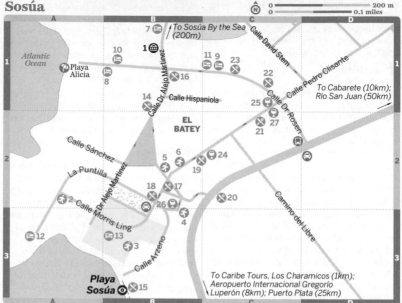

and deep-sea fishing (US$50 to US$100) are hard to fake, and are generally good value.

Melissa Tours (☎809-571-2567; www.melissa tours.com.do; Calle Duarte 2) Also sells plane tickets.

Mel Tours (☎809-571-2057; ww.mel-tour.com) On the road to Playa Sosúa.

🛏 Sleeping

Sosúa Bay Resort & Victorian House   RESORT $$$
(☎809-571-4000; www.sosuabayresort.com; Calle Dr Alejo Martínez 1; all-incl r US$80-200; ⓟ❋@⚊) Set on a bluff overlooking the bay, virtually every inch of this sprawling resort affords picturesque views and easy access to a bar. There are two sister properties with very different personalities – the Sosúa Bay Resort looks as if it was furnished by a Caribbean version of Crate & Barrel, while the Victorian House is more upscale and looks like, well, a Victorian house. They share facilities, including a large pool area and access directly to the bay below.

PierGiorgio Palace Hotel   HOTEL $$$
(☎809-571-2626; www.hotelpiergiorgio.com; La Puntilla; r incl breakfast US$95; ❋ⓟ⚊) Understandably popular with wedding planners, the PierGiorgio is built on a rocky cliff overlooking the ocean, ornately constructed with a white gingerbread facade and a grand red-carpeted staircase that spirals to the top floor. The room furnishings are aging and don't match the magnificent sea views – ask for a room on the 3rd floor. Room rate includes breakfast, and the cliffside restaurant (mains from US$7 to US$32) is an undeniably romantic spot.

Hotel Casa Cayena Club   HOTEL $$
(☎809-571-2651; www.hotelcasacayena.com; Calle Dr Rosen 25; s/d US$65/85; ⓟ❋🛜⚊) This well-managed hotel contains 24 rooms on two floors, connected by broad breezy corridors. All rooms have red-tile floors, clean modern bathrooms with hot water, cable TV and security boxes. There's a nice pool area, and Playa Alicia is just down the street. A small outdoor restaurant serves breakfast. Expansion plans call for a spa, conference rooms and suites.

Hotel Casa Valeria   HOTEL $$
(☎809-571-3565; www.hotelcasavaleria.com; Calle Dr Rosen 28; r/apt US$50/65; ❋🛜⚊) All nine rooms at this cozy hotel are slightly different, whether in size, furnishings or decor. Three units have kitchens (with gas burners), the others are hotel-like rooms

with comfortable beds, attractive furnishings and painted pink. Rooms are set around a leafy courtyard with a kidney-shaped pool in the middle; all have cable TV, fans and ceramic-tiled bathrooms.

Hotel El Rancho HOTEL **$$**
(☏809-571-4070; www.hotelelranchososua.com; Calle Dr Rosen 36; r from US$40; P✳❄) The rather pleasant leafy pool and garden area is the centerpiece of this small centrally located hotel only a block from Playa Alicia. A three-story modern concrete building decorated with vaguely Mexican murals and topped with a palapa-style roof for show, El Rancho has clean, well-kept rooms.

Sosúa By the Sea RESORT **$$**
(☏809-571-3222; www.sosuabythesea.com; cnr Calles B Phillips & David Stern; s/d incl breakfast US$70/110; P✳@❄) Set on a coral spit on the aptly named Playa Chiquita, this hotel's rooms are minimally furnished in an attractive way. Unfortunately, however, the pool area out back could use some attention, even just a tree or two to break up the concrete. All rooms do have mini refrigerators and an all-inclusive service is available for a US$20 surcharge. The restaurant **Josef's Grill & Grape** (mains RD$400) is part of the complex.

Casa Marina Beach Resort RESORT **$$$**
(☏809-571-3690; www.amhsamarina.com; Calle Dr Alejo Martínez; all-incl s/d US$150/200; P✳@❄) Where the Sosúa Bay Resort has little in the way of grounds, the Casa Marina is a large complex with three pools, five restaurants, almost 400 rooms arranged in three-story buildings and direct access to Playa Alicia, though it's no great shake of a beach. The rooms are classic all-inclusive: clean and comfortable but not memorable in any way, with cable TV and a balcony, and most looking onto the pool.

Rocky's Rock & Blues Bar Hotel BUDGET HOTEL **$**
(☏809-571-2951; www.rockysbar.com; Calle Dr Rosen 22; r with fan/air-con US$25/30; ✳@❄) Probably not the best for couples, the five rooms at Canadian-owned Rocky's are a good deal for undemanding travelers. All are clean, breezy and have cable TV. Resembling a fraternity rec room, a mellow lounge with a large-screen TV, couches and tables spills into the bar-restaurant area, where locals and travelers hang out most of the afternoon and evening.

New Garden Hotel HOTEL **$$**
(☏809-571-1557; www.newgardenhotel.com; Calle Dr Rosen 32; r incl breakfast US$90; P✳❄❄) Not especially good value; however, the

clean, modern rooms at this two-story hotel are what you might find at any good-quality chain motel in North America. A bar area and pool are in front.

🍴 Eating

There's no shortage of good restaurants in town – a handful are within a block of Parque Central. The path along Playa Sosúa is lined with restaurants and bars, as is Pedro Clisante, and most of the hotels have their own eateries.

La Finca   CONTINENTAL $$$
(📞809-571-3925; cnr Calles Dr Rosen & Dr Alejo Martínez; mains from RD$600; ⊘5-11pm; 🕾) This longtime Sosúa culinary landmark with a colonial-era design scheme takes its cuisine seriously, both in the presentation and price. But if you're after the very best, then La Finca is it. Steak and seafood are the rock stars here – there's chateaubriand, surf and turf, and a mixed seafood platter for two (US$50). It has an amazing cocktail list, and the menu is in five languages, including Russian.

Marua Mai   DOMINICAN $$
(cnr Calles Pedro Clisante & Arzeno; mains RD$450; ⊘breakfast, lunch & dinner) Right smack in the middle of things, this two-level, tropical-themed restaurant is a solid midrange choice. Its burgers are great, but it also does lobster by the kilo and sometimes has seafood specials. There's a pleasant bar to sit for a quiet drink before or after. Good breakfasts, too.

Bailey's   INTERNATIONAL $$
(Calle Dr Alejo Martínez; mains RD$450; ⊘breakfast, lunch & dinner) A favorite among expats, this Austrian-owned restaurant is set around a large horseshoe-shaped bar, and its specialties include chili burgers and enormous schnitzel sandwiches. The decor includes lots of rattan furniture, and there's a small play area with a slide and jungle gym to keep the kids amused.

Restaurante El Cultivo   DOMINICAN $
(Calle Pedro Clisante 10; mains RD$130) More campo than the campo, this cute-kitsch place announces its personality like a Times Sq theme restaurant: checkered tablecloths, rocking chairs, hammocks and even a tire swing, and waiters wear straw hats. The indoor dining room has plenty of character too, packed to the brim with knick-knacks. A filling *plato del día* will set you back only RD$130 and all-you-can-eat barbecue Sundays are RD$350.

Oh La Vache   PIZZERIA $$
(Calle Pedro Clisante; pizzas RD$375; ⊘lunch & dinner) Decorated whimsically in a cow theme, this pizza joint makes some of the best crispy-crust pizzas on the north coast. Owned by a French couple, this is also a pleasant place to while away the early evening with a beer.

Rocky's Rock
& Blues Bar Hotel   DOMINICAN, AMERICAN $$
(Calle Dr Rosen 24; mains RD$250; ⊘7am-late; @🕾) Rocky's is a Sosúa institution. The sign outside says 'World Famous Ribs,' but that's just the beginning – the breakfasts, served until 3pm, are great value, the steaks are Dominican beef (not imported), and the beers are some of the cheapest in town. Pizza is served after 5pm and the music, like the name suggests, is pure rock and blues.

Scotch & Sirloin   STEAKHOUSE $$
(Calle Dr Rosen; mains RD$300; ⊘breakfast, lunch & dinner) A pleasant and modern open-air pavilion, Scotch & Sirloin specializes in what you might think: burgers, steaks and baby back ribs (RD$600).

La Roca Argentine   STEAKHOUSE $$
(Calle Pedro Clisante; mains RD$375; ⊘lunch & dinner) Try to make it for the Sunday all-you-can-eat lobster, shrimp, fish, calamari and more or Friday's barbecue feast.

Playero Supermarket (⊘8am-10pm), on the main highway, offers a good selection of local produce and imported, hard-to-find delicacies.

🍸 Drinking

Sosúa's nightlife is packed with bars and clubs, many catering to prostitutes and their customers. Calle Pedro Clisante is Sosúa's main drag and is lined with bars and restaurants; restaurants, wherever they are in town, are often a better choice for a drink than the bars along the main drag.

El Flow Latin Bar   BAR
(cnr Calles Pedro Clisante & Dr Rosen) Dominicans come here for the merengue, *bachata* and the occasional reggaeton that is blasted, as well as the cheap beer.

Rose & Thistle   BAR-RESTAURANT
(Beachway Plaza; ⊘9am-late) Owned by an expat English couple, this small bar in a narrow alleyway also does an excellent all-day English breakfast, sausage rolls and pork pies.

Britannia Pub
BAR

(Calle Pedro Clisante; ⊘10am-late) Popular with expats, this is a pleasant spot for a quiet drink. There's a good book exchange at the back, and the cheap bar food, like burgers and wings, isn't bad.

Rumba Bar
BAR

(Calle Pedro Clisante) Open-air bar in the thick of things with TV for sports. Tuesday and Friday are karaoke nights.

ℹ Information

Banco Popular (cnr Calles Dr Alejo Martínez & Sánchez)

Banco Progreso (Calle Pedro Clisante)

Book Nook (Beachway Plaza; ⊘10am-4pm Mon-Sat) Used books in several languages.

Caribe Internet (Calle Duarte 5; per hr RD$70; ⊘9am-9pm Mon-Sat, 10:30am-5pm Sun) Modern internet cafe and call center; also has webcams and scanners.

Family Laundry (cnr Calles Dr Rosen & Dr Alejo Martínez; per kilo RD$50)

Farmacia KH3 (☑809-571-2350; Calle Pedro Clisante)

Plaza Médica (☑809-571-3007, emergency 809-854-1633; Calle Pedro Clisante 30; ⊘24hr) English, French, Spanish and Italian spoken.

Scotiabank (Calle Pedro Clisante)

V@net (Calle Dr Rosen 24; per hr RD$50; ⊘9:30am-midnight)

ℹ Getting There & Away

AIR Sosúa is much closer to the **Aeropuerto Internacional Gregorío Luperón** (POP; ☑809-586-0107) than Puerto Plata, although it's commonly referred to as 'Puerto Plata airport.' We're guilty of the same bias – see the Puerto Plata section for more info. A taxi from the airport to Sosúa is US$15. You can also walk 500m from the terminal to the highway and flag down a passing *gua-gua* (RD$15, 10 minutes).

BUS Metro Tours (☑809-571-1324; cnr Av Luperón & Calle Dr Rosen) has its depot right in the middle of town. It runs services to Santiago (RD$170, two hours) and onward to Santo Domingo (RD$320, five hours, 8:20am, 10:20am, 1:20pm and 5:50pm). **Caribe Tours** (☑809-571-3808; Carretera a Puerto Plata) has a bus depot on the highway at the edge of Las Charamicos neighborhood, 1km southwest of the city center. It offers service from Sosúa to Santo Domingo (RD$330, hourly from 5:15am to 6:20pm). Grab the same bus for Puerto Plata (RD$35, 20 minutes), Santiago (RD$150) and La Vega (RD$200). **El Canario** (☑809-291-5594) is a Puerto Plata-based bus that leaves daily to Samaná (RD$250, three hours) at 7am

from the main *parada* (bus stop). Be sure to call the day before to reserve your seat.

GUA-GUA For eastbound destinations along the coast, go to the highway and flag down any passing *gua-gua*. They pass every 15 minutes or so, with services to Puerto Plata (RD$30, 30 minutes), Cabarete (RD$20, 20 minutes) and Río San Juan (RD$90, 1½ hours).

ℹ Getting Around

You can walk just about everywhere in Sosúa, except the hotels east of the center, which are better reached by *motoconcho* or taxi. The former are easy to find around town, while shared taxis for intercity travel along the coast can be located at a **taxi stand** (☑809-571-3027) on the corner of Calles Morris Ling and Arzeno.

To rent a car, make your way to the airport (8km away).

CABARETE
POP 17,000

This one-time farming hamlet is now the adventure-sports capital of the country, booming with condos and new development. You'll find a sophisticated, grown-up beach town, with top-notch hotels, and a beach dining experience second to none (not to mention the best winds and waves on the island). Cabarete is an ideal spot to base yourself for exploring the area – you're within two hours' drive of the best that the coast has to offer, and if you want to go surfing, or windsurfing, or kitesurfing, heck, you don't even need to leave town. You'll hear a babble of five or six languages as you walk Cabarete's single street, where the majority of the hotels, restaurants and shops are located.

◉ Sights & Activities
PARQUE NACIONAL EL CHOCO

Part of the park, the **caves of Cabarete** are walking distance from town. Here you can take a two-hour **tour** (US$15; ⊘9am-3:30pm) of a number of privately managed caves and the surrounding forest. Bring a swimsuit – the crystal-stalactite caves 25m below the surface offer two opportunities to swim in small clear pools, provided the guide can still see you with his flashlight. The caves are padlocked by management and cannot be visited independently.

Follow the access road to El Choco a further 9km for **Monkey Jungle** (www.monkeyjungledr.com; ⊘9am-5pm), a working organic farm, sanctuary for capuchin monkeys and a thrilling 4400ft **zip line** (adult/child RD$2000/1000). All proceeds

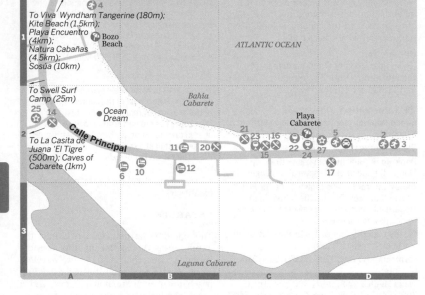

To Viva Wyndham Tangerine (180m);
Kite Beach (1.5km);
Playa Encuentro (4km);
Natura Cabañas (4.5km);
Sosúa (10km)

To Swell Surf Camp (25m)

To La Casita de Juana 'El Tigre' (500m); Caves of Cabarete (1km)

Bozo Beach

ATLANTIC OCEAN

Bahía Cabarete

Ocean Dream

Playa Cabarete

Calle Principal

Laguna Cabarete

go to medical and educational charitable projects in the DR and Haiti.

KITESURFING

Cabarete is one of the top places in the world for kitesurfing, and the sport has eclipsed windsurfing as the town's sport *du jour*. Kite Beach, 2km west of town, has ideal conditions for the sport, which entails strapping yourself to a modified surfboard and a huge inflatable wind foil then skimming and soaring across the water. Bozo Beach at the west end of the city beach is also a good spot and typically less crowded. A number of kitesurfing schools offer multiday courses for those who want to learn – just to go out by yourself you'll need at least three to four days of instruction (two to three hours' instruction per day). The learning curve for the sport is quite steep – you'll need several weeks to get good enough to really enjoy yourself.

Expect to pay US$150 to US$180 for a three-hour beginner lesson, or anywhere from US$300 to US$500 for a three- to four-day course (around eight hours total). Schools and instructors vary considerably in personality, so spend some time finding one where you feel comfortable. Kitesurfing is a potentially dangerous sport and it is

extremely important that you feel free to ask questions and voice fears or concerns, and that you receive patient, ego-free answers in return. The **International Kiteboarding Organization** (www.ikointl.com) has a new feature listing student ratings for schools and instructors.

About half of the schools are located on Kite Beach.

Dare2Fly   KITESURFING
(☑809-571-0805; www.dare2fly.com) Owned by Vela Windsurf Center, Dare2Fly has a center next to Agualina Kite Resort on Kite Beach (but its offices are on the main street). You can also inquire at Vela about classes and equipment.

Kite Club   KITESURFING
(☑809-571-9748; www.kiteclubcabarete.com) This well-run club is at the top of Kite Beach, and has a fantastic atmosphere for hanging out and relaxing between sessions. The tiny kitchen delivers delicious fresh ahi tuna salads and sandwiches.

Kitexcite   KITESURFING
(☑829-962-4556; www.kitexcite.com; Kite Beach) This award-winning school uses radio helmets and optional offshore sessions to maximize instruction.

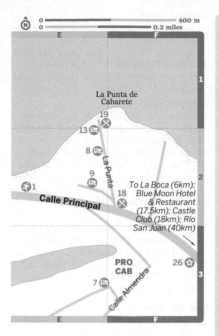

La Punta de
Cabarete

To La Boca (6km);
Blue Moon Hotel
& Restaurant
(17.5km); Castle
Club (18km); Río
San Juan (40km)

Calle Principal

Calle Almendra

PRO
CAB

Laurel Eastman Kiteboarding KITESURFING
(☑809-571-0564; www.laureleastman.com)
Friendly, safety-conscious shop located on
Bozo Beach and run by one of the world's
top kiteboarders. Offers lessons in five languages. If you're walking along the beach
from Cabarete, look for the canvas-sail
roof of the restaurant next door.

Luciano Gonzalez Kite School KITESURFING
(☑809-986-6454; lucianocabarete@hotmail
.com) Two-time winner of the Master of
the Ocean, Luciano now runs this small
school opposite Kite Beach. Very patient
with beginners. Offers a three-day, US$300
introductory course.

SURFING
Some of the best waves for surfing on the
entire island – up to 4m – break over reefs
4km west of Cabarete on Playa Encuentro.
The waves break both right and left and are
known by names like Coco Pipe, Bobo's
Point, La Derecha, La Izquierda and most
ominously, Destroyer. Several outfits in town
and on Playa Encuentro rent surfboards
and offer instruction. Surfboard rental
for a day is around US$25 to US$30; a
three-hour course costs US$45 to US$50 per
person, and five-day surf camps cost US$200
to US$225 per person. All the surf schools
have small offices on Playa Encuentro.

Ali's Surf Camp SURFING
(☑809-571-0733; alissurfcamp.com) Part of the
hotel of the same name. Frequent shuttle
service from Cabarete to Encuentro for
surfers.

Bobo Surf's Up School SURFING
(☑809-882-5197; www.bobossurfsup.com)

Cabarete Buena Onda SURFING
(☑829-877-0768; www.cabaretebuenaonda.com;
Playa Encuentro)

Pau Hana Surf Center SURFING
(☑809-975-3494; Playa Encuentro)

Swell Surf SURFING
(www.swellsurfcamp.com)

(☎809-963-7873; www.321takeoff.com; Playa Encuentro) The German owner also organizes the Master of the Ocean competition.

WINDSURFING

The combination of strong, steady winds, relatively shallow water and a rockless shore creates perfect conditions for windsurfing here.

Board and sail rentals average US$30 to US$35 per hour, US$60 to US$65 per day or US$280 to US$300 per week. For a bit more, shops offer 'nonconsecutive rentals' so you get multiday prices but you don't have to go out every day. Renters are usually required to purchase damage insurance for an additional US$50 per week. Private lessons cost around US$50 for an hour, US$200 for a four-session course, with discounts for groups. **Vela Windsurf Center** (☎809-571-0805; velacabarete.com), on the main beach, uses excellent gear and works in conjunction with kitesurfing school Dare2Fly. It also rents sea kayaks (per hour US$10 to US$15).

SAILING

With more than 20 years' experience, the **Carib Bic Wind Center** (☎809-571-0640; caribwind.com) is for those who prefer an actual boat attached to your sail. It rents Lasers and provides instruction.

WAKEBOARDING

Kitesurfers swear that this is a great way to develop your board skills, and on windless days you'll find more than a few at La Boca going out for a tow or two. The river mouth at La Boca has more than 2km of flat, smooth water to play with, and attracts devoted wakeboarders from around the world.

Cabwake School (☎829-866-3929; www.cabwake.com; ⏱9am-6pm), 6km east of town, is the only operator licensed to tow on the river. A 20-minute tow will set you back US$35, and week-long 'wake camps' – 10 to 15 tows in a week – are available at significant discount.

DIVING

The well-respected Sosúa-based dive shop **Northern Coast Diving** (☎809-571-1028; www.northerncoastdiving.com) has a representative in the offices of Iguana Mama and can organize excursions from Río San Juan in the east to Monte Cristi in the west. You can also pop over to Sosúa to compare prices and services.

MOUNTAIN BIKING

If strapping a GPS and a machete to your bike and going out bush is your idea of a good time, hook up with **Max 'Maximo' Martinez** (☎809-882-5634; maxofthemt@yahoo.es; per person from US$25), a passionate and experienced mountain-bike guide (see p179).

PADDLEBOARDING

Increasing in popularity is this somewhat meditative, less athletic method of boarding. **Paddle Board Cove** (☎809-849-2147; methodlodge@gmail.com) rents equipment for RD$700 and offers instructional tours through the lagoon here. Look for the office on the main coastal highway across the street from the Kite Beach Hotel.

HORSEBACK RIDING

The fully equipped **Rancho Mirabal** (☎809-912-5214) riding stables are situated right on Playa Encuentro. A one-hour ride on the beach is US$25, two hours US$40 and a longer half-day ride in the mountains is US$75 including food.

✎ Courses

Tony Vargas (☎809-916-4551; www.a-bailar.net; 3 1hr lessons per person US$45) offers salsa, merengue and *bachata* (popular guitar music based on bolero rhythms) lessons in the dance studio in his home.

☞ Tours

TOP CHOICE **Iguana Mama** OUTDOOR ADVENTURES (☎809-571-0908; www.iguanamama.com) The leading adventure-sports tour operator on the north coast is in a class of its own. Its specialties are mountain biking (from easy to insanely difficult, US$65) and cascading. It is one of the few operators that take you to the 27th waterfall at Damajagua (US$85), and it pioneered a cascading tour to Ciguapa Falls, which only Iguana Mama offers. There's also a variety of hiking trips, including a half-day walk (US$45) into the hills behind Cabarete (Parque Nacional El Choco), and a full-day trip to Mount Isabel de Torres (US$80), just outside Puerto Plata. Its Pico Duarte trek is expensive, but handy if you want transportation to and from Cabarete (per person US$450). Iguana Mama can also arrange a number of half-day and full-day canyoning opportunities in the area (US$90 to US$125). Action and adventure junkies should ask about the one-week 'Mama Knows Best' tour – seven days of nonstop adrenaline.

Cabarete's beaches are its main attractions, and not just for sun and sand. They're each home to a different water sport, and are great places to watch beginner and advanced athletes alike.

» Playa Cabarete Main beach in front of town, the best place for watching windsurfing, though the very best windsurfers are well offshore at the reef line. Look for them performing huge high-speed jumps and even end-over-end flips.

» Bozo Beach On the western downwind side of Playa Cabarete, and so named because of all the beginner windsurfers and kiteboarders who don't yet know how to tack up wind and so wash up on Bozo's shore. There are more kiteboarders at Bozo than at Playa Cabarete and the surf here is better for boogie boarding.

» Kite Beach Two kilometers west of town, a sight to behold on windy days, when scores of kiters of all skill levels negotiate huge sails and 30m lines amid the waves and traffic. On those days there's no swimming here, as you're liable to get run over.

» Playa Encuentro Four kilometers west of town, the place to go for surfing, though top windsurfers and kiteboarders sometimes go there to take advantage of the larger waves. The beach itself is a long, narrow stretch of sand backed by lush tropical vegetation and palm groves as it curves east toward Cabarete; strong tides and rocky shallows make swimming here difficult. To find the beach look for the yellow archway with a small hand-painted sign that says 'beach'.

» La Boca At the mouth of the Río Yásica, 7km east of town, an ideal spot for wakeboarding – more than 2km of straight, flat river water to practice your latest trick.

NORTH COAST EAST OF PUERTO PLATA

Fun Tours   OUTDOOR ADVENTURES
(☑809-571-0250) With these tours you get less than Iguana Mama (which is next door), but you also get charged a lot less. It offers the usual range of package tours, including a day trip to Cayo Arena (US$55), and an abridged version of the Damajagua Falls tour (you go only as far as the seventh waterfall).

Cabarete Coffee Company   FARM TOURS
(☑809-571-0919; www.cabaretecoffee.com) Organizes trips to the Finca Alta Gracia coffee farm outside Jarabacoa, as well as to an organic cocoa farm near Río San Juan.

☆✦ Festivals & Events

Master of the Ocean   WATER SPORTS
(☑809-963-7873; www.masteroftheocean.com) A triathlon of water sports – surfing, windsurfing and kitesurfing – held in the final week of February. From the beach you can watch some spectacular performances.

International Sand Castle Competition   SAND CASTLES
Also in the last week of February, sand-sculpture enthusiasts convene in Cabarete.

Dominican Jazz Festival   MUSIC
(www.drjazzfestival.com) Held in Santiago and Cabarete in early November, this festival attracts top musical talent from around the country and even abroad. A large stage and a beer tent are set up at the western end of the beach, and the players trumpet jazz into the night.

🛏 Sleeping
In low season you can pick up great deals on long-term rentals, but in high season – when condo owners return – hotel rooms can be hard to find. **L'Agence** (☑809-571-0999; www.agencerd.com), located in monster condo development Ocean Dream, can help you find a condo rental. New buildings are emerging on either end of town and on the inland side of Calle Principal.

IN TOWN

Velero Beach Resort   HOTEL, RESORT **$$$**
(☑809-571-9727; www.velerobeach.com; La Punta 1; r from US$170; P❄@☒) Distinguished by boutique-style rooms, the nicest in Cabarete, and its location down a small lane at the relatively traffic-free eastern end of town, Velero is an excellent choice. True to its four-star rating in service, professionalism and maintenance of the property, the Velero's only downside is it's on a small spit of a beach, but the pool and lounge area more than make up for this.

WHO'S YOUR MAMA – MAMAJUANA

You're on the beach, and some old guy is holding a bunch of empty bottles filled with leaves in your face asking you if you want to buy them.

A bottle full of leaves? What, are you kidding me?

Nope – it's *mamajuana*, the national hooch. Take a bottle, fill it with a variety of herbs and dried bark (the exact mixture depends on who's doing the mixing), top it up with rum, wine and a bit of honey, and let it steep for a month or so.

Mamajuana is reputed to enhance male virility, and packs a punch. Most bars have a bottle somewhere, and quality can range from the revolting to the eye-poppingly good.

TOP CHOICE Ali's Surf Camp BACKPACKER **$$**
(☎809-571-0733; www.alissurfcamp.com; s US$29-44, d US$33-66, apt US$75-120; P✱🔊🛜🏊) The closest thing Cabarete has to a backpacker, Ali's is ideal for groups of friends or couples looking to learn how to surf or kitesurf or who already know the drill. It's a fun, social scene, encouraged by the German owner who serves up great barbecue dinners on picnic tables sitting at the edge of a lagoon, only a five-minute walk inland. Most of the accommodations are in small but colorfully painted rustic cabins; a two-story Victorian-style building has somewhat nicer rooms with kitchenettes. The property is lush and shaded and includes a nice pool. Surf school on site.

Hotel Villa Taína HOTEL **$$$**
(☎809-571-0722; www.villataina.com; incl breakfast s US$109-142, d US$119-142; P✱@🛜🏊) This appealing boutiquey hotel at the western end of town has 55 tastefully decorated rooms, each with balcony or terrace, air-con, comfortable beds and modern bathroom. There is a small, clean pool and a nice beach area fringed by palm trees. Suites and deluxe suites are also available.

Swell Surf Camp SURF HOTEL **$$**
(☎809-571-0672; www.swellsurfcamp.com; week-long incl breakfast and 4 dinners dm/s/d US$425/635/1000; P✱🔊🛜🏊) Recently constructed and designed with the discerning surfer in mind,

this new hotel is far from a crash pad. The spare clean lines, plush bedding, modern photographs and funky furniture say 'boutique' but the pool and ping-pong table and social vibe suggest otherwise. Provides shuttle service to Playa Encuentro and other spots and airport transfers included in rates. Week-long packages are available for those who want to learn how to kitesurf or surf.

Viva Wyndham Tangerine RESORT **$$$**
(☎809-571-0402; www.vivawyndhamresorts.com; all-incl r from US$150; P✱@🛜) A bit of a fish out of water in this independent traveler enclave, this resort, part of the Wyndham chain, offers a by-the-numbers all-inclusive experience. It is only a few hundred meters west of town so if you tire of the food, whose reputation isn't stellar, it's only a few minutes to Cabarete's restaurants. The 222 rooms are tastefully decorated, the bathrooms are spacious and modern and it has all the facilities you'd expect.

Albatros Hotel & Condos HOTEL, APARTMENTS **$$**
(☎809-571-0841; www.hotel-cabarete.com; r US$45-70, apt US$96-145, penthouse US$145-165; P🛜🏊) Set back from the road at the western end of town, the Albatros offers clean and cheerful rooms amid a palm-tree-laden garden. Standard rooms come with a sitting area, a ceiling fan and a fridge. Studios and apartments come in various sizes: the smallest is a regular-sized room with a kitchenette; the largest is a two-story condo. A welcoming pool is the centerpiece of the grounds.

Hotel Alegría HOTEL, APARTMENTS **$$**
(☎809-571-0455; www.hotel-alegria.com; Callejón 2; r US$35, with ocean view US$55, studio/apt US$55/110; P🛜) Hidden down one of Cabarete's few side streets, the Alegría may not have beach access, but from the wooden deck that towers from the top of the hotel you have an unrivalled view out over the ocean. There's a small gym with treadmill and weights, and the studios and apartment each have kitchens, but more importantly the owner and staff are friendly, informative and professional.

Hotel Kaoba HOTEL, APARTMENTS **$$**
(☎809-571-0300; www.kaoba.com; r/bungalows/apt from US$32/32/70; P✱@🛜) A large complex at the eastern end of town, Kaoba is sandwiched between the Calle Principal and the Laguna Cabarete. Not especially recommended for its level of personal attentive-

ness, Kaoba has a wide range of accommodations to choose from, including ones with full kitchenettes, and all are simply designed with access to good light. The pool welcomes guests as they enter the complex and a restaurant-bar at the front of the hotel is often hopping.

Caribe Surf Hotel
HOTEL $$

(☎809-571-0788; La Punta; r US$35; ❋ 🖅) Down a quiet lane at the western end of town is this good-value hotel. The beach is obscured by the adjoining Velero Beach Resort but there is a small pool in a garden absolutely overgrown with lush vegetation, and a restaurant, Dolce Italian, which is sometimes open. Rooms are simple with few frills but some have small refrigerators where you can stock goods bought at the grocery around the corner.

OUT OF TOWN

TOP
CHOICE **Natura Cabañas**
RESORT $$$

(☎809-571-1507; www.naturacabana.com; s/d incl breakfast US$130/180; 🅿@🖅) Think rustic-chic. Luxurious facial scrub or yoga? Jungly garden or white-sand beach? You don't have to choose at this collection of marvelously designed thatched-roof bungalows about halfway between Cabarete and Sosúa. True to its name, everything is constructed from natural materials – mahogany, bamboo and stone – and a gravel path leads to a secluded beach. Owned and designed by a Chilean husband-wife team, this is what all-inclusive should look like. The two open-air restaurants serve exquisitely created and plated dishes (US$15 to US$30).

TOP
CHOICE **Hooked Cabarete**
BUNGALOWS $$

(☎809-935-9221; www.hookedcabarete.com; Playa Encuentro; s/d/tr US$48/64/75; 🅿❋🖅) If a beachfront location isn't a priority, then this small property down a dirt road only 200m or so from Playa Encuentro is a nice place to ensconce yourself – especially if you're a surfer. A handful of modern bungalow-style studio apartments with kitchenettes and attractive wooden porches surround a quiet garden courtyard and small pool. Expect to get to know your neighbors. It also rents scooters so you can get into town easily.

Hideaway Beach Resort
HOTEL $$

(☎809-571-4300; www.hideawaybeachresort.com; per person incl breakfast from US$40; 🅿❋🖅) True to its name, this whitewashed Mediterranean-style property feels like a

secret. Occupying a spectacular stretch of the western end of Playa Encuentro, Hideaway is best for those looking for a low-key vacation. Restaurant Chez Antonio serves up a wide variety of Dominican and Italian dishes in its pool-side dining room or on a table out on the perfectly manicured lawn under a towering palm tree. Friday nights' special is 6oz filet mignon or 1lb lobster for RD$400. Look for a sign marking the access road off the highway. Villas for rent as well.

You can't go wrong choosing either one of the two hotels next to one another directly on Kite Beach. Both offer prime beachfront access and views of kitesurfers struggling to get airborne, pools and casual ocean-front restaurants. Rooms at the **Agualina Kite Resort** (☎809-571-0787; www.agualina .com; Kite Beach; r US$80; 🅿❋🖅) are somewhat more stylishly decorated with more luxurious bathrooms and all rooms have sea views. The larger **Kite Beach Hotel** (☎809-571-0878; www.kitebeachhotel.com; Kite Beach; s/d incl breakfast US$60/66, studio s/d US$70/80, apt US$90-240; 🅿❋🖅) is better for those looking for front-desk concierge service and rates include a nice breakfast; be sure to book a room with a view.

✖ Eating

Dining out on Cabarete's beach is the quintessential Caribbean experience – paper lanterns hanging from palm trees, a gentle ocean breeze and excellent food (even if it does cost the same as you'd pay back home). After your meal, dig your toes into the sand and kick back with a cocktail. While we've only listed three restaurants on the beach, many of the bars listed in the drinking and entertainment section serve good food as well.

Casanova
INTERNATIONAL $$

(mains RD$350; ⊙breakfast, lunch & dinner) You'll think you're on a beach in southern Thailand. Casanova is lavishly decorated with Buddha statues and other Asian-inspired trinkets – the usual suspects like surf and turf make an appearance, as do fresh salads, pizza and inventive surprises.

Pomodoro
ITALIAN $$

(mains RD$300; ⊙lunch & dinner) Run by an Italian jazz fiend, this pizza joint makes the best crispy-crust pizza on the beach. It uses only quality toppings – including pungent,

OUT OF TOWN EATS

If you should ever grow tired of the beachside scene, both of the following restaurants are wonderfully unique options. Even if it weren't for the excellent food, they would be worthy destinations simply for the chance to get out into the countryside.

Blue Moon Hotel & Restaurant

INDIAN $$$

(☎809-757-0614; www.bluemoonretreat.net; Los Brazos; mains RD$600; ⊙dinner) Set in the mountains a short drive from Cabarete, this bungalow-style hotel and restaurant hosts family-sized Indian dinners (minimum eight people, reserve in advance). Food is quality South Asian fare, including two different veggie dishes, a main course such as tandoori or curried chicken or fish, rice, salad, coffee, tea and dessert. The bungalows (US$50 to US$60 per bungalow) include breakfast in the price, and are cool and comfortable, with inventive Indian-style decor. To get here from Cabarete, head east on the highway to Sabaneta and turn right on the road to Jamao al Norte. Proceed a few kilometers and you'll pass a bridge in the town of Los Brazos, where you should look for a sign to your left as you climb the hill.

Castle Club

FUSION HAUTE CUISINE $$$

(☎809-357-8334; www.castleclubonline.com; Los Brazos; per person excl drinks US$35; ⊙dinner) Just 200m past the Blue Moon on your left is this rambling, eccentric home – a castle of sorts. The owners grow much of their own food on the property, and serve this super-fresh produce in their restaurant, one of the very best in the country. Expect dishes like coconut sea bass, exquisite salads and cold lemon soufflé. Their schedule can be erratic, though – book at least two days in advance. They can cater for groups from six to 100.

---

imported Italian cheese – and there's live jazz on Thursday nights.

Blu Cabarete Restaurant

INTERNATIONAL $$

(mains RD$250; ⊙lunch & dinner) Blu Cabarete has comfy, thick couches on the beach. Dinner prices are double lunchtime; the lunch menu includes good, healthy wraps.

TOP
CHOICE **Otra Cosa**

FRENCH $$$

(☎809-571-0607; La Punta; mains RD$500; ⊙dinner Wed-Mon; 🛜) Simply a must, this romantic French-Caribbean restaurant just across from the Velero Resort guarantees an incredible dining experience. From a secluded spot with marvelous sea breezes at dusk, you can listen to the surf and watch the moon rise over the water while sipping wine and feasting on *très délicieux* expertly prepared dishes like seared tuna in ginger flambéed in rum (RD$650). An *amuse-bouche* of eggplant caviar and shot of *mamajuana*, both complimentary, serve as bookends to the meal. Reservations recommended.

Bliss

FRENCH, CARIBBEAN $$$

(Callejón de la Loma; mains RD$500; ⊙4pm-midnight Mon-Sat) It may not be on the beach, but sitting around the crystal-blue pool with a top-shelf cocktail in your hand, you can be forgiven for not caring. The food here is creative – think rack of lamb with thyme and bitter caramel sauce, shrimp with passionfruit sauce, or roasted duck breast with green pepper sauce.

La Casita de Juana 'El Tigre'

DOMINICAN $

(Callejón de la Loma; set meals RD$150; ⊙dinner, lunch in high season, closed Tue) The irrepressibly warm owner of this Dominican restaurant makes Dominican food memorable (no small challenge). Choice of chicken, goat or fish with rice, beans and salad. The specialty of the house is *arepita de yucca* (aniseed-flavored yucca pancakes).

Hexenkessel

GERMAN $$

(mains RD$200; ⊙24hr) After a night of debauchery, nothing hits the spot like a monstrous schnitzel (US$5) at this never-closed German eatery. Clients sit side by side at picnic tables. Other house specialties include potato pancakes with ground beef and fried Bavarian bratwurst.

Panadería Repostería Dick

BAKERY $

(set breakfasts RD$150; ⊙7am-3pm Thu-Tue) The undisputed champion of breakfast in Cabarete, Dick serves large set breakfasts with juice and strong coffee. The bakery does wholewheat bread and mind-blowing vanilla-cream Danish pastries.

Aki Sushi JAPANESE $$
(☏809-571-0075; Hotel Agualina, Kite Beach; sushi rolls RD$215) If you're staying on Kite Beach and don't want to head into town, this unassuming Japanese restaurant serves top-notch sushi and the service is friendly and attentive. The ten-piece combination special (RD$700) is enough for two.

There are three supermarkets in Cabarete. The biggest and best is **Janet's Supermarket** (Calle Principal) in the east end of town.

🍸 Drinking & Entertainment

Cabarete nightlife is centered on the bars and restaurants that spill out onto the beach.

Nikki Beach BAR, NIGHTCLUB
(☺9am-late) St Tropez comes to the DR in this swish club with its own sommelier; DJs get the party started late.

Lax BAR, NIGHTCLUB
(www.lax-cabarete.com; ☺9am-1am) This mellow bar and restaurant serves food until 10:30pm, when the DJ starts to spin. In many ways it's the social headquarters of Cabarete.

Onno's RESTAURANT, NIGHTCLUB
(☺9am-late) This edgy, Dutch-owned restaurant and nightclub is a European and hipster hangout and serves good-value food on the beach. At night a DJ spins a decent set.

Bambú BAR, DISCO
(☺6pm-late) Just 100m west of Onno's, this bar and disco plays loud house music and reggaeton, and the crowd spills out onto the beach.

Voy Voy CAFE, BAR
(☺6pm-late) Vela Windsurf Center by day, bar by night, this small, hip cafe also serves sandwiches and snacks. Monday karaoke is a mandatory part of Cabarete beach life.

Latino Lounge NIGHTCLUB
(Callejón de la Loma; ☺6pm-late) Just inside Callejón de la Loma, this spot is the best place in Cabarete to dance merengue or *bachata*.

Ocean Sands Casino NIGHTCLUB
(☏809-571-0050; disco cover charge RD$150; ☺4pm-very late) The on-site disco plays loud merengue and reggaeton, and doesn't begin to fill up till way past midnight.

It's one of your few options after the bars close. The adjoining strip club means a moderate presence of sex workers.

ℹ Information

Active Cabarete (www.activecabarete.com) A website with a range of information including activities and events, weather, and 'special stuff.'

All City (per hr RD$35; ☺9am-9pm Mon-Sat, 10am-6pm Sun) Fast connection and head-phones. There's also a small bank of phones for domestic and international calls.

Banco Popular (Calle Principal)

Family Lavandería (per kg RD$50; ☺8am-6pm Mon-Sat) Eastern end of town, opposite Janet's Supermarket.

Fujifilm Digital (per hr RD$60) Fast internet connection and headphones.

Politur (tourist police; ☏809-571-0713) At the eastern entrance to town.

Scotiabank (Calle Principal)

Servi-Med (☏809-571-0964; ☺24hr) Highly recommended; English, German and Spanish are spoken and it carries out house calls. Travel medical insurance and credit cards accepted.

ℹ Getting There & Around

BUS None of the main bus companies offer a service to Cabarete – the closest bus depots are in Sosúa.

CAR If you want to rent a car the best place to do so is at the Puerto Plata airport when you arrive. If you're already in town, you can take a *gua-gua* (30 minutes) to the airport road (just past Sosúa), walk 500m to the terminal and shop around at the numerous car-rental agencies there.

GUA-GUA Heaps of *gua-guas* ply this coastal road, including east to Río San Juan (RD$80, one hour) and west to Sosúa (RD$20, 20 minutes) and Puerto Plata (RD$50, 45 minutes). Hail them anywhere along Cabarete's main drag.

MOTOCONCHO Transportation in town is dominated by *motoconchos,* who will attempt to charge you two to three times the price you'd pay for a similar ride in Puerto Plata. Don't be surprised if you can't haggle them down. A ride out to Encuentro should cost RD$100.

SCOOTER A popular option for the many visitors who stay a week or longer is to rent a scooter or a motorcycle. Expect to pay around US$20 per day, less if you rent for a week or more. There are lots of scooter-rental shops along the main drag, and some hotels rent two-wheeled transportation too. Be aware that helmets are pretty much nonexistent in this country, so if that's important to you consider bringing your own.

NORTH COAST EAST OF PUERTO PLATA

TAXI The motorcycle-shy can call a **taxi** (☎809-571-3819), which will cost RD$250 to Encuentro, US$20 to US$25 to the airport, and US$35 to Puerto Plata. There's also a taxi stand in the middle of town.

RÍO SAN JUAN
POP 9000

Only an hour east of Cabarete, this sleepy Dominican town is distinct because of its location on a mangrove lagoon and its proximity to several of the north coast's better beaches. There's good diving and snorkeling nearby (although you'll need to organize it with a dive shop in Sosúa before you come).

◉ Sights

Laguna Gri-Gri   LAGOON
This lagoon (it shares the same ecosystem as Los Haitises south of Península de Samaná) at the northern end of Calle Duarte was once Río San Juan's claim to fame, drawing tourists from near and far for boat rides through its tangled mangrove channels. Unfortunately, overuse and pollution mean the lagoon is no longer pristine and swimming is no longer recommended. It's still fairly picturesque and a dozen or more boatmen still offer **tours**, which typically cost US$35 for up to seven people and last around an hour, with visits to the mangrove forests, some interesting rock formations and a cave populated by hundreds of swallows. Look for a small shack next to the public bathrooms down by the Laguna – you'll find it easier to join a group on weekends, when Dominicans come to take this trip.

You can also visit the lagoon on foot – there's a path on the far side of the Hotel Bahía Blanca along the water's edge into the mangroves.

Playa Caletón   BEACH
Located about 1km east of town, this small bay is a peaceful and beautiful place to spend an afternoon. The tawny sand is lapped by teal waters, and almond trees interspersed with towering palms provide plenty of shade. Food stands are near the entrance. The easiest way to get here is to take a *gua-gua* (RD$15) or a *motoconcho* (RD$35) to the turn-off (a fading and difficult-to-spot sign is painted on a wall), from which it's a 200m walk down a rocky access road past a goat farm to the beach. If you have a car, you can make it all the way to the beach, but take it slow on the rough parts.

Playa Grande   BEACH
Just 8km east of Río San Juan is Playa Grande, one of the most beautiful beaches in the DR. Here, the long, broad, tawny beach has aquamarine water on one side and a thick fringe of palm trees on the other, with stark white cliffs jutting out into the ocean in the distance. It's a picture postcard everywhere you look. There are facilities at the entrance – food stands selling snacks and beer; vendors renting beach chairs (per day RD$100), umbrellas (per day RD$175), snorkel equipment (full day RD$800), body boards (per hour RD$150) and surfboards (full day RD$800); plus a smattering of vendors selling shell necklaces, bikinis and sunscreen. An afternoon repast of pina coladas (RD$150) and lobster (per pound RD$600) cooked to order is highly recommended. If you don't want to be hassled, walk east or west of the entrance – the beach goes on for ages and you're sure to find plenty of secluded spots.

A word about safety: Playa Grande has heavy surf and a deceptively strong undertow. Riptides – powerful currents of water flowing out to sea – do form occasionally, and tourists have drowned here in the past. Be conservative when swimming at Playa Grande, and children and less-experienced swimmers should probably not go in at all unless the surf is very low. If you do get caught in a riptide, swim parallel to the shore until you get out of the current and then swim in to shore.

If you take a *gua-gua* from town, most drivers will drive you right to the beach if you ask – it's not a detour for them as the beach road reconnects with the highway a couple of kilometers past the beach. You can also hire a *motoconcho* (RD$75) or a taxi (RD$300) to bring you directly to the beach.

Playa Preciosa   BEACH
Off the same access road to Playa Grande but 100m east of it (look for a tiny dirt parking area) is a narrow and unmarked beach known as Playa Preciosa. This spectacular stretch of sand is pounded by serious waves and few attempt to play in the surf. Those who do – typically surfers at dawn – do so for the thrill. Much of the beach is covered during high tide.

🏃 Activities
DIVING & SNORKELING

Río San Juan has a great variety of nearby dive sites, including **Seven Hills**, a collection of huge coral heads descending from 6m to 50m, and **Crab Canyon**, with a series of natural arches and swim-throughs. Twenty minutes east of Río San Juan is **Dudu Cave**, one of the best freshwater cavern dives in the Caribbean, where the visibility is almost 50m. Most dive shops require an Advanced Diver certificate or at least 20 logged dives to do these trips.

There's no dive center in Río San Juan; your best bet is to organize something in Sosúa, where you'll pay roughly US$100 to US$120 per person for a full day of diving (minimum three people). You can also organize half-day snorkeling trips here (per person US$70 to US$85).

GOLF

Playa Grande Golf Course   GOLF
(✆809-582-0860; www.playagrande.com; Carretera a Nagua; 9/18 holes US$80/140; ☺7am-4:30pm) This par-72 course built on a verdant cliff before Playa Grande is part of a planned development involving Aman resorts and a group of bold-faced Americans led by a former New York City banker with utopian ambitions – the original blueprint called for an artist's colony and science research center. It is a well-tended course that boasts a spectacular ocean view from almost every hole. Caddies and carts are obligatory but not included in the rate (US$20 extra for 18 holes). Multigame discounts are also available. Be sure to call ahead.

☞ Tours

The small **Campo Tours** (✆809-589-2550; Calle Duarte 17) agency sells predigested package tours to guests at the local all-inclusive Bahía Principe Hotel, including a glass-bottomed boat tour (US$20) of the *laguna*, and a three-hour deep-sea fishing trip (US$70).

🛏 Sleeping

Bahía Blanca Hotel   HOTEL $
(✆809-589-2563; bahia.blanca.dr@codetel.net.do; Calle Deligne; r US$35; ☜) Perched on a rocky spit over turquoise-blue waters, the Bahía Blanca has undeniably beautiful ocean views. Rooms are decent – clean, tile-floored and with private bathroom – but are showing their age. All but two have at least partial ocean views, and wide balconies on each of the three floors provide plenty of opportunities to enjoy the beauty. Rooms on the 3rd floor are the most spacious and have small private balconies.

The hotel is also flanked by two calm bays, which are great for swimming.

✗ Eating & Drinking

Directly in front of the lagoon is **La Orquidea** (Calle FR Sánchez; mains RD$300; ☺breakfast, lunch & dinner) and a few blocks up from the lagoon is **Estrella Bar & Restaurant** (Calle Duarte; mains RD$300; ☺breakfast, lunch & dinner; ☜), both of which serve French/Caribbean fare.

Cheo's Café (Calle Billini 6; mains RD$250; ☺lunch & dinner) and **La Casona** (Calle Duarte 6; mains RD$200; ☺lunch & dinner) are friendly informal Dominican restaurants; the latter has especially good empanadas. Cheo's does familiar beef, chicken and pasta dishes.

❶ Information

Banco Progreso (Calle Duarte 38) Just off the main coastal highway.

Con@net (cnr Calles Rufino Bulbuena & Capotillo; internet per hr RD$50)

Farmacia Reyes (✆809-589-2234; Calle Duarte 36)

Politur (tourist police; ✆809-754-3241) Located on the highway, 300m west of Calle Duarte.

Tourist office (cnr Calles FR Sánchez & Lorenzo Adames) Not very helpful but you may find a few maps and brochures on hand.

❶ Getting There & Around

BUS Caribe Tours (✆809-589-2644), just west of Calle Duarte on the coastal highway just outside town, provides bus service between Río San Juan and Santo Domingo (RD$330, 4½ hours) and stops along the way at Nagua (RD$65, 45 minutes) and San Francisco de Macorís (RD$75, 2½ hours). Buses depart at 6:30am, 7:30am, 9:30am, 2pm and 3:30pm.

WESTBOUND GUA-GUA These come and go from the intersection of Calle Duarte and the coastal highway, known around town as simply *la parada* (the stop). Westbound *gua-guas* line up at the northwest corner of the intersection, departing every 15 minutes from 6am to 5pm for Cabarete (RD$80, 1½ hours), Sosúa (RD$90, 1½ hours) and Puerto Plata (RD$100, two hours).

EASTBOUND GUA-GUA These line up on the northeast corner of Calle Duarte and the coastal highway and leave every 10 minutes from 6:30am to 6pm for Playa Caletón (RD$17, 5 minutes), Playa Grande (RD$34, 15 minutes) and Nagua (RD$76, 1¼ hours). From Nagua you can catch *gua-guas* to Samaná or 1st-class buses to Santo Domingo.

TAXI There's a **taxi stand** (✆809-589-2501) on Calle Duarte between Calles Luperón and

Dr Virgilio García. Some sample fares are Playa Caletón RD$100, Playa Grande RD$400, Cabarete RD$1800, Aeropuerto Puerto Plata RD$2500 and Las Terrenas on the Península de Samaná RD$3000.

CABRERA

East of Playa Grande is Cabrera, a sleepy town of distinctive stone houses with green shutters, colorful flower boxes and well-kept gardens, as well as lavish vacation homes owned by Dominicans and expats. Within the private Orchid Bay Estates development is Orchid Bay Beach. Also nearby is Playa Diamante with shallow water good for children; Playa El Breton, within Parque Nacional Cabo Francis, has excellent snorkeling; and Playa Entrada, one of the longest beaches on the north coast.

The area is beginning to be colonized by high-end villas for rent; surely one of the nicest is the eight-bedroom **Sunrise Villas** (villas from US$1350; ☎866-998-4552; www .sunrise-villa.com). Otherwise travelers can head to **Hotel La Catalina** (☎809-589-7700; www.lacatalina.com; Cabrera; s/d incl breakfast US$78/98, apt USD$118-224; ❋🐾P🐾), perched on a lush hill several kilometers inland. It offers charming and airy rooms with fresh white linens and wicker furniture, as well as spectacular views from the restaurant and pool area. Free shuttles take guests to and from Playa Grande.

NAGUA
POP 34,000

On the coastal highway 36km northwest of Sánchez and 54km southeast of Río San Juan, Nagua is a hot, dusty town whose interest to tourists is strictly as a transportation hub. It is the main transfer point for *gua-guas* heading in either direction along the coastal highway. The inland road to San Francisco de Macorís, Moca and Santiago begins here as well, meaning you can catch a *gua-gua* to just about anywhere. To catch one, simply walk to the highway and wave down a *gua-gua* going in the direction you want – ones on the coastal road pass every 15 minutes, while inland buses can take up to half an hour.

Caribe Tours (☎809-584-4505; Calle Mella at Emilio Conde) has almost a dozen buses running to Santo Domingo (RD$320, 3½ hours) every half-hour to hour from 7:30am to 5pm and four buses to Samaná (RD$60, 7am, 9:30am, 1:30pm and 4pm).

West of Puerto Plata

The coastal area west of Puerto Plata remains largely undeveloped, and sees few foreign visitors. Inland villages are surrounded by sugarcane fields and cattle country. There's a couple of good day-trips – the highly recommended Damajagua waterfalls and Cayo Arena. History buffs might like to visit Parque Nacional La Isabela, where Columbus founded the second settlement in the New World. Boaters will already know of Luperón – famous as a 'hurricane hole' – but landlubbers have little reason to visit. If you're on your way to Haiti, Monte Cristi is worth a day, but the lack of tourist infrastructure makes it difficult to visit the outlying islands, where pristine coral lurks. The twice-weekly Haitian market at Dajabón may be of interest, if only to see how strikingly different are the lives of the two peoples who share this island.

LUPERÓN
POP 4500

Luperón is famous among boaters as a 'hurricane hole' – a safe haven from rough seas. There are two marinas here – plans for a larger third development with villas and condos and a marina that could accommodate cruise ships seem to be perpetually on hold – and on average there are anywhere from 40 to 70 craft in the harbor. Unless you're a boater, though, or a guest at the nearby all-inclusive resort, the town holds little allure. Deeply rutted and dusty streets are quiet during the day and in near total darkness at night.

The road from Imbert enters Luperón from the south. Staying to your left, the highway becomes Calle Duarte and eventually intersects with Calle 27 de Febrero, Luperón's main east-west drag. This intersection is the commercial center of town. The town park is a few blocks east of there, the marinas a kilometer west and Parque Nacional La Isabela beyond that.

◉ Sights & Activities

Luperón doesn't have much in the way of sights and activities, but it is the nearest town to Parque Nacional La Isabela.

Playa Grande is fronted by an all-inclusive resort, and as far as Dominican beaches go, is subpar. There are two entrances – one is a path running beside the Hotasa Beach resort and the other is at the end of a well-marked dirt road off the

Travelers routinely describe the tour of the waterfalls at Damajagua as 'the coolest thing I did in the DR.' We agree. Guides lead you up, swimming and climbing through the waterfalls. To get down you jump – as much as 8m – into the sparkling pools below.

It's mandatory to wear a helmet and a life jacket, and guides are trained in first aid and CPR. It wasn't always that way, however. Flashback to 2004. A handful of unofficial guides led tours at the waterfalls. There were no safety measures, no visitors center, and the occasional minor injury. Then a young boy drowned. Peace Corps volunteer Joe Kennedy – grandson of Robert F Kennedy and great-nephew of JFK – had just arrived. And there was nothing here. 'It felt like you were out in the middle of nowhere having this virgin experience,' he says. 'There was no visitors center, no restaurant, nothing. There simply wasn't any money for helmets or life jackets and training.' Kennedy applied for and received grant money from both USAID (US$50,000) and the UN Development Program (US$30,000). 'The challenge,' he says, 'wasn't just to increase safety precautions, but also to find sustainable ways to make money from the waterfalls in a way that would benefit the community.'

The grant money was used to build the **visitors center** (☎809-635-1722; www.27charcos.com) and restaurant that are there now. With the help of several Puerto Plata area resorts, Kennedy raised upward of US$10,000 to purchase life jackets and helmets.

These days it's mandatory to go with a guide, but there's no minimum group size, so you can go by yourself if you wish. You'll need around four hours to make it to the 27th waterfall and back. The falls are open from 8:30am to 4pm, but go early, before the crowds arrive, and you might just have the whole place to yourself.

To get to the falls, go south from Imbert on the highway for 3.3km (and cross two bridges) until you see a sign on your left with pictures of a waterfall. From there it's about 1km down to the visitors center. Alternatively, take a *gua-gua* from Puerto Plata and ask to get off at the entrance.

You can go up to the 7th, 12th or 27th waterfall. Most 'jeep safari' package tours only go to the 7th waterfall. You should be in good shape and over the age of 12. The entrance fee varies depending on your nationality and how far you go. Foreigners pay RD$460 to the highest waterfall and less to reach the lower ones.

US$1 of every entrance fee goes to a community development fund. Eight people sit on the board, including the Secretary of Environment, to make sure the money gets spent wisely. Considering that an average of 3000 tourists go through the falls every month, the bank account is going well – plans are underway to build a library for the local school, fix a local church and build footbridges over a nearby river. Other Peace Corps volunteers are continuing the project Kennedy began.

The big Texaco station at Imbert serves as a crossroad for the entire area. There is a frequent *gua-gua* service to Santiago (RD$80, 1¼ hours) and Puerto Plata (RD$40, 30 minutes).

NORTH COAST WEST OF PUERTO PLATA

highway another 700m further west. A *motoconcho* ride costs about US$1.80.

With enough time and patience it's possible to arrange a **boat trip** at Marina Puerto Blanco, 1km east of town. There are no official tours, but if you put the word out that you're interested someone is bound to turn up sooner or later. Prices vary widely depending on the captain, but expect to pay US$40 to US$60 for a half-day trip, or US$70 to US$120 for a full day.

🛏 Sleeping

Hotasa Luperón Beach Resort   RESORT **$$**
(☎809-571-8303; www.hotasa.es; Carretera de las Américas; all incl per person US$65-110; P❄@☲) The rotating hot dog warmer out by the pool bar says it all. You are a long way from Punta Cana. After an ownership change and consolidation with a neighboring resort, Luperón's only all-inclusive still manages to attract a small number of mostly European vacationers. Rooms have balconies facing the ocean and Playa Grande or more likely the sprawling grounds – the fact that the chairs

are cheap plastic is telling. Windsurfing, boat trips, horseback riding and scuba clinics in the pool are available.

La Casa del Sol HOTEL $
(☎809-712-4293; www.casadelsol.de.ms; Calle 27 de Febrero; r with fan/air-con US$24/30; ✳) Management of this hotel seems to be in a state of flux. Set on a leafy lot about 100m west of La Yola Bar Restaurant, it features seven basic rooms with old furniture and TVs, each with large beds, some with sofas or chairs and tables.

Pension Alfonso Guesthouse GUESTHOUSE $
(☎809-963-1623; r RD$300) There's something intimate about sleeping above a beauty salon. When the generator powering the two old-fashioned blow-dryers goes silent in the early evening, the handful of small, 2nd-floor rooms at Alfonso's feel like a cozy lair. There's just enough room for a fan, a TV and a bed and cold-water showers in equally cramped bathrooms. Give Alfonso a call or ask Steve of Captain Steve's Place, who is a friend, to put you in touch. It's on a side street a handful of blocks from Parque Central.

✗ Eating & Drinking

Captain Steve's Place AMERICAN, DOMINICAN $
(Calle Duarte 47; mains RD$150; ☉7am-9pm; @🛜❄) Owned and operated by an American-Dominican husband-wife team, Steve's is the hangout of choice for the small community of expats who make Luperón a regular pit-stop on their Caribbean cruising. The large menu includes omelets, burgers, stir-fry, really anything you can think up – Steve, a former charter boat captain, will take orders and the lunch special of fish, rice and salad (RD$100) can't be beat for value. Good, strong coffee, free wi-fi, laundry (per pound RD$20) and a small pool at the back (per person US$5) mean it's a good place to while away a day.

A few kilometers from town in the same general direction as the Hotasa Luperón Beach Resort and perched on a small hill above the lagoon is the **Yacht Club Marina Luperón** (mains RD$250; ☉breakfast, lunch & dinner). Unfortunately, the wonderful views are offset by desultory management and an uncertain future. A little further down the same dirt road is **Puerto Blanco Marina** (mains RD$200), a small outdoor restaurant and bar on a deck at the water's edge.

❶ Information

The town's sole ATM is notorious for being frequently out of cash or not functioning; it's best to withdraw as much money as you think you'll need before venturing out this way.

BanReservas (Calle Duarte) Across the street from Politur.

Farmacia Danessa (☎809-571-8855; Calle Independencia) West side of the park.

Politur (tourist police; ☎809-581-8045; cnr Calle Duarte & 16 de Agosto)

Post office (Calle Luperón) East side of the park.

Thornless Path (www.thornlesspath.com) Luperón resident and Caribbean cruiser Bruce Van Sant's website tribute to Luperón.

❶ Getting There & Away

Gua-guas to Imbert (RD$50, 30 minutes, every 15 minutes 5am to 6:30pm) leave from a stop on Calle Duarte at 16 de Agosto, four blocks south of Calle 27 de Febrero. From Imbert you can pick up *gua-guas* headed south to Santiago or north to Puerto Plata.

If you're driving, pick up the turn-off near Imbert on the Puerto Plata–Santiago highway.

A taxi from Puerto Plata should cost around US$90 (around one hour).

PARQUE NACIONAL LA ISABELA

This historically significant **national park** (admission RD$100; ☉8am-5pm) marks Columbus' second settlement on Hispaniola. When he arrived at the first settlement at Cap-Haïtien in Haiti on his second voyage to the New World, he found it destroyed, so he shifted 110km east and set up a new camp here; the foundations of several oceanfront buildings are all that remain.

A small, fairly lackluster museum visited frequently by groups of Dominican primary-school students marks the occasion. Exhibits in Spanish include sociopolitical explanations of the Taíno communities Columbus encountered, some old coins, rings, arrowheads and a small-scale replica of Columbus' house.

Across the road from the park is the mildly impressive **Templo de las Américas** (☉9am-6pm; admission free). It's a loose replica – though much larger – of La Isabela's original church and was built as part of the settlement's 500th anniversary celebrations.

Also nearby is **Playa Isabela**, a broad outward-curving beach with coarse sand and calm water. There are a couple of small beach restaurants and usually at least one knick-knack stand that rents snorkeling gear (RD$150) – ask the vendor to point you in the direction of the best coral patches. When swimming or wading, be alert for sea urchins lurking in the rock patches in the shallows.

Located where the main road dead ends before the entrance to the national park, **Hostelería Rancho del Sol** (☑809-696-0325; s/d incl breakfast with fan RD$700/1400, with air-con RD$1200/1900; P❋⊠) is a rambling, idiosyncratic little hotel. All eight rooms have a terrace with rocking chairs looking out over an ungroomed plot of land and the ocean beyond. On the plus side, rooms are spacious enough to contain a couch, desk and chairs – the downside is they're a haphazard mix of styles and age.

❶ Getting There & Away

FROM LUPERÓN Only 20 minutes or so away. Drive 11km west until you come to a T-junction. To your right lies Playa Isabela (1km), directly ahead is Rancho del Sol, left down an access road is the museum and the site itself (100m), and left on the main road is the church (500m). A taxi from Luperón will set you back US$60 return (if the driver waits), and a *motoconcho* around RD$250 one way.

FROM MAIN HIGHWAY It's possible, but somewhat harder, to get to La Isabela from the main highway between Santiago and Monte Cristi. Turn off at Cruce de Guayacanes and head north 25km to Villa Isabela, passing through Los Hidalgos on the way. (The signs can be a little confusing, so ask for 'El Castillo' – as you go.) The park is 7km from Villa Isabella, but the road is dirt and you have to cross two broad rivers that are often impassable; ask at a *motoconcho* stand in Villa Isabela how high the water is and if the car you're driving will make it across. After crossing the second river, turn right on the main road and you'll drive past the park – look for Templo de Las Américas on your right.

PUNTA RUSIA
POP 200

This remote outpost exists solely to service the package tours coming to **Cayo Arena** (aka 'Paradise Island'), a picturesque sandbar around 10km northwest of Punta Rusia. Tour groups are shuttled by speedboat for a couple of hours here, before returning via a fairly humdrum mangrove plantation (where you might spot a manatee). The corals around the atoll are pristine and the snorkeling tops; however, the throngs in the water can detract from the experience. On weekends, hundreds of people, primarily Dominicans from Santiago, occupy the beach.

Lots of agents sell this tour, but the actual operator is **El Paraíso Tours** (☑809-320-7606; www.cayoparaiso.com). Expect to pay roughly US$50 per person (drinks and buffet lunch included); if you're coming from the Puerto Plata region be prepared to spend three hours each way in the back of a truck. If you're already in Punta Rusia it's US$35 per person. If you want to avoid the package tourists, hop on the service and supply boat, which leaves Punta Rusia around 8:15am. You'll have the island to yourself for more than an hour. Otherwise, go on an afternoon boat, when there are fewer people.

A German-French couple runs **Casita Mariposa** (☑809-325-2378; s/d incl breakfast US$15/24), a handful of rustic cabins set on a bluff overlooking the ocean not far from town. Halfway between town and Playa Enseñada 3km away is Tortuga Hotel, a foreign-owned, orange concrete building, just off the beach.

For food, you can join one of the tour-group buffets for US$14, including drinks. There is also a number of modest **restaurants** (mains RD$200) and beachside fish stands that serve basic, cheap meals.

❶ Getting There & Away
There is no public transportation here, and the road is a muddy, rutted nightmare. While the beach is pleasant enough, and you'll spot some wild orchids on a dirt track leading inland (5km west of town), the amount of effort required to get here doesn't really pay off once you arrive.

FROM VILLA ISABELA A 25km dirt road leads from Villa Isabela, which can be reached by paved roads from either Imbert or Hwy 1 (turn off at Cruce de Guayacanes). You have to ford two rivers on this route, so ask in Villa Isabela about conditions.

FROM HWY 1 The easier route is from Villa Elisa, 20km west of Laguna Salada on Hwy 1. From there, the road north is paved for 8km and deteriorates steadily for the next 12km, but does not require you to cross any rivers.

MONTE CRISTI
POP 17,000

A dusty frontier town originally founded by the Spanish crown in 1750, Monte Cristi's allure, if it can be said to have one, lies principally in its end-of-the-road feel. Most travelers who come this way are passing through on their way to Haiti. Its formerly prosperous incarnation as the base of the Grenada Fruit Company can be seen in the wide streets and dilapidated Victorian homes in the immediate vicinity of the Parque Central. Some have been partially restored enough to appreciate their one-time glory. Residents continue to make their living fishing and tending livestock, just as they've done for generations; another source of revenue is salt harvested from evaporation ponds north of town and sold in the US by Morton Salt.

Monte Cristi celebrates what is considered the most brutal Carnival in the country – participants carry bullwhips and crack each other as they walk through the streets.

◉ Sights & Activities

Calle San Fernando, which runs along the far side of the park, leads to the beaches and El Morro.

El Morro MOUNTAIN

Part of the 1100-sq-km **Parque Nacional Monte Cristi** (◷8am-5pm, admission free) that surrounds Monte Cristi on all sides, El Morro (The Hill) sits 5km northeast of town – follow Av San Fernando north of town to the beach and continue to your right until the road dead-ends. Opposite the ranger station, 585 wooden stairs lead to the top (239m). If you manage to safely scramble over the rotting planks and loose gravel, you'll be rewarded with excellent views. It's about an hour return.

Parque Central PARK

Monte Christi's city park is notable for the 50m clock tower at its center designed by French engineer Alexandre Gustave Eiffel. The clock tower, which was imported from France in 1895, was allowed to deteriorate, but in 1997 the Leon Jimenez family, of Aurora cigar and Presidente beer fortune, financed the tower's restoration.

🏖 Beaches

Tucked behind the hill in the national park and backed by a towering precipice, **Playa Detras del Morro** is the prettiest beach in the area. There's only a long sliver of tan sand as much of it is made up of rocks. Just past the ranger station where the road dead-ends is a short dirt path down to the beach. **Playa Juan de Boloños** is the main public beach, 1km north of town.

Only if you have time and a 4WD, **Playa Popa** is a little strip of sand 16km from town down a rough road – it's difficult to find so ask directions. It's not especially beautiful but is little-visited.

☞ Tours

Most of the hotels in town organize snorkeling tours (per person US$50), trips to the isolated beach at **Isla Cabra** (US$30 up to four people), and boat trips to **Los Cayos de los Siete Hermanos** (US$300 up to 12 people), a collection of seven uninhabited islands inside the national park.

So few people come here, though, that it can be expensive and difficult to arrange any of these tours – your best bet is to come on weekends in the high season (November to March) and ask at your hotel. Alternatively, ask Politur to recommend a boatperson and haggle with them directly.

Hostal San Fernando also runs a small dive center, and charges US$150 per person per day. Northern Coast Diving in Sosúa may also be willing to take you out this way. The corals here make excellent diving, but then there are equally good corals more easily accessible elsewhere. Fortune-hunting wreck divers work this coastline, but the many wooden galleons that sank here have long since rotted away, leaving very little for the recreational diver to see.

🛏 Sleeping

Chic Hotel HOTEL $

(☎809-579-2316; Benito Monción 44; r with fan/air-con RD$650/1100; P❄☒☞) The front desk person is dressed sharply and the entranceway is marked by Doric (or is it Corinthian?) columns; however, this hotel is a far cry from chic. Good news is the 50 or so rooms are kept clean and you can pop out for a bite to eat at its neighboring restaurant and ice-cream store with street-side seating. Many of the rooms are windowless and street noise can be a problem in front. Check out the mango tree the hotel was built around – you'll pass the trunk in the hallway.

Hotel Los Jardines BUNGALOWS $$

(☎809-853-0040; r with fan/air-con RD$1700/2000; P❄☒) The perfectly manicured grounds punctuated with a towering palm tree or two feel like something of a sanctuary – Monte Cristi feels far away. The five basic rooms are something of a letdown but each has a porch with chairs. To find Los Jardines, head north out of town toward El Moro and turn left onto the waterfront dirt road – if you've passed Restaurant Cocomar and Hotel Montechico you've gone too far; just past Cayo Arena.

Cayo Arena APARTMENTS **$$**
(📞809579-3145; www.cayoarena.com; ste RD$2500; 🅿✳@❄) Especially recommended for families or small groups, this is an excellent base if you're interested in exploring the area. It's a two-story modern building with a handful of two-bedroom suites with full kitchens, living rooms and balconies. A small pool and restaurant are on site. Follow driving instructions for Los Jardines; Cayo Arena is on the same dirt road along the water.

Hotel Montechico HOTEL **$**
(📞809-579-2565; r RD$1500; 🅿✳) There's something very Soviet-era about this institutional-looking building occupying prime oceanfront real estate. Even the cavernous, barely furnished lobby is evocative of a Politburo ministry. High-ceilinged concrete hallways lead to no-frills rooms with cold-water showers, yet all have balconies with uninterrupted ocean views. A non-functioning restaurant occasionally is the site for concerts. It's on the road north of town on the way to El Morro, about a 20-minute walk away.

Hostal San Fernando BUNGALOWS **$$**
(📞809-866-4511; www.ecomarinamontecristi.com; s/d RD1500/3000; 🅿✳@❄) Pleasant bungalows with high, sloped ceilings, white-washed walls, firm beds, clean bathrooms and tile floors. From here it's a short walk to both the beach and El Morro. There's a restaurant on site, but it's nothing special.

🍴 Eating & Drinking
A result of the fact that goats feed on oregano plants, the *chivo* here is renowned for its spiciness. Ask to try different varieties: *ripiado* (pulled goat), *horneado* (partly blackened, firm on the inside) and *picante* (traditional stew).

Comedor Adela DOMINICAN **$**
(Alvarez 41; set meals RD$170) This popular family-owned joint has a menu, but ignore it, and go for the day's special – rice and beans, salad and some very tasty *chivo* (goat).

Restaurant Cocomar DOMINICAN **$$**
(mains RD$250; ⊙9am-midnight) Look for this restaurant with oceanfront outdoor seating just before the green monstrosity of the Hotel Montechico.

El Bistrot Restaurant DOMINICAN **$$**
(Calle San Fernando 26; mains RD$300; ⊙noon-2:30pm & 6pm-midnight Mon-Fri, noon-midnight Sat & Sun) The Hotel Los Jardines owners have this restaurant serving fresh seafood and Dominican fare three blocks north of the park in the direction of El Morro.

Ocean DOMINICAN **$$**
(Calle Benito Monción 1; mains RD$300; ⊙9am-midnight) Four blocks south of Calle Duarte – look for the prominent red stairway and thatched roof – this open-sided restaurant and discotheque offers loads of choices, from chicken dishes to lobster.

Lilo Supermercado (Calle Alvarez), one block south of Duarte, is the place to stock up on drinks and other supplies.

Super Fria Nina (cnr Calle Duarte & Colón) and **Terraza Fedora** (Calle San Fernando), five blocks north of Duarte, are large beer gardens that are crowded most evenings, but especially on weekends. Also check out **New York New York** (opposite Parque 14 de Julio) to bump and grind the night away.

ℹ Information
Just about everything you'll need is on or within a block or two of Calle Duarte.

BanReservas (Calle Duarte) Next to the post office.

Hospital Padre Fantino (Av 27 de Febrero; ⊙24hr) Located two blocks north of Calle Duarte, this modest hospital has a 24-hour emergency room.

Politur (tourist police; 📞809-579-3980) Office on the main beach.

Post office (cnr Calle Duarte & Colón; ⊙8am-5pm Mon-Fri)

Super Farmacia Maria (📞809-579-2315; cnr Calles Duarte & Alvarez)

ℹ Getting There & Away
BUS Caribe Tours (📞809-579-2129; cnr Mella & Carmargo) has a depot a block north of Calle Duarte. Buses to Santo Domingo (RD$350, 4½ hours) leave at 7am, 9am, 1:45pm, 2:45pm and 4pm, with a stop in Santiago (RD$180, 2¼ hours).

CAR It's hard to get lost – Hwy 1 enters Monte Cristi from the east, where it turns into Calle Duarte and becomes the main east–west road through town. Av Mella becomes Hwy 45 to Dajabón. The latter is potholed and rough in parts. Avoid at night, as assaults on cars have occurred in the past.

GUA-GUA The terminal is on Calle Duarte near 27 de Febrero. *Gua-guas* can take you to Dajabón (RD$50, 40 minutes, every 20 minutes from 7:30am to 10pm); for Puerto Plata, take any Santiago-bound *gua-gua* and get off at the junction in Navarrete (RD$130, 1½ hours, every 20 minutes), where you can change for a

MOUNTAIN ROAD – DAJABÓN TO HWY 1

If you're making the trip out here you might as well drive in a loop so as not to retrace your steps. Take Hwy 1 from Santiago out to Monte Cristi, spend the night and head to Dajabón the following day, preferably a market day. On the return, head south on 18, which takes you through small villages, country towns and pastoral scenery. You pass through Sabaneta and Mao before meeting up again with Hwy 1 – from there you can head to the north coast or south.

Puerto Plata *gua-gua* (RD$140, one hour, every 20 minutes).

DAJABÓN
POP 16,500

Most foreigners here are on their way to or from Haiti. Every Monday and Friday is the **Haitian market** – when the border bridge opens, Haitians pour across to buy fruit and vegetables from the DR and sell just about everything else. Crowds push and shove wheelbarrows, motorcycles burrow through the throng, crates of eggs are piled high on women's heads and your hands are pressed hopelessly at your sides, trying to escape the crush of people advancing an inch a minute across the narrow bridge.

If you're planning an early-morning border crossing, the best place to spend the night is **Super Hotel Brisol** (☎809-579-8703; Calle Padre Santa Anna 18; s/d with fan RD$500/750, with air-con RD$700/1000; 🅐🛜🅟), only a few blocks from the border. Rooms in this modern four-story building are sparkling clean, have hot water and even bright colored paintings for decoration. A sliver of a restaurant serving substantial meals of

Dominican fare is attached. Or try the equally acceptable **Gran Hotel Raydan** (☎809-579-7366; F Valerio 32; r with fan/air-con RD$400/700; 🅐🅟): the plain rooms have balconies facing the street and there's a small patio and decent restaurant.

Lots of vendors sell grilled corn and hot dogs on the main park, and there are a few undistinguished eateries on the main road coming into town.

Several major banks with ATMs are located around a circle at the northern entrance to town.

❶ Getting There & Away

BUS Caribe Tours (☎809-579-8554; cnr Calles Carrasco & Henríquez) has a depot five blocks from the border. Buses to Santo Domingo (RD$350, five hours) with stops in Monte Cristi and Santiago (RD$190, 2½ hours) leave at 6:45am, 7:45am, 9:30am, 1pm, 2:15pm and 3:15pm. On market days the 9:30am bus leaves at 9:15am.

GUA-GUA Expreso Liniero (☎809-579-8949) goes to Monte Cristi (RD$50, 40 minutes) and Santiago (RD$190, 2½ hours). The terminal is just beyond the arch at the entrance to town on the east side of the road.

FROM BORDER There are taxis and *motoconchos* near the crossing point every day until the time the border closes. After that, taxis and *motoconchos* may still be found on the main road.

TO BORDER Reaching the border is simple; coming from Monte Cristi on Hwy 45, as most people do, you'll come to a huge arch (the formal entrance to town) and a short distance afterward the Parque Central on the east side of the street. Just past the park is Calle Presidente Henriquez; turn right (west) and the border is six blocks ahead. If you're arriving by Caribe Tours bus, the bus station is on Calle Presidente Henriquez. Just walk west from the bus station five blocks to get to the border. For information on crossing the border (open 9am to 5pm, except Monday and Friday market days 8am to 4pm), see p252.

Central Highlands

Best Places to Stay

» Rancho Baiguate (p182)

» Alto Cerro (p188)

» Gran Almirante (p172)

Best Places to Eat

» Camp David (p173)

» Il Pasticcio (p173)

» Hotel Gran Jimenoa (p183)

Why Go?

Even diehard beach fanatics will eventually overdose on sun and sand. When you do, the cool mountainous playground of the Central Highlands is the place to come; where else can you sit at dusk, huddled in a sweater, watching the mist descend into the valley as the sun sets behind the mountains? Popular retreats, roaring rivers, soaring peaks and the only white-water rafting in the Caribbean beckon. Below, on the plains in the Valle del Cibao, is where merengue spontaneously erupted onto the musical landscape, and where you'll find some of the best Carnival celebrations in the country. Economic life in the Central Highlands revolves around Santiago, the DR's second-largest city and the capital of a vast tobacco- and sugarcane-growing region.

When to Go

Some of the most raucous Carnival (Carnaval) celebrations in all the DR are held in Santiago and La Vega at the end of February and beginning of March. It tends to be dry from January to March and June to August in the area around Santiago in the center of this region. Rains can be torrential in May and again September to November. Meanwhile, the temperatures in the mountain towns like Jarabacoa and Constanza are cooler year-round and nighttime temperatures in the latter can even fall below freezing.

ⓘ Getting There & Around

Santiago's **Aeropuerto Internaciónal del Cibao** (☎809-233-8000; www.aeropuertocibao.com.do) is the third-largest airport in the country, and offers frequent international air service to major destinations. There's a good selection of car rental agencies at the airport too.

Santiago sits on the main trunk highway that runs north from Santo Domingo to Puerto Plata, and has plenty of efficient bus service to all points of the compass. There's regular, first-class bus service to all destinations listed in this chapter, except for Constanza – you'll need to hop on a *gua-gua* (local bus) to get up into the mountains. As always, renting

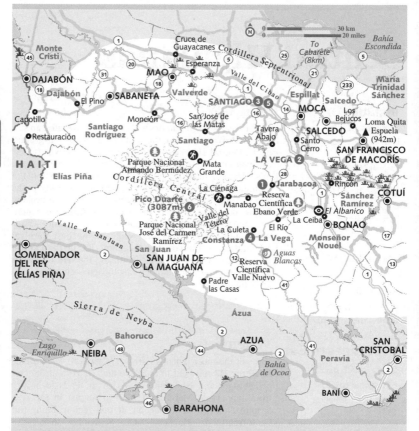

Central Highlights Highlights

❶ Go **white-water rafting** (p178) on the Caribbean's only raftable river, the turbulent Río Yaque del Norte near Jarabacoa

❷ Party hearty with the locals in little La Vega in February, when it throws the country's biggest **Carnival celebrations** (p177)

❸ Visit the **Centro León** (opposite) in Santiago, an exceptional museum with more than a century's worth of works by the very best Dominican artists

❹ Watch the sunset as the mist descends into the valley in high-altitude **Constanza** (p187)

❺ Dance merengue and party till the wee hours at one of the bars surrounding the Monument in **Santiago** (p174)

❻ Linger at the top of **Pico Duarte** (p184), taking in the views of the Atlantic and the Caribbean

a car, preferably an SUV, will give you more freedom to explore the countryside.

Santiago

POP 623,000

One of the oldest settlements in Spain's New World empire, Santiago is the country's second-largest city, spilling over its original border, the Río Yaque del Norte. This sprawling city churns out rum and cigars, feeding off the large-scale tobacco and sugarcane plantations that make up much of the topography of the surrounding valley floor. The Cordillera Central to the west and Cordillera Septentrional to the north hem in the city, which is bifurcated by Highway Duarte, the country's primary north-south thoroughfare.

Overlooked by most travelers, Santiago is a good place to familiarize yourself with the ordinary Dominican's way of life. Typical of poor barrios throughout the country, Santiago's are a maze of haphazardly constructed homes made with corrugated iron roofs. Meanwhile, just east of downtown is the neighborhood of Cerros de Gurabo – surely one of the wealthiest in the DR – where the roads are lined with enormous mansions concealed behind high walls. But all strata of society cheer for the hometown baseball team and come together around the Monument, the city's raucous nightlife center.

History

Santiago was founded in 1495 by Christopher Columbus' elder brother, Bartholomew. But the earthquake of 1562 caused so much damage to the city that it was rebuilt on its present site beside the Río Yaque del Norte. It was attacked and destroyed several times by invading French troops, as part of long-simmering tension between Spain and France over control of the island. Santiago also suffered terribly during the DR's civil war in 1912.

The years immediately following the civil war were some of the city's best. WWI caused worldwide shortages of raw tropical materials, so prices soared for products such as sugar, tobacco, cocoa and coffee – all of which were being grown around Santiago. From 1914 through the end of the war and into the 1920s, Santiago's economy boomed. Lovely homes and impressive stores, electric lighting and paved streets appeared throughout town. In May 1922, Highway Duarte opened, linking Santiago with Bonao, La Vega and Santo Domingo to the south.

◉ Sights & Activities

The center of town is Parque Duarte, a usually crowded, leafy park with a gazebo, the cathedral to its south and Palacio Consistorial to its west.

TOP CHOICE ⟩ **Centro León**   MUSEUM

(☎809-582-2315; www.centroleon.org.do; Av 27 de Febrero 146, Villa Progreso; adult/child RD$100/70, free Tue; ⊙10am-7pm Tue-Sun, closed Mon) This large, modern museum built by the tobacco wealth of the León Jimenez family is a world-class institution with an impressive collection of paintings that trace the evolution of Dominican art in the 20th century. There are three **exhibition rooms** in the main building: one focuses on the island's biodiversity, Taino history and cultural diversity; the upstairs room displays a permanent collection of Dominican art and photography; and the third houses temporary art exhibits (see p233 for more information on Dominican painting).

There's a working **cigar factory** on site, where you can watch a dozen cigar rollers making Aurora Preferidos, its premium brand. The adjoining cigar shop sells the complete range of smokes, including the Preferidos (a box of 25 costs US$375). English is spoken and staff on hand can answer any cigar-related questions.

Guided tours of the property are available in Spanish (RD$200 per person), English, French and German (RD$250 per person) and last about 1½ hours. Reservations for tours are required three days in advance.

An excellent **gift shop** sells books on Dominican history, art, culture and food, and there's an equally appealing modern **cafeteria** serving up sandwiches and drinks. During the evenings, the center offers an ever-changing schedule of art appreciation classes, arthouse cinema and, sometimes, live musical events.

The Centro León is a few kilometers east of downtown. A taxi there will cost around RD$100, or pick up a Ruta A *concho* (private car that follows a set route; RD$12) along Calle del Sol – not all Ruta A *conchos* go as far as the Centro León, though, so be sure to ask.

Museo Folklórico don Tomás Morel MUSEUM
(☎809-582-6787; Av Restauración 174; admission free; ⊙9am-noon & 3:30-7pm Mon-Fri) Re-

nowned poet and cultural critic Tomás Morel founded this eclectic, eccentric folk art museum in 1962, and helped operate it until his death in 1992. Considered by many to be the father of Santiago's modern Carnival, Morel was a tireless promoter and chronicler of the yearly celebration. He was especially fond of the distinctive *caretas* (masks), and the museum displays the best of these for visitors to enjoy. There's always someone around to give a quick tour of the rooms (Spanish only), which are chaotically arranged with barely an inch of free space. With at least a week's notice you can organize **mask-making classes** (US$150 per group) at Carnival time, and **dance classes** (US$50 per group for two hours) the rest of the year. The brightly colored clapboard building is hard to miss.

Monumento a los Héroes de la Restauración de la República   MONUMENT

(Av Monumental; admission free; ☉9am-6pm Tue-Sun) On a hill at the east end of the downtown area is Santiago's most visible and recognizable sight, the Monument to the Heroes of the Restoration of the Republic. This eight-story boxy behemoth was originally built by Trujillo to celebrate Trujillo, but was rededicated after his assassination to honor the Dominican soldiers that fought the final war of independence against Spain. The site boasts life-sized museum exhibits of Dominican history, and is often visited by large groups of uniformed primary-schoolers (the spire is closed due to safety concerns). Large bronze statues of the celebrated generals gaze down upon Santiago from the steps.

Estadio Cibao   BASEBALL STADIUM

(☎809-575-1810; Av Imbert) Santiago's Águilas (www.aguilas.com.do) baseball team is one of six in the country, and watching local fans root for the home side is almost as fun as the games themselves, played at this stadium northwest of the city center; they're held two to three times a week in winter, and tickets start at RD$150. It's wise to book in advance – stadium capacity is a mere 18,000 people, and the Águilas are the most successful team in the league's history. To get there, take a taxi or hop on any Ruta A *concho* westbound on Calle del Sol.

Casa del Arte   ART GALLERY

(☎809-471-7839; Benito Monción 46; admission free; ☉9am-7pm Mon-Sat) This small gallery displays Dominican painting, photography and sculpture. Some nights of the week a film club meets to screen arthouse and

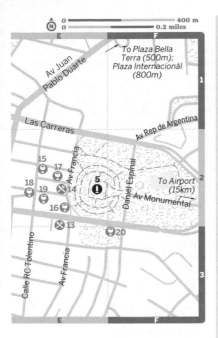

good-quality Hollywood flicks (free admission). There's sometimes live music (from RD$100) and, on Saturdays, live theater (RD$100). Pass by for a copy of the gallery's latest monthly event calendar.

Galería la 37 por las Tablas   ART GALLERY
(☎809-587-3033; 37porlastablas.blogspot.com; Benito Monción 37; admission varies; ⊙9am-7pm Mon-Sat) Across the street from the Casa del Arte, La 37 also hosts local art shows in its foyer, and has an outdoor stage for live music, dance and theater performances, both amateur and professional.

Fortaleza San Luis   MUSEUM
(cnr Calle Boy Scouts & San Luis; ⊙9am-5pm) Built in the late 17th century, the Fortaleza San Luis operated as a military stronghold until the 1970s, when it was converted into a prison. Today it houses a small museum, with a strong emphasis on Dominican military history, including ancient rusty weapons, a collection of 20th-century tanks and artillery. There's a small collection of Taíno pottery, some paintings, and outdoors, in the middle of the fort, there are a few pleasant shady benches where you can sit and ponder the many busts of bygone Dominican generals.

Catedral de Santiago Apóstol   CHURCH
(cnr Calles 16 de Agosto & Benito Monción; ⊙7-9am Mon-Sat, to 8pm Sun) Santiago's cathedral, opposite the south side of Parque Duarte, was built between 1868 and 1895 and is a combination of Gothic and neoclassical styles (undergoing restoration at time of research). The cathedral contains the marble tomb of the late-19th-century dictator Ulises Heureaux, an elaborately carved mahogany altar and impressive stained-glass windows by contemporary Dominican artist Dincón Mora.

Held in February, Carnival is big all over the country, but especially so in Santiago. The city is famous for its artistic and fantastical *caretas* (masks) and hosts an annual international *careta* competition in the lead-up to the big event.

The Carnival parade here is made up of rival neighborhoods: La Joya and Los Pepines. Onlookers watch from overpasses, apartment buildings, even the tops of lampposts. Costumes focus on two images: the *lechón* (piglet), which represents the devil, and the *pepín*, a fantastical animal that appears to be a cross between a cow and a duck. The most obvious difference between the two is that *lechón* masks have two smooth horns and those of the *pepínes* have horns with dozens of tiny papier-mâché spikes. Participants swing *vejigas* (inflated cow bladders) and hit each other – and onlookers – on the behind.

If you decide to come to Santiago for Carnival, be sure to make reservations – rooms fill up fast this time of the year.

Palacio Consistorial　MUSEUM
(Parque Duarte; admission free; ⊘9am-noon and 2-5pm Mon-Sat) On the west side of Parque Duarte you'll find the former town hall and a small museum devoted to the city's colorful history. If you're here during Carnival, don't miss the huge and stunning display of masks and *fichas* (posters), part of a yearly competition that draws entries from the top artists and maskmakers in Santiago and from across the country.

☞ Tours

Camping Tours (☏809-583-3121; www.camping tours.net; Calle Two 2, Villa Olga) offers the cheapest trek to Pico Duarte. Expect Spanish-speaking guides and groups of 20 to 25 people. Prices per person are US$220 on foot, US$255 with a shared mule and US$290 for your own mule (mules are recommended).

🛏 Sleeping

Gran Almirante　HOTEL $$$
(☏809-580-1992; www.hodelpa.com; Av Estrella Sadhalá; r/ste　US$205/285;　P✹@🛜🏊) Referencing Columbus, the Grand Admiral, signals this plush hotel's ambitions. The obvious choice for business travelers on an expense account, Gran Almirante's sundeck, spa and gym also entices tourists looking for extra comfort. The rooms are top-notch, there's a variety of restaurants and bars and an on-site casino. It's several kilometers from downtown but the surrounding neighborhood has a handful of good restaurants within walking distance.

Hotel Platino　HOTEL $$
(☏809-724-7576; www.hotelplatinord.com.do; Av Estrella Sadhalá; s US$33-73, d US$61-106, ste US$97-124; P✹🛜) Set at the back of the Plaza Platinum shopping center, a short drive from town, this is an excellent-value midrange option. A large gazebo marks the entrance and another one is out the back on a groomed lawn. While rooms with a good dose of natural light are scarce, the beds are comfortable and most rooms have a small desk and even a mini-bar with a sink; ones on the executive floor have plasma TVs and attractive wood floors. Avoid the claustrophobic basement standard rooms.

Hodelpa Centro Plaza　HOTEL $$
(☏809-581-7000; www.hodelpa.com; cnr Mella 54 & Del Sol; r incl breakfast US$100; P✹🛜) The fact that this business-class hotel, part of the Hodelpa chain, is located only a block from the primary commercial artery in the heart of the city means that lower floors suffer from street noise. Expect courteous, professional service but fairly plain rooms, some dimly lit. There's a restaurant, tapas bar, lounge and small casino attached.

Camp David　HOTEL $$
(☏809-276-6400;　www.campdavidranch.com; Carretera Luperón Km 71/2; s/d US$40/45; P✹🛜) On a mountain ridge about 30 minutes outside Santiago, at 923m Camp David offers sweeping vistas out over the city and the valley below. It was founded by an admirer of Trujillo – the lobby holds three of the former dictator's vintage cars – and while the rooms in general are drab, some are large enough for their own car or two. As it's set several kilometers off the main

road, you'll need a car to get here (or helicopter – it has its own heliport), or take a taxi (RD$400).

Hotel Aloha Sol   HOTEL $$
(☏809-583-0090; www.alohasol.com; Calle del Sol 50; s/d incl breakfast from RD$1900/2700, ste RD$3700; P❄@🖙) This centrally located hotel is a good deal if you don't mind the mildly stale quality of the furnishings, both in the rooms and the common areas. Be sure to ask for a room with window exposure and check out several before committing – the lighting situation varies. Breakfast buffet is better than average.

Hotel Colonial   BUDGET HOTEL $
(☏809-247-3122; colonialdeluxe@yahoo.com; Salvador Cucurullo 113-115; s/d RD$500/790; ❄) If price is an object, the Colonial is an acceptable hotel in the center. But staying beyond a night or two can't be recommended. Hallways reminiscent of a military barracks lead to no-frills rooms, some lit by single light bulbs; all have small TVs with cable and some have fridges. The rooms in the hotel's ambitiously named **Colonial Deluxe** building next door are basically of a similar quality.

✖ Eating

Quality eating options in the downtown area are few and far between. There's a handful of Dominican fast-food joints on and around Calle del Sol and hole-in-the-wall *comedors* in the surrounding blocks. Virtually all the bars and lounges around the Monument serve good food as well.

TOP CHOICE Camp David   DOMINICAN $$
(☏809-276-6400; www.campdavidranch.com; Carretera Luperón Km 71/2; mains RD$400; ⊙breakfast, lunch & dinner) Sitting outside on the restaurant balcony, piano music on the stereo, and the city spread out at your feet... This is easily the most romantic spot around, though you'll need a car to make it up the mountain where it's perched outside of town. Service is worthy of a resort called Camp David; beef is the specialty here – go for the *filete generalissimo*, 8oz of Angus beef (RD$550). Good wine list.

Il Pasticcio   ITALIAN $$
(☏809-582-6061; Calle 3 & Av Del Llano, Cerros de Gurabo; mains RD$350; ⊙noon-3.30pm &

7-11pm Tue-Fri, noon-11pm Sat & Sun) Long on character and style, Paolo the Italian owner has been welcoming Santiago's powerful and bohemian since 1995. Curiously decorated with a range of objets d'art, the restaurant is a reflection of his personality, and the menu of fresh pasta, meat and seafood is truly satisfying; we enjoyed the salmon carpaccio.

Montezuma   MEXICAN $$
(cnr Av Francia & Beller; mains RD$350; ⊙11am-2am) Facing the Monument, this popular restaurant specializes in Mexican dishes, from tacos and burritos to filet of grouper grilled with chili and garlic. Prices are a bit high for the main dishes, but the smaller orders are reasonable and the restaurant itself – spread over three levels with patio seating, long bar tables and rusted steel stools – is worth a look. There's live mariachi music every Friday starting at 10pm.

Bioö Light   DOMINICAN $$
(Calle Cuba 92; mains RD$220; ⊙breakfast, lunch & dinner; 🖙) Something of a surprise, Bioö Light qualifies as hip in this somewhat run-down part of the city. As the name suggests, there are a few healthy choices on the menu (salads RD$215), but they're hardly the norm. Burgers (RD$300) and brownie a la mode (RD$150) are just as representative. Happy hour is from 5-8pm and there are a few wicker chairs and some window-side stools if you just want a coffee and wi-fi.

El Rinconsito D'Dona Carmen   DOMINICAN $
(Sabana Larga; mains RD$65; ⊙breakfast, lunch & dinner) The façade of this no doubt formerly elegant colonial-era home, all wrought-iron filigree and clapboards, suggests something quite different to what you find inside – a cramped dining room serving simple *plato del dias* from heated buffet trays. However, an espresso (RD$5) taken at the wooden bar that runs along the outside of the front porch is highly recommended.

Marisco Centro   SEAFOOD $$
(cnr Calle del Sol & Av Francia; mains RD$350; ⊙9am-midnight, to 2am Fri & Sat; 🖙) Amid all the nearby Monument action, this classy restaurant serves grilled fish and seafood in an elegant indoor dining room or breezy outdoor garden.

Francepan (Av 27 de Febrero; ☺breakfast, lunch & dinner) and La Campagna (Av Juan Pablo Duarte; ☺breakfast, lunch & dinner) are similar restaurants in the Los Jardínes neighborhood east of downtown. Both are relatively upscale cafes with attractive outdoor patio seating areas and large menus, with everything from healthy smoothies (RD$110) and salads (RD$200) to burgers (RD$180) and heavy soups (RD$300).

🍷 Drinking & Entertainment

Clustered around the Monument are a dozen or so bars, restaurants and late-night eateries (and one pool hall), making this Santiago's best place for general revelry. Most also serve more than passable food. Vendors sell beer from coolers and locals blast music from their car stereos till dawn. While not especially dangerous, the center can be dodgy in the wee hours so it's best to take a taxi home. Monday to Wednesday nights are generally subdued. Hotel Almirante and Hotel Matum (Av Las Carreras 1) have dance clubs of their own.

TOP CHOICE Ahi-Bar   BAR
(cnr Calle RC Tolentino & Av Restauración; ☺4pm-late) This is the biggest of a string of similarly chic bars on Calle RC Tolentino, with a large patio set above street level featuring high bar tables and stools. Most people come to drink, but in case you miss dinner the food here is actually pretty good. There's live outdoor jazz on Mondays and a sister dance club across the street on Av Restauración.

Wind Restaurant & Bar   LOUNGE
(cnr Calle del Sol & Daniel Espinal; ☺4pm-late; 📶) A cross between a VIP airport lounge, sports bar and downtown NYC nightclub, this sleek and chic establishment stretches along the southern side of the Monument. More than ten large-screen plasma TVs cover the back wall, while the three other sides are open to the street. Good mixed cocktails and a stylish vibe.

Tipico Monte Bar   DANCE CLUB
(📞809-575-0300; Av 27 de Febrero 18; www.tipicomontebar.com; admission varies; ☺5pm-late, closed Tue) For a taste of real merengue music and dancing, head to the Monte Bar, which draws a diverse mix including locals, dom-yors (Dominicans who live in New York City) and even a celebrity baseball player or

two. There's frequent live music, and you'll spot some of the best dancers in town. It even broadcasts its musical events live on its website. The club is set amid a series of auto-repair shops in the Las Colinas neighborhood, north of the city, so you'll want a cab there and back (RD$100 one way).

El Carrito de Marchena   RESTAURANT, BAR
(Av Estrella Sadhalá; ☺24 hours; 📶) This open-air pavilion, only 25m before the Hotel Platino and a few kilometers from the Monument, is where groups of friends roll up after a night of dancing and boozing. A few large-screen TVs tuned to sports and an extensive menu, which includes tacos (RD$100), burritos (RD$180) and mofongo (RD$240), mean the party doesn't have to stop until sleep calls.

Las 3 Café   BAR
(Calle RC Tolentino 38; ☺5pm-late) If a quiet drink with friends is what you're after, this is the place to go. The music is kept to a dull roar, although there's still enough space to dance merengue or bachata and if you get peckish, the kitchen can set you up with picaderas – literally 'munchies' – a sampling of meats, cheeses and olives, perfect for sharing.

Oscar Billiard Club   POOL HALL
(Beller btwn Calle RC Tolentino & Av Francia; tables per hr RD$70; ☺2pm-4am) This club has 18 pool tables scattered through a large room with a bar fronting onto the street. The music is earplug-worthy loud.

Also recommended – all open late and on Av Francia on the western side of the Monument – are Barajanda Bar and La Brasa, two informal spots next to one another, and Kukara Macora Country Bar & Restaurant, a sprawling and kitschy western themed place, and fun for a meal or drink.

🛍 Shopping

Calle del Sol, the primary commercial artery in the downtown area is lined with mostly unremarkable clothing shops, banks, hair salons and small department stores. There is, however, a two-story indoor market (btwn Calle España & Av 30 de Marzo) worth visiting if you're looking for souvenirs like cigars, mamajuana and rum. Directly behind this building, on several small side streets, is a covered outdoor market, with stall after stall of secondhand clothes, shoes and other items.

Santiago has several shopping malls, including the upscale **Plaza Bella Terra** (Av Duarte; 🕑8am-11pm) and the older **Plaza Internacional** (Av Duarte; 🕑8am-11pm), near one another east of the Monument, and **Las Colinas Mall** (Av 27 de Febrero; 🕑8am-11pm) anchored by the aptly named Supermercado Jumbo. All three have **food courts** and **movie theaters** (🕑7pm-late Mon-Fri, 4pm-late Sat & Sun) showing mostly contemporary Hollywood fare for around RD$100.

🛈 Information

BanReservas (Calle del Sol 66)

Centro de Internet Yudith (Calle 16 de Agosto near Mella; per hr RD$35; 🕑8:30am-8:30pm Mon-Fri, to 5pm Sat)

Clínica Unión Médica (📞809-226-8686; Av Juan Pablo Duarte 176; 🕑24hr)

Farmacia Jorge (📞809-582-2887; cnr Calle España & Av Gómez)

Hospital Metropolitano de Santiago (📞809-947-2222; www.homshospital.com; Autopista Duarte Km 2.8; 🕑24hr) Large and modern hospital.

Nin@Net (Calle Cuba; per hr RD$35; 🕑8am-8pm Mon-Sat; 📞) Doubles as a call center.

Post office (cnr Calle del Sol & San Luis) Three blocks east of Parque Duarte.

Scotiabank (cnr Calle del Sol & 30 de Marzo)

🛈 Getting There & Away

AIR Santiago's **Aeropuerto Internacionál del Cibao** (📞809-233-8000; www.aeropuertocibao .com.do), around 12km south of downtown, is serviced by the following airlines:

Air Turks and Caicos (📞809-233-8262; www .airturksandcaicos.com)

American (📞809-200-5151; www.aa.com) JFK and Miami.

American Eagle (📞809-583-0055; www.aa .com) San Juan, Puerto Rico and Puerto Prince, Haiti.

Copa Airlines (📞809-200-2772; www.copaair .com) Panama City, Panama.

Delta (📞809-200-9191; www.delta.com) JFK.

Jet Blue (📞809-200-9898; www.jetblue.com) JFK.

Spirit Airlines (📞809-587-9326; www.spirit .com) Extremely early morning flight to Fort Lauderdale, Florida.

Taxis are your only option to the airport (US$20 one way).

BUS Caribe Tours (📞809-241-1414) has two terminals in Santiago (all buses, except the one for Haiti – from Las Colinas station only – stop at both stations): in Las Colinas on Av 27 de Febrero about 3km north of the center, and more conveniently in the Los Jardínes neighborhood at Maimon and 27 de Febrero, just steps from the competing **Metro Buses** terminal (📞809-587-3837; cnr Av Duarte & Maimón). All three terminals are on or near the Ruta A *concho* line, or take a taxi. Some of the destinations:

DESTINA-TION	FARE	DURA-TION	FRE-QUENCY
Cap-Haïtien, Haiti	RD$900	4hr	noon daily
Dajabón	RD$190	2½hr	take Monte Cristi bus
La Vega	RD$70	45min	take Santo Domingo bus
Monte Cristi	RD$180	1¾hr	6 times daily, 8:45am-6:15pm
Puerto Plata	RD$110	1¼hr	hourly, 8:15am-9:15pm
Santo Domingo	RD$280	2½hr	26 times daily, 6am-8:15pm
Sosúa	RD$150	2hr	take Puerto Plata bus

CAR The airport has a good selection of reliable international car rental companies, all open from 7am to 11pm.

Alamo/National (📞809-233-8163)

Avis (📞809-233-8154)

Europcar (📞809-233-8150)

Hertz (📞809-233-8555)

🛈 Getting Around

CONCHO These are private cars that follow set routes around town and charge RD$12 (up to six passengers per vehicle). *Concho* drivers pay a weekly fee for a permit to slap a letter on their windshield and drive the route. After dark, however, the unlicensed *piratas* take over, and you should exercise caution before hopping into some random person's car.

TAXI Regular radio taxis ply the streets looking for passengers – the in-town fare when we were there was around RD$100.

STRAIGHT TO THE STOAGIE SOURCE

Many of the world's top cigar brands are made in and around Santiago – Aurora, Monte-cristo, Arturo Fuente, to name a few. Many of those name brands contract the work to local, Dominican cigar-makers, who then offer the 'label-less' cigar to locals and travelers at half the price. It's critical when buying cigars to test whether they've been made well and stored properly. Pick up the cigar: it should have a springy tightness, indicating solid construction. If it's too soft or too hard it won't draw well. It shouldn't crackle under your fingers either; that means it's too dry, and will smoke like kindling.

Besides the museum-quality workshop on the grounds of Centro León, other producers offer free tours of their factories. Reservations are preferred; most open Tuesday through Friday. The village of Tamboril is northeast of Santiago at the foot of the Cordillera Septentrional.

» **E León Jimenes Tabacalera** (☑809-563-1111; Av 27 de Febrero, Villa Progresso)

» **Fabrica Anilo de Oro** (☑809-580-5808; in Tamboril)

» **Tabacalera Jacagua** (☑809-580-6600, in Tamboril)

» **Pinar del Rio Tabacalera** (in Villa Gonzales)

La Vega

POP 220,000

Pressed hard up against the highway halfway between Santo Domingo and Santiago, La Vega is known primarily as a transportation hub and the site of the country's most boisterous Carnival celebrations. And while in most respects it's a lackluster town – dusty and noisy during the day – La Vega's origin story is an interesting one. In the 1490s, Christopher Columbus himself ordered a fort built in the area to store gold mined nearby. Over the next 50 years, the first mint in the New World was established, the nation's first commercial sugar crop was harvested, and the first royally sanctioned brothel in the western hemisphere opened its doors for business in La Vega. But this prosperity came to an abrupt end in 1562, when an earthquake leveled the city. The damage was so severe that the city was moved several kilometers to its present site on the banks of the Río Camú. You can visit what remains of the old city near the town of Santo Cerro.

◉ Sights & Activities

Make your way to La Vega during Carnival if at all possible. Otherwise, a few worthwhile sights lie outside the city, only really easily accessible in a private vehicle.

Santo Cerro   CHURCH
Legend has it that Columbus placed a cross he received as a bon-voyage gift from Queen Isabella atop this hill, which commands fantastic sweeping views of the Valle del Cibao. During a battle between Spaniards and Taínos, the latter tried to burn the cross but it wouldn't catch fire. The Virgen de las Mercedes appeared on one of its arms and the Taínos are said to have fled in terror.

Today the cross is gone – supposedly in private hands, although it's unclear as to whose – but you can still see the Santo Hoyo (Holy Hole) in which the cross was allegedly planted. The hole is inside the **Iglesia Las Mercedes** (◷7am-noon & 2-6pm), covered with a small wire grill and tended by nuns and Jesuit priests. The beige-and-white church, with its red-tile roof, is a major pilgrimage site, drawing thousands of believers every September 24 for its patron-saint day. Be sure to look for a fenced-off tree near the steps leading to the church – it is said to have been planted in 1495.

Santo Cerro is northeast of La Vega, several kilometers east of Highway Duarte, up a steep winding road. It's somewhat confusing to find your way leaving the city, so ask for directions.

La Vega Vieja   HISTORICAL SITE
(admission RD$100; ◷8am-5pm) What's left of the original site of the city are the ruins of the fort Columbus ordered built and a church. After the great earthquake of 1562, most of what remained of the structures was taken to the latter-day La Vega, where it was used in construction. With some imagination and the help of a guide (Spanish speaking only), it's possible to begin to grasp the historical implications of what you're seeing.

A small museum in the back of the site contains both Taíno and Spanish tools, weapons and ceramics. The cost of admission and guide seems open to negotiation and depends on the number in your party.

To get here, continue around 4km past the turn-off for Santo Cerro and look for an old and battered sign on the left-hand side of the road.

Catedral de la Concepción   CHURCH
(cnr Av Guzman & Adolfo; ⊙varies) La Vega's infamous cathedral is a fascinating eyesore that looks more like a cross between a medieval fortress and a coal plant than a place of worship. It is an odd mixture of Gothic and neoindustrial styles, constructed of concrete and decorated with sculpted metal bars and pipes alongside random ornamental windows. The large interior looks more contemporary and is easier on the eyes. The cathedral faces the main park, where families and young people gather in the evenings and weekends, and is impossible to miss.

🛏 Sleeping & Eating

Unless you're in La Vega for Carnival, there is no real reason to stay overnight. There's one good, regular hotel and lots of little love motels whose principal business is *de paso* – a few hours' rental – but which may rent you a room for the night. The main street is Av Antonio Guzman, which runs north-south and intersects Highway Duarte on the north side of town.

Hotel Rey   HOTEL **$$**
(☑809-573-9797; Calle Restauración 3; r from RD$1500; P🕸🛜) The most respectable choice in the city, Hotel Rey is close to the highway and a half dozen or so blocks from the cathedral. It caters to business travelers, so expect clean rooms and friendly and attentive service. Standard rooms are unfortunately dark and sparsely decorated; the deluxe rooms, with king-sized beds, flat-screen plasma TVs and better lighting, are definitely worth the extra RD$500. There's an on-site **restaurant** (mains RD$200) that serves uninspiring if decent Dominican fare – a good thing if you pull in after dark and don't want to wander the streets looking for a meal.

Rarus   DOMINICAN **$**
(mains RD$250) Worth the drive, especially for live-music Sunday nights, Rarus is further along the same road that brings you to Santo Cerro and even higher above the valley floor. This open-air thatched-roof perch takes advantage of the fantastic views, with a long wooden bar that runs along its outer edge – food can be ordered up as well. Signs pointing the way to Rarus begin to appear near Santo Cerro.

Food stands serving fried chicken and *pastelitos* (flaky fried dough stuffed with meat, cheese or veggies) can be found in front of the cathedral. Otherwise, there are several large open-air *comedors* and Dominican fast-food restaurants scattered along the highway near the city.

ℹ Information

BanReservas (Adolfo 24) A half-block from the cathedral.

Red Cross (☑809-277-8181; ⊙24hr) Your best bet in a medical emergency.

ℹ Getting There & Away

La Vega is a regular stop on the well-traveled Santo Domingo–Santiago route. **Caribe Tours** (☑809-573-2488; Av Rivera) has its terminal on the main highway, 1.5km from the center of La Vega.

CENTRAL HIGHLANDS LA VEGA

DON'T MISS

LET THERE BE LENT

La Vega hosts the largest and most organized Carnival celebrations in the country. Townspeople belong to one of numerous Carnival groups, which range from 10 to 200 members and have unique names and costumes. The costumes (which can cost up to US$1000) are the best part of Carnival here – colorful baggy outfits (supposed to be princes but they look more like clowns), capes and fantastic diabolical masks with bulging eyes and gruesome pointed teeth.

Groups march on a long loop through town, and spectators either watch from bleachers set up alongside or march with them. The latter do so at their own risk – the costumes also include a small whip with an inflated rubber bladder at the end, used to whack passersby on the backside.

BEST HIKES

Central Highlands has some great walking trails, both longer treks and day hikes.

» **Pico Duarte** (p184) This is the most popular multiday trek in the country. It can be walked in as little as two days or as many as five days, including some spectacular side trips.

» **Loma Quita Espuela** (see boxed text, p190) Rising out of the flat plains near San Francisco de Macorís, Loma Quita Espuela is surrounded by organic cocoa plantations and swimming holes. There's even a rustic cabin owned by a local farmer where you can stay the night.

» **El Mogote** (p181) This small mountain outside Jarabacoa makes for a challenging and strenuous day climb. Hoof it past a Salesian monastery up to the top of the hill for great views of the surrounding mountain range.

DESTINA-TION	FARE	DURA-TION	FREQUENCY
Jarabacoa	RD$70	1hr	buses from Santo Domingo pass by at 7 & 10am, 1:30 & 4:30pm
Puerto Plata	RD$150	2hr	take the Sosúa bus
Santiago	RD$70	40min	take the Sosúa bus
Santo Domingo	RD$210	1½hr	every 30-60 min, 6:30am-7:45pm
Sosúa	RD$200	2½hr	hourly, 7:30am-8:30pm

Another option for the trip to Santiago is to catch one of the *gua-guas* (RD$65, 50 minutes) that leave from a terminal on the main road into town, about five blocks from Parque Central. Alternatively, *gua-guas* and pickups for Jarabacoa (RD$65) leave whenever they're full from a stop called Quinto Patio (about a kilometer from the center, RD$70 in a taxi) from 7am to 6pm.

FOR CONSTANZA: There are two direct buses (RD$200, two to three hours) leaving from the *mercado público* (public market) at around 8am and 2pm, though the actual departure times can vary widely. Otherwise, you can catch a Bonao-bound *gua-gua* on Av Gregorio Riva south to El Albanico (RD$84, 45 minutes), and hail a passing *gua-gua* there (RD$100, 1½ hours).

Jarabacoa

POP 57,000/ELEV 488M

Nestled in the low foothills of the Cordillera Central, Jarabacoa maintains an under-the-radar allure as the antithesis to the clichéd Caribbean vacation. Nighttime temperatures call for light sweaters, a roiling river winds past forested slopes that climb into the clouds, and local adventurers share their exploits over a beer in the handful of bars or nightclubs near the town's Parque Central. The fact that thousands of well-to-do Dominicans from Santo Domingo and Santiago have built summer homes here is a testament to Jarabacoa's laid-back charm as the 'City of Eternal Spring'. With a number of good hotels outside town, this is the place to base yourself if you want to raft, hike, bike, horseback ride, go canyoning or simply explore rural life.

🏃 Activities
White-Water Rafting

Promising and delivering thrills, chills and, for the unlucky, spills, a rafting trip down the Río Yaque del Norte is an exhilarating ride. A typical rafting excursion begins with breakfast, followed by a truck ride upriver to the put-in. You'll be given a life vest, a helmet and a wetsuit, plus instructions on paddling and safety. Then everyone clambers into the rafts and sets off downriver. You're usually only asked to paddle part of the time; in the rapids to keep the boat on its proper line, and occasionally in the flat water areas to stay on pace. You'll stop for a small snack about two-thirds of the way downriver, and then return to Jarabacoa for lunch.

The rapids are rated 2 and 3 (including sections nicknamed 'Mike Tyson' and 'the Cemetery') and part of the fun is the real risk of your raft turning over and dumping you into a rock-infested, surging river. A cameraman leapfrogs ahead of the group along the riverbank to film you going over each rapid, so you can watch (and purchase, as a cherished keepsake) the instant replay afterwards over a beer.

The Río Yaque del Norte has level 4, 5 and 6 rapids much further up in the mountains. No official tours go that far, but some intrepid guides raft it for fun on their own time. Ask around at **Rancho Baiguate** (p182) – if you don't mind paying a premium you might be able to organize something.

A lot of people come from the north coast to raft and then head straight back. This involves at least four hours each way on a bus. Consider spending a couple of nights in Jarabacoa – you'll enjoy your trip much more if you do.

Canyoning

For those whose adrenaline fix isn't satiated by white-water rafting, a few hours rappelling, jumping, sliding, zip-lining and swimming down a mountain river will have you feeling like a Navy Seal or Hollywood stunt person. Rancho Baiguate's standard canyoning trip (US$50, all gear provided) ends with a rappel down Salto Baiguate.

Waterfalls

The falls are easy to visit if you've got your own transportation. If not, a *motoconcho* tour to all three will set you back around RD$700, and a taxi US$60 to US$80.

SALTO DE JIMENOA UNO

So picturesque are these waterfalls near Jarabacoa that an opening scene of the movie *Jurassic Park* was filmed here. It's definitely the prettiest – a 60m waterfall pouring from a gaping hole in an otherwise solid

---

LOCAL KNOWLEDGE

MAXIMO MARTINEZ: MOUNTAIN BIKER

Maximo Martinez has been exploring mountain bike trails all over the DR for the last twenty years. Based in Cabarete, Martinez created the **Mountain & Beach Bike Course**, an advanced and technical 45km bike ride from Jamao (near Moca), alongside the Jamao river ending at the isolated Magante Beach near Rio San Juan, near the north coast.

According to Martinez, the Central Highlands are the outdoor sports gem of the country and the Cordillera Septentrional running along the north coast has the most trails of high difficulty.

Some tips:

» Santo Domingo and the surrounding area are open to riders of all levels of experience.

» A not-to-miss ride for those interested in easy-going terrain is through the sugarcane fields around La Romana in the southeast.

» The best times are when you're deep in the mountains and local villagers allow you access to their trails.

» My new gem is the 'Cibao Valley Loop' which begins in Cabarete, taking the road to Sabaneta de Yásica, 40km through the mountains down to Moca, heading to the west of Santiago, then north to Puerto Plata and back to Cabarete. It's just a wonderful six to seven hours' biking experience.

» The Septentrional range possesses the most technical rides, especially around Cabarete. The descents are down rocky, shady trails, best during summertime. These are perfect teaching trails.

Favorite Ride

From Jánico to Jarabacoa to La Vega. It's 77km, very advanced, very hilly, very fast with technical downhills. It's like an exam for riders. If you make it then you're ready for any hardcore ride.

Other Recommended Rides

Jarabacoa to Constanza to San José de Ocoa to Santo Domingo, aka Tour del Sufrimiento (The Suffering Tour), has been held the last weekend in January since 1997. It's one of the most demanding rides in the entire country.

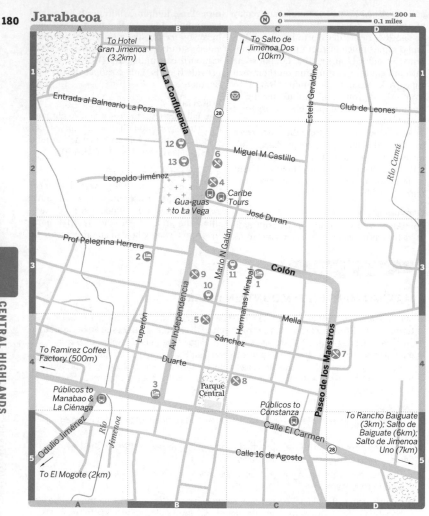

rock cliff. There's a sandy beach and nice swimming hole, but the water is icy cold and potentially dangerous; if you do swim, stay far away from the swirling currents. The trailhead to the waterfall is 7km from the Shell station in Jarabacoa along the road to Constanza. Look for a small shed by the side of the road housing the 'office' for this community project – admission (RD$100) comes with a bottle of water. The steep path down can be slippery after rain and sweat-inducing all other times (expect each way to take between 15 minutes and half an hour).

SALTO DE BAIGUATE

In a lush canyon, Baiguate is not as visually impressive as the others, but it's the most accessible for swimming. To get there, take Calle El Carmen east out of Jarabacoa for 3km until you see a sign for the waterfalls on the right-hand side of the road. From there, a badly rutted dirt road, which at one point is crossed by a shallow creek, leads 3km to a parking lot. A lovely 300m trail cut out of the canyon wall leads from the parking lot to the salto – canyoning trips end here with a rappel down the falls.

Jarabacoa

SALTO DE JIMENOA DOS

Generally just referred to as Salto Jimenoa (admission RD$50), come here for the views only since access to bathing pools at the foot of this 40m cascade is fenced off. The turn-off to the falls is 4km northwest of Jarabacoa on the road to Highway Duarte. Coming from town, you'll reach a major fork in the road with a large bank of signs; the falls are to the right. From there, a paved road leads 6km past the golf course to a parking lot. The waterfall is a 500m walk from there, over a series of narrow suspension bridges and trails flanked by densely forested canyon walls.

Hiking

In addition to the trek to Pico Duarte, there are a number of shorter half-day and full-day walks you can take in the area.

You can get a taste of the ecology of **Parque Nacional Armando Bermúdez** (see p184) with a one-day hike. Rancho Baiguate can arrange the trip, which involves a four-hour walk up and another four hours back down for US$100 per person (minimum two) or you can make your way to the park yourself, pay the entrance fee of RD$200 and negotiate with guides; this should cost no more than RD$1000 per person.

A challenging steep hike is to **El Mogote**, a peak west of town; to get to the trailhead 5km away, hop in a taxi (one way RD$400). You'll encounter a Salesian monastery where the monks have taken a vow of silence, and support themselves with a small pasta factory. From here it's a stiff five-hour hike to the summit – only to be attempted by the aerobically fit. Start early, wear boots if you have them, and bring plenty of water. It's a slippery walk (or slide) down from the top (at least the first half).

There are a couple of other shorter walks you can do in the area, including to **La Jagua** (around four hours; we estimate it's about 6km in distance) and **Los Tablones** (seven hours; about 10km). These trails are poorly marked and it's highly recommended to go with a local guide (US$35). You can also join a hiking group with Rancho Baiguate, which offers all of these excursions, ranging in price from US$25 to US$100 per person.

Paragliding

If launching yourself off a cliff sounds like fun then you've come to the right place. Make a point of looking up Antonio Rosario Aquino, otherwise known as **Tony** (www .paraglidingtonydominicanrepublic.com; tandem flights RD$2500), a native of Jarabacoa, one of the most experienced pilots on the island and a guide for Rancho Baiguate. After the initial take-off, it really only requires an ability to sit in a comfortable contraption. See if you can hold your lunch after a series of high-speed 360-degree whirls. Remember to bring your camera – it's an opportunity for fantastic panoramic photos. Can be arranged on short notice.

☞ Tours

Jarabacoa's biggest and best tour operator dominates the stage. A few smaller outfits come and go, but for safety and reliability we recommend only **Rancho Baiguate** (☏809-574-6890; www.ranchobaiguate.com; Carretera a Constanza). While its main clientele are Dominican groups from the capital and foreign guests from the all-inclusive resorts near Puerto Plata, independent travelers are more than welcome to join any of the trips, usually by calling a day or two in advance (except for Pico Duarte, which should be arranged with more notice). Overnight guests can pop in to the office in the afternoon and see what adventure is on the next day.

Activities have the following prices (all include breakfast and lunch): **rafting** (US $50), **canyoning** at Salto Baiguate (US$50), **mountain biking** (US$18 to US$50 depending on trail). Rancho Baiguate also offers **horseback/jeep** tours to the waterfalls (US$16 to US$21 with lunch, US$9 to US$11 without lunch). Its Pico Duarte trips range in price depending on the number of people and the side trips you take; a group of four people for three days with no side trips costs US$300 per person.

A popular excursion, often done by groups on a whistle-stop tour of the area, but also easily arranged by independent travelers with a little notice, is a visit to two nearby organic coffee farms where you can learn about the labor-intensive art of turning beans into your daily caffeine fix.

Ramirez Coffee Factory   COFFEE FARM

(☎809-574-2618; www.gbr.com; Rte 94) The 8000-sq-km family-run farm is near Manabao, at an elevation of between 213m and 430m, but the processing factory itself, which you can tour, is just outside the center of Jarabacoa (cross the bridge over the river). You can sample a cup of their Monte Alto brand in a little cafe-cum-shop in the parking lot.

Finca Alta Gracia   COFFEE FARM

(in US ☎802-398-2776; www.cafealtagracia.com) Owned by Julia Alvarez, author of *In the Time of the Butterflies* (see p234) and her husband, this coffee plantation, 17km west of Jarabacoa near Sonido del Yaque, also accepts volunteers (see p249). Coffee here is exported to Vermont, US, for roasting.

★彡 Festivals & Events

Newly inaugurated in 2010, the **Master de la Cordillera** is an Outward Bound version of a race that would have found a time slot on a US nationwide sports network. Scheduled to be held yearly, in the last weekend in October, the 39km-long event involves canyoning, hiking, biking, tubing, zip-lining and running. Contact Rancho Baiguate for more information.

🛏 Sleeping

IN TOWN

Hotel Brisas del Yaque II   HOTEL $

(☎809-574-2100;   hotelbrisasdelyaque@hotmail .com; Av Independencia 13; r from RD$1500; P✹) A step up from its sister hotel, the low-slung Yaque II has larger rooms and front-desk staff better able to answer travel-related questions. The twin rooms are distinctive in having two bathrooms, one for each guest. Ask for a mountain-facing room, if only to avoid the noisy streetside market.

Hostal Jarabacoa   HOTEL $

(☎809-574-4697; Calle Hermanas Mirabal; r with fan/air-con RD$900/1300; P✹) A good-value option if staying in town is a priority. There's no real lobby or public spaces to speak of, only clean rooms with small bathrooms and TVs lining a long hallway. Even though it feels like a hospital, the owners are friendly and welcoming.

Hotel Brisas del Yaque   HOTEL $

(☎809-574-4490;   hotelbrisasdelyaque@hotmail .com; cnr Luperón & Prof Pelegrina Herrera; RD$1300; ✹) This small hotel offers eight compact rooms, all with balconies, air-con and mini fridges. Ask for one facing west – the view of the surrounding mountains is excellent.

OUT OF TOWN

TOP CHOICE Rancho Baiguate   RESORT $$

(☎809-574-6890;   www.ranchobaiguate.com; Carretera a Constanza; all-incl s US$77-107, d US$126-163, tr US$170-220, q US$252; P🛜🏊) A wonderful base to explore the mountains, Baiguate is a rustic resort set in enormous 72-sq-km leafy compound. Ask for a room in the low-slung building along the river – large, comfortable, tile-floored rooms have private patios with wicker chairs. There's a pool on the other side of the river that runs through the complex, a beach volleyball court, Ping-Pong and pool tables, and good bird life for those who just want to sit still and chill. Large groups of students pack the place on weekends and holidays but mid-week low-season you might have it all to yourself. An on-site veggie garden supplies the competent Dominican cook, and a worm farm and a gray-water treatment plant reduce the resort's impact on the environment. The friendly staff speak English; the best adventure tour company in the area is here. The hosts can pick you up from town.

Jarabacoa River Club   HOTEL $$

(☎809-574-2456;   www.jarabacoariverclub.com; s/d incl breakfast RD$2035/3670; P✹@🏊) This rambling multilevel fun-for-all-ages complex sits on both sides of the roaring Río Yaque del Norte, around 26km south of town on the way to Manabao. White-water rafting trips put-in the river north of here; you can hang out at the riverside restaurant or cafe, or at one of the pools and see them pass below. The low-slung two-story building has spacious, modern rooms but it's the views that are special.

SONIDO DEL YAQUE

A short walk down a very steep hill brings you to **Sonido del Yaque** (☎809-846-7275; per person RD$400), a community tourism project initiated by the women of the village of Los Calabazos, around halfway between Jarabacoa and Manabao. It's a handful of wood and concrete cabins set amid lush jungle above the roaring Yaque del Norte river, each with bunk beds and a porch. There's electricity, cold-water showers (hot water in the future) and mosquito nets. Meals can be made with advanced notice upon request. A two-story lodge-restaurant with views of the surrounding mountains was being built at the time of our visit. The coffee farm Alta Gracia is nearby. Ask for Esperanza Marte.

Hotel Gran Jimenoa   HOTEL **$$**
(☎809-574-6304; Av La Confluencia; www.gran jimenoahotel.com; s/d/tr incl breakfast RD$1650/ 2425/3150; 🅿❄@🛜🏊) Set several kilometers north of town directly on the roaring Río Jimenoa, this is the Cordillera Central's most upscale hotel. It's neither on the beach nor an all-inclusive hotel, but you could easily spend a week here without leaving the extensive grounds, which include a footbridge to a bar on the far bank of the river.

✕ Eating

Restaurant Del Parque Galería DOMINICAN **$$**
(Hermanas Mirabal; mains RD$300; ⊙breakfast, lunch & dinner) Built directly around a tree and miniature children's playground overlooking Parque Central, this is the nicest place to eat in town. The large menu includes Dominican specialties like *conejo criollo* (rabbit prepared Creole-style, RD$400) and the *cabrito al vino* (goat in wine sauce, RD$350) as well as international favorites.

Hotel Gran Jimenoa   DOMINICAN **$$$**
(Av La Confluencia; mains RD$500; ⊙7am-11pm) Jarabacoa's best hotel also offers one of the town's most notable dining experiences. The restaurant here occupies an open-air deck perched right alongside the roaring Río Jimenoa. Tables along the edge are so close you may even feel some errant spray. Dishes cover the standard Dominican, Italian and French, as well as guinea hen and rabbit in wine sauce.

Pizza & Pepperoni   PIZZA **$$**
(☎809-574-4348; Paseo de los Maestros; pizza RD$210) The straightforward name isn't entirely accurate: excellent pepperoni pizzas are on the menu, along with more than a dozen other varieties, but so are calzones, burgers, pasta, grilled meat and fish dishes.

It's a relatively modern outdoor dining area with TVs tuned to sports. Delivers.

Panadería La Fleca   BAKERY **$**
(Av Independencia & Duarte; mains RD$110; ⊙breakfast, lunch & dinner; 🛜) This charming, tiny spot with a few street-front tables is across from the Esso gas station at the northern part of town. Freshly baked bread, pastries, simple sandwiches and excellent espresso are on the menu. Only two doors down from the Caribe Tours and *gua-gua* station, it's a great place to get your bearings upon arrival.

Caleu   DOMINICAN **$$**
(Av Independencia 1; mains RD$250; ⊙breakfast, lunch & dinner; 🛜) Formerly Restaurante El Rancho, this latest iteration of the Baiguate empire is a combination of a BBQ joint and piano bar. Independent travelers can inquire here about trips with Rancho Baiguate, or any other information about the region.

Supermercado Jarabacoa (Av Independencia; ⊙8am-10pm Mon-Sat, 9am-1pm Sun) is a good-sized supermarket and the **Mercado Municipal** (Av Mario N Galán) sells fresh fruit, vegetables and other foodstuffs.

🍷 Drinking

Social life in Jarabacoa revolves around Parque Central: the church, the casino and restaurants are all here. At night, the numerous *colmados* pump loud merengue and beery customers onto the sidewalk, where the party really gets going.

El Viejo Jack   BAR
(cnr Av Marío N Galán & Mella; ⊙10.30am-10.30pm Sun-Thu, to midnight Fri & Sat) This liquor-store-cum-bar is full of enormous glass cases of dust-free premium booze. Balloon wine glasses give a certain panache to sharing an entire bottle of cognac with friends. The beer is icy cold.

Entre Amigos DANCE CLUB
(Colón 182; ⏰9pm-late Fri-Sun) This thumping bar is the best party in town – expect merengue, salsa and reggaeton, and elbow-to-elbow service at the bar. There's often karaoke early in the evening, ending at 11pm.

Two other nightspots next to one another, across from the Esso petrol station at the northern end of town, are **Venue Bar & Lounge** (Av La Confluencia) and **Liquor Bar & Grill** (Av La Confluencia); the latter has outdoor seating on the second-floor balcony.

ℹ Information

Banco BHD (Galán, near Carmen)

Banco Popular (cnr Av Independencia & Colón)

Banco Progreso (Calle Uribe, near Av Independencia)

Centro de Copiado y Papelería (cnr Duarte & Av Independencia; per hr RD$35) An internet cafe.

Centro Medico Dr Abad (☎809-574-2431; Calle El Carmen 40)

Clínica Dr Terrero (☎809-574-4597; Av Independencia 2A)

Farmacia Miguelito (☎809-574-2755; Calle Marío N Galán 70) Will deliver.

New York Net Café (Plaza Ramirez; per hr RD$30; ⏰8am-midnight)

Politur (☎809-754-3216; cnr José Duran & Marío Galán) Tourist police, behind the Caribe Tours terminal.

Post office (Av Independencia) On the northern edge of town.

Western Union/Call Center (Av Independencia 43; ⏰8am-5.30pm, closed Sun)

ℹ Getting There & Away

TO SANTO DOMINGO Caribe Tours (☎809-574-4796; José Duran, near Av Independencia) offers the only first-class bus service to Jarabacoa. Four daily departures to Santo Domingo (RD$250, 2½ hours, at 7am, 10am, 1:30pm and 4:30pm) include a stop in La Vega (RD$75, 45 minutes).

TO LA VEGA A *gua-gua* terminal (cnr Av Independencia & José Duran) provides frequent service to La Vega (RD$70, 30 minutes, every 10 to 30 minutes from 7am to 6pm). If you prefer to hire a cab, the ride costs around US$25.

TO CONSTANZA *Públicos* (cnr Deligne & Calle El Carmen) leave from diagonally opposite the Shell petrol station at around 9am and 1pm daily (RD$150, 40 minutes). The new road should make this spectacularly scenic drive

less taxing on your car's shock absorbers; once you hit El Río, the remaining 19km passes through a lush valley.

TO LA CIÉNAGA *Públicos* (RD$85, 1½ hours) leave roughly every two hours from Calle Odulio Jiménez near Calle 16 de Agosto. The road is 42km long, of which the first 33km are paved. Returning can be more of a challenge, especially if you return from a hike in the afternoon. Don't hesitate to hail down any truck heading toward Jarabacoa: chances are the driver will allow you to hop aboard.

ℹ Getting Around

To get to outlying hotels and sights you can easily flag down a *motoconcho* on any street corner during the day. If you prefer a cab, try **Jaroba Taxi** (☎809-574-4640) next to the Caribe Tours terminal or hail one at the corner of José Duran and Av Independencia.

There are several **car-rental agencies** in Jarabacoa, but we strongly recommend that you bring a car with you if you need one (preferably an SUV).

Parques Nacionales Bermúdez & Ramírez

In 1956 the Dominican government established Parque Nacional Armando Bermúdez with the hope of preventing the kind of deforestation occurring in Haiti. The park encompasses 766 sq km of tree-flanked mountains and pristine valleys. Two years later, an adjoining area of 764 sq km to the south was designated Parque Nacional José del Carmen Ramírez. Between them, the parks contain three of the highest peaks in the Caribbean, and the headwaters of 12 major rivers, including the Río Yaque del Norte, the country's only white-water, and most important, river.

🏃 Activities
Climbing Pico Duarte
Pico Duarte (3087m) was first climbed in 1944, as part of a celebration commemorating the 100th anniversary of Dominican independence. During the late 1980s, the government began cutting trails in the parks and erecting cabins, hoping to increase tourism to the country by increasing the accessibility of its peaks. These days, about 3000 people a year ascend Pico Duarte.

For all the effort involved to reach the summit, there actually isn't a great deal to see. Up to around 2000m, you travel through rainforest, passing foliage thick with ferns

CENTRAL HIGHLANDS

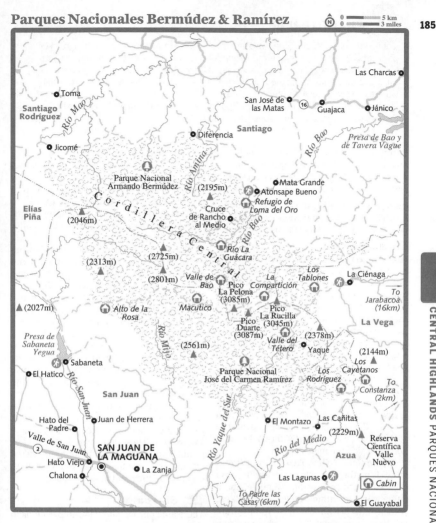

and some good bird life. You quickly pass above this limit, however, and spend most of the trip in a wasteland of burnt-out *pino caribeño* – a monoculture plantation that looks suspiciously like Monterey pine (the stuff loggers like because of its spindly, knot-free branches). Numerous forest fires have left the landscape barren, and the only animals you're likely to see are marauding bands of cawing crows. Although amid the bleakness you may see the occasional colorful epiphyte.

You'll enjoy this trip more if you spend part of the journey on the back of a mule.

TOURS & GUIDES

The easiest way to reach the summit of Pico Duarte is to take an organized tour. Prices vary widely and depend on how many people are going and for how long. Expect to pay roughly US$80 to US$100 per person per day. Be sure to book at least a month in advance.

Rancho Baiguate (p182) is the best overall choice for non-Spanish speakers, as it is based in Jarabacoa, and also offers a detour through Valle del Tétero.

Camping Tours (p172) in Santiago is the cheapest, as it caters primarily to

CENTRAL HIGHLANDS PARQUES NACIONALES BERMÚDEZ & RAMÍREZ

ℹ WHAT TO BRING

Cold- and wet-weather clothing are musts for anyone intending to spend a night in either park. While the average temperature ranges between 12°C and 20°C most of the year, lows of -5°C are not uncommon, especially in December and January. Rainstorms can happen at any time during the year. While the soil is sandy and drains well, you'll still want a good raincoat, plus sturdy shoes or boots.

If you're not climbing Pico Duarte as part of an organized tour, you'll also need to discuss with your guide what supplies to bring.

Dominicans, but the guides speak only Spanish. This is your only option if you want to walk Mata Grande to Pico Duarte and exit at La Ciénega.

Iguana Mama (p152) in Cabarete is good if you're in a hurry and want transportation to and from the north coast.

SELF-ORGANIZED TOURS

Your other option – assuming you speak good Spanish and you're not in a hurry – is to go to the trailhead in person and organize mules, food and a guide on your own. Mules and muleteers go for around US$15 per day each, and the lead guide around US$30 per day (minimum one guide for every five hikers). Be aware also that if you walk out a different entrance to where you came in, you'll have to pay several days' extra wages for your guides to get back to the starting point (where they live). Guides can organize basic provisions for you. There is a small spring of drinking water halfway up the trail from La Ciénega, but you're well advised to pack your own water (water-cooler-sized bottles, which the mules carry).

Attempting to climb Pico Duarte without mules is neither possible nor desirable – you can't enter the park without a guide, and a guide won't go without mules. And walking with a full pack in this heat would drain whatever enjoyment you might get from the walk. Mules are also essential in case someone gets injured.

ROUTES TO THE TOP

There are two popular routes up Pico Duarte. The shortest and easiest (and by far the most used) is from La Ciénega via Jarabacoa. It is 23km in each direction and involves approximately 2275m of vertical ascent en route to the peak. It's recommended to do this route in three days – one long day to arrive at the La Comparatición campground, one easy day to hike up and enjoy the views, and one long day back out again. The trip can be done in

two days by getting up at 4am for a dawn summit, but afterward it's a grueling, hot slog down the mountain. Consider also adding a fourth day to do the side trip to the Valle del Tétero, a beautiful valley at the base of the mountain. Camping Tours, Rancho Baiguate and Iguana Mama offer the hike from La Ciénega.

The second most popular route is from Mata Grande. It's 45km to the summit and involves approximately 3800m of vertical ascent, including going over La Pelona, a peak only slightly lower than Pico Duarte itself. You'll spend the first night at the Río La Guácara campground and the second at the Valle de Bao campground. You can walk this route in five days (return), but it's far more interesting to walk out via the Valle del Tétero and La Ciénega (also five days). Camping Tours offers the hike from Mata Grande.

It is also possible to reach the peak from Sabaneta (via San Juan de la Maguana), Las Lagunas (via Padre las Casas) and Constanza. These routes are little traveled, significantly more difficult, and not offered by any tour companies – you'll need to organize a guide and mules yourself.

🛏 Sleeping

There are approximately 14 campgrounds in the parks, each with a first-come-first-served cabin that hikers can use free of charge. Each cabin can hold 20 or more people and consists of wood floors, wood walls, a wood ceiling, but no beds, cots, mats or lockers of any kind. That wouldn't be so bad, except that the most-frequented cabins have developed a somewhat unnerving rat problem – if you have a tent, consider bringing it along so you can avoid using the cabins altogether.

Most of the cabins also have a stand-alone 'kitchen': an open-sided structure with two or three concrete wood-burning stoves. Fallen dead wood is usually abundant near the campgrounds – be sure you or your guide bring matches and some paper to get the fire started.

ℹ Information

There are **ranger stations** (park admission RD$200; ⊙8am-5pm) near the start of the major trails into the parks – at La Ciénaga, Sabaneta, Mata Grande, Las Lagunas and Constanza. As a safety precaution, everyone entering the park, even for a short hike, must be accompanied by a guide.

San José de las Matas

POP 36,000/ELEV 518M

This small mountain town 45km southwest of Santiago is a jumping-off point for two major hiking trails in the Parque Nacional Armando Bermúdez. It's a pleasant-enough town – with nice mountain views, several rivers and *balenarios* to swim in; a place to linger the day before or after a long hike. If you do happen to be out here, follow the trail that starts behind the post office on Calle 30 de Marzo. It leads to a cliff-top park with great views of the surrounding mountains. It's about an hour return.

Only **Camping Tours** (p172) offers the trek to Pico Duarte starting from Mata Grande. From there, it's a five-day trek to the summit and then down to Valle del Tétero and out at La Ciénega.

There are two good accommodations options: **The Mansion Hotel & Villas** (☎809-571-6868; www.hotellamansionsajoma .com; r RD$2000), a former Trujillo retreat, is an enormous complex with panoramic views, a large pool area, bar and **restaurant** (mains RD$300; ⊙9am-11pm); when it hosts live music events it comes alive. Or the more rustic **Ventana Rio Lindo** (☎809-214-4430; www.ventanariolindohotel.com; r from RD$500) perched over the Inoa river, a short drive from the center of town. Run by a Canadian family, it offers basic, homespun rooms with wonderful views from private balconies; food is served as well.

Gua-guas for Santiago (RD$65, one hour, from 6am to 7pm) leave from opposite the Texaco station at the entrance of town. Buses leave roughly every 15 minutes in the mornings, but you may have to wait an hour or more in the middle of the day. By car it's only 40 minutes from Santiago.

Constanza

POP 43,000/ELEV 1097M

There's a saying here in the mountains: 'God is everywhere, but he lives in Constanza'. Set in a fertile valley and walled in by towering mountains, you can see why – it's a breathtaking spot. Dusk, especially, is awesome – as the sun sets behind the peaks, a thick mist sinks down into the valley floor. This is the capital of industrialized agriculture – 80% of fruits and vegetables (mainly potatoes, strawberries, apples, lettuce and garlic) and 75% of flowers are grown on farms around here. During the week you're likely to have the hotel to yourself, but Dominicans from the lowland cities journey here for weekend getaways. There isn't a whole lot to do here, though, and the tourist attractions are of far less interest than the cooler climate and the sheer remoteness of it all.

Also calling Constanza home are a couple of hundred Japanese farmers who arrived during the 1950s at dictator Rafael Trujillo's invitation. In return for providing superior farmland at dirt-cheap prices to 50 Japanese families, Trujillo hoped the Japanese would convert the fertile valley into a thriving agricultural center, which they did.

◎ Sights & Activities

Aguas Blancas   WATERFALLS

These impressive waterfalls are a beautiful but difficult 16km drive from Constanza, and are reputedly the largest in the Greater Antilles. The falls – actually one cascade in three different sections – crash some 135m down a sheer cliff into a pretty pool. You'll need a 4WD to get there: turn north at the Isla gas station and continue past Colonia Japonésa. The way through the mountains passes by a couple of extremely poor communities of Haitian and Dominican farm workers. If you haven't got your own vehicle, many hotels can take you there for around US$35 per person.

Ebano Verde   NATURE RESERVE

Look for the entrance to this 23-sq-km reserve on the road from Santiago just before the Sanctuario de la Virgen de Altagracia. If time is limited, there's an easy 2km-long nature trail through tropical forest where you might spot Dominican magnolias, the Green Ebony tree and bird life like red-tailed hawks. A more difficult 6km path leads to a pool you can swim in at the base of a small waterfall.

Valle Nuevo NATURE RESERVE

Also known as Parque Nacional Juan Pérez Rancier, this remote park begins around 17km southeast of Constanza. **Las Pirámides**, a monument marking the geographic center of DR, is 46km away. The area records the coldest temperatures in the country, sometimes reaching -8°C during the night and, at 2438m, is the highest plain in the Caribbean. In theory, you can drive all the way to San José de Ocoa, around 90km to the south (though you might need a military vehicle).

Piedras Letradas CAVE ART

Meaning 'Inscribed Stone,' Piedras Letradas is a shallow cave containing scores of Taíno petroglyphs and pictograms, mostly depicting animals and simplistic human-like figures. The site is a good 30km northwest of Constanza via the town of La Culeta. The road to La Culeta is paved, but it deteriorates quickly after that. Ask for directions in La Culeta, as the road is easy to miss. You'll need a 4WD.

Sanctuarío de la Virgen de Altagracia CHURCH

If you're driving the primary road to Constanza – turning off Highway Duarte at El Albanico – look for this small church perched at the top of the highest pass (1300m), where devout travelers frequently stop to light a candle and utter a few words of prayer. The less devout will still welcome the views and the opportunity to stretch their legs or take a bathroom break. It's about 38km east of Constanza.

On weekends, Constanza's Parque Central comes alive with locals drinking at the end of the day – a sociable place to hang out for an hour or two. **Softball games** are held almost every night at 7pm at the field a few blocks west of here.

☞ Tours

The main sights are all quite distant and require a 4WD. Most hotels in the area can organize ad hoc tours in their own vehicles, or call **Safari Constanza** (✉809-539-3839; www.safariconstanza.com).

⚜ Festivals & Events

Every September – the date varies – Constanza goes nuts during **Fiestas Patronales**, a nine-day-long party that is nominally in honor of the Virgen de las Mercedes, the town's patron saint. There are live music events, beer tents in the park, and the whole shebang culminates in the crowning of the new *reina* – a Miss Constanza pageant, of sorts.

🛏 Sleeping

Only two to three hours from Santo Domingo by car, Constanza fills up on weekends and holidays and empties during the week. The center of town is noisy, with the constant din of motorcycles and scooters.

IN TOWN

Hotel Vistas del Valle HOTEL $

(✉829-689-9808; socratesgp@hotmail.com; Calle Antonio Maria Garcia; s/d with fan RD$450/700; P) Granted, the competition is less than fierce, but this well-maintained family-owned hotel on the western side of town offers the most comfortable accommodations. The second-floor rooms even have views outside their front doors.

Mi Cabaña Resort VILLAS $$

(✉809-539-2930; Carretera Antonio Duverge; s/d incl breakfast RD$1400/2400; P❄☲) South of town, just before the turn-off for the Colonia Japonesa, is this development of nine villas. When Dominican families and groups aren't in residence, it resembles a Floridian townhouse retirement community under foreclosure. That being said, tile-floored rooms are spotless and there's a pool and restaurant.

Hotel Restaurant Mi Casa HOTEL $

(✉809-539-2764; cnr Luperón & Sánchez; r RD$800; P) A block west from the Isla gas station, rooms here are basic and clean. Some are tiled but all have private bathrooms. Request one with an outward-facing window for a breeze. The on-site restaurant is decent for breakfast.

OUT OF TOWN

TOP CHOICE Alto Cerro HOTEL $$

(✉809-539-6192; www.altocerro.com; s/d/tr incl breakfast RD$1500/1800/2100, villas for 2/5/7 people RD$1900/3900/5800, camping per person RD$335; P🛜) Easily the best accommodations in Constanza, this large, family-owned complex is 2km east of town off the road toward Highway Duarte (look for the turn-off just past the airport on your right). More than half a dozen buildings line a hillside perched partway up a high bluff. The rooms themselves are unremarkable, but they have balconies with terrific views of the whole valley, and the large suites and two-story villas are equipped with kitchens. The hotel's **restaurant** is recommended and there's a small **store** with basics for a simple meal. Behind the main building is a well-maintained **campground**, popular with Dominican families and big groups. A full-service spa and convention center were in the works at the time of research.

✖ Eating

Alto Cerro DOMINICAN **$$**
(mains RD$300; ⓡ) Constanza's version of a destination restaurant, primarily for the breathtaking views from the second-floor balcony, which frames the mountains across the valley like a picture postcard. The kitchen turns out Dominican and European-style dishes pushed in a cart to your tablecloth-covered table by well-dressed wait staff.

Lorenzo's Restaurant DOMINICAN **$$**
(Luperón 83; mains RD$250; ☺breakfast, lunch & dinner) You'll find solid Dominican fare and heaping portions at this restaurant on the western edge of town. Crowded at lunchtime, especially on Sundays when few other restaurants are open, Lorenzo's professional wait staff scurry about the room doling out sandwiches, pasta, pizza, fish and hearty *sancocho* (RD$150) – a stew of meat, sausage, plantain and potato. The *plato del dia* (RD$100) is always a good deal.

Antojitos d' Lauren PIZZA **$$**
(☎809-539-3839; Duarte 15; pizza RD$250; ☺lunch & dinner) Even though this restaurant has all the stripped-down allure of eating in a dark warehouse, Antojitos serves tasty pizzas – choose from over a dozen different varieties, including the vegetarian, loaded with produce from area farms. The owner, a friendly and knowledgeable man, is happy to share advice for travel around Constanza. Delivers.

Restaurant Aguas Blancas DOMINICAN **$$**
(Espinosa 54; mains RD$200; ☺lunch & dinner) The cozy log-cabin-like dining room qualifies as fine dining in Constanza. Along with usual Dominican fare are a few simple pasta dishes and the specialty, *guinea guisada*.

Across from Isla petrol station is **Super El Económico** (Luperón; ☺7:45am-noon & 1:45-8pm Mon-Sat, 9am-noon Sun), a medium-sized grocery. For locally grown produce try the

Mercado Municipal (cnr Gratereaux & 14 de Julio; ☺7am-6pm Mon-Sat, to noon Sun).

❶ Information

Banco Léon (Luperón 19) On the main drag. Also exchanges traveler's checks.

BanReservas (Luperón 18) Next door to Banco Léon.

Constanza Information Center (☎809-539-1022; www.constanza.com.do) In the airport parking lot. Ask for Milena Delgado. English and Spanish spoken.

Copy Centro (Calle Sanchez 9; per hr RD$30; ☺8am-10pm Mon-Fri, to 5pm Sat; @)

Farmacia San José (☎809-539-2516; Miguel Abreu 87) At the northeast corner of the park.

Farmacia Yazdana (☎809-539-1142; Luperón 38) Two blocks east of the Isla petrol station.

Hospital Pedro Antonio Cespede (☎809-538-2420, 809-539-3288; Calle Antonio Isacc; ☺24hr) Fully equipped emergency room. On your right as you come into town, just past the airport.

Politur (☎809-539-3020) Tourist police – opposite the airport, 2km east of town.

❶ Getting There & Away

AIR You'll pass a small airstrip as you come into town; plans are for charter flights from Santo Domingo, as well as further abroad, to arrive here regularly one day.

GUA-GUA Transporte La Cobra (☎809-539-2119) services Santiago (RD$300, 2 hours) and Santo Domingo (RD$300, 2½ hours). Other *gua-guas* travel to Jarabacoa (RD$150, 40 minutes). *Gua-guas* also regularly service El Albanico (RD$160, 40 minutes), where you can change for a *gua-gua* to Santo Domingo and La Vega.

CAR The long-awaited Jarabacoa–Constanza highway was opened several months after we visited; the road was once jaw-rattlingly bad. In theory, travel times between the two towns will be dramatically shortened to an easy 40-minute drive in a compact car. If you're coming from Highway Duarte, the turn-off at El Albanico is 89km north of Santo Domingo, and from there it's 51km on a well-paved, twisty mountain road that passes through lush scenery and a handful of small villages. You'll enjoy your time in Constanza more if you come in an SUV, though, as the roads outside town are pretty bad.

East of Santiago

The country town of **Moca** has prospered in recent decades as a result of its production of coffee, cocoa and tobacco. The tallest building in town is also its only tourist

RESERVA CIENTÍFICA LOMA QUITA ESPUELA

The 'Mountain of the Missing Spur' – a reference to the dense underbrush that ripped boot spurs from cowboys – is a remote and lovely national park, containing the largest rainforest on the island. It is full of endemic species that are on the point of extinction. The NGO **Fundación Loma Quita Espuela** (☏809-588-4156; www.flqe.org.do; Urbanización Almánzar, cnr Calle Luis Carrón & Av del Jaya; ☺8am-noon & 2-5pm), is actively involved in developing sustainable ways for the local farmers to use this natural resource.

The Foundation offers a number of tours, including the hike to the top of Loma Quita Espuela (942m, 2½ hours, RD$1050 for up to five people, plus RD$50 park entrance fee), where an observation tower commands excellent views over the Valle del Cibao. A guide is mandatory (Spanish only).

There's also a shorter walk that tours several cocoa plantations, where you can buy *bola de cacao* – crude chocolate balls that are used to make hot chocolate. The tour ends at a local *balenario* (swimming hole), where you can take a dip. There are several Taíno caves nearby, too, and, if you're driving, the Foundation staff can take you there for free (or, if not, for the price of the petrol).

Simple accommodations are available at **Rancho Don Lulú** (r RD$350), just 1km from the Loma Quita Espuela trailhead. There's one double bed in a rustic cabin a couple of hundred meters from the owners' home, where you eat (meals RD$150). Contact the Foundation at least a day or two in advance for reservations.

The entrance to Loma Quita Espuela is 14km (30 minutes) northeast of San Francisco de Macorís on a rough road that gets progressively worse. From the center of town, take Calle Salcedo to Av Libertad and turn left. Continue three blocks until you see the *mercado municipal* (municipal market) on your left. Then turn right on Calle Castillo and follow the road out of town as it bends around to the east. The entrance will be on your left, and from there it's two rough kilometers to the trailhead, including crossing a small river. Don't try this without a good 4WD.

attraction, the **Iglesia Corazón de Jesus** (admission free; ☺varies), with a panel of beautiful stained glass imported from Turin, Italy.

During the 18th century, Moca was one of the Spanish colony's chief cattle centers. In 1805 an invading Haitian army took Moca, killed virtually the entire population and burned the town to the ground. Moca struggled back, and in the 1840s began to raise tobacco as a commercial crop; now, some of the world's finest cigars contain tobacco grown on the hillsides around the town.

East of Moca and around 4km east of the town of Salcedo is the **Museo de Hermanas Mirabel** (☏809-587-7075; admission RD$20; ☺9am-5pm Mon-Fri, to 5:45pm Sat & Sun). The home of the Mirabel sisters, Patria, Minerva and María, assassinated by agents of Trujillo because of their opposition to his regime, has been turned into a time-capsule museum. Everything in the rooms – from bedrooms to kitchen to study – is presented as if they had just left; even the garments they were wearing when they were killed are displayed. Price of admission includes guided tour (Spanish only).

There's not much point coming out this way if you haven't got your own car.

SAN FRANCISCO DE MACORÍS
POP 157,000

San Francisco de Macorís is a bustling, prosperous place in the heart of the Valle del Cibao. It draws much of its prosperity from the fields of cocoa and rice that grow around it in all directions. There are a number of colonial buildings about the place, and a large, pretty plaza. San Francisco is also home of one of the DR's six baseball teams, the Gigantes (Giants).

Probably the best reason to venture out this way is a day trip to **Loma Quita Espuela** (see box text). Another is to tour a chocolate farm. Currently, the DR is the number-one producer of organic cacao worldwide. **Sendero del Cacao** (☏809-547-2166; www.cacaotour.com; La Paja; tour without transportation US$45) offers two-hour tours (Spanish, English and French) of a working plantation, including explanations and demonstrations of the entire process; the tours end with a large lunch. Independent travelers can join up with a group and reservations are required. With your own vehicle, it's only a ten-minute drive from Parque Duarte.

Hotel Las Caobas (Mahogany Hotel; ☎809-290-5858; cnr Calle Carrón & Av San Diego; s/d RD$2500/2900; P🌸🔁📶) only seems true to its name in the lobby and restaurant's furniture and paneling; otherwise, the property looks decidedly non-arboreal from the outside. The hotel's rooms are up to the standards of business travelers, the pleasant cafe and restaurant is open all day, and a large pool and lounge area is out the back. It's also conveniently located just a few hundred meters from the offices of Fundación Loma Quita Espuela.

On the southern side of Parque Duarte is **Buffalo Steak House** (San Francisco 63; mains RD$200; ⊘breakfast, lunch & dinner), a Western-themed restaurant with a relatively upscale open-air dining area and excellent burgers, seafood and, of course, steaks.

The turn-off from Highway Duarte is about 15km (10 minutes) south of La Vega. It's possible but much more difficult (and on much worse roads) to come south from the coast via Nagua. **Caribe Tours** (☎809-588-2221; cnr Calle Castillo & Hernández) runs more than a dozen buses daily to Santo Domingo (RD$260, 6am to 6:30pm).

The Southwest & Península de Pedernales

Best Places to Eat

» Casa Bonita (p204)

» Hotel Casablanca –
Campo Suizo (p204)

» Rincón Mexicano (p198)

» Rancho Tipico (p208)

Best Places to Stay

» Casa Bonita (p204)

» Cachóte (p205)

» Hotel Casablanca –
Campo Suizo (p204)

» Rancho Platón (p205)

Why Go?

Talk about criminally undervisited. Few travelers make it to the southwest: it's remote, its treasures yield themselves only to those who apply the effort and its highlights don't exactly roll off the traveler tongue – and that's exactly the reason to turn right out of Santo Domingo instead of left. The stunning coastline of the Península de Pedernales offers miles of pristine, empty beaches and otherworldly swirls of turquoise sea; there's a soundtrack set to twittering birdsong in the cloud forests of the mountains, and the striking dry desert landscape of cactus stretching all the way to the Haitian border will jar your preconceived Caribbean perceptions to the point of disbelief. Like the astounding Bahía de Las Águilas, a 10km deserted stretch of postcard-perfect beach in the far-flung corner of the southwest, you can have this region all to yourself – a notion long-harnessed but long-forgotten in most other parts of the world.

When to Go

Laguna Oviedo's biodiversity is in full swing in March and April, the best time for nature lovers and ecotourists to witness the area's impressive migratory feast. December to February offers up sunny skies and seemingly endless fiestas on every corner, the busiest time for the DR as a whole, with North American and European holidays in overdrive. But caffeine fiends will want to hold off until June: the first week sees the Polo Organic Coffee Festival percolating inland – yes, the coffee is *that* good.

The Southwest & Península de Pedernales Highlights

1 Taking the spectacular boat ride to **Bahía de Las Águilas** (p208), the most remote and beautiful beach in the country

2 Spotting flamingos and turtles on a boat tour to super-salty **Laguna Oviedo** (p207)

3 Leaving the stereotypical Caribbean behind in the coolness and tranquility of the cloud forest at the remote cabins of **Cachóte** (p205)

4 Spotting cactus flowers, butterflies and beefy iguanas on **Isla Cabritos** (p210), the lowest point in the Caribbean

5 Killing a day cooling off in the idyllic freshwater pool at **Los Patos** (p204) near Paraíso

6 Renting some wheels and riding one of the most beautiful unheard-of coastal drives in the Americas along the eastern shoreline of the **Península de Pedernales** (p200)

7 Becoming a miner for a day and sourcing your own semiprecious stone at the **Larimar Mine** (p206), the only one of its kind in the world

ⓘ Getting There & Around

Although there's one nominally international airport just outside of Barahona, no commercial airlines fly there, so your only way to get here is by bus or car. Caribe Tours has regular service to Barahona and San Juan de la Maguana, but after that only *gua-guas* (small buses) transit the rest of the region. Because of union agreements, *gua-guas* plying the coastal highway do not stop at every town along the way, even though they pass right through them. Be careful to get on the right bus, or else you'll be let off outside of town and you'll have to walk or catch another ride in.

WEST OF SANTO DOMINGO

Heading west from the city takes you not only in the opposite direction to the beach resorts to the east but also to a different DR – one whose landscape isn't defined by tourism but by the more haphazard demands of ordinary life. From Santo Domingo Hwy 2 cuts inland to the provincial capital of San Cristóbal and from there it continues south to the city of Baní. Hwy 41, north to San José de Ocoa, takes you into the foothills of the Cordillera Central.

San Cristóbal

POP 220,000

During his authoritative and brutal rule, which lasted from 1930 until his assassination in 1961, Rafael Trujillo showered his hometown with generosity and monuments to his excess, including a never-lived-in mansion and a US$4-million church, a paragon of Latin American Caudillo high kitsch (see boxed text, opposite). The city's name was officially changed in 1934 to 'Meritorious City.' (It was changed back after Trujillo died.) An appropriate symbol and reminder of Trujillo's regime is the empty pedestal across from the church – it used to support a statue of the *commandante* on horseback but was pulled down by enraged Dominicans after Trujillo's death.

Today, most visitors heading west from the capital pass through this traffic-clogged provincial capital just 30km from Santo Domingo. There are a few beaches nearby – Playa Palenque and Playa Najayo, popular with families on weekends – and it's also

ⓘ CAR RENTAL

If you're thinking of renting a car, two thoughts: there are no rental car agencies of any kind in the southwest, so rent something in Santo Domingo; and two, unless you insist on taking your DIY ethos to the extreme, a 4WD is not necessary. Save one or two, all of the southwest's main attractions are reachable in an economy rental.

the nearest town to Reserva Antropológica El Pomier, a series of caves that contain the country's largest collection of Taíno cave paintings.

Because of its proximity to Santo Domingo and dearth of quality accommodations, San Cristóbal is not a popular choice for staying overnight. The nearby **Rancho Campeche** (✆809-686-1053; www.ranchocampeche.com; Calle Leonor de Ovando 1; tent & 3 meals per person RD$1225), however, offers one of the few opportunities to camp in the country. At the end of a rough road west of San Cristóbal, you can set up tents on this property overlooking the Caribbean. Toilets and shower facilities as well as meals are provided. Definitely arrange in advance since it's not uncommon for the property to be booked by groups or reserved for special occasions. Playa Palenque and Playa Najayo are nearby.

The culinary claim to fame of San Cristóbal is the *pastel en hoja,* literally 'pastry in paper,' basically a doughy empanada stuffed with cheese or meat wrapped in a piece of butcher paper. They cost around RD$90 a piece and can be found at most eateries. **Pasteleria Chichita** (Calle General Leger; ⊙breakfast, lunch & dinner), one block east of Parque Colón, has been churning them out for more than 50 years. San Cristóbal's main **market**, along Calle María Trinidad Sánchez, is two blocks west of Av Constitución. All of San Cristóbal's services are on those two streets, most within a few blocks of Parque Colón, where you'll be dropped if you arrive by bus.

Buses for San Cristóbal leave Santo Domingo from Parque Enriquillo. In San Cristóbal, *gua-guas* for the capital (RD$70, 45 minutes, every 15 minutes from 6am to 8pm) leave from a stop at the southeast edge of the park. *Gua-guas* to Baní (RD$70, 45 minutes, every 25 minutes from 7am to

8:20pm) leave from beside Isla gas station on Calle María Trinidad Sánchez, 600m west of Parque Colón. For towns further west, you have to go out to the Isla gas station, 4.3km north of Parque Colón on the main highway, and flag down a passing bus: to Ázua (RD$120) and Barahona (RD$225), for example.

There are taxis and *motoconchos* in the vicinity of Parque Independencia from sunrise until late at night.

Reserva Antropológica Cuevas del Pomier

Visiting the Reserva Antropológica Cuevas del Pomier is like reading a history book written in stone. There are 55 limestone caves (admission Dominican/foreigner RD$50/100; ☺8am-5pm) in the area just 10km north of central San Cristobal, five of which are open to the public, with Cave 1 carrying the

mother lode, some 590 prehistoric paintings. The caves contain thousands of drawings and carvings that constitute the most extensive example of prehistoric art yet discovered in the Caribbean, including works by Igneri and Caribs as well as the Taínos. The faded drawings, painted with a mix of charcoal and the fat from manatees, depict birds, fish and other animals, as well as figures that may be deities. Relatively little is known about Hispaniola's earliest inhabitants, though the paintings here, believed to be as much as 2000 years old, provide some tantalizing clues. Sir Robert Schomburgk, who left his name and that of his companions on the wall, first discovered the principal cave in 1851.

The caves were closed as a safety precaution because of nearby explosives blasting, part of a marble-mining operation, and to re-stabilize Cave 1, from 2004 to 2010, but are now once again open to the public and

195

THE SOUTHWEST & PENÍNSULA DE PEDERNALES RESERVA ANTROPOLÓGICA CUEVAS DEL POMIER

CAUDILLO KITSCH

You can visit San Cristobal's strangest sight providing you adhere to the dress code (shirts and closed-toe shoes required). The **Castillo del Cerro** (☎809-480-8633; admission free; ☺9am-5pm), now being used as the National Penitentiary School, was built on Trujillo's orders for himself and his family in 1947 (at a cost of US$3 million) but he reportedly hated the finished product and never spent a single night there. The name means 'Castle on the Hill,' which is pretty accurate – it overlooks the city – but the imposing concrete-and-glass structure looks like a medieval office building. Inside, though, huge dining rooms, ballrooms and numerous bedrooms and salons have fantastic ceilings and wall decorations made of plaster and painted in gaudy colors. The bathrooms – of which there must be 20 – have tile mosaics in reds, blues and even gold leaf. There are six floors in all, and you can spend a half-hour or more just wandering through the once-abandoned structure. There is also a small museum detailing various atrocities of Trujillo's iron fist, including a few original instruments of torture and murder, a replica electric chair and – huh? – loads of exquisite bed frames.

Any taxi driver or *motoconchista* (motorcycle taxi driver) can take you there – it probably makes sense to ask the driver to come back in 30 to 60 minutes to pick you up. If you've got a vehicle, from Parque Independencia take Calle María Trinidad Sánchez west for 700m. Take a left onto Calle Luperón near the Isla gas station. Follow Calle Luperón for 500m until you reach a fork in the road. There, veer right and head up the hill another 700m to the entrance gates.

Also interesting and slightly strange is the informal **Museo Jamas El Olvido Será tu Recuerdo** (☎809-474-8767) in the home of local resident José Miguel Ventura Medina, known to some as 'El Hippi.' The museum's name translates literally to 'Forgetfulness will never be your remembrance,' or simply 'You will never be forgotten.' The 'you' in this case is none other than Generalísimo Trujillo, who, along with John F Kennedy, was Ventura's favorite world leader. Most will not agree with Ventura's assessment of Trujillo as a 'good dictator,' but the extensive collection of photos and other memorabilia – plus a slew of random antiques – is worth poking around. The museum is free and open whenever Ventura is home; if he's not there, give him a call. It's located on Calle General Leger, 6½ blocks north and one block east of Parque Colón – look for a small white car perched on the rooftop.

well worth a visit. The guided tour can last anywhere from 30 minutes for an average tourist to a full day for blossoming anthropologists.

It's a challenge to get to the caves on your own, even with a slew of new signs. The easiest way there is to take a taxi or *motoconcho*. Round-trip with an hour wait should cost around RD$500 on a *motoconcho*. If you're driving, follow Av Constitución north to La Toma, a small community across the highway from San Cristobal, where there is an easy-to-spot sign just over the bridge. From there, it's 300m until a right turn on Carratera La Toma. Follow this road 2.6km to a prominent and signed T-intersection, where you turn left and proceed up the hill on a gravelly, eventually paved road for several more kilometers. Just past the DoCALsa factory entrance, turn right (it will seem as though you are turning into a mining quarry, which you are). Stay straight another 600m to the signed entrance. Ask as you go, as the turn-offs are easy to miss. Be alert for giant dump trucks coming down the road from the mine – there are a number of blind curves.

Baní

POP 73,800

Notable mainly as a convenient stopping point for those driving between Santo Domingo and Barahona, Baní also marks the turn-off for the beach and sand dunes of **Las Salinas**, 25km to the southwest. Its historical claim to fame is as the birthplace of Generalísimo Máximo Gómez y Báez who, after serving in the Spanish army in Santo Domingo, moved to Cuba to become a farmer. During the 1860s, Gómez joined the insurgents opposed to Spanish rule and the heavy taxation it imposed, rose to the rank of general of the Cuban forces and, together with José Martí, led the revolution of 1868–78 that culminated in Cuba's independence from Spain.

◉ Sights

Monumento Natural Dunas de las Calderas   NATURE RESERVE

(admission RD$20, guide per groups of 10 RD$200; ◎8am-6pm) This protected reserve, part of the Península de las Salinas, is 20 sq km of gray-brown sand mounds, some as high as 12m. A guided tour offers views of the dunes and beaches beyond and is well worth a look

if you want to see a unique landscape in the Caribbean, completely contrary to sparkling seas and floury sands. The brown sandy beach near here gets crowded with Dominican families and windsurfers on Sundays and is not kept especially clean. Weekdays, you'll have it all to yourself. To get to Las Salinas, take Av Máximo Gómez 400m west of Parque Duarte and turn left at the Isla gas station onto Av Fernando Deligne; this eventually bears right onto a single, surprisingly decent paved road that passes through several small 'towns,' at least one of which has an ATM. There's a naval station at the end of the road; continue past the guard's pillbox and turn left. Follow this road into town. The entrance to the dunes is 1.5km east of Salinas Hotel & Restaurant, a great place to bed down if you come.

🛏 Sleeping & Eating

Hotel Caribani   HOTEL $$

(☏809-522-3871; hotelcaribani@gmail.com; cnr Calles Sánchez 12 & San Tomé; s/d RD$1200/1400; 🅿❄🛜) Adequate as a place to lay your head for the night, the Caribani is conveniently located only one block from the northwestern edge of Parque Duarte. The basic, dim rooms have cable TV, air-con and the standard safe box in the bathroom – however, the front desk isn't helpful, so bring your patience and don't expect them to move a muscle if something isn't working.

Pala Pizza   ITALIAN $$

(cnr Calles Duarte & Sánchez; mains RD$200-275, pizzas RD$255-715; ◎lunch & dinner) Yes, it's a chain, but this is Baní and locals swear it's better than anything else nearby. Think of it as a Dominican Pizza Hut: there's perfectly decent pizza, but also loads more, like tacos, calzones, pasta, burgers and a surprisingly good brownie with ice cream. Staff even apologized for not having a lime for our margarita – try getting that at Pizza Hut.

Supermercado Daneris (cnr Calle Mella & Vladislao Guerrero; ◎7:30am-9pm Mon-Sat, 8am-noon Sun), a small grocery for food and other supplies, is two blocks south of Parque Central.

ℹ Information

Banco León (cnr Hwy Sánchez & Calle Mella)

BanReservas (cnr Calle Sánchez & Señora de Regla) One block east of the park; another is half a block east of the *gua-gua* stop for Barahona.

WORTH A TRIP

SALINAS HOTEL & RESTAURANT

You'll feel like you need a passport to visit this lovely **hotel** (☎809-866-8141; www.hotel salinas.net; 7 Puerto Hermosa; d RD$3000, d all-incl RD$6000; **P ❀ ☎ ☎**), located at the near-literal end of the road on the peninsula, 20km southwest of Baní, amid semi-arid dunes and desert, striking mountains and a postcard-blue bay – it looks more like the American southwest than the DR. All the rooms in this surprising four-story hotel with thatched roof have stunning views of the mountains across the bay, as does the restaurant – easily the best place to eat in town, with lobster (RD$700), fresh fish (RD$350) and chicken (RD$280). It's all decked out very shabby-chic with rustic furnishings and kitschy paraphernalia and antiques. The trendy new Ibiza Café even offers home-theater recliners for kicking back with a beer and a flick. Try to avoid the yellow annex across the street, which isn't nearly as charming but offers two-bedroom apartments for groups; on the other hand, you can have the full white villa (also across the street) to yourself for the same price if you're lucky – but none of the views. Sailboats are docked at the attached marina and the hotel has its own helipad, in case you plan on flying in. Otherwise, it's most easily reached by car, but there are gua-guas to Baní (RD$50, 40 minutes) that pass the hotel hourly. In Baní, they depart from the 'Asomicaba' terminal at the southern end of Av Fernando Deligne.

Centro Médico Regional (cnr Presidente Billini & Restauración) A recommended hospital four blocks east of Parque Duarte.

Farmacia Santa Ana (cnr Calles Presidente Billini & Mella; ⊙8am-11pm Mon-Sat, to 10pm Sun) On the southeast corner of the park.

Punto Net (Plaza Santana; per hr RD$25; ⊙9am-10pm Mon-Sat, to 8pm Sun) Internet cafe hidden away in Plaza Santana, half a block south of the park on Calle Mella.

❶ Getting There & Away

There are express gua-guas to Santo Domingo (RD$100, 1¼ hours, every 15 minutes from 4am to 8pm) leaving from a terminal half a block west of the main park.

Passengers wait for gua-guas to Barahona (RD$180, two hours) at the corner of a small orange food stall called Cafeteria La Paradita about 650m west of the park on Av Máximo Gómez. They pass roughly every 30 to 60 minutes from 8am to 8pm – they're coming from Santo Domingo and don't have a fixed schedule for Baní. They don't linger long here, so be sure to be on the lookout.

INLAND

Three highways lead west to the Haitian border. Fifteen kilometers west of Ázua the highway branches west to San Juan de la Maguana and the border at Elías Piña, and south to Barahona. At Barahona the road splits again – the interior road runs past Lago Enriquillo to the busy Jimaní border

post, and the southern road hugs the coast before dead-ending at Pedernales and the residential border crossing to Haiti.

Ázua

POP 88,000

Ázua is the first and largest town you'll encounter as you approach the southwest from the east, but unless you are incapacitated, sleeping here would be a quirky choice. For those on a trajectory to or from the Haitian border at Comendador/Elías Piña, Ázua might be a transit hub for buses to the interior west. Otherwise, Baní is a much more pleasant place to spend the night.

Express gua-guas to Santo Domingo (RD$150, 1¾ hours, hourly from 6am to 5pm) and regular gua-guas (RD$140, two hours, every 10 minutes from 5:15am to 7pm) leave from a terminal on Calle Duarte, on the corner opposite the park. For San Juan (RD$100, 1½ hours, every 15 minutes from 5:40am to 7pm) and the path to the Haitian border, gua-guas depart from a small 'Asodumas' terminal beside Parque 19 de Marzo, three blocks from Parque Central. Gua-guas to Barahona (RD$100) also stop here on no fixed schedule from 6:40am to 5:30pm – it's infinitely better to pick up a gua-gua for Barahona at points east of here.

Caribe Tours buses running between Santo Domingo and Barahona stop in Ázua, arriving and departing from Parque Central. If you're already in Ázua and headed to Santo

Domingo, buses depart at 7:15am, 7:30am, 10:45am, 11:15am, 2:45pm, 6:15pm and 6:30pm (RD$180).

San Juan de la Maguana

POP 73,000

San Juan de la Maguana is known as *La Ciudad de los Brujos,* the City of Shamans. Haitians are increasingly taking the places of Dominicans who move to the big city, and the Vodou influence lurks just under the Dominican-Catholic exterior. That said, if you really want to put a hex on your ex, you might have to do a little digging – most shamans live in the hills outside the city, and are definitely not tourist attractions. Otherwise, San Juan isn't a bad place to kill a night in transit. If it's your first stop, the manageable city is pleasant though certainly not typical of the country's coastal Caribbean vibe; and it's definitely not shy with its monuments – there are several worth a look at the eastern entrance to town and beyond.

✦ Festivals & Events

Sometime in May – the date varies according to the date Easter falls – San Juan's faithful mount a unique procession that showcases, among other things, the strong Haitian influence in this region. Beginning in the small town of El Batey, a procession carries a small religious figurine to San Juan, some 15km away. The procession includes drumming and chanting, and it's not uncommon for marchers to become possessed by either the Holy Spirit or Taíno ghosts, and to suddenly begin dancing around or speaking in tongues or to collapse on the ground. The festival continues for another day or so in San Juan, mostly in the plaza around the church.

◉ Sights

El Corral de los Indios   HISTORICAL SITE
Despite being lavished with such grandiose praise as 'the Stonehenge of the Dominican Republic,' this pre-Colombian site – one of the few in the Antilles – offers more theoretical shock and awe than visual. The site is composed of a circular clearing some 235m in diameter, with a 1.5m-long gray stone with a face carved on one end in the center. Research here is thin, but it's said to have originally contained two rows of block stones forming two concentric circles around the center. One theory is that it was formerly a ceremonial place for the Caonabo and Anacaona Indians as well as an astronomical instrument. Today, the only thing surrounding the center is a football and baseball field. It's located 5km north of Calle Independencia.

🛏 Sleeping & Eating

Hotels in San Juan are generally full of Dominican business travelers, and for this reason are mildly good value.

Hotel Maguana   HOTEL $
(☎809-557-2244; alejandrosuero1@hotmail.com; Av Independencia 72; s/d/tr/ste incl breakfast on weekends RD$1000/1500/1900/2000; ⓟ❋🛜) Built at dictator Trujillo's request in 1947, the Maguana's imposing facade and under-utilized interior courtyard suggest a grandeur that has now faded, but that doesn't mean it's not interesting. All the rooms have hot water and TV, although some lack windows – look before you leap – and singles are cramped. There's a great (but noisy) alfresco bar in the parking lot and a quieter interior bar. If you can afford it, ask for the Trujillo suite, where his highness used to lay his head. Breakfast is weekends only.

Hotel Nuevo Tamarindo   HOTEL $
(☎809-557-6408; hoteltamarindosjm@hotmail.com; Calle Dr Cabral 26; s/d with air-con RD$600/950, without air-con RD$400/600; ⓟ❋🛜) It's very hard to beat this hotel for value: clean, simple rooms; free coffee, international cable TV, a wi-fi signal that covers the place; a small but charming courtyard breakfast area and a location right across the street from Caribe Tours. And you can practically skip over to Maguana's popular bar.

⎡TOP⎤
CHOICE Rincón Mexicano   MEXICAN $
(☑cnr Calle 27 de Febrero & Capotillo; mains RD$65-485; ❂dinner) Owned by a real live Mexican, this large, airy restaurant pumps out authentic Mexican tacos (RD$65) that come in flour (pretty big, two should do it unless you come from a country where there is little or no good Mexican) or yellow maize tortillas (smaller, better make it three or four) filled with beef, chicken or pork. Sides include a spicy salsa that hurts it's so good. The generous sides of guacamole (RD$40) are a bargain, too. Chase it all back with an ice-cold beer and toast to your good fortune that a place this good exists in San Juan.

Il Bocconcino ITALIAN $$
(☎809-557-1616; Calle 2 No 13; mains RD$232-377, pizzas RD$174-406; ☺lunch & dinner Fri-Wed) This top-shelf pizzeria hidden (well) in a residential neighborhood near Supermercado El Detallista also runs a public swimming pool next door, where you can sit around in your swimsuit eating pizza and drinking beer. There's a quieter, more refined dining area on the second floor, where you can enjoy quality pasta. It delivers (RD$30 extra; a better option unless you have a GPS!), and charges RD$100 per person to use the pool.

D'Rojas Empanadas FAST FOOD $
(cnr Calle Independencia & Mariano Rodriguez; ☺breakfast, lunch & dinner) Quick, cheap and good, this glorified stand dishes out empanadas (RD$20) and so many fresh juices (RD$20), they didn't even want to rattle all of them off to us.

For groceries, **Hotel y Supermercado El Detallista** (☎809-557-1200; cnr Calle Trinitaria & Puello; s/d RD$900/1300/1600; [P]✳) is one-stop shopping: the best grocery store, an ATM, a Western Union branch and lodging. The downside is that it's a few blocks east of the action.

ⓘ Information

Banco León (cnr Calle Independencia & Mariano Rodríguez) This bank is two blocks west of the arch.

BanReservas (cnr Calle Independencia & 27 de Febrero) Non-fee ATMs.

Cetecom (Calle 16 de Agosto 49A btwn Mella & Colón; per hr RD$25; ☺7am-9:30pm Mon-Sat) This rambling copy shop has a few computers with internet access.

Claro/Codetel (cnr Calles 16 de Agosto & Anacaona; ☺8am-8pm Mon-Sat, to 5pm Sun) Provides telephone services.

Data Center (cnr Capotillo & Colon; per hr RD$25; ☺8am-10pm) Biggest and fastest internet cafe in town, two blocks south of Calle Independencia.

Farmacia Centro (cnr Calle Trinitaria & Dr Cabral; ☺8am-10pm) The best pharmacy in town, attached to the Centro Medico San Juan, a good bet for medical help.

Lavandaria Montillo 2 (Calle Independencia; ☺8am-11pm Mon-Sat) Same-day service laundromat.

Policia Nacional (national police; ☎809-557-2380; cnr Calle Independencia & Dr Cabral;

☺24hr) Located one block west of the large white arch at the east entrance of town.

Post Office (Calle Mella btwn Calles Independencia & 16 de Agosto)

ⓘ Getting There & Around

When the highway hits the town, it splits into two one-way streets – the westbound street is Calle Independencia, and the eastbound is Calle 16 de Agosto. A large white arch modeled on the Arc de Triomphe in Paris stands dramatically at the eastern entrance of the city. At the western end of town is San Juan's large plaza, with a pretty cream-colored church on one side and a school of fine arts on the other.

Caribe Tours (☎809-557-4520) has a terminal 75m west of Hotel Maguana next to Pollo Rey. Buses to Santo Domingo (RD$260, 2½ hours) depart at 6:30am, 10:15am, 1:45pm and 5:30pm.

Gua-guas for Santo Domingo (RD$250, 3½ hours, every 25 minutes from 3am to 6:30pm) leave from the 'Tenguerengue' terminal three blocks east of the arch, just west of the Shell gas station. There are three express buses (RD$250, 6:30am, 9:30am and 3pm), which make the trip a half-hour faster because they don't make a food stop along the way.

Transporte de Valle (☎809-557-6200) runs a bus (RD$230) at 3am to Santo Domingo, arriving around 6:30am, and can pick you up from your hotel, in addition to departures every 30 minutes from 7am to 6pm.

If you are going to Barahona, you can take any of the four Caribe Tours buses to Ázua (RD$80, one hour) and catch a Barahona-bound bus there. Alternatively, take a Santo Domingo *gua-gua* and get off at Cruce del Quince (RD$100, 50 minutes), the main highway intersection 15km west of Ázua, and catch a southbound *gua-gua* from there.

For Comendador/Elías Piña, express (RD$120, 1½ hours) and regular (RD$100, 2½ hours) buses depart every 20 minutes from 7am to 6pm from the *gua-gua* stop at the far western end of town, past the Mesopotamia bridge. You can walk with a pack, but probably not with luggage. Head out of town west on Calle Caonabo, four blocks north of Calle Independencia. Additionally, make absolutely sure your bus is going all the way to Elías Piña: if there aren't enough passengers, they may dump you halfway (at Las Matas) and you'll have to wait for another bus to come through (or pay a premium for a taxi). A taxi direct to the border for up to five passengers costs RD$1800.

Taxis and *motoconchos* may be found near Parque Central. You can also call a *taxi* (☎809-557-6400).

Comendador del Rey (Elías Piña)

POP 26,000

Comendador del Rey, or Comendador for short, is the official name of the border town west of San Juan. However, almost everyone who doesn't live there calls it Elías Piña, which is the name of the state, and you'll have more luck using that name anywhere but in town. Comendador is best known for the Haitian market held there every Monday and Friday, when hundreds of Haitians arrive on donkeys and on foot to sell their wares.

Comendador also has a major military base and a police headquarters, and security (aimed at preventing illegal Haitian immigration) is tight. Even foreign travelers may find themselves detained and questioned if not carrying their passport (it has happened to us).

For more information on crossing the border see p252.

◉ Sights

The **Haitian market** is impossible to miss; just stay on the main road through town until you run into it. Vendors lay their goods out on the ground, shaded by large plastic tarps suspended from every available tree, road sign and telephone pole. Cooking utensils, clothing, shoes, fruits and vegetables are the primary items, sold for as little as 50% of the normal price. There's not much in the way of handicrafts, since few tourists attend the market, but just wandering around and taking in the scene is worthwhile. (And who knows, maybe you'll see a colander you like.)

⬛ Sleeping

If you get stuck here there's one serviceable hotel-cum–hardware store.

Casa Teo Hotel y Ferretería HOTEL **$**
(☑809-345-9532; cnr Calles Santa Teresa & Las Mercedes; s/d with fan RD$300/500, tr with aircon RD$1000; ❋) Every border town should have one of these places – for all your holiday hardware needs! It faces the park and is predictably prison cell–like.

❶ Information

For emergencies, contact the **Policía Nacional** (☑809-527-0290; cnr Calles 27 de Febrero & Las Mercedes; ☺24hr). There is no tourist police office here. BanReservas has a 24-hour ATM at its branch office located at a traffic circle near the market on the west end of town. There is a public hospital at the eastern entrance of the town, near the military base, but really, you are better off moving on to San Juan unless you're at death's door. There's a small **taxi service** (☑809-839-4420; ☺8am-midnight).

❶ Getting There & Away

The highway splits into two one-way streets when it enters town. The westbound street is Calle Santa Teresa and the eastbound is Calle 27 de Febrero. Almost everything you need is on or near those two streets. The park is at the eastern end of town, between Calles Las Carreras and Las Mercedes. There's a large traffic circle at the western end of town, at which point the roads merge again and lead to the Haiti-DR border, about 2km away.

The main *gua-gua* terminal is on Av 27 de Febrero, at the eastern end of the main park. Buses leave from here for Santo Domingo (RD$400, four hours) every 30 minutes from 2am to 6pm. If you're just going to San Juan (RD$120, one hour), take one of the *gua-guas* parked just outside the terminal, as the Santo Domingo bus doesn't officially stop in San Juan. For Barahona, take a Santo Domingo bus to Cruce del Quince (the main highway intersection 15km west of Ázua; RD$200, two hours) and then catch a southbound bus from there. Or use Caribe Tours – see p199 for details.

PENÍNSULA DE PEDERNALES

The Península de Pedernales contains some of the most outstanding attractions of the Dominican Republic: Bahía de Las Águilas, Laguna Oviedo and Parque Nacional Jaragua; Cachóte; and world-class birdwatching in the Parque Nacional Sierra de Bahoruco. Tourism in this part of the country is shockingly low, so much so that conspiracy theorists in the area think a southeastern tourism mafia somehow controls the lack of flights into Barahona's airport. If you do come – and you absolutely should – you will quickly feel their pain.

The peninsula was originally a separate island, but tectonic movement pushed it north and upward into Hispaniola, closing the sea channel that once ran from Port-au-Prince to Barahona, and creating many of the unique geographical features you'll see today.

The southwest is the best place on the island to go birdwatching, as you can see nearly all the endemics here. At last count, there are roughly 306 known birds in the DR and 31 endemic birds on the island. Half of these birds are migratory, making winter the best time to spot them.

☞ Tours

TOP CHOICE **Ecotour Barahona** ECOTOURS
(☏809-856-2260; www.ecotourbarahona.com; apt 306, Carretera Enriquillo 8, Paraíso) This experienced, professional French-owned tour company has been pioneering tourism in the southwest since 2004. It offers good day trips to Bahía de Las Águilas, Isla Cabritos, Laguna Oviedo, Cachóte and Hoyo de Pelempito. It also offers a handful of day hikes in the hills around Paraíso, and can organize one-day and multiday horseback-riding tours. The owners and their small group of guides are trilingual. All day trips cost US$75 and include an excellent three-course picnic lunch.

Those seeking to leave the beaten path in the dust will be interested in the 14-day hikes, which take you to some of the most remote and beautiful portions of the southwest, places that require several days' walk or mule-ride to get to. These run three to four times a year (usually Christmas, February and Easter), and aren't cheap, but they will give you a comprehensive survey of all the best of the southwest. Ecotour Barahona also offers a number of shorter, three- to four-day trips, including one to Isla Beata.

Tody Tours BIRDWATCHING
(☏809-686-0882; www.todytours.com; Santo Domingo) The only birdwatching tour company based in the DR. The expatriate American owner lives in Santo Domingo but runs tours on demand to the southwest. She has more than 10 years' experience as a guide and charges US$200 per day plus expenses; all transportation, food and accommodations are organized for you. A minimum booking of a week is preferred. The company also owns and runs a remote birdwatching camp, Villa Barrancoli.

Barahona

POP 78,000
Barahona is an unavoidable eyesore on an otherwise dramatically beautiful coast, full of industrial smokestacks and of little interest to travelers. A growing number of quality, good-value accommodations sit along the coastal road between here and Paraíso,

making it somewhat unavoidable when exploring the region. It's home to the only ATM until Pedernales, so, you'll need to come here to get cash; and it's also a necessary transfer point if you're traveling by bus, but that doesn't mean you need to wear out your welcome.

History

By Dominican standards, Barahona is a young city, founded in 1802 by Haitian general L'Ouverture as a port to compete with Santo Domingo. For over a century, residents mostly made their living taking what they could from the Caribbean Sea, but today fishing accounts for only a small part of Barahona's economy. The dictator Rafael Trujillo changed everything when he ordered many square kilometers of desert north of town converted into sugarcane fields for his family's financial benefit. More than three decades after his assassination, the thousands of hectares of sugarcane continue to be tended, only now they are locally owned and benefit the community.

🛏 Sleeping

Unless you're after dirt-cheap budget accommodations, there's no reason to stay in the city itself. Far better are the numerous hotels that string themselves along the coast south of Barahona on the road to Paraíso.

TOP CHOICE **Hotel Loro Tuerto** GUESTHOUSE $$
(☏809-524-6600; www.lorotuerto.com; Av Delmonte 33; s/d RD$1300/1500; ❉🖥) Rooms at this charming nine-room guesthouse aren't notably less simple than elsewhere, but it runs circles around the competition in character. Frida Kahlo reproductions dot the walls and rooms empty out into a peaceful courtyard with hammocks. There's a seriously charismatic cafe in the front (mains RD$150 to RD$250) that does breakfast, too. The one downside is it's on noisy Av Delmonte.

Hotel Cacique GUESTHOUSE $
(☏809-524-4620; Calle Peña Gómez 2; s with fan RD$350, s/d/tr with air-con RD$750/1100/1250; ❉🖥) A good-value cheapie, especially if you're traveling solo and willing to forgo air-con, though it's a doubtful fit for the *cacique* (headman of the tribe). Expect fairly clean rooms, cable TV, hot water (in the afternoon, when you least need it), precariously balanced shower curtains,

ℹ CASH

Stock up on cash in Barahona – it's the last ATM for more than 100km. But if you have to return from the south for cash, you don't have to come all the way into town. There is a BanReservas at the Isla gas station on the southern entrance to town.

dreadfully sweet (though free) coffee and wi-fi. There is a little too much local foot traffic from family and friends for our tastes, though the night stayed surprisingly quiet. Good location.

Gran Hotel Barahona HOTEL **$**
(☎809-524-2415; Calle Jaime Mota 5; s/d/tr RD$1107/1392/1566; P❄🏊🌐) Near Parque Central and several restaurants, banks and internet cafes, it's a step up from Cacique – but not by much – other than the considerably nicer bathrooms. There's a restaurant on the premises.

✗ Eating

Los Robles CARIBBEAN, SEAFOOD **$$**
(cnr Nuestra Senora del Rosario & Av Enriquillo; mains RD$135-600; ⊘dinner Mon-Sat, lunch & dinner Sun) Among the best value in town for size, taste and price; you can have sit-down service at picnic tables on a pleasant outdoor patio, or order hefty grilled sandwiches (serious business in Barahona) from a stand-alone to-go shack. There's something for everyone – including pizzas (RD$132 to RD$500), grilled beef and chicken plates (RD$120 to RD$400) and a long list of *mofongos* (RD$135 to RD$600). The giant outdoor TV screen becomes sort of a modern outdoor movie theater.

Brisas del Caribe SEAFOOD **$$**
(Av Enriquillo 1; mains RD$275-750; ⊘breakfast, lunch & dinner) Probably Barahona's nicest option, the kitchen here dishes out fresh seafood as the seasons dictate. The perfectly sized seafood soup appetizer (RD$150) has more seafood than broth; and the fish medallions *al ajillo* (RD$350) are tasty as well, though not medallions. Its location, on a small rise about 500m north of Av Delmont, obstructs views of the green-blue Caribbean somewhat (and they are mostly of smoke stacks from nearby processing plants, anyway), so come for the *comida* not the *vista*.

Restaurant Pizzería D'Lina ITALIAN **$**
(cnr Av 30 de Mayo & Calle Anacaona; mains RD$125-550; ⊘breakfast, lunch & dinner) Has a loyal clientele who come for good pizza and friendly family service. Cheap sandwiches (RD$60 to RD$175) and various meat, chicken and seafood dishes. Filling egg breakfasts are good value, too.

Stock up on rations for travels further south at **Supermercado H y M** (cnr Peña Gómez & Padre Billini; ⊘8am-8pm Mon-Sat, till 1pm Sun).

☆ Drinking & Entertainment

Los Robles (cnr Nuestra Senora del Rosario & Av Enriquillo; ⊘5pm-late) and other nearby open-air restaurants are popular spots for a beer.

There are two discos duking it out around Parque Central. The old standby, **Lotus** (cnr Calle Padre Billini & Nuestra Senora del Rosario; cover Fri RD$50; ⊘to 1am Sun, Wed & Thu, to 3am Fri & Sat), spins the latest merengue, salsa and *bachata* hits and gets very crowded. **Atlantic Café** (Calle Jaime Mota 20; ⊘to 4am Wed, to 3am Fri & Sat, to 1am Sun) is slightly more relaxed but with enough shine to explode a disco ball. Karaoke Wednesdays are popular. Everybody goes to both, including prostitutes.

ℹ Information

Banco Popular (cnr Calles Jaime Mota & Padre Billini) Right at Parque Central. Has a 24-hour ATM.

BanReservas (cnr Calles Peña Gómez & Padre Billini) Two blocks around the corner from Banco Popular. Has a 24-hour ATM.

Centro de Llamadas (Calle Nuestra Señora del Rosario; per hr RD$35) Internet and telephone; behind Lotus.

Centro Médico Regional Magnolia (cnr Calle Peña Gómez & Fransisco Vásquez; ⊘24hr emergency room) Medical services; serious cases generally get sent to Santo Domingo.

Farmacia Dotel (cnr Av Delmonte & Duverge)

GigaNet (cnr Mota & Móntez; per hr RD$50; ⊘8am-9pm Mon-Sat, to 6pm Sun) Biggest and best internet cafe in town.

Lavandaria Barahona (Calle Maria Trinidad Sanchez 16; ⊘8am-4pm Mon-Sat; per piece RD$20) Hard to find, but cheap, fast and extra-friendly laundromat – they even lump all your socks and underwear into one 'piece.'

Post Office (Parque Central)

❶ Getting There & Away

The highway enters town from the west; after a large traffic circle with a prominent square arch, it becomes Av Luís E Delmonte and Barahona's main drag.

Air

Aeropuerto Internacional María Móntez is located 10km north of town. There were no commercial flights when we were there.

Bus

There is frequent *gua-gua* service to all points of the compass during daylight hours. Many *gua-guas* leave near the corner of Av Delmonte at Calle Padre Billini. You can also pick up southbound *gua-guas* at a stop on the highway at the southern end of town. *Gua-guas* generally leave every 15 to 30 minutes during daylight hours.

There's frequent express service to Santo Domingo (RD$250, 3½ hours, hourly from 6:30am to 6pm) leaving from the 'Sinchomiba' terminal on Av Casandra Damirón near the northwestern entrance to town. Regular service (RD$225, four hours, every 20 minutes from 4am to 7pm) also departs from here. For routes south and west along the coastal highway to Paraíso (RD$100, one hour) and Pedernales (RD$180, two hours, until 5pm), *gua-guas* depart from the corner of Calle 30 de Mayo and Av Delmonte. *Gua-guas* head west to the border at Jimaní from Calle María Móntez just north of Calle Colón (RD$170, two hours, every 45 minutes from 7am to 4pm). It's also possible but difficult to visit Isla Cabritos via *gua-gua* – take any bus to Neyba (RD$100, 1¾ hours, every 20 minutes from 6am to 6pm) from the corner of Calle Padre Billini and Av Delmonte and transfer for a La Descubierta-bound bus (RD$100, 40 minutes).

For San Juan de la Maguana, take any non-*expreso* Santo Domingo–bound *gua-gua* and get off at the Cruce del Quince (15km west of Ázua; RD$100), and wait at the junction for a westbound bus to San Juan (RD$100, 1½ hours).

Caribe Tours (☑809-524-4952; cnr Peña Gómez & Calle Apolinar Perdomo) has 1st-class service to Ázua (RD$60, one hour) and Santo Domingo (RD$260, 3½ hours) departing at 6:15am, 9:45am, 1:45pm and 5:15pm.

❶ Getting Around

Barahona is somewhat spread out, though the area around the center is navigable by foot. For points further afield, taxis and *motoconchos* can be found beside the Parque Central and along Av Delmonte, or call the local **taxi association** (☑809-524-4003).

Don't take *motoconchos* after dark along the coastal road – that's just asking for trouble.

South of Barahona
◉ Sights & Activities

Bahoruco & La Ciénaga   VILLAGES

The adjoining seaside villages of Bahoruco and La Ciénaga are 17km south of Barahona, and are typical of the small communities along the east coast of the Península de Pedernales, with friendly local residents and a gravelly beach used more for mooring boats than bathing.

Especially in La Ciénaga, after dark almost any night of the week you're likely to find small, no-name *colmados* (small bars) and discos pumping the merengue out to the stars, and people drinking and dancing out of doors. If you decide to join them you'll likely be the only gringo in the place.

San Rafael   SWIMMING HOLE

Three kilometers south of Bahoruco and La Ciénaga is the town of **San Rafael** (population 5300), notable for several awesome highway **vista points** on either side of town, and for Balneario San Rafael – natural and artificial swimming holes in the river, which are popular with local kids and families. You'll see one set of pools right alongside the highway at the rather fancy Comedor Josefa – 100m north (downhill) from there is an unmarked dirt road leading to a second set of pools nearer the ocean. Fifty meters in the other direction, a steep paved road leads to **Villa Miriam** (⊙8am-6pm; admission RD$100), another swimming area that has several natural pools (with some help from sandbags) and a regular swimming pool.

Paraíso   BEACH

About 35km south of Barahona is the aptly named town of Paraíso (population 13,500), with a spectacular beach and mesmerizing ocean – who knew there could be so many shades of blue? Paraíso is a good budget alternative to Barahona, and is walking distance (or *motoconcho* distance) to the *balneario* (swimming hole) at Los Patos. If you're driving, be sure to check out the mirador (lookout) just north of town – the views of the beach and ocean are jaw-dropping.

The **beach** directly in front of town has a fair amount of litter and numerous boats moored there. There are much better spots several hundred meters outside of town – follow the shady coastal road south and look for small paths through the brush. As elsewhere, much of the beach is covered in

WHERE TO FIND THE BLUE STUFF

There are two small artisan shops selling handmade larimar jewelry along the coastal road. **C & A Larimar Gift Shop** (☎829-266-1670; ☺8am-6pm) is located just off the main coastal highway as you drive south, about 17km south of Barahona, near Bahoruco. It's just before the little baseball 'diamond,' just off the turn-off for Casa Bonita.

The other, **Vanessa's Gift Shop** (☎809-842-2713; ☺vary), is along the beachside road that goes through Bahoruco and La Ciénega. Once you enter Bahoruco on the main highway, you'll pass the baseball 'diamond,' cross a bridge and there will be an unsigned road that goes to your left along the beach. Follow that road to the beach for a half-mile, pass Restaurant Luz on your left, and you'll come to the gift shop on your right.

In addition to the handmade larimar jewelry they both have for sale, they'll admit you to their workshop out back and let you make your own larimar souvenir. An artisan will use a wet saw to cut a general shape to your taste, then guide you in shaping and polishing the stone. The cost ranges from RD$500 to RD$700 depending on the size of the raw piece.

Beachcombers may also find their own larimar stones on the beach. The river that runs near the mine meets the sea at Playa Bahoruco, a short walk from town. After heavy rains especially, there's a good chance you'll find a larimar stone or two washed up onto the sand.

white stones, but there are several patches of fine sand where you can lay out a towel.

TOP CHOICE Los Patos
BEACH, SWIMMING HOLE

If humans coveted polished-stone beaches rather than those of floury sands, the small hamlet of Los Patos would be Eden. **Playa Los Patos,** a pretty white-stone beach, and its adjacent *balneario,* larger and more attractive than Balneario San Rafael, are idyllic traveler finds. The water here flows clear and cool out of the mountainside, forming a shallow lagoon before running into the ocean. Small shacks serve good, reasonably priced food and cold *cerveza,* making this an easy place to kill a day. On weekends it's crowded with Dominican families, but is much less busy midweek.

🛏 Sleeping & Eating

Given the overall sense of isolation in this part of the country, it makes sense that most of the hotels along the Barahona–Paraíso coastal highway also have their own restaurants, which are generally excellent and open to nonguests.

TOP CHOICE Casa Bonita
HOTEL $$$

(☎809-476-5059; www.casabonitadr.com; Carretera Km 17; r incl breakfast US$252; P❄@🛜🏊) Formerly the vacation retreat of a wealthy Dominican family – and now run by the daughter along with her American husband, a former New York City chef – Casa Bonita

is set on a hill with stunning Caribbean and mountain views in all directions. It is easily the most remarkable hotel in the southwest and is vying with Peninsula House (p129) for the best in the country. Rooms aren't lavish but are modestly stylish, all with views, and are just a short walk to the stunning infinity pool, Jacuzzi and hammock-strung gardens. The restaurant is steeped in sustainability, with everything plated coming from its own organic vegetable garden or sourced locally. Specialties include a remarkable baked artisanal cheese (RD$350) from Polo and organic lemongrass filet of beef (RD$650); and there's a stunning cocktail menu (RD$250 to RD$300). Of course, organic coffee from Polo is standard. There's a new spa treatment and yoga pavilion tucked deep in the forest, set to a soundtrack of a small stream. Refined. Personal. Perfect!

Hotel Casablanca – Campo Suizo
B&B $

(☎809-471-1230; www.hotelcasablanca.com.do; Carretera Km 10, Juan Esteban; s/d/tr US$45/ 60/80; P🛜) This small, Swiss-owned B&B offers this coast's most personalized style and service in this price range. Six simple but comfortable rooms are set in a well-tended garden. All rooms have a fan, a clean bathroom and either a king-size bed or a queen and twin, decked out in unobtrusive pastels. Fifty meters away a beautiful curving cliff provides a dramatic view of the Caribbean, and stairs down one side lead to a narrow beach that's mostly rocky but has some nice sandy spots. The included breakfast is one of the best you'll have in the entire country. Ditto for dinner – even if you aren't staying here, consider phoning ahead in the morning to reserve a spot – the owner is one of the peninsula's best cooks!

Rancho Platón RANCH $$$
(☎809-683-1836; www.ranchoplaton.com; all-incl d US$170-195; P⛵♨) If you're looking for the anti–Punta Cana experience, this is it. This wonderful rustic country retreat sits about 7km west of Paraíso on a rough road that crosses several rivers. A 20m-high waterfall drops right next to the main building, where an artificial pool has been built. There are enormous stands of bamboo throughout the property and it's perfect for families – there's a 25m-high water slide and several swing ropes in addition to activities like horseback riding, tubing and hiking. Rooms are rustic-luxe, built log cabin-style and tied together with coiled rope for support. A new renovation offers at least two 15m-high villa treehouses surrounded by a massive palm forest. It was closed when we came through, but set to reopen in 2011. Transportation and three meals included in price. Bring mosquito repellent.

Playazul RESORT $$
(☎809-454-5375; playazulbarahona@hotmail.com; Carretera Km 7; s/d/tr incl breakfast RD$1500/ 2200/2900; P✳☀♨) This French-run mini-resort is good value but comes across as too casual, with the front desk staff exuding a sense of nonchalance that borders on untrained. Still, rooms are tastefully decorated and floored in blue tile, the beds comfortable and the shower has reliable hot water. The hotel is built on a bluff with great ocean views, and sturdy concrete slabs lead down to a pretty (though rocky) private beach. Room price includes breakfast in the French-influenced restaurant (mains US$5 to US$15), which is also popular with nonguests.

Hotel Comedor Calibre HOTEL, RESTAURANT $
(☎809-243-1192; Calle Arzobispo Meriño 16, Paraíso; s/d with fan RD$800/1200, with air-con RD$1200/1600; P✳) This small budget hotel in the center of Paraíso is two blocks from the beach and offers a significant step up from Hotel Paraíso. The family splits the duties: Mom runs the simple but good seafood-heavy restaurant (mains RD$310 to RD$450), daughter handles the hotel, with well-kept rooms and bathroom, hot water and cable TV. There's a pleasant courtyard and TV room poolside and

CACHÓTE – FOGGY MOUNTAIN BREAKDOWN

About 25km (1½ hours' drive) west of Paraíso on an impressively bad road – you ford the same river half a dozen times – sit the remote cabins of Cachóte. At 1400m you're in the heart of Caribbean cloud forest. It's here that seven rivers spring from the ground to supply the coastal towns below.

In order to protect the water supply, coffee-growing was ended in the 1990s, and today, with the help of Peace Corps volunteers, cabins have been constructed and short trails built in the regenerating forest.

The cabins themselves are rustic but comfortable, and each has one large queen-size bed and a triple-decker dormitory-style bunk. Prices are skewed toward large groups – one to four people pay RD$1500 per cabaña per night, RD$3000 per cabaña per night for groups of five to nine, and RD$4500 per cabaña per night for groups of up to 12. You can camp for RD$200 per person per night. Transportation and meals (RD$200 to RD$500) are not included in the price. Contact **Ecoturismo Comunitario Cachóte** (☎829-721-9409; soepa.paraiso@yahoo.com); be sure to give them at least two weeks' notice that you're coming, but even then they are not the most accommodating. You are better off contacting Ecotour Barahona (p201), which runs a day-trip to Cachóte (US$75), stopping at the small communities along the way. You'll pass from dry coastal plains up through a large coffee-, citrus- and mango-growing region into cloud forest at the top. It can also arrange overnight stays.

Unless you're a professional off-road rally driver we don't recommend trying to drive here yourself. Those sufficiently foolhardy, however, should look for the turn-off in the village of La Ciénega. There is no sign but it's the only road leading west into the mountains.

ℹ PLANNING

Fifteen kilometers south of Paraíso (and 54km south of Barahona) is the typical Dominican town of Enriquillo, notable for having the last few hotels and gas station until Pedernales, some 82km away.

hospitality here is without a doubt more appreciative and welcoming.

Hotel Paraíso   HOTEL $
(☏809-243-1080; dohasa@hotmail.com; Carretera Km 34, Paraíso, cnr Av Gregorio Luperón & Calle Doña Chin; r with fan RD$800, with air-con RD$1200; P☀☲) Color us unimpressed. This old standby is resting on its laurels but with so few likable options in Paraíso, it apparently can. Rooms are fine – clean, comfortable and new bathrooms (half with hot water) – until you realize nothing works. Our cable was out, the tepid shower barely registered above a trickle and the air-con wasn't even hooked up. They do, however, mean well – the owner is a hospitable dude – and get points for prompt and friendly coffee service and good pillows.

⎡TOP⎤ Hotelito Oasi Italiana   ITALIAN $
(☏829-926-9796; www.lospatos.it; Carretera Km 37, Los Patos, Calle José Carrasco; mains RD$250-500; P☀☲☎) While this Italian-owned hotel does offer a few rooms (doubles including breakfast from RD$1200), the real star of the show here is the food. It's not gourmet, but simple food, well prepared – great pastas, some made here (lasagna), some imported from Italy; fresh fish, pizza priced Italian-style (according to size, not ingredients), and even homemade polenta (the owner-chef is from Verona). Our lovely penne *matriciana* was a tad salty, but in a 'Holy shit, salt is good!' sort of way. Set on a rise a few hundred meters from the beach, there are choice views over the sea, but the rooms, despite a retro Italian/funky vibe, don't capitalize on the same money shot.

Restaurante Luz   SEAFOOD, DOMINICAN $
(mains RD$180-400; ⊙breakfast, lunch & dinner) On the coastal road in the adjoining villages of Bahoruco and La Ciénaga, this good option has a tidy second-floor dining room overlooking the shore, and a nice ocean breeze. It's old school Dominican, with three portly ladies running the show. Seafood is the main option here, including grilled fish

and *lambi* (conch). All dishes come with rice and beans.

ℹ Information

One of the few reliable places for internet outside of Barahona, **Guanaba.net** (Calle Duarte 35, La Ciénaga; www.guanaba.net; per hr RD$40; ⊙8am-8pm Mon-Sat, to 9:30pm Sun) has 10 computers with a good satellite link, plus a few headphones. **Paradi-Net** (Calle Gaston Deligne, Paraíso; per hr RD$40; ⊙8am-10pm), several blocks up the hill from the sea, has a few computers and a laptop cable. For medical emergencies, there's the **Clínica Amor el Prójimo** (Calle Arzobispo Noel), also in Paraíso, with a doctor and nurse on call 24 hours per day.

ℹ Getting There & Away

The *gua-gua* stop in Paraíso is on the highway at Calle Enriquillo, 1km uphill from the beach. From here you can get buses north to Barahona (RD$100, 40 minutes, every 20 minutes). Southbound *gua-guas* to Enriquillo (RD$50, 15 minutes), Laguna Oviedo (RD$100, 45 minutes) and Pedernales (RD$150, 1½ hours) pass by roughly every 30 minutes between 7am and 7pm. Santo Domingo–bound express buses from Pedernales pass through here at 4am and 2:30pm (RD$300, four hours). If you want a guaranteed seat on either, you'll need to put your name on a list at the office of **Transportes Cuchi** (☏809-243-1270; Calle Arzobispo Noel 41, Paraíso) in town near the Orange shop. The morning bus will pick you up at your hotel, the afternoon loads at the *malecón*.

Larimar Mine

All larimar in the DR – and, indeed, the world – comes from this one mine. Discovered in 1974 by Miguel Méndez, the name comes from Larissa (Méndez's daughter) plus *mar* (sea). Its scientific name is blue pectolite.

The mining operations are done not by a large mining concern but by a small collective of individual miners. You can visit the mines and even go down some of the mine shafts. A small group of basic shacks sells cut-rate larimar jewelry at the mine, and a few no-name eateries sell food and drink to the miners.

To get there, look for the turn-off in the small hamlet of El Arroyo, 13km south of Barahona (3km north of Bahoruco). There's no sign, but there is a European Commission sign referring to the mine. It's an hour's drive on a rough road (4WD absolutely required). Ecotour Barahona offers a tour here (US$75). Alternatively, take a *gua-gua* to the turn-off early in the morning; you may be able to hitchhike in with one of the miners.

Oviedo and Pedernales buses can drop you at the park entrance. The last bus back to Barahona passes by around 4pm, but try not to cut it that close.

Parque Nacional Jaragua

The largest protected area in the country, **Parque Nacional Jaragua** (admission Dominican/foreigner RD$50/100; ☻8am-5pm) is 1400 sq km. The park includes vast ranges of thorn forest and subtropical dry forest and an extensive marine area that spans most of the southern coastline, including Laguna Oviedo, Bahía de Las Águilas and the islands of Isla Beata and Alto Velo.

LAGUNA OVIEDO

This hypersalinic lake, separated from the ocean by a thin 800m-wide strip of sand, is a popular birdwatching destination, and home to a small colony of flamingos, which swells in population during winter. You're also likely to spot ibis, storks and spoonbills, especially in late spring and early summer. The enormous, 1-ton *tinjlare* turtle comes here from April to June to lay and hatch its eggs, but can mostly be seen only very late at night.

You can take a boat tour from the **visitors center** (☎829-305-1686; ☻6am-6pm). A 2½-hour tour costs RD$2000 per boat (up to eight people), including a Spanish-speaking guide, plus there's the national park entrance fee (Dominican/foreigner RD$50/100). The tour includes a brief visit to a small Taíno cave, plus a short walk across the dividing strip to the ocean and the beach there, a beautiful yellow strand marred by an unbelievable quantity of plastic flotsam and jetsam – broken buckets, empty bleach bottles and the occasional light bulb. Wear shoes. If you're especially interested in turtles, arrange a tour with **Francisco Saldaña Cuevas** (☎829-808-8924).

There are two viewing platforms – one at the shore behind the visitors center, another on the biggest of the 24 or so islands in the lake, where you'll also find lots of big, beefy iguanas. So salty is the lake that in the dry season you'll see crystallized salt mixed with the sand on the islands.

Ecotour Barahona offers a day-trip here (US$75).

There's a well-marked entrance to the park and lagoon off the coastal highway about 3km north of the town of Oviedo.

Isla Beata & Alto Velo

These are end-of-the-world spots, difficult to access but seductive because of their remoteness. They are challenging for independent travelers to visit, and can be enjoyed more fully by taking a tour.

Isla Beata, once home to a prison for political dissidents under the dictatorship of Trujillo in the 1950s, remains under joint management of the military and the Parque Nacional Jaragua. The small fishing village of **Trudille** sits directly on **Playa Blanca**, a 40km-long white-sand beach full of iguanas. The prison was destroyed after Trujillo's assassination but you can still visit the ruins.

Alto Velo is a smaller, uninhabited island 1½ hours further south of Isla Beata. It's the southernmost point in the DR. Windswept and covered in bird droppings (from the swarms of seagulls that live there), there's a lighthouse at the highest point of the island (250m). It's a two-hour return walk (about 2.5km each way) with amazing views. There's no beach though.

The best way to visit the islands is to take a tour with Eco Tour Barahona, which offers a day-trip to Isla Beata (US$140 per person, minimum six), with the option of adding a night in Las Cuevas; and trips to Alto Velo on a private basis.

Pedernales

POP 14,000

The coastal highway dead-ends in Pedernales. Haiti is reachable through a residential street and border post about 1.5km from central Pedernales. Otherwise, this end-of-the-road town is principally of interest to those wanting to linger at Bahía de Las Águilas or in the national parks nearby.

The **Asociación de Guias de Natu-raleza de Pedernales** (AGUINAPE; ☎809-214-1575) will be of most interest to travelers without their own vehicles, as the group can organize transportation to and from both Bahía de Las Águilas (RD$1800 up to six people) and Hoyo de Pelempito (RD$3000 up to 12 people).

DON'T MISS

BAHÍA DE LAS ÁGUILAS

If you believe in fairy-tale utopian beaches, like those championed in such fictional tales as Alex Garland's *The Beach*, or films like *The Blue Lagoon* or *Y Tu Mamá También*, Bahía de Las Águilas fits the bill. It is a pristine masterpiece located in the extremely remote southwestern corner of the DR – not on the way to anything else – but those who do make it are rewarded with 10km of nearly deserted beach forming a slow arc between two prominent capes.

To get there, take the paved (and signed!) road to Cabo Rojo, about 12km east of Pedernales. You'll reach the port of Cabo Rojo after 6km. Continue following the signs to Bahía de Las Águilas (the road turns nasty after Cabo Rojo but it's manageable – *slowly* – in a normal car) to a tiny fishing community called Las Cuevas 6km after that. Note the namesake cave in the middle of the settlement – fishing folk used to live inside it. There are two ways to get to Las Águilas from here. One is to have a really good 4WD (and a driver with significant off-road experience) and attempt to drive there on a steep, pockmarked track through the coastal cactus forest. The far more spectacular alternative is to go by boat, where the ride itself is every bit as jaw-dropping as the beach. In fact, sailing past these gorgeous cliffs, with cacti clinging to the craggy edges and sea-diving pelicans, might just leave you underwhelmed by the time you touch toes to sand.

The gorgeously located restaurant **Rancho Tipico** (☎809-753-8058; rodriguez santiago3@hotmail.com; mains RD$250-700; ☺breakfast, lunch & dinner) in Las Cuevas offers tours. Prices are as follows: for groups of one to five, RD$1800 per boat; six to eight, RD$325 per person; nine to 10, RD$300 per person; 11 to 15, RD$250 per person; 16 to 20, RD$225 per person and so on. The owner also rents goggles and fins at outrageous prices: groups of one to five, US$150; six to eight, US$30 per person; nine to 12, US$25 per person. It's also an excellent restaurant, specializing in seafood and fantastic *mofongos* (try the *pulpo*) and sits on the edge of aquatic perfection.

There are also two guide associations that have sprung up. The **Pedernales guide association** (AGUINAPE; ☎809-214-1575; ☺8am-6pm), which gathers around the national park ranger station just off the parking lot in Las Cuevas, takes groups of one to five for RD$1800 per boat. For larger groups, you just pay again in increments of five people. Then there's the local **Las Cuevas guide association** (ASOTUR; ☎809-507-2294), which will take up to five people for RD$1500. You can find them milling about the small pier a few meters past Ranch Tipico. Both associations claim to include snorkeling gear in their prices, though we didn't see any. Bring your own if you can.

With all choices, you'll also need to pay the national park entrance fee (Dominican/foreigner RD$50/100). If you arrive here on your own, grouping up with others here is also a possibility, especially on weekends.

Ecotour Barahona runs a day trip here (US$75). It organizes all the logistics, picks you up and drops you off at your hotel, supplies lunch, and can show you where the best corals are to go snorkeling.

There's a very small shelter with bathrooms on the beach, and a small lookout tower, but otherwise no facilities. Camping is permitted, but be sure to bring plenty of water, food and insect repellent, and take your garbage out with you.

The wonderful **Hostal Doña Chava** (☎809-524-0332; www.donachava.com; Calle P N Hugson 5; r/tr with fan RD$750/850, with air-con RD$850/900; P✳@☎) offers simple rooms with tidy bathrooms and cable TV and wonderful common areas: there's a jungly courtyard (bring repellent) and sustainable touches all over, including organic coffee; and breakfast (RD$140 to RD$160) is available. You'll often run into biologists and NGO staff here.

Another great option nearby is **Hostal D'Óleo Méndez** (☎809-524-0414; Calle Antonio Duvergé 9; s/d RD$800/1000; P✳☎), which comes with a sense of humor. When asked if breakfast was included, the answer was, 'No, only *Buenos Días* and *Buenos Noches* is included.' Rooms have new flooring, TVs and mattresses and there's a good restaurant serving three meals. Pricier singles with pleasant balconies go for RD$1000.

There are a couple of good seafood restaurants in town. **King Crab** (Calle Dominguez 2; mains RD$195-450; ☺breakfast, lunch & dinner) and **Jalicar** (Calle Libertad; mains RD$125-250; ☺breakfast, lunch & dinner) are both recommended.

BanReservas (Calle Duarte) has the only ATM in town, but it empties out fast, especially on weekends.

Gua-guas go back and forth between Pedernales and Barahona (RD$180, two hours, hourly from 2am to 3pm). Calle 27 de Febrero leads to the Haitian border and the small village of Anse-à-Pitres, approximately 1km from the intersection near BanReservas. For more information on crossing the border, see p252.

Parque Nacional Sierra de Bahoruco

This **national park** (admission Dominican/foreigner RD$20/50; ☺8am-5pm) directly west of Barahona covers 800 sq km of mostly mountainous terrain and is notable for the rich variety of vegetation that thrives in its many different climates, from lowland desert to cloud forest. Valleys are home to vast areas of broad-leafed plants, which give way to healthy pine forests at higher elevations. In the mountains the average temperature is 18°C, and annual rainfall is between 1000mm and 2500mm. Together with Parque Nacional Jaragua and Lago Enriquillo, Parque Nacional Sierra de Bahoruco forms the Jaragua-Bahoruca-Enriquillo Biosphere Reserve, the first Unesco Biosphere Reserve in the country.

Within the national park there are 166 orchid species, representing 52% of the country's total. Around 32% of those species are endemic to the park. Flitting about among the park's pine, cherry and mahogany trees are 49 species of bird. These include the white-necked crow, which can only be seen on Hispaniola. The most common birds in the mountains are La Selle's thrush, white-winged warblers, Hispaniolan trogons and narrow-billed todies. At lower elevations, look for white-crowned pigeons, white-winged doves, Hispaniolan parakeets, Hispaniolan lizard cuckoos and Hispaniolan parrots.

Tody Tours runs a birdwatching camp near Puerto Escondido called **Villa Barrancoli** (☎809-686-0882; www.todytours

.com; Santo Domingo; camping US$2-10, food per day US$20 per group). When the camp is not otherwise in use independent travelers are welcome – be sure to give several days' notice. You'll want a good 4WD (and to know how to use it). To get there from Barahona, head to the town of Duvergé along the southern side of Lago Enriquillo. In town, turn left just past a Kenworth Parts sign and before the Yolanda Furniture store about four corners after the gas station. Follow this to Puerto Escondido (30 minutes). You'll see the park office on your right as you enter. Continue to a 'T' intersection, then turn left, following the sign to Rabo de Gato. Turn right and cross the canal. At the next fork turn right again and follow the signs to Rabo de Gato until you come to the campsite.

HOYO DE PELEMPITO

Part of Parque Nacional Sierra de Bahoruco, the 'hole' at Pelempito is actually a deep gorge formed when the Península de Pedernales jammed itself up into Hispaniola umpteen million years ago. The visitors center, perched on the edge of a cliff at 1450m, offers breathtaking views, north and east, of completely untouched national park. The cliff itself is a 600m drop.

The visitors center has information (in Spanish) on the various flora and fauna in the area, and a number of short nature walks have small signs identifying the various plants. Serious birdwatchers scoff that this is a poor birdwatching location, but for the casual tourist the views make it worth the drive.

Pelempito sits on the south side of the Sierra de Bahoruco. The turn-off is about 12km east of Pedernales. Shortly after the turn-off to Bahía de Las Águilas, you'll cross a small bridge. Immediately after, you turn left on a dirt road that swings around to the paved road north to Hoyo de Pelempito (it actually ends up being same road that leads to Bahía de Las Águilas but you'll need the opposite direction). Around 14km later, you'll come to a **ranger station** (admission RD$50; ☺9am-4:30pm). From here, the paved highway-like road continues for 6km, turning into a rutted dirt track for the last 7km. Rains frequently destroy this part of the road, so you'll need a 4WD or a very high vehicle.

WORTH A TRIP

THE POLO ORGANIC COFFEE FESTIVAL

Started in 2004, the **Festival de Café Orgánico de Polo** (Festicafé; ☏809-682-3386; www.festicafe.org) is held on the first weekend in June. From Friday to Sunday local coffee-growers celebrate the end of the coffee-harvesting season. There's live merengue and *bachata* in the evenings, and during the day stands sell coffee and typical southwestern arts and crafts. There's a 'coffee parade,' and lots of (decaffeinated) games for the kids. The organizers also lead hiking trips to remote coffee plantations in the mountains.

There's no real hotel in town, but during the festival the organizers can put you up in a spare room in someone's house – be sure to call several weeks ahead, as rooms fill up fast. You can also drive out from Barahona; it's about an hour each way.

Polo

POP 9500

The small town of Polo, nestled on the south slopes of the Sierra de Bahoruco, is the center of a major coffee- and vegetable-growing region. It's principally famous for the optical illusion on the highway 20km north of town (see opposite), and more recently for the Festival de Café Orgánico (Festicafé), which happens on the first weekend of June (see the boxed text, above).

Even if the festival's not on, various shops around town sell the coffee packaged to go – it's excellent if you take your caffeine seriously and worth the side trip if you have wheels.

From Barahona, drive 12km west to Cabral and look for the marked southbound turn-off in the middle of town (there's a flashing traffic light). From there it's about a 20km (30-minute) drive to Polo.

NORTH OF PEDERNALES

Lago Enriquillo & Isla Cabritos

Parque Nacional Isla Cabritos (☏809-880-0871; admission Dominican/foreigner RD\$30/50; ⊙8am-6pm) is named after the 12km-long desert island in the center of Lago Enriquillo, an enormous saltwater lake 40m below sea level – the lowest point of any ocean island. The lake is the remains of an ancient channel that once united the Bahía de Neyba to the southeast (near Barahona) with Port-au-Prince to the west. The accumulation of sediments deposited by the Río Yaque del Sur at the river's mouth on the Bahía de Neyba, combined with an up-ward thrust of a continental plate, gradually isolated the lake. Today it is basically a 200-sq-km inland sea with no outlet.

The park includes, oddly, just the island, and not the rest of the lake, where fishermen cast nets for tilapia, an introduced fish. The highlights are the lake's creatures, including an estimated 200 American crocodiles that can be seen at the edge of the lake. From December to April you'll also see flamingos and egrets.

The island, which varies in elevation from 40m to 4m below sea level, is a virtual desert, supporting a variety of cacti and other desert flora. In summer, temperatures of 50°C have been recorded – go early. It is home to Ricord iguanas and rhinoceros iguanas, some more than 20 years old and considerably beefier than most house cats. The island also has lots of scorpions, not to mention plenty of cacti, so wear covered shoes if possible.

There is a small visitors center here, with information on the history and geology of the island. From March to June you'll see a blooming of cactus flowers, and June sees a small swarm of butterflies.

The park entrance is about 3km east of La Descubierta. The local **guide association** (AGELE; ☏809-816-7441 for English & French) offers boat tours of the park for RD\$3500 for up to 15 people – expect a sore, wet bum (and salt stains). Be sure to call ahead – if a tour group has the boat reserved (or if a particularly festive bout of drinking took place the night before), you might be out of luck. The boat will take you to the mouth of the Río de la Descubierta – where the most crocodiles and flamingos are visible – and Isla Cabritos. The tour usually lasts two hours and the last boat departs at noon. Bring a hat and plenty of water.

A short distance east of the park entrance, look for **Las Caritas** (The Masks). On the north side of the highway, bright yellow handrails lead up to a small rock overhang with what are believed to be pre-Taíno petroglyphs. A short but somewhat tricky climb up the hillside – you'll need shoes or decent sandals – affords a close look at the pictures and a fine view of the lake. Very little is known about the meaning of the figures. Note that much of the rock here is actually petrified coral, remnants of the time the entire area was under the sea.

Ecotour Barahona offers a popular day trip to Isla Cabritos (US$75), including lunch at the swimming hole at La Descubierta and a visit to Las Caritas, the Haitian market at Jimaní, though at the time of research this was suspended due to the 2010 cholera outbreak in Haiti.

Sleeping & Eating

About 3km west of the park entrance lies the small town of La Descubierta, which is popular for its large swimming hole right in the middle of town. There's not much reason to spend the night here, but if you get stuck, **Hotel Iguana** (809-958-7636; r/ tw RD$400/500; P), on the main road west of the park, will do at a pinch. Rooms are small and simple, but also clean and quiet, with private bathrooms and better-than-expected beds. The Iguana's friendly proprietor prepares excellent home-cooked meals at a day's notice, but she will also offer to cook the day you arrive if you don't check in too late. Otherwise, there are food shacks in town, near the park and swimming hole.

Getting There & Away

You're better off driving if you're coming out this way, but you can also grab a *gua-gua* from Barahona to Neyba, and then change for any westbound *gua-gua* to the ranger station. Be sure to tell the driver that that's where you want to go, or he'll drive right past it.

Jimaní

POP 6700

This dusty border town is on the most direct route from Santo Domingo to Port-au-Prince, and is therefore the busiest of the four official border crossings. Dominicans from as far away as Santo Domingo come here for the Monday and Friday markets, where they can buy humanitarian aid (giant sacks of rice and beans and jugs of cooking oil), meant for Haitians, at rock-bottom prices. There are also a few *tiendas* selling Haitian beer (Prestige) and rum (Rhum Barbancourt), both arguably better than their Dominican counterparts. The market is just past the Dominican border post in no-man's-land. This area – including immigration posts and other border control facilities – was seriously flooded in 2010 due to the alarmingly expanding shoreline of Etang Saumâtre, Lago Enriquillo's twin lake on the Haitian side (also known as Lake Azuéi), whose southeast end sits just 1km from the border post under normal conditions. When we passed through, makeshift damming was keeping the water at bay, but it was all of 10m from the through-point.

For information on crossing the border see p252.

Sleeping & Eating

Hotel Jimaní   HOTEL $
(809-248-3139; Calle 19 de Marzo 2; r RD$1000;) On the right side of the road as you enter town from La Descubierta, this border crashpad looks a little like a small high school. Each of the 10 rooms has both twin and queen-size beds, plus cable TV (no remote) and a private cold-water bathroom, but there's no internet, no breakfast included and, quite frankly, nothing to justify the price when compared with others in the southwest. Except one minor detail: lack of competition. Who are they kidding? We checked in, checked right back out.

The hotel has a somewhat popular **restaurant** (breakfast, lunch & dinner). Otherwise, the eating options are slim, limited to

DON'T MISS

POLO MAGNÉTICO

Twelve kilometers west of Barahona is the town of Cabral and the turn-off south for nearby Polo. About 11km south of the turn-off you'll encounter a famous mirage. Put your car in neutral, let go of the brake and watch your car get 'pulled' uphill. The effect is best between the towns of El Lechoso and La Cueva, and works on a smaller scale, too – get out of the car and put a water bottle on the road. It, too, will show a mysterious desire to climb uphill.

several small, forgettable eateries along the road to Duvergé.

❶ Information

BanReservas has a 24-hour ATM and is at the west end of Calle 19 de Marzo, the main road from Neyba just before it leaves town for the Haitian border. A Banco Popular ATM is right across the street from **Farmacia Melenciano** (☺8am-10pm), on the uphill road to/from Duvergé.

❶ Getting There & Away

Jimaní is served by *gua-guas* from Santo Domingo, passing La Descubierta, Neyba and Baní along the way; and from Barahona via Duvergé and the south side of Lago Enriquillo. Both bus stops are on the sloping road that enters town from the Duvergé side. The Santo Domingo route has a proper terminal near the bottom of the hill (RD$380, five hours, every 30 to 45 minutes from 7am to 5pm). For La Descubierta, it's RD$50 and takes 30 minutes. *Gua-guas* to Barahona (RD$200, two hours, every 45 minutes from 4am to 3pm) leave from a shady corner about 200m up the hill, across from a small supermarket. Caribe Tours has a direct service from Santo Domingo to Port-au-Prince, with a stop in Jimaní (see p72).

Understand Dominican Republic

>

population per sq mile

DR   USA   UK

ŤŤ   Ť   ŤŤŤŤ
        ŤŤŤŤ

Ť ≈ 83 people

Dominican Republic Today

The Mood

» Gallon of gas: RD$160

» First-class bus Santo Domingo to Puerto Plata: RD$320

» Coconut from street vendor: RD$20-25

» Unemployment rate: over 15%

Young and old alike groan equally about corruption and lack of opportunities, though those who are hopeful of reform can take heart in the fact that the current president, Leonel Fernandez, has announced he will not pursue the constitutional changes he had been seeking that would allow him to run for a fourth term in 2012. Reformists had argued that because the judiciary branch is fairly inactive, there is already little significant check on executive power.

The Other Half

Many Dominicans still refer angrily to the Haitian occupation of their country over 160 years ago. Haitians are typically blamed for overburdened schools, insufficient healthcare and rising crime rates, especially guns, drugs and prostitution, and for taking Dominican jobs. In the aftermath of the devastating earthquake that struck Haiti in January 2010, the Dominican government provided medical and humanitarian assistance and much of the aid from other countries was shipped overland through the DR. However, the thaw in relations only lasted so long. Haiti's cholera epidemic that erupted the following year (as of April 2011, 650 people in the DR had been diagnosed with cholera and seven had died) led to the temporary closure of some border crossings, which ignited more conflict: several Haitians were killed and scores injured in protests. A rising number of incidents at the end of 2010 and beginning of 2011 left dozens of Haitians dead and hundreds injured in clashes in poor barrios around the country. Some Dominicans claiming they were trying to evict illegal Haitians say they were justified by the threat of cholera and crime. And in the beginning of February 2011, the Dominican government initiated a

Top Books

» *Dead Man in Paradise* – Canadian journalist JB Mackinnon, the nephew of a priest murdered during the Trujillo regime, tries to piece together the unsolved crime.

» *Fiesta del Chivo* (*Feast of the Goat*) – Peruvian novelist Mario Vargas Llosa's imaginative

telling of dictator Rafael Trujillo's final days.

» *The Wondrous Life of Oscar Wao* – Junot Diaz's inventive story of a self-professed Dominican nerd in New Jersey and the tragic history of his family in the DR.

Keep in Mind

» *Colmados*, an institution in Dominican life, are combination corner stores, groceries and bars.

» Car washes in the DR combine two typical local passions – automobiles and beer. These facilities serve drinks throughout the afternoon and evening.

belief systems
(% of population)

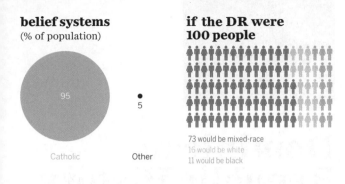

95 — Catholic

5 — Other

if the DR were 100 people

73 would be mixed-race
16 would be white
11 would be black

---

widespread crackdown, deporting 'illegal' Haitians back over the border. Haitians continue migrating to the DR in large numbers to work on the vast sugar plantations or construction (the average income is six times that of Haiti's), risking violence, discrimination and poor living conditions.

Strengths

With a past filled by strong-man dictators and corrupt politicians, the average Dominican who has learned to live through hardships approaches the present with a healthy skepticism – why should things change now? Despite this, there's a general equanimity, or at the very least an ability to appreciate the good things: family, togetherness, music and laughter. The DR earns more tourism dollars than any other country in Latin America except Mexico and Brazil. Unsurprisingly, the service industry, primarily tourism but the prosperous free-trade zone areas as well, is the largest employer and earner in the DR. Another major revenue source is remittances from Dominicans living abroad (mostly in the US) – more than one million people collectively send over US$1 billion to the DR yearly. Families are large and children are expected to help care for elders, but with so many young Dominicans leaving for the US, this creates a unique domestic stress, albeit offset somewhat by the remittances sent home.

Struggles

Many Dominicans lack electricity, while the remainder experience regular blackouts. Nearly 40% of the population lives below the poverty line, and the wealthiest 10% control 40% of the country's total economy. Women, who make up less than one-third of the DR's paid workforce, are poorly represented in government and politics as well, making up just 10% to 15% of legislator and top- or middle-level cabinet officer positions.

» Most workers on sugarcane plantations only have work during the *zafra*, the four- to six-month harvest period.

» Hammocks *(hamacas)*, canoe *(canoa)*, barbecue *(barabacoa)*, hurricane *(huracán)* are derived from words of the Taíno, the native inhabitants of Hispaniola.

Dos & Don'ts

» Do take things slowly and practice patience. Dominicans take leisurely meals and it's considered rude for a waiter to bring your bill before being asked.

» Don't confuse small buildings with signs saying 'Banca' for banks; these are where tickets for the lottery are sold.

» Don't dress down in public places – Dominicans tend to take pride in their appearance and if you do the same you'll attract less unwanted attention.

Top Films

» *Sugar* – Story of a Dominican baseball prospect's journey to minor leagues in middle America.

» *Ladrones a Domicilio* (Robbers of the House) – A political satire and slapstick comedy involving a robbery and kidnapping and corruption in everyday life.

Dominican Republic History

The rival of any country in terms of its roller-coaster history, the Dominican Republic has endured a long struggle to independence and nationhood. From 1492 when Columbus landed on the island of Hispaniola seeking a route to the East Indies as well as gold, the DR has seen wave after wave of foreign interlopers.

The destruction of the native population (see p325 for an explanation of the country's pre-colonial history) led to periods of intermittent neglect and conflicts between the French and Spanish colonial systems and their peculiar distinctions in how they went about exploiting the land and people.

One of the most important strands winding its way through Dominican history, which has shaped its identity and self-understanding more than anything, is its relationship with Haiti, its onetime invader and neighbor sharing the island of Hispaniola. More recently, decades of dictatorial and general misrule have left scars, both physical and psychological; all of these factors combined mean history feels like a constant force impinging on the country's future.

The Columbus Brothers

In 1492 Christopher Columbus sailed from Spain with 90 men in the *Pinta,* the *Niña* and the *Santa María,* bound for Asia. He sailed west rather than east, expecting to circumnavigate the globe, instead discovering the New World for the Old. After stops at the small Bahamian island of Guanahaní and present-day Cuba (which Columbus initially mistook for Japan), a mountainous landscape appeared before the explorers. Columbus named it 'La Isla Española,' 'the Spanish Island,' later corrupted to 'Hispaniola.' He made landfall at Môle St-Nicholas in modern Haiti

TIMELINE	1496	1500	1510
	Nueva Isabela founded by the Spanish. Rebuilt as Santo Domingo after a 1502 hurricane, it quickly receives a royal charter, making it the oldest European city in the New World.	Santo Domingo governor captures Christopher Columbus and returns him to Spain in shackles; Queen Isabella orders him released soon after.	King Ferdinand of Spain issues first royal charter to import slaves to Hispaniola. Demand booms, to supplement rapidly crashing Taíno workforce.

on December 7, and days later ran the *Santa María* onto a reef. Here on Christmas Day he established Villa La Navidad, the first settlement of any kind made by Europeans in the New World.

Columbus was greeted with great warmth by the Taínos, who impressed him further with their gifts of gold jewelry. Capturing a handful to impress his royal patrons, he sailed back to Spain to be showered with glory. He returned within a year, leading 17 ships of soldiers and colonists.

La Navidad had been razed by the Taínos in reprisal for the kidnappings by the settlers, so Columbus sailed east and established La Isabela on the north coast of the DR, named for Spain's queen; the first church in the Americas was erected here. However, La Isabela was plagued with disease, and within five years the capital of the new colony was moved to Santo Domingo, where it has remained.

Columbus' early administration was a disaster and appointing his brother Bartholomé proved no better. Their haphazard rule soon had the colonists up in arms, and a replacement sent from Spain returned the brothers home in chains. The colony would now be run with military harshness.

The Taínos were the ones to bear the brunt of this. They were already stricken by European illnesses that sent their numbers crashing, but on top of this Spain introduced *encomienda,* forced labor requiring the natives to dig up quotas of gold. The Spanish broke up Taíno villages, killed their chiefs and put the entire population to work. Within three decades of their first meeting with Europeans, the Taínos were reduced to a shadow of their previous numbers.

European Competition & Colonization

As Taíno civilization collapsed, so did the gold mines, and no amount of imported African slaves could make up the shortfall. Spain dropped Hispaniola as quickly as it had found it, turning its attention instead to the immense riches coming from its new possessions in Mexico and Peru. Santo Domingo was reduced to a trading post for gold and silver convoys, but couldn't even hold onto that position with the opening of new trade routes via Cuba. After the English admiral Sir Francis Drake sacked Santo Domingo in 1586, it was effectively abandoned for the next 50 years, further signaling the decline of Spanish Hispaniola.

For the next three centuries, Europe was riven by war. Imperial Spain slipped into a slow decline, and the English and French took advantage, competing not just in the Old World but in North America and the Caribbean. Hispaniola was considered a great prize. The colony was stagnating under Spanish rule. Both the English and French encouraged piracy against the Spanish, even licensing the pirates as 'privateers.' For

Christopher Columbus, Hernán Cortés, Francisco Pizarro, Juan Ponce de León and Vasco Nuñez de Balboa all spent time in what is now the DR.

COLUMBUS

1519–1533		1586	1605
A Taíno *cacique* named Enriquillo leads a rebellion against the Spanish in the Bahoruco mountains near the present-day DR-Haiti border.		Following the outbreak of war between England and Spain, Sir Francis Drake leads a devastating naval raid against Santo Domingo, leaving the city virtually razed.	Spain sends the army to relocate most of its colonists to Santo Domingo city by force, to prevent contraband trade with foreign merchants, effectively abandoning claims to western Hispaniola.

» The Alcazar de Colon

ALFREDO MAQUEZ/LONELY PLANET IMAGES©

Colonial Sites

» Zona Colonial, Santo Domingo

» Castillo de San Felipe, Puerto Plata

» La Vega Vieja, La Vega

» La Isabela, North Coast

security, the Spanish convoys sailed en masse once a year, a system that effectively cut Hispaniola off from trade with the mother country – not only were visiting ships far and few between, but the colonists were banned from trading with non-Spaniards. The colony shrank to the area around Santo Domingo, leaving the rest of the island open for the taking.

Isolated pockets of settlers were followed by soldiers. The English attempted to come in through the front door in 1655, but their army of 13,000 soldiers was somehow repelled at the gates of Santo Domingo. Years of neglect meant the 125,000-person colony missed out on the sugar rush for now (Spanish investors had preferred to put their money into booming Cuba), relying primarily on cattle ranching for its lifeblood. Slave imports had never been high, as they simply couldn't be afforded, and slaves made up less than 1% of the population.

Separation Anxiety

While France and Spain's power in Europe waxed and waned, so, too, did their imperialist ambitions. And conflict within the colonies became an avenue for waging proxy wars against their rivals. So when the enslaved African population of western Hispaniola's Saint-Domingue rose up in bloody revolt, Spain supported the revolution. However, once the French agreed to abolish slavery, the former slaves turned their attention to liberating the entire island – the Spanish colony had about 60,000 slaves of its own. Lacking the appetite, will and ability to forcefully oppose the uprising, Spain and France haggled over the details, one of which involved the injunction that Spanish colonists abdicate their lands in exchange for ones in Cuba.

In 1801, frustrated by the slow pace of negotiations, François Dominique Toussaint Louverture, a former slave and leader of the rebel forces, marched into Santo Domingo and, without French authority, declared that the abolition of slavery would be enforced throughout the island. At odds with French leaders, who now viewed him as a loose cannon, he was betrayed to the French, who sent him in chains to France, where

PIRATES OF THE CARIBBEAN

The purported remains – mostly pieces of cannons, anchors and wood – of the *Quedagh Merchant*, which belonged to the Scottish privateer Captain William Kidd, were found in the waters off Isla Catalina near the shores of the Casa de Campo resort. The ship was scuttled and set on fire after Kidd returned to England to face charges of piracy. Despite the fact that he was often acting under the authority of the English navy, he was convicted of piracy and hanged in London in 1699.

1655	1664	1821–22	1844
English military expedition dispatched by Oliver Cromwell to conquer Santo Domingo. Although beaten back, the navy saves face by managing to grab Jamaica as a permanent Caribbean foothold.	Spain cedes the western third of the island of Hispaniola to France; exact boundaries aren't established until 1929.	Colonists of Santo Domingo, known as Spanish Haiti, declare independence from Spain in November 1821, only to be invaded by Haiti nine weeks later and incorporated into a united Hispaniola.	Coalition of Santo Domingo intellectuals and rebel Haitian soldiers spark a largely bloodless coup and the Dominican Republic declares its independence from Haiti, after 22 years of occupation.

he died of neglect in a dungeon in April 1803. Jean-Jacques Dessalines, who had been one of Toussaint's chief lieutenants, crowned himself emperor of the Republic of Haiti with the clearly stated ambition of uniting Hispaniola under one flag.

For the Spanish colonists in Santo Domingo, this new imperialist threat compelled them to ask Spain to reincorporate them into the empire. But through neglect and mismanagement Spain completely bungled its administration of Santo Domingo and on November 30, 1821, the colony declared its independence once again. Colonial leaders intended to join the Republic of Gran Colombia (a country that included present-day Ecuador, Colombia, Panama and Venezuela) but never got the chance – Haiti invaded and finally achieved its goal of a united Hispaniola.

Dominicans chafed under Haitian rule for the next 22 years, and to this day both countries regard the other with disdain and suspicion. Resistance grew until February 27, 1844 – a day celebrated as Dominican Independence Day – when a separatist movement headed by Juan Pablo Duarte captured Santo Domingo in a bloodless coup. The Puerto del Conde in Santo Domingo marks the spot where Duarte entered the city. Despite the reversal of fortunes of the two countries in the 20th century, many Dominicans still view Haiti as an aggressive nation with territorial ambitions.

Fearing another invasion and still feeling threatened by Haiti in 1861, the Dominican Republic once again submitted to Spanish rule. But ordinary Dominicans did not support the move and, after four years of armed resistance, succeeded in expelling Spanish troops in what is known as the War of Restoration. (Restauración is a common street name throughout the DR, and there are a number of monuments to the war, including a prominent one in Santiago.) On March 3, 1865, the Queen of Spain signed a decree annulling the annexation and withdrew her soldiers from the island.

The *trinitaria*, a bougainvillea that blooms purple, red and magenta, also refers to Juan Pablo Duarte, Francisco de Rosario Sánchez and Ramón Mella, the three fathers of the republic, and to the secret cells of three that were organized in 1838 to struggle for independence from Haiti.

Big Sugar

After the island's gold reserves were quickly exhausted and the native population decimated, Spanish colonists harvested the first sugar crop in 1506. While the tropical climate and topography rendered it an ideal physical environment, labor was in short supply. Slaves imported from Africa rebelled and fled to the western part of the island – soon after Spain discovered sugar was being sold to France and Holland and so decided to burn all they could.

It wasn't for another several hundred years, when in the mid-19th century prosperous Cuban plantation owners began to seek out new territory, that sugar took root once again in the DR. Cuba's failed 10-

INDEPENDENCE

1849	1860s	1865	1880–1884
Buenaventura Baez begins the first of five terms – between 1849 and 1878 – as president of the DR. One of his first acts was an attempt to have his country annexed by the USA.	American businessmen in Cuba introduce the baseball game on the island and it soon becomes a Cuban pastime.	Two years after initial uprising in Santiago, triggered by the Spanish authority's continual erosion of Dominican rights, the DR gains independence by defeating Spanish troops in the War of Restoration.	A handful of modern sugar mills begin operating in San Pedro de Macorís, the start of the Dominican sugar industry.

SUGAR

year war of independence only accelerated the migration, and only when slavery was abolished in other Spanish colonies like Cuba and Puerto Rico in the 1870s could the DR begin to compete in terms of production costs.

The first steam-powered sugar mill *(ingenio)* was opened in 1879 near San Pedro de Macoris on the southeast coast. This commercial port town was soon booming, with more than a half-dozen modern plants in operation by 1920. San Pedro, which would later become synonymous with baseball, became a relatively elegant and cosmopolitan town known for its poets as well as sugar wealth. When the European sugar industry was destroyed by WWI, Caribbean suppliers stepped into the void. Sugar became the DR's leading export and the US its leading buyer.

But Dominicans, able to survive with their own small plots of land, were largely uninterested in the backbreaking, low-paying work. Companies started turning to workers from the British-speaking Caribbean islands, who were more eager for seasonal labor and disinclined to push for better pay or improved working conditions. These migrant workers from the eastern Caribbean came to be called *cocolos* and where they lived *bateys*. A backlash was inevitable – in 1919 a law was passed banning non-Caucasians from immigrating to the DR. Though thousands of *cocolos* and their families remained around San Pedro working for the mills, Haitians began to replace them during the harvest in part because it was easier for the companies to 'repatriate' them when the work was over.

When the bottom dropped out of the price of sugar on the world market in the 1930s, around the same time Trujillo came to power, the financial well-being of the industry in the DR was inextricably tied to quotas obtained through negotiations with the US. Just as he did in other sectors of the economy, Trujillo consolidated control and ownership in his family and coterie and was able to influence many members of the US Congress into supporting his regime through continued trade in sugar.

Power from the North

With no strong central government, the newly independent Dominican Republic was a fractured nation, divided up among several dozen caudillos and their militias. From 1865 until 1879 there were more than 50 military uprisings or coups and 21 changes in government. In 1869, after Buenaventura Báez, the leader of a coalition of plantation owners, mahogany exporters and a significant portion of residents of Santo Domingo, was installed as president, he attempted to sell the country to the US for US$150,000. Even though the treaty was signed by Báez and US president Ulysses S Grant, the agreement was defeated in the US Senate.

Alan Cambeira's *Azucar! The Story of Sugar* is a fascinating novel that portrays the human toll of sugar production in the DR, with much of the information, descriptions and events based on real events.

Between 1844 and 1916, the Dominican Republic had 40 different governments.

1886	1904–1905
American and Cuban sugar mill owners encourage baseball games in San Pedro de Macorís in the DR.	US Marines are sent to Santo Domingo to assist the Dominican government fighting rebels; customs collections are turned over to the US.

» Cathedral of Santa Maria la Menor, Santo Domingo

But the US was to involve itself once again in Dominican affairs, this time at the invitation of General Ulises Heureaux, who stabilized the musical chairs of political and military leadership from 1882 until his assassination in 1899. The general, known as Lilí, borrowed heavily from American and European banks to finance the army, infrastructure and sugar industry. But after a sharp drop-off in world sugar prices, Lilí essentially mortgaged the country to the US-owned and -operated San Domingo Improvement Company just before his death. Because the Dominican government was bankrupt, the US government intervened in 1905 by taking control of the customs houses and guaranteeing repayment of all loans, stopping just short of ratifying President Theodore Roosevelt's plan to establish a protectorate over the DR.

Despite some economic growth, after the assassination of another president in 1911, Dominican politics mostly remained chaotic, corrupt and bloody. In 1916, under the dual pretext of quelling yet another coup as well as guarding the waters from German aggression during WWI, President Woodrow Wilson sent the marines to the DR – they remained for the next eight years. Though deeply imperialistic, the US occupation did succeed in stabilizing Dominican politics and the economy. Once the DR's strategic value to the US was no longer important, and a new strain of isolationism had entered American discourse, the occupation ended and the troops were sent home.

Trujillo titles: Benefactor of the Fatherland, Founder and Supreme Chief of the Partido Dominicana, Restorer of Financial Independence, First Journalist of the Republic, Doctor Honoris Causa in the Economic Political Sciences.

Trujillo nicknames: Hot Balls, the Goat, the Chief, the Butcher.

The Rise of the Caudillo

Like the calm before the storm, the years from 1924 to 1930 were in many ways positive, led by a progressive president, Horacio Vásquez, whose administration built major roads and schools and initiated irrigation and sanitation programs. Vásquez did extend his four-year term to six, a constitutionally questionable move that was nevertheless approved by the Congress. When a revolution was proclaimed in Santiago, Rafael Leónidas Trujillo, chief of the former Dominican National Police (renamed the National Army in 1928), ordered his troops to remain in their barracks, effectively forcing Vásquez and his vice president from office. After a sham election in which he was the sole candidate, Trujillo assumed the presidency. Within weeks he organized a terrorist band, La 42, which roamed the country, killing everyone who posed any threat to him. An egomaniac of the first degree, he changed the names of various cities – Santo Domingo became Ciudad Trujillo, for example – and lavished support on San Cristobal, the small city west of the capital where he was born; a never-used palace Trujillo had built can still be visited.

Trujillo ruled the Dominican Republic with an iron fist from 1930 to 1961, lavishing over 21% of the national budget on the ever-expanding

1910	1916–24	1930	1937
San Pedro de Macorís baseball team Estrellas Orientales (Eastern Stars) is founded.	After years of civil wars, the US occupies the Dominican Republic under the pretense of securing debt payments owed by the defaulting Dominican government.	After six years of relatively stable government, Rafael Trujillo, the chief of the Dominican National Police, declares himself president after an election in which he was the sole candidate.	In the culmination of his xenophobia, paranoia, racism and tyranny, dictator Rafael Trujillo orders the extermination of Haitians along the border; tens of thousands are killed in a matter of days.

Guardia Nacional and creating a handful of intelligence agencies dedicated to suppressing any dissent. The torture and murder of political prisoners was a daily event in Trujillo's DR. Two of the more infamous incidents were the kidnapping and murder of a Spanish professor teaching in New York City, who had criticized his regime, and plotting to assassinate the Venezuelan president Rómulo Betancourt. Trujillo, in spite of being part black, was deeply racist and xenophobic; he sought to 'whiten' the Dominican population by increasing European immigration and placing quotas on the number of Haitians allowed in the country.

During these years, Trujillo used his government to amass a personal fortune by establishing monopolies that he and his wife controlled. By 1934 he was the richest man on the island. Today there are many Dominicans who remember Trujillo's rule with a certain amount of fondness and nostalgia, in part because Trujillo did develop the economy. Factories were opened, a number of grandiose infrastructure and public works projects were carried out, bridges and highways were built, and peasants were given state land to cultivate.

Life in Santo Domingo during the Trujillo regime was regimented: begging was allowed only on Saturdays, laborers were awakened with a siren at 7am while office workers were given an extra hour to sleep in; their siren was at 8am.

Border Bloodbath

The zenith of the Haiti xenophobia was Trujillo's massacre of tens of thousands of Haitians in 1937. After hearing reports that Haitian peasants were crossing into the Dominican Republic, perhaps to steal cattle, Trujillo ordered all Haitians along the border to be tracked down and executed. Dominican soldiers used a simple test to separate Haitians from Dominicans – they would hold up a string of parsley (*perejil* in Spanish) and ask everyone they encountered to name it. French- and Creole-speaking Haitians could not properly trill the 'r' and were summarily murdered. Beginning on October 3 and lasting for several days, at least 15,000 – and some researchers claim as many as 35,000 – Haitians were hacked to death with machetes and their bodies dumped into the ocean.

Trujillo never openly admitted a massacre had taken place, but in 1938, under international pressure, he and Haitian president Sténio Vicente agreed the Dominican Republic would pay a total of US$750,000 as reparation for Haitians who had been killed (US$50 per person). The Dominican Republic made an initial payment of US$250,000 but it's unclear if it ever paid the rest.

The Dictator Next Door: The Good Neighbor Policy and the Trujillo Regime in the Dominican Republic, 1930-1945, by Eric Paul Roorda, details the compromises the US government made with Trujillo's regime and its complicity in its survival.

False Starts

When Trujillo was assassinated by a group of Dominican dissidents on May 30, 1961, some hoped that the country would turn a corner. The promise of change, however, was short-lived. President Joaquín Balaguer officially assumed the office. He renamed the capital Santo Domingo. After a groundswell of unrest and at the insistence of the USA, a seven-member Council of State, which included two of the men who'd taken part in Trujillo's deadly ambush, was to guide the country until elections were held in December 1962. The first free elections in many years in the DR was won by the scholar-poet Juan Bosch Gaviño.

Nine months later, after introducing liberal policies including the redistribution of land, the creation of a new constitution and guaranteeing civil and individual rights, Bosch was deposed by yet another military coup in September 1963. Wealthy landowners, to whom democracy was a threat, and a group of military leaders led by Generals Elías Wessin y Wessin and Antonio Imbert Barreras installed Donald Reid Cabral, a prominent businessman, as president. Bosch fled into exile but his supporters, calling themselves the Constitutionalists, took to the streets and seized the National Palace. Santo Domingo saw the stirrings of a civil war; the military launched tank assaults and bombing runs against civilian protesters.

The fighting continued until the USA intervened yet again. This time the Johnson administration, after losing Cuba, feared a left-wing or communist takeover of the Dominican Republic despite the fact that Bosch wasn't a communist and papers later revealed US intelligence had identified 54 individuals that were part of the movement fighting the military junta. The official reason was that the US could no longer guarantee the safety of its nationals and so over 500 marines landed in Santo Domingo on April 27, 1965. A week later and only 40 years since the previous occupation, 14,000 American military personnel were stationed in the Dominican Republic.

The Last Playboy: The High Life of Porfirio Rubirosa, by Shawn Levy, tells the life story of the DR's most famous womanizer and Trujillo intimate.

Caudillo Redux

Elections were held in July 1966. Balaguer defeated Bosch. Many voters had feared a Bosch victory would lead to civil war. Bosch would go on to contest elections in 1978, 1982, 1986, 1990 and 1994, always losing. Balaguer, meanwhile, would outlast every Latin American ruler except Fidel Castro. Not the typical authoritarian dictator, Balaguer was a poet and a writer – in one book he argues against interracial marriage – who lived in the servant's quarters of his female-dominated home.

Taking a page from Trujillo's playbook, Balaguer curtailed opposition through bribes and intimidation and went on to win reelection in 1970 and 1974. Despite economic growth, in part fueled by investment and aid from the USA, who saw Balaguer as a staunch anticommunist ally, Balaguer lost the 1978 election to a wealthy cattle rancher named Silvestre Antonio Guzmán. The transfer of power wouldn't come easily, however; Balaguer ordered troops to destroy ballot boxes and declared himself the victor, standing down only after US president Jimmy Carter refused to recognize his victory.

After losing power to revolutionaries led by Fidel Castro, Cuban dictator Fulgencio Batista fled to Trujillo City.

1965 Lyndon Johnson ultimately sends 42,000 US Army personnel and Marines to invade the DR, ostensibly to prevent a civil war. The troops remain until October 1966.

1966 Trujillo's former vice-president Dr Joaquín Balaguer is elected president.

» Punta Cana became popular with tourists in the '70s

As a result of plunging sugar prices and rising oil costs, the Dominican economy came to a standstill under Guzmán's administration; he committed suicide shortly before leaving office in 1982. His successor, Salvador Jorge Blanco, adhered to a fiscal austerity plan under pressure from the International Monetary Fund, measures that were far from popular with many ordinary Dominicans. (Blanco, who passed away in 2011, is the only president in the DR to have been prosecuted for corruption.) But old dictators don't go easily and Balaguer, 80 years old and blind with glaucoma, returned to power in the 1986 election.

For the next eight years Balaguer set about reversing every economic reform of the Blanco program; the result was five-fold devaluing of the Dominican peso and soaring annual inflation rates. With little chance of prospering at home, almost 900,000 Dominicans, or 12% of the country's population, had moved to New York by 1990. After Balaguer won the 1990 and 1994 elections (amid accusations of electoral fraud), the military grew weary of his rule and he agreed to cut his last term short, hold elections and, most importantly, not be a candidate. But it wouldn't be his last campaign – he would run once more at the age of 92, winning 23% of the vote in the 2000 presidential election. Thousands would mourn his death two years later, despite the fact that he prolonged the Trujillo-style dictatorship for decades. His most lasting legacy may be the Faro a Colón, an enormously expensive monument to the discovery of the Americas that drained Santo Domingo of electricity whenever the lighthouse was turned on.

Moving Away From the Past

The Dominican people signaled their desire for change in electing Leonel Fernández, a 42-year-old lawyer who grew up in New York City, as president in 1996; he edged out three-time candidate José Francisco Peña Gómez in a runoff. Still, the speed of his initial moves shocked the nation. Fernández forcibly retired two dozen generals, encouraged his defense minister to submit to questioning by the civilian attorney general and fired the defense minister for insubordination – all in a single week. In the four years of his presidential term, he presided over strong economic growth and privatization, and lowered inflation and high rates of unemployment and illiteracy – accusations of endemic corruption, however, remained pervasive.

Hipólito Mejía, a former tobacco farmer, succeeded Fernández in 2000 and immediately cut spending and increased fuel prices, not exactly the platform he ran on. The faltering US economy and September 11 attacks ate into Dominican exports, as well as cash remittances and foreign tourism. Corruption scandals involving the civil service, unchecked spending, electricity shortages and several bank failures, which cost the

In honor of the Mirabal sisters, Minerva, Paria and Maria Teresa, activists who were murdered by Trujillo's agents, the UN declared November 25, the day of their death, International Day for the Elimination of Violence Against Women.

ACTIVISTS

February 1973	1982	1983	1986
A state of emergency is declared by Balaguer after a small guerilla invasion fails; Bosch goes into hiding after Balaguer implicates him in insurgency.	Distraught over revelations of financial corruption and improprieties, incumbent President Silvestre Antonio Guzman commits suicide, with just over a month left in term.	Juan Marichal becomes the first and only Dominican player to be elected to the baseball Major League Hall of Fame.	After an eight-year hiatus, Joaquín Balaguer, 80 years old and blind, is elected to his fifth term as president despite his previous administration's corruption and dismal human rights record.

government in the form of huge bailouts for depositors, all spelled doom for Mejía's reelection chances.

More of the Same

Familiar faces reappear again and again in Dominican politics and Fernández returned to the national stage by handily defeating Mejía in the 2004 presidential elections. Though he's considered competent and by some even forward-thinking, it's common to hear people talk about him unenthusiastically as a typical politician beholden to special interests. The more cynical observers claim that the Fernández administration is allied with corrupt business and government officials that perpetuate a patronage system different from Trujillo's rule in name only.

In May 2008, with the US and world economies faltering and continued tensions with Haiti, Fernández was reelected for another presidential term. He avoided a runoff despite mounting questions about the logic of spending US$700 million on Santo Domingo's subway system, rising gas prices, the fact that the DR still has one of the highest rates of income inequality in Latin America and the government's less-than-stellar response to the devastation wrought by Tropical Storm Noel in late October 2007. Over 66,000 people were displaced from their homes and around 100 communities were completely isolated, some for over two weeks, because of damaged roads and bridges. There were massive layoffs in the agricultural industry after crop production took a major hit.

Why the Cocks Fight, by Michele Wucker, examines Dominican-Haitian relations through the metaphor of cockfighting.

THE HUNTER BECOMES THE HUNTED

For divers, the main attraction in the Parque Nacional Submarino La Caleta is the *Hickory*, a 39m-long steel ship that was scuttled in 1984. Once a vessel that carried treasure hunters, the tables have now turned and the *Hickory* has become a sought-after underwater destination.

The *Hickory* was the primary vessel used in the recovery of artifacts from the Spanish galleons *Nuestra Señora de Guadalupe* and *El Conde de Tolosa*, both of which sank in the Bahía de Samaná on August 25, 1724. Both of these galleons were en route to Mexico when a violent storm forced them away from the shore and toward a treacherous coral reef. The captains were unable to steer the galleons to safety and the ships were torn apart and sank, taking the lives of over 600 passengers.

The remains of the ships – and their cargo – were left untouched until 1976 when fishermen discovered the *Guadalupe*. Curious about the wreck, the Dominican government hired a salvage company from Texas to explore the sunken galleon using the *Hickory*.

Among the thousands of items discovered at the two wreck sites were hundreds of silver and gold coins minted in Spain during the early 18th century, a cache of jewelry and hundreds of crystal glasses.

1996	2003–04	2007	2008
After massive election fraud and widespread national and international pressure, Balaguer agrees to step down after two years and Leonel Fernández is elected president.	A growing financial crisis sparks widespread public unrest and protests, including a general strike in which several people are killed and scores injured by police.	Tropical Storm Noel devastates much of the country, destroying roads and bridges, stranding communities for weeks and killing over 120 people. The government's response is questioned.	In May Leonel Fernández convincingly wins reelection to his third presidential term; a 2002 constitutional amendment allows him to again run for office.

The Dominican Republic: A National History, by Frank Moya Pons, is the most comprehensive book on the country's colorful history.

COLORFUL

Crossings

Haitians have few legal protections; in 2005 the Dominican Supreme Court ruled that the children of visitors 'in transit' were not afforded citizenship. This ruling defines illegal immigrants, which virtually all Haitian workers are, as 'in transit', meaning that even those Haitians who were born in the DR and have lived their entire lives in the DR are denied citizenship.

By the end of 2007 there were 200 UN soldiers, mostly from other Caribbean countries, to help buttress the DR army's attempts to stop the flow of drugs and arms across the Haitian border. In early 2008 there were increased tensions along the border over accusations of cattle rustling and reprisals, and Dominican chickens being turned away because of fears over avian flu.

While almost four million people, the majority foreign tourists, visited the country in 2009, more than any other island in the Caribbean, Dominicans continue to migrate in the other direction, seeking better lives abroad, mostly in the US. The US coast guard continues to intercept hundreds of Dominicans attempting the dangerous crossing from the Mona passage to Puerto Rico; many lose their lives in the attempt. The DR has also become a major transshipment hub for drugs; hundreds of flights and an even larger number of boats arrive yearly on the DR's shores, transporting mostly cocaine from elsewhere in South America, most notably Columbia, on its way to the US and Europe.

2010	2011	April 2011	May 2011
Haiti's cholera epidemic, following the devasting earthquake, spreads into the DR, reigniting border conflicts.	La Romana's Los Toros del Este sweep the Estrellas of San Pedro in five games to win only their second DR winter baseball pennant.	President Leonel Fernández announces he will not pursue constitutional reforms in order to seek a fourth presidential term.	Former president Hipólito Mejía officially announces his candidacy for presidential elections scheduled for the end of May, 2012.

Music & Dance

Life in the Dominican Republic seems to move to a constant, infectious rhythm, and music has always been an important part of Dominican heritage. Despite, or perhaps in part because of, the country's tumultuous history of bitter divisions, revolutions and dictatorial rule, the Dominican Republic has made significant contributions to the musical world, giving rise to some of Latin music's most popular and influential styles.

Merengue

Merengue is the national dance music of the Dominican Republic. From the minute you arrive until the minute you leave, merengue will be coming at you full volume: at a restaurant, in public buses or taxis – it's there; at the beach or walking down the street – more merengue. And if you attend a dance club here and take a shine to the music, you may want to pick up some CDs before leaving the country. There are many merengue bands in the Dominican Republic; the nation's favorites include Johnny Ventura, Coco Band, Wilfredo Vargas, Milly y Los Vecinos, Fernando Villalona, Joseito Mateo, Rubby Perez, Miriam Cruz, Milly Quezada and, perhaps the biggest name of all, Juan Luis Guerra.

Dominicans dance merengue with passion and flair. Rhythmically driven and heavy on the downbeat, merengue follows a common 2-4 or 4-4 beat pattern. But what sets it apart from other musical forms is the presence of traditional signature instruments and how they work within the two- or four-beat structure. Merengue is typically played with a two-headed drum called a *tambora*, a guitar, an accordion-like instrument known as a *melodeon*, and a *güira* – a metal instrument that looks a little like a cheese grater and is scraped using a metal or plastic rod.

If you have a chance, go to a nightclub or dance hall where merengue is played. Even if you don't dance – something Dominicans will find very peculiar – you'll be impressed by the skill and artfulness of the way even amateur dancers move their feet and hips in perfect time to the music. The *merengue típico*, or traditional folk genre, is a fast two-step dance characterized by the close proximity of the dancers. The most prevalent of the folk styles, called *perico ripiao*, originated in the northern valley region of Cibao and is still commonly played today.

From its humble rural beginnings in the countryside, merengue evolved into a more modernized orchestral 'big band' style, largely due to its elevated status as a national symbol, embraced by former president Rafael Leónidas Trujillo in the 1930s. During his term, Trujillo ordered many merengues to be composed in his honor. While the earlier traditional forms established the complexities of the rhythm and the development of the dance, it was the orchestral style, called *orquesta merengue* or *merengue de salon*, that saw merengue's rise to prominence by the 1980s, becoming a worthy competitor of salsa. By the 1990s, contemporary merengue had incorporated electronic drum beats and synthesizers,

Since 1986 merengue and *bachata* superstar Juan Luís Guerra has won almost every major music award possible, including a Grammy, three Latin Grammy's, five Billboard Latin Music Awards and two Premios Soberanos.

MERENGUE

and this new sound was heard blaring out of cars, stereos and nightclubs from Puerto Rico to New York City.

The origins of merengue are up for debate. For most Dominicans, to discuss merengue's origins is to discuss the Dominican national and racial identity. Dominican merengue didn't emerge as its own distinct genre until the mid 19th century. Earlier versions existed in Cuba and Haiti, but Dominicans are often disinclined to admit African and Haitian influences on their culture. Many origin theories point to European-derived ballroom-dance styles. According to one popular myth, merengue originated in 1844, the year that the Dominican Republic was founded, to poke fun at a Dominican soldier who had abandoned his post during the Battle of Talanquera in the War of Independence. The Dominicans won the battle and, while celebrating the victory at night, soldiers mocked the cowardly deserter in song and dance. So it all depends on who you ask: Eurocentric thinkers emphasize merengue's European elements; Afrocentric scholars may emphasize its African and Haitian elements; and those who celebrate racial amalgamation point to its synergistic nature. No matter which way you look at it, merengue is an expression of Dominican identity.

The *güira*, a musical instrument in merengue music, was originally used by the indigenous Taíno for ceremonial songs. However, the earlier version was made from dried, hollowed-out gourds and sticks.

Bachata

Whereas merengue might be viewed as urban music, *bachata* is definitely the nation's 'country' music. This is the music of love, of broken hearts, of life in the country. Born in the poorest of Dominican neighborhoods, *bachata* emerged in the mid 20th century as a slow, romantic style played on the Spanish guitar. The term initially referred to informal, sometimes rowdy backyard parties in rural areas, finally emerging in Santo Domingo shanties.

'*Bachata*' was meant as a slight by the urban elite, a reference to the music's supposed lack of sophistication. Often called 'songs of bitterness', *bachata* tunes were no different to most romantic ballad forms, such as the Cuban bolero, but were perceived as low class, and didn't have the same political or social support as merengue. In fact, *bachata* was not even regarded as a style until the 1960s – and even then it was not widely known outside the Dominican Republic.

Bachata: A Social History of Dominican Popular Music, by Deborah Pacini Hernandez, and *Merengue: Dominican Music and Dominican Identity*, by Paul Austerlitz, are academic examinations of the DR's two most important musical contributions and obsessions.

But widespread interest in and acceptance of the style grew largely due to the efforts of musician and composer Juan Luis Guerra, who introduced international audiences to this rich and sentimental form. Already credited with developing a more modern and socially conscious merengue, Guerra nearly single-handedly brought *bachata* out of obscurity, paving the way for many Dominican artists to come.

While merengue continues to be the more popular style, *bachata* has witnessed a recent rise in popularity, particularly in New York City's Dominican community. Among the big names of *bachata* are Raulín Rodríguez, Antony Santos, Joe Veras, Luis Vargas, Quico Rodríguez and Leo Valdez. *Bachata Roja* is a compilation of classic bachata from the early 1960s to late 1980s; the pre-electric era when the music was entirely guitar based and drew on a variety of musical traditions, including Mexican *ranchera*, Puerto Rican *jíbaro*, Cuban bolero, guaracha and

TOP MUSIC FESTIVALS

» Carnaval – end of February
» Santo Domingo Merengue Festival – last week in July/first week in August
» Puerto Plata Merengue Festival – third week in October
» Santiago and Cabarete Jazz Festival – last week in October

son. The record includes legendary musicians like Edilio Paredes and Augusto Santos.

Salsa

Salsa, like *bachata*, is heard on many Caribbean islands, and is very popular in the DR. Before they called it salsa, many musicians in New York City had already explored the possibilities of blending Cuban rhythms with jazz. In the 1950s, the Latin big-band era found favor with dancers and listeners alike, and in the mid-1960s, Dominican flutist, composer and producer Johnny Pacheco founded the Fania label, which was exclusively dedicated to recording 'tropical Latin' music.

With Cuba cut off from the United States politically as well as culturally, it was no longer appropriate to use the term 'Afro-Cuban'. The word 'salsa' (literally 'sauce') emerged as a clever marketing tool, reflecting not only the music but the entire atmosphere, and was the perfect appellation for a genre of music resulting from a mixture of styles: Cuban-based rhythms played by Puerto Ricans, Dominicans, Africans and African Americans.

By the 1970s, salsa was hot, hot, hot – not only in the US, but also in South America and Central America. Even European, Japanese and African audiences were treated to this new sound. In the 1980s, salsa evolved into a bland version of itself – the so-called 'salsa romántica' genre – and during this time Dominican merengue served up some worthy competition. Since the 1990s, however, salsa has rebounded and has spread throughout the globe, living on in new generations of players and dancers alike.

If you like the music, it may interest you to know that the following individuals and groups enjoy particularly favorable reputations in the DR: Tito Puente, Tito Rojas, Jerry Rivera, Tito Gómez, Grupo Niche, Gilberto Santa Rosa, Mimi Ibara, Marc Anthony and Leonardo Paniagua.

Reggaeton & Rap

Reggaeton, a mix of American-style hip-hop and Latin rhythms, has exploded onto the Dominican scene. Reggaeton has a distinctly urban flavor, and its fast-paced danceable beats, street-life narratives and catchy choruses make it the party music of choice for many young Dominicans. In terms of origins, Panama claims it was the first country to bring Spanish-influenced reggae to the underground scene in the late 1970s. But it was Puerto Rico that gave the music a whole new beat and name in the 1980s and '90s.

Since that time, reggaeton has become increasingly popular throughout the DR, and Dominican artists have made their own stamp on the genre. Like hip-hop in the US, reggaeton has evolved from a musical genre to an entire culture, with its own brand of fashion and commerce. Artists to look out for include the well-known reggaeton duo Wisin & Yandel, Pavel Nuñez, an established star whose music is a mix between folk and Latin, and Kat DeLuna, a 23-year-old pop singer whose music is a hodge-podge of styles and rhythms.

MUSIC & DANCE

Hit Songs

» Joseito Mateo – 'El Negrito de Batey' (merengue)

» Luis Vargas – 'Volvia el Dolor' (merengue)

» Antony Santos – 'Voy pa'lla' (*bachata*)

» La Fabrica – 'En Cuatro Gomas' (reggaeton)

COCOLOS

Cocolos (English-speaking immigrants from the Eastern Caribbean who primarily settled in the region around San Pedro de Macorís) have their own distinctive musical and dance culture. A good time to experience this hybrid of African and Caribbean rhythms is February 27, the national holiday celebrating Dominican independence from Haiti.

In 1818 the Spanish colonial governor ordered nighttime dancing in the street without a permit to be illegal.

Rap Dominicano, a relatively new musical sub-genre, is now pounding unapologetically out of the Dominican barrios, and taking its place alongside reggaeton as a popular form of music among Dominican youth. Although rap is an imported genre and the sounds blasting from the speakers don't resemble the typical sounds of the DR, Dominican rap artists have managed to weave the sounds of *bachata* and merengue into their tracks, rapping about an urban upbringing that is uniquely their own. Among those spitting rapid-fire artists on their way to the limelight are El Lapiz Conciente, Vakero, Joa, Toxic Crow, Punto Rojo and R1.

Baseball: A Dominican Passion

Not just the USA's game, *beísbol* is part of the Dominican social and cultural landscape. So much so that Dominican ballplayers that have made good in the US major leagues are without doubt the most popular and revered figures in the country. Over 400 Dominicans have played in the major leagues (today, Dominicans make up around 17% of major and minor leaguers), including stars like David Ortiz, Moises Alou, Julio Franco, Pedro Martinez, Albert Pujols and, maybe most famously, Sama Sosa. Two dozen major league teams have training facilities here.

Needless to say, the quality of play is high, but even if you're not a fan of the sport, it's worth checking out a game or two. It's always a fun afternoon or evening. Fans are decked out in their respective team's colors waving pennants and flags, as rabidly partisan as the Yankees–Red Sox rivalry, and dancers in hot pants perform to loud merengue beats on top of the dugouts between innings. Games usually don't start on time and the stands aren't filled in until several innings have passed.

Getting to First Base

The origin of baseball in the DR is intertwined with the beginnings of the sugar industry, first in Cuba and later in the DR. Around the same time that American business ambitions were directed toward the Caribbean, particularly Cuba, baseball was being established in the states. When Cuban plantation owners fled their country during a failed war of independence in 1868, they brought with them their passion for the game, which they learned from the Americans (where and when the game was originally established is open for dispute).

Workers from the English-speaking Caribbean who were brought to the DR to work in the cane fields were already skilled cricket players, bringing a familiarity with the general concepts of batting, pitching and fielding. With few leisure activities available, plant owners encouraged baseball rather than cricket and organized competitive teams into a 'sugar league'. Cubans, Americans and Dominicans in Santo Domingo, La Vega and near Santiago also formed their own teams.

But it was the US embargo of Cuba that began in 1962 (as well as free agency that began in the 1970s) that really accelerated the recruitment of Dominican players since fewer Cubans were willing to defect – a requirement imposed by the government. Major-league scouts turned to other Caribbean countries including the DR to pick up the slack and Dominicans, unlike Puerto Ricans who are American citizens, were not subject to draft rules at the time.

The Eastern Stars: How Baseball Changed the Dominican Town of San Pedro de Macorís, by Mark Kurlansky, is a comprehensive history of baseball in the DR, with a focus on San Pedro de Macorís, known as the 'city of shortstops'.

The movie Sugar tells the story of a young Dominican baseball prospect drafted to play in the US minor leagues, and the loneliness and dislocation he and other players experience.

» Tigres de Licey (Santo Domingo)
» Leones del Escogido (Santo Domingo)
» Aguilas Cibeanas (Santiago)
» Estrellas Orientales (San Pedro de Macorís)
» Los Toros del Este (La Romana)
» Gigantes del Cibao (San Francisco de Macorís)

SANDINO

Santiago's base-
ball team was
originally named
'Sandino' in
honor of Augusto
César Sandino,
the leader of
Nicaragua who
was deposed by
the US invasion.
After Trujillo
came to power he
forced the team
to change its
name.

One in six of the
471 Dominicans
who played at
least one game in
the major leagues
came from San
Pedro de Macorís.

Drafting Dilemmas

For a young prospect in the Dominican Republic the financial incen-
tives of just being drafted, let alone actually playing a single game, in
the major leagues are considerable. The average bonus (US$180,000)
alone can provide a down payment on a home and provide for family
members. However, the odds are overwhelmingly against success – only
3% of those signed make it to the majors - and when a young teenager
pins their hopes on baseball (players are eligible for recruitment at 16),
education usually falls by the wayside.

Over the past several years a series of high-profile issues have
arisen, complicating the often incestuous relationship between
Dominican baseball and the major leagues, whose teams have academies
here that are a mix of university dormitory, work camp and health club.
Problems include steroid use, which isn't technically illegal in the DR,
fake birth certificates intentionally misstating a player's age (younger to
overstate potential and older to allow recruitment) and the increasingly
questionable role that *buscones* play in the whole system. Taken from
the Spanish verb '*buscar*,' to look for, *buscones* are more than merely
scouts. They train, feed, house and educate promising players, grooming
them to be signed by the majors in the hopes of one day gaining a large
percentage of whatever signing bonus their prospects earn.

Take Me Out to 'El Partido de Beísbol'

The Dominican professional baseball league's season runs from October
to January, and is known as the Liga de Invierno (Winter League; the
winner of the DR league competes in the Caribbean World Series against
other Latin-American countries). The country has six professional teams.
Because the US and Dominican seasons don't overlap, many Dominican
players in the US major leagues and quite a few non-Dominicans play in
the winter league in the DR as well.

From June to August there is also a Liga del Verano (Summer League)
if you're in the DR outside of regular season. Various major-league
franchises – the San Francisco Giants, the Toronto Blue Jays, the
Arizona Diamondbacks and the NY Yankees, to name a few – maintain farm teams in the DR, and summer-league play is a semiformal
tournament between these teams. Games are held at smaller stadiums
around town.

Art & Architecture

Literature

The Dominican Republic's literary history dates to the Spanish colonial period (1492–1795). It was then that Bartolomé de Las Casas, a Spanish friar, recorded the early history of the Caribbean and pleaded for fair treatment of the Taínos in his famous *Historia de las Indias* (History of the Indies). In the same era, Gabriel Téllez, a priest who helped to reorganize the convent of Our Lady of Mercy in Santo Domingo, wrote his impressive *Historia general de la Orden de la Mercéd* (General History of the Order of Mercy).

During the Haitian occupation of Santo Domingo (1822–1844), a French literary style became prominent, and many Dominican writers who emigrated to other Spanish-speaking countries made names for themselves there. With the first proclamation of independence in 1844, Félix María del Monte created the country's principal poetic form – a short, patriotic poem based on local events of the day.

Dominican poetry flourished in the late 19th century, primarily through the three figures of Salome Ureña, Joaquín Pérez and Gastón Fernando Deligne. Pérez's collection, *Fantasías Indíginas* (Indian Fantasies), imagines encounters between Spanish conquistadores and the native Taíno. Pedro Mir established himself while living in exile in Cuba during the Trujillo regime and was later named Poet Laureate in 1984.

During the late 19th and early 20th centuries, three literary movements occurred in the DR: *indigenismo*, *criollismo* and *postumismo*. *Indigenismo* exposed the brutalities the Taínos experienced at the hands of the Spaniards. *Criollismo* focused on the local people and their customs. And *postumismo* dealt with the repression that Rafael Trujillo's iron-fist leadership brought. Some writers, such as Manuel and Lupo Fernández Rueda, used clever metaphors to protest against the regime.

San Pedro de Macorís is also known for its poets: Gastón Fernando Deligne, Pedro Mir and René del Risco Bermúdez, among others, were either born here or drew their inspiration living in this city.

AN UNLIKELY MAN OF LETTERS

Balaguer, president of the DR from 1960 to 1962, 1966 to 1978, and from 1986 to 1996, was a writer as well as a strong-man ruler. He published over 50 works, from poetry and biographies to criticism and one novel. Maybe his most infamous work was his autobiography *Memorias de un Cortesano de la Era de Trujillo* (Memoirs of a Courtesan in the Era of Trujillo). In it he includes a blank page, which refers to the murder of outspoken Dominican journalist Orlando Martinez Howley in 1975. Balaguer apparently intended the page to be a memorial to Howley and assigned someone to reveal the details of the assassination – Balaguer denied he gave the orders – after his death. He died in 2002 and no one has come forward.

Juan Bosch Gaviño, writing from exile, penned numerous stories that openly attacked Trujillo. Bosch, who held the presidency for only seven months in 1963, is one of the more influential literary figures in the DR, both as an essayist tackling social problems and as a novelist and short-story writer.

Only a few Dominican novels have been translated into English. Viriato Sención's *They Forged the Signature of God,* winner of the DR's 1993 National Fiction award (after realizing that the book was critical of both Trujillo and himself, Balaguer rescinded the prize) and the country's all-time best seller, follows three seminary students suffering oppression at the hands of both the state and the church. Though slightly preachy, it provides another perspective on the Trujillo regime.

Less well known than Junot Diaz's *The Brief Wondrous Life of Oscar Wao,* but perhaps a more devastating picture of the Dominican diaspora's rejection of the conventional American Dream, is Maritza Pérez's *Geographies of Home.* For Spanish readers, other recommended young Dominican authors are Pedro Antonio Valdés *(Bachata del angel caído, Carnaval de Sodoma),* Rita Indiana Hernández *(La estrategia de Chochueca, Papi)* and Aurora Arias *(Inyi's Paradise, Fin del mundo, Emoticons).*

In the Time of the Butterflies is an award-winning novel by Julia Álvarez, about three sisters slain for their part in a plot to overthrow Trujillo. Also by Álvarez is *How the García Girls Lost Their Accents,* describing an emigrant Dominican family in New York. Other well-known contemporary Dominican writers include José Goudy Pratt, Jeannette Miller and Ivan García Guerra.

Painting

The Dominican art scene today is quite healthy, thanks in no small part to dictator Rafael Trujillo. Although his 31 years of authoritarian rule in many ways negated the essence of creative freedom, Trujillo had a warm place in his heart for paintings, and in 1942 he established the Escuela Nacional de Bellas Artes (National School of Fine Arts). Fine Dominican artwork predates the school, but it really wasn't until the institution's doors opened that Dominican art underwent definitive development.

If the artwork looks distinctly Spanish, it's because the influence is undeniable. During the Spanish Civil War (1936–1939), many artists fled Franco's fascist regime to start new lives in the Dominican Republic. Influential artists include Manolo Pascual, José Gausachs, José Vela-Zanetti, Eugenio Fernández Granell and José Fernández Corredor.

In the late 1960s in Santiago, Grupo Friordano, as well as other small groups of socially engaged artists, began politically conscious and ideological aesthetic movements. Painters like Daniel Henriquez, Orlando Menicucci and Yori Morjel considered their work as engaged critiques of society; Morjel painted traditional rural scenes and helped develop a distinctly Dominican vernacular style.

If you visit any of the art galleries in Santo Domingo or Santiago, keep an eye out for paintings by Adriana Billini Gautreau, who is famous for portraits that are rich in expressionist touches; the cubist forms of Jaime Colson, emphasizing the social crises of his day; Luis Desangles, considered the forerunner of folklore in Dominican painting; Mariano Eckert,

ICONIC

Those colorful and bright canvases of simple rural scenes lined up on virtually every street corner and piece of pavement where tourists are expected are actually reproductions of iconic Haitian paintings; these are often churned out with house paint.

BEST ART MUSEUMS

» Centro León, Santiago
» Museo de Arte Moderno, Santo Domingo
» Museo Bellapart, Santo Domingo

» Museo Alcázar de Colón, Santo Domingo
» Catedral Primada de América, Santo Domingo
» Basilica de Nuestra Señora de la Altagracia, Higuey
» Catedral de la Concepción, La Vega

representing the realism of everyday life; Juan Bautista Gómez, whose paintings depict the sensuality of the landscape; Guillo Pérez, whose works of oxen, carts and canefields convey a poetic vision of life at the sugar mill; Ivan Tovar's surrealist Dali-esque works; the traditional realist paintings of Ada Balcacer; Mariam Balcacer, a photographer who lives in Italy; the steel sculptures of Johnny Bonnelleg Ricart; and, finally, the enigmatic and dream-like paintings of Dionisio Blanco.

Also well represented is what's known as 'primitive art' – Dominican and Haitian paintings that convey rural Caribbean life with simple and colorful figures and landscapes. These paintings are created by amateur painters – some would say skilled craftsmen – who reproduce the same painting hundreds of times. They are sold everywhere there are tourists; you're sure to get an eyeful regardless of the length of your trip.

A good resource on Dominican art is the authoritative *Enciclopedia de las Artes Plásticas Dominicanas* (Encyclopedia of Dominican Visual Arts) by Cándido Gerón. Illustrations and Spanish text are followed by English translations; look for copies at used bookstores in the Zona Colonial.

Architecture

The quality and variety of architecture found in the Dominican Republic has no equal in the Caribbean. Santo Domingo's Zona Colonial, a well-preserved grid of Spanish colonial buildings, is a showcase of landmarks. An imposing fortress – the oldest still intact in the Americas – stands adjacent to mansions and Dominican and Franciscan convents. The Americas' oldest functioning cathedral, the Catedral Primada de América, whose construction began in 1514, stands in the center. You'll see plenty of the Baroque, Romanesque, Gothic and Renaissance styles which were popular in Europe during the colonial times.

Elsewhere in Santo Domingo and Santiago you can see examples of Cuban Victorian, Caribbean gingerbread and art deco. The buildings in Puerto Plata vary between the vernacular Antillean and the pure Victorian; sometimes English, sometimes North American. Sugar magnates in San Pedro de Macorís built late-Victorian style homes with concrete (it was the first city in the DR to use reinforced concrete in construction). And rural clapboard homes – Monte Cristi in the far northwest has these in spades – have a charm all their own: small, square, single-story and more colorful than a handful of jelly beans, you'll find yourself slowing down to take a longer look.

More contemporary and postmodern architecture is best seen in homes commissioned by wealthy Dominicans, in upscale neighborhoods in Santo Domingo and Santiago. Elsewhere, including Jarabacoa in the central highlands, along the southeastern coastline around Punta Cana, and around Puerto Plata on the north coast, are enclaves of vacation homes; these communities are worth a look for creative and high-concept design.

Easily the best book on architecture in the country is *Arquitectura Dominicana: 1492–2008*, edited by Gustavo Luis More (available at the gift shop at the Centro León in Santiago). Another excellent resource is *Interiors*, a book of photographs by Polibio Diaz, which shows glimpses into the homes of ordinary Dominicans with respect and care.

ART & ARCHITECTURE ARCHITECTURE

The Eduardo León Jimenes Art Contest in Santiago began in 1964 and is the longest-running privately sponsored art competition in Latin America.

Dominican Landscapes

The Land

If wealth were measured by landscape, the DR would be among the richest countries in the Americas. Hispaniola is the second-largest island in the Caribbean, after Cuba, with a landmass of around 76,000 sq km, a dynamic country of high mountains, fertile valleys and watered plains, and an amazing diversity of ecosystems.

The island's geography owes more to the Central American mainland than its mostly flat neighboring islands. The one thing that Hispaniola has in spades is an abundance of mountains. Primary among mountain ranges is the Cordillera Central that runs from Santo Domingo into Haiti, where it becomes the Massif du Nord, fully encompassing a third of the island's landmass. The Cordillera Central is home to Pico Duarte, the Caribbean's highest mountain (at 3087m), which is so big it causes a rain shadow that makes much of southwest DR very arid. Other ranges include the Cordillera Septentrional, rising dramatically from the coast near Cabarete, and the Cordillera Orientale, along the southern shoreline of Bahía de Samaná.

Between the ranges lie a series of lush and fertile valleys. Coffee, rice, bananas and tobacco all thrive here, as well as in the plains around Santo Domingo. In comparison, sections of southwest DR are semi-desert and studded with cacti.

The unique landscape of Hispaniola is due to the 90-million-year-old movements of the earth's crust. As it slowly ground past North America, the Caribbean Plate cracked and crumpled to form the islands stretching from Cuba to Puerto Rico. Further collisions formed the Lesser Antilles, the coastal mountains of Venezuela and much of Central America. The plate is still moving at 1cm to 2cm per year, and continues to elevate Hispaniola.

Wildlife

The Dominican Republic's rich landscape is matched by an equally rich biodiversity. There are over 5600 species of plants and close to 500 vertebrate species on the island, many of these endemic.

The problems of colonizing an island are clear, with plants heavily reliant on seeds and roots arriving on floating rafts of vegetation, often with animal hitchhikers. Reptiles make the best long-distance voyagers and over 140 species are found on the island, compared to around 60 amphibians and 20 land mammals (only two of which survived the arrival of Europeans). The rest of the country's fauna is made up of a rich variety of birds, marine mammals and bats.

When British monarch George III asked one of his admirals to describe Hispaniola, he was given a crumpled piece of paper – to demonstrate how mountainous the island was.

Updated in 2006, *Birds of the Dominican Republic & Haiti*, by Steven Latta et al, is the most recent book on birds in the DR.

An overview of Caribbean coral reefs can be found in the eye-opening *A Guide to the Coral Reefs of the Caribbean*, by Mark Spalding.

Birds

Over 300 species of bird have been recorded in the DR, including more than two dozen found nowhere else in the world. Abundant, colorful species include the white-tailed tropicbird, magnificent frigatebird, roseate spoonbill and greater flamingo, plus unique endemic species such as the Hispaniolan lizard-cuckoo, ashy-faced owl and Hispaniolan emerald hummingbird.

Travelers are most likely to encounter birds on beaches and coastal waterways – specifically herons, egrets, ibis, rails, pelicans and gulls. Some of the best spots for twitchers in the DR are Parque Nacional Jaragua, Parque Nacional Los Haitises, Parque Nacional Monte Cristi and Laguna Limón. More determined travelers taking the time to wander into some of the rich wildlife areas in the DR's interior can expect to encounter a tremendous variety of forest birds. Depending on the season and habitat, you will find a full range of North American warblers, or local birds like Hispaniolan trogons, woodpeckers, parakeets and parrots. Some of these are common and widespread, while others are highly secretive and require specialized knowledge or a guide to locate.

Favorites among birdwatchers include the odd palmchat, DR's national bird, which builds large apartment-like nests where each pair sleeps in its own chamber.

The Birds of the West Indies, by Herbert Raffaele et al, covers birds across the West Indies, including migratory species you may see in the DR.

Land Mammals

The arrival of Europeans, who introduced many disruptive species of their own, proved disastrous for Hispaniola's land mammals. Rats, cats, pigs and mongooses all tore through the local wildlife with severe consequences.

Just two native mammal species remain, clinging to survival in scattered pockets throughout Haiti and the DR. These are the hutia, a tree-climbing rodent, and the solenodon, an insectivore resembling a giant shrew. The solenodon is particularly threatened, and both species are nocturnal, making sightings extremely difficult.

Marine Mammals

The DR is world famous for its marine mammals, with manatees and humpback whales the star attractions. Travelers, however, are more likely to see dolphins unless they arrive in the right season or make a special trip to the right habitat.

Bats are the only nonendangered, protected species on the island. They eat as many as 2000 mosquitoes a night, helping to reduce the transmission of dengue and other mosquito-borne diseases.

Several thousand humpback whales migrate south from frigid arctic waters to breed and calve in the tropical waters of the DR each winter (with their numbers peaking in January and February). The Bahía de Samaná is one of the foremost places in the world for boat-based whale-watching, and the Banco de Plata (Silver Banks) is one of only two places in the world where you can swim and snorkel (under supervision, on week-long live-aboard trips) with these truly magnificent creatures.

Manatees feed on the seagrass meadows surrounding Hispaniola, hence their alternative name of 'sea cow' (their closest relative is, in fact, the elephant). Weighing up to 590kg and reaching 3.7m in length, manatees are shy, docile creatures; Parque Nacional Monte Cristi is the best place to try to spot them.

Most of the humpbacks visiting the DR spend the winter gorging on krill in the feeding grounds of the Gulf of Maine, off the US coast. They don't eat during their entire Caribbean stay.

Fish & Marine Life

The shallow coastal waters and coral reefs that surround the DR are home to a tremendous variety of sea life. So many species of tropical fish, crustaceans, sponges and corals can be found here that it takes a specialized field guide to begin to sort them out. Where they remain intact and unfished – such as at Sosúa and Monte Cristi – they are stupendously

NATIONAL PARKS OF THE DR

Parque Nacional Armando Bermúdez (p184) This 766-sq-km park in the humid Cordillera Central is blanketed in pine trees, tree ferns and palm trees, and is home to the hawk-like Hispaniolan trogon.

Parque Nacional del Este (p89) Located in the southeastern part of the country, this park consists of dry and subtropical humid forest, with caves featuring Taíno petroglyphs, as well as the sandy beaches of Isla Saona. Look out for manatees and dolphins off the coast.

Parque Nacional Isla Cabritos (p210) In the southwest, this park is a 24-sq-km island surrounded by the saltwater Lago Enriquillo. It is a refuge for crocodiles, iguanas, scorpions, flamingos, crows and cacti.

Parque Nacional Jaragua (p207) At 1400 sq km, this is the largest park in the DR. It is made up of an arid thorn forest, an extensive marine area and the islands of Beata and Alto Velo. The park is rich in birdlife, particularly sea and shore birds, and its beaches are nesting grounds for hawksbill turtles.

Parque Nacional José del Carmen Ramírez (p184) This 764-sq-km park is home to the Caribbean's tallest peak – Pico Duarte – and the headwaters of three of the DR's most important rivers: Yaque del Sur, San Juan and Mijo. Although there is occasional frost, the park is considered a subtropical humid mountain forest.

Parque Nacional La Isabela (p162) Located on the north coast, this park was established in the 1990s to protect the ruins of the second European settlement in the New World. An on-site museum contains many objects that were used by the earliest European settlers.

Parque Nacional Los Haitises (p108) Situated on the Bahía de Samaná, this park's lush hills jut out of the ocean and are fringed with mangroves, tawny beaches and several Taíno caves. Bamboo, ferns and bromeliads thrive, along with the Hispaniolan parakeet.

Parque Nacional Monte Cristi (p164) This 530-sq-km park in the extreme northwest contains a subtropical dry forest, coastal lagoons and seven islets. It is home to many seabirds, including great egrets, brown pelicans and yellow-crowned night herons. American crocodiles also inhabit the park's lagoons.

Parque Nacional Sierra de Bahoruco (p209) Located in the southwest, this 800-sq-km park stretches from desert lowlands to 2000m-high tracts of pine. Along with the broad range of plant life (orchids abound), it's rich in birds, including the endemic white-necked crow and the Hispaniolan parrot.

Parque Nacional Submarino La Caleta (p77) Only 22km from Santo Domingo, this 10-sq-km park is one of the country's most visited. Containing several healthy coral reefs and two shipwrecks, it is one of the top diving spots in the country.

beautiful. Some of the more colorful Caribbean reef fish include fluorescent fairy basslet, queen angelfish, rock beauty and blue tang, but each visitor will quickly find their own favorite.

The warm waters are also home to four species of sea turtle: green, leatherback, hawksbill and loggerhead. You may have occasional encounters with these turtles while snorkeling, but from May to October they can be viewed in places such as Parque Nacional Jaragua, coming ashore at night to lay their eggs on sandy beaches.

The Dominican Republic has the highest mountain in the Caribbean – Pico Duarte (3087m) – and the lowest point in the Caribbean – Lago Enriquillo, a lake 40m below sea level.

Reptiles & Amphibians

Reptiles were Hispaniola's most successful vertebrate colonists. You can expect to see lots of lizards (geckos in particular), but also keep your eye out for snakes, turtles and even the American crocodile (or caiman), found in sizable numbers in the brackish cross-border lake of the DR's Lago Enriquillo and Haiti's Lac Azueï.

There is also a Hispaniolan boa, its numbers now reduced by mongoose predation. At opposite ends of the spectrum are the Jaragua lizard, which is the world's smallest terrestrial vertebrate (adults measure only 2.8cm), and the massive 10kg rhinoceros iguana. Frogs are the most numerous amphibians.

Plants

Hispaniola presents a bewildering assortment of plants. In every season there is something flowering, fruiting or filling the air with exotic fragrances, and it makes the place truly magical. Nearly a third of the 5600-odd species are endemic, spread across more than 20 discrete vegetation zones, ranging from desert to subtropical forest to mangrove swamp.

Of these vegetation zones, by far the most prevalent is the subtropical forest, which blankets the slopes of many of the DR's valleys and is found throughout the Península de Samaná. This is a majestic landscape, dominated by royal palms with large curving fronds, and native mahogany trees.

True tropical rainforest is rare, both because areas receiving enough rainfall are scarce and because the grand trees of this forest type have been extensively logged. Green-leaved throughout the year, these dense humid forests support a wealth of tree ferns, orchids, bromeliads and epiphytes. Examples can still be found in the Vega Real, which is located in the eastern end of the Valle de Cibao, adjacent to the Samaná region.

Above 1830m, the habitat gives way to mountain forests characterized by pines and palms, as well as ferns, bromeliads, heliconias and orchids. Although threatened by coffee plantations and ranching, large tracts still exist in Parques Nacionales Armando Bermúdez and José del Carmen Ramírez.

Thorn and cacti forests abound in the southwest corner of the DR. Parque Nacional Jaragua, the country's largest protected area, consists largely of thorn forest, cacti and agaves, and receives less than 700mm of rain a year.

Mangrove swamps are a characteristic feature along the coast around the DR's Bahía de Samaná. They're hugely important wildlife habitats, serving as nurseries for many marine species and nesting grounds for water birds. Mangrove stands also play a critical ecological role by buffering the coast against the erosive power of storms and tides.

National Parks

The DR is home to some of the largest and most diverse parks in all the Caribbean. The DR has set aside over 10% of its land as *parques nacionales* (national parks) and *reservas científicas* (scientific reserves) and is doing a reasonably good job of protecting these important local resources in the face of external pressures. This is especially important in coastal areas, where beach resorts are devouring open spaces like they were candy and destroying fragile coral reefs with huge numbers of tourists. Enforcement has been less effective in the DR's central mountains, where logging and encroachment by farmers continues in many areas. Together, Parque Nacional Jaragua, Lago Enriquillo and Parque Nacional Sierra de Bahoruco form the Jaragua-Bahoruco-Enriquillo Biosphere Reserve, the first Unesco biosphere reserve in the country.

Environmental Issues

The DR has a rapidly growing population and millions of tourists a year, all of whom put severe pressure on the land. Water use, damage to marine ecosystems and, most of all, deforestation, present acute environmental challenges. Despite the government's continual efforts in setting aside pristine land, and at times banning commercial logging, parks

---

DOMINICAN LANDSCAPES PLANTS

Not-to-be-Missed Waterfalls

» Salto de Jimenoa Uno, Jarabacoa (p179)

» Cascada El Limón, Las Terrenas (p123)

» Damajagua, south of Puerto Plata (p161)

» Aguas Blancas, Constanza (p187)

Want to put a name to that frog or gecko? Consult *Amphibians and Reptiles of the West Indies*, by Robert Henderson and Albert Schwartz.

Living in salt water mangroves is a challenge, and some species require a healthy dose of fresh water at least once a year in order to survive. Their source? Hurricanes.

HURRICANE ALLEY

Caribbean hurricanes are born 3000km away off the west coast of Africa, where pockets of low pressure draw high winds toward them and Earth's rotation molds them into their familiar counterclockwise swirl. The strongest and rarest of hurricanes, Category 5, typically build up in July and August and pack winds that exceed 250km/h. Hurricane Katrina, which devastated New Orleans in 2005, was a Category 5 hurricane. Hispaniola has often been hit hard by hurricanes. In 1979, Hurricane David killed over a thousand people; in 1998 the destruction wreaked by Hurricane Georges left around 340,000 people homeless. In 2007, Hurricane Noel was the deadliest hurricane of the year, arriving in November (well past the traditional hurricane season). Severe flooding, particularly in the DR, killed around 160 people, and knocked out electricity for a third of the country. Haiti got off comparatively lightly, with 400 houses destroyed. If you're near the coast when a hurricane is approaching, head inland, preferably to a large city where there are modern buildings and emergency services. Large resorts in the DR have sturdy hurricane shelters and evacuation procedures. Stay away from the beach, rivers, lakes and anywhere mudslides are a risk. Avoid standing near windows, as flying debris and sudden pressure changes can shatter the glass. The **National Hurricane Center** (www.nhc.noaa.gov), run by the US National Oceanic and Atmospheric Administration, is the place to head for current tropical storm information.

One of the coldest parts of the country is Reserva Científica de Valle Nuevo, southeast of Constanza on the way to San Jose de Ocoa, with temperatures as low as -8°C and vegetation similar to the European Alps.

and reserves remain chronically underfunded, and illegal logging and agricultural encroachment remain a problem, especially in the central highlands. It's estimated that the DR has lost 60% of its forests in the last 80 years, and only 5% of Haiti's remain.

Coastal resorts and villages also have a tremendous impact on the very seas that provide their livelihood. Pollution, runoff and other consequences of massive developments have destroyed many of the island's foremost reefs. Overfishing and the inadvertent destruction caused by careless humans transform reefs into gray shadows of their former selves.

In the DR – country of the megaresorts – there is an increased emphasis on low-impact tourism and environmental monitoring, and outside funding has helped support critical infrastructure for ecotourism and parks.

Vertebrate species particularly endangered on Hispaniola include the Caribbean manatee, Caribbean monk seal, Atlantic spotted dolphin, American crocodile, rhinoceros iguana, Hispaniolan ground iguana, sea turtles, three species of freshwater turtle and dozens of bird species.

Survival
Guide

Directory A–Z

Accommodations

Compared to other destinations in the Caribbean, lodging in the Dominican Republic is relatively affordable. That said, there is a limited number of options for independent travelers wishing to make decisions on the fly and for whom cost is a concern.

In some places, such as Santo Domingo, you can stay in restored colonial-era buildings with loads of character with comfortable accommodations for less money than you would spend for a night at a bland international-chain-style hotel. Most have websites where you can make reservations in advance and you can often pay with a credit card, though it's a good idea to check in advance. A good number of all-inclusives, especially outside the holidays and the high season, fall into this category and can be remarkably good deals considering what you get. It's important, however, to keep in mind the peculiar nature of this style of accommodations; see opposite for more details.

From US$200 and up (the ceiling is high for the most exclusive resorts) there's a big jump in terms of the quality of furnishings, food and service, and in the Dominican Republic, maybe more than elsewhere, you truly get what you pay for.

Pay budget room rates and you won't necessarily feel like you're on vacation, especially in the cities, but there are some exceptions. The DR has no proper hostels, and very little backpacker culture of the sort found in the rest of Latin America, Europe and elsewhere. The walled compounds generically called 'cabañas turisti-cas', with names suggestive of intercourse or romantic love, on the outskirts of most large towns are short-time hotels for couples seeking privacy. Note that some budget options may not be able to guarantee hot water. Across this book, prices for budget options are up to US$40, midrange are generally between US$40 and US$80 and top end are over US$80. Following are some guidelines on room rates:

» Room rates quoted in this book are for the high season (generally from December to March and July to August) and include bathroom unless otherwise stated.

» Sometimes a price range is indicated where the low- or medium-season rates are significantly reduced (otherwise assume that low-season rates are from 20% to 50% less than high-season rates).

» Rooms booked a minimum of three days in advance on the internet are shockingly cheaper (especially so at the all-inclusive resorts) than if you book via phone or, worst-case scenario, simply show up without a reservation.

» Be sure the rate you are quoted already includes the 23% room tax. We've experienced sticker shock when paying the bill after making reservations and booking online.

PRACTICALITIES

» *El Listín Diario* (www.listin.com.do), *Hoy* (www.hoy.com.do), *Diario Libre* (www.diariolibre.com) and *El Nacional* (www.elnacional.com.do), plus *International Herald Tribune*, the *New York Times* and the *Miami Herald* can be found in many tourist areas.

» There are about 150 radio stations, most playing merengue and *bachata* (popular guitar music based on bolero rhythms); and seven local TV networks, though cable and satellite programming is very popular for baseball, movies and American soap operas.

» The DR uses the metric system for everything except gasoline, which is measured in gallons, and at laundromats, where laundry is measured in pounds.

SORTING THROUGH ALL THE ALL-INCLUSIVES

Consider the following questions if you're trying to choose an all-inclusive resort:

» **Location**: What part of the country is the resort in? What sights are nearby?

» **The fine print**: Are all the restaurants included and if so, any variety other than buffet? How about alcoholic beverages? Motorized water sports?

» **Ocean front**: Is the resort on the beach, across the street, a bus ride away?

» **Children**: Is this a kid-friendly resort? Is there a kids' club? Babysitting service?

» **Entertainment**: Are there nightly performances or live-music venues? How about a disco?

All-Inclusive Resorts

Easily the most popular form of lodging in the DR is the all-inclusive resort. Much of the prime beachfront property throughout the country is occupied by all-inclusives. The largest concentrations are at Bávaro/Punta Cana in the east and Playa Dorada in the north, though their numbers are growing in other areas including the Península de Samaná which until recently was considered relatively hard to get to. Boca Chica and Juan Dolio, both within easy driving distance of Santo Domingo, have small concentrations as well.

If you're looking for a hassle-free vacation, it's easy to understand the appeal of the all-inclusive. The majority offer at least one all-you-can-eat buffet and several stand-alone restaurants (these sometimes require reservations once you've arrived and sometimes cost extra) and food is usually available virtually around the clock. Drinks (coffee, juice, soda, beer, wine, mixed drinks) are also unlimited and served up almost 24/7 from restaurants, beach and pool bars, cafes, discos etc. Most are located on the beach and have lounge chairs and towels, as well as several pools. A variety of tours

are on offer daily, including snorkeling, diving, trips to parks and sights in the surrounding area, city tours and horseback riding. If there isn't a golf course on the property, no doubt the concierge can arrange a tee time.

Several companies dominate the resort landscape in the Dominican Republic. Names like Melia, Barcelo and Wyndham are plastered on signs everywhere from Puerto Plata to Bávaro. Often there will be several Melias, Barcelos or Wyndhams in the same area, ranging widely in terms of quality and costs – it can get confusing. While choosing the best resort for you or your family requires some homework, it's well worth the effort. Too often people's vacations are ruined by unrealistic expectations fostered by out-of-focus photos and inaccurate information found online.

And if it's your first time visiting the Dominican Republic, it's difficult to have a sense of the geography of the

area you're considering. For example, the Bávaro/Punta Cana region is quite large, and while some resorts are within walking distance of one another and local restaurants and shops, others are isolated and without a rental vehicle you might end up feeling stranded. Websites like dr1. com (www.dr1.com) and Debbie's Dominican Republic Travel Page (www.debbies dominicantravel.com) can be useful, with detailed, first-person reviews from travelers who have stayed recently at various resorts.

In this book, reviews for all-inclusive options will include a mention of 'all-incl' in the practicalities details where costs are shown.

Camping

Other than the basic free cabins en route to Pico Duarte, there are only a handful of formal campgrounds. You'll have the most luck in rural mountain areas or along deserted beaches – inland, you should ask the owner of the plot of land you are on before pitching a tent, and on the beach ask the Politur (tourist police) or local police if it is allowed and safe.

Rental Accommodations

If you'll be in the Dominican Republic for long – even a couple of weeks – renting an apartment, condo or villa can be a convenient and cost-effective way to enjoy the country. There are a number of homes that can be rented by the week or month; alternatively, look for 'apartahotels,' which have studio, one-bedroom and two-bedroom apartments, usually with fully

---

BOOK YOUR STAY ONLINE

For more accommodations reviews by Lonely Planet authors, check out hotels.lonelyplanet.com/Dominican -Republic. You'll find independent reviews, as well as recommendations on the best places to stay. Best of all, you can book online.

equipped kitchens. This book lists a number of apartahotels in areas where long-term units are popular, such as Cabarete. Some hotels have a small number of units with kitchens – such cases are also indicated in the listings.

Business Hours

The following are normal business hours. Reviews don't include hours unless they differ from these standards.

» **Banks** 9am-4:30pm Mon-Fri; to 1pm Sat

» **Bars** 6pm-late; to 2am in Santo Domingo

» **Government offices** 7:30am-2:30pm Mon-Fri

» **Restaurants** 8am-10pm Mon-Sat (some closed btwn lunch & dinner)

» **Shops** 9am-7:30pm Mon-Sat; some open half-day Sun

» **Supermarkets** 8am-10pm Mon-Sat

Children

All-inclusive resorts can be a convenient and affordable way for families to travel, as they provide easy answers to the most vexing of travel questions: when is dinner? Where are we going to eat? What are we going to do? Can I have another Coke? For independent-minded families the DR is no better or worse than most countries – its small size means no long bus or plane rides, and the beaches and outdoor activities are fun for everyone. At the same time, navigating the cities can be challenging for parents and exhausting for children. For excellent general advice on traveling with children, check out Lonely Planet's *Travel with Children*.

Practicalities

All-inclusive resorts have the best child-specific facilities and services, from high chairs in the restaurants to child care and children's programming. That said, not all

Climate

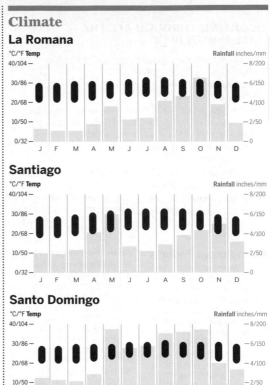

resorts cater to families with young children, so be sure to ask before booking. Independent travelers will have a harder time finding facilities designed for children.

Child safety seats are not common, even in private cars, and are almost unheard of in taxis or buses. Seatbelts are required by law, however, so if you bring your own car seat – and it's one that can adapt to a number of different cars – you may be able to use it at least some of the time.

Breastfeeding babies in public is not totally taboo, but nor is it very common. It is definitely not done in restaurants, as in the US and some other countries. Nursing mothers are recommended to find a private park bench and use a shawl or other covering.

Major grocery stores sell many of the same brands of baby food and diapers (nappies) as in the US.

Customs Regulations

Customs regulations are similar to most countries, with restrictions on the import of live animals, fresh fruit or vegetables, weapons and drugs, and the export of ancient artifacts and endangered plants or animals.

Other than the obvious, like weapons and drugs, there are only a few specific import restrictions for foreigners arriving in the Dominican Republic. Visitors can bring up to 200 cigarettes, 2L of alcohol and gifts not exceeding US$100 duty-free. It's best to carry a prescription for any medication, especially psychotropic drugs.

It is illegal to take anything out of the DR that is over 100 years old – including paintings, household items and prehistoric artifacts – without special export certificates. Mahogany trees are endangered and products made from mahogany wood may be confiscated upon departure. Black coral is widely available but although Dominican law does not forbid its sale, international environment agreements do – avoid purchasing it. The same goes for products made from turtle shells and butterfly wings – these animals are facing extinction. It is illegal to export raw unpolished amber from the DR, though amber jewelry is common and highly prized.

Most travelers run into problems with the export of cigars, and it's not with Dominican customs as much as their own. Canada, European countries and the US allow its citizens to bring in up to 50 cigars duty-free.

Electricity

110v/60hz

Food

Some visitors to the Dominican Republic never experience a meal outside of their all-inclusive resort and when all the food you can eat is calculated into the room price, eating can seem like a bargain. For travelers hoping to eat out on their own, food can be surprisingly expensive. Of course, prices tend to be much higher in heavily touristy areas, such as the Zona Colonial in Santo Domingo (comparable to US and European prices), and cheaper in small towns and isolated areas. However, outside of informal food stands and cafeteria-style eateries, a meal without drinks at most restaurants will cost a minimum of RD$250 or US$7 (after the 16% ITBIS tax and 10% service charge have been added on). Many restaurants have a range of options, from inexpensive pizza and pasta dishes to pricey lobster meals.

Dinner is the biggest meal, though neither breakfast nor lunch are exactly light. All three meals usually consist of one main dish – eggs for breakfast, meat for lunch and dinner – served with one or more accompaniments, usually rice, beans, salad and/or boiled vegetables.

The most typically Dominican meal is known as *la bandera* (the flag); it consists of white rice, *habichuela* (red beans), stewed meat, salad and fried green plantains, and is usually accompanied by a fresh fruit juice. Red beans are sometimes swapped for small *moros* (black beans), *gandules* (small green beans) or *lentejas* (lentils).

Bananas *(guineos)* are a staple of Dominican cuisine and served in a variety of ways, including boiled, stewed and candied. But the main way Dominicans eat bananas is boiled and mashed, like mashed potatoes. Prepared the same

way, but with plantains, the dish is called *mangú;* with pork rinds mixed in it is called *mofongo.* Both are very filling and can be served for breakfast, lunch or dinner, either as a side dish or as the main dish itself.

It should be no surprise that seafood is a central part of Dominican cuisine, especially along the coast where it is sure to be fresh. The most common plate is a fish fillet, usually *mero* (grouper) or *chillo* (red snapper), served in one of four ways: *al ajillo* (with garlic), *al coco* (in coconut sauce), *al criolla* (with a mild tomato sauce) or *a la diabla* (with a spicy tomato sauce). Other seafood like *cangrejo* (crab), *calamar* (octopus), *camarones* (shrimp), *pulp* (squid) and *lambí* (conch) are prepared in the same sauces, as well as *al vinagre* (in vinegar sauce).

Two other common dishes are *locrio,* the Dominican version of paella – rice is colored with achiote – with a number of different variations, and Dominican sweet bean soup – *habichuela con dulce,* a thick soup with root vegetables. Goat meat is also extremely popular and two of the best dishes are *pierna de chivo asada con ron y cilantro* (roast leg of goat with rum and cilantro) and *chivo guisado en salsa de tomate* (goat stewed in tomato sauce).

One of the DR's favorite drinks, among locals and foreigners alike, is *batidas* (smoothies), made from crushed fruit, water, ice and several tablespoons of sugar. A *batida con leche* contains milk and is slightly frothier. Popular varieties include *piña* (pineapple), *papaya* (known as *lechoza*), *guineo* (banana) and *zapote* (sapote). Some *batidas* have strange local names, such as *morir soñando* (literally, 'to die dreaming'), made of the combination of orange juice, milk, sugar and crushed ice.

EMBASSIES & CONSULATES

All of the following are located in Santo Domingo.

EMBASSY	CONTACT DETAILS	ADDRESS
Canada	☎809-685-1136	Av Eugenio de Marchena 39
Cuba	☎809-537-0139	Calle Hatuey 808
France	☎809-695-4300	Calle Las Damas 42
Germany	☎809-542-8949	Torre Piantini, 16th fl, Av Gustavo A Mejía Ricart 196
Haiti	☎809-412-7112	Calle Juan Sánchez Ramírez 33
Israel	☎809-472-0774	Calle Pedro Henriquez Ureña 80
Italy	☎809-682-0830	Calle Rodríguez Objío 4
Japan	☎809-567-3365	Torre BHD office Bldg, 8th fl, cnr Calle Luís Thomen & Av Winston Churchill
Netherlands	☎809-262-0320	Calle Max Henriquez Ureña 50
Russia	☎809-620-1471	Diamond Plaza, 2nd fl, Los Proceres
Spain	☎809-535-6500	Av Independencia 1205
UK	☎809-472-7671	Hotel Santo Domingo, Ste 1108, cnr Av Independencia & Lincoln
US	☎809-221-2171	cnr Av César Nicolás Penson & Av Máximo Gómez

Coffee, grown in six different regions by over 60,000 growers, is a staple of most Dominicans' diets. It's typically served black in an espresso cup with sugar; a *café con leche* is a coffee with hot milk.

Quick Eats

» *Agua de coco* Fruits like oranges, bananas and pineapples mixed with sliced coconuts and sugarcane juice.

» *Chimi* Sandwich of seasoned ground meat, cooked cabbage, carrots, red onions and tomatoes; typically served in a plastic bag to catch the juices.

» *Frío-frío* Shaved ice and syrup, the local snow cone.

» *Frituras de batata* Sweet-potato fritters.

» *Fritos maduros* Ripe plantain fritters.

» *Helados* Ice cream.

» *Pastelito* By far the most common snack in the DR – these fried patties usually contain beef or chicken, which has first been stewed with onions, olives, tomatoes and a variety of seasonings, and then chopped up and mixed with peas, nuts and raisins.

» *Tostones* Fried plantain slices.

» *Yaniqueques* Johnny cakes.

Gay & Lesbian Travelers

As a whole, the Dominican Republic is quite open about heterosexual sex and sexuality, but still fairly closed-minded about gays and lesbians. Gay and lesbian travelers will find the most open community in Santo Domingo, though even its gay clubs are relatively discreet. Santiago, Puerto Plata, Bávaro and Punta Cana also have gay venues, catering as much to foreigners as to locals. Everywhere else, open displays of affection between men or women are rare and quite taboo. Two men may have trouble getting a hotel room with just one bed, even though you'll pay more for a room with two. Two good websites with gay-specific listings and information for the Dominican Republic are **Guia Gay** (www.guiagay.com, in Spanish) and **Planetout. com** (www.planetout.com).

Health

From a medical standpoint, the DR is generally safe as long as you're reasonably careful about what you eat and drink. The most common

RESTAURANT PRICE RANGES

The listing categories in this book refer to the cost of a main dish with tax.

Budget $ less than RD$180 or US$5

Midrange $$ RD$180 to RD$540 or US$5 to US$15

Top end $$$ RD$540 or US$15 and above

travel-related diseases, such as dysentery and hepatitis, are acquired by consumption of contaminated food and water. Mosquito-borne illnesses are not a significant concern, although there is a small but significant malaria risk in the western provinces and in La Altagracia (including Punta Cana). Medical care is variable in Santo Domingo and limited elsewhere, although good care can be found in many of the more heavily touristed towns. Many doctors and hospitals expect payment in cash, regardless of whether you have travel-health insurance.

Some internet resources:

Lonely Planet (www.lonely planet.com) A great place to start.

MD Travel Health (www .mdtravelhealth.com) Another website of general interest which provides complete travel health recommendations for every country, updated daily, at no cost.

World Health Organization (www.who.int/ith) Available online at no cost as well as in book form – *International Travel and Health* – which is revised annually.

Internet Access

The Dominican Republic has a surprisingly limited number of internet cafes; most charge RD$35 to RD$70 per hour, more for additional services like printing or burning CDs. Most of these cafes also operate as call centers.

Wi-fi access is becoming more and more prevalent, especially in cafes and restaurants, as well as at midrange and top-end hotels and resorts throughout the country. Travelers with laptops won't have to go far before finding some place with a signal. However, the majority of the all-inclusives, as opposed to most midrange and even budget hotels, charge daily fees (around US$15 and up) for access. Many hotels that offer the service free for guests only have a signal in public spaces like the lobby and not in guest rooms.

Legal Matters

The Dominican Republic has two police forces – the Policía Nacional (national police) and the Policía Turística (tourist police, commonly referred to by its abbreviation 'Politur').

Politur officers are generally friendly men and women whose job is specifically to help tourists. Many speak a little bit of a language other than Spanish. They wear white shirts with blue insignia and can usually be found near major tourist sights and centers. You should contact Politur first in the event of theft, assault or if you were the victim of a scam, but you can equally ask them for directions to sights, which bus to take etc. Many cities have a Politur station, which you will find listed in the destination chapters throughout this book.

It's best to have as little interaction with the Policía Nacional as possible. If a police officer stops you, be polite and cooperate. They may ask to see your passport – you're not required to have it on you, but it's always a good idea to carry a photocopy.

Prostitution is big business in the DR. Tourists picking up willing men or women is common and, evidently, there is no law that is enforced against it, even if money changes hands. But there is no law expressly legalizing prostitution, either. It is definitely illegal to have sex with anyone under the age of 18, even if the offender didn't know the prostitute's real age. Encouraging or aiding prostitution is illegal, and the law, while targeted at pimps or brothel owners, is interpreted in various ways. The Dominican consulate will tell you that prostitution in all forms is illegal. In any case, walking the line between what is legal and illegal, especially as a foreigner, is definitely risky.

Money

The Dominican monetary unit is the peso, indicated by the symbol RD$ (or sometimes just R$). Though the peso is technically divided into 100 centavos (cents) per peso, prices are usually rounded to the nearest peso. There are one- and five-peso coins, while paper money comes in denominations of 10, 20, 50, 100, 500 and 1000 pesos. Many tourist-related businesses, including most midrange and top-end hotels, list prices in US dollars, but accept pesos at the going exchange rate. We've listed prices in the currency they are most commonly quoted on the ground – either RD$ or US$. See p21 for a list of exchange rates.

ATMs

ATMs are common in the Dominican Republic and are, without question, the best way to obtain Dominican pesos and manage your money on the road. Banks with reliable ATMs include Banco Popular, Banco Progreso, Banco de Reservas, Banco León and Scotiabank. Most charge ATM fees (around RD$115 on average), but some don't depending on the card you use; it's worth checking with your domestic bank before you travel. As in any country, be smart about where and when you withdraw cash – at night on a dark street in a bad part of town is not the ideal spot. Most ATMs are not in the bank itself, but in a small booth accessible from the street (and thus available 24 hours). Unless otherwise indicated all banks listed have ATMs.

Credit Cards

Credit and debit cards are more and more common among Dominicans (and more widely accepted for use by foreigners). Visa and MasterCard are more common than Amex but most cards are accepted in areas frequented by tourists. Some but not all businesses add a surcharge for credit-card purchases (typically 16%) – the federal policy of withdrawing sales tax directly from credit-card transactions means merchants will simply add the cost directly to the bill. We've had reports of travelers being excessively overcharged when paying by credit card so always check the bill before signing.

Moneychangers

Moneychangers will approach you in a number of tourist centers. They are unlikely to be aggressive. You will get equally favorable rates, however, and a much securer transaction, at an ATM, a bank or an exchange office.

Taxes & Tipping

There are two taxes on food and drink sales: a 16% sales tax (ITBIS) and a 10% service charge. The latter is supposed to be divided among the wait and kitchen staff; some people choose to leave an additional 10% tip for exceptional service. There's a 23% tax on hotel rooms – ask whether the listed rates include taxes. It's customary to tip bellhops for carrying your bags and to leave US$1 to US$2 per night for the housecleaner at resorts. You should also tip tour guides, some of whom earn no other salary.

Safe Travel

Tensions along the Haitian border flare up from time to time so it's recommended that you check on the current situation before planning to cross the border.

In light of the threat of cholera at the time of research, it's highly recommended that only purified water be used for drinking, brushing your teeth as well as hand washing.

Telephone

Remember that you must dial ☎1 + 809 or 829 for all calls within the DR, even local ones. There are no regional codes. Local calls cost US$0.14 per minute and national calls are US$0.21 per minute. Toll-free numbers have ☎200 or ☎809 for their prefix (not the area code).

The easiest way to make a phone call in the DR is to pay per minute (average rates per minute: to US US$0.20; to Europe US$0.50; to Haiti US$0.50) at a Codetel Centro de Comunicaciones (Codetel) call center or an internet cafe – virtually all operate as dual call centers.

Cell Phones

Cell (mobile) phones are very popular and travelers with global-roaming-enabled phones can receive and make cellphone calls. It's worth checking with your cell-phone carrier for details on rates and accessibility – be aware that per-minute fees can be exorbitant. If you have a GSM phone, and you can unlock it, you can use a SIM card bought from Orange or Claro (prepaid startup kit US$10). If it's CDMA, it will work with Claro or Tricom. New cell phones can be bought at Orange with a prepaid SIM card for less than US$30; used phones at Claro can be bought for US$10.

Phonecards

These can be used at public phones and are available in denominations of RD$50, RD$100, RD$150, RD$200 and RD$250.

Time

The DR is four hours behind Greenwich Mean Time. In autumn and winter it is one hour ahead of New York, Miami and Toronto as well as Haiti – extremely important to keep in mind if heading to or from the border. However, because the country does not adjust for daylight saving time as do the USA and Canada, it's in the same time zone as New York, Miami and Toronto from the first Sunday in April to the last Sunday in October.

Tourist Information

Almost every city in the DR that's frequented by tourists has a tourist office, and a number of less-visited towns do as well. Whether they are actually helpful is another question entirely. In general, treat the information you get at tourist offices skeptically and double-check with other sources. Some tourist offices offer maps, bus schedules or a calendar of upcoming events, which can be handy.

Travelers with Disabilities

Few Latin American countries are well suited for travelers with disabilities, and the Dominican Republic is no different. On the other hand, all-inclusive resorts can be ideal for travelers with mobility impairments, as rooms, meals and day- and nighttime activities are all within close proximity, and there are plenty of staff members to help you navigate around the property. Some resorts have a few wheelchair-friendly rooms, with larger doors and handles in the bathroom. And, it should be said, Dominicans tend to be extremely helpful and accommodating people. Travelers with disabilities should expect some curious stares, but also quick and friendly help from perfect strangers and passersby.

Visas

The majority of would-be foreign travelers in the Dominican Republic do not need to obtain visas prior to arrival. Tourist cards (you don't need to retain this for your return flight) are issued for US$10 upon arrival to visitors from Argentina, Australia, Austria, Belgium, Brazil, Canada, Chile, Denmark, France, Germany, Greece, Ireland, Israel, Italy, Japan, Mexico, the Netherlands, Portugal, Russia, South Africa, Spain, Sweden, Switzerland, the UK and the US, among many others. Whatever your country of origin, a valid passport is necessary.

Tourist Card Extensions

A tourist card is good for up to 30 days from the date of issue. If you wish to stay longer, it's unnecessary to formally extend – instead you'll be charged RD$800 when you depart the country for any stay up to 90 days. Another way to extend your time is to leave the DR briefly – most likely to Haiti – and then return, at which point you'll be issued a brand-new tourist card. (You may have to pay entrance and departure fees in both countries, of course.)

To extend your tourist card longer than three months, you must apply in Santo Domingo at the **Dirección General de Migración** (☑809-508-2555; www .migracion.gov.do; cnr Av 30 de Mayo & Héroes de Luperón; ☉8am-2:30pm Mon-Fri) at least two weeks before your original card expires. You'll be required to fill out a form – usually available in Spanish only – and to present your passport, a photocopy of your passport's information page(s) and two passport-size photos of yourself. The fee is US$10; your passport

and new tourist card will be ready for pickup at the same office two weeks later. The process is a good way to blow an entire day.

Volunteering

Many NGOs operating in the DR are primarily community networks attempting to develop sustainable ecotourism. Formal volunteering programs may be nonexistent, but if you speak good Spanish and don't mind some elbow grease (or office work), you may be of some use to them. Be sure to contact them well ahead of time. There is occasionally some wildlife volunteering on offer – helping biologists hatch turtle eggs, for instance – and the best months for field work are February, April, May, August and October. Several of the more established organizations that accept volunteers include the following:

CEDAF (Centro para el Desarrollo Agropecuario y Forestal; ☑809-565-5603; www.cedaf .org.do; José Amado Soler 50, Ensanche Paraíso, Santo Domingo) This nationwide NGO helps local farmers develop sustainable ways to use the land.

DREAM Project (Dominican Republic Education & Mentoring; ☑809-571-0497; www.dominicandream.org; Plaza de Patio, Cabarete) Nonconformists will want to avoid this rigidly managed NGO, which otherwise does excellent work in the Cabarete schools.

Fundación Taigüey (☑809-537-8977; offices in Barahona & La Ciénaga) This is a network of small NGOs, several of which focus on ecotourism.

Grupo Jaragua (☑809-472-1036; www.grupojaragua .do) The largest and oldest NGO in the southwest. Based in Santo Domingo, it

concentrates on biodiversity and conservation through microfinancing as little as US$300 to assist locals with bee farming etc.

Punta Cana Ecological Foundation (☑809-959-9221; www.puntacana.org) One of the pioneers of sustainable development in the DR; projects targeted at restoring and preserving the natural environment in the Punta Cana area.

REDOTOR (Red Dominicana de Turismo Rural; ☑809-487-1057; www.redotur.org) Promotes alternative and sustainable tourism projects.

SOEPA (☑809-899-4702) Its biggest project is maintenance and development at Cachóte (see boxed text, p205).

Women Travelers

Women traveling without men in the Dominican Republic should expect to receive a fair amount of attention, usually in the form of stares and comments like 'Hola, preciosa' (Hello, beautiful). Although the attention may be unwanted, it's more of a nuisance than anything else. If you don't like it, dressing conservatively and ignoring the comments are probably your best lines of defense.

But that is not at all to say that women travelers shouldn't take the same precautions they would in other countries, or ignore their instincts about certain men or situations they encounter. Robbery and assaults, though rare against tourists, do occur and women are often seen as easier targets than men. Beyond that, simply follow basic common-sense precautions when traveling by yourself: avoid isolated streets and places, especially at night, and don't hitchhike or camp alone.

Transportation

GETTING THERE & AWAY

Entering the Country

The vast majority of tourists entering the Dominican Republic arrive by air. Independent travelers typically arrive at the main international airport outside of Santo Domingo, Aeropuerto Internacional Las Américas. Passing through immigration is a relatively simple process. Once disembarked, you are guided to the immigration area where you must buy a tourist card (US$10). You're expected to pay in US dollars. Euros and GBP are accepted, but you lose out substantially on the rate; a few people report that DR pesos (RD$) are accepted, though this is not official policy. Once you've filled in the card, join the queue in front of one of the immigration officers. You're allowed up to 30 days on a tourist card. The procedure is the same if you arrive at one of the other airports like Puerto Plata or Punta Cana; the latter is easily the busiest airport in the country

in terms of tourist arrivals. Officers are even less scrutinizing there, but the queues may become backed up as you are asked to pause for an obligatory photograph with two woman dressed in some kind of garish island costume reminiscent of the Chiquita Banana mascot.

Flights, tours and rail tickets can be booked online at lonelyplanet.com/bookings.

Passport

All foreign visitors must have a valid passport to enter the DR. Be sure you have room for both entry and exit stamps, and that your passport is valid for at least six months beyond your planned travel dates. See p249 for information on visas.

Air

Airports

The DR has 10 international airports, though at least three of them are primarily used for domestic flights.

Aeropuerto Internacional Arroyo Barril (ABA; ☎809-248-2718) West of Samaná, a small airstrip used mostly during whale-watching season (January to March)

that handles only propeller aircraft.

Aeropuerto Internacional Cibao (STI; ☎809-581-8072) Serves Santiago and the interior.

Aeropuerto Internacional El Catey (AZS; ☎809-338-0094) Forty kilometers west of Samaná; handles international flights from various European cities and San Juan, Puerto Rico.

Aeropuerto Internacional El Portillo (EPS) Airstrip only a few kilometers from Las Terrenas that gets busiest during whale-watching season. Used for domestic flights.

Aeropuerto Internacional Gregorio Luperón (POP; ☎809-586-1992) Serves Playa Dorada and Puerto Plata.

Aeropuerto Internacional La Isabela (JBQ or AILI; DR Joaquin Balaguer, Higuero; ☎809-826-4003) Located 16km north of Santo Domingo in Higuero, this airport services domestic airlines.

Aeropuerto Internacional La Romana (LRM; Casa de Campo; ☎809-689-1548) Modern airport near La Romana and Casa de Campo; handles primarily charter flights from the US, Canada and Europe. American and American Eagle have flights from Miami and Puerto Rico.

Aeropuerto Internacional Las Américas (SDQ; ☎809-947-2220) Located 20km east of Santo Domingo. The country's main international airport, with modern facilities, including a strong wi-fi signal once past security.

Aeropuerto Internacional María Montez (BRX; ☎809-524-4144) Located 5km from Barahona; does not have a regular commercial passenger service.

Aeropuerto Internacional Punta Cana (PUJ; ☎809-959-2473) Serves Bávaro and Punta Cana, and is the busiest airport in the country.

AIRLINES FLYING TO/ FROM THE DOMINICAN REPUBLIC

Aeropostal (www.aeropostal .com)

Air Berlin (www.airberlin .com) Charter flights from Germany

Air Canada (www.aircanada .ca)

Air Europa (www.aireuropa .com)

Air France (www.airfrance .com)

Air Jamaica (www.airjamaica .com)

Air Tran (www.airtran.com) Direct flights to Punta Cana.

Air Turks & Caicos (www .flyairtc.com)

American Airlines (www .aa.com) Flies to Samaná via San Juan (Puerto Rico); also flies to Santo Domingo, Santiago and Puerto Plata.

Blue Panorama (www .blue-panorama.com) Charter flights from Italy.

Condor (www.condor.com)

Continental Airlines (www .continental.com)

COPA Airlines (www.copaair .com) Several flights a week from Santo Domingo to Havana, Kingston and Port of Spain (Trinidad).

Cubana Air (www.cubana.cu) Twice-weekly direct flights between Santo Domingo and Havana.

Delta (www.delta.com)

Iberia (www.iberia.com)

Jet Blue (www.jetblue .com; hub) Nonstop service between JFK and Puerto Plata, Santiago and Santo

Domingo. Also nonstop service from Orlando to Santo Domingo.

Lan Chile (www.lan.com)

LTU (www.ltu.com) Flights from Germany and Austria to Samaná.

Lufthansa (www.lufthansa .com)

Martinair Holland (www .martinair.com) Flights from Amsterdam and Frankfurt to Puerto Plata and Punta Cana.

Mexicana (www.mexicana .com)

Spirit Airlines (www.spiritair .com; Fort Lauderdale) Non-stop flights from Fort Lauderdale to Santo Domingo and Punta Cana.

Thomson Airways (www .flights.thomson.co.uk) Charter flights from the UK.

US Airways (www.usair.com)

USA 3000 (www.usa3000 .com) Nonstop flights between Punta Cana and Baltimore, Chicago, Cleveland, Pittsburgh, Philadelphia and St Louis.

Varig (www.varig.com)

Sea

International cruise ships on Caribbean tours commonly stop in Santo Domingo, Cayo Levantado in the Península de Samaná and elsewhere. Sans Souci, the Santo Domingo port where Royal Caribbean's *Legend of the Seas* docks, has amenities geared towards disembarking passengers.

Caribbean Fantasy, now run by **America Cruise Ferries** (www.acferries.com) Santo Domingo (☎809-688-4400); Mayagüez, Puerto Rico (☎787-832-4800); San Juan, Puerto Rico (☎787-622-4800) offers a passenger and car ferry service between Santo Domingo and San Juan and Mayagüez, Puerto Rico. The trip takes about 12 hours and departs three times weekly; see p75 for more information.

GETTING AROUND

Air

Airlines in the DR

The DR is a fairly small country, so in theory at least it's easy to drive or take public transportation from one side of the country to the other. In practice, however, the inadequate road network will behoove some with limited time to consider flying. It's a more expensive option, but often a convenient and logical one that can save you an entire day of road rage. Most one-way flights cost US$35 to US$170. The main domestic carriers and air-taxi companies include the following:

AeroDomca (☎809-826-4141; www.aerodomca.com) Scheduled flights between La Isabela outside Santo Domingo to El Portillo near Las Terrenas (US$80); one daily flight stops at Santo

---

CLIMATE CHANGE & TRAVEL

Every form of transportation that relies on carbon-based fuel generates CO_2, the main cause of human-induced climate change. Modern travel is dependent on aeroplanes, which might use less fuel per kilometer per person than most cars but travel much greater distances. The altitude at which aircraft emit gases (including CO_2) and particles also contributes to their climate-change impact. Many websites offer 'carbon calculators' that allow people to estimate the carbon emissions generated by their journey and, for those who wish to do so, to offset the impact of the greenhouse gases emitted with contributions to portfolios of climate-friendly initiatives throughout the world. Lonely Planet offsets the carbon footprint of all staff and author travel.

DOMINICAN REPUBLIC BORDER CROSSINGS

These are the four points where you can cross between Haiti and the DR.

Jimaní-Malpasse This, the busiest and most organized crossing, is in the south on the road that links Santo Domingo and Port-au-Prince. Open to 7pm.

Dajabón-Ouanaminthe Also busy is this northern crossing, which is on the road between Santiago and Cap-Haïtien (only a six-hour drive); however, you should try to avoid crossing on market days (Monday and Friday) because of the enormous crush of people and the risk of theft.

Pedernales-Ainse-a-Pietre In the far south; there's a small bridge for foot and motorcycle traffic, cars have to drive over a paved road through a generally shallow river. A small blue building on the other side is Haitian immigration. Relatively easy and calm crossing.

Comendador (aka Elías Piña)-Belladère Least busy and certainly the dodgiest. No doubt your presence will draw attention. On the Haiti side, the immigration building is several hundred meters from the actual border. Transportation further into Haiti is difficult to access.

Practicalities

Immigration offices on the Dominican side are usually open 8am to 6pm, and 9am to 6pm on the Haitian side. It's always a good idea to arrive as early as possible, so you are sure to get through both countries' border offices and onto a bus well before dark. When deciding between either crossing in the late afternoon or staying an extra night and crossing in the morning, choose the latter. Also, long lines and immigration officials who leave early or take long lunch breaks can cause delays at the border.

Leaving the DR You will be asked to produce your passport and are likely to be asked more questions than if you were leaving via an airport. However, this shouldn't be a concern since it's usually only out of curiosity that a tourist would travel this way. Officially, you are supposed to pay US$25 to leave the DR, which gives you the right to reenter at the same point for no extra charge. However, border officials have been known to ask for an extra US$5 to US$10 to leave and the full US$25 to reenter for no other reason than they can. It's worth politely pointing out that you have already paid the full fee. In the end, however, you may have to cough up the extra cash. If you're only interested in leaving without returning the fee should be US$10. For more information on leaving Haiti, see p356

Entering Haiti Pay a US$10 fee (US dollars only).

Public Transportation Caribe Tours and Capital Coach Lines service the Santo Domingo-Port-au-Prince route daily (see p74); it's the most convenient way to reach Haiti via public transportation. Caribe Tours also has daily departures at noon from Santiago for Cap-Haïtien (see p175). From the north coast it's easy enough to reach Dajabón, but then you have to transfer to a Haitian vehicle on the other side.

Private Transportation Rental vehicles are not allowed to cross from one country into the other, and you need special authorization to cross the border with a private vehicle. For specific information about the border facilities and services in individual towns, check the relevant destination chapters in this book.

Domingo's Aeropuerto Internacional Las Américas. Charter flights can be booked to almost any airport.

Air Century (☎809-826-4222; www.aircentury.com) Twice-daily flights from La Isabela outside Santo Domingo to Punta Cana (US$99).

Caribbean Air Sign (☎809-696-7460; www.caribbeanairsigns.com) Daily evening flights between Santo Domingo's Aeropuerto Internacional Las Américas and Punta Cana.

Dominican Shuttles (☎809-738-3014; www.dominicanshuttles.com)

Flights between La Isabela outside Santo Domingo and Punta Cana (US$99); two daily flights (US$99) between La Isabela and El Portillo near Las Terrenas.

Take Off (☎809-552-1333; www.takeoffweb.com) Offers the widest selection of scheduled flights, including

La Isabela outside Santo Domingo to El Portillo near Las Terrenas ($80), Punta Cana to El Portillo (US$116) and Puerto Plata to La Romana (US$170). A small, efficient office with English speakers is in the Plaza Brisas in Bávaro.

Volair (☑809-826-4068; www.govolair.com) Daily flights from La Isabela outside Santo Domingo to Punta Cana, Puerto Plata, Santiago and Arroyo Barril west of Samaná.

Bicycle

The DR's highways are not well suited for cycling, and Dominican drivers are not exactly accommodating to people on bikes. Add to that the high number of motorcycles (which move faster than bikes but slower than cars), and *gua-guas* (local buses) and *públicos* (private cars operating as taxis) making frequent unannounced stops, and the situation on the side of the road is hectic to say the least. However, mountain biking on the DR's back roads and lesser-used highways can be very rewarding, and a number of recommended tour companies operate in Jarabacoa and Cabarete. If you're planning a multiday ride, definitely consider bringing your own bike. If you're joining a bike tour, most tour operators will provide you with one.

Boat

The only regularly scheduled domestic passenger boat route in the DR is the ferry service between Samaná and Sabana de la Mar, on opposite sides of the Bahía de Samaná in the northeastern part of the country (see p116). The journey is subject to weather and departures are frequently canceled. There is no car ferry service here, so unfortunately, if you arrive in Sabana de la Mar with a rental vehicle, you'll have to leave it behind

and return by the same route you arrived.

Bus

The DR has a great bus system, with frequent service throughout the country. And since it's relatively small in size, there are none of the epic overnight journeys travelers often encounter in places like Mexico or Brazil. There are two classes of bus service in the DR: *primera* (first class) utilizes large air-conditioned buses similar to Greyhound buses in the US. Virtually all first-class buses have toilets in the back and TVs in the aisles showing movies en route. Air-conditioning is sometimes turned up to uncomfortable levels. Fares are low – the most expensive first-class ticket is less than US$10 – you must buy your ticket before boarding. Unfortunately, there are no central bus terminals in the majority of cities and each company has its own station location. They almost never stop along the road to pick up passengers but drivers are often willing to drop passengers off at various points along the way; they will not, however, open the luggage compartment at any point other than the actual terminal.

Reservations aren't usually necessary and rarely even taken. The exceptions are the international buses to Port-au-Prince, Haiti, operated by Caribe Tours and Terra Bus. During Dominican holidays you can sometimes buy your ticket a day or two in advance, which assures you a spot and saves you the time and hassle of waiting in line at a busy terminal with all your bags.

First-class carriers include the following:

Capital Coach Lines (☑809-531-0383; www.capital coachline.com; Plaza Lama, cnr Avs 27 de Febrero & Winston Churchill, Santo Domingo) Air-con service from Santo

Domingo to Port-au-Prince, Haiti.

Caribe Tours (☑809-221-4422; www.caribetours.com.do; cnr Avs 27 de Febrero & Leopoldo Navarro, Santo Domingo) The most extensive bus line, with service everywhere but the southeast. Fares given in destination chapters are for Caribe Tours.

Metro (☑809-566-7126; www.metrotours.com.do; Calle Francisco Prats Ramírez, Santo Domingo) Located behind Plaza Central Shopping Mall in Santo Domingo, Metro serves nine cities, mostly along the Santo Domingo–Puerto Plata corridor. Fares tend to be slightly more expensive than Caribe Tours.

Gua-Guas

Wherever long-distance buses don't go, you can be sure a *gua-gua* does. *Gua-guas* are typically midsize buses holding around 25 to 30 passengers. They rarely have signs, but the driver's assistant (known as the *cobrador,* or 'charger', since one of his jobs is to collect fares from passengers) will yell out the destination of the bus to potential fares on the side of the road. Don't hesitate to ask a local if you're unsure which one to take. *Gua-guas* pick up and drop off passengers anywhere along the route – to flag one down simply hold out your hand – the common gesture is to point at the curb in front of you (as if to say 'stop right here') but just about any gesture will do. Most *gua-guas* pass every 15 to 30 minutes and cost RD$35 to RD$70, but unless you have the exact amount some *cobradors* may pocket the change of unwary foreigners. It's a good idea to carry change or small bills and to find out the exact cost in advance by asking a local waiting with you at the stop.

Gua-guas are divided into two types – the majority are *caliente* (literally 'hot'), which don't have air-conditioning, naturally. For every four or five *caliente* buses there is usually an *expreso*, which typically has air-conditioning, makes fewer stops and costs slightly more. Within these two categories there's a virtual rainbow of diversity in terms of vehicle quality and reliability.

El Canario (*☑*809-291-5594) and **Papagayo** (*☑*809-802-3534) both offer daily service between Samaná and Puerto Plata (RD$250, 3½ to 4 hours), with stops in Nagua and Sánchez.

Expreso Santo Domingo Bávaro (*☑*809-682-9670; cnr Juan Sánchez Ruiz & Máximo Gómez, Santo Domingo) connects Santo Domingo and Bávaro with a stop in La Romana.

Car & Motorcycle

Though the DR's bus and *gua-gua* system is excellent, having your own car is invariably faster and more convenient. Even if renting a car isn't in your budget for the entire trip, consider renting one for a select couple of days, to reach sights that are isolated or not well served by public transportation.

Driver's License

For travelers from most countries, your home country driver's license allows you to drive in the DR. Be sure it's valid.

Fuel & Spare Parts

Most towns have at least one gas station, typically right along the highway on the outskirts of town. There are a couple of different companies, but prices are essentially the same for all. The base price of gasoline is regulated by the federal government; at the time of research, gas prices were fluctuating between RD$160 to RD$170 per gallon. Most gas stations do not accept credit cards, however many do have ATMs.

Play it safe and always keep your gas tank at least half full. Many *bombas* (gas stations) in the DR close by 7pm, and even when they are open they don't always have gas. If you're traveling on back roads or in a remote part of the country, your best bet is to buy gas from people selling it from their front porch. Look for the large pink jugs sitting on tables on the side of the road.

The most common car trouble is to end up with a punctured or damaged tire caused by potholes, speed bumps and rocks or other debris in the road. The word for tire is *goma* (literally 'rubber') and a tire shop is called a *gomero*. These are even more common than gas stations. If you can make it to one on your busted tire, the guys there can patch a flat (RD$180 to RD$280), replace a damaged tire (RD$360 to RD$1800 depending on type of tire and whether you want a new or used replacement), or just put the spare on for you (RD$70).

Insurance

The multinational car-rental agencies typically offer comprehensive, nondeductible collision and liability insurance for fairly small daily fees. Smaller agencies usually offer partial coverage, with a deductible ranging from US$100 to US$2000. Several credit-card companies, including Amex, offer comprehensive coverage for rentals, but you should check your own insurance policy before declining the rental company's.

Maps

If you rent a car, it's worth buying a good map to the area you'll be driving in. In Santo Domingo, **Mapas GAAR** (*☑*809-688-8004; www .mapasgaar.com.do; Espaillat; *☉*8:30am-5:30pm Mon-Fri) publishes and sells the most comprehensive maps of cities and towns in the DR. Borch produces a high-quality map of the DR available online and in bookstores.

You should also get in the habit of asking directions frequently. Not only will this prevent you from getting off track, but it's also a good time to ask about road conditions – in some cases rain or construction have made the roads very difficult to pass, especially if you're driving a compact car. The easiest way to ask directions if you're going to, say, Punta Rusia is to ask '*¿Para Punta Rusia?,*' literally 'For Punta Rusia?' To ask about conditions, you can say '*¿El camino está bien o malo?*' ('Is the road good or bad?') or '*¿Se puede pasar mi carro?*' ('Will my car be able to pass?'). Of course, understanding the directions you're given is half the battle; some key words to listen for are *derecho* (straight), *derecha* (right), *izquierdo* (left), *desvío* (turn-off), *letrero* (sign), *mucho pozo* or *mucha olla* (lots of potholes or holes) and *vaya preguntando* (ask along the way).

Rental

Familiar multinational agencies like Hertz, Avis, Europcar, Alamo and Dollar all have offices at Aeropuerto Internacional Las Américas (and pickup service at airports like Punta Cana), as well as in Santo Domingo and other cities. Not only are their rates usually much less than those of local or national agencies, but their vehicles are of much better quality and they provide reliable and comprehensive service and insurance. If you plan to do any driving outside major cities, a 4WD is recommended. Rates typically cost US$40 to US$120 per day, but if you make a reservation in advance via the internet discounts are substantial. Motorcycles can also be rented, but only experienced riders should do so because of poor road conditions.

Road Conditions

Roads in the DR range from excellent to awful, sometimes along the same highway over a very short distance. The *autopista* (freeway) between Santo Domingo and Santiago has as many as eight lanes, is fast moving and is generally in good condition. However, even here, always be alert for potholes, speed bumps and people walking along the roadside, especially near populated areas. On all roads, large or small, watch for slow-moving cars and especially motorcycles. Be particularly careful when driving at night, as potholes and speed bumps are harder to spot and many motorcycles and pedestrians don't have lights or reflectors. Better yet, *never drive at night*. Even the most skilled person with the reflexes of a superhero will probably end up in a ditch by the side of the road.

Some of the highways, including Hwy 3 heading out of Santo Domingo to the east and Hwy 2 leaving the city to the west, have toll fees of fairly nominal amounts (RD$35), while the Santo Domingo–Samaná highway (DR-7) is a relatively whopping RD$347. For the former it's best to have exact change that you can simply toss into the basket and quickly move on. If not, there are booths and collectors who can give change.

Road Rules

The first rule is there are none. In theory, road rules in the DR are the same as for most countries in the Americas, and the lights and signs are the same shape and color you find in the US or Canada. Seatbelts are required at all times. That said, driving in the DR is pretty much a free-for-all, a test of one's nerves and will, a continuous series of games of chicken where the loser is the one who decides to give way just before the moment of impact.

In small towns, nay in all towns, traffic lights – when working – are frequently ignored, though you should always plan to stop at them. Watch what other drivers are doing – if everyone is

going through, you probably should, too, as it can be even more dangerous to stop if the cars behind you aren't expecting it. Many city streets are one way and often poorly marked, creating yet another hazard.

Hitchhiking

Though hitchhiking is never entirely safe anywhere in the world, Dominicans, both men and women, hitch all the time, especially in rural areas where fewer people have cars and *gua-gua* service is sparse. It's also very common in resort areas like Bávaro, where a large number of workers commute to Higüey or other towns nearby every morning and evening. That said, it is rare to see foreigners hitchhiking, and doing so (especially if you have bags) carries a greater risk than for locals.

Local Transportation

Bus

Large cities like Santo Domingo and Santiago have public bus systems that operate as they do in most places around the world. Many of the larger city buses are imported from Brazil, and are the kind which you board in the back and pay the person sitting beside the turnstile. Other city buses are more or less like *gua-guas*, where you board quickly and pay the *cobrador* when he comes around. In general, you will probably take relatively few city buses, simply because *públicos* follow pretty much the same routes and pass more frequently.

Metro

See p74 for information on Santo Domingo's metro system.

Motoconcho

Cheaper and easier to find than taxis, *motoconchos*

(motorcycle taxis) are the best, and sometimes only, way to get around in many towns. An average ride should set you back no more than RD$30. That being said, you might have to negotiate to get a fair price and we've even heard of travelers being unknowingly dropped off far short of their intended location. Accidents resulting in injuries and even deaths are not uncommon; ask the driver to slow down *(¡Más despacio por favor!)* if you think he's driving dangerously. Avoid two passengers on a bike since not only is the price the same as taking separate bikes but the extra weight makes most scooters harder to control. For longer trips, or if you have any sort of bag or luggage, *motoconchos* are usually impractical and certainly less comfortable than the alternatives.

Públicos

These are banged-up cars, minivans or small pickup trucks that pick up passengers along set routes, usually main boulevards. *Públicos* (also called *conchos* or *carros*) don't have signs but the drivers hold their hands out the window to solicit potential fares. They are also identifiable by the crush of people inside them – up to seven in a midsize car! To flag one down simply hold out your hand – the fare is around RD$12. If there is no one else in the car, be sure to tell the driver you want *servicio público* (public service) to avoid paying private taxi rates.

Taxi

Dominican taxis rarely cruise for passengers – instead they wait at designated *sitios* (stops), which are located at hotels, bus terminals, tourist areas and main public parks. You can also phone a taxi service (or ask your hotel receptionist to call for you). Taxis do not have meters – agree on a price beforehand.

Language

The official language of the Dominican Republic is Spanish, and it's spoken by every Dominican. Some English and German is also spoken by individuals in the tourist business. If you don't already speak some Spanish and intend to do some travel outside Santo Domingo or Puerto Plata, it's worth learning at least some basics in the lingo.

Dominican Spanish is very much like Central America's other varieties of Spanish. Note though that Dominicans tend to swallow the ends of words, especially those ending in 's' – *tres* will sound like 'tre' and *buenos días* like 'bueno día.'

Spanish pronunciation is relatively straightforward as the relationship between what's written and how you pronounce it is clear and consistent – each written letter is always pronounced the same way. Also, most Spanish sounds are similar to their English counterparts. Note that the kh in our pronunciation guides is a throaty sound (like the 'ch' in the Scottish *loch*), v and b are similar to the English 'b' (but softer, between a 'v' and a 'b'), and r is strongly rolled.

If you read our pronunciation guides as if they were English, you will be understood. In our guides, we've also indicated the stressed syllables in italics.

Spanish nouns (and the adjectives that accompany them) are marked for gender (masculine or feminine). Where necessary, both forms are given for the phrases in this chapter, separated by a slash and with the masculine form first, eg *perdido/a* (m/f).

When talking to people familiar to you or younger than you, use the informal form of 'you', *tú*, rather than the polite form *Usted*, which is the one to use when talking to strangers, people older than you, officials and service staff. The polite form is used in the phrases provided in this chapter; where both options are given, they are indicated by the abbreviations 'pol' and 'inf'.

Talking like a local

Here are a few typical regionalisms you might come across in the Dominican Republic:

apagón	power failure
apodo	nickname
bandera dominicana	rice and beans (lit: Dominican flag)
bohío	thatch hut
bulto	luggage
carros de concho	routed, shared taxi
chichi	baby
colmado	small grocery store
fucú	a thing bringing bad luck
guapo	bad-tempered
guarapo	sugarcane juice
gumo	(a) drunk
hablador	person who talks a lot
papaúpa	important person
pariguayo	foolish
pín-pún	exactly equal
una rumba	a lot
Siempre a su orden.	You're welcome.
tiguere	rascal
timacle	brave

BASICS

Hello.	Hola.	o·la
Goodbye.	Adiós.	a·dyos
How are you?	¿Qué tal?	ke tal
Fine, thanks.	Bien, gracias.	byen gra·syas
Excuse me.	Perdón.	per·don
Sorry.	Lo siento.	lo syen·to
Please.	Por favor.	por fa·vor
Thank you.	Gracias.	gra·syas
You're welcome.	De nada.	de na·da
Yes.	Sí.	see
No.	No.	no

My name is ...
Me llamo ...   me ya·mo ...

What's your name?
¿Cómo se llama Usted?   ko·mo se ya·ma oo·ste (pol)
¿Cómo te llamas?   ko·mo te ya·mas (inf)

Do you speak English?
¿Habla inglés?   a·bla een·gles (pol)
¿Hablas inglés?   a·blas een·gles (inf)

I understand.
Yo entiendo.   yo en·tyen·do

I don't understand.
Yo no entiendo.   yo no en·tyen·do

ACCOMMODATIONS

I'd like to book a room.
Quisiera reservar una habitación.   kee·sye·ra re·ser·var oo·na a·bee·ta·syon

How much is it per night/person?
¿Cuánto cuesta por noche/persona?   kwan·to kwes·ta por no·che/per·so·na

Does it include breakfast?
¿Incluye el desayuno?   een·kloo·ye el de·sa·yoo·no

campsite	terreno de cámping	te·re·no de kam·peeng
hotel	hotel	o·tel
guesthouse	pensión	pen·syon
youth hostel	albergue juvenil	al·ber·ge khoo·ve·neel

I'd like a ... room.	Quisiera una habitación ...	kee·sye·ra oo·na a·bee·ta·syon ...
single	individual	een·dee·vee·dwal
double	doble	do·ble

air-con	aire acondicionado	ai·re a·kon·dee·syo·na·do
bathroom	baño	ba·nyo
bed	cama	ka·ma
window	ventana	ven·ta·na

To get by in Spanish, mix and match these simple patterns with words of your choice:

When's (the next flight)?
¿Cuándo sale (el próximo vuelo)?   kwan·do sa·le (el prok·see·mo vwe·lo)

Where's (the station)?
¿Dónde está (la estación)?   don·de es·ta (la es·ta·syon)

Where can I (buy a ticket)?
¿Dónde puedo (comprar un billete)?   don·de pwe·do (kom·prar oon bee·ye·te)

Do you have (a map)?
¿Tiene (un mapa)?   tye·ne (oon ma·pa)

Is there (a toilet)?
¿Hay (servicios)?   ai (ser·vee·syos)

I'd like (a coffee).
Quisiera (un café).   kee·sye·ra (oon ka·fe)

I'd like (to hire a car).
Quisiera (alquilar un coche).   kee·sye·ra (al·kee·lar oon ko·che)

Can I (enter)?
¿Se puede (entrar)?   se pwe·de (en·trar)

Could you please (help me)?
¿Puede (ayudarme) por favor?   pwe·de (a·yoo·dar·me) por fa·vor

DIRECTIONS

Where's ...?
¿Dónde está ...?   don·de es·ta ...

What's the address?
¿Cuál es la dirección?   kwal es la dee·rek·syon

Could you please write it down?
¿Puede escribirlo, por favor?   pwe·de es·kree·beer·lo por fa·vor

Can you show me (on the map)?
¿Me lo puede indicar (en el mapa)?   me lo pwe·de een·dee·kar (en el ma·pa)

at the corner	en la esquina	en la es·kee·na
at the traffic lights	en el semáforo	en el se·ma·fo·ro
behind ...	detrás de ...	de·tras de ...
far	lejos	le·khos
in front of ...	enfrente de ...	en·fren·te de ...
left	izquierda	ees·kyer·da
near	cerca	ser·ka
next to ...	al lado de ...	al la·do de ...
opposite ...	frente a ...	fren·te a ...
right	derecha	de·re·cha
straight ahead	todo recto	to·do rek·to

EATING & DRINKING

What would you recommend?
¿Qué recomienda?   ke re·ko·*myen*·da

What's in that dish?
¿Que lleva ese plato?   ke *ye*·va e·se *pla*·to

I don't eat ...
No como ...   no *ko*·mo ...

That was delicious!
¡Estaba buenísimo!   es·*ta*·ba bwe·*nee*·see·mo

Please bring the check/bill.
Por favor nos trae   por fa·*vor* nos *tra*·e
la cuenta.   la *kwen*·ta

Cheers!
¡Salud!   sa·*loo*

I'd like to book a table for ...	Quisiera reservar una mesa para ...	kee·*sye*·ra re·ser·*var* oo·na *me*·sa pa·ra ...
(eight) o'clock	las (ocho)	las (o·cho)
(two) people	(dos) personas	(dos) per·*so*·nas

Key Words

appetizers	aperitivos	a·pe·ree·*tee*·vos
bar	bar	bar
bottle	botella	bo·*te*·ya
bowl	bol	bol
breakfast	desayuno	de·sa·*yoo*·no
cafe	café	ka·*fe*
children's menu	menú infantil	me·*noo* een·fan·*teel*
(too) cold	(muy) frío	(mooy) *free*·o
dinner	cena	*se*·na
food	comida	ko·*mee*·da
fork	tenedor	te·ne·*dor*
glass	vaso	*va*·so
highchair	trona	*tro*·na
hot (warm)	caliente	kal·*yen*·te
knife	cuchillo	koo·*chee*·yo
lunch	comida	ko·*mee*·da
main course	segundo plato	se·*goon*·do *pla*·to
market	mercado	mer·*ka*·do
menu (in English)	menú (en inglés)	oon me·*noo* (en een·*gles*)
plate	plato	*pla*·to
restaurant	restaurante	res·tow·*ran*·te
spoon	cuchara	koo·*cha*·ra
supermarket	supermercado	soo·per·mer·*ka*·do
vegetarian food	comida vegetariana	ko·*mee*·da ve·khe·ta·*rya*·na
with/without	con/sin	kon/seen

Signs

Abierto	Open
Cerrado	Closed
Entrada	Entrance
Hombres/Varones	Men
Mujeres/Damas	Women
Prohibido	Prohibited
Salida	Exit
Servicios/Baños	Toilets

Meat & Fish

beef	carne de vaca	*kar*·ne de *va*·ka
chicken	pollo	*po*·yo
duck	pato	*pa*·to
fish	pescado	pes·*ka*·do
lamb	cordero	kor·*de*·ro
pork	cerdo	*ser*·do
turkey	pavo	*pa*·vo
veal	ternera	ter·*ne*·ra

Fruit & Vegetables

apple	manzana	man·*sa*·na
apricot	albaricoque	al·ba·ree·*ko*·ke
artichoke	alcachofa	al·ka·*cho*·fa
asparagus	espárragos	es·*pa*·ra·gos
banana	plátano	*pla*·ta·no
beans	judías	khoo·*dee*·as
beetroot	remolacha	re·mo·*la*·cha
cabbage	col	kol
carrot	zanahoria	sa·na·o·rya
celery	apio	*a*·pyo
cherry	cereza	se·*re*·sa
corn	maíz	ma·*ees*
cucumber	pepino	pe·*pee*·no
fruit	fruta	*froo*·ta
grape	uvas	*oo*·vas
lemon	limón	lee·*mon*
lentils	lentejas	len·*te*·khas
lettuce	lechuga	le·*choo*·ga
mushroom	champiñón	cham·pee·*nyon*
nuts	nueces	*nwe*·ses
onion	cebolla	se·*bo*·ya
orange	naranja	na·*ran*·kha
peach	melocotón	me·lo·ko·*ton*
peas	guisantes	gee·*san*·tes

(red/green) pepper	pimiento (rojo/verde)	pee·*myen*·to (ro·*kho*/ver·de)
pineapple	piña	pee·nya
plum	ciruela	seer·*we*·la
potato	patata	pa·*ta*·ta
pumpkin	calabaza	ka·la·*ba*·sa
spinach	espinacas	es·pee·*na*·kas
strawberry	fresa	*fre*·sa
tomato	tomate	to·*ma*·te
vegetable	verdura	ver·*doo*·ra
watermelon	sandía	san·*dee*·a

Other

bread	pan	pan
butter	mantequilla	man·te·*kee*·ya
cheese	queso	*ke*·so
egg	huevo	*we*·vo
honey	miel	myel
jam	mermelada	mer·me·*la*·da
oil	aceite	a·*sey*·te
pasta	pasta	*pas*·ta
pepper	pimienta	pee·*myen*·ta
rice	arroz	a·*ros*
salt	sal	sal
sugar	azúcar	a·*soo*·kar
vinegar	vinagre	vee·*na*·gre

Drinks

beer	cerveza	ser·*ve*·sa
coffee	café	ka·*fe*
(orange) juice	zumo (de naranja)	*soo*·mo (de na·*ran*·kha)
milk	leche	*le*·che
tea	té	te
(mineral) water	agua (mineral)	*a*·gwa (mee·ne·*ral*)
(red/white) wine	vino (tinto/blanco)	*vee*·no (*teen*·to/*blan*·ko)

EMERGENCIES

| Help! | ¡Socorro! | so·*ko*·ro |
| Go away! | ¡Vete! | *ve*·te |

Call a doctor!
¡Llame a un médico!   *ya*·me a oon *me*·dee·ko

Call the police!
¡Llame a la policía!   *ya*·me a la po·lee·*see*·a

I'm lost.
Estoy perdido/a.   es·*toy* per·*dee*·do/a (m/f)

Question Words

How?	¿Cómo?	*ko*·mo
What?	¿Qué?	ke
When?	¿Cuándo?	*kwan*·do
Where?	¿Dónde?	*don*·de
Who?	¿Quién?	kyen
Why?	¿Por qué?	por ke

I had an accident.
He tenido un accidente.   e te·*nee*·do oon ak·see·*den*·te

I'm ill.
Estoy enfermo/a.   es·*toy* en·*fer*·mo/a (m/f)

It hurts here.
Me duele aquí.   me *dwe*·le a·*kee*

I'm allergic to (antibiotics).
Soy alérgico/a a (los antibióticos).   soy a·*ler*·khee·ko/a a (los an·tee·*byo*·tee·kos) (m/f)

SHOPPING & SERVICES

I'd like to buy ...
Quisiera comprar ...   kee·*sye*·ra kom·*prar* ...

I'm just looking.
Sólo estoy mirando.   *so*·lo es·*toy* mee·*ran*·do

May I look at it?
¿Puedo verlo?   *pwe*·do *ver*·lo

I don't like it.
No me gusta.   no me *goos*·ta

How much is it?
¿Cuánto cuesta?   *kwan*·to *kwes*·ta

That's too expensive.
Es muy caro.   es mooy *ka*·ro

Can you lower the price?
¿Podría bajar un poco el precio?   po·*dree*·a ba·*khar* oon *po*·ko el *pre*·syo

There's a mistake in the check/bill.
Hay un error en la cuenta.   ai oon e·*ror* en la *kwen*·ta

ATM	cajero automático	ka·*khe*·ro ow·to·ma·*tee*·ko
credit card	tarjeta de crédito	tar·*khe*·ta de *kre*·dee·to
internet cafe	cibercafé	see·ber·ka·*fe*
post office	correos	ko·*re*·os
tourist office	oficina de turismo	o·fee·*see*·na de too·*rees*·mo

TIME & DATES

What time is it?	¿Qué hora es?	ke *o*·ra es
It's (10) o'clock.	Son (las diez).	son (las dyes)
It's half past (one).	Es (la una) y media.	es (la *oo*·na) ee *me*·dya

Numbers

1	uno	oo·no
2	dos	dos
3	tres	tres
4	cuatro	kwa·tro
5	cinco	seen·ko
6	seis	seys
7	siete	sye·te
8	ocho	o·cho
9	nueve	nwe·ve
10	diez	dyes
20	veinte	veyn·te
30	treinta	treyn·ta
40	cuarenta	kwa·ren·ta
50	cincuenta	seen·kwen·ta
60	sesenta	se·sen·ta
70	setenta	se·ten·ta
80	ochenta	o·chen·ta
90	noventa	no·ven·ta
100	cien	syen
1000	mil	meel

morning	mañana	ma·nya·na
afternoon	tarde	tar·de
evening	noche	no·che
yesterday	ayer	a·yer
today	hoy	oy
tomorrow	mañana	ma·nya·na

Monday	lunes	loo·nes
Tuesday	martes	mar·tes
Wednesday	miércoles	myer·ko·les
Thursday	jueves	khwe·ves
Friday	viernes	vyer·nes
Saturday	sábado	sa·ba·do
Sunday	domingo	do·meen·go

January	enero	e·ne·ro
February	febrero	fe·bre·ro
March	marzo	mar·so
April	abril	a·breel
May	mayo	ma·yo
June	junio	khoon·yo
July	julio	khool·yo
August	agosto	a·gos·to
September	septiembre	sep·tyem·bre
October	octubre	ok·too·bre
November	noviembre	no·vyem·bre
December	diciembre	dee·syem·bre

TRANSPORTATION

Public Transportation

boat	barco	bar·ko
bus	autobús	ow·to·boos
plane	avión	a·vyon
train	tren	tren
first	primero	pree·me·ro
last	último	ool·tee·mo
next	próximo	prok·see·mo

I want to go to ...
Quisiera ir a ...   kee·sye·ra eer a ...

Does it stop at ...?
¿Para en ...?   pa·ra en ...

What stop is this?
¿Cuál es esta parada?   kwal es es·ta pa·ra·da

What time does it arrive/leave?
¿A qué hora llega/   a ke o·ra ye·ga/
sale?   sa·le

Please tell me when we get to ...
¿Puede avisarme   pwe·de a·vee·sar·me
cuando lleguemos   kwan·do ye·ge·mos
a ...?   a ...

I want to get off here.
Quiero bajarme aquí.   kye·ro ba·khar·me a·kee

a ... ticket	un billete de ...	oon bee·ye·te de ...
first-class	primera clase	pree·me·ra kla·se
second-class	segunda clase	se·goon·da kla·se
one-way	ida	ee·da
return	ida y vuelta	ee·da ee vwel·ta

airport	aeropuerto	a·e·ro·pwer·to
aisle seat	asiento de pasillo	a·syen·to de pa·see·yo
bus stop	parada de autobuses	pa·ra·da de ow·to·boo·ses
canceled	cancelado	kan·se·la·do
delayed	retrasado	re·tra·sa·do
platform	plataforma	pla·ta·for·ma
ticket office	taquilla	ta·kee·ya
timetable	horario	o·ra·ryo
train station	estación de trenes	es·ta·syon de tre·nes
window seat	asiento junto a la ventana	a·syen·to khoon·to a la ven·ta·na

Driving & Cycling

I'd like to rent a ...	Quisiera alquilar ...	kee·sye·ra al·kee·lar ...
4WD	un todo-terreno	oon to·do·te·re·no
bicycle	una bicicleta	oo·na bee·see·kle·ta
car	un coche	oon ko·che
motorcycle	una moto	oo·na mo·to
child seat	asiento de seguridad para niños	a·syen·to de se·goo·ree·da pa·ra nee·nyos
diesel	petróleo	pet·ro·le·o
helmet	casco	kas·ko
hitchhike	hacer botella	a·ser bo·te·ya
mechanic	mecánico	me·ka·nee·ko
gas/petrol	gasolina	ga·so·lee·na
service station	gasolinera	ga·so·lee·ne·ra
truck	camion	ka·myon

Where can I rent a bicycle?
¿Dónde se puede alquilar una bicicleta? don·de se pwe·de al·kee·lar oo·na bee·see·kle·ta

I have a puncture.
Se me ha pinchado una rueda. se me a peen·cha·do oo·na rwe·da

Is this the road to ...?
¿Se va a ... por esta carretera? se va a ... por es·ta ka·re·te·ra

(How long) Can I park here?
¿(Por cuánto tiempo) Puedo aparcar aquí? (por kwan·to tyem·po) pwe·do a·par·kar a·kee

The car has broken down (at ...).
El coche se ha averiado (en ...). el ko·che se a a·ve·rya·do (en ...)

I have a flat tyre.
Tengo un pinchazo. ten·go oon peen·cha·so

I've run out of gas/petrol.
Me he quedado sin gasolina. me e ke·da·do seen ga·so·lee·na

I need a mechanic.
Necesito un/una mecánico/a. ne·se·see·to oon/oo·na me·ka·nee·ko/a (m/f)

GLOSSARY

bahía – bay

cobrador – conductor who takes money for fares on *gua-guas*

concho – private car that follows a set route

gua-gua – local bus

isla – island

motoconchos – motorcycle taxis

playa – beach

público – a form of public transportation service, usually small vans or trucks

Haiti

Haiti

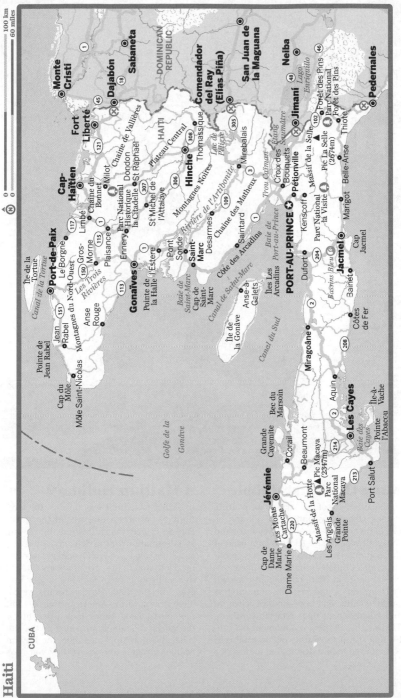

CUBA

100 km
60 miles

Pointe de
Jean Rabel

Cap du Môle
Môle Saint-Nicolas

Île de la
Tortue
Canal de la Tortue

Port-de-Paix

Jean
Rabel
(151)

Montagnes du Nord-Ouest

Anse
Rouge

Le Borgne
Gros-
Morne
(150)
Plaisance
(115)
Ennery

Limbé
(1)
Chaîne du
Bonnet /

Milot
Parc National
Historique
la Citadelle

(1)

Dondon
St Raphaël

St Michel de
l'Attalaye

Chaîne de Vallières

(121)

(45)

Fort
Liberté

Dajabón
(18)

Sabaneta

Monte
Cristi

DOMINICAN
REPUBLIC

(1)

San Juan de
la Maguana

Comendador
del Ray
(Elías Piña)

Neiba

Pedernales

Lago
Enriquillo

(46)

(48)
Jimani
(002)

Forêt des Pins
Parc National
Forêt des Pins

Thiote

Belle-Anse

Pic La Selle
(2674m)
Massif de la Selle
(305)

Haiti

Plateau Central

Thomassique

Hinche
(306)
(308)

Mirebalais

(3)

Lac de
Péligre

Montagnes Noires

Saint-
Marc

Desarmes
Pont
Sondé

Saintard

Chaîne des Matheux
(109)

(1)

Croix des
Bouquets
Trou Caïman

Étang
Saumâtre

Pétionville

PORT-AU-PRINCE

Parc National
la Visite
Kenscoff

Baie de
Port-au-Prince

Bassins Bleu

(204)

Dufort

Jacmel

Cap
Jacmel

Margot

Côte des Arcadins

Îles Les
Arcadins

Anse-à-
Galets

Île de
la Gonâve

Canal du Sud

Cap de
Saint-
Marc

Canal de Saint-Marc

Baie de
Saint-Marc

Cap à
Foux

Pointe de
la Halle

Gonaïves

(113)

Les Trois
Rivières

St L'Estere

(1)

Rivière de l'Artibonite

Bainet

Côtes
de Fer

(2)

Miragoâne

(208)

Aquin

(2)

Les Cayes

Île-à-
Vache

Pointe
l'Abacou

Baie des
Cayes

Corail

Grande
Cayemite

Beaumont

Pic Macaya
(2347m)
Parc
National
Macaya

Port Salut

(214)

(213)

Jérémie

Les Monts
Cartache
(220)

Massif de la Hotte

Les Anglais

Grande
Pointe

Cap de
Dame
Marie

Dame Marie

Golfe de la
Gonâve

welcome to
Haiti

More than Just Rubble

In the aftermath of the earthquake of 2010, Barack Obama appointed Bill Clinton as one of his special envoys to the country, and the ex-president later became joint head of the commission tasked to oversee reconstruction. Clinton is hardly an uncontroversial figure in Haiti, but one little-known fact surfaced – that his long-time interest in the country had been sparked when he and Hillary spent their honeymoon there. That's right – forget for a moment the rubble that still clogs swathes of Port-au-Prince – Haiti used to be a destination for lovers.

A Haitian Holiday?

In actual fact, Haiti was once at the forefront of Caribbean tourism. In the 1950s, Port-au-Prince was rivaled only by Havana as a destination for the rich and famous; its jazz clubs and casinos a favored getaway for the Hollywood elite. Twenty years later, it was still cool enough for Mick Jagger, and even into the 1980s Haitian resorts were a huge drawcard for American tourists. But the tourist good times took place under the veneer of stability provided by the Duvalier dictatorship. Since then, the Haitian people's struggle to reassert their voice has

Haiti is still struggling with the aftermath of the devastating January 12, 2010 earthquake. But this is a proud country, born of revolution, and its people are determined to rebuild for a better future

(below) Colonial architecture of the Hotel Florita
(left) Rue du Commerce, Jacmel

been repeatedly stifled by coups, insecurity, foreign intervention and, now, a natural disaster of terrible proportions.

With a modicum of stability, Haiti could yet become the Caribbean's alternative travel destination par excellence: it has palm-fringed beaches to rival any of its neighbors. But lazing on the sand with a rum punch isn't really the point of Haiti (although you can do that, too). The richness of the country lies in its history and culture. The slave revolution left behind a wealth of historic sites, including the Citadelle la Ferrière – a fortress that easily holds its own against anything similar in the Americas.

Haiti's history has meant that it's kept closer to its African roots than any other Caribbean nation, a legacy that's ever present in its vibrant art and music scenes.

Haiti isn't the easiest country to travel in. You frequently need to keep an ear out for the news, and it can be more expensive than you'd expect. However, once you're there, travel is not only possible, but also incredibly rewarding. It's an addictive country to visit: once in Haiti, there's something about the people, the history, and even the air, that can get in your blood and draw you back time and again.

need to know

When to Go

Cap-Haïtien
GO Mar-Jul

Port-au-Prince
GO Nov-Jul

Jacmel
GO Nov-May

 Dry climate
Tropical climate, wet-dry season

High Season
(Nov–Mar)

» Hot and dry; added attractions are Carnival in Port-au-Prince and Jacmel (Feb), and the countrywide Fet Gédé Vodou festival.

» The north is frequently rainy.

Shoulder
(Apr–Jun)

» Rain in the south

Low Season
(Aug–Oct)

» Hurricane season, but travel is perfectly feasible if there are no storms.

» Often heavy daily rainfall; humid.

Your Daily Budget

Budget less than
US$50

» Hotel room: US$40

» Cheap street food and markets for self-catering

» Public transportation

Midrange up to
US$100

» Room in midrange hotel: US$70

» Lunch and dinner in decent restaurants

» Internal flights: around US$85

Top end over
US$100

» Room in a top-end hotel: from US$90

» Meal at a top restaurant: US$30

» 4WD rental: around US$150 a day

Money

» ATMs mostly restricted to Port-au-Prince. Credit cards accepted in many hotels. Cash in US$ widely used.

Visas

» Generally not required for stays of up to 90 days.

Cell Phones

» Local SIM cards can be used in American and European phones, or set your phone to roaming.

Driving

» Drive on the right; steering wheel is on the left side of the car.

Websites

» **Lonely Planet** (www .lonelyplanet.com /haiti) Destination information, traveler forum and more.

» **Haitian Footsteps** (www.haitianfootsteps .com) Coverage of Haitian travel, culture and history.

» **Association Touristique d'Haiti** (www.haiticherie.ht) Basic tourist information site.

» **Haiti News** (www .haitinews.net) Useful news aggregator.

» **Haitian Today** (www .haitiantoday.com) Haitian news and entertainment.

Exchange Rates

Australia	A$1	HTG43
Canada	C$1	HTG42
Dominican Republic	RD$1	HTG1
Europe	€1	HTG60
Japan	¥100	HTG50
New Zealand	NZ$1	HTG32
UK	UK£1	HTG67
US	US$1	HTG40

For current exchange rates see www.xe.com

Important Numbers

Haiti doesn't have separate area codes, so always dial the full 8-digit number.

Country code	☑509
International access code	☑00
Police	☑122
Fire	☑115
Minustah	☑113

Arriving in Haiti

» **Aéroport International Toussaint Louverture**
Taxis: US$20 to US$40, around 30 minutes to central Port-au-Prince (see p290)
Taptap: HTG10 per trip

Is Haiti Safe?

Many governments advise against recreational travel to Haiti, but the realities on the ground are actually far better than popular media coverage might lead you to expect. Although crime can be a worry, Port-au-Prince, and Haiti in general, has a far lower violent crime and murder rate than nearby Jamaica with its prosperous tourist industry. Discontent against the government and the UN is rife, so it's wise to keep abreast of the political scene and keep away from demonstrations, which can be regular occurrences.

Although the country's poverty and broken infrastructure makes traveling here more akin to visiting the Developing World than the Americas, the vast majority of visitors are pleasantly surprised at how calm and welcoming Haiti really is.

if you like...

Art & Music

Haiti can make a strong case for being the artistic capital of the Caribbean. From its painted buses and street art to stylish galleries and works of the great masters, there's plenty of color to draw the eye.

Croix des Bouquets Beautifully styled metal artworks are hammered out in this unique artists' village, from high concept pieces to pocket-sized souvenirs (p292)

Grand Rue Artists Wood, scrap metal and found objects turned into mind-boggling Vodou cyberpunk art, a world away from the posh collectors' image of tropical Haiti (p279)

Jacmel artisans Bright arts and crafts in wood and papier-mâché from Haiti's handicrafts capital, with huge Carnival masks a specialty (p302)

RAM The best house-band in Haiti, serving up Vodou-styled roots and rythm every Thursday at Port-au-Prince's Hôtel Oloffson (p283)

Festivals

Both locally and nationally, Haiti has plenty of big days (and nights) out. Some of the most popular festivals are those associated with Vodou. Color, music and spectacle are all guaranteed.

Carnival Haiti's biggest street celebrations – a time for music and dancing. Head to Port-au-Prince (p282) or Jacmel (p300)

Fet Gédé Nationwide Vodou festival marking All Saints' Day – a festival for the dead – held in cemeteries everywhere

Saut d'Eau Haiti's biggest Vodou pilgrimage, with thousands of adherents bathing in the pools of a sacred waterfall every July (p293)

Souvenance Held near Gonaïves after Good Friday – a huge Vodou festival, its ceremonies originating from the camps of runaway slaves (p318)

Landscapes

Visitors may be surprised at how picturesque Haiti can be, and from old forts to beaches and waterfalls, there's plenty to capture your attention.

The Citadelle & Sans Souci One of the most dramatic historic sites in the Americas, this fortress atop a mountain crest, with a ruined palace at its feet, will leave you agog (p314)

Parc National la Visite Limestone crags sprinkled with pine forests – ideal for hiking and easily reached from Port-au-Prince (p292)

Bassins Bleu In wooded hills above Jacmel, this series of grottos and waterfalls makes a perfect swimming hole, and is home to magical spirits (p299)

Port Salut Haiti can do picture-postcard Caribbean as well as anywhere, as this miles-long palm-fringed beach shows (p304)

month by month

Top Events

269

1 **Carnival,** February

2 **Fet Gédé,** November

3 **Saut d'Eau,** July

4 **Souvenance,** April

5 **Soukri,** August

January

Haiti's year begins with two important anniversaries.

Independence Day

New Year's Day, a public holiday, marks Haitian independence – proclaimed in Gonaïves in 1804. *Soup jomou* (pumpkin soup) is traditionally eaten.

Earthquake commemoration

The anniversary of the January 12, 2010 earthquake. A day of remembrance, and likely to become a public holiday in future.

February

Many towns have local saints' day celebrations, but the country's biggest party is Carnival: a highlight of the Haitian year.

Carnival

After Ash Wednesday, two huge Carnivals are held: the glitzy parades and organised music of Port-au-Prince and, a week later, the more earthy and surreal street theatre of the Jacmel Carnival.

March/April

Souvenance

A week-long Vodou festival held near Gonaïves, just after Good Friday (Easter, late March). The Vodou spirit of Ogou is particularly celebrated here, honoring his role in the Haitian Revolution.

July

Saut d'Eau

The biggest Vodou pilgrimage in Haiti, held at a sacred waterfall just outside Mirebelais.

August

August is the traditional start of Haiti's hurricane season, which typically blows itself out by the end of October. If you're visiting at this time, expect outbursts of strong winds and heavy rains.

Soukri

Mammoth two-week Vodou festival, honoring the Kongo Vodou spirits, held near Gonaïves.

November

The hurricane season should have finished by now, although you still run the risk of tropical storms.

Fet Gédé

All Saints' Day marks Vodou's biggest national celebration. Held in cemeteries and peristyles (temples) across the country in honour of the Gédé, the Vodou trickster spirits of the dead.

Anniversary of the Battle of Vertières

At the final battle of the Haitian Revolution, Dessalines definitively trumped the French army at Vertières, just outside Cap-Haïtien. The anniversary is now a public holiday.

itineraries

Whether you've got six days or 60, these itineraries provide a starting point for the trip of a lifetime. Want more inspiration? Head online to lonelyplanet .com/thorntree to chat with other travelers.

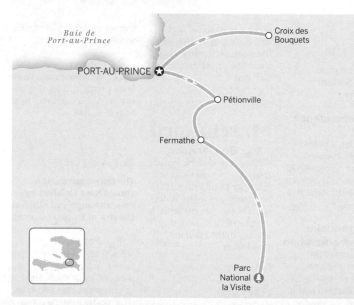

One Week
Port-au-Prince & Around

The gravitational pull of Port-au-Prince inevitably sucks in both Haitians and foreign visitors alike. The traditional place to start getting your bearings is **Champs de Mars**, where the extent of post-earthquake reconstruction is most visible. Eat in the restaurants in **Pétionville**, and swing by the many art galleries. The artists' village of **Croix des Bouquets** is a good half-day trip, but if you really want to get out of the city for some fresh air, head uphill to **Fermathe** and on to **Parc National la Visite** for a day's hiking. Back in the city, visit the Vodou art cooperative of the **Grand Artists**, contrasting this earthquake-battered part of the city with the **gingerbread houses** of the Pacot and Bois Verna districts. Finish with a last visit to the Pétionville **art galleries**, then time the close of your stay so you can call in at the Oloffson Hotel on a Thursday night to see a **RAM concert** and have one last rum punch.

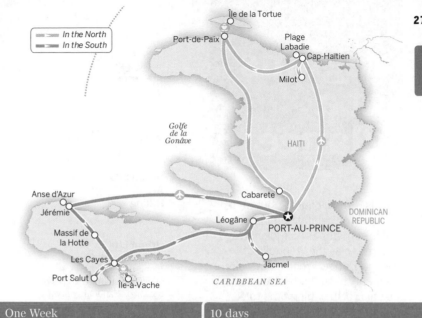

Legend:
- In the North
- In the South

One Week
In the North

From Port-au-Prince, catch an internal flight up to **Cap-Haïtien**. Take a full day to make a tour out to the **Citadelle** and the ruined palace of **Sans Souci** – you can even spend the night at the cultural center in **Milot**. Back in Cap-Haïtien, explore the **architecture** of the old city and walk along the coast to the cliff-bound remains of **Fort Picolet**. The following day, take a vehicle and boat-taxi to **Labadie**, possibly stopping en route at **Cormier Plage** – for the Atlantic coast scenery and beaches. If you're after some real adventure, drive overland to **Port-de-Paix** and arrange a boat trip to **Île de la Tortue**, Haiti's pirate island. On the way back to Port-au-Prince, pause in **Cabarete** to stock up on *tablet* (local peanut brittle).

10 days
In the South

Take a short flight (or a long day's drive) from Port-au-Prince to **Jérémie**, in the far southwest. Explore the town, and beaches west such as **Anse d'Azur**. Head south on the new road over the **Massif de la Hotte** mountains, and break for the night in **Les Cayes**. You've done the hard traveling now, so enjoy your pick of Haiti's best beaches. It's a short boat trip out to the gorgeous **Île-à-Vache**, or an equally short drive to **Port Salut**. Either way, all your Caribbean clichés of white sand, palm trees and grilled fish on the beach will be easily fulfilled. When you're done, turn east. The Port-au-Prince highway splits near Léogâne, so let it take you to **Jacmel**. Check out the town's **historic quarter**, and fill up on souvenirs with the **handicrafts** the town is famed for. And with that, you're ready to return to the capital.

regions at a glance

Haiti is a small country, but densely packed. The capital dominates, and is sometimes half-jokingly referred to as the 'Republic of Port-au-Prince'. While most visitors inevitably base themselves there, it's still worth finding time to explore the provinces.

Cap-Haïtien, the country's second city, is the hub of the north, and relatively isolated from Port-au-Prince by bad roads. The south is better connected – greener and more lush, it's home to the country's best beaches – but the north coast holds many historical sites worth exploring. Mountains dominate the landscape wherever you head, with several good hikes to tempt you when the towns become too much.

Port-au-Prince & Around

Urban Life ✓✓
Art ✓✓
Hiking ✓✓

Urban Life
Port-au-Prince's fabric was rent asunder by the earthquake. The toppled domes of the Palais National symbolize the damage done; its gradual rebuilding and the rehousing of people from surrounding tent camps are a good barometer for measuring the progress made in the country's reconstruction.

Art
Despite everything, Haitian artists continue to produce new work. There's a lot to see – and buy – from the Vodou-cyberpunk Grand Rue artists and the open-air street paintings of Port-au-Prince to the upscale galleries of Pétionville and, outside the city, the metal-artists of Croix des Bouquets.

Hiking
Port-au-Prince can feel like being in a pressure cooker, but fresh air is still viable for city visitors. The forests of Parc National la Visite and Parc National Forêt des Pins are both within easy reach, and offer long and short hiking opportunities.

p276

Southern Haiti

Culture ✓✓
Beaches ✓✓
Wilderness ✓✓

Culture
The old coffee port of Jacmel is one of Haiti's most important cultural centers. From its historic 19th-century quarter and artisans to its raucous annual carnival, this is a town that punches above its weight.

Beaches
The south has all the Caribbean beaches you could want. Whether it's the long stretches of white sand at Port Salut or the tiny island of Île-à-Vache – just two of many options – there are plenty of opportunities for sun and beach.

Wilderness
The mountainous Massif de la Hotte bisects southwestern Haiti, and contains Parc National Macaya, the last area of original cloud forest in the country. There are hiking and bird-watching opportunities here, but there's no infrastructure, making this one for the most adventurous.

p296

Northern Haiti

History ✓✓
Vodou ✓✓
Beaches ✓✓

History
At Milot near Cap-Haïtien are the two grandest reminders of Haiti's history: the imposing fortress of the Citadelle and the ruined palace of Sans Souci. Elsewhere along the coast there are French forts and the old pirate island of Île de la Tortue.

Vodou
Northern Haiti has many minor sites associated with Vodou, but it is also where you'll find two of the biggest annual festivals. Souvenance and Soukri are both held near Gonaïves and are huge gatherings of Vodou followers.

Beaches
With Atlantic waves crashing ashore, the north coast is more dramatic than the south, but you can still find places to relax with the sand and surf. One of the most charming is Labadie, near Cap-Haïtien – also a place where Haiti's only cruise passengers come to play.

p308

Look out for these icons:

  Our author's recommendation

 A green or sustainable option

FREE No payment required

See the Index for a full list of destinations covered in this book.

On the Road

Port-au-Prince & Around

Best Places to Stay

» St Joseph's Home for Boys Guest House (p282)

» Les Palmiers (p282)

» Hôtel Oloffson (p283)

Best Places to Eat

» Papaye, Pétionville (p285)

» Assiette Creole, Pétionville (p285)

» Café Terrasse, Pétionville (p287)

Why Go?

Let's admit the obvious: Port-au-Prince doesn't have the image of somewhere you'd visit purely for fun. A true city of the developing world, just an hour by air from Miami, the city is preceded by a reputation for impoverished chaos, even before the 2010 earthquake literally shook it to its foundations. The infrastructure is compromised, the gulf between rich and poor remains as wide as ever, and the quake's rubble and tent camps are acquiring a terrible sense of permanence.

And yet, the city remains one of the most vibrant and exciting in the Caribbean. Like a bottle of local *klerin* rum, Port-au-Prince takes all the raw energy of Haiti and distils it into one buzzing shot, and witnessing the self-sufficiency and spirit of its people might be the most life-affirming experience you will have on your travels. It's a chaotic, exhilarating and compelling place. We encourage you to jump right in.

When to Go

Just before Ash Wednesday (around February), Port-au-Prince hosts the largest and liveliest Carnival celebrations in the country. The first week of November is a great time to experience celebrations for the Vodou festival of Fet Gédé.

Port-au-Prince & Around Highlights

1 Discovering the mind-bending recycled artworks of the **Grand Rue artists**, Port-au-Prince (p279)

2 Dancing to Vodou rock 'n' roots music until the small hours at a **RAM concert**, Port-au-Prince (p288)

3 Shopping for metal artwork at **Croix des Bouquets** (p292)

4 Lazing on the sand at the beaches of **Côte des Arcadins** (p294)

5 Stretching the legs and enjoying the views while hiking in **Parc National la Visite** (p292)

PORT-AU-PRINCE

History

Port-au-Prince was founded in 1742 during the boom years of French rule, and was given its royal charter as capital seven years later. Its name is taken from the French ship *Prince*, which had first moored there in 1706.

During the slave revolution, Port-au-Prince was a key strategic target, although the slave armies saw it as a mulatto stronghold. When Haiti was reunited in 1820, Port-au-Prince regained its capital status and has dominated the country ever since.

The initial site of the city was confined to the modern Bel Air district. During the 19th century Port-au-Prince grew rapidly, its expansion only occasionally halted by the periodic fires that razed it to the ground. Wealthier residents created the suburbs of Turgeau and Bois Verna, where many of Port-au-Prince's best 'gingerbread houses' are found. The poor found themselves pushed to the less salubrious marshy areas of La Saline in the north.

The US occupation of 1915 improved the city's infrastructure and there was further modernisation in the 1940s, to celebrate the city's bicentennial. During the Duvalier period (1957–1986), anarchic growth was more the order of the day. The model development of Cité Simone (named for 'Papa Doc' Duvalier's wife) lapsed into slums, and was subsequently renamed Cité Soleil.

A third of Haitians now live in Port-au-Prince, and the uncontrolled expansion of poor quality buildings left the city grievously exposed to the 2010 earthquake (see p344).

◉ Sights

Champs de Mars   NEIGHBORHOOD

The once-neat order of **Champs de Mars** (pronounced *Chanmas*) is the starkest reminder of the damage wrought by the earthquake. A series of parks split by wide boulevards that collectively make up the **Place des Héros de l'Independence**, with the **Palais National** at its center, this broken heart of Port-au-Prince is no longer a place to linger – its wide spaces have been replaced by a series of sprawling tent cities.

The most potent symbol of destruction is the ruined **Palais National**. The focus of national politics, and traditional host to coups d'état, it had already been destroyed during political unrest in 1869 and 1912. January 12, 2010 laid it low for the third time – its beautiful white domes collapsed like a clumsily dropped wedding cake.

Several statues of Haiti's founding fathers dot Champs de Mars: Toussaint Louverture, Jean-Jacques Dessalines, Alexandre Pétion and Henri Christophe. Of these, only the horsebacked Dessalines, high on his plinth, is currently visible above the tent camps. The **Marron Inconnu**, the iconic statue of an unknown slave blowing a conch-shell trumpet, is similarly beset. The only monument that stands apart and untouched is Aristide's bicentenary statue – an ugly gray monolith resembling an oil derrick. The 2004 coup meant it was never finished, nor is it likely to be.

Champs de Mars speaks strongly of the travails of post-earthquake reconstruction. At the time of research, the remains of the Palais National had not yet been torn down to allow rebuilding to commence. The state of the tent camps – and hopefully the reappearance of the statues of the revolutionary heroes – will provide a barometer for future progress.

Musée du Panthéon National   MUSEUM

(Mupanah; Map p280; ☎2222-8337; Place du Champs de Mars; adult/student US$1.40/0.70; ⊙8am-4pm Mon-Thu, to 5pm Fri, 12-5pm Sat, 10am-4pm Sun) A modern, mostly subterranean museum set in its own gardens. The unusual design echoes the houses of Haiti's original Taíno inhabitants; a motif repeated by the conical central 'well', bringing light to illuminate the gold monument that recreates the cannons and banners found on the national flag. The bodies of Haiti's founding fathers are interred below, and the names of other heroes of the independence struggle are marked on the surrounding walls.

The museum's permanent exhibition chronicles Haiti's history, from the Taínos and slavery to independence and the modern era. There are some fascinating exhibits. Exquisite Taíno pottery faces the rusting anchor of Columbus' flagship, the *Santa María;* slave shackles nod toward a copy of the fearsome *Code Noir* that governed the running of the plantations; while the silver pistol with which Christophe took his life leads past Emperor Faustin's ostentatious crown to 'Papa Doc' Duvalier's trademark black hat and cane. A further gallery holds a good cross-section of modern Haitian art, but it suffers from poor labeling.

Musée d'Art Haïtien MUSEUM
(Museum of Haitian Art; Map p280; ☎2222-2510; 16 Rue Légitime; admission US$1.40; ◷10am-5pm Mon-Sat, to 4pm Sun) This museum, on the southern edge of Champs de Mars, is something of a curate's egg. It holds probably the largest collection of Haiti's naive art, with masters like Hector Hyppolite, Préfète Duffaut, Philomé Obin and Robert St Brice well represented. Unfortunately the works aren't hung well, the permanent collection isn't always on display, and you have to take potluck as to what's on show.

Grand Rue Artists ART SPACE
(Map p280; www.atis-rezistans.com; 622 Grand Rue) While most of Haiti's artists are represented in the rarified air of Pétionville's galleries, a collective of sculptors and installation artists is producing spectacular work in the unlikeliest of settings, squeezed into the cinderblock houses backing onto the mechanics and body workshops on Grand Rue. The Grand Rue artists are unlike anything you've seen in Haiti, turning scrap and found objects into startling Vodou sculpture. The results are a heady mix of spirit, sex and politics – a Caribbean junkyard gone cyberpunk – but also very much grounded in the preoccupations of daily Haitian life.

André Eugène is the founder and elder member, sculpting in wood, plastic and car parts to produce his vision of the *lwa* (Vodou spirits). Dolls' heads and human skulls abound, alongside the earthy humor of highly phallic Gédé pieces. Jean Hérard Celeur, another of the artists, trained as a sculptor, and has done many of the largest pieces: life-sized statues of twisted wood and parts of car chassis, hubcaps, old shoes and a liberal application of twisted nails.

Local children are also involved in making art, through the spin-off organisation Ti Moun Rezistans.

This hub of creativity is near Ciné Lido, set slightly back from the road. Look for the giant Gédé statue made from car parts and with a giant spring-loaded penis guarding the way. Just beyond this, Eugène's house-museum is surrounded by statues, with the motto 'E Pluribus Unum' ('out of many, one') hung over the door.

Grand Cimetière de Port-au-Prince CEMETERY
(Map p280; Bel Air) A vast necropolis of raised tombs, the capital's **Grand Cimetière de**

Some official street names don't match the names used by locals. The following are some of the most common:

OFFICIAL NAME	COLLOQUIAL NAME
Ave Jean Paul II	Turgeau
Ave John Brown	Lalue
Ave Lamartinière	Bois Verna
Ave Martin Luther King	Nazon
Blvd Harry Truman	Bicentenaire
Blvd Jean-Jacques Dessalines	Grand Rue
Blvd Toussaint Louverture	Rte de l'Aéroport
Delmas 105	Fréres
Rue Paul VI	Rue des Casernes

Port-au-Prince sprawls between Grand Rue and Silvio Cator Stadium, bound by walls with often lurid Vodou murals. It's a fascinating but weird place, littered with broken graves and old beer bottles left behind from late-night offerings to Baron Samedi and Maman Brigitte, guardians of the deceased.

The cemetery is the focus for the Fet Gédé celebrations every 1 and 2 November (see p269) and is well worth checking out. It's best to attend with a local.

Pétionville NEIGHBORHOOD
The suburb of Pétionville was founded by President Boyer, although it never became the replacement capital he hoped for. Urban sprawl has long since incorporated Pétionville into greater Port-au-Prince, but the district has maintained its own identity as the center of gravity for Haiti's elite, and a hub for many businesses and banks.

Place Saint-Pierre is the heart of Pétionville; at the time of research it was home to a post-quake tent camp. The action flows downhill from here, with streets laid out in a grid (surprisingly well signed for Haiti). This is where you'll find the best restaurants, galleries and upmarket shops. At the bottom of the hill a chaotic street market spills along Rue Grégoire toward Rte de Delmas.

Port-au-Prince

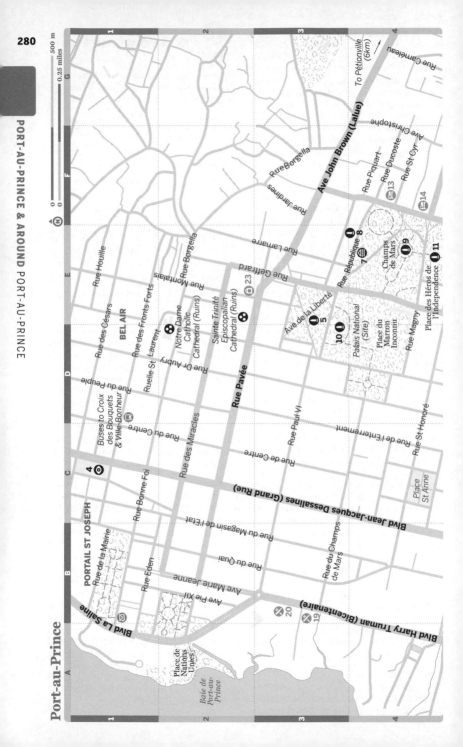

0 | 500 m
0 | 0.25 miles

Baie de
Port-au-
Prince

Place de
Nations
Unies

Blvd La Saline

PORTAIL ST JOSEPH

Rue de la Mairie

Rue Eden

Rue Bonne Foi

Ave Pie XII

Ave Marie Jeanne

Rue du Quai

Blvd Harry Truman (Bicentenaire)

❌ 20
❌ 19

BEL AIR

Rue des Césars

Rue des Fronts Forts

Ruelle St Laurent

Rue Dr Aubry

Rue Houille

Rue du Peuple

Rue du Centre

Rue des Miracles

Buses to Croix
des Bouquets
& Ville-Bonheur

④ ⊚ 4

Rue Bome Foi

Rue du Magasin de l'Etat

Rue du Champs
de Mars

Blvd Jean-Jacques Dessalines (Grand Rue)

Rue de Centre

Rue Paul VI

Rue de l'Enterrement

Rue St Honoré

Place
St Anne

Notre Dame
Catholic
Cathedral (Ruins)

Sainte Trinité
Episcopalian
Cathedral (Ruins)

Rue Pavée

Rue Montalais

Rue Borgella

Rue Geffrard

Rue Lamarre

🔲 23

Ave de la Liberté

① 5

10 ⓭ ①

Palais National
(Site)

Place du
Marron
Inconnu

Rue Magny

Champs
de Mars

① 7

① 8

⑪ 9

Place des Héros de
l'Independence

① 11

Rue République

Ave John Brown (Lalue)

Rue Borgella

Rue Jardines

Rue Piquant

Rue Ducoste

Rue St Cyr

Ave Christophe

🏨 13

🏨 14

To Petionville
(6km)

Rue Camileau

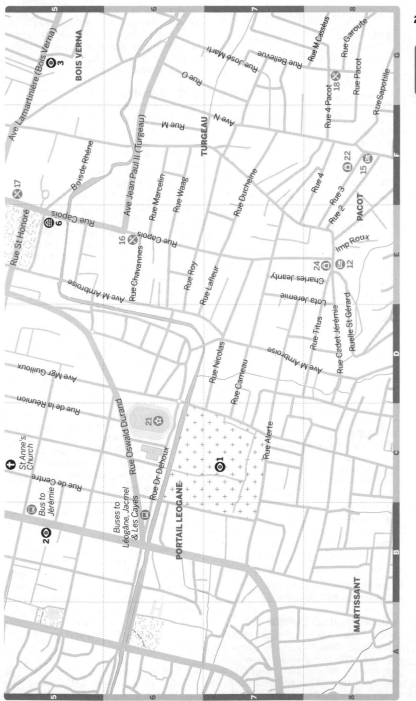

BOIS VERNA

Ave Lamartinière (Bois Verna)

3

Rue M Casseus

Rue Garoute

Rue Bellevue

Rue Pacot

Rue José Marti

18

Rue Pacot

Rue Sapotille

Rue O

Rue N Ave

TURGEAU

Rue M

Bois de Rhêne

Ave Jean Paul II (Turgeau)

Rue Duchesne

Rue 4

Rue 3

Rue 2

22

15

PACOT

17

6

Rue Capois

Rue Marcelin

Rue Waag

Rue St Honoré

Rue Chavannes

16

Rue Capois

Rue Roy

Rue Lafleur

Imp Roux

24

12

Charles Jeanty

Ave M Ambroise

Lota Jeremie

Rue Titus

Rue Cadet Jérémie

Ruelle St Gérard

Ave M Ambroise

Rue Nicolas

Rue Camieau

St Anne's Church

Ave Mgr Guilloux

Rue de la Réunion

Rue de Centre

Bus to Jérémie

2

Rue Oswald Durand

21

Rue Dr Dehoux

Buses to Léogâne, Jacmel & Les Cayes

PORTAIL LÉOGÂNE

1

Rue Alerte

MARTISSANT

Port-au-Prince

Tours

For guided tours around Port-au-Prince, and excursions beyond the capital:

Tour Haiti (☏2510-2223, 3711-1650; www.tour haiti.net; 31 Rue Casseus, Pacot, Port-au-Prince)

Voyages Lumière (☏3607-1321/3557-0753; voyageslumierehaiti@gmail.com)

Festivals & Events

Carnival takes place during the three days before Ash Wednesday in February. The highpoint is the huge parade of floats, music and carnival queens that winds its way downtown through an immense crush of people, before climaxing at Champs de Mars.

Taking most of the afternoon, the revelries continue late into the night. Carnival bands are fiercely competitive, each devising new songs that they hope will become the theme to the entire festival, played on the radio in the run-up to the parade.

Sleeping

There's one main decision to make when choosing a bed for the night: whether to stay downtown or above it all in Pétionville.

PORT-AU-PRINCE

TOP CHOICE **St Joseph's Home for Boys Guest House**   GUESTHOUSE **$**
(☏2257-4237/3449-9942; www.sjfamly.org; opp Radio Haiti Inter, Delmas 91; full board, shared r per person US$40; 🖉) Rebuilding with great fortitude after their original house collapsed in the earthquake, this home for ex-street boys still offers a fantastic Haitian experience. The new building will evolve during the life of this guide; expect either twin rooms or sharing with bunks, buckets for showering and toilet flushing, but great food and company (meals are taken together).

TOP CHOICE **Les Palmiers**   BOUTIQUE HOTEL **$$$**
(off Map p280; ☏3702-9648; www.lepalmierguest hotel.com; 16 Rue Lamothe, Puits Blain 4, Frères; s/d US$100/160; ▣🕸🖉🌊) Near Djoumbala nightclub but tucked down a quiet lane, this new house-turned-hotel is the last thing you'd expect to find in Port-au-Prince: a bizarre Aztec-meets-Star Wars confection. There's just a clutch of rooms around the circular core of the building, furnished with great attention to detail (such as the Croix des Bouquets-made bedheads). A great addition to the scene.

TOP CHOICE **Inn at Villa Bambou** BOUTIQUE HOTEL **$$$**
(☏2245-3513/2813-1724; www.villabambouhaiti .com; 1 Rue Marfranc, Pacot; r US$200-250 half-board; ▣🕸🖉🌊) A 1920s house rebuilt since the earthquake, this is a truly gorgeous boutique hotel. There are half a dozen rooms, each named for a herb and beautifully decorated. The quality of the food is a particular selling point, along with the leafy garden – and if there's a guesthouse offering better views of Port-au-Prince, we'd like to know about it.

TOP CHOICE **Karibe Hôtel**   HOTEL **$$**
(☏2256-9808; www.karibehotel.com; Juvenat 7; s/d from US$130/150, ste fromUS$230; ▣🕸@🖉🌊)

PORT-AU-PRINCE'S GINGERBREAD ARCHITECTURE

The vast majority of Haiti's unique gingerbread buildings are in Port-au-Prince, almost entirely the product of just three Parisian-trained Haitian architects: Georges Baussan, Léon Mathon and Joseph-Eugèe Maximilien. There are a couple of hundred gingerbreads, and although many are now falling into disrepair, being expensive to maintain, they withstood the 2010 earthquake much better than many modern concrete buildings.

The key gingerbread characteristics are brick-filled timber frames adorned with lacy wooden latticework, high ceilings, and graceful balconies set over wide porches – all designed to take advantage of the prevailing winds. The old Palais National, built in 1881 (and blown up in 1912), was an early model, and its style was quickly appropriated as the height of bourgeois tropical living. The residential areas of **Pacot** and **Bois Verna** saw gingerbread houses reach their zenith during a 30-year spree that ended in 1925, when Port-au-Prince's mayor stifled the construction of wooden buildings due to their potential fire hazard.

Hôtel Oloffson (below) is Port-au-Prince's most photographed example of gingerbread style. Built in 1887, it served as the family home to the son of President Sam, then as a military hospital during the American Occupation, before being converted to a hotel in 1936. A walk along **Ave Lamartinière** in Bois Verna reveals a parade of great gingerbreads, while LaLue has the famous Le Manoir at 126.

There are few gingerbreads in Pétionville. The loveliest by far is the **Hotel Kinam** (p284), although this was built in the 1950s, long after the original gingerbread boom.

Preserving Haiti's Gingerbread Houses, a post-earthquake report by the **World Monument Fund** (www.wmf.org), is an excellent introduction to the challenges facing this unique aspect of Haitian heritage.

By some degree the fanciest big hotel in Haiti, this hotel-cum-conference-centre is where you'll find the richest businessmen, international consultants and even presidents putting their bills on expenses (Bill Clinton and 'Baby Doc' Duvalier have been recent guests). Rooms and service are impeccable.

Hôtel Oloffson   HOTEL $$
(Map p280; ☎2223-4000; www.hoteloloffson.com; 60 Ave Christophe; s/d from US$85/100; [P][❀][@][🛜][🏊]) If Haiti has an iconic hotel, it's the Oloffson. Immortalized as Hotel Trianon in Graham Greene's *The Comedians,* the elegant gingerbread building is one of the city's loveliest, further tricked out with paintings and Vodou flags. There's a very sociable bar for your rum punches, and every Thursday the house band RAM plays up a storm until the small hours. Sadly, the Oloffson isn't beyond trading on its name, and the rooms, fixtures and service don't quite live up to the tariff. Still, it remains a lively scene.

Wall's Guest House   GUESTHOUSE $
(off Map p280; ☎3703-4788/3622-0684; www.walls guesthouse.org; 8 Rue Mackandal, Delmas 19; shared r per person incl breakfast & dinner, with fan or aircon US$40; [P][❀][🛜]) A friendly guesthouse run with a strong Christian ethic; you're likely to find yourself sharing with missionaries and aid workers, and adopting families. Rooms are basic and bathrooms shared. There's a tiny pool and everyone eats together. Heavily damaged in the earthquake, but happily thriving again.

Park Hotel   HOTEL $$
(Map p280; ☎2940-1453; www.parkhotel.home stead.com/park2.html; 23 Rue Capois; s/d US$52/ 69; [P][❀][🛜]) An old townhouse-hotel facing Champs de Mars, the Park aspires to faded grandeur but ends up just feeling a bit sleepy. Rooms are simple but well turned out, set around the empty pool at the back or in the block alongside. The gardens are shady, adding to the quiet atmosphere. Good value for downtown.

Coconut Villa Hôtel   HOTEL $$$
(off Map p280; ☎2510-4901/2246-0234; www .coconutvillahotel.com; 3 Rue Berthold, Delmas 19;

WANT MORE?

Head to Lonely Planet (www.lonelyplanet .com/haiti/port-au-prince) for planning advice, author recommendations, traveler reviews and insider tips.

DON'T MISS

MARCHÉ DE FER

Several of Haiti's cities have iron markets, but Port-au-Prince's is the original and best. The **Marché de Fer** (Map p280; Grand Rue; ☉daily) is an exuberant red-metal structure dating from 1889, which looks more akin to something from the *Arabian Nights* than tropical Haiti. It was originally destined to be the main hall of Cairo Train Station (hence the minarets), but was bought by President Hyppolite as part of his plan to modernize Port-au-Prince.

The Iron Market burnt down after the earthquake, but has been magnificently and speedily restored, reopening on the one-year anniversary. The southern hall is the food market, a full-on assault on the senses; the stifling air buzzing with the noise of traders and the tang of fruit, vegetables, meat and unknown scents. The northern hall is given over to a giant craft market, with the biggest selection of local arts in the country. The market is especially rich in Vodou paraphernalia.

Be prepared for plenty of bustle, and a little hustle too – you'll attract plenty of would-be guides. Keep a close watch on your possessions.

s/d US$100/150; P✳❄☒) The Coconut Villa is set in large and leafy grounds, with quick and easy access to Route de Delmas. Rooms in the main block are comfy, with the green calm of the surroundings (and the cool blue of the pool) making this hotel a welcome retreat.

Prince Hotel   HOTEL **$$**
(Map p280; ☎2223-0100, 2245-2764; princehotel ha@yahoo.com; 30 Rue 3, Pacot; s/d from US$77/91; P✳☒) Placing yourself in Pacot should give the advantage of views across Port-au-Prince, and this hotel doesn't disappoint. A charming-enough option, with pool, bar and restaurant, although some of the rooms are in need of a refit.

Le Plaza   HOTEL **$$$**
(Map p280; ☎3701-9303/2940-9800; www.plaza haiti.com; 10 Rue Capois; s/d US$115/126; P✳ ☒❄) The unobtrusive main entrance opposite Champs de Mars (you'll walk past it twice) hides the fact that this is downtown's largest and most high-class hotel. Rooms have balconies facing inward to a central quadrangle and, while well fitted out with all the mod-cons, are best described as business-class bland. A second home for visiting international media.

PÉTIONVILLE
Be aware that some of Pétionville's budget hotels tread an uneasy line between cheap and cheerful, and are used by local sex workers.

Belle Etoile Hôtel   HOTEL **$**
(Map p286; ☎2256-1006; Rue C Perraulte; s/d US$40/45)
The Belle Etoile is the best of the budget hotels for travellers purposes – threatening to be grimy from the outside, but actually hosting bright and clean rooms that have been recently kitted out; friendly staff.

Doux Sejour Guest House   GUESTHOUSE **$$**
(Map p286; ☎2257-1533, 2257-1560; www.doux sejourhaiti.com; 32 Rue Magny; s/d from US$65/74; ✳❄) A fun little guesthouse painted lobster pink, the Doux Sejour has a series of airy rooms, interestingly laid out (ascending the balcony terrace feels like climbing into the trees). Staff are helpful and the attached restaurant, **Le Bistro** (mains US$8 to US$10) serves tasty, filling meals.

Hotel Kinam   HOTEL **$$$**
(Map p286; ☎2944-6000/2955-6000; www .hotelkinam.com; Place Saint-Pierre; s/d from US$92/103; P✳@☒) A large gingerbread hotel right in the center of Pétionville, the Kinam is a good option. Rooms are well sized and modern, while the hotel as a whole offers good quality. The whole effect is charming, particularly on evenings when the pool is lit up and guests congregate for the renowned rum punches.

Ibo Lele   HOTEL **$$$**
(Map p286; ☎2257-8500, 2257-8509; Rue Ibo Lele; s/d US$100/140; P✳☒❄) The Ibo Lele was a big player in the 1960s tourist-heavy years, but today it feels a bit lifeless. Rooms still maintain quality, and the huge pool can be a draw for nonguests to use (if you

have transportation to get here). There are stunning views, as the hotel is perched high on the slopes above Pétionville proper.

La Villa Creole
HOTEL $$$
(Map p286; ☎2257-1570, 2257-0965; www.villa creole.com; Rue El Rancho; s/d from US$148/192; P❄🛜❄) Although it lost a hotel block in the earthquake, the Villa Creole carries a slightly more relaxed air than its competitors. It's nicely laid out, with the open reception area flowing down to the exceedingly pleasant bar and pool area. Rooms are medium to large, superbly appointed and comfortable, and the staff are well known for their service and attention to detail.

La Reserve
HOTEL $$$
(Map p286; ☎2510-5026; www.lareservehaiti.com; 2 Rue Marcel Toureau, Berthé; s/d from US$140/140; ❄🛜P) In a secluded part of Pétionville, this hotel is the old home of 1920s president Borno, and a one-time Dominican monastery. In shady grounds, it's now been kitted out as a more than comfortable hotel. Recently refurbished rooms are swish, and the open-air **restaurant** is a great place to eat.

Eating

There's a wide range of restaurants in Port-au-Prince. The default menu is Creole, with a smattering of French and American dishes. If you're downtown, you should also consider the hotel restaurants – many restaurants close on Sundays and lots of places only open in daytime hours during the week (lunch is the big meal of the day). For a wider range of eating options, head up the hill to Pétionville – the post-quake influx of foreigners has actually led to a mini boom of new places opening up.

PORT-AU-PRINCE

Hôtel Oloffson
FUSION $$
(Map p280; ☎2223-4000; 60 Ave Christophe; snacks/mains from US$4/8; ⊙7am-11pm) A lazy lunch on the veranda of the Oloffson is one of central Port-au-Prince's more pleasurable dining experiences, and lit up at night it's equally charming. A mixed international and Creole menu, dishes can sometimes be a bit hit and miss, although the salads and club sandwiches are always reliable. On Thursdays, stay to watch the owner's band, RAM, play from around midnight.

Arc-en-Ciel
CREOLE $
(Map p280; 24 Rue Capois; mains around US$5; ⊙9am-2am) This is a decent no-frills sort of a place, serving up healthily large portions of Creole standards. Along with platters of *griyo* (pork), plantain and the like, there's good jerked chicken and a dash of American fast food. Later in the evening, diners compete with dancers as the music and atmosphere crank up a pitch.

Chez Rose
CREOLE $
(Map p280; ☎2245-5286; cnr Rues 4 Pacot & Bellevue; mains from US$8; ⊙11am-9pm) The service and setting in this converted ginger-bread are worth a detour. The menu is the expected mix of Creole and French dishes, nicely presented, with accompanying ambiance.

Le Tiffany
FRENCH $$
(Map p280; ☎2943-4496; 12 Blvd Harry Truman; mains around US$11; ⊙9am-6pm Mon-Sat) This well-regarded restaurant has a cool, dark interior that attracts a slightly more well-heeled crowd, making this one of the few higher end downtown restaurants to hold its own against the gravitational pull of the Pétionville dining scene. The French-influenced menu and good wine list are equally attractive draws here.

Épi d'Or
FAST FOOD $
(☎2246-8560; Rte de Delmas, Delmas 56; sandwiches around US$2.50; ⊙6am-9pm) This place is always busy; be warned of big queues at lunchtime. As well as great sandwiches, it also serves crepes, pizza and 'MacEpi' burgers, and there's an inhouse patisserie, all in bright surroundings and with aircon. Pay first, then present your ticket to complete the order.

Big Star Market
SUPERMARKET $
(Map p280; Rue Capois) This is the most central supermarket for downtown hotels, with several other options along Lalue.

PÉTIONVILLE

TOP CHOICE Assiette Creole
CREOLE $
(Map p286; 6 Rue Ogé; meals around US$3-4; ⊙noon-9pm, closed Sun) Tremendously popular with local office workers, this place serves up very generous portions of excellent quality Creole cuisine. You can take away or sit at the tables with umbrellas.

TOP CHOICE Papaye
FUSION $$$
(Map p286; ☎3513-9229; 48 Rue Métellus; mains around US$18-28; ⊙noon-2:30pm & 7-11pm, closed Sun-Mon) 'Caribbean fusion' aren't words you expect to see written in a Haitian restaurant

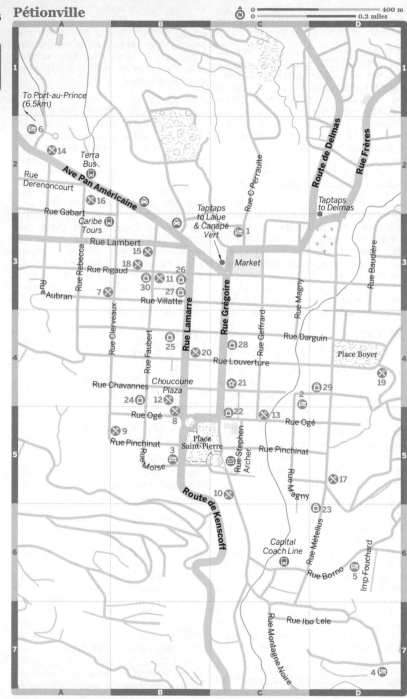

N 0 _____ 400 m
0 _____ 0.2 miles

To Port-au-Prince
(6.5km)

Terra Bus

Rue Derenoncourt

Ave Pan Américaine

Rue Gabart

Caribe Tours

Rue Lambert

Rue Rebecca

Rue Rigaud

Rue Cleveaux

Rue Aubran

Rue Villatte

Rue Faubert

Rue Lamarre

Rue Grégoire

Rue C Perraulte

Route de Delmas

Rue Frères

Taptaps to Lalue & Canapé Vert

Taptaps to Delmas

Market

Rue Baudière

Rue Geffrard

Rue Magny

Rue Darguin

Place Boyer

Rue Louverture

Choucoune Plaza

Rue Chavannes

Rue Ogé

Place Saint-Pierre

Rue Pinchinat

Rue Morse

Route de Kenscoff

Rue Stephen Archer

Rue Ogé

Rue Pinchinat

Rue Magny

Rue Métellus

Capital Coach Line

Rue Borno

Imp Fouchard

Rue Ibo Lele

Rue Montagne Noire

review, but Papaye carries off the idea with considerable aplomb, taking Creole dishes and jamming them up against Asian, European and other culinary influences. Somehow it works, producing one of Haiti's classiest restaurants.

Anba Tonel CREOLE **$$**
(Map p286; ☎2257-7560; cnr Rues Clerveaux & Villatte; mains US$8-15; ⏰5-11pm, closed Mon-Wed) Most people hit Pétionville's restaurants for an alternative to Creole cuisine, but Anba Tonel may be the place to change minds. *Kibby* (fried stuffed meatballs) is the highlight here, along with the winning (and unlikely) conch kebabs. It's all served amid wonderfully kitsch decor, quite unmissable.

Quartier Latin CONTINENTAL **$$**
(Map p286; ☎3455-3325; 10 Place Boyer; mains US$5-22; ⏰10:30am-11pm) An established mainstay, Quartier Latin throws French, Italian and Spanish dishes into the mix, and serves up generous and tasty dishes as a result. There are a few tables outside in the garden and a generally relaxed atmosphere. There's regular live jazz music too.

Café Terrasse CONTINENTAL **$$**
(Map p286; ☎2256-0825; 81 Rue Grégoire; sandwiches US$7, mains US$12-24; ⏰11am-11pm; ☎) Formerly located downtown, Café Terrasse is a regular haunt for the NGO and embassy set. It's open layout and art-covered yellow walls give a chilled atmosphere; service is prompt and the food is good. There's a small arts and crafts shop at the back.

Harry's BAR-RESTO **$**
(Map p286; ☎2257-1885; 97 Ave Pan Américaine; mains around US$5; ⏰10am-4am) A popular extended bar-resto, Harry's is always good value. Lunchtime offerings include good-value Creole plat du jour, while pizzas seem more popular in the evening, when the place fills up with diners and drinkers.

Fior di Latte ITALIAN **$$**
(Map p286; ☎2256-8474; Choucoune Plaza; salads from US$5, mains US$9-17; ⏰11am-10pm, closed Mon) Fior di Latte is not particularly well signed (it's next to the American Airlines office). This restaurant's vine-covered canopy is a lovely place to take an extended lunch break. The menu is Italian, with great plates of pasta and pizza, and some really tasty quiches thrown in too. Finishing a meal with a bowl of homemade ice cream is a must.

Presse Café CAFE **$$**
(Map p286; ☎2257-9474; 28 Rue Rigaud; light bites US$3-7, buffet US$10, mains US$10-13; ⏰7:30am-midnight Tue-Sat, to 7pm Mon, closed Sun; ☎) We like Presse Café for its casual bistro air. Decorated with old newspapers and photos of jazz heroes, it's a great place for a relaxed snack and drink, and even better for its lunchtime buffet. On Thursday and Friday evenings there's usually live music.

Tropic CREOLE $
(Map p286; cnr Rues Lamarre & Louverture; mains from US$4; ⊘24hr) This bar-resto with its bright yellow-and-purple frontage claims to never close. We're not too sure, and expected that while the Prestige beer may always flow, it's best to turn up at something approaching normal dining hours if you want a plate of good Creole fare.

Mun Cheez FAST FOOD $
(Map p286; ✆2256-2177; 2 Rue Rebecca; burgers/pizza from US$2.50/6; ⊘11am-11pm Mon-Sat, 2-10pm Sun) A long-established and popular first-floor fast-food joint with good food, overlooking the junction with Ave Pan Américaine. You can sit with a beer and burger and watch the world go by.

Épi d'Or FAST FOOD $
(Map p286; ✆2257-5343; 51 Rue Rigaud; sandwiches around US$2.50; ⊘6am-9pm) This branch of the popular Haitian franchise serves up more of its successful mix of sandwiches, burgers, crepes and pastries to the Pétionville crowd.

Giant Supermarket SUPERMARKET $$
(Map p286; cnr Rues Ogé & Geffrard; Ⓟ) There are plenty of supermarkets in Pétionville; this is by far the biggest. On two levels, it even has an elevator.

☆ Entertainment

You don't have to go far to hear music in Port-au-Prince: many taptaps have their own mega soundsystems. If you want something a little more organized, look out for the billboards posted on major junctions advertising forthcoming concerts. Cover charges cost about US$7 to US$20 for really big names. As well as venues in Port-au-Prince (most bands play in Pétionville), large concerts and music festivals are regularly held at Canne á Sucre (p293) just outside the city.

Bear in mind that taxis can be extremely hard to find late at night.

Hôtel Oloffson LIVE MUSIC
(Map p280; ✆2223-4000; 60 Ave Christophe, Port-au-Prince; every Thursday) Once a week, from about 11pm, crowds gather here to dance until the small hours to the Vodou rock 'n' roots music of RAM – the hotel band. A potent blend of African rhythms, rara horns, guitar and keyboards, the shows have an irresistible atmosphere. At the center of everything is band leader (and Oloffson owner) Richard A Morse.

Xtreme CLUB
(Map p286; ✆2257-0841; 64 Rue Grégoire, Pétionville) Ever-popular Pétionville club, with live music and plenty of compas, rapkreyol and R&B sounds, tailor-made to get everyone dancing.

Djoumbala CLUB
(off Map p286; ✆2257-4368; cnr Ave Boisand Canal & Rue Frères, Pétionville) A large and always popular open-air club, leaning heavily on *compas*, with regular live bands.

Institut Français CULTURAL CENTER
(Map p280; ✆2244-0016; accueil@haiti-ifh .org; 99 Ave Lamartinière, Port-au-Prince) Holds regular concerts of classical, folk and modern Haitian music.

Sylvio Cator Stadium SPORT
(Map p280; cnr Rue Oswald Durand & Ave Mgr Guilloux, Port-au-Prince) Hosts Port-au-Prince's two biggest soccer clubs: Racing Club Haïtien and Violette Athletic.

There are plentiful bar-restos that often feature live music on the weekend. Rue Capois, off Champs de Mars, has several decent places – head for **Arc-en-Ciel** (Map p280; 24 Rue Capois, Port-au-Prince; ⊘9am-2am), or just follow your ears. There's also good live music most Friday and Saturday nights at **Presse Café** (Map p286; ✆2257-9474; 28 Rue Rigaud, Pétionville; ⊘7:30am-midnight Tue-Sat, to 7pm Mon, closed Sun). There's no admission fee for these shows.

🛍 Shopping

Port-au-Prince is Haiti's marketplace. For a full-on sensory shopping experience, head for the **Marché de Fer** (p284), where you'll find everything from paintings and artisanat (handicrafts) to Vodou flags. Alternatively, try some of the following:

Crafts

As well as the places below, if you want to buy the best metalwork, head straight to the source at the artisan's village at **Croix des Bouquets** (p292). Some crafts are also sold streetside: along the top of Lalue for painted metal animals and, closer to Christmas, vendors of *fanal* (houses made of festive paper and card made to be illuminated by candles).

Haitizana CRAFTS
(Map p286; ✆2256-2282; 6 Rue Ogé, Pétionville) Run by the umbrella body of the Institut de Recherche pour la Promotion de l'Artisanat

Impromptu open-air art galleries can be found throughout Port-au-Prince, with canvases hung on fences and walls; all quickly executed copies of the Haitian masters. Large congregations are found along the wall of the Hotel Kinam in Pétionville and along Delmas 33. Prices should never really top US$20.

If you're after something more specific, try the following galleries, all in Pétionville. Staff are knowledgeable and will be able to give more information about specific artists and schools of painting. Prices range from reasonable to astronomical, depending on the artist.

» **Galerie Marassa** (Map p286; ☎2257-5424; galeriemarassa@hotmail.com; 17 Rue Lamarre, Pétionville) A specialized and exclusive gallery exhibiting a good base of contemporary and naive Haitian artists, as well as metalwork, crafts and Vodou flags.

» **Galerie Monnin** (Map p286; ☎2257-4430; www.galeriemonnin.com; 23 Rue Lamarre, Pétionville; ⊙Tue-Sat) Port-au-Prince's oldest private art gallery, in a lovely building. Lots of landscapes, but with a wide selection of different Haitian schools.

» **Galerie Nader** (Map p286; ☎2257-5602; www.galeriendartader.com; 50 Rue Grégoire, Pétionville; ⊙Mon-Sat) A huge gallery over two floors, with a large collection of mostly moderns and some naives. The Nader family are possibly Haiti's biggest art collecting family.

» **Galerie Flamboyant** (Map p286; ☎3555-9398; 9 Rue Darguin, Pétionville) A small gallery with a nice mix of naives and moderns.

» **Expressions** (Map p286; ☎2256-3471; www.galeriendartader.com; 55 Rue Métellus, Pétionville) A well-regarded Pétionville gallery, with one of the largest and most wide-ranging selections of Haitian artists.

Haïtien (IRPAH), you'll find a comprehensive selection of Haitian crafts here at very reasonable prices. Every October, IRPAH organises the *Artisanat en Fête*, the largest craft fair in the country, at Canne á Sucre (p293).

Galata CRAFTS
(Map p286; ☎2256-2282; Choucoune Plaza, Pétionville; ⊙closed Sun) In a small gingerbread house, this has an interesting mix of traditional and eclectic crafts, including unusual items such as taptap-styled mouse mats, and (if your luggage allowance permits) painted rocking chairs.

Comité Artisanat Haïtien CRAFTS
(Map p280; ☎2222-8440; 29 Rue 3, Pacot; ⊙closed Sun) Established in 1972, this craftmakers' cooperative has worked to promote Haitian crafts and provide fair wages for its artisans. The shop here is strong on well-priced metalwork, stone sculptures, lively painted boxes and miniature taptaps.

Books & Music

Asterix BOOKS
(Map p286; ☎2257-2605; cnr Rues Grégoire & Ogé, Pétionville) Has a large selection of French-language books and magazines, plus some in English.

J'Imagine BOOKS
(Map p286; ☎2257-2605; 49 Rue Chavannes, Pétionville) Also known as Maison Henri Deschamps, this has French (and some English) books and magazines, and also a great coffee shop serving drinks, sandwiches and light lunches.

Le Mélodisque MUSIC
(Map p286; cnr Rues Rigaud & Faubert, Pétionville) Has the best selection of Haitian music CDs in Pétionville. Also sells concert tickets.

ℹ Information

Emergency
Fire Brigade (☎emergency 115)

Minustah (☎emergency 113)

Police Port-au-Prince (☎2222-1117, emergency 122; 4 Rue Légitime); Pétionville (☎2257-2222; emergency 122; Place Saint-Pierre)

Red Cross (☎emergency 2510-4103)

Internet Access
Most hotels have wi-fi, but internet cafes are plentiful and cost around HTG50 per hour

DNS Computer (Rue Capois, Port-au-Prince; per hr HTG40; ⊙8am-9pm)

Semicom (Rue Capois, Port-au-Prince; per hr US$1; ⊙7am-9pm)

Medical Services

Hôpital du Canapé Vert (☎2245-0984/0985; 83 Rte de Canapé Vert, Port-au-Prince) Excellent doctors and emergency service, recommended by expats.

Hôpital Français (☎2222-2323, 2222-4242; 378 Rue du Centre, Port-au-Prince)

Hôpital François de Sales (☎2223-2110, 2222-0232; 53 Rue Charéron, Port-au-Prince)

Hôpital de la Communaute Haitienne (☎2812-1212/2213-3400; Rue Audant, Rte de Frères, Port-au-Prince).

Money

ATMs are increasingly widespread. To beat bank queues, head to supermarkets to change money; most have dedicated counters.

Promobank (cnr Ave John Brown & Rue Lamarre, Port-au-Prince)

Scotiabank (cnr Rues Geffrard & Louverture, Pétionville)

Sogebank Port-au-Prince (Rte de Delmas 30); Pétionville (Rue Lamarre)

Unibank (118 Rue Capois, Port-au-Prince)

Post

DHL (☎2812-9400; Rte de l'Aéroport, Port-au-Prince)

Post office Delmas (Delmas 45); Pétionville (Place Saint-Pierre)

UPS (☎2511-8181; Rue Geffrard, Pétionville)

Travel Agencies

Agence Citadelle (☎2940-5900; www .agencecitadelle.com; 35 Place du Marron Inconnu, Port-au-Prince)

🛈 Getting There & Away

Air

International flights depart from **Aéroport International Toussaint Louverture** (off Map p280; ☎2250-1120) and domestic flights from **Aérogare Guy Malary** (off Map p280; ☎2250-1127), both on the northern outskirts of Port-au-Prince.

The following airlines have offices in Port-au-Prince:

Air Canada (☎2250-0441/0442; www .aircanada.ca; Aéroport International Toussaint Louverture)

Air France (☎2222-1078/2222-4262; www .airfrance.com; 11 Rue Capois, Port-au-Prince)

American Airlines (☎2246-0100/3510-7010; www.aa.com; Choucoune Plaza, Pétionville)

Insel Air (☎2813-0401/0403; www.fly-inselair .com; Belvédère Plaza, Pétionville)

Salsa d'Haiti (☎2813-1222/3717-6455; www .flysalsa.com; Aérogare Guy Malary)

Tortug Air (☎2250-2555/2556; tortugair@yahoo.com; Aérogare Guy Malary)

Bus & Taptap

Port-au-Prince has no central bus station; instead, there is a series of mildly anarchic departure points according to the destination. Timetables are generally absent, with buses and taptaps leaving when full – exceptions are for Cap-Haïtien and Jérémie, which you can buy seats for in advance.

For destinations in the south and southwest, go to **Estasyon Portail Léogâne** (Map p280). Buses and taptaps go to Jacmel (US$3, three hours), Les Cayes (US$8, four hours) and all points in between.

For Jérémie (US$12, nine hours) there are bus offices on Grand Rue near the Ciné Lido (Map p280). Buses usually depart early.

For Cap-Haïtien (US$12, seven hours) go to **Estasyon O'Cap** (Map p280). Transportation to Gonaïves (US$6, three hours) and the Côte des Arcadins also leaves from here.

For Croix des Bouquets (US$1, 30 minutes), buses depart from the junction of Rue des Fronts Forts and Rue du Centre. For Kenscoff (HTG20, 30 minutes), taptaps leave from Place Saint-Pierre in Pétionville.

For Santo Domingo in the DR: **Caribe Tours** (Map p286; ☎2257-9379; cnr Rues Clerveaux & Gabart, Pétionville), **Terra Bus** (Map p286; ☎2257-2153; Ave Pan Américaine, Pétionville) and **Capital Coach Line** (off Map p286; ☎2512-5989; www.capitalcoachline.com; 8 Rue Borno, Pétionville and Rte de Tabarre, nr US Embassy). All have daily departures at around 8am, arriving in Santo Domingo nine hours later, with tickets costing around US$40 plus border taxes. For more on the border, see p356.

Car

Many of the car-rental companies are near the airport.

Budget (☎2813-1094; www.budgethaiti.com; Rte de l'Aéroport)

Dollar (☎2250-1800; www.dollarhaiti.com; Rte de l'Aéroport)

Secom (☎2942-2941; www.secomhaiti.com; Delmas 68, Rte de Delmas, Pétionville)

🛈 Getting Around

TO/FROM THE AIRPORT It takes around 30 to 45 minutes to reach the airport from the city center, depending on the time of day. Airport taxis are run by the **Association des Chauffeurs Guides d'Haïti** (ACGH; ☎2222-1330, 3402-7706). Fares should be between US$20 and US$40. You can take a taptap to or from the airport (HTG10); they wait outside the terminal and drop passengers off at the corner of Blvd Toussaint Louverture and Rte de Delmas.

MOTO-TAXI Useful for weaving through traffic jams. They cost around HTG30 to HTG40 for short trips, haggle for longer distances.

TAPTAP Port-au-Prince's taptaps run along set routes and are a very cheap and convenient way of getting around. The usual fare is HTG10 per trip. Routes are painted on the side of the cab doors. All stop on request. Shouting 'Merci chauffeur!' or banging on the side of the vehicle will stop the driver. Particularly useful routes include Lalue to Pétionville, Rte de Delmas to Pétionville and Canapé Vert to Pétionville. Routes running north-south include Aéroport to Nazon (crossing Delmas and Lalue), and Saline to Martissant (along Grand Rue).

TAXI Collective taxis running set routes are called *publiques*, recognizable from the red ribbon hanging from the front mirror. Hail as you would a taptap. Fares are set at HTG25. If you get into an empty *publique* and the driver removes the red ribbon, he's treating you as a private fare and will charge accordingly – up to US$20 if you're going a long way. State clearly if you want to ride *collectif* and share the ride with others. *Publiques* don't tend to travel between Port-au-Prince and Pétionville, so hiring is often the best option. There are a couple of radio-taxi firms, especially useful if you're out late: **Nick's Taxis** (☎2257-777) and **Taxi Rouge** (☎3528-1112). Both charge around US$10 between downtown and Pétionville, or US$15 per hour.

SOUTH OF PORT-AU-PRINCE

Route de Kenscoff

The main road from Pétionville's Place St-Pierre winds steeply uphill toward the cool of the mountains. After just a few kilometers you're in a rich agricultural area, with steep terraced fields clinging to the sides of the mountains, and the fug of the city replaced by sweet cool breezes.

❶ Getting There & Away

Taptaps (local buses or minibuses) leave throughout the day from Pétionville's Place St-Pierre to Kenscoff, departing when full (HTG20, 30 minutes), and pass through Fermathe. Change at Kenscoff for Furcy.

FERMATHE

The small town of Fermathe is 13km above Pétionville. The main attraction is **Fort**

Jacques (admission HTG25; ☉sunrise-sunset), erected during the burst of fort-building following independence in 1804. Built by Pétion and named for Jean-Jacques Dessalines, it was slightly damaged in the 2010 earthquake. The ruined **Fort Alexandre** is a short walk away. Overlooking Port-au-Prince, they offer grand views. The forts are a 3km walk from the main road – take the sharp uphill road opposite Fermathe's covered **market**.

Fermathe also has the **Mountain Maid Gift Shop** (☉8.30am-5pm, closed Sun) located near the entrance to the town. Run as part of the Baptist Mission, it sells crafts and produce from local cooperatives and self-help groups – everything from greeting cards and carvings to jams and cakes. There's a decent cafeteria attached. Next door is an interesting **museum** (donation requested; ☉8.30am-5pm, closed Sun), with a large and well-labeled array of artifacts from Haitian history, and a small ethnographic collection.

KENSCOFF

The cool of Kenscoff makes it a popular weekend destination for city dwellers – at 1980m above sea level, it's often referred to as the Switzerland of the Caribbean (there are even a few weird Caribbean–Alpine architectural hybrids). With sweeping views everywhere you look and the brooding cloud-capped backdrop of Massif de la Selle behind you, it's tailor-made for day walks. Coffee and vegetables are grown in great quantities here, giving Kenscoff an interesting local market.

Le Florville (☎3512-3535; 19 Rte de Kenscoff, Kenscoff; s/d US$40/60; **P**) is a popular hotel and restaurant on the left as you drive up from Pétionville. There are only a couple of rooms, tidily appointed, but eating here is the big drawcard, with the restaurant's well-set tables serving a mix of French and Creole dishes (mains US$12 to US$22). The terrace offers fine views, and there's often live music on weekends.

FURCY

To continue to the smaller and even more picturesque village of Furcy, turn left at Kenscoff Commissariat, then right after the fast-food places and continue uphill. Locals will rent out horses here (around US$3 per hour), making it easy to reach the Bassins Bleu waterfall, 1½ hours above the village by foot. Continuing on from Furcy, you reach the entrance to Parc National la Visite, from where you can hike over the mountains to

Seguin. Whatever your plans, don't forget some warm clothes – temperatures drop once the sun starts to dip.

A Canadian-style stone-and-wood cottage seems incongruous in Haiti, but the **Lodge** (☎3510-9870; www.thelodgeinhaiti.com; Furcy; s/d/tr incl breakfast US$60/90/120; P❋@), set amid the trees, has been furnished with a keen eye for details. As well as standard rooms, there are a couple of apartments, some with saunas. The restaurant is of high standard, making a big deal of imported food items like crab and salmon.

Parc National la Visite

The Massif de la Selle, a series of spectacular ridges still dotted with pine forest, divides Haiti's southeast. You can do one of Haiti's best hikes here – a day of trekking that takes you across the western section of the mountains toward the Caribbean. The route traverses four mountains and takes in some truly beautiful terrain, from wooded slopes to almost-rolling green hills, as well as lovely views out to sea. Once you reach Seguin you'll find the weird *kraze dan* (broken teeth) rock formations – great slabs of karst jutting up from the ground like so many discarded giant dentures.

A decent degree of fitness is required to do the trek, which usually takes six to eight hours. Take plenty of water and some food, as well as suitable clothing: the altitude ascends above 2000m in places, so there can be strong sun and wind, as well as unexpected rain and chill. You won't always be alone on the trek, however; although this is a rugged terrain, the route is also a well-used pedestrian highway, traveled primarily by women on their way to market, balancing produce on their heads. The sight of foreigners walking for fun always seems to raise a friendly smile.

To reach the trailhead, take a taptap from Pétionville to Kenscoff, and change for Furcy. From there, you can walk to Carrefour Badyo, then bear left to follow the track to Seguin. By 4WD, it's a 15-minute drive to Badyo, and then you have to start hiking. Once at Seguin, you descend to Marigot (a further couple of hours), and from here it is a taptap ride to Jacmel (US$1, one hour). At Furcy it's possible to hire horses with guides, but you'll have to pay for the return trip from Seguin.

In Seguin, the **Auberge de la Visite** (☎2246-0166; tiroyd@yahoo.com; r full board US$50) is a delightful place to rest up after the trek. There are two low stone buildings with cozy rooms and porches, where you can sit in a rocking chair and enjoy views to the Caribbean. The owner is Haitian-Lebanese, a fact further reflected in the food served. The Auberge can also arrange guides and horses for further exploration of the area.

EAST & NORTH OF PORT-AU-PRINCE

Plaine du Cul-de-Sac

The fertile Plaine du Cul-de-Sac runs east from Port-au-Prince toward the Dominican Republic. Once the heart of the colonial plantation system, it's of interest to visitors for its metalworking community in Croix des Bouquets, its bird-watching sites at Trou Caïman, and the brackish waters of Lac Azueï, which straddles the border. To the northwest, the road leads into Haiti's central district, where every year the village of Saut d'Eau becomes the focus of a major Vodou pilgrimage.

CROIX DES BOUQUETS

Almost sucked in by Port-au-Prince's inexorable urban sprawl, Croix des Bouquets is the setting for one of Haiti's most vibrant art scenes. It's Noialles district is home to the *boss fè* (ironworkers), who hammer out incredible decorative art from flattened oil drums and vehicle bodies.

☉ Sights

Croix des Bouquets's metal-art tradition was begun by the blacksmith George Liautaud, who made decorative crosses for his local cemetery. In the early 1950s, he was encouraged by the American De Witt Peters to make freestanding figures and incorporate Vodou iconography into his work. The result was an explosion of creativity, with Liautaud and his apprentices creating a uniquely Haitian form of art: carved iron. Although Liautaud died in 1991, his legacy is the thriving community of artists in Croix des Bouquets.

Steel drums are the most common material for the art. They're cut in half and flattened, the designs chalked and then cut out with chisels. Once free, the edges are

In 1847 a vision of the Virgin Mary in Ville-Bonheur drew pilgrims, who were convinced of its healing abilities, to the town. A church was built on the site of the vision, but local devotees soon spiritually associated it to the nearby waterfalls of Saut d'Eau, which was sacred to Erzuli Dantor – a *lwa* often represented as the Virgin. As a result, both Catholic and Vodou adherents now make the pilgrimage in huge numbers. A Catholic mass is said in the church and a statue of the Virgin Mary is carried around town. Vodou pilgrims then trek 4km to the Saut d'Eau waterfalls, a series of shallow pools overhung by greenery, where they bathe in the sacred waters, light candles and whisper requests to those lucky enough to become possessed by Erzuli herself.

smoothed and relief work beaten out. The smallest pieces are the size of this guidebook; the most gloriously elaborate can stand over 2m. Popular designs include the Tree of Life, the Vodou *lwa* La Siren (the mermaid), birds, fish, musicians and angels.

It's worth spending time in Noailles wandering between artists' workshops to get an idea of what different artists are producing. The first workshop you pass belongs to Serge Jolimeau, the current master of the scene. His designs are frequently sold in American galleries. Many pieces depict particular *lwa* (Vodou spirits), so don't be afraid to ask about specific meanings.

There's a complete absence of trying to hard sell. The smallest pieces can be picked up for US$3 to US$4, while pieces from the most celebrated artists can stretch into hundreds or thousands.

❶ Getting There & Away

Taptaps from Port-au-Prince (HTG20, 30 minutes) leave from Carrefour Trois Mains near the airport. Get out at the police post, where the road splits left to Hinche and right to the DR. Take the right-hand road, then turn right at Notre Dame Depot. For Noailles, turn right at the Seventh Day Adventist Church, and follow the sound of hammered metal: the artist's village is signed.

PARC HISTORIQUE DE LA CANNE À SUCRE

At the outbreak of the Haitian Revolution, the Plaine du Cul-de-Sac was one of the richest parts of Saint-Domingue. Little remains of this period, but one important sugar mill constructed at the end of the 19th century now stands as a **museum** (☑2298-3226; Blvd 15 Octobre, Tabarre; admission U$7; ☉9am-1pm Mon-Fri, to 5pm Sat & Sun). Exhibits are mainly open air, surrounded by low colonial-style buildings that comprised factories and shops, plus a collection of sugarcane presses, boilers

and part of the aqueduct used to drive the mills. There's also a train for the narrow-gauge railway laid to carry sugarcane to the factories.

The park is also a popular outdoor venue for music concerts, and every October hosts the *Artisanat en Fête*, Haiti's largest crafts fair. Held over two days, artisans gather from across the country, along with Haitian fashion designers and food producers. There's live music too.

VILLE-BONHEUR

An otherwise unprepossessing town, Ville-Bonheur becomes the focus of Haiti's largest Vodou pilgrimage every July 16. True to form, elements of Catholicism and Vodou have been blended to produce something uniquely Haitian (see boxed text, above).

During the pilgrimage, the area around the Church of Our Lady of Mt Carmel is turned into a huge campground for pilgrims. The few guesthouses are inundated. A decent option is the bright and clean **Hotel Villa Marie Robenson & Georges** (☑2245-2212; www.sautdeauinfo.com; Rue Clerveaux, Saut d'Eau; r US$40; P❋@), in the town center. Alternatively, there are accommodations in nearby Mirebalais. The **Wozo Plaza Hôtel** (☑4455-07730; wozoplazahotel@yahoo.fr; Rte National 3, Mirebalais; s/d incl breakfast US$70/100; P❋@☀) on the outskirts of town gets consistently good reviews for its service.

Buses and taptaps leave from Estasyon Mirebalais in Port-au-Prince (US$2.50, 2½ hours) between Grand Rue and the cathedral, at the junction of Rue des Fronts Forts and Rue du Centre. Taptaps run throughout the day between Ville-Bonheur and Mirebalais (HTG20, 45 minutes).

PARC NATIONAL FORÊT DES PINS

When you're sweltering in Port-au-Prince, the idea of cool mountain pine forests can seem a world away, but driving three hours east to the Massif de la Selle near the Dominican border can have you pleasingly reaching for another layer to ward off the cool.

The road is very poor as it winds up the mountains, but the views are spectacular. Sadly, it's also a textbook illustration of deforestation and erosion; many towns beyond Forêt des Pins are regularly damaged during hurricanes. Although the forest is nominally protected under law, cutting for wood and charcoal continues to be a problem.

From Fond Parisien on the Croix des Bouquets-Dominican Republic highway, the road turns south. It's a 50km drive to the village of **Fond Verettes** (which has a market on Tuesdays), and as the road climbs the climate gets colder and mistier. Four hours' drive from Port-au-Prince, the park entrance is just beyond the suitably named village of Terre-Froide. A checkpoint for the **Ministry of Agriculture, Natural Resources and Rural Development** (MARNDR; ✆2250-0867) is here. There is no entrance fee to the park. Just past the entrance, there is a cluster of basic cabins (US$11 per person). Prebooking with MARNDR is advisable, and you should be self-sufficient down to your (warm) bedding. The village of **Forêt des Pins** is a short walk beyond the cabins and has an interesting Saturday market.

The park is perfect for hiking. The denser parts of the forest are cool and tranquil, with birdsong and sunlight filtering through the trees. Good hikes from the park entrance include the gentle 5km walk to Chapotin, where views stretch to the sea, and to Lake Enriquillo in the Dominican Republic, or the stiff climb to Do Gimbi ridge for more fantastic views of the mountains, forest and sea (around four hours' walk round-trip). You'll meet plenty of locals on the tracks along both routes, so you shouldn't get lost.

Côte des Arcadins

From Port-au-Prince, Rte National 1 stretches north along the coast before turning inland toward Gonaïves and Cap-Haïtien. The area is named for the Arcadins, a trio of sand cays surrounded by coral reefs in the channel between the mainland and Gonâve.

The first main town after leaving the capital is **Cabarete**, 'Papa Doc' Duvalier's modernist construction, built as a symbol of his regime and ruthlessly satirized for its pretensions in Graham Greene's novel, *The Comedians*. Look out for the merchants selling delicious local *tablet* (peanut brittle) to passengers in passing vehicles. Just beyond is **Arcahaie**, where Dessalines created the Haitian flag from the rags of the Tricolor in 1804.

Beyond Arcahaie are the beach resorts. The beaches themselves aren't too inspiring, but they offer safe, shallow swimming and snorkeling in clear water. On weekends they come alive with visitors from the capital; it's worthwhile booking accommodations in advance. The coast is also good for diving – **Pegasus at Kaliko Beach Club** can arrange dives (see below).

The **Plage Publique** (Km 62, Rte National 1; admission US$1) is tucked in between the Kaliko Beach Club and Wahoo Bay. There are basic facilities, food sellers, sound systems and booze – it's a great place to see regular Haitians at play.

North of Montrouis, at Moulin sur Mer, is the **Musée Colonial Ogier-Fombrun** (✆2278-6700; Km 77, Rte National 1; admission free; ◷10am-6pm) in a restored colonial plantation and sugar mill. At the entrance is a framed letter from Toussaint Louverture to the present owner's ancestors. If you visit during the week, you'll probably have to ask for it to be opened.

🛏 Sleeping & Eating

Beach hotels are the order of the day along the Côte des Arcadins, and are listed here in order of their distance from Port-au-Prince.

Kaliko Beach Club   HOTEL $$$

(✆3513-7548; www.kalikobeachclub.com; Km 61, Rte National 1; s/d full board US$110/150, day pass US$35; P❄@🌊) A modern all-inclusive-style resort, with a series of linked pools and cute octagonal bungalows set amid shady grounds. There are various water sports options along the pebbly beach. Also based at Kaliko, **Pegasus** (✆3624-9486/ 9411/4775; nicolemarcelinroy@yahoo.com) can arrange diving charters for qualified divers.

Ouanga Bay   HOTEL $$

(✆2257-6347; ouanga@hotmail.com; Km 63, Rte National 1; r incl breakfast US$80; P❄🌊) A relatively small hotel, but with a cute and immaculate beach and breezy rooms. The

Barren Île de la Gonâve has always been set slightly apart from the mainland. A refuge for Taínos from the Spanish and for runaway slaves from the French, it was on its reefs that the ghost ship *Marie Celeste* was abandoned in 1884. But the island's strangest story came with the US occupation in 1915, when a Polish-American marine sergeant named Faustin Wirkus was appointed administrator of the island. Popular with the locals, he came to be seen as the reincarnation of Emperor Faustin Soulouque, who ruled in the mid-19th century. At his police station he was crowned King Faustin II with great ceremony, and decorated with hummingbird and macaw feathers. He ruled for four years until 1929, when he was faced with an army transfer; he resigned his commission and left Haiti for the more prosaic occupation of bond broker. Wirkus wrote a regal memoir, *The White King of La Gonâve*, and died in 1945.

A daily **ferry** (US$6, one hour) crosses to Île de la Gonâve from a jetty 500m north of **Ouanga Bay hotel** (opposite), departing early in the morning for the port of **Anse-á-Galets** and returning late afternoon. There's a very basic hotel here and not much else, but some good beaches on the west side of the island.

palm-thatched restaurant extends over the water, making it an ideal place to laze over fresh seafood (mains US$12 to US$16) and watch the boats go by.

Moulin sur Mer HOTEL $$$
(☎2222-1918; www.moulinsurmer.com; Km 77, Rte National 1; s/d full board US$120/170, day pass US$9; P✱@✾) This large charming complex has a nice selection of rooms – 'gingerbreadized' rooms near the beach, and more Spanish-hacienda style ones further back. There's the beachside **Boucanier** (mains US$10-18) seafood restaurant, and gardens full of sculptures. The **Musée Colonial Ogier-Fombrun** is in the same grounds, a (complimentary) golf-buggy ride away.

Club Indigo HOTEL $$$
(☎3442-9999; www.clubindigo.net; Km 78, Rte National 1; s/d US$121/176, day pass US$35; P✱@✾) Everything at this former Club Med hotel is bright and breezy, with huge grounds and whitewashed buildings centered on the pool and restaurant-bar area.

The beach is lovely but the rooms are tiny. On weekends, Club Indigo heaves with UN staff and Port-au-Prince's hip set.

Xaragua Hôtel HOTEL $$$
(☎3510-9559; Km 80, Rte National 1; s/d full board US$71/128; P✱✾) Big rooms all offer sea views here. Rates are very reasonable, so you can happily ignore the tired 1970s architecture and decor inside. Instead, look to the pool terrace and the beach. The hotel is owned by a local aid organization, and all profits go toward running five rural hospitals in Haiti.

ℹ Getting There & Away

Catch a **bus** or **taptap** to Gonaïves or Saint-Marc (US$3.50, 2½ hours) from Estacyon O'Cap beside the Shell petrol station, at the corner of Blvd Jean-Jacques Dessalines (Grand Rue) and Blvd La Saline in Port-au-Prince. Advise the driver where you want to be dropped. Return transportation is a lot more hit and miss; you're reliant on flagging down passing buses.

Southern Haiti

Best Places to Eat

» Cyvadier Plage Hôtel, Jacmel (p301)

» Congo Beach, Jacmel (p301)

» Beach Bars, Port Salut (p305)

Best Places to Stay

» Cyvadier Plage Hôtel, Jacmel (p301)

» Dan's Creek Hotel, Port Salut (p304)

» Tamarin Place Charmant, Jérémie (p306)

Why Go?

Haiti's south is about taking it easy. Pulling out of Port-au-Prince, the urban hustle is soon replaced by a much more relaxed air as you head towards the Caribbean Sea.

Of the southern coastal towns Jacmel is the gem. It's an old port full of pretty buildings, with a friendly welcome. Some hit the handicrafts shops to load up on local art, while others time their visit for the famous Carnival.

Further west, things get pretty sleepy. The town of Les Cayes is an embarkation point for the gorgeous beaches of Île-à-Vache, while there are more palm-fringed sandy delights for all budgets in nearby Port Salut.

The southern 'claw' is bisected by the Massif de la Hotte, home to Haiti's last remaining cloud forest. After a spectacular mountain crossing, the road terminates at Jérémie, the sometime City of Poets.

When to Go

Jacmel enjoys its biggest day of the year – and Haiti's most surreal street-theatre – during its colourful annual Carnival celebrations in February. The hurricane season means the heaviest rainfall and strongest winds are during August to October, but between November and March there's little annual fluctuation in temperature, and these months are the driest and least humid.

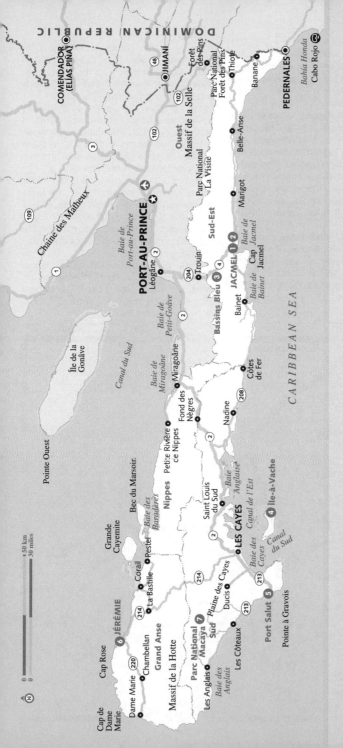

Southern Haiti Highlights

1 Exploring the architecture of **old Jacmel** (299)

2 Having your mind blown by the street theater of Jacmel **Carnival** (p300)

3 Diving into the cool waters of **Bassins Bleu waterfall** (p299)

4 Getting away from everything by heading to **Île-à-Vache** (p304)

5 Lazing on miles of sandy beaches at **Port Salut** (p304)

6 Finding the city at the end of the road in **Jérémie** (p305)

7 Cutting an adventurous trail into remote **Parc National Macaya** (p305)

JACMEL

POP 40,000

Sheltered by a beautiful 3km-wide bay, the old port of Jacmel is one of the most friendly and tranquil towns in Haiti, and host to one of its best Carnivals.

Part of Jacmel's charm is down to its old town center, full of mansions and merchants' warehouses with a late-Victorian grace poking out from behind the wrought-iron balconies and peeling facades. Unfortunately, many of these buildings were damaged in the 2010 earthquake. Jacmel as a whole was badly hit by the earthquake, with as many as 500 people killed, and many buildings destroyed.

The town is the undisputed handicrafts capital of Haiti, with dozens of workshops producing hand-painted souvenirs, from wall decorations to the elaborate papier-mâché masks produced for the Carnival festivities.

History

Founded by the French in 1698 near the old Arawak settlement of Yaquimel, Jacmel was a prosperous port by the close of the 18th century, when the town's large mulatto population began demanding equality with the whites. Soon after, under André Rigaud's leadership, Jacmel became an important battleground in the Haitian independence struggle, and Jacmel remained a center of mulatto power when Haiti split into two following Dessaline's death in 1806.

Jacmel also played a small role in the South American independence movement. Pétion hosted Simón Bolívar here in 1816 when the Venezuelan revolutionary leader was assembling his army, hospitality that Bolívar returned by abolishing slavery after liberating his country.

By the middle of the 19th century, Jacmel was serving as a major Caribbean loading point for steamships bound for Europe. Jacmel was the first town in the Caribbean

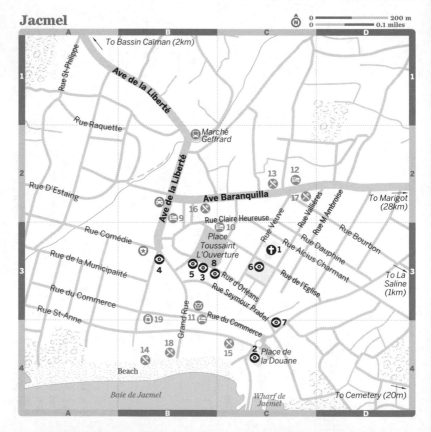

Jacmel

to have telephones and potable water, and (in 1895) the first to have electric light. The town center was destroyed by a huge fire in 1896 and then rebuilt in the unique Creole architectural style that remains to this day. Port trade, however, began to dry up following WWII and the Duvalier era, leaving the annual Carnival the one time of year when Jacmel truly recreates its glory days.

◉ Sights

Old Jacmel   NEIGHBORHOOD
Running parallel to the seafront, Rue du Commerce is the heart of old Jacmel and has many splendid (albeit shabby) examples of 19th-century warehouses and merchants' residences. Key characteristics are the high-shuttered doors and windows, shaded by wide balconies with filigree railings. Of these, the house of the influential Vital trading family has been turned into the **Hôtel Florita**. At the eastern end of the street are some of the oldest surviving buildings, including the **Customs House** next to the wharf on Place de la Douane, and the 18th-century **prison**.

The Vital family also owned the **Manoir Alexandre**, between Rue du Commerce and Place Toussaint L'Ouverture, during WWI. Other key buildings to look out for are the grand **Maison Cadet** (cnr Ave de la Liberté & Grand Rue), with its red-iron 'witch's hat,' and **Maison Boucard**, near Rue Seymour Pradel, which has an intricate wrought-iron gallery facade.

Near Maison Boucard is the **Salubria Gallery** (⌨2288-2390; 26 Rue Seymour Pradel; ⊙by appointment), an eclectic gallery in a blue-and-white fin-de-siècle house. The walls are packed with paintings, even the bathrooms and bedrooms; you trail around the whole house, looking at a collection that includes most of the masters of Haitian art.

East of Place Toussaint L'Ouverture is the red-and-green baroque **Marché de Fer**, built in 1895 as a scaled-down version of the grand iron market in Port-au-Prince. Closed Sundays, at all other times local produce spills out of every side of the market, jamming the surrounding streets.

The pretty white **Cathédrale de St Phillippe et St Jacques** (Rue de l'Eglise) built in 1859 is close to the market. The ostentatious tombs in the rambling **cemetery** at the eastern end of Rue Alcius Charmant, one block north of Rue de l'Eglise, include those of many early European settlers.

Bassins Bleu   WATERFALLS
Bassins Bleu is tucked into the mountains 12km northwest of Jacmel, a series of three cobalt-blue pools linked by waterfalls that make up one of the prettiest swimming holes in the country.

The three pools are Bassin Clair, Bassin Bleu and Bassin Palmiste. Bassin Clair is the most beautiful of the three, deep into the mountain at the bottom of the waterfall, sheltered and surrounded by smooth rocks draped with maidenhair and creeper ferns. Local kids may delight you by lunging into the pool from the higher rocks. You're sadly less likely to see the nymphs that according to legend live in the grottoes, although be warned that they've been known to grab divers attempting to discover the true depth of the pool.

Any guide in Jacmel can arrange a trip to Bassins Bleu, which takes about two hours each way, usually by horse. Expect to pay around US$20. The road is accessible by 4WD and (when it's dry) by moto-taxi. There is a small hamlet close to the pools, where you pay the entrance fee (US$2.50); a local

CARNIVAL IN JACMEL

Every year, thousands of partygoers descend on Jacmel to take part in Carnival, one of Haiti's most fantastic spectacles. At this time, Jacmel turns into one giant street theater: it's a world away from the sequins and sparkle of Carnival in Rio de Janeiro.

The Carnival season starts its buildup on Epiphany (January 6), with events every Sunday leading up to the giant celebrations and procession on the Sunday of the week before Shrove Tuesday (it's held a week earlier than other Carnivals so it doesn't clash with Port-au-Prince's party). The streets suddenly swell and everywhere you look are strange figures in fantastical papier-mâché masks – the signature image of Jacmel Carnival. You can see the masks being made and on display in the ateliers year-round. Jungle animals jostle with mythical birds, giant fruit and *lwa* (Vodou spirits). Mixed in with the procession are celebrants dressed as Arawaks and colonists, and horned figures covered in molasses and soot, who tease revelers with their sticky grab. St Michael and his angels ritually fight the devil, while gangs of *chaloskas* – monsters caricaturing military misrule – growl scarily at the crowds. There's even (an old Carnival favorite, this) a donkey dressed up in peasant clothes and sneakers. Music is everywhere, from bands on organized floats to *rara* (one of the most popular forms of Haitian music) outfits on foot. It's an enormous party. The procession kicks off roughly around noon, with celebrations continuing late into the night.

guide then escorts you to the pools. The path is a little uneven, and at one point you must climb down a steep rock face (with carved footholds) by rope. From here, you're ready to dive in.

While the mineral-rich waters of Bassins Bleu are a delight at most times of the year, they turn a muddy brown after heavy rainfall.

🏖 Beaches

The beachfront along Jacmel is sandy but also a little dirty – it's worth making the effort to head a little further out to enjoy more pleasant surroundings. Note that the undertow is especially strong along this coastline; don't venture out too far.

The closest beach is **La Saline**, a small cove that's a 30-minute walk from the town center past the cemetery (25HTG by moto-taxi). If you're lucky, you might find a fisherman here who'll catch and grill you a lobster and sell you some cold beer to boot. You can also arrange a lift from here (or from Jacmel's wharf) across the bay to the large sand-and-pebble beach of **Baguette** (30 minutes by boat), where there are also ruins of an old French fort.

Heading east, there's a succession of fine beaches. A taptap (local bus or mini-bus) heading in the Marigot direction will be able to drop you off at any of them. **Cyvadier Plage** is about 10km outside of Jacmel, down a small track leading from the

Cayes Jacmel road. The beach is part of the Cyvadier Plage Hôtel. The small half-moon-shaped cove flanked by rocky cliffs has no undertow.

About 13km from Jacmel is the popular **Plage Raymond-les-Bains**. This is another long stretch of sand, with palm trees and mountains as a backdrop. It can get crowded at weekends, although eating freshly caught seafood here surrounded by holidaying Haitians can make for a great time.

In the small fishing village of **Cayes Jacmel**, about 14km east of Jacmel, the beach spreads a further 3km to **Plage Ti Mouillage**, a gorgeous white-sand stretch fringed with coconut palms, plus a beach bar for drinks and seafood. Cayes Jacmel is known for making the rocking chairs seen throughout Haiti.

🎪 Festivals

Jacmel's Carnival celebrations are famous across Haiti, and people come from across the country and the diaspora to join in the party.

Since 2004 **Jacmel Film Festival** (www.festivalfilmjakmel.com) has been one of Haiti's biggest cultural events. Taking place over a week every November, Jacmel hosts movie screenings by Haitian and international directors as well as film-making workshops run by Jacmel's **Ciné Institute** (www.cineinstitute.com).

🛏 Sleeping

Despite its obvious tourist attractions, Jacmel isn't over-endowed with hotel beds. Many of the midrange and top-end hotels are actually outside Jacmel, heading east from Ave Baranquilla. If you plan on visiting during Carnival, advance booking is absolutely essential. In a potential tourism boost, two US hotel chains announced plans in 2010 to build in Jacmel.

Hôtel Florita HOTEL $$$
(☎2288-2805; www.hotelflorita.com; 29 Rue du Commerce; s/d US$80/100; ❄@) Damaged in the earthquake but rebuilt, this converted mansion from 1888 oozes charm. There are polished floorboards and period furniture, while rooms are whitewashed and airy, with mosquito nets and balconies. The bar is great, and chock-full of art.

Cyvadier Plage Hôtel HOTEL $$
(☎2288-3323; www.hotelcyvadier.com; Rte de Cyvadier; s US$65-75, d US$82-104, tr US$158; P❄@≋) Off the main highway, this is the furthest of the beach hotels from the center of Jacmel, but also one of the best. Rooms in a cluster of buildings face the terrace restaurant and out to the private cove of Cyvadier Plage (nonresidents are welcome). Rooms are good; the cheaper ones have fans rather than air-con.

La Cascade Auberge GUESTHOUSE $
(☎3695-0453; cascadeauberge@yahoo.fr; 63 Ave Baranquilla; r US$40; ❄) This guesthouse is a great deal: the large and spotless rooms have gleaming private bathrooms. The management speaks some English; the only drawback is that some rooms don't have external windows, making them a bit gloomy.

Guy's Guesthouse HOTEL $
(☎2288-2569, 2288-9646; Ave de la Liberté; s US$30-40, d US$50-60, tr US$65) There are invariably a few NGO workers staying at Guy's and it's easy to see why it remains popular. Although bathrooms are shared, everything is kept very clean, the rooms are comfy, and the staff friendly and helpful. Breakfasts are huge, and the restaurant out the front is a good place for lunch or dinner.

Le Rendez Vous Guesthouse GUESTHOUSE $
(☎3541-3044; lerendez_vousrestobar@yahoo.fr; Rte de Cyvadier; r US$35; P@) Outside Jacmel opposite the airstrip, you'll find this friendly, simple place. There are nine uncluttered rooms, an open-sided bar-restaurant, and lots of greenery with chickens and ducks pecking about. The manager also has a house to rent that sleeps four (per night US$200).

Hôtel de la Place GUESTHOUSE $$
(☎2288-3769; 3 Rue de l'Eglise; s/d US$50/75; P❄) A pleasant old building overlooking Place Toussaint L'Ouverture, and a popular place to enjoy Carnival. Rooms are modern, although some are a little on the small side; most manage a view. The ground-floor terrace bar seems designed for hours of people-watching.

Cap Lamandou Hôtel HOTEL $$$
(☎3720-1436, 3920-9135; www.lamandouhotel.com; Rte de Lamandou; r US$98; P❄@🛜≋) On the edge of Jacmel but a bit of a hike off the main road, the Cap Lamandou is Jacmel's glitziest hotel. Rooms are immaculate, with wi-fi throughout and all with possibly the best views over the bay in Jacmel. The bar leads onto the central terrace and pool, which has more steps descending to the sea if you're in need of a further dip.

Jaclef Plaza Hôtel HOTEL $$
(☎3757-6818; www.jaclefplazahotel.com; Rte de Cyvadier; s/d US$65/75; P❄@≋) A hotel just outside town with a good range of facilities, a bar and conference rooms. Guest rooms are very well sized but a shade characterless, something that's overcompensated for with a reckless love of chintz.

Ozana Hôtel HOTEL $$
(☎3703-7463, 3542-0487; Rue St Cyr Imp Prophéte; r US$80; P❄@≋) A bright, clean and very modern hotel, with nice rooms, satellite TV, a restaurant and everything kept spotlessly clean. The drawback? The location, down a long dirt track off the highway, makes your own vehicle pretty much essential.

🍴 Eating

Congo Beach CREOLE $
(Jacmel beach; mains around US$5; ⏰noon-midnight) Right on the beach, this is a collection of two dozen beach shacks, each serving up plenty of beer and cheap food, with accompanying sound systems. Fish, chicken and plantains are all filling staples, with plenty of lime chili dressing.

Cyvadier Plage Hôtel SEAFOOD $$
(☎2288-3323; Rte de Cyvadier; mains US$13-20; ⏰11am-11pm) The lobster at this hotel-restaurant is worth making a detour for,

served up on a terrace that catches a cool sea breeze. There are plenty of other good fish dishes to choose from, although we'd recommend you go easy on the lethal house rum punch.

La Crevette SEAFOOD $$
(☎2288-2834; Rue St-Anne; mains US$6-14; ☺noon-late) This place has a long covered dining area that overlooks the wharf and sea, so you'll be unsurprised to find seafood playing heavily on the menu. It's particularly busy at weekends, when locals also come for the cocktails and the dance floor to get the party going.

Le Buffet Resto-Bar CREOLE $
(Ave Baranquilla; mains US$5; ☺9am-11pm) Typical of the bar-restos along Ave Baranquilla, Le Buffet is a hole-in-the-wall place serving simple but satisfying Creole dishes. Ask what's available that day – usually chicken, *griyo* (pork) or *kabrit* (goat) with plantains, undoubtedly washed down with a cold Prestige and accompanied by a tomato and avocado salad.

Guillano's Pizza PIZZA $$
(☎2288-2695; Ave de la Liberté; pizzas US$5-15) Part of Guy's Guesthouse, this place does better-than-average pizzas, coming in very generous sizes. If you want a smaller snack, the sandwiches are good too.

Petit Coin Restaurant HAITIAN $$
(☎2288-3067; Rue Bourbon; mains around US$7; ☺noon-11pm) A cozy little restaurant, with a hint of French bistro. Three tables on a tiny terrace allow you to catch the last of the day's sun and people-spot, before retiring to the interior. The menu is Creole, with a couple of French dishes, all of it tasty.

Hôtel de la Place INTERNATIONAL $$
(☎2288-2832; 3 Rue de l'Eglise; mains US$3-9; ☺10am-10pm) The menu at this hotel inclines to Western fast food with a few Creole dishes thrown in. The main reason to eat here is to sit on the terrace and watch life unfold on the town square before you.

Yaquimo Restaurant & Bar CREOLE $$
(Grand Rue; mains US$5-10; ☺11am-11pm) Another beach bar, the Yaquimo has a bit of everything, mixing good food with decent music and plenty of drinks. It's a popular place for bands to play at weekends, when there's an admission charge of around US$6.

Ambians Restaurant CREOLE $
(Ave Baranquilla; mains US$4-11) A bar-resto with a terrace to relax with a drink and take the town's temperature. It has a varied Creole-French menu; the food is good, but can sometimes take a while to materialize.

For self-caterers, the markets in the streets around the Marché de Fer are the place to head for; a local specialty is tiny sweet *ti malice* (bananas). There's plenty of street food around here, too. Between July and January look out for women selling *pisquettes,* tiny fish sautéed in huge numbers.

🛍 Shopping

Jacmel is a souvenir-buyer's paradise. Its most famous output is the papier-mâché Carnival masks, unique to the town. More portable handicrafts include hand-painted placemats and boxes, wooden flowers, and models of taptaps, jungle animals and boats. Prices are cheap, and there's a complete absence of hard sell. Most of the shops can be found on Rue St-Anne near the Hôtel la Jacmelienne sur Plage, along with a number of galleries showcasing Jacmel's art scene. One of the better artisanat-galleries is **Moro** (21 Rue du Commerce), although it's not the cheapest.

ℹ Information

Banque Nationale de Crédit (Grand Rue)

CC Net (Ave Baranquilla; internet per hr HTG50; ☺9am-10pm)

Dola Dola (cnr Aves Baranquilla & de la Liberté) Moneychanger.

Hôpital St Michel (☎2288-2151; Rue St-Philippe) For emergencies, but not brilliant.

Jacmel Cybernet (Ave Baranquilla; internet per hr HTG50; ☺7am-10pm Mon-Sat, 9am-10pm Sunday)

Pharmacie St-Cyr (48 Ave Baranquilla)

Philippe Agent de Change (Ave Baranquilla) Changes euros and Canadian dollars.

Police (Ave de la Liberté)

Post office (Rue du Commerce; ☺8am-4pm Mon-Sat)

Unibank (Ave de la Liberté) Gives Visa advances.

ℹ Getting There & Around

Buses (HTG80, three hours) and taptaps (HTG100, 2½ hours) to Port-au-Prince leave from the Bassin Caïman station 2km out of town. Some taptaps also leave from Marché Geffrard, closer to the town center. From either place, transport runs from before dawn until about 5pm, departing when full. The ride along Rte National 4 (Rte de l'Amité) is particularly scenic. At Carrefour Dufort the road joins Rte National 2 to the capital. If you want to travel west, get off here by the Texaco gas station and flag down passing buses before noon, as there are no direct buses from Jacmel in this direction.

The **airport** (☎2288-2888; Rte de Cyvadier) is about 6km east of town, but there are currently no scheduled flights.

A moto-taxi around town costs around HTG20. Even trips as far as Cyvadier Plage should give change from HTG40. Taptaps run all day along Ave Baranquilla.

THE SOUTHWEST

From Port-au-Prince, Rte National 2 runs the length of Haiti's southern 'claw' to Les Cayes. After crawling through **Carrefour**, the road winds through a succession of medium-sized towns along the coast: **Léogâne**, which is known for its distilleries and stone sculptors; **Petit-Goâve**, famous for its sweet *dous macoss* (a type of peanut brittle); and the port of **Miragoâne**, its streets brimming over with imported (and often smuggled) goods, and home to a large cathedral. This region was the hardest hit by the 2010 earthquake, whose epicenter was just outside Léogâne. Around 80% of the buildings in that town were damaged or destroyed, with great loss of life. Petit-Goâve was almost as badly hit.

The coastal road used to be popular for weekend beach visits from the capital before snarling traffic made the resorts of Côte des Arcadins a more attractive prospect. From Miragoâne the road cuts inlands and heads across the mountains westward to Les Cayes.

Buses and taptaps ply the highway all day between Port-au-Prince and Les Cayes.

Les Cayes

POP 46,000

You'd be hard-pressed to find a sense of urgency in Haiti's fourth-largest city. More popularly known as Aux Cayes, Les Cayes is an old rum port sheltered by a series of reefs that has sent many ships to their graves (its first recorded victim was one of Columbus' ships on his final voyage to Hispaniola). Pirates were another threat, notably from

nearby Île-à-Vache. Today Les Cayes has little to offer the visitor, although it's a good stopping-off point for other destinations in the south.

Les Cayes is laid out in a grid. Rte National 2 turns into Ave des Quatre Chemins upon entering the town, bisected by Rue Général Marion. Two main roads lead south from here to the town center – Rue Nicholas Geffrard and Rue Stenio Vincent. The former leads to the wharf, while the latter takes you to the main square and Notre Dame Cathedral.

🛏 Sleeping & Eating

Le Meridien des Cayes   HOTEL $$
(☎2286-0331; info@hotelmeridiendescayes.com; 15 Rte National 2; s/d with fan US$45/55, with air-con US$65/85; ✳@) A fair if slightly bland choice. Rooms vary but are mostly spacious; some face onto the internal courtyard and restaurant, and lack external windows. Staff are brisk rather than friendly, although the restaurant is reasonable, both for the breakfasts and the Creole dinner menu.

Concorde Hôtel   HOTEL $$
(☎2286-0079; Rue Gabions des Indigenes; s/d with fan US$42/46, with air-con US$70/80; P✳@☲) Centrally located, the Concorde has two buildings set in large and pleasant gardens. Rooms are slightly quaint but decent enough (those in the main building are nicer), there's a pool, and the manager is helpful. Dinner is available.

Cliff Hôtel   HOTEL $
(☎3919-3679; Rue Capitale; s/d US$25/50; P) A quiet and clean bungalow with a handful of rooms, this is a decent budget option. Breakfast isn't included, and some rooms share a bathroom with adjoining doors.

Cayenne Hôtel   HOTEL $$
(☎3814-2594; lacayenneht@yahoo.fr; Rue Capitale; r with fan/air-con US$77/88; P✳@☲) This is the closest thing Les Cayes gets to a beach hotel: the sea is on the other side of the Cayenne's boundary wall. There's nothing wrong here – rooms are standard, and there's plenty of space and a pool – but nothing spectacular either.

Pen Doré   FAST FOOD $
(Rue Stenio Vincent; mains US$3-6; ⊙9am-10pm) A red-fronted snack place opposite the cathedral, this is a good place to come for sandwiches, burgers or a pizza, or just a fruit juice or bottle of cold Prestige.

La Cayenne CREOLE **$$**
(✆2286-1114; cnr Rue Geffrard & Mgr Maurice; mains US$6-9; ⊙10am-10pm) With its walls decked out in bright murals, La Cayenne is a trusty restaurant serving big platters of chicken, *griyo* or *kabrit*, fries, plantains and rice plus fast-food options. There's a good *plat du jour* served from 10am to 3pm, and the fruit juices are great.

❶ Getting There & Around

Voyageur (✆2942-7025; Meridien Hôtel) and **Transport Chic** (✆3630-2576; 227 Ave des Quatre Chemins) have luxury air-conditioned minibuses running daily to Port-au-Prince (US$10, four hours). Buy tickets the day before, and take photo ID.

Buses and taptaps leave from the area around Carrefour des Quatre Chemins, departing when full. Port-au-Prince transport is the most common (US$8, four hours), stopping at Petit-Goâve and Léogâne. Get off at the former to change for Jacmel, or just before at Carrefour Dufort. There are taptaps to Port Salut (US$1, 30 minutes) To get to Jérémie (US$10, eight hours) you have to wait for the bus from Port-au-Prince to pass through around mid-morning, or go to Camp Perrin (US$2, 1½ hours) and hope to get something from there.

Moto-taxis around town cost HTG20, charging around HTG120 to Port Salut.

Île-à-Vache

The so-called 'Island of Cows,' Île-à-Vache lies about 15km south of Les Cayes. In the 16th century it was a base for the Welsh pirate Henry Morgan as he terrorized Santo Domingo and Colombia. Three centuries later Abraham Lincoln tried to relocate emancipated black American slaves here, but it was a short-lived and ill-provisioned experiment. The island today is scattered with rural houses, plantations, mangroves, the odd Arawak burial ground and some great beaches.

The only accommodation options are two contrasting upmarket resorts, although some islanders in the village of Madame Bernard have been known to rent rooms to foreigners for around US$10.

Abaka Bay Resort (✆3721-3691; www.abaka bay.com; Anse Dufour; s/d incl full-board US$125/ 200; ❄@) must have one of the most fabulous beaches in the Caribbean, a smooth white curve of a bay, met by lush foliage and a series of pleasant bungalows and villas. The atmosphere is laid-back, but the service manages good attention to detail.

Served by a yacht harbor, **Port Morgan** (✆3921-0000; www.port-morgan.com; Cayes Coq; s/d incl full board from US$225/420, 2-night min; P❄@☀) is all bright-and-breezy gingerbread chalets with lovely views out to sea. There's a small beach, a really excellent restaurant serving French-influenced cuisine, and various kayaks and other water-sports equipment for rent.

Both resorts include transfers from Les Cayes wharf in their rates. Otherwise, *bateaux-taxis* (water taxis) leave from the wharf several times daily (US$2, 30 minutes) for Madame Bernard. Getting around by foot is easy; you can do a pleasant day walk in a loop between the two resorts via Madame Bernard, taking in the viewpoints of Pointe Ouest and Pointe Latanier.

Port Salut

A picturesque road leads west from Les Cayes to the spectacular beaches of Port Salut. A one-street town strung for several kilometers along the coast, the beach is the main reason to come here: kilometers of palm-fringed white sand with barely a person on it, and the gorgeously warm Caribbean to splash around in.

🛏 Sleeping & Eating

Dan's Creek Hotel HOTEL **$$$**
(✆3664-0404; r US$120; P❄@☀) A delightful brand-new seafront hotel with more than a hint of gingerbread about it. Charming rooms have balconies overlooking the sea, and there's an outdoor restaurant.

Hôtel du Village BEACH CHALETS **$$**
(✆3779-1728; portsaluthotelduvillage@yahoo.fr; s/d US$75/95; P❄) A government-owned hotel comprising a series of chalets. The rooms are nicely turned out, although you're not likely to spend much time in them since the front doors open straight onto the sand.

Auberge du Rayon Vert GUESTHOUSE **$$$**
(✆3713-9035; www.aubergedurayonvert.com; s/d US$80/110; P❄@) Stylish and immaculate rooms are the order of the day here, with locally made furniture and very modern bathrooms, and the beach seconds away. The restaurant-bar is the best in Port Salut.

Chez Guito SEAFOOD **$$**
(mains US$4-10) Opposite Hôtel du Village, this decent beach bar (albeit sitting on the opposite side of the road) is the place

to head for fish and *lambi* (conch), a cold Prestige and a sweet *compas* soundtrack.

Beach Bars SEAFOOD **$$**
(mains US$4-15) A group of candy-colored beach bars sit opposite the Coconut Breeze. Fish, lobster and *lambi* are all cooked up on demand, and washed down with beer and rum punch. Caribbean-slow during the day, but lively at weekends.

Coconut Breeze RESTAURANT, HOTEL **$$**
(☑3727-4885; r US$50; [P][❄]) A funky, low-slung sort of place with a clutch of rooms, with further beach bars across the road.

❶ Getting There & Around

Taptaps to Les Cayes (US$1, 45 minutes) leave throughout the day, while moto-taxis zip up and down the length of the town.

Camp Perrin

At the foot of the Massif de la Hotte range en route to Parc National Macaya and Jérémie, Camp Perrin is where the tarmac stops: from here roads are rough and bumpy. The town is little more than two streets with a few shops and bar-restos. It was founded in 1759 by the French, who left behind a network of irrigation canals. A different watery attraction not to be missed is the beautiful **Saut Mauthurine waterfall** *('les chutes')* with its deep green pool, a 15-minute moto-taxi ride away.

Auberge La Distribution (☑2286-0899; Zone Lévy; d with fan/air-con US$25/40; [P][❄]) is a number of buildings set in a large and rambling garden, with tidy rooms and a palm-shaded terrace bar and restaurant.

Taptaps to Les Cayes (US$2, 1½ hours) leave several times daily, picking up passengers along the main street. Buses to Jérémie usually pass through in the middle of the day.

Parc National Macaya

The 5500-hectare Parc National Macaya contains Haiti's last region of cloud forest, spread across the mountain ridges of the Massif de la Hotte. It has an extremely rich biodiversity, particularly birds and amphibians, with a high number of endemic species. One in every 10 plants is only found inside the park, with orchids notably represented. The near-permanent cloud cover brings around 4000mm of rain per year.

The region is not immune to the pressures of tree felling for charcoal and land clearance. The **Critical Ecosystem Partnership Fund** (www.cepf.net) is working to promote the long-term conservation of the park.

Macaya has several potential treks. The most challenging, taking four days there and back, is to the top of Pic Macaya (2347m). You must cross over a 2100m ridge and descend another 1000m before attempting the mountain itself. The trails are barely existent, so a knowledgeable guide and a machete to cut the way are both essential.

The main starting point for entering the park is Formond. You'll need a 4WD with high clearance, a couple of spare tires and at least four hours. Along the way you'll pass the overgrown Citadelle des Platons, one of Dessalines' network of defensive forts built after independence.

A good guide based in Camp Perrin is **Jean-Denis Chéry** (☑3766-4331). Tents are necessary, as are food, water-purification paraphernalia and wet-weather gear.

Jérémie

Jérémie, the capital of Grand Anse Département, is about as close to the end of the road as you can get in Haiti. The journey here amply demonstrates its isolation, although the terrible mountain road is under improvement. Once here, it seems to fulfill the cliché of a forgotten tropical port, with abandoned warehouses, little traffic and a sense of torpor in the air.

By contrast, Jérémie has a rich history. In 1793 it was the landing point for Britain's short-lived invasion of Haiti. After independence it was a major center for mulatto power, and its inhabitants grew rich on the coffee trade, sent their children to be educated in Paris and wore the latest French fashions. Jérémie was known as the 'City of Poets' for its writers. Its most famous sons are Alexandre Dumas, whose son wrote *The Three Musketeers,* and the poet Emile Roumer. In 1964 the town was the focus of an attempt to overthrow 'Papa Doc' Duvalier, who responded in murderous fashion by ordering the massacre of virtually Jérémie's entire mulatto population of around 400 men, women and children, leaving the city politically and economically isolated.

Jérémie is a sleepy, pretty place to spend a few days. The town is centered on Place Alexandre Dumas, with its red-and-white cathedral. Rue Stenio Vincent runs parallel to the sea, with many interesting old buildings and coffee warehouses, almost all sadly neglected. Continuing past the grubby beach takes you to Fort Télémargue, a crumbling fort that makes an excellent spot to watch the sunset.

About 5km northwest of Jérémie is the beach of **Anse d'Azur**, a gorgeous sandy bay with several caves that any Caribbean country would envy. A return moto-taxi will cost around US$3 to US$4.

🛏 Sleeping

There are several insalubrious cheapies on Rue Stenio Vincent near Place Alexandre Dumas.

TOP CHOICE Tamarin Place Charmant
GUESTHOUSE **$$**
(📞3722-5222; tamarin_jeremie@hotmail.com; 2 Calasse; r incl half-board from $US65; P@☀) Slightly out of town and with great views out to sea, this is a wonderful home-from-home. There are a variety of rooms from bungalows to new guest apartments, but the real welcome is in the great food and genial hosts.

Auberge Inn
GUESTHOUSE **$$**
(📞3727-9678, 3465-2207; aubergeinn@netscape .net; 6 Ave Emile Roumer; s US$45-54, d US$72-84, tr US$90-108; P☀@) The decor makes the Auberge Inn feel as much a home as a guesthouse. Dinner on request is excellent, and there's a selection of books, maps and handicrafts on sale, but the fact that all rooms share a single bathroom is a real drawback.

Hôtel La Cabane
HOTEL **$$**
(📞2284-5128; Ave Emile Roumer; s/d with fan US$50/70, with air-con $60/80; P☀@) A bright pink hotel. Some rooms are a little small, or maybe they just feel that way because of the ostentatious dark-wood furniture squeezed in. The airy restaurant is decorated with paintings of Jérémie's famous literary and political sons.

Hôtel le Bon Temps
HOTEL **$$**
(📞2943-5030; hotelbontemps@yahoo.fr; 8 Ave Emile Roumer; s/d from US$50/65; P☀@) Next door to the Auberge Inn, this is a modern if lifeless hotel. The whole place is spotless, although some of the (cheaper) rooms have skylights rather than windows.

✖ Eating

Depanneur
CREOLE **$**
(Rue La Source Dommage; meals US$3-10; ☺9am-9pm) A decent restaurant in a two-storey blue-and-white building with a supermarket downstairs. The *plat du jour* (usually meat with plantain and rice) is good value at US$3. The red-and-yellow-fronted Mme Dodo bar-resto next door is also worth a visit.

Chez Patou
CREOLE **$**
(Rue Monseigneur Boge; snacks/mains from US$2/4; ☺8am-3pm & 6-9pm) A great place to fill up, this airy red-and-white building has a decent range of sandwiches and burgers, along with hearty servings of Creole standards, spaghetti and the like.

Le Boucanier
CREOLE **$$**
(Rue Stenio Vincent; mains from US$5; ☺6-11pm) A typical bar-resto, Le Boucanier has a wide-ranging Creole menu, but there are usually only one or two dishes available, typically barbecued chicken or *griyo* (pork) served with plantain and salad.

L'Oasis Restaurant
CREOLE **$**
(Rue Adrien Brus; mains around US$7-10; ☺6pm-late) Popular with Jérémie's youth, this large restaurant is a lively place at weekends, when the drinks flow and the sound system is cranked up (there's often live music). Expect no surprises from the menu (although the fish and *lambi* are good), but go for the atmosphere.

You can buy fruit, vegetables and bread at the market north of the main square, along Rue Alexandre Pétion and Rue Monseigneur Boge.

ⓘ Information

Alliance Française (📞2286-6573; 110 Rue Stenio Vincent; internet per hr US$1.70; ☺9am-1pm & 4-8pm) Excellent internet connection. Also hosts concerts, films and an annual cultural festival every April.

Martha Cybernet (Place Alexandre Dumas, 1st fl; internet per hr US$1.40; ☺9am-8pm)

Soleil Levant (Ave Emile Roumer) Money-changers inside small supermarket.

Unibank (Place Alexandre Dumas)

ⓘ Getting There & Around

The quickest way in and out is the daily **Tortugair** (📞3610-0520; Rue Dr Hyppolyte) flight from Port-au-Prince (US$90, 35 minutes).

Demand is high, so book as far in advance as possible. The grassy airstrip is 5km northwest of Jérémie.

Buses leave every afternoon for Port-au-Prince (US$12, 11 hours) from a lot on the southern outskirts. Buses stop at all main towns en route, but you'll be asked to pay the full Port-au-Prince fare irrespective of your destination.

A ferry sails from Jérémie wharf every Friday evening to Port-au-Prince (US$14, 12 hours), although the boat is very creaky and often dangerously overloaded.

Moto-taxis ply the streets, charging around US$0.40 for most rides.

Around Jérémie

About 20km west of Jérémie is the startlingly beautiful cove of **Anse du Clerc**. It's pretty much as far as the road goes and you need a 4WD to get here, although a moto-taxi can just do it if it hasn't rained recently (US$8.50, one hour). There's a small village on the pebble beach, and a charming hotel. **Anse du Clerc Beach Hotel** (☑2246 3519; per person incl half-board US$65) has half a dozen thatched bungalows surrounded by lawns and palm trees right on the beach.

An appallingly rough road continues west from here to Dame Marie and Anse d'Hainault, but there is no public transport.

Pestel

The port village of Pestel is four hours east of Jérémie along the Grand Anse coast. It's a charming place once you're here, with its French fort, old wooden houses and some of Haiti's most wonderful (and wonderfully untouched) beaches. The main businesses are fishing and charcoal. **Hotel Louis & Louise** (☑2284-6191; r US$55) is a yellow-and-blue gingerbread-style building with cozy rooms and home-cooked food.

The easiest way to get to Pestel from Jérémie is by boat (US$7), but they're often worryingly overloaded. There's daily transport, but the road is terrible.

Northern Haiti

Best Places to Eat

» Lakay, Cap-Haïtien (p311)

» Kokiyaj, Cap-Haïtien
(p313)

» Cormier Plage Resort,
west of Cap-Haïtien (p316)

Best Places to Stay

» Hostellerie du Roi
Christophe, Cap-Haïtien
(p311)

» Lakou Lakay, Milot (p315)

» Norm's Place, Labadie
(p316)

Why Go?

If you're interested in how Haiti came to be as it is today, head north. From Columbus' first landfall on Hispaniola to the key events of the slave revolution, it all happened here.

Base yourself at Cap-Haïtien, Haiti's second city. Once one of the richest colonial ports in the world, it's the ideal base to visit the magnificent Citadelle la Ferrière, a true castle perched high on a mountain, with the ruined palace of Sans Souci sitting below, looking like something from a tropical Hollywood adventure movie. There are plenty of smaller forts along the coast, while Île de la Tortue evokes memories of the golden age of piracy.

The crashing Atlantic waves give the north some spectacular coastline and great beaches. Cormier Plage and Labadie are a stone's throw from Cap-Haïtien and are ideal places to unwind.

When to Go

The Vodou festival of Souvenance is a major highlight of Haiti's religious calendar, taking place just after Good Friday in March/April. The important Vodou festival and pilgrimage of Soukri is held near Gonaïves in July.

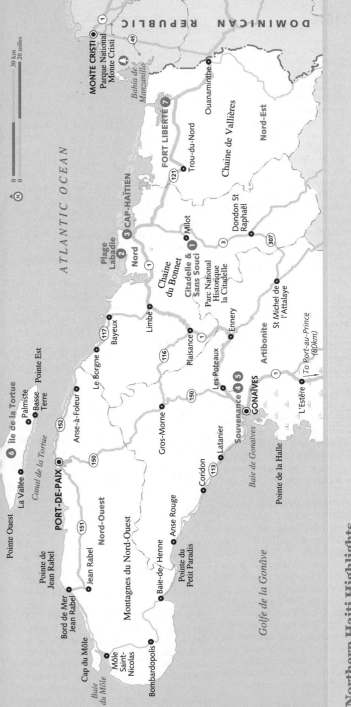

Northern Haiti Highlights

1 Reliving Haitian history at the **Citadelle** and ruins of **Sans Souci** (p314)

2 Letting the waves lap at your feet at **Plage Labadie** (p316)

3 Exploring the backstreets of Haiti's second city, **Cap-Haïtien** (p310)

4 Joining the pilgrimage to the **Souvenance Vodou festival** (p318)

5 Feeling the Vodou rhythms of the **Soukri Vodou festival** (p318)

6 Looking for pirates at **Île de la Tortue** (p318)

7 Finding the remains of France's colonial history at **Fort Liberté** (p316)

CAP-HAÏTIEN

POP 150,000

Haiti's second city feels a world away from the throng and hustle of Port-au-Prince. During the French colonial era it was the richest city in the Caribbean, and even if that grandeur has long since faded, the city still maintains a relaxed atmosphere, and the old port architecture of high shop fronts and balconies makes it a pleasant place to wander. Most people refer to the city simply as 'Cap', or 'O'Kap' in the high-lilting local Creole accent of its residents.

Despite its rich history, there is still plenty of poverty in Cap-Haïtien, although recent efforts to improve municipal facilities are slowly beginning to have their effect.

There isn't too much to do in Cap-Haïtien beyond enjoy the atmosphere, but it's an ideal place to base yourself to enjoy the nearby attractions, including the Citadelle la Ferrière and the beaches around Plage Labadie.

History

Razed to the ground five times by man and nature alike, Cap-Haïtien has a turbulent history, inextricably linked to Haiti's colonial past and independence struggle.

Cap-François was founded in 1670 by Bertrand d'Ogeron, who recognized the superb natural harbor of its location. As Saint-Domingue grew as a colony, the port was renamed Cap Français, and sat at the hub of the booming plantation economy. Sugar, coffee, cotton and indigo – and the slave trade – swelled its coffers. By the middle of the century, Cap Français was so rich it was dubbed the 'Paris of the Antilles.'

This Paris was destined to burn in revolutionary fire. Early rebellions had been squashed here, the inhabitants witnessing the executions of Mackandal in 1758, Vincent Ogé, who had agitated for mulattos' rights, in 1790 and the Vodou rebellion of Boukman a year later. The city was sacked when revolution erupted, and completely torched in 1803 on the orders of Toussaint Louverture, lest it fall into the hands of Napoleon's invading army. At Vertières on its outskirts, Dessalines won the final victory that brought independence, and renamed the city Cap-Haïtien as a symbol of freedom. When Christophe became king he renamed it Cap Henri, but the name reverted on his death in 1820.

Leveled by an earthquake in 1842, Cap-Haïtien has arguable never fully recovered. Its central political and economic role has been long-ceded to Port-au-Prince, and even today the road to the capital is poorly maintained.

◉ Sights

City Center
NEIGHBORHOOD

Cap-Haïtien is centered on **Place d'Armes**, a wide square between Rues 18 and 20 guarded by a large statue of Dessalines. It's a popular hang-out for students from the Roi Christophe University, on the southeast corner of the square. The **Cathédrale Notre Dame** otherwise dominates proceedings, an airy white basilica with abstract stained-glass windows.

The earthquake of 1842 left few colonial-era buildings in Cap-Haïtien, and its streets are now lined with an amalgam of styles. Most common are the old commercial buildings, with high shop fronts and tall shuttered doors and windows. The floors above are residential and support wide balconies with ornate iron railings that give the sidewalks shade at almost all times of day.

The best architectural gems are in the immediate vicinity of the cathedral. On the corner of Rue 16F is a tremendous (if slightly worn) red-brick Gothic mansion built in 1898, while on Rue 15 behind the cathedral are some charming gingerbread houses. The oldest accessible building is the Hostellerie du Roi Christophe, now a hotel, whose oldest parts were built in 1724.

Like Port-au-Prince and Jacmel, Cap-Haïtien has a **Marché de Fer** (Iron Market). This forms the hub of commercial activity, with market vendors spilling out in the streets around it and bringing traffic to a halt.

Forts
RUINS

As a major port, Cap-Haïtien has had a number of important, mostly French-built forts to defend its harbor. All are ruins, but offer nice views and a chance to get out of the city center.

Following Blvd de Mer through Carenage, you'll quickly arrive at **Fort Etienne-Magny**, about 500m past the Hôtel Les Jardins de l'Ocean. Only the foundations remain, but five cannons are still in place. Several benches have also been installed there, and the spot is a popular place for Haitian kids to meet and kick a football around. The next is **Fort St Joseph**, on the right on the edge of the cliff.

If you continue until the road peters out at Plage Rival, then along the pebble beach, you'll reach **Fort Picolet**, about a mile from Fort Etienne-Magny. Built by Dessalines and perched on a cliff, it's the most intact fort, with an amazing array of cannons. The view is perfect, and the spot is often deserted. It's a peaceful place to watch the sunset, although it's a dark walk home.

🛏 Sleeping

Cap-Haïtien still has a shortage of midrange beds. Rooms fill fast at the weekend, so advance booking is advised.

Beau Rivage Hôtel HOTEL $$
(📞2262-3113; beaurivage@yahoo.com; 25 Blvd de Mer; s/d US$60/80; P✳️🛜) Facing the seafront, the Beau Rivage is a good choice, though it lacks a sign to help find it: look for the big red brick and cream balustrades next to Kokijaj. If some rooms are a little on the small and boxy side, they're all well appointed with modern fixtures and fittings.

TOP CHOICE **Hostellerie du Roi Christophe** HOTEL $$$
(📞2262-0414; Rue 24B; s/d US$86/120; P✳️🛜🏊) Cap-Haïtien's most charming hotel, this French colonial building has something of the Spanish hacienda about it. There's an elegant, leafy central courtyard with plenty of rocking chairs, and a terrace restaurant. The rooms are large, with plenty of period furniture and art; many have balconies. The story that Henri Christophe worked in the kitchens is sadly apocryphal.

NAME & NUMBER

Cap-Haïtien is laid out in a grid pattern, with streets running north–south lettered Rue A through Q, and those running east–west numbered Rue 1 to 24. It wasn't always this way: the utilitarian system dates from the US occupation. Arriving in the city in 1915, US marines couldn't pronounce the original French street names, so changed everything to numbers and letters. If you look on street corners, however, you can still sometimes see plaques with the old street names, although their usage has sadly fallen out of fashion.

Auberge du Picolet HOTEL $$$
(📞2262-5595; Blvd de Mer; s/d US$90/110; P✳️🛜) A popular hotel. Spacious rooms are uncluttered and centered on a small shady courtyard. Sympathetically designed, it feels more Dominican colonial than brand-new Haitian.

Universal Hotel HOTEL $
(📞2262-0254; Rue 17B; r US$25-30, with shared bathroom US$20; ✳️) Definitely one of the better budget options. A large hotel with several terraces, its rooms are simple and clean. Bible passages remind guests that the meek shall inherit the earth, but less-than-Godly guests often check in for just an hour with a 'friend'.

Hôtel Rival HOTEL $$
(📞2262-0977; hotelrival@hotmail.com; Rte de Rival; r with fan/air-con US$60/75; P✳️🛜🏊) On the outskirts of the city by the sea near Fort Picolet, you can't miss this orange hotel. It's a bright option, and agreeably self-contained given its location. Rooms are fine (ask for a sea view), and it's the one place in Cap where you can happily dip your toes in the sea.

Hôtel Les Jardins de l'Ocean HOTEL $$
(📞2262-2277; 90 Carenage; r US$65-95; P✳️🛜) This French-run hotel seems to ramble up the side of the hill it sits on, so there's no shortage of terraces offering sea views (the rooms themselves have none). Rooms come in a variety of shapes and sizes, all individually decorated to the owner's taste – we loved the one with the mosaic wall of broken mirror. Its restaurant is recommended.

Hôtel Mont Joli HOTEL $$$
(📞2262-0300; www.hotelmontjoli.com; Rue B, Carenage; s/d US$122/150; P✳️🛜🏊) On a hill overlooking Cap, the Mont Joli easily has the best views in the city. Once the place to go, it's let itself go to seed of late. Rooms are generously sized, there's a restaurant with bar, and a pleasant pool and terrace to chill out on, but it's terribly over-priced.

🍴 Eating

TOP CHOICE **Lakay** CREOLE $$
(📞2262-1442; Blvd de Mer; mains from US$8; ⏰5-10pm) One of the busiest restaurants in Cap-Haïtien, and it's not hard to see why. There are tables facing the seafront where you can enjoy a drink, otherwise you step inside to eat under bamboo thatch and

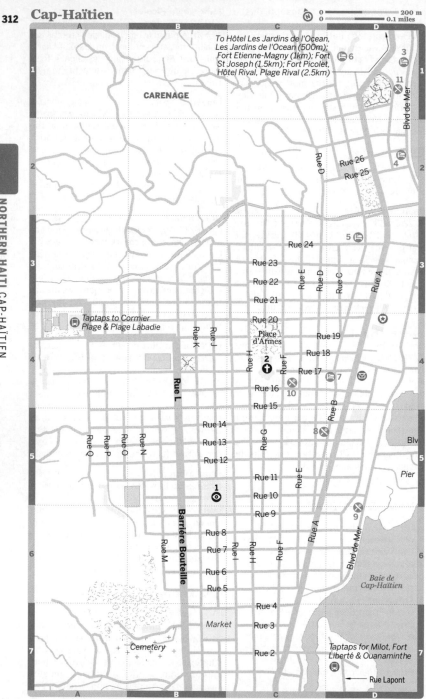

0   200 m
0   0.1 miles

To Hôtel Les Jardins de l'Ocean,
Les Jardins de l'Ocean (500m);
Fort Etienne-Magny (1km); Fort
St Joseph (1.5km); Fort Picolet,
Hôtel Rival, Plage Rival (2.5km)

CARENAGE

Blvd de Mer

Rue D
Rue 26
Rue 25

Rue 24

Rue 23
Rue E
Rue D
Rue C
Rue A
Rue 22
Rue 21

Taptaps to Cormier
Plage & Plage Labadie

Rue K
Rue J
Rue 20
Place
d'Armes
Rue H
Rue F
Rue 19
Rue 18
Rue 17

Rue L

Rue 16
Rue 15

Rue 14
Rue G
Rue 13
Rue B
Rue N
Rue O
Rue P
Rue Q
Rue 12

Rue 11
Rue E
Rue 10
Rue A
Rue 9

Rue 8
Rue M
Rue 7
Rue I
Rue H
Rue F
Rue 6
Rue 5

Rue 4

Market
Rue 3

Barrière Bouteille

Cemetery
Rue 2

Blv

Pier

Baie de
Cap-Haïtien

Blvd de Mer

Taptaps for Milot, Fort
Liberté & Ouanaminthe

Rue Lapont

Cap-Haïtien

load up on generous plates of Creole food, or pizza. The atmosphere is lively, and at weekends there are often bands (an admission charge of US$4 applies).

TOP CHOICE **Kokiyaj** INTERNATIONAL **$$**
(Blvd de Mer; mains US$8-15; � 10.30am-11pm) A self-styled sports bar above a supermarket sounds unimpressive, but this restaurant is actually a cut above. As well as Creole classics there are some good continental and American mains, good service and a well-stocked bar.

Croissant d'Or BAKERY **$**
(Rue 8 Blvd; ☺8am-4pm Mon-Sat) This small bakery sells fresh baguettes, cakes and savory pastries. It always seems packed out and one visit will explain why – it's the best bakery in town. Fill up on sticky treats, or go for the quiche or pizza slices as filling snacks.

D Corner FAST FOOD **$**
(Rue D17; dishes US$2-6; ☺7am-10pm) This bright yellow and blue-fronted fast-food place is always busy. It's easy to see why, as there's a wide range on offer, from pizza and pasta to huge sandwiches, burgers, pastries and ice cream. Cheap and filling.

Akenssa Plaza Restaurant CREOLE **$**
(Rue 14B; mains US$5-8; ☺6am-11pm) A good bar-resto in the town center, although busier during the day than in the evening, when beer tends to win out over food in the ordering stakes. All the Creole standards

are here, such as *griyo* (pork) and *lambi* (conch), piled high with rice and plantain. Pasta dishes and burgers cater to other tastes.

Les Jardins de l'Ocean CONTINENTAL **$$**
(☎2262-2277; 90 Carenage; mains US$8-15; ☺noon-3pm & 6-10pm) The menu here is decidedly Gallic. The menu is ambitious, including lamb with green herbs, Provençal shrimp and carpaccio of *lambi*, but you're better off asking what's available before drooling over the menu too much. The resulting meals, however, are delicious.

Le Roi Christophe Restaurant CONTINENTAL **$$**
(☎2262-0414; Rue 24B; mains US$6-11; ☺11am-3pm & 6-10.30pm) Relaxing on the terrace of this hotel restaurant is a great way to spend a meal. There are some tasty sandwiches that make ideal lunchtime fillers, and a good range of pasta dishes. French and Creole round out the menu, along with a decent wine list.

🛍 Shopping

There is a recently refurbished **Tourist Shopping Center** (Blvd de Mer) near the port entrance, with stalls selling paintings, metalwork and other handicrafts. There aren't many tourists, so attention from vendors is guaranteed.

❶ Information

There's a useful cluster of banks along Rue 10-11A. When the banks are closed, you can change money on the street outside the Universal Hotel – moneychangers call to attract your attention.

Alliance Français (☎2262-0132; Rue 15B-C; ☺8am-4:30pm Mon-Fri) Runs regular cultural events.

Banque de L'Union Haïtienne (BUH; Rue 17A)

Bureau du Tourisme (☎262-0870; cnr Rue 24 & Blvd de Mer) Rarely open.

Cybertronique (Rue D17; per hr US$1.25; ☺8am-10pm)

Discount Cybercafé (Rue 14H; per hr US$1.15; ☺8am-9pm)

Hôpital Justinien (☎2262-0512/0513; Rue 17Q) Cap-Haïtien's main hospital.

Police (☎122; Rue A)

Post Office (Rue 16-17A)

Rien Que Pour Vos Yeux (82 Rue 17Q) Well-stocked pharmacy.

Sogebank (Rue 11A) Has an ATM open during banking hours.

Unibank (cnr Rue 11 A)

Up 2 Date Travel (✆2262-5545; Rue 17L) Useful for domestic flight tickets.

ℹ Getting There & Away

The airport is 3.5km east of the city (US$5/1.25 by taxi/moto-taxi). Both **Tortugair** (✆2250-2555) and **Salsa d'Haiti** (✆3717-6455; Rue 16B) have several daily flights to Port-au-Prince (US$85, 30 minutes).

Buses for Port-au-Prince (US$12, seven hours) leave from Barrière Bouteille on Rue L from around 5am. Travel early, as buses terminate in La Saline on the edge of Cité Soleil – not recommended after dark. Buses travel via Gonaïves (US$6, three hours) and Saint-Marc (US$7, four hours).

For Cormier Plage and Plage Labadie, taptaps (local buses or minibuses) leave regularly from Rue 21Q (HTG25, 30 minutes). For the Citadelle, taptaps to Milot (HTG20, one hour) leave from Stasyon Pon near the main bridge. Transportation to Fort Liberté (HTG30, two hours) and Ouanaminthe (HTG60, three hours) also leaves from here.

Caribe Tours (✆3444-5585, Rue 29A) runs a direct coach service to Santiago in the Dominican Republic twice weekly from the Hôtel Mont Joli. Buy tickets at the hotel shop.

ℹ Getting Around

Publiques (collective taxis) have a set rate of HTG15 anywhere in town – a few are signed as taxis, otherwise look for the red ribbon hanging from the front windshield mirror. Taptaps (HTG5) run two main routes along Rue L (also called Rue Espanole) from Rue 15L to the Barrière Bouteille, and along Rue A from Rue 10A to the airport.

Moto-taxis here should never cost more than HTG20. The Akenssa Plaza Hôtel runs a metered taxi service, **Akenssa Taxi** (✆2262-4934).

AROUND CAP-HAÏTIEN

The Citadelle & Sans Souci

The awe-inspiring mountain fortress of La Citadelle la Ferrière is a short distance from Cap-Haïtien on the edge of the small town of Milot. Built to repel the French, it's a monument to the vision of Henri Christophe, who oversaw its construction. A visit here is an essential part of any trip to Haiti, and actually takes in two sites – the Unesco World Heritage–listed fortress itself and the palace of Sans Souci.

◉ Sights

Sans Souci   HISTORICAL SITE

Built as a rival to Versailles in France, Henri Christophe's palace of Sans Souci has lain abandoned since it was ruined in the 1842 earthquake. The years of neglect have left it an elegant monument, slightly alien against its tropical backdrop.

Finished in 1813, Sans Souci was more than just a palace, designed to be the administrative capital of Christophe's kingdom, housing a hospital, a school and a printing press, as well as an army barracks.

The palace is approached by a grand staircase once flanked by bronze lions. You enter a series of rooms – the throne room, banqueting halls and private apartments. Although the walls are now bare brick they would have been hung with rich tapestries and paintings, all designed to show that although Haitians had once been slaves, they were now a cultured nation. The palace originally had four stories and huge French picture windows. From his apartments, Christophe maintained correspondences with the Czar of Russia and the English abolitionist William Wilberforce.

Behind the palace are the remains of the King's and Queen's ornamental gardens. To one side are the remains of the hospital and, opposite, the old barracks, home to the Royal Corps of freed slaves from Dahomey.

Just above the palace site, a roughly paved road winds up the mountain to the Citadelle.

LOOKING FOR COLUMBUS

Although La Isabela and Santo Domingo in the DR are celebrated for their connections to Columbus, the site of La Navidad, the first attempted Spanish settlement in the Americas, remains unknown and a holy grail for archaeologists. It's believed to be close to Cap-Haïtien in Haiti, probably built on the site of a Taíno village around Bord de Mer de Limonade. If you don't want to dedicate yourself to archaeology, the easiest way to get close to La Navidad is at Musée du Panthéon National in Port-au-Prince, where you can see the anchor of the *Santa María*, whose wood was salvaged to build the settlement in 1492.

If you fancy yourself as Indiana Jones, head well off the beaten track to the caves of Dondon St Rafaël. This small town surrounded by coffee, cocoa and vanilla plantations is home to a series of caves once used by the Taínos for refuge. From Dondon it's a two-hour hike up the mountain to the caves (Des Grottes), but you'll probably require a local guide to show you the way, and possibly rent you a horse. The caves are now home to large numbers of bats, but the Taínos have left their mark on many of the stalagmites, the tops of which have been carved to resemble skulls. It's one of the most intriguing – and remote – Arawak sites in the country.

It takes a 4WD one hour to reach Dondon St Rafaël from Cap-Haïtien; there are daily taptaps from Rue Lapont (US$1.50, two hours).

La Citadelle la Ferrière
FORTRESS

Haitians call the Citadelle the eighth wonder of the world and, having slogged to the 900m summit of Pic la Ferrière, you may be inclined to agree. This battleship-like fortress gives commanding views in every direction. It was completed in 1820, employed 20,000 people over 15 years and held enough supplies to sustain the royal family and a garrison of 5000 troops for a year. With 4m-thick walls that reach heights of 40m, the fortress was impenetrable, although its cannons were never fired in anger.

Inside the ramparts the fort has a series of drawbridges and blind corners to fox attackers. These lead through a gallery containing the first of several cannon batteries. The Citadelle contains over 160 cannons, mostly captured in battle from the English, the Spanish and the French. Throughout the fort are huge piles of cannonballs – 50,000 in total.

At the heart of the fort is the central courtyard, with its officers' quarters. Christophe himself was buried here after his suicide – his grave is under a huge boulder that forms part of the mountain. On the level above is the whitewashed tomb of his son Prince Noel.

It's easily possible to spend a couple of hours exploring the site, which constantly reveals hidden passages, halls and new views from its ramparts. Sheer drops protect the Citadelle from every angle except its rear, where you can look south to Site des Ramiers, a huddle of four small forts protecting its exposed flank.

In the main courtyard there's a small shop that sells postcards and drinks; the caretaker will open it for you.

🛏 Sleeping & Eating

Most people visit the Citadelle as a day trip from Cap-Haïtien, but if you're here overnight there's one good sleeping and eating option.

Lakou Lakay
GUESTHOUSE **$**

(✆2262-5189, 3667-6070; Milot; r per person US$30, meals US$10) This cultural community center is a delight. Run by guide Maurice Etienne and his family, visitors are welcomed by traditional dancing and serenaded with folk songs and drumming while enjoying a huge Creole feast. Rooms for visitors are simple.

ℹ Information

The site entrance is at the far end of Milot, next to the huge dome of Église Immaculée Conception de Milot, facing the ruins of Sans Souci. Opposite this is the **ticket office** (admission Sans Souci/Sans Souci plus Citadelle US$12.50/25, horse rental US$50; ⊘8am-5pm). There are many guides and horse wranglers here. One that comes recommended is **Maurice Etienne** (✆3667-6070), who also runs the Lakou Lakay cultural center. A reasonable fee for a good guide is US$20 to US$30, plus the hire of his horse.

Horses are the normal method of reaching the Citadelle. Each generally comes with two handlers (both of whom expect a tip of US$4 to US$5). From Sans Souci to the Citadelle takes a couple of hours by horse, although a 4WD can make it to a parking area 30 minutes' walk short of the top.

ℹ Getting There & Away

Taptaps from Cap-Haïtien (one hour, HTG20) drop you a short walk from Sans Souci. Don't leave the return too late, as transport dries up by late afternoon.

Beaches West of Cap-Haïtien

A rough road leads west from Cap-Haïtien, winding along the northwest coast of the cape toward some of the loveliest coastal scenery in the country, where green hills tumble straight into the Atlantic, the two divided by sheer cliffs or stretches of delicious golden sand.

The road hits the north coast of the cape near **Cormier Plage**, the picture of a Caribbean beach and resort, where white breakers roll in to shore and rum punches are the order of the day. Further around the point is **Plage Labadie** (also called Coco Plage), a walled-off peninsula rented by Royal Caribbean Lines for its cruise-ship guests, who arrive three or four times a week.

If you've been in Haiti for any length of time, the sight of a giant white ship with up to several thousand passengers – a sight common anywhere in the Caribbean – seems like a surreal event. Ferries shuttle guests back and forth all day, and the sea buzzes with jet skis and holidaymakers leaping from giant inflatable toys.

Royal Caribbean Lines are the single biggest contributor to Haitian tourism, paying the government US$10 for every passenger landed, and have recently invested over US$55 million in their Labadee operation here. Although the company contributes to local education projects, little of the revenues are spent locally – the nearby Labadie village lacks decent electricity and the road to Cap-Haïtien remains a complete nightmare.

From Plage Labadie, *bateaux-taxis* (water taxis) ferry passengers to the beaches further west. Just around the cape is **Plage Belli**, from where the view of ocean-washed headland after headland fading into the far distance is spectacular. The village of **Labadie**, a small collection of rural dwellings, is a nice place to wander around watching kids playing basketball and women washing clothes. There are a few small shops, places to buy drinks and snacks, and fishermen selling their catch.

🛏 Sleeping & Eating

Norm's Place GUESTHOUSE $
(✆810-5988, 3780-5680; normsplacelabadee @yahoo.com; Labadie; r per person US$30; P❋@⬤) A *bateau-taxi* hop between Plage Belli and Labadie village (ask for 'Kay Norm'),

this charming guesthouse was built from a restored French fort. Large rooms have four-poster beds with mosquito nets, there's a garden for lounging and a warm welcome throughout. Meals are home-cooked on request.

Cormier Plage Resort HOTEL $$$
(✆3702-0210; cormier@hughes.net; Route de Labadie; s/d incl half-board US$110/180; P❋@) Dotted amid palm trees, this pleasant resort has 36 big and airy rooms looking out to sea, and is meters from the gently shelving golden beach. The restaurant is great for seafood, but service can be very slow.

Belli Beach Bar HOTEL $
(✆2262-2338; Plage Belli; s/d US$25/40) As the road west of Plage Labadie peters to an end, follow the narrow, steep steps leading down to Plage Belli. The tiny beach is lovely, but the hotel is exceedingly basic, with spartan rooms and frequent problems with water supply. A restaurant serves seafood and Creole dishes.

❶ Getting There & Away

Taptaps going to Cormier Plage and Plage Labadie (both HTG25, 30 and 40 minutes respectively) leave from Rue 21Q in Cap-Haïtien. Taptaps terminate (and leave from) the western side of Plage Labadie by the boundary fence of the Royal Caribbean Lines compound, from where brightly painted *bateaux-taxis* (HTG25) ferry passengers to Plage Belli and Labadie village.

THE NORTHEAST

The Nord-Est Department borders the Dominican Republic. In the colonial era it was a major plantation area, and remains an important coffee-producing district. In addition to the border area, there are a few colonial forts of interest to visitors.

Fort Liberté

Fort Liberté was once one of France's most strategically important bases in Saint-Domingue, at the center of a wide bay with a natural harbor. Named Fort Dauphin by the French in 1731, a huge fortress was built here, one of several bases that guarded the bay like beads on a string. When Toussaint Louverture captured the port in 1796 he named it Fort Liberté. The area is now economically depressed, the huge sisal plantations it once sustained long closed; donkey traffic is as likely as the motorized version.

Fort Français (the fort's current name) is largely intact, with its ramparts, batteries and magazines. If the guardian is there, you'll be asked to pay a US$0.70 entrance fee. The remains of the fort surrounding the Baie de Fort Liberté can also be visited in a couple of hours – the easiest way is by moto-taxi. Fort Labouque and the Batterie de l'Anse are on the eastern lip of the bay guarding its entrance. Between here and the town are Fort St-Charles and Fort St-Frédéric.

The **Hôtel Bayaha** (cnr Rues Vallières et Bourbon; s/d US$35/60) is the best option if you wish to stay, overlooking the bay. It has reasonablerooms and a restaurant. Fort Liberté can be visited as a day trip from Cap-Haïtien (HTG30, two hours).

Ouanaminthe

A dusty border town, Ouanaminthe is an important trading centre across the Massacre River from Dajabón in the Dominican Republic. It's alive with small traders hurrying across to the Dominican side to buy goods, particularly on the market days of Monday and Friday. The contrast between the rubbish-strewn anarchy of Ouanaminthe and the paved streets and order of Dajabón is striking.

The border is open from 8am to 4.30pm. On arrival in Ouanaminthe, continue until the road splits in two. The left road leads to the bridge across the river that marks the border; the right to the customs and passport office. For more on crossing between the two countries, see p356.

Hôtel Paradis (Rue St-Pierre; s/d US$10/16) is just about bearable if you get stranded in town. You're better off sleeping in Dajabón if you can.

Taptaps to Cap-Haïtien (HTG60, three hours) are plentiful.

THE NORTHWEST

Heading north from the Côte des Arcadins, you'll find the departments of Artibonite and Nord-Ouest. This is the birthplace of Haitian independence, but its history extends to the

earliest European contacts – Columbus first set foot on Hispaniola here, and the island of Île de la Tortue (Tortuga) was a free port during the golden age of piracy.

Gonaïves

At first glance, Gonaïves looks like any other large town in Haiti, but it holds a very close place in the nation's heart. On January 1, 1804, Dessalines signed the act of Haitian independence here, creating the world's first black republic, and his wife, Claire Heureuse, is buried in the local cemetery. Gonaïves has played a revolutionary role in more recent years as well – it was rioting here in 1985 that showed the writing was on the wall for 'Baby Doc' Duvalier, while the rebel capture of Gonaïves in 2004 marked the beginning of the end for Aristide. Gonaïves was badly flooded in 2008, and its infrastructure has taken a long time to recover.

The town is a handy breaking point when traveling between Port-au-Prince, Cap-Haïtien and Port-de-Paix. Place de l'Indépendence is the town's focus, with its striking triangular modernist cathedral. In front of this is a martial statue of Dessalines in the prow of a ship, as if willing independence by the force of his presence alone.

🛏 Sleeping & Eating

There are several cheap bar-restos near the main bus station and on Rue L'Ouverture. Some other recommendations:

Family Hotel HOTEL $$
(☑2274-0600; Ave des Dattes; d with fan/air-con US$35/50; P☀) This is a decent medium-sized hotel, with a restaurant. Rooms are good value, although the service can be a bit poor.

Chachou Hôtel HOTEL $$
(☑3547-0172; 145 Ave des Dattes; s/d US$60/80; P☀@☎) Gonaïve's best hotel, and frequently full of international workers. Rooms are large and comfortable, with satellite TV, and the restaurant is well recommended.

❶ Getting There & Away

Gonaïves is roughly halfway between Port-au-Prince and Cap-Haïtien. The bus station is east of the main square next to the Texaco gas station on the main highway. There are regular buses to Port-au-Prince (US$7, 3½ hours) and Cap-Haïtien (US$6, three hours). The highway

SOUVENANCE & SOUKRI

Souvenance and Soukri are major dates on the Vodou calendar. People from all over Haiti congregate near Gonaïves to take part in these marathon ceremonies, used by celebrants for spiritual cleansing and revival.

Souvenance begins on Good Friday, and continues for a week, to the constant sound of *rara* music. Prayers are offered to a sacred tamarind tree, initiates bathe in a sacred pond and bulls are sacrificed for the Vodou spirits. The ceremonies include singing and dancing and go on every night, while the celebrants rest by day. The rituals are said to have originated in the maroon camps, the secret communities of runaway slaves. Ogou, the warrior *lwa* who helped inspire slaves during the revolution, is particularly revered here.

Soukri is a ritual dedicated to the Kongo *lwa*. The service is divided into two branches: 'the father of all Kongo' takes place on January 6, and the second, larger ceremony, 'the mother of all Kongo,' occurs on August 14. The rituals last a mammoth two weeks each, a true test of endurance. Many of the celebrations are similar to those in Souvenance. If you wish to visit these ceremonies, you should introduce yourself to the head of the Vodou society when you arrive.

Souvenance is held off the road between Gonaïves and Cap-Haïtien, about 20km north of Gonaïves. The festival has become well known enough that the place where it is held is also now known as Souvenance. As you leave Gonaïves on the road to Cap-Haïtien, you cross over the Rivière Laquinte on a bridge called Mapou Chevalier. The first immediate right after the bridge will take you to Souvenance. There are small houses for rent around the temple, although many of the participants just sleep on straw mats in the shade.

Soukri takes place off the same road from Gonaïves to Cap-Haïtien. Continue northward past the turnoff for Souvenance until you reach a small market town, Les Poteaux. A turning opposite the Saint-Marc Catholic Church leads to the *lakou* (a collection of dwellings) known as Soukri.

to Cap-Haïtien is a microcosm of environmental climates. Having followed the road from the capital through banana plantations and the beaches of Côte des Arcadins, around Gonaïves the land turns to semidesert, with cacti the size of trees. Turning inland from here the road climbs through green mountains before finally descending to the coast. The highway is in definite need of improvement, but the ever-changing views are always interesting.

Buses to Port-de-Paix (US$8, five hours) also leave from the bus station. The road is poor.

Port-de-Paix & Île de la Tortue

Nord-Ouest Department, of which Port-de-Paix is the capital, is the most deforested and arid part of Haiti. The main reason to come here is to visit Île de la Tortue, the sliver of an island that forever seems to be on the cusp of development as the Caribbean's next big tourist thing. Although the island is covered with rocky hills, it also holds some glorious beaches, particularly the truly gorgeous Pointe-Ouest (although you really need your own boat to get there).

Île de la Tortue is famous for its piratical associations (see p325). The contraband heritage continues into the 21st century, as the island (and Port-de-Paix) are well-known smuggling transshipment points to Miami, from duty-free goods to cocaine.

Boats sail every morning from Port-de-Paix to Basse-Terre on Île de la Tortue (US$4, one hour). From here you can get transport to the capital, Palmiste. Unfortunately there is no accommodation on the island. The **Hôtel Brise Marina** (☎2239-4648; Rte de St-Louis-du-Nord; r US$60; P✳☀), just outside Port-de-Paix, is the best accommodation option in the region. Decent rooms have sea views and there's a restaurant.

There's regular transport to Gonaïves (US$8, five hours), from where you must change for onward travel.

Understand
Haiti

Haiti Today

» Country area:
27,560 sq km

» Population:
9.72 million

» Population
under 14 years
old: 38%

» Life expec-
tancy at birth:
62 years

» GDP per
capita:
US$1200

Haiti is a country that is frequently viewed by outsiders in clichés, as if the country was little more than a grab-bag of negative images: 'voodoo', coups, boat people and a peculiar idea that somehow the country is doomed to failure. For some, the earthquake of January 12, 2010, only compounded this picture. But while they recognize their country's travails, for Haitians, their national identity is something they are equally proud of. Haiti's history as the first independent black republic is something to be continuously celebrated, and that original struggle for independence remains a powerful wellspring of national inspiration.

The Great Population Divide

Life in Haiti has always been sharply divided between the tiny urban elite and the poor rural bulk of the population.

Most Haitians are peasants practicing subsistence farming. Beans, rice, sweet potatoes, maize, bananas or coffee are grown on small plots, while along the coast fishermen take their catch from simple sailboats. Rural life is hard. Electricity is often a distant aspiration and food is cooked over charcoal, the production of which is a major cause of environmental damage. Food insecurity is high, and usually only two meals a day are eaten. Community spirit isn't wanted for, and large-scale jobs are tackled by communal work teams called *kombits*.

According to city dwellers, the rural poor live in the *peyi andeyò* (outside country), totally removed from the economic and political levers of power. Peasants are either mocked as yokels or mythologized in folkloric art and dances as the noble poor. But as demands on the exhausted land have reached breaking point, increasing numbers of peasants have sought a better life in Port-au-Prince. The result is the

Top Books

» *Breath, Eyes, Memory* is a moving debut novel by Edwidge Danticat, the queen of Haitian letters.

» *The Comedians,* by Graham Green, is an acid-sharp satire of Haiti under 'Papa Doc' Duvalier.

» *Bonjour Blanc,* by Ian Thomson, remains one of the best travelogues to Haiti published.

Top Food Tips

» A bottle of Barbanourt Five Star rum always impresses as a present for friends.

» Haiti's 'Madam Francis' mango is one of the sweetest and juiciest.

» Add some chili heat with Ti-Malice sauce.

belief systems
(% of population)

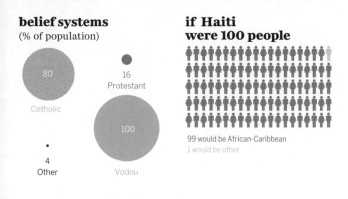

80
Catholic

16
Protestant

100
Vodou

4
Other

if Haiti were 100 people

99 would be African-Caribbean
1 would be other

---

teeming *bidonvilles* (shanties) of cinder-block houses, where drinking water has to be brought in on tankers, and open ditches serve for sewers. Such rapid uncontrolled urbanization had terrible consequences when the earthquake hit.

For the elite 1% of the population who own half the country's wealth, life could hardly be more different. The mainly mulatto family oligarchies disdain Creole in favor of speaking French, dominate manufacturing and import/export, and have traditionally been the powers that stood behind the president's throne. Behind the high walls of Pétionville are the best French restaurants and boutiques and riches unimaginable by the vast majority of Haitians.

Economic Realities

Haiti is the poorest country in the Western hemisphere and even before the earthquake was a major recipient of international aid.

In the 1980s Haiti became a major center for assembly factories, producing sporting goods, clothing and electronic components for the US market. Despite the work being generally very low paid, these factories were important job creators, many of which pulled out during the turmoil of the 1990s. Revival of these industries and the creation of free-trade zones are official government reconstruction policy, aided by the US HOPE II Act for duty-free access to American markets. Removal of tariffs in the opposite direction has damaged local economies further – rice farming has been devastated by cheap imported rice from subsidized US farmers.

The majority of urban Haitians are underemployed and scraping by on minimal incomes. Even the *bouretye,* the cart pullers in every city working as beasts of burden, have to rent their handcarts, while the lack

---

Top Films

» *Heading South* (2005) is a drama about power relationships and sex tourism in Baby Doc Duvalier's Haiti.

» *The Agronomist* (2003), a documentary about the life (and murder) of Haitian journalist-activist Jean Dominique.

» *Ghosts of Cité Soleil* (2006) presents a slick (if partisan) documentary about gangs in the aftermath of Aristide's 2004 ouster.

of access to capital means that the *marchands* (female market vendors) find it hard to expand their businesses.

The huge number of Haitians living outside Haiti are important contributors to the economy, with remittances to families helping more directly than much international aid.

Political Aftershocks

In many ways, the earthquake didn't just create new challenges, it laid bare fault lines in Haitian society and the body politic. The UN mission, Minustah, has provided some basic security, but progress in political stability and social reform has been largely absent. The parliamentary system allows the easy and frequent sacking of prime ministers, while presidents are forbidden from serving consecutive terms, virtually guaranteeing political gridlock. Major issues, such as attempts to raise the minimum wage, protect agriculture or decentralize services away from Port-au-Prince, have repeatedly run into the buffers.

These problems, and what many Haitians perceive as the slow pace of earthquake recovery and an indifferent UN, came to the fore with the presidential elections in November 2010. Widely seen as important to bring in a new administration that would handle the billions of reconstruction dollars, the process was marked by the banning of the most popular political party (Fanmi Lavalas), a controversial recount process, and the re-appearance from exile between rounds of voting of ex-presidents 'Baby Doc' Duvalier and Jean-Bertrand Aristide. Right-wing Singer Michel 'Sweet Mickey' Martelly eventually emerged as victor, but the path to reconstruction will be a long one indeed.

Culture

» Not all earthquake survivors want to discuss their experience, so exercise your judgment.

» French will get you only part of the way in Haiti – Creole is the language of most Haitians.

» It's Vodou, not 'Voodoo': a rich and complex religion that has nothing to do with sticking pins in dolls.

» Restaurants and hotels automatically provide jugs of treated drinking water.

» Travel between towns is quickest by taptap – very cheap but almost always packed to bursting.

Haitian History

Haiti's earliest inhabitants called their island Quisqueya – 'cradle of life.' Despite its size, it's often played a key role in world history: Christopher Columbus founded the first European settlement in the Americas here and under French slavery it became the richest colony – an iniquity that led to two firsts: the only successful slave revolution in history and the founding of the world's first black republic. Unfortunately, modern Haiti has suffered from self-serving leaders, foreign interventions and natural disasters, preventing it from living up to the promise of its revolutionary heroes.

The Taínos

Hispaniola had been inhabited for three millennia before Christopher Columbus sailed into view, colonized by a successive wave of island-hopping incomers from South America. Most notable were the Arawaks, and then the Taínos ('the friendly people'), who prospered on the island for around 700 years until the clash of civilizations with Europe brought their ultimate downfall.

The Taínos were both farmers and seafarers, living in chiefdoms called *caciques,* with a total population of around 500,000 at the time of Columbus' arrival. Each chiefdom comprised several districts with villages of 1000 to 2000 people.

Comparatively little of Taíno culture has survived to the modern age. Pottery and stone tools form the most common artifacts, along with jewelry of bone, shell and gold that was panned from rivers. Clothing was made of cotton or pounded bark fibers. While Taíno artifacts are relatively few, the crops they bequeathed to the world were revolutionary, from tobacco to yams, cassava and pineapples. Hispaniola's inhabitants, however, were barely to survive their first encounter with Europe.

TIMELINE

4000 BC	1200 BC	AD 500–1000
Earliest evidence of human colonization of Hispaniola. Stone-flaked tools found at archaeological digs are thought to have been brought by hunter-gatherers migrating from the Yucatan peninsula in Mexico.	Ancestral Arawaks arrive in Hispaniola, via the Lesser Antilles. Dubbed 'the Saladoid culture,' they live in settled agricultural communities, and are best known for their sophisticated pottery.	A third wave of migrations arrives in Hispaniola with the rich seafaring culture of the Taínos. The population expands rapidly, and is divided into a series of interdependent but competing chiefdoms.

Columbus' New World

In 1492 Christopher Columbus sailed from Spain with 90 men in the *Pinta*, the *Niña* and the *Santa María*, bound for Asia. He sailed west rather than east, expecting to circumnavigate the globe, but ended up 'discovering' the New World. After stops at the Bahamas and present-day Cuba (which Columbus initially mistook for Japan), a mountainous landscape appeared before the explorers. Columbus named it 'La Isla Española,' 'the Spanish Island,' later corrupted to 'Hispaniola'. He made landfall at Môle St-Nicholas in modern Haiti on December 7, and days later ran the *Santa María* onto a reef. Here on Christmas Day he established Villa La Navidad, the first settlement of any kind made by Europeans in the New World.

Columbus was greeted with great warmth by the Taínos, who impressed him further with their gifts of gold jewelry. Capturing a handful to impress his royal patrons, he sailed back to Spain to be showered with glory. He returned within a year, leading 17 ships of soldiers and colonists.

La Navidad had been razed by the Taínos in reprisal for kidnappings by the settlers, so Columbus sailed east and established La Isabela, in the modern Dominican Republic.

Hispaniola was ruled with an iron fist and an eye for gold, and the Taínos bore the brunt. Stricken by European illnesses that sent their numbers crashing, forced labor required the natives to dig up quotas of gold. Within three decades of their first meeting with Europeans, the Taínos were reduced to a shadow of their previous numbers.

Pirates & Colonists

After a hundred years, Hispaniola fell into stagnation. Spanish attention turned to Cuba and Mexico, while the French and English encouraged piracy against them. As Spanish influence shrank, the island became open for the taking.

The 17th century was the golden age for Caribbean piracy, and the rugged coast and mountainous interior of Hispaniola made it an ideal base for operations. Although a few captains became notorious raiders, most divided their time between hunting the wild cattle and pigs that thrived on the island and plundering for booty. The lack of any governmental control also made the island a haven for runaway slaves.

Isolated pockets of settlers were followed by soldiers. French tobacco farmers grabbed more and more territory until France had formed a de facto colony. The Spanish could do nothing, especially as France was beating it on the battlefields of Europe. At the close of the 17th century, Paris had managed to grab the western two-thirds of Hispaniola, christening them the colony of St-Domingue.

Top Historical Sites

» La Citadelle la Ferrière, Milot
» Sans Souci Palace, Milot
» Historic quarter, Jacmel
» Gingerbread houses, Port-au-Prince
» Fort Jacques, Fermathe

1492	1503	1640s	1640–70
Christopher Columbus makes landfall on Hispaniola on Christmas Day and founds the settlement of La Navidad (Nativity) near modern-day Cap-Haïtien in Haiti, before returning to Spain with Taíno captives.	Queen Anacaona of the Taíno kingdom of Xaragua in central Hispaniola is arrested by the Spanish governor and publicly executed, effectively marking the end of Taíno independence on the island.	The sugar plantation system is introduced to the West Indies. Highly profitable and labor-intensive, it causes a massive increase in demand for slaves from Africa. France establishes a formal claim on Hispaniola.	Tortuga (Île de la Tortue) is a major base for Caribbean piracy. Nominally ruled by a French governor, its buccaneers effectively form an independent republic, plundering Spanish ships for treasure.

Blood, Sugar & Slaves

Sugar and slavery helped the French turn St-Domingue into the richest colony in the world. The European taste for sugar had been growing steadily for years, and at the start of the 18th century the colonial powers turned much of the Caribbean over to its production. Molasses, a by-product of sugar production, was turned into cheap rum for export.

The fertile lowlands of northern St-Domingue were soon turned over to sugar plantations, centered on the port of Cap Français (modern Cap-Haïtien). Plantations were both farm and factory – huge fields of sugarcane with a mill and refining house at their heart. Surrounding quarters consisted of the planter's house, workshops, food crops and slave quarters.

Sugar cultivation was very hard, labor-intensive work. Field slaves worked in gangs, with even children required to work. Ten- and 12-hour days were the norm, and punishments for stepping out of line were governed by the bloody *Code Noir*. Owners were never slow to apply the whip.

ÎLE DE LA TORTUE – A REAL PIRATE'S ISLAND

When Captain Jack Sparrow (Johnny Depp) needs safe harbor in the film *Pirates of the Caribbean* he sets sail for the port of Tortuga. In the mid-17th century, so did a lot of other freebooters. Tortuga is the Spanish name for Île de la Tortue, named for its resemblance to a sea turtle. French settlers, who found it rich in timber and wild cattle, first made the island their home, and sold meat and hides to passing traders. From the 1620s the settlers began supplementing their income by piracy and were christened 'buccaneers,' from the *boucan* grills they used to smoke the meat that they sold.

The French, then at war with Spain, welcomed the redistribution of wealth from Spanish galleons, and appointed a governor who strengthened the island's defenses against Spanish reprisals. He oversaw a peculiarly democratic attempt at creating a society, with loot shared out equitably, compensation paid to injured buccaneers and, due to a shortage of women, same-sex marriages with rights of inheritance.

The buccaneer experiment was relatively short-lived. It reached its peak in the 1660s, but as the French increased their stake on Hispaniola, raids began to be suppressed. A later governor imported prostitutes for the buccaneers, who eventually married and settled down, turning to growing sugar and tobacco. Those that couldn't give up the Jolly Roger moved to Petit-Goâve in southern St-Domingue, and Port Royal in Jamaica. Ironically, present-day Île de la Tortue is an important smuggling station for drugs heading from Colombia to the USA, showing that the lure of contraband is yet to fully disappear from the island.

1697	1749	1757	1789
The Treaty of Ryswick settles the nine-year pan-European War of the Grand Alliance. As a result, Hispaniola's colonial borders are finally settled, dividing the island into Spanish Santo Domingo and French St-Domingue.	Port-au-Prince is founded by French governor Charles Burnier. Its wide bay and central location make it the ideal candidate for the capital of increasingly prosperous St-Domingue.	François Mackandal leads a band of Maroons in a long-planned open rebellion to gain freedom for the slaves of St-Domingue. Betrayed by a confidante, he is burned at the stake by the French.	Revolutionary fervor sweeps France, with the masses demanding *liberté, égalité* and *fraternité*. Calls for liberation are heard as far away as St-Domingue, leading to independence for the colonies in Hispaniola.

Mortality rates were high, and there was a constant decline in numbers that could only be met by importing more African captives. It's estimated that around one in five slaves (one in three in some areas) died within three years of arrival on a sugar plantation.

Slaves who lived in towns, such as the new colonial capital of Port-au-Prince, fared a little better. Wealthy planters ran extravagant numbers of servants, even poor whites kept a slave if they could afford it.

The Musée Colonial Ogier-Fombrun near Port-au-Prince, built on an old sugar plantation, gives an insight into the harsh realities of sugar production.

Stirrings of Revolt

If you were a white planter in St-Domingue in 1789, life was good. Around half the world's sugar and coffee came from the colony. The produce of 8000 plantations was providing 40% of France's foreign trade – the envy of Europe. Around 40,000 whites lorded it over half a million slaves, although there was an increasing number of free blacks and mulattoes (mixed race) who were allowed to own property but were forbidden many political and legal rights.

THE ATLANTIC SLAVE TRADE

When the Portuguese first rounded the coast of Africa in the 1450s, they were astounded by the wealth of the continent. Gold was a driving force in their early interactions with Africa, but this was swiftly overtaken by a trade in slaves. The settlement of the Americas and development of the sugar industry turned this into an international money machine, mining Africa for its human resources.

The Atlantic slave trade was dubbed 'the triangular trade.' European merchants sailed to Africa with goods to exchange for slaves. From Senegal to Mozambique, domestic slavery was already an established part of most African societies. The demand for trade goods – horses, firearms and gunpowder being the most sought after – turned African states into asset-strippers for the Europeans, sucking in slaves in insatiable numbers.

Traders packed hundreds of captives – often shackled in pairs by the wrist and leg – into the bowels of their ships. Around one in eight died from dysentery and scurvy during the passage, which lasted two to three months. The slaves were sold for sugar, which was then exported back to Europe – the third profitable leg of the trade.

The Portuguese and the British were the most avid slave traders, followed by the French and the Dutch. Lisbon, Liverpool, Bristol, Nantes, Marseilles and Bordeaux all boomed as a result of the trade. Some African kingdoms (such as Benin) also became rich, but the majority of societies were impoverished by the repeated harvest of their most economically productive members. During the lifetime of the trade, around 12 million slaves were brought to the Americas. Such was the reach of the trade's tentacles, slaves were often from tribes living 1000 miles from African slave ports. But few records were kept regarding the origin of the Africans brought to Hispaniola or nearby islands, and it remains almost impossible to trace the exact origins of most present-day African Caribbeans.

1791	1793	1794–96
A Vodou ceremony held by slaves at Bois Caïman near Cap-Haïtien preaches the message of emancipation, sparking a slave rebellion that sets St-Domingue's plantations ablaze.	Toussaint Louverture, Henri Christophe and Jean-Jacques Dessalines lead slave armies against the French and mulattoes. Amid the confusion, Britain invades, hoping to grab the island for itself.	Slavery is abolished in the colony, and Toussaint Louverture rejoins French forces to repel the British. After bringing St-Domingue under his control, Toussaint is appointed governor-general.

TONY WHEELER/LONELY PLANET IMAGES©

»Toussaint Louverture

FREEDOM

Small-scale slave revolts were bloodily suppressed, but slaves regularly absconded and formed bands that sought refuge in the mountainous hinterland between the two colonies. Dubbed 'Maroons,' they set up their own communities to try to re-create the African life they had lost. Others were more ambitious yet. Charismatic Maroon leader François Mackandal set up a network to agitate among plantation slaves and poison the planters. His revolt was short-lived, but France itself was on the cusp of revolution, and when the Bastille was stormed in 1789, the struggle for *liberté* opened the door for Haitian slaves to grab their independence.

The Haitian Slave Revolution

The French Revolution tore St-Domingue apart. White colonists divided into revolutionaries and royalists, while mulattoes sailed to Paris to demand political representation. A mulatto uprising led by Vincent Ogé was crushed, but the revolutionary fires had spread beyond the slave owners to their slaves. At Bois Caïman, the Vodou priest Boukman led a ceremony that saw the north erupting into a full-blown slave revolt that lasted two years.

Out of the chaos stepped Toussaint Louverture. His slave army had sought support from Spanish Santo Domingo, which sought to weaken France's hold on the island. St-Domingue's planters were so wedded to slavery that they turned to the hated British for support against the revolution, who landed a massive invasion force from Jamaica. But when Revolutionary France formally abolished slavery, Toussaint allied his slave army to the motherland. With his generals Jean-Jacques Dessalines and Henri Christophe, he crushed the British and brought the colony under his firm control.

Toussaint didn't stop there, and in 1801 he invaded Santo Domingo to free the Spanish slaves. Napoleon, who had taken control in France, saw that as a step too far. He wanted a return to slavery instead, and a year later the French invaded. The guerrilla war was immensely costly. Over half the soldiers died of tropical diseases before a truce was agreed. Toussaint was arrested and shipped to France.

Dessalines raised the country in anger again, promising full independence as the slaves' reward. He beat the French for a final time at Vertières, and on New Year's Day 1804 in Gonaïves proclaimed independence for Haiti (an old Taíno name for the island), the world's first black republic.

Haiti was ravaged – in 13 years of war the economy was shattered and nearly a third of the population dead or displaced. Dessalines declared himself emperor and massacred the remaining whites, for fear of being reconquered. Free, educated mulattoes were spurned, and the laborers forced back onto the plantations to rebuild the economy. His rule

'The freedom of the negroes, if recognized in St-Domingue and legalized by France, would at all times be a rallying point for freedom-seekers of the New World'. – Napoleon Bonaparte

The Louverture Project (http:// thelouverture -project.org) is a highly useful online resource covering the history of the Haitian revolution.

1802	1804	1807	1820
France invades St-Domingue. Invited to a parley with the French general Leclerc, Toussaint Louverture is clapped in irons and shipped to prison in France, where he dies of neglect the following year.	Following his victory at the Battle of Vertières, Jean-Jacques Dessalines declares Haitian independence, and symbolically rips the white from the French Tricolore to create the new country's flag.	Haiti splits in two. Henri Christophe crowns himself ruler of the new Kingdom of Haiti in the north, while Alexandre Pétion is declared president of the southern Republic of Haiti.	Henri Christophe commits suicide in Sans Souci. The president of the south, Jean-Pierre Boyer, reunites the country as one republic.

was brutal, and the reaction inevitable. In 1806, Dessalines died in an ambush outside Port-au-Prince.

North Against South

On Dessalines' death, Haiti split in two. General Alexandre Pétion grabbed Port-au-Prince, becoming president of the mulatto-dominated southern Republic of Haiti. Henri Christophe retreated to the north and crowned himself king.

Christophe ruled with absolute power, but was an enlightened and effective monarch. Within a year, he had stabilized the economy, reformed the judicial system, and built schools and a state printing press. He built a splendid palace at Sans Souci and the awesome Citadelle la Ferrière near Cap-Haïtien.

All this was supported by serfs, who weren't particularly happy that Christophe had kept them tied to the hated plantations, even if they were now earning a wage. As time went on his nobles began to plot against him. But as revolt sparked, Christophe suffered a massive stroke and rather than face the dual indignities of infirmity and rebellion he shot himself in the heart.

Pétion faced black guerillas, a secessionist movement in the far southwest and a restive army. A political liberal, his answer was massive land

TOUSSAINT LOUVERTURE

The son of an African chief, yet born into slavery near modern Cap-Haïtien, François Dominique Toussaint Louverture was one of the most remarkable figures of the 18th century. He worked as a steward but read voraciously. When the fires of rebellion reached St-Domingue he was ready to grab their ideals and lead the slaves to liberty.

He was a naturally gifted tactician and inspired great successes against the colonist militias, and English and French armies. Toussaint was astute enough to try to keep the valuable plantations intact and went out of his way to woo the white planters to his cause, and for a while was feted by revolutionary whites, blacks and mulattoes alike. But he could be ruthless, too – ordering the torching of Cap-Français to prevent it falling into enemy hands, and enacting forced labor to prop up the economy (thus alienating many of his followers).

Toussaint was a product of the French Revolution as much as Robespierre was. For a long time he saw a free St-Domingue as part of France, and only late in the day saw that independence was the only option for the slaves. It took the more ruthless Dessalines to declare a free Haiti, one reason why he, rather than Toussaint, is often more celebrated in modern Haiti. But Toussaint was the real architect of the revolution. Even as Napoleon was deriding him as 'the gilded African' and leaving him to rot in jail, the poet Wordsworth was dedicating sonnets to him. Today Toussaint's statue stands aptly in Port-au-Prince between the National Palace and the statue of the Marron Inconnu, 'Unknown Slave'.

1825	1844	1847	1915
France finally recognizes Haitian independence, after Port-au-Prince agrees to reparations for French slavers' losses incurred during the revolution. The sum amounts to 10 times Haiti's annual revenue.	Santo Domingo takes advantage of the confusion following the ouster of President Boyer, and declares independence as the Dominican Republic.	Head of the presidential guard Faustin Soulouque crowns himself emperor, in imitation of Jean-Jacques Dessalines. His failed attempts to conquer the DR bank-rupt the state and, in 1860, cost him his crown.	The USA invades Haiti, starting a 20-year occupation. Aimed at stabilizing the country, US marines introduce forced labor gangs to build infrastructure and realign the economy toward American interests.

reform. Recognizing the plantation system was no longer feasible, he divided and distributed the land into small plots, allowing him to resettle his soldiers and, even more importantly, placate the peasantry. Liberty became associated with the possession of a small plot of land, and Pétion is still remembered as 'Papa Bon-Coeur' ('Papa Good-Heart') for his actions.

However, the move to subsistence peasant farming meant loss of revenues for the state. The mulattoes became mercantilists and frequently saw government as a way of enriching their own pockets. Haiti's two classes began to take separate paths.

United but Not Free?

It took the deaths of both Pétion and Christophe for Haiti to be joined again under one flag and one president, Jean-Pierre Boyer, Pétion's chosen successor. Unfortunately, Boyer's rule laid many of the foundations of Haiti's current problems.

To consolidate mulatto rule, Boyer dismantled Christophe's education system and (given a shortage of soldiers to enforce it) the northern plantation system. Sugar cultivation virtually disappeared, but the demand for land increased, opening the door to forest clearance, soil erosion and ultimately environmental degradation.

Foreign powers had refused to accept Haiti's independence; Boyer sought rapprochement with France. The old colonial planters sought compensation of 60 million francs, enforced by a French naval blockade. Haiti was forced to take out huge loans (from French banks) to pay the debt. It took until 1947 to pay off the loan. The USA only recognized Haiti in 1862, when American slave emancipation was finally on the cards.

Boyer was overthrown in 1843, having presided over Haiti's bankruptcy, a weakening of state machinery and the entrenchment of the rich mulatto/poor black divide. Haiti slipped into a political morass, with a revolving door of short-lived presidents, political generals and even 10 years as an 'empire.' Of the 22 heads of state between 1843 and 1915, only one served his full term in office; the others were assassinated or forced into exile.

American Occupation

In the early 20th century, Haiti's strategic proximity to the new Panama Canal and increased German interests in the country reignited American interest. When President Sam was killed by a mob in 1915, the US sent in the marines.

During its nearly 20-year occupation of the country, the US replaced the Haitian constitution and built up the country's infrastructure by instituting the hated *corvée*, labor gangs of conscripted peasants, roped

> When Henri Christophe became king he created an instant nobility among his followers, including such luminaries as the Count of Limonade and the Duke of Marmalade, each with their own coat of arms.

> 'In overthrowing me, you have cut down in St-Domingue only the trunk of the tree of liberty. It will spring up by the roots again for they are numerous and deep.' – Toussaint Louverture

1928–31	1937	1957	1971
The novel *Ainsi parla l'oncle (Thus Spoke the Uncle)* by Jean-Price Mars and the writings of Jacques Roumain spark the politically important Noiriste movement to reclaim Haiti's African heritage.	Dominican dictator Rafael Trujillo orders the massacre of 20,000 Haitian migrant workers in the Dominican Republic. After an outcry, compensation is later paid to the Haitian state at US$29 per victim.	François 'Papa Doc' Duvalier becomes president, and begins his project to turn Haiti into a totalitarian dictatorship, using a blend of terror, patronage, Vodou and economic cronyism.	François Duvalier dies. His son Jean-Claude 'Baby Doc' Duvalier is inaugurated as president for life at the age of 19, with the national treasury as his personal piggy bank.

together. Reminiscent of slavery, it provoked the two-year Chacos Rebellion led by Charlemagne Péralute, in which thousands of Haitians were killed before the assassination of Péralute effectively put an end to the uprising.

US businesses flooded in and American dime-store novels and Hollywood movies played up Haiti as primitive, black and Vodou-ridden. Haiti's black middle classes responded with the development of the Noirisme (or Indigeniste) movement. Rejecting the 'European' values of the mulatto elite, it took pride in Haiti's African heritage. Creole and Vodou became sources of inspiration and cultural identity.

The US pulled out in 1934, and there followed a string of pro-American presidents and military leaders. Most Haitians remained no better off than before, and thousands migrated to seek work in sugarcane fields in the Dominican Republic. Competition for jobs and institutional racism culminated in the killing of around 20,000 Haitians by the Dominican army in 1937.

Papadocracy: Haiti & the Duvaliers

In 1957 a black country doctor named François 'Papa Doc' Duvalier swept to victory in national elections on a Noiriste platform. Power was Duvalier's raison-d'être, and his soft-spoken demeanor belied a ruthless streak. He set up his own paramilitary force that eventually evolved into the feared Tonton Macoutes militia. The Government fell apart, with local rule devolved to loyal section chiefs who acted as feudal lords over the population. The Tonton Macoutes enforced Chevalier's rule. Thousands were killed or simply disappeared in the 'nightmare republic' of Graham Greene's novel *The Comedians*.

Things became worse in 1971 when Papa Doc died, leaving his son Jean-Claude as his successor. Baby Doc (as he was inevitably dubbed) realigned himself with the traditional elite through his marriage to Michele Bennet. He made some token concessions to human rights long enough to attract foreign factories back to Haiti, but followed up with periodic bouts of brutal repression.

In the mid-1980s protests began to erupt against the regime. The handling of a swine-fever outbreak that led to the eradication of the Creole pig, which peasants depended on, was only one spark to the fire. Mass protests toppled Baby Doc from power, who fled to a life of exile in Paris.

Aristide's Rise & Fall

Despite the optimism following Baby Doc's ousting, it soon became clear that even without the Tonton Macoutes it was business as normal – Duvalierism without Duvalier, with the army in charge. But a young

Two great books on the Haitian revolution: *The Black Jacobins* by CLR James, and *Avengers of the Free World* by Laurent Dubois

Edwidge Danticat's novel *The Farming of Bones* movingly recreates the events around the 1937 massacre of Haitians in the Dominican Republic.

Papa Doc's feared militia was named after Tonton Macoute ('Uncle Knapsack'), the child-snatching bogeyman of Haitian folklore.

1986	1990	1991	1994
Popular protests force Jean-Claude Duvalier to flee Haiti into exile in France. A turbulent period of *dechoukaj* (uprooting) follows, to remove the influence of Duvalierism from the Haitian body politic.	Jean-Bertrand Aristide wins a landslide presidential election with support from his grassroots Lavalas movement, promising economic reform for the poor and plans to strip the Haitian army of its political powers.	A military coup overthrows Aristide, followed by violent repression against the population. An international embargo is declared against the junta, while thousands of Haitians attempt to flee in boats to the USA.	Backed by US Marines, Aristide returns to office, although his social reforms are hobbled by the economic deals he struck to win international support for his return.

priest named Jean-Bertrand Aristide, influenced by Latin American liberation theology, had begun advocating a rebalancing of power away from the elites toward the poor.

In the face of increasing unrest, the generals were persuaded to hold presidential elections. Aristide stood with the slogan 'Lavalas' (Flood) and won a landslide victory. But just seven months into his term, an alliance of rich mulatto families and army generals staged a bloody coup. General Raoul Cédras seized the reins of power.

International condemnation was swift, but it wasn't until floods of Haitian boat people started arriving in the US a year later that efforts to resolve the situation stepped up. Although American support for Aristide was crucial, it wasn't unconditional. Many had seen the priest as a radical socialist, so when a plan was finally brokered for his return, it was only on his agreement to sign up to an economic restructuring plan that eviscerated his original ideas for reform. Aristide signed, after three years of exile, and was returned cheering, backed by a UN mandate and 20,000 US army troops.

Coups & Interventions, Redux

Back in office, Aristide choked on implementing the imposed economic reforms and the promised foreign aid vanished as a result. Constitutionally barred from two successive presidential terms, Aristide returned to opposition in 1995.

The privatization of state utilities and lowering of tariffs to allow cheap imports (particularly of rice) devastated the economy. Aristide's new party, Fanmi Lavalas, split parliament and left the government without a prime minister for almost two years, but after the 2001 elections Aristide returned to the presidential palace.

Aristide's second term was hardly a success. The opposition refused to accept the result and the country again looked chaos in the face. The police were ineffectual against violence from both sides: opposition agitators, and the *chimeres,* armed gangs loyal to Aristide. Haiti's bicentennial in 2004 was marked by bloodshed.

The end came just a month later, when rebels captured Gonaïves and Cap-Haïtien. For the second time Aristide's presidency ended in exile, as he fled to the Central African Republic and finally South Africa. Claims about his flight vary – Aristide himself maintains he was effectively kidnapped by US agents and bundled out of Port-au-Prince; the US denies this but maintains that his overthrow was necessary to return stability to Haiti. Either way, the US favorite Gerard Latortue took power and formed an interim administration, with peacekeepers from the UN Stabilization Mission for Haiti (Minustah) sent to the island.

'When [Haitians] ask me, 'Who is our Mother?' I tell them, 'The Virgin.' But when they ask, 'Who is our Father?' then I must answer, 'No one – you have only me'.' – 'Papa Doc' Duvalier

Amy Wilentz's *The Rainy Season* is essential reading for an eyewitness account of the fall of Jean-Claude Duvalier and the rise of Aristide

In the 1990s President Aristide campaigned (unsuccessfully) for France to repay the 'blood money' it demanded for recognition of Haiti's independence in 1825.

HAITIAN HISTORY COUPS & INTERVENTIONS, REDUX

2001	2004	2006	2008
Aristide wins a second term as president, against a backdrop of increasing instability and an opposition boycott of the election. Chaos paralyses Haiti, making effective government impossible.	Armed rebels force Aristide from office, in disputed circumstances. Violence continues under the interim government, made worse by the havoc wreaked by Hurricane Jeanne later in the year.	René Préval is re-elected as president. In response to gang warfare and kidnappings, UN-mandated troops assail Port-au-Prince gangs, improving security but resulting in civilian deaths.	Rocketing worldwide food prices provoke violent demonstrations in Port-au-Prince, costing the prime minister her job. Meanwhile, Gonaïves is devastated by Hurricane Hannah.

The Road Ahead

The instability of the coup period continued throughout Latortue's government. Repression against Lavalas supporters was matched by the violence of the *chimeres*. Port-au-Prince, in particular, was hit by a rash of gang violence and kidnappings. It wasn't until René Préval returned to office in 2006 that things started to calm down. Minustah launched a controversial but largely successful military campaign to uproot the gangs, and finally brought a modicum of normality to the streets of the capital.

The path ahead has remained tricky. In early 2008 violent demonstrations against rocketing food prices shook the government. But the destruction caused by the earthquake of 2010 (see p344) has Haiti facing arguably its greatest set of challenges since the revolutionary war.

Michael Deibert's *Notes from the Last Testament* and Peter Hallward's *Damming the Flood* both detail the 2004 coup against Aristide

2010
A massive earthquake on January 12 results in over 200,000 deaths between Port-au-Prince and Jacmel. Reconstruction is slowed by inefficiency, a cholera outbreak and a chaotic presidential election.

2011
After a frequently controversial months-long electoral process, Michel 'Sweet Micky' Martelly is elected as Haitian president.

TONY WHEELER/LONELY PLANET IMAGES©

» Notre Dame Cathedral before the 2010 earthquake

Haitian Arts

It doesn't take long for the visitor to Haiti to realize that this is a country rich in color, sound and beauty. Despite, or perhaps because of, its relative poverty, Haitian art is an outpouring of creative force unmatched in the Caribbean, often drawing on the deep spiritual well of Vodou for inspiration.

Painting

Haiti's streets can seem like one continuous gallery, from the painted advertisements on buildings, and the myriad canvases hung on fences, to the brightly decorated taptaps (buses). The roots of Haitian painting are deep indeed.

While early Haitian elite art of the 19th century followed the European portrait tradition, the Haitian peasantry were forging their own path: painting murals to decorate the walls of Vodou temples and making elaborate sequined flags to use in ceremonies. This link to the *lwa* (Vodou spirits), with their visual language of *vévé* (sacred symbol) signs, is central to Haiti's artistic vision.

Gérald Alexis's monumental *Haitian Painters* is a comprehensive and gorgeously illustrated book about the Haitian art scene.

This tradition was brought front and centre in the 1920s by parallel literary and visual art movements. Modern Haitian literature was born through Noirisme (see p335), while visual artists founded the Indigéniste movement. Both sought to reclaim Haiti's African roots from the Francophilia of the elite. Subject matter switched from literal representation to idealized subjects, such as peasant life and landscapes. This style of art is often dubbed 'naive' or 'primitive,' partly due to its simple style and avoidance of classical perspective.

The Indigénistes paved the way for the arrival of the American, De Witt Peters, in Port-au-Prince. Trained in the arts, Peters recognized the extraordinary flavor of the primitivist work, and helped artists to develop their skills by setting up the Centre d'Art in Port-au-Prince in 1944. Here he discovered Hector Hyppolite, a Vodou priest now considered Haiti's greatest painter. A flood of brilliant artists soon arrived at the Centre d'Art, untutored but producing incredible work that stunned the international art world. As one critic noted, 'generous nature was their one and only instructor.' At the same time, Peters also discovered Georges Liautaud, the carved-iron sculptor of Croix des Bouquets (p292). Through its work, the Centre d'Art helped give painters such as Hyppolite, Philomé Obin and Wilson Bigaud the recognition they deserved, and was of such importance in the development of Haitian art that its opening is often referred to as 'the miracle of 1944.'

Throughout the 1950s, naive art became standard, pressed into easily recognizable images to serve the booming tourist market (the same paintings are still offered today). The Foyer des Arts Plastiques movement, led by Lucien Price, reacted against this by injecting a social ethic into Indigénisme: artists moved away from magic realism to portray the harsh realities of Haitian life.

PAINTERS

BIENNALE

Held every December in Port-au-Prince since 2010, the Ghetto Biennale invites international artists, film-makers, musicians and scholars for collaborative art projects with local communities.

The next great theme arose with the Saint-Soleil group of the 1970s. Spontaneity was key for artists like Louisianne St Fleurant and Tiga, who often painted *lwa* as abstract forms or bursts of energy.

Modern Haitian art continues to go from strength to strength, including painters such as Frantz Zéphirin, Magda Magloire and Pascal Monnin, and the inspired junkyard Vodou sculptures of the Grand Rue artists (p279).

Music

Haitian music has been used for many things: an accompaniment to Vodou ceremonies, a form of resistance in politics, and also just to dance the night away.

One of the most popular forms is *rara*. During Carnival, Port-au-Prince and Jacmel fill with rivers of people who come to hear *rara* bands moving through the streets on floats. Most bands compete for the song prize with a special composition, which has been recorded and played constantly on the radio during the lead up to Carnival. In the country, *rara* bands march for miles, with percussionists and musicians playing *vaskins* and *kònets* (bamboo and zinc trumpets). Each instrument plays just one note but, together with the drummers, they combine to create mesmerizing riffs.

Dance music has always taken in foreign sounds. Cuban *son* has influenced the troubadour bands that entertain in restaurants and hotels, singing and gently strumming guitars. Merengue, the Dominican big-band sound (see p227), has always been played enthusiastically on dance floors, and in the 1950s evolved into *compas direct* (or just *compas* for short), with its slightly more African beat. A joy to dance to, its greatest exponents are Nemours Jean-Baptiste and the late Coupé Cloué.

Racines (roots) music grew out of the Vodou-jazz movement of the late 1970s. Vodou jazz was a combination of American jazz with Vodou rhythms and melodies. For many, this new music reflected the struggle for change in Haiti. The lyrics were a clarion call for the revival of long-ignored peasant culture. *Racines* was propelled by Vodou rhythms over-

VODOU FLAGS

Brightly sparkling Vodou flags are one of Haiti's more unusual and eye-catching forms of art. Used during Vodou services, the flags *(drapo)* are magnificent affairs, made of thousands of beads and sequins sewn onto sacking, which catch the light from every angle. Each flag is dedicated to a particular *lwa* (Vodou spirit), often depicted through its Catholic saint counterpart or with its individual *vévé* (sacred symbol). A Vodou peristyle (temple) will usually have a pair of flags, one dedicated to the *lwa* Ogou, and the other to the peristyle's patron *lwa*.

Flags are highly collectable, and many of the most celebrated artists' flags are sold in Pétionville's art galleries and in the US. Some of the best artists are female; women who sought new outlets for their creativity, after having worked during the textile sweatshop boom of the 1980s and '90s. The best known include Evelyne Alcide and Mireille Délismé, who both produce highly intricate tableaux on their flags.

The Bel Air district is the traditional center of Vodou flag production, and it's possible to go direct to the artists themselves. A guide is recommended, however, as many of the *ateliers* (workshops) are down narrow alleys and impossible to find alone, and some were destroyed in the earthquake. The Hôtel Oloffson, which also sometimes sells flags, is a good place to ask (see p283). Artists to look out for are Silva Joseph, a Vodou priest (at the top of Rue Houille), and Yves Telemacque (on Rue Tiremasse). There are also a couple of good flag artists in the district of Nazon, such as Ronald Gouin (off Rue Christ Roi) and Georges Valris (in the same area).

The earthquake of January 12, 2010 didn't just take lives, it also tore down some of the country's most cherished icons. The loss of buildings such as the Sainte Trinité Episcopalian Cathedral was symbolic of the damage done to Haiti's cultural history: the inside of the cathedral had been covered with exuberant religious murals, executed by the great masters of Haitian painting, including Wilson Bigaud, Philomé Obin and Préfète Duffaut – artists commissioned by the Centre d'Art. Only three of its 15 murals survived the collapse.

The Centre d'Art itself was leveled and thousands of paintings were destroyed. An equally grievous loss was the private Musée Galerie d'Art Nader, which held one of the largest collections of Haitian art in the world. While Port-au-Prince's gingerbread houses came through relatively unscathed, Jacmel's historic quarter was badly damaged; the Fondasyon Sant d'A Jakmel (FOSAJ) art center was destroyed. Many artists lost their homes – and their lives. In total, it's estimated that 250,000 works of art and public monuments were damaged or destroyed.

The Haiti Cultural Recovery Project (http://haiti.si.edu), led by the Smithsonian Institution, and working with the Haitian Ministries of Culture and Tourism, has been at the forefront of attempts to conserve what was left in the wreckage. As well as working at Sainte Trinité, the Centre d'Art and the Musée Galerie d'Art Nader, it has launched a program to train local conservators.

Haitian artists have responded to the earthquake in their own ways: painter Frantz Zéphirin has produced astounding canvases depicting the earthquake in surreal quasi-mythical forms; Vady Confident, in Jacmel, has thickened his pigments with rubble dust, and paints straight onto ruined concrete; and graffiti artist Jerry has produced one of the most iconic post-quake images – a map of Haiti with an eye shedding a tear alongside a pair of praying hands. Even Préfète Duffaut, now in his late 80s, has responded with a new series of paintings, and a promise that when Sainte Trinité is rebuilt, it will be covered with murals even more glorious than before.

---

laid with electric guitars, keyboards and vocals. The most notable *racines* bands are Boukman Eksperyans, Boukan Ginen and RAM (see p283). During the military dictatorships of the late 1980s and the coup years of the 1990s, many of these bands endured extreme harassment and threats from the military.

Haitian popular music and politics seem destined to be intertwined: in the 2010 presidential election, musician Wyclef Jean was only disqualified from running for office on a technicality, while *compas* singer Michel 'Sweet Micky' Martelly went on to win the vote for high office. The influence of Wyclef (and fellow ex-Fugees member Pras Michael) has also helped refresh Haitian music – given the proximity to the USA, it's no surprise that *rapkreyol* (Haitian hip-hop) is a growing genre, with early exponents such as Torch blazing a musical trail.

Song and dance are integral to any Vodou ceremony, with the *lwa* greeted and saluted by their own songs, and constant drumming marking out the pace of ritual.

Literature

Haiti's literary scene is almost as rich as its visual arts one. The American occupation, from 1915 to 1934, was its main creative spur, as black Haitians sought to create a strong independent cultural identity through literature. The resulting Noiriste movement had a big impact on Haitian politics (see p329). Important novels were *Ainsi parla l'oncle* (Thus Spoke the Uncle) by Jean-Price Mars, which sought to reclaim the voice of the Creole peasantry, and Jacques Roumain's *Les gouverneurs de la rosée* (Masters of the Dew), generally recognized to be Haiti's finest work of literature.

Writers like Roumain were influenced by the international Surrealist movement, which in the late 1940s was responding to the

For the freshest *compas* sounds, check out T-Vice and Djakout Mizik, the two biggest *compas* bands, who regularly play in Port-au-Prince and beyond.

newly discovered Haitian naive painters. Novelist Stéphen Alexis and poet René Depestre thrived in this environment.

The rise of the ostensibly Noiriste 'Papa Doc' Duvalier saw intellectual and literary life come under attack. Alexis was murdered by Duvalier's henchmen and Depestre went into exile. Probably the most famous book about Haiti, *The Comedians* by Graham Greene, was a horrifically comic response to Papa Doc's vicious rule.

Many of the best contemporary Haitian writers have come from the diaspora. Most celebrated is Edwidge Danticat, author of *Breath, Eyes, Memory*, *The Farming of Bones* and *Krik? Krak!* Lionel Trouillot (*Streets of Lost Footsteps, Children of Heroes*) and Dany Laferrière (*An Aroma of Coffee*) are other novelists worth checking out, while 2011's *Haiti Noir* anthology offers a good introduction to a wider range of Haitian writers.

Away from more formal literary circles, Haiti has a rich oral storytelling culture. *The Magic Orange Tree*, an anthology of folktales collected by Diane Wolkstein, is a particularly worthwhile introduction to the tradition.

Unsurprisingly, Papa Doc Duvalier hated Graham Greene's satirical novel, *The Comedians*, banning it and raging against the author, who he dubbed 'a conceited scribbler' and 'a chimerical radicalist.'

Architecture

Very few examples of French colonial architecture have survived Haiti's tempestuous history. The best are found in the north, such as at Fort Liberté (p316). Many forts were also built in the years immediately following independence, the most stupendous of which is easily the Citadelle (p315), along with the palace of Sans Souci (p314), both built during the reign of Henri Christophe.

In the late 19th century, Parisian style met the requirements of tropical living in the so-called 'gingerbread' houses and mansions, characterized by their graceful balconies, detailed wooden latticework and neo-Gothic designs. For a walk through Port-au-Prince's gingerbread architecture, see p283. Fine examples can also be found in Cap-Haïtien and Jacmel. The traditional building techniques employed in gingerbreads resulted in many of them surviving the 2010 earthquake intact. More modern structures failed to pass this test: two of the earliest large reinforced concrete buildings erected in Haiti – the National Palace and the Notre Dame Catholic Cathedral – both collapsed.

Gingerbread Houses: Haiti's Endangered Species, by Anghelen Arrington Phillips, contains dozens of beautiful line drawings of the best gingerbreads in Port-au-Prince, Cap-Haïtien, Jacmel and Jérémie.

Haitian Landscapes

The Land

When British monarch George III asked one of his admirals to describe Hispaniola, he was given a crumpled piece of paper – to demonstrate how mountainous it was. The island is the most mountainous in the Caribbean. Three ranges dominate the landscape: the central Massif du Nord, extending into Cordillera Central in the DR; the southwestern Massif de la Hotte, noted for the rich biodiversity of its cloud forests; and the Massif de la Selle in the southeast, containing some of the country's last remaining pine forests.

Between the ranges lie a series of lush and fertile valleys. Coffee, rice, bananas and tobacco all thrive here. Most important of these is the Artibonite Valley, descending from the Central Plateau of the Massif du Nord, where Haiti's only major river, the Artibonite, rises. The plains around Cap-Haïtien (Plaine du Nord) and Les Cayes are equally important for agriculture, and it was the plantations of the former that drove the wealth on which French colonial St Domingue thrived. By comparison, the Côte des Arcadins, north of Port-au-Prince, is semi desert and studded with cacti.

Plate tectonics account for Haiti's dramatic landscape. For 90 million years, the grinding movements of the Caribbean Plate against North America has caused the rise of the Antilles from Cuba to Puerto Rico, including the island of Hispaniola. Haiti itself was once split from the rest of the island by a strait. When it became connected, it left behind the Cul-de-Sac plain and the brackish lakes (once the ocean) of Lac Azueï and the DR's Lago Enriquillo.

Unfortunately, the movement of the earth's crust can be a destructive force as well as a creative one. Haiti has been beset by a number of huge earthquakes throughout its history: in 1842, an earthquake in the north leveled Cap-Haïtien and several other towns; and on January 12, 2010 a quake of possibly even greater magnitude struck just outside Port-au-Prince, with the loss of over 200,000 lives (see p344).

Thirty of the 133 orchid species found in Hispaniola are endemic to the cloud forests of Haiti's Parc National Macaya.

ORCHIDS

Wildlife

Hispaniola's rich landscape is matched by an equally rich biodiversity. There are over 5600 species of plants and close to 500 vertebrate species on the island, many of these endemic. Despite this, Haiti is not a wildlife destination, and many animal species are hard to spot, or under pressure from the extreme environmental challenges faced by the country. Birdwatchers will get the most out of Haiti. Species are shared with the DR – for more information see p236.

BIRDS

Environmental Issues

Haiti is a crowded country. It occupies one third of Hispaniola, but has about half the total population. This fact alone could account for many of the environmental challenges facing the country. Nowhere are these challenges more starkly illustrated than when flying between Haiti and the DR. The border cuts the the countries like a knife, dividing the green forested hills of the DR from the brown slopes of Haiti. Today, just 1% of Haiti's natural forest remains, compared with 28% of the DR's across the border.

Bird lovers will want *A Guide to the Birds of the West Indies,* by Herbert Raffaele, to answer all their ornithological questions.

The different paths that Haiti and the DR have taken are a result of history, economics and politics. Land clearance was an early priority in French St-Domingue, while Spanish Santo Domingo languished as a colonial backwater; at independence Haiti was economically far more developed than its neighbor. But the isolation it suffered in the 19th century saw the country return to a largely peasant economy and increasingly unstable central government – a pattern extending to the present. Stronger government in the DR, notably under the Trujillo dictatorship, allowed it to avoid Haiti's ruinous path –pristine land was set aside and commercial logging was, at times, banned.

In the 19th century, much of Haiti's big tropical hardwood forests were logged for financial gain, but today clearance for subsistence farming and charcoal burning (still the main form of fuel) are the main drivers of deforestation. Charcoal production is a local cottage industry in forested areas, with vast quantities exported to the towns and cities; many people, unable to afford the investment in gas or other alternatives, buy a handful of charcoal a day to cook with. Môle Saint-Nicholas in the north and Pestel in the southwest are both important charcoal ports for

CONCH

What Haitians call *lambi* is known to scientists as *Strombus gigas,* in Taíno as *cohobo* and in English queen conch. No matter what you call it, this hefty snail-like creature is the largest mollusc in the Caribbean (growing up to 35cm long and weighing up to 3kg). It's a vital part of the underwater ecosystem and popular in Haitian (and Dominican) cuisine.

Conch (pronounced 'konk') live in shallow waters near coral reefs and are found throughout the Caribbean, as well as along the Mexico, Florida, Bahamas and Bermuda coastlines, and as far south as Brazil. They feed on algae that can asphyxiate coral if not kept in check.

Conch shells were used by the Arawaks and Taínos in tool-making, and carved into fine necklaces and other jewelry. Taínos also used ground conch shell as an ingredient for a hallucinogenic powder used in religious ceremonies. Centuries later, blowing the conch became the emblematic call to arms of the Haitian slave rebellion, still commemorated in popular art.

Conch has been an important food source on Hispaniola, and throughout the Caribbean, for centuries. *Lambi* is found on almost every restaurant menu in both Haiti and the DR; typically it's chopped into small morsels and fried or served with a spicy tomato sauce. As a by-product, conch shells are still used in jewelry and other crafts. One out of every 10,000 conches also forms a pearl – highly prized, ranging from pale pink to fiery red.

Conch take three to five years to mature, and are easily caught as they prefer clear, shallow water. A valuable fishery resource, conch populations have shrunk considerably in most areas of the Caribbean due to over-harvesting and degradation of the seagrass meadows used as conch nurseries. As a result, the Convention on International Trade in Endangered Species of Wild Fauna and Flora (CITES) introduced quota-based export restrictions on conch in 2003. While the DR (previously the largest exporter in the Caribbean) has implemented these restrictions, instability across the border has meant that Haiti has lagged behind.

» **Parc National Historique la Citadelle** (p314) An hour from Cap-Haïtien, this small park hosts the imposing mountain fortress of La Citadelle la Ferrière, one of the most stupendous historic sites in the Caribbean.

» **Parc National la Visite** (p292) Within easy reach of Port-au-Prince, this mountainous park offers good hiking through pine forests, with views to the Caribbean.

» **Parc National Macaya** (p305) Located in the Massif de la Hotte, this remote park has Hispaniola's best cloud forest and some of its richest biodiversity.

Port-au-Prince. Haiti's exploding population – two thirds of which occupies one third of its space – also creates pressure to clear further land.

Deforestation has led to erosion, decreased soil fertility and lower rainfall, and has left Haiti far more exposed than the DR to the same hurricane weather systems. In recent years, the city of Gonaïves has been particularly badly hit – by Hurricane Jeanne in 2004, and Hurricane Hanna four years later. The storms raised sea levels, flooding the low-lying city, and further damage was done by mudslides from the surrounding denuded mountains – caused by rain that would otherwise have been caught by forested slopes. Both hurricanes resulted in the loss of hundreds of lives. Governmental plans to reforest the region have yet to take root.

The loss of Haiti's forests is just the latest chapter in centuries of human activity that have forever altered Hispaniola's landscape. Introduced mammal species, from rats and mongooses to pigs, have wreaked havoc on native ecosystems, while swaths of land were cleared for commercial plantations such as sugar (even the iconic coconut palm is an import from the Indian Ocean islands).

Rivers and waterways are frequently used as garbage dumps, and many rivers and beaches are strewn with trash and plastic bags. Garbage is even a problem in towns and cities, where trash bins are few and collection sporadic. An insatiable appetite for disposable items results in many of them ending up in overflowing garbage pits or scattered elsewhere in the environment. The problem is especially pressing as the majority of the population lacks adequate sanitation and access to clean water. Such conditions create breeding grounds for diseases such as cholera, which ravaged the country in late 2010.

But it's not all bad news. In early 2011, a team of researchers from Conservation International (www.conservation.org) working in the Massif de la Hotte rediscovered six species of frog previously thought extinct. Frogs are regarded by ecologists as a 'barometer' species, as their presence gives a good indication of the general health of the ecosystem. This proves that the country's remaining intact forests are in good shape and worth preserving. Nevertheless, environmental protection must go hand in hand with social and economic development – both goals toward which Haiti continues to take baby steps.

Coconut palms have huge leaves divided into narrow segments, so they don't tear like cotton sheets in powerful tropical storms.

HAITIAN LANDSCAPES

COCONUT PALMS

Vodou

It's hard to think of a more maligned and misunderstood religion than Vodou. Even its name sparks an instantly negative word-association game of voodoo dolls, zombies and black magic – less a religion than a mass of superstitions. The truth is somewhat distant from the hype. Vodou is a sophisticated belief system with roots in Haiti's African past and the slave rebellion that brought the country to independence in 1804. Central to Haiti's national identity, these roots have also led to the demonization of Vodou in the West. For three centuries, slaves were shipped to Haiti from the Dahomey and Kongo kingdoms in West and Central Africa. As well as their labor, the slaves brought with them their traditional religions; Vodou is a synthesis of these, mixed with residual Taíno rituals and colonial Catholic iconography.

Vodou played a large part in both the inspiration and organization of the struggle for independence. The Vodou ceremony at Bois Cayman in 1791, presided over by the slave and priest Boukman, is considered central to sparking the first fires of the Haitian slave revolution. However, Vodou's relationship to power has always been a rocky one. Both Toussaint Louverture and Jean-Jacques Dessalines outlawed Vodou during their reigns, fearing its political potential. Overseas, the 'bad example' of slaves emancipating themselves led to Vodou being castigated in the US and Europe throughout the 19th century. The bad press went into overdrive during the 1915–1934 US occupation. Coinciding with the advent of Hollywood and the dime-store pulp novel, concocted stories of darkest Africa in the Caribbean – all witch doctors and child sacrifice – were eagerly eaten up by the Western public.

Haitian governments have played their part too, with several ruthless antisuperstition campaigns in the 20th century egged on by the Catholic Church. In the 1930s and early 1940s Vodou altars were burned and mapou trees (sacred trees where spiritual offerings are made) cut down. 'Papa Doc' Duvalier chose to co-opt the Vodou priests, which led to a violent backlash after his son's fall from power in 1986. By this time, however, progressive Catholics in the Haitian church had begun to reach an accommodation with Vodou. In 1987 a new constitution guaranteeing freedom of religion was put in place, and in 1991 Vodou was finally recognised as a national religion alongside Christianity.

Practice & Ceremonies

Vodou is not an animist religion of spirit worshipping. Followers of Vodou worship a god, who they call 'Gran Met' (Great Master). As Gran Met is distant from the physical plane, lesser spirit entities called *lwa* are approached in ceremonies as interlocutors. Summoned through prayer, song, drumming and dance, the *lwa* are the spirits that help followers on their journey back to the divine. During ceremonies, the *lwa* possess, or 'mount', participants. Being possessed is central to a ceremony and is the ultimate purpose for initiates as they experience absolute communication with the god and their ancestors. Possession is analogous to Christian spiritualism's speaking in tongues, or the rapture of Sufism. *Lwa* possession manifests itself in song, dance, the offering of advice or healing of illnesses.

There are many branches (or houses) of *lwa*, which are called upon in different orders according to ritual. The most popularly invoked *lwa* are the Rada, also known as the 'sweet' or 'cool' spirits. Rada summoning accounts for more than 90% of Vodou ceremonies. The 'hot' or 'angry' Petro *lwa*, by comparison, are rarely invoked due to their links with black magic. Those that summon the Petro are said to practice their religion with the left hand. Other families of *lwa* include the Gédé, spirits associated with death and the transition to the next world, and the *lwa* of the African nations, such as the Ibo, Senegal and Kongo.

Ceremonies are generally held in dedicated temples, called peristyles. Each peristyle contains an altar decorated with paintings of *lwa* and images of Catholic saints alongside bottles of liquor and other offerings. At the center of the peristyle is a *poto mitan*, a pole representing a tree, providing a focus for ceremonies. Peristyles are dedicated to a particular house of *lwa*, and decorated accordingly with wall paintings and bunting. Peristyles are maintained by a priest – either a *houngan* (male) or a *mambo* (female), each carrying an *asson* (ceremonial rattle) as a symbol of their priesthood.

Initiation

There are different levels of participation in Vodou ceremonies and religions. An uninitiated adherent, known as a Vodouisant (a general term such as Christian or Muslim), can attend ceremonies, seek advice and medical treatment from a *houngan* or *mambo*, and take part in Vodou-related activities.

For a Vodouisant to become a *houngan* or *mambo*, he or she must first go through a series of initiations. Those preparing for the first level of initiation are sometimes called *hounsi bossale*. All wear white clothing in ceremonies to show humility. Forming a choir, the *hounsis* can be possessed by *lwa*. After their first mounting, initiates are regarded as *serviteurs* or *hounsi kanzo*, marked by a ritual washing of the head (*lave tet*).

Those willing or able to progress take the *asson* at a *si pwen* ritual, held in secret, where the *serviteur* becomes a *houngan* or *mambo*. These practitioners lead prayers and songs, conduct rituals and are most likely to be possessed by *lwa*. They often act as choirmasters in ceremonies, and may become leaders of their own temples. The final level of initiation is *Asogwe*. These are the ultimate human authority, with the power to initiate Vodouisants, and are called upon when others are unable to summon a particular *lwa*.

Beating the Drums

Vodou services are highly developed rituals to pleasure, feed, and ultimately summon the *lwa* through the possession of a human body. Ceremonies are called to order through singing and drums, struck in tattoos of 13 beats. These symbolize knocking on the door of Ginen (ancestral Africa), with the entire congregation matching the beat with handclaps. After this, the Priye Ginen (prayer of Africa) is sung, beginning with Catholic hymns in French, segueing into Creole prayers and lists of ancestors and *lwa*, and finishing in *langaj,* the forgotten tongues of the 21 African nations.

Before any *lwa* can be summoned, Legba, the spirit of the crossroads, must open the gates to the spirit world. Then the four cardinal points are saluted, acknowledging the rising and setting sun, birth and death.

DIVINE SPIRIT

Vodou derives from the Fon word *vodu* (divine spirit) from modern-day Benin, where Vodou remains a national religion. The Anglicized spelling 'voodoo' is avoided because of its lurid associations in popular culture.

The ceremony first honors Papa Loko Attisou (the ancestral spirit of Vodou's original priest), who is greeted through song. The *houngan* then traces out the *vévé* (sacred symbol) for Ayizan (the first Vodou priestess) in cornmeal or flour on the floor. Thought to be a legacy of the Taínos, the ephemeral and delicate *vévés* are pounded into the earth by dancers' feet. These spirits preside over the ceremony as a whole, rather than manifesting through mounting. Next, Damballah may be greeted – a participant possessed by Damballah will writhe around the floor in a serpentine manner. The congregation then continues to salute a host of spirits with individual rhythms and songs.

The first group of *lwa* is the Rada. This is the most disciplined and re-strained part of the ceremony, as participants seeking particular services make their requests. The ceremony then transitions through the Doubja *lwa,* the Ibo, Senegal and Kongo before arriving at the Petro *lwa*. Their ceremonial color of red reflects their fierce, magical and aggressive characters, and creates a fast-paced and exciting atmosphere.

The last family to appear is the Gédé, which includes Baron and Maman Brigitte, the keepers of the dead. With instantly distinguish-able colors of violet and black, they appear in any order they like and their degenerate and bawdy behavior instantly changes the mood of any ceremony. When the last repetitions of the final song are finished, the ceremony is over. Sometimes, however, enthusiastic participants

THE VODOU PANTHEON

There are a dizzying number of *lwa*, each with well-defined characteristics, including sacred numbers, colors, days, ceremonial foods and ritual objects. These are some of the most important:

» **Legba** The master of passageways, who guards entrances and crossroads, and the doors between the physical and spirit worlds. Often portrayed as a crippled wanderer, he can both direct and misdirect. Counterparts: St Peter and St Lazarus. Offerings: green bananas, bones, toys, cigars.

» **Damballah** A snake biting its tail, the master of the sky represents the ordering of chaos and the creation of the world, and the dualities of death/rebirth, sickness/health and male/female. Counterpart: St Peter. Offerings: white chickens, eggs, rice, milk.

» **Baron** Also known as Baron Samedi, this *lwa* is master of the dead and keeper of cemeteries. His powers are responsible for both procreation of the living and putre-faction of the dead. Often depicted as a skeleton with top hat, cane and purple cape. Counterpart: St Gerard. Offerings: black roosters, rum, cigars and black coffee.

» **Maman Brigitte** The wife of Baron, Maman Brigitte has similar curative powers and is a foul-mouthed *lwa* with sexually suggestive dances. She's known to press hot peppers on her genitals, the test to which women suspected of 'faking' possession are subjected. Counterpart: St Brigitte. Offerings: same as Baron.

» **Erzuli Dantor** Comparable to Venus, Erzuli Dantor is the *lwa* of love. She's also represented as La Siren, a mermaid who enchants with her beauty and her trumpet. Counterpart: Virgin Mary. Offerings: perfume, wine, cakes and jewelry.

» **Erzuli Freda** The heart and the knife are the symbols of Erzuli Freda, the *lwa* of motherhood. She is voiceless, and carries facial scars from her African homeland. Counterpart: the Black Madonna. Offerings: Creole pigs and rum.

» **Ogou** This warrior spirit of steel and iron was invoked by slaves fighting for free-dom; people call on his strength for support in physical and legal struggles. Counterparts: St James and St Jacques. Offerings: all things red, especially roosters.

» **Zaka** Zaka the farmer is the *lwa* of agriculture and harvest, depicted as a peasant in denims and red scarf, with a *macoute* (straw bag). Counterpart: St Isodor. Offerings: bread, sugar, tobacco and *klerin* rum.

Many Haitians believe in the existence of the *zombi* (the Creole spelling): a person brought back from the grave to do the bidding of another. The practice is the alleged province of a *bokor* (sorcerer), who serves the *lwa* 'with both hands'. A potion is secretly given to a victim, which induces such a deathlike state that they are actually given a funeral. The *bokor* then exhumes and revives the victim, inducing a trance under which they can be controlled (usually to do manual labor). Fact or horror story? Researchers have claimed that the poison tetrodotoxin, capable of inducing such deathlike states, is the key ingredient in the potion used. Vodouisants claim that the potion causes the victim to lose their *ti-bonanj* (a person's 'good angel', similar to the conscience), turning them into a shell. Salt apparently can revive a *zombi*. Modern reports of *zombis* are incredibly uncommon and rarely verified, but zombification remains a criminal offence under Haitian law.

VODOU

may continue singing and dancing along to songs that relate to the *lwa*. This is the party that follows the service, called a *bamboche* in some parts of the country, and it can last until dawn.

Attending a Ceremony

There are various levels of participation in a Vodou ceremony. Anyone may enter the peristyle and join a ceremony, and singing and dancing are encouraged. Most Vodou practitioners also welcome tourists, in the hope that they will take a more positive view of the practice back to their home country (although it's essential to check first instead of turning up unannounced).

It's advisable to arrive with a guide – most ceremonies take place without fanfare in locations that would be hard to stumble upon randomly. You should treat the *houngan* or *mambo* with respect by offering a gift, traditionally a bottle of Barbancourt rum or a few good cigars. When you're introduced to the *houngan* or *mambo,* show appropriate reverence and, should you want to take photos or join in with the dancing, obtain permission beforehand. You may also be asked for a cash donation – to make an offering to the *lwa,* to pay the drummers and the *houngan* or *mambo,* and to contribute to the upkeep of the peristyle.

Certain elements of ceremonies are extremely secret and take place behind closed doors. Once they have advanced into the open they can still remain very intimate affairs, and in many cases it may be best to sit on the sidelines. It's definitely worth being aware that most services also involve animal sacrifice of some kind, usually a chicken. The killing of an animal releases life, which the *lwa* receive to rejuvenate themselves during the rapture of the ceremony.

Ceremonies are commonly held at night, starting any time from sunset and often lasting until dawn. You might want to pace yourself, although it's acceptable to wander in and out of the sidelines. If you're staying late, try to arrange transport home before attending, as taxis start drying up late at night.

In *The Serpent and the Rainbow,* ethnobotanist Wade Davis searches for the truth behind Haiti's *zombi* phenomenon. A gripping mix of science and travelogue.

ZOMBIES

Haiti Earthquake

At 4.53pm on January 12, 2010 Haiti was shaken to its core. Shockwaves from a fault line 13km below the earth's surface caused a 7.0 magnitude earthquake. The epicenter was just outside the southern town of Léogâne, close to the densely crowded capital Port-au-Prince. It took just 35 seconds for the earthquake to do its terrible work. The damage in lives lost and buildings destroyed was horrific, and although the tremors subsided relatively quickly, the social, political and economic aftershocks will be with Haiti for years to come.

» Striking at the heart of what was already the poorest country in the Americas, *Godou-Godou* is one of the largest natural disasters on record.

The Scale of the Destruction

Haitians quickly dubbed the earthquake *Godou-Godou*, named for the sound it made as the buildings collapsed. Others, more wary to give a name to something of almost unimaginable scope, refer to it simply as *bagay la* – 'the thing'. The raw statistics are shocking. It's thought that 230,000 people were killed, with 300,000 injured. In the immediate aftermath, 2.3 million people were displaced; either made homeless or vacating Port-au-Prince and other affected towns to move to the provinces. Over 180,000 buildings were either damaged or destroyed. Included in that total was 80% of schools in the earthquake zone, and over half of the hospitals. The Haitian government was effectively decimated: nearly a fifth of all federal employees lost their lives and 60% of government buildings were damaged or destroyed outright. The Palais National was reduced to rubble, along with 27 of the 28 government ministries, the National Assembly, Supreme Court, central prison, Port-au-Prince's two cathedrals and the headquarters of the UN. The towns of Léogâne and Petit-Goâve were leveled, and even Jacmel was badly damaged. Striking at the heart of what was already the poorest country in the Americas, *Godou-Godou* is one of the largest natural disasters on record.

The Humanitarian Response

Logistics in the immediate aftermath of the quake were challenging: it took several days to reopen the damaged airport to bring in supplies, and nearly a fortnight to get the port functioning. This heavy lifting was done by the US army, although they were criticized by some for initially prioritizing security over an emergency response. The urbanized nature of the disaster and the rubble-strewn roads meant that access to affected areas was slow for all.

The earthquake prompted an enormous humanitarian response, with assistance flooding in from across the world. By the time a fundraising conference of international donors was held in New York in March, US$5.5 billion had been pledged for recovery, including debt relief. The two biggest pledges came from Venezuela and the US. Mobile hospitals were pressed into service and huge numbers of tents and tarpaulins were distributed. Under the auspices of the UN, NGOs devised the 'Cluster' system to help coordinate responses in a dozen sectors, such as health, water sanitation and hygiene, protection and, for the myriad impromptu tent camps that sprang up, camp coordination and management. Many smaller NGOs, such as church groups and 'Mom and Pop' outfits (often people who had just got on a plane with a desire to help), operated independently.

The Road to Recovery

A famous Haitian proverb seems to sum up the task of rebuilding the country: *Deye mon gen mon* (beyond the mountains there are more mountains). The mountains of rubble are just the start – around 10 million cubic meters of it; the equivalent of 10 World Trade Center sites.

By the one-year anniversary, just under 10% of the rubble had been cleared (by comparison, the World Trade Center site was cleared in around nine months). Around 800,000 people were still recorded as living in tents, down from a peak of 1.5 million. The building of transitional shelters was hampered not only by the rubble, but by complications over land rights. Many records were lost in the earthquake, and disputes between land owners and tent camp residents have been common. The site for the international 'model' reconstruction camp, Corail Cesselesse, was poorly chosen, and flooded during hurricane season. Progress has been equally dogged in other areas: only a quarter of the population has access to proper sanitation, and even fewer to potable water: problems that became even more acute with a deadly cholera outbreak in November 2010 (Nepalese UN troops were blamed for importing the disease, following an outbreak in that country). Security in the tent camps was also a problem, with Amnesty International reporting an 'epidemic of rape'.

In April 2010 the Interim Haiti Recovery Commission (IHRC) was set up to coordinate reconstruction efforts, led by Bill Clinton and the then Haitian Prime Minister Jean-Max Bellerive. Its mandate was to 'build back better'; no easy task when, even before the earthquake, Haiti's infrastructure was so battered.

A year later, of the $4.46 billion pledged for both 2010 and 2011 combined, just 28.7% had been disbursed. Nearly 3000 temporary schools and 32,000 transitional shelters had been built, with much of the progress outside the capital in towns like Léogâne. Major reconstruction had yet to start, however, and further delays were caused by the political limbo following the disputed presidential election in November.

While many in the humanitarian community judged the immediate disaster response phase as having proceeded relatively well, the longer road to reconstruction has been more open to criticism.

Where to Next?

Even before the earthquake, Haiti had more aid organizations per capita than any other nation; it was disparagingly referred to by some as the 'Republic of NGOs'. With no governmental requirement to register, it's impossible to know how many NGOs operate in the country – the most common number cited is 10,000.

The high media visibility of the Haitian earthquake, and the difficulties faced in the response effort, prompted a healthy debate on the limits of aid in a disaster situation. Certainly, aid is just one aspect of the response – the Haitian government has been much criticized for failing to take the lead in directing rebuilding. But the scope of the disaster has simply proved overwhelming for many. The destructive force of the 2004 Asian Tsunami was unleashed on a densely populated area smaller than the US state of Connecticut. Ultimately, only Haitians themselves can rebuild their country – as they did after the 13 years of revolutionary war that led to the country's independence. Recovering from January 12 is a challenge of equal magnitude.

» Magnitude: 7.0 M_w

» Casualties: 530,000 (230,00 deaths)

» Buildings damaged or destroyed: 180,000

» Pledged relief funding January 2011: $US4.46 billion

» Funding disbursed January 2011: 28.7%

Survival Guide

Directory A–Z

Accommodations

Most levels of accommodation are available in Haiti, from top-end hotels and beach resorts to complete fleapits. Port-au-Prince naturally has the widest choice, along with Cap-Haïtien and Jacmel. You should be able to find the right accommodation for you, although there is often a shortage of midrange beds.

We have defined budget as up to US$40, midrange as between US$40 and US$80 and top end as anything above this. Rooms are with private bathroom unless noted in the text. As a general rule, only expect breakfast to be included in midrange and top-end places. Even cheap hotels usually have a ceiling fan, with air-conditioning more or less standard for midrange and above.

Bringing a torch (or candles) is recommended. Power cuts can be both frequent and long. Many hotels add an electricity surcharge of US$5 to US$10 to the daily rate to cover running their generators, included in the prices listed where possible. Midrange and top-end rates also include the 10% government tax added to the bill.

Camping

Pitching a tent isn't really an option in Haiti, and most Haitians would find the idea of voluntarily sleeping under canvas eccentric in the extreme, particularly in light of the tens of thousands sleeping under canvas following the 2010 earthquake. On top of this, finding a private pitch is nigh on impossible.

BOOK YOUR STAY ONLINE

For more accommodations reviews by Lonely Planet authors, check out hotels.lonelyplanet.com. You'll find independent reviews, as well as recommendations on the best places to stay. Best of all, you can book online.

Guesthouses

Port-au-Prince has a number of small private guesthouses that cater primarily to visiting church groups, volunteers and aid workers. They offer a homey alternative to hotels, with a modest price tag attached. Standard rates are around US$40, including breakfast and dinner, eaten together to give a sociable atmosphere. Bathroom facilities are invariably shared. These places often have a strong Christian ethic attached, and may operate night curfews.

Hotels

In comparison to the DR, rooms in Haiti can feel expensive, particularly in the midrange bracket where you're not even always guaranteed hot water.

At the budget end, hotels can be dreary, although we've tried to pick the best of the bunch. Many hotels cater to prostitutes and clients (or just couples seeking privacy), so you may be asked if you want to pay for a 'moment' rather than the whole night. As a result, some hotels aren't particularly female friendly, although the turnover of guests means that their rooms are cleaned more regularly and efficiently than others. At the other end of the market, wi-fi access is becoming standard. Expect good fixtures and a decent electricity supply.

Most hotels of all ranges have attached restaurants or bars. Mosquito nets are rare. Room rates don't change according to season, although at peak times – Jacmel during Carnival, for example – prices go up with demand.

Resorts

Beach resorts don't feature in Haiti to the extent they do in the DR, but there are a string of them along the Côte des Arcadins, north of Port-au-Prince. Prices are all-inclusive, usually with a couple of bars and restaurants to choose from, along with water sports and other activities. If you arrive during the week, you'll virtually have them to yourself, while the city's well-heeled inhabitants descend en masse at weekends.

Activities

Compared to the DR, Haiti isn't a very activity-based destination. However, there are a few good options if you want a particular focus for your trip.

Scuba diving and snorkeling Côte des Arcadins and the Atlantic coast

Hiking Parc National La Visite and Parc National Forêt des Pins

Birdwatching Trou Caïman and Parc National Macaya

Business Hours

Banks 8.30am to 1pm weekdays, but some of the more central branches also open from 2pm to 5pm.

Offices 7am to 4pm weekdays, but many close earlier on Fri; Government offices close for an hour at noon.

Shops 7am to 4pm weekdays, but many close earlier on Fri; most also open on Sat.

Many restaurants and most businesses close on Sun.

Climate

Port-au-Prince

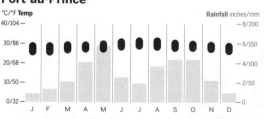

Customs

Customs regulations are similar to most countries, with restrictions on the import of live animals, weapons and drugs, and the export of ancient artifacts and endangered plants or animals. You can bring in 1L of liquor and one carton of cigarettes or 50 cigars. Those bringing in large amounts of medical supplies independently have frequently been faced with large importation fees.

Electricity

110v/60hz

110v/60hz

Embassies & Consulates

All of the embassies and consulates listed following are in Port-au-Prince or Pétionville. Australia, New Zealand and Ireland do not have diplomatic representation in Haiti.

Brazil (☎2256-7556; ppinto@mr.gov.br; 168 Rue Darguin, Place Boyer, Pétionville)

Canada (☎2249-9000; www.port-au-prince.gc.ca; btwn Delmas 71-75, Rte de Delmas, Port-au-Prince)

Cuba (☎2256-3811; ecuhaiti@hainet.net; 3 Rue Marion, Pétionville)

Dominican Republic (☎2257-9215; embrepdomhai@yahoo.com; 121 Ave Pan Américaine, Pétionville)

France (☎2222-0951; www.ambfrance.ht; 51 Rue Capois, Port-au-Prince)

Germany (☎2257-6131; fax 2257-4131; 2 Impasse Claudinette, Bois Moquette, Pétionville)

Mexico (☎2257-8100; embmxhai@yahoo.com; 2 Musseau, Delmas 60, Port-au-Prince)

UK (☎3744-6371; florence.boucard-hon@fconet.fco.gov

350

DIRECTORY A–Z FOOD

PRACTICALITIES

» Newspapers: *Le Matin*, *Le Nouvelliste*, *Haiti Progrés* (has an English section), *Haiti en Marche* and *Libète* (Creole). International press is available in Port-au-Prince.

» Radio stations include Radio Haiti Inter, Radio Soleil and Radio Ibo. French and US TV available on satellite/cable.

» Haiti uses the metric system, although gasoline is sold in gallons.

.uk; 367 Rte de Delmas, Face ERF, Port-au-Prince) Honorary consulate only.
US (☎2229-8000; http://haiti.usembassy.gov; 41 Rte de Tabarre, Tabarre, Port-au-Prince)
Venezuela (☎2222-0971; embavenzhaiti@hainet; 2 Blvd Harry Truman, Port-au-Prince)

Food

You can eat on any budget in Haiti; spending just a few gourdes on filling *fritay* (fried street food), eaten on the hoof, or dining in the posh restaurants of Pétionville, where a main course might set you back US$20. The most typical experience is eating in a bar-resto (a bar-restaurant, less formal than a proper restaurant), with a plateful of fried pork or chicken with plantains, salad and a beer, all for around US$4. Vegetables aren't high on the agenda, but there's plenty of fresh fruit. Excellent seafood abounds along the coast.

PRICE RANGES

Prices are based on the average cost of a mains dish and include tax.
Budget $ less than US$5
Midrange $$ US$5 to US$15
Top end $$$ over US$15

Gay & Lesbian Travelers

Haiti isn't as homophobic as some other places in the Caribbean, including macho Spanish DR. There are no dedicated gay venues, however; these were clamped down on in the 1980s following negative publicity about HIV and AIDS in Haiti. While you may commonly see friends of the same sex holding hands and being openly affectionate with each other, any tourists doing this will attract attention. Same-sex couples sharing a room should have no problem, although some discretion, especially in the more religious establishments, is advisable.

Health

Travel in Haiti is generally safe as long as you're reasonably careful about what you eat and drink. The most common travel-related diseases, such as dysentery and hepatitis, are acquired by consumption of contaminated food and water. There is a small but significant malaria risk in certain parts of both countries, and you should check before travel as to required prophylaxis. Following the 2010 earthquake, Haiti suffered a widespread cholera outbreak.

Insurance

It's always unwise to travel without insurance. Policies vary widely, but it's essential to have as much medical cover as possible (including emergency evacuation cover). Medical services insist on payment on the spot, so collect all the paperwork you can when being treated so you can claim later. Some policies ask you to call them (they'll usually call you back) so that an assessment of your problem can be made. Check excess fees for lost, stolen or damaged luggage.

An important point to note is that some governments issue travel warnings advising against nonessential travel to Haiti. Some insurance policies (or certain areas of their cover) may be invalidated in such circumstances, so discuss this with your broker before signing up.

Internet Access

Online access isn't a problem in any decently sized Haitian town, and internet cafes open and close frequently. Broadband connections are increasingly standard, along with webcams, CD burning and USB connections for uploading digital photos. Prices cost around 50HTG (US$1.25) per hour. The more expensive the joint, the better the electricity supply is likely to be. If you're bringing in a laptop, wi-fi access is increasingly widespread.

Legal Matters

One of the key tasks of the UN presence in Haiti has been to train and reorganize the Haitian National Police (HNP). It's a mammoth task, as the police are spread thin and corruption is rife (the judiciary is burdened with similar problems).

Drugs are illegal in Haiti, and you will be jailed for possession. If you are involved in a car accident, the law requires you to stop your car and call the police as soon as possible. In general, Haitian law presumes innocence until guilt is proven, and it's unlikely that you'll actually be arrested unless there are supportable charges against you. Always try to contact your embassy without delay, and keep its contact details on you. If the problem is an imaginary one, being extremely patient may eventually see the issue disappear.

Maps

Of most use to travelers is the *Haïti Carte Touristique*, which can be found in Port-au-Prince bookshops. On one side there is a detailed country map with lots of tourist information, and on the reverse there are street plans of Port-au-Prince, Cap-Haïtien, Jacmel and all the other departmental capitals.

A decent alternative is the map produced by the Association of Haitian Hoteliers, which is available for free from most car-rental companies and includes a map of Port-au-Prince. Guides Panoramas produces the best up-to-date map of Port-au-Prince (US$5), as well as a street plan of Jacmel (available from Tour Haiti, see p356).

Money

The Haitian currency is the gourde, usually written as 'GDE' or 'HTG'. The gourde is divided into 100 centimes, although the smallest coin you're likely to see is the 50 centimes, followed by the one and five gourde coins. Bank notes come in denominations of 10, 25, 50, 100, 250, 500 and 1000 gourdes, all with a revolutionary hero on one side and a historic fort on the other. There are still a few very grubby one,

two and five gourde notes in circulation, although these are no longer issued.

In practice, most Haitians refer to the Haitian dollar (H$) when quoting costs. The gourde used to be tied to the US dollar at a rate of one to five, with the result that five gourdes is universally known as one Haitian dollar. It's a system seemingly designed to perplex short-term visitors. When buying something, always check what people mean when quoting the price, eg whether a hundred is in gourdes or dollars (in which case it's 500 gourdes). To make things even more confusing, prices for expensive goods (or tourist souvenirs) are sometimes listed in US dollars.

The way to minimize headaches is to choose one system, either the Haitian dollar or the gourde, and stick with that. If you choose to work in Haitian dollars, you must divide prices in gourdes by five; if you choose to think in gourdes, you must multiply all Haitian dollar prices by five. You'll eventually be able to make price comparisons to your home currency, which is nearly impossible if you keep slipping between the two systems.

In this book, we present most costs in US$; however some smaller items/services, eg local transport costs, may be presented in the local currency.

ATMs

Automated teller machines are increasingly common in Port-au-Prince and Pétion-ville, but yet to catch on elsewhere in the country (there's one in Cap-Haïtien). They're the simplest way to manage your money on the road, although obviously you'll need to make sure you're liquid when heading out of the capital. Most ATMs are directly on the street, with some in secure booths. Always be aware of your surroundings when using an

ATM and pocketing a wad of cash.

Cash

Cash is king in Haiti. With the exceptions noted for credit cards (below), almost everything you buy will be with folding stuff. Traveling outside Port-au-Prince, you're likely to be carrying plenty of money, but there are a few precautions to reduce the risk of losing your stash to misadventure.

It's unwise to carry wads of money in your wallet, and you're similarly more prone to being robbed if you carry valuables in a shoulder bag, which can easily be snatched. Keep a small amount of money for the day in a handy but concealed place (eg in an inner pocket), and the bulk of your resources more deeply hidden. A well-concealed money belt is one of the safest ways to carry your money as well as important documents, such as your passport. It's also a good idea to have emergency cash (say US$100 in small bills) stashed away from your main hoard, as a backup.

For many purchases – hotel rooms, for instance – it's acceptable to pay in US dollars instead of gourdes.

Credit Cards

Most midrange and all top-end hotels (and Port-au-Prince restaurants) will happily let you flash the plastic. Visa, MasterCard and (to a slightly lesser extent) American Express will all do nicely. With an accompanying passport, cash advances on credit cards can be made in the larger banks.

Moneychangers

Haiti must be one of the few countries where if you want to change money, the simplest option is to go to a supermarket. These generally have a separate counter near the cashier where you can top up your gourdes. The US dollar rules supreme, although Canadian dollars and euros are usually accepted, along with Dominican pesos. Don't bring any other currency. Where there are street moneychangers, they're only interested in US dollars.

Traveler's Checks

These are a complete nonstarter in Haiti. Bank tellers will almost look at them with some curiosity before pushing them back over the counter for you to take elsewhere, possibly mumbling something about having to go to the 'head office.' Don't bother.

Photography

As in many developing countries, taking photos of airports and police buildings is forbidden. It's a bad idea to snap a policeman without obtaining permission first, and UN soldiers can be similarly sensitive.

Haitians are well aware of their country's poverty, and often hate to be photographed in work or dirty clothes. Always ask permission – whether you're in a market or the countryside, producing a camera out of the blue can occasionally provoke a reaction. This goes double at Vodou ceremonies, where you should always check with the *houngan* or *mambo* (respectively male or female Vodou priest) before you start clicking away.

Post

There are post offices in every town. Postcards to North America cost 25 gourdes (US$0.60) to send, or 50 gourdes (US$1.25) to Europe and Australia. It's generally better to send from a postbox, although the larger towns also have mailboxes dotted around. The service is reasonably reliable, although hardly superfast.

If you're in Haiti long term and want to receive mail, you can have it addressed to Poste Restante at the central post office where you're based. Senders should underline your name and you should bring your passport identification when collecting mail. A better, although more pricey, alternative is to set up a *boîte postale* (post box) at your local post office. Receiving mail is never fast in Haiti.

Faster in both directions are the international couriers. DHL, UPS and TNT are all represented in Port-au-Prince and Pétionville, with a few offices elsewhere noted throughout this book.

Public Holidays

Government offices and most businesses will be closed on the following days:

Independence Day January 1

Ancestors' Day January 2

Carnival February (three days before Ash Wednesday)

Good Friday late March/early April

Agriculture and Labor Day May 1

Flag and University Day May 18

Anniversary of Jean-Jacques Dessalines' Death October 17

Anniversary of Toussaint Louverture's Death November 1

Anniversary of the Battle of Vertières November 18

Christmas Day December 25

Safe Travel

Haiti has rarely enjoyed a popular media image abroad. Poverty and regular political turmoil play their part, and many governments currently advise against nonessential travel to the country. And yet, for the traveler, Haiti really can seem like one of the friendliest and most welcoming countries in the Caribbean. Navigating these apparently contradictory states is the key to getting the most out of your visit.

The presence of large numbers of UN troops under the auspices of the Stabilization Mission for Haiti (Minustah) have done much to bring stability to Haiti, especially in dealing with the large-scale gang and kidnapping problems. But you should always keep your ear to the ground for current developments before traveling – trouble generally occurs around elections, although it's incredibly rare for foreigners to get caught up in it. Avoid demonstrations, and if you come across one, turn in the opposite direction. In the event of real trouble, listen to the advice of embassy and hotel staff and follow it.

A weak state and high poverty levels can foster street crime. Take advantage of hotel safes and don't carry anything you're not willing to lose (or money in your back pocket). There are plenty of people on the streets during the day, and should you encounter trouble it's quite likely that someone will come to your aid.

For all this, the main annoyances travelers are likely to face are the poor electricity supply and crazy traffic. A lack of street lights is as good a reason not to walk at night as any risk of being mugged – no one wants to fall into a sewer hidden in the darkness. Beggars can be persistent in some places, and at tourist spots, such as the Citadelle, expect persistent attention from faux guides. Try to discourage them before you set off – their only function seems to be to tell you how much tip you're going to have to pay at the end – as it's very hard to not pay them after they've run up a mountain alongside you.

On a less obtrusive note, all foreigners should get used to being stared at out of curiosity. You'll be called *blanc* a lot, too. This is the generic word for a foreigner and is not color-specific. If someone gestures to you with what looks like a throat-slitting action, they're telling you they're hungry and want food – not that you're for the chop.

Finally, while taking care to be sensible, it's important not to get too hung up on Haiti's bad name. Many travelers fear the worst and avoid the country; those who do make it here are more likely to come away with positive impressions than horror stories.

Shopping

With its renowned arts scene, Haiti is filled with enough interesting handicrafts and souvenirs to have you worrying about your baggage allowance on the plane home. Port-au-Prince has the widest choice, with good shopping areas including the Marché de Fer and the Pétionville galleries. Jacmel, the so-called handicrafts capital of Haiti, also offers a comprehensive (and more laid-back) shopping experience. Often you'll be able to buy direct from the artists or artisans.

Except in galleries and a few shops, prices are never fixed, so be prepared to haggle. There's no rule on how much to offer, but it's best to treat the deal-making as a game rather than become obsessed with driving the price into the ground.

Telephone

Landlines Connections can sometimes be patchy. Most businesses list several numbers on their cards and many people carry two cell phones on different networks.

Cell Phones Haiti uses the GSM system. The two main

operators are Digicel and Voila. Coverage is generally good. The providers have international roaming agreements with many foreign networks, but it can be cheaper to buy a local handset on arrival in Haiti for about US$20, or a sim-card for about US$5. Take a copy of your passport to the dealer for identification.

Costs Within Haiti: around US$0.10 per minute according to the network. Overseas: around US$0.90 per minute. Top-up scratch cards are available from shops and ubiquitous street vendors.

Codes International telephone code: 🖉509. No area codes. To make an international call, dial 🖉00.

Calling The quickest option is to find a phone 'stand' – usually a youth on the street with a cell phone that looks like a regular desk phone, who will time your call and charge accordingly.

Haiti Business Directory (www.haiti-business.com) Useful for tracking down numbers (updated annually).

Time

Haiti runs on Eastern Standard Time (GMT minus five hours), putting it in the same time zone as New York, Miami and Toronto. Haiti doesn't adjust for daylight savings, so from the first Sunday in April to the last Sunday in October it's actually an hour ahead of eastern US and Canada.

Tourist Information

Haiti's moribund tourist industry has left visitors to the country scrabbling around for information. Port-au-Prince's main information center, the **Maison de Tourisme** (🖉2222-8659; Rue Capois, Champs de Mars, Port-au-Prince; ⊗8am-4pm Mon-Fri), had been closed for some time when we visited, with no plans to reopen. You may have more luck contacting the **Ministry of Tourism** (🖉2223-2143; 8 Rue Légitime, Champs de Mars, Port-au-Prince) direct, but we make no promises. There's an occasionally staffed information booth at the international airport, Aéroport International Toussaint Louverture. Alternatively, the country's private tour operators (see p356) are probably your best source of up-to-date information.

Outside the capital, the **Associations des Micro-Enterprises Touristiques du Sud'Est** (Amets; 🖉2288-2840; amets_service@yahoo.fr; 40 Rue d'Orléans;⊗8am-4pm Mon-Fri, to 2pm Sat) in Jacmel can be a good source of information for tourists, and the **Bureau du Tourisme** (Map p312; 🖉2262-0870; cnr Rue 24 & the Blvd, Cap-Haïtien) can also sometimes help. There are no tourist offices abroad.

TRAVEL ADVISORIES

The following government websites offer current travel advice for Haiti:

» **US State Department** http://travel.state.gov

» **British Foreign Office** www.fco.gov.uk/countryadvice

» **Canadian Department of Foreign Affairs** www.dfait-maeci.gc.ca

» **Australian Department of Foreign Affairs** www.smartraveller.gov.au

Toilets

There are no public toilet facilities in Haiti, but you can use the toilets in hotels or restaurants. The Haitian sewerage system is overstretched so, where supplied, dispose of toilet paper in a bin. Many Haitians think nothing of urinating in the streets and, on long journeys, relieving oneself at the side of the road is usually the only option. For women, this is more easily accomplished if you're wearing a loose-fitting skirt or dress, although you'll see plenty of local women pulling down their trousers in such situations.

Travelers with Disabilities

Haiti is going to be hard going for travelers with disabilities. Crowded and broken streets, anarchic traffic and the absence of wheelchair-accessible buildings all pose serious problems. However, travel is possible for those with plenty of stamina and the willingness to adapt to whatever hurdles present themselves. Traveling with an able-bodied companion can help immensely in overcoming these obstacles. At the very least, hiring a vehicle and a guide will make moving around a great deal easier. Travelers with disabilities shouldn't be surprised at stares from Haitians, but they'll often also receive offers of assistance where needed. For more information, consider contacting **Mobility International USA** (MIUSA; www.miusa.org),

which offers general travel advice for travelers with physical disabilities.

Visas

Unless you're a citizen of the DR, Colombia, Panama or Taiwan, no visa is needed to visit Haiti; just a valid passport and a return ticket. Your entry stamp entitles you to stay for up to 90 days.

If you wish to stay longer, you must apply for a visitor/resident visa at your nearest embassy before you travel; a process that can take several months, involving letters of support from your employer or a Haitian resident.

Women Travelers

It's easier for a woman to travel alone in Haiti than in many countries in the region (for travel in the DR, see p249). The catcalls, whistles and leering that women may experience in other places seem to be at a minimum. Haitian men do enjoy flirting and complimenting, but it usually isn't too overbearing and should be taken in good humor.

Haitian roads are abysmal and, as public transport is extremely bouncy, consider wearing a sports bra, especially on longer journeys (where you should also wear a skirt to allow for roadside toilet breaks). It's not a problem for women to wear modest shorts or sleeveless tops in and around town. A sarong is recommended for wrapping over a swimsuit at a hotel pool or the beach.

Work

Paid work is in short supply in Haiti. Official unemployment estimates mask far higher figures, and wages are desperately inadequate. Competition for jobs is enormous, so to find work you need to be able to demonstrate you have skills that no one in the domestic market possesses. Fluency in French and/or Creole is virtually essential. After you've been in the country for 90 days you must register as a resident with the **Department of Immigration** (171 Ave John Brown, Port-au-Prince), for which you'll need a letter from your embassy and your employer, a health check and a Haitian bank account proving solvency.

Many foreigners working in Haiti and not in business are involved in aid and development. **ReliefWeb** (www .reliefweb.int) and **DevNet** (www.devnetjobs.org) are good places to look for jobs in the development sector in Haiti. The country also attracts many volunteers. Haiti doesn't lack for unskilled labor, so unless you have skills that can't be gotten locally, do your research on local organizations and consider raising funds or public awareness instead: many organizations can offer understanding and a possibly life-changing experience for volunteers, but the prime objective must be to provide sustainable benefits for the local population. The website **Good Intentions Are Not Enough** (www.goodintents .org) is a good place to start to dissect this thorny issue.

Transportation

GETTING THERE & AWAY

Flights and tours can be booked online at lonely planet.com/bookings.

Entering Haiti

Most travelers enter Haiti by air through Port-au-Prince, with the most common flight routes all being from the US – Miami, Fort Lauderdale and New York. The international airport at Cap-Haïtien also handles a small number of incoming flights.

By land, there are several border crossings with the Dominican Republic, and direct bus services link Port-au-Prince with Santo Domingo, and Cap-Haïtien with Santiago. There are no international boat services to Haiti.

Passport

All foreign visitors must have a valid passport to enter Haiti. Be sure you have room for both entry and exit stamps, and retain the green entry card you're given on arrival, as you must give this up on departure. See (p354) for information on visas.

Air

Airports & Airlines

Haiti has just two international airports.

Aéroport International Toussaint Louverture (PAP; ☑2250-1120) The main international airport, in Port-au-Prince.

Aéroport International Cap-Haïtien (CAP; ☑2262-8539) Limited international flights but scheduled for expansion.

AIRLINES FLYING TO/ FROM HAITI

International carriers with services to Haiti:

Aerocaribbean (7L; ☑2222-5004; www.aero-caribbean .com) Flights from Havana and Santiago, and Punta Cana (DR) and Port-au-Prince.

Air Canada (AC; ☑2250-0441, 2250-0442; www.air canada.com) Direct flights from Montreal.

Air France (AF; ☑2222-1078, 2222-4262; www.airfrance.com) Flights from Paris via Pointe-á-Pitre, Guadeloupe or Miami.

Air Santo Domingo (EX; ☑2244-4897; http://airsanto domingo.com.do)

Air Turks & Caicos (JY; ☑2942-6711; www.airturksand caicos.com)

American Airlines (AA; ☑2246-0100, 3510-7010; www .aa.com) Direct flights from Miami, Fort Lauderdale and New York.

Continental (CO; www .continental.com) Flights from Newark due to start soon after this guide went to press.

IBC Travel (II; ☑2813-1099; www.ibcairways.com) Scheduled and charter flights to

---

CLIMATE CHANGE & TRAVEL

Every form of transport that relies on carbon-based fuel generates CO_2, the main cause of human-induced climate change. Modern travel is dependent on aeroplanes, which might use less fuel per kilometer per person than most cars but travel much greater distances. The altitude at which aircraft emit gases (including CO_2) and particles also contributes to their climate change impact. Many websites offer 'carbon calculators' that allow people to estimate the carbon emissions generated by their journey and, for those who wish to do so, to offset the impact of the greenhouse gases emitted with contributions to portfolios of climate-friendly initiatives throughout the world. Lonely Planet offsets the carbon footprint of all staff and author travel.

Cap-Haïtien from Miami and Fort Lauderdale.

Insel Air (7I; ☑2813-0401; www.fly-inselair.com) Flights from Curaçao, St. Maarten and Miami.

Lynx Air (LY; ☑3513-2597, 2257-9956; www.lynxair.com)

Spirit Airlines (NK; ☑2940-4421; www.spiritair.com)

Tortug'Air (TA; ☑2812-8000; www.tortugair.com) Flights from Santo Domingo, Nassau and Providenciales.

Tours

Haiti has three local tour operators, all offering excellent packages and services if you don't want to strike out on your own.

DOA/BN (☑3510-2223; www .haititravels.org)

Tour Haiti (☑2510-2223, 3711-1650; info@tourhaiti.net, www.tourhaiti.net; 31 Rue Casseus, Pacot, Port-au-Prince)

Voyages Lumière (☑3607-1321, 3557-0753; voyages lumierehaiti@gmail.com; www .voyagelumierehaiti.com)

GETTING AROUND

Air

Domestic flights operate from **Aérogare Guy Malary** (☑2250-1127), near the international terminal. The following airlines have their offices there:

Salsa d'Haiti (☑2813 1222; www.flysalsa.com) Four daily flights to Cap-Haïtien.

Tortug'Air (☑2812 8000; www.tortugair.com) Twice-daily flights to Cap-Haïtien, daily to Jérémie and Port-de-Paix.

Missionary Fights International (☑3791-9209; www .missionaryflights.org) Flights to all major cities, plus many smaller towns with airstrips only. Flights are for affiliated organisations only, although this is often flexibly interpreted on the ground.

Haiti's small size means that flights are short (no flight is longer than 40 minutes), saving hours on bad roads.

The planes are small, typically carrying 16 passengers or fewer. One-way tickets usually cost around US$100.

A reliable small-plane charter service is run by **Frantz Gabriel** (☑3861-4161; frangabri2004@yahoo.fr). Profits support a foundation providing training for local engineers and pilots.

Bus

Getting around Haiti by bus isn't always terrifically comfortable, but it's the cheapest way to travel within the country, and services run to most places you'll want to get to. Sturdy beasts, buses have the advantage of taking you to places that you'd usually need a 4WD to reach. They are mostly secondhand American school buses, colorfully repainted, with more Haitian liveries for bus lines like L'Ange de Dieu and Dieu Qui Decide.

Seating is designed to squash in as many people as possible, with six across being the norm. Your space is numbered, however, so look for the numerals painted above your head as you clamber through the bus over the assembled passengers and their bags (and occasionally chickens, too). When buying your ticket it's worth asking for a window seat to give yourself some extra air. Try not to sit too far back either – passengers sitting behind the rear axle are regularly bounced unceremoniously into the air. The front cab has several seats next to the driver, attracting a premium of around two-thirds of a standard ticket.

With a few exceptions noted in the text, there are no timetables; buses leave instead when they've collected their quota of passengers. Buying a ticket in advance is possible for long distances (Port-au-Prince to Cap-Haïtien or Jérémie, for example), but be advised that the hour you're

HAITI BORDER CROSSINGS

The Haitian-Dominican border has three official crossing points. Most useful to travelers is the Malpasse-Jimaní crossing between Port-au-Prince and Santo Domingo, followed by the northern Ouanaminthe-Dajabón crossing on the road between Cap-Haïtien and Santiago. A third, and little-used, crossing is from Belladère to Comendador (aka Elías Piña).

There are direct coach services linking the two capitals, and Cap-Haïtien to Santiago; see p290 and p314 respectively for more details. Included in the cost of the tickets are border fees that all travelers have to pay. Entering the DR you must pay US$10 for a tourist card. The situation with fees entering and leaving Haiti by land is fluid – these are meant to have been abolished, but border officials may still ask for US$10 to stamp you in or out. It remains unclear whether this is a legitimate fee or just a 'gratuity.'

The Haitian border can be slightly chaotic if you're traveling independently, particularly at Ounaminthe with its sprawling local market. Onward transport is plentiful, however, along with the occasional hustle – any tourist is going to stand out in this scenario. For more on the Dominican side of the border, see p252.

told to be at the bus station will invariably be at least an hour before the bus pulls onto the road. Overhead racks and space below the seats should be sufficient for most bags, otherwise they'll have to go on the roof (the baggage handler will want his tip). Although baggage is usually covered, rainstorms can still soak through, so keeping your belongings in plastic bags inside your luggage is a good idea.

Each town has a departure point for buses, known as 'estasyon' followed by the destination name (Estasyon Port-au-Prince, for example). They're not proper bus stations, rather sprawling, chaotic and noisy conglomerations of vehicles and people and market stalls: Haiti in microcosm. Touts shout out destinations, which are also painted on bus fronts. While you're waiting for the bus to leave, there's a constant procession of hawkers and street-food vendors, so you won't go hungry. Some even travel with the bus – traveling goods salesmen selling everything from toothpaste to miracle cures (we've experienced pitches lasting a good hour into a journey).

Upon arrival in their destination, buses turn into pseudo-taxi services, stopping at the roadside at passengers' request. This can be done by pressing a buzzer or yelling 'merci, monsieur' to the driver. While this may be great for getting dropped right outside your chosen hotel, it can be maddeningly frustrating as the bus stops every 50m or so to drop off yet more people and their assorted baggage.

Breakdowns aren't uncommon, but can sometimes provide relief from the terrible roads, or allow a much-needed food or toilet stop (it's not uncommon to need to squat by the roadside occasionally). Otherwise food or rest stops can be rare, although brave food

and drink vendors do hang perilously from the windows and doors as buses pass through towns and villages. When road conditions allow it, buses love to get up a head of steam, forcing all comers to scatter before them.

Car & Motorcycle

Although having your own wheels is a convenient way of seeing Haiti, be aware that you need both nerves of steel and a sense of humor. Terrible roads, a lack of road signs, and the perils of wayward pedestrians and oncoming traffic are all part of the mix. But if you're up for the challenge, you might find yourself driving with a flair and aplomb you never knew you possessed before.

Driver's License

In order to drive or rent a vehicle in Haiti, you need either a valid International Driving Permit or a current license from your home country. It is an offense to drive without a valid driver's license on your person. Carry your passport with you at all times, as the police will want to see it if they stop you for any reason.

Rental

Many international car-rental companies operate in Haiti, mostly based near Port-au-Prince's international airport; see p290. Rates are pricey due to the high rate of accidents and road conditions that cause a lot of wear and tear. Although fees vary from company to company, don't be surprised to be quoted around US$80 for a saloon, or US$150 for a 4WD per day. Although insurance is offered, it isn't always comprehensive and often carries high deductibles; furthermore, foreign drivers are often held liable for accidents whether they are at fault or not.

Road Conditions

It's best not to come with high hopes of Haiti's roads. With the notable exception of the well-maintained highway from Port-au-Prince to Jacmel, the main roads are potholed and cracked. Secondary roads are worse, with some becoming impassable, especially after rain, except in a 4WD. Wherever tarmac allows drivers to get some speed up, accidents are common, so it's sometimes worth thinking of the broken roads as an efficient traffic-calming system.

Avoid driving at night if at all possible. Many drivers are allergic to using headlights, and animals and pedestrians are hard to see in the dark.

Road Rules

Road rules are extremely lax, but most vehicles at least aspire to drive on the right. Drivers rarely signal, so expect cars to swerve out in front of you suddenly, usually to avoid a hole. When overtaking, use your horn liberally. Many drivers far prefer the horn instead of the brakes, so take heed. Always beep to warn people walking that you're coming, and they will make way – even in the most congested street, you can usually miraculously slip through.

If you have an accident, you must stop your car and call the police as soon as possible.

In cities, watch out for parking restrictions. Instead of issuing tickets, police are liable to remove your license plates, returnable from the local police station on payment of a fine. When parking, kids or men may approach you to be a gardien and watch your vehicle for you for a small fee.

Hitchhiking

It's extremely unusual to see foreigners hitchhiking in Haiti, but due to the low rate of car ownership and unreliable transport systems, Haitians are used to asking for a *rue libre* (free ride). As with hitchhiking anywhere in the world, there's a small but potentially serious risk in flagging down a ride. If you do get picked up, don't be surprised if the driver asks for some money – keep public-transport fares in mind so that, should you strike someone trying to extort silly amounts from you, you'll know what not to give and what you'll be expected to pay for the ride. However, some Haitians will be baffled by the sight of a foreigner without a vehicle and will just pick you up out of curiosity.

Local Transportation

Moto-taxis

The quickest and easiest way to get around any town is to hop on the back of a moto-taxi (motorcycle taxi), often just referred to as a 'moto'. As with *publiques* (collective taxis), these have transport license plates, and in some towns the drivers wear colored bibs. A trip will rarely cost more than about US$0.75, although rates can climb steeply if you want to travel any serious distance. Motos in Port-au-Prince are more expensive than elsewhere.

Moto-taxis can have two passengers riding pillion, although it's not recommended. If you have luggage, get the driver to place it between his handlebars, rather than unbalancing yourself with it on your back. Although pot-holed roads don't always allow the bikes to attempt high speeds, many drivers seem to have a fatalist's view of their own mortality, so don't be afraid to tell them to slow down.

Taxi

Port-au-Prince and Cap-Haïtien operate collective taxis called *publiques* for getting around town. You might find them hard to spot initially, as they look like any other battered car, but look for the red ribbon hanging from the front mirror and license plates starting with 'T' for transport. Once you spot one, they're everywhere. Charging set fares (usually about US$0.70), they roughly stick to particular routes. After you hail a *publique,* the driver will let you know if he's going your way (minor detours are usually fine). The usual tight seating arrangement is two in the front and four in the back.

When you get into an empty *publique,* the driver will sometimes remove the ribbon, indicating a private hire with resulting increased charge. If you want to ride *collectif* (with other passengers), now is the time to let him know. Alternatively, settle the fee before he drives off, not on arrival.

Most major towns have radio-taxi firms with meters.

Taptap & Camionette

Smaller vehicles than buses ply the roads carrying passengers. A taptap is a converted pick-up, often brightly decorated, with bench seats in the back. Fares are slightly cheaper than a bus. The same rules for buses apply to taptaps, which leave from the same *estasyon*: they go when full, the comfy seats next to the driver are more pricey, and you can hail one and get off where you like. They're usually packed like sardines (the answer to how many people you can fit in a taptap is invariably 'one more'), so carrying luggage places you at a disadvantage. Expect a few bruises from the hard bench seats, bouncy roads and sharp elbows.

Taptaps are better suited for short trips, and in many areas are likely to be the only feasible way of getting around. In Port-au-Prince, taptaps run within the city along set routes and are by far the cheapest and easiest way of getting from A to B: fares are usually US$0.25.

Halfway between a taptap and a bus is the *camionette*. This is a larger truck designed primarily for transporting goods, but which also takes human cargo. Often open sided, or with crude windows cut out of the truck body, these are very cheap and as basic as they come. There are no seats, just a few ropes dangling from the ceiling for people to hold on to. A foreigner riding in a *camionette* will get such looks of incredulity from a Haitian that it's worth trying one for the response alone. Certainly, don't do it for a smooth ride.

ART ON WHEELS

Haitian art isn't just found on the walls of galleries – it weaves through the streets picking up passengers. Painted taptaps are one of Port-au-Prince's delights. While some owners are content to just paint their routes on the doors, others really go the distance by adding extra bumpers and mirrors and repainting the whole vehicle until it looks like a fairground ride. Slogans and Biblical verses typically decorate the windshield, while the rear serves as a canvas for paintings both sacred and profane: in five minutes between downtown and Carrefour we spotted the Nativity, Daniel in the lion's den, two Ché Guevaras, Tupac Shakur and a Ronaldinho!

Language

While for many years French has been considered the official language of Haiti, only 15% of the population can speak it, mainly the educated elite, who these days also have very good English. The majority of the population speaks only Creole – also called Kreyol (Haitian Creole) – and beyond the major centers it's the only sure means of communication.

Language in Haiti deepens the divisions between social classes, as the government and the judicial system operate in French. The Creole-speaking and often illiterate masses are in this way excluded from civil society, leaving the control in the hands of the upper and middle classes. Most schools teach in French, which further disadvantages those who only speak Creole.

Since the 1980s there has been a movement toward the increased use of Creole in civil society. Politicians have begun to make more speeches in Creole, musicians sing in it – *rapkreyol* (Haitian hip-hop) is a growing genre – more radio stations broadcast in it and there is a weekly Creole-language paper, *Libète* (Liberty).

There is some debate as to the roots of the Creole language. The vocabulary is predominantly French, with some English and Spanish thrown in, but the structure is considered closer to that of West African languages. The most popularly held belief is that it's the synthesis of 18th-century French with many African languages, Spanish and English.

With the ever increasing number of aid and church workers traveling throughout the country, and Haitians repatriated from the US,

the number of English-speaking Haitians is on the rise. While you won't find them everywhere, they will seek you out and, in the larger cities, a combination of English and pidgin French will get you from A to B and enable you to order a beer when you get there.

Nonetheless, knowing a few basics in Creole might come in handy and surely will enhance your travel experience.

PRONUNCIATION

Creole pronunciation is fairly intuitive. There are no silent consonants – every letter you see written is pronounced. This is also the case for the letter *e*: all instances of *e* are pronounced as acutes (*é*) unless they have a grave accent (*è*). For example, *pale* (to speak) is pronounced like *palé* ('pa-lay'). The word *mèsi* (Thanks) sounds more like 'me-si'.

The word for 'me' is *m* and is pronounced 'um'.

Note also that the letter *g* is always pronounce as a hard 'g' as in 'go'.

BASICS

Polite greetings when out and about are very important in Haiti. When you are addressing people you don't know, you should always say *bonjou* (good morning) or *bonswa* (good afternoon/evening). Also use the various polite forms of address which are given in this chapter.

When you're introduced to someone, don't forget to you give them your name and say *anchante* (pleased to meet you).

To get someone's attention you say 'psst.' This isn't rude, but clicking your fingers to someone is. Using 'psst' is also the best way to stop a taxi or a taptap.

BASICS

Good day ...
Bonjou .... (used before noon)

Good afternoon/evening ...
Bonswa .... (used after 11am)

Good night ...
Bonnwit .... (used when taking your leave at the evening's end)

Sir	*Msye*
Madam	*Madam*
Gentlemen	*Mesye*
Ladies	*Medam*
Ladies and Gentlemen	*Mesye e Dam*

See you later.	*Na wè pita.*
Yes.	*Wi.*
No.	*Non.*
Please.	*Silvouple.* *Souple.*

(In the capital you'd use *silvouple* whereas *souple* is used more in the provinces.)

Thank you.	*Mèsi anpil.*
Sorry.	*Pàdon.*
Excuse me.	*Pàdon.*
How are you?	*Ki jan ou ye?*
Not bad.	*M pal pi mal.*
I'm going OK.	*M-ap kenbe.*
What's your name?	*Ki jan ou rele?*
My name is ...	*M rele ...*

I'm ...	*Mwen se ...*
American	*ameriken* (male) *amerikenn* (female)
British	*anglèz* (male & female)

I'm from ...	*Mwen sòti ...*
Australia	*ostrali*
France	*lafrans*

PRACTICALITIES

Do you speak English?	*Eske ou ka pale angle?*
I don't understand.	*M pa konprann.*
May I take your photograph?	*Eske m ka fè foto ou?*

What's the time?	*Kilè li ye?*
I'm looking for ...	*M'ap chache ...*
Where is ...?	*Kote ... ye?*
Where does the bus leave from?	*Kote taptap pati?*

I'd like to change money.	*Mwen ta vle chanje lajan.*
Is that local dollars or US dollars?	*Eske se dola ayisyen ou dola ameriken?*
How much is it?	*Konbyen?*
How many?	*Konbyen?*

I'd like to go visit ...	*M ta vle ale vizite ...*
I'd like to go speak with ...	*M ta vle ale pale ak ...*
Let's go.	*Ann ale.*

to stop	*rete*
to wait	*tann*

EMERGENCIES

I'm lost.	*M pèdi.*
Help!	*A mwen!*
Can you help me, please?	*Eske ou kap ede mwen silvouple/souple?*
Where are the toilets?	*Kote twalèt yo?*
Where is the hospital?	*Kote lopital la?*

I have (a) ...	*M gen ...*
chills	*lafièv*
cramps/diarrhea	*vant fè mal*
fever	*fyèv*
headache	*tèt fè mal*

I keep vomiting.	*M'ap vomi.*

Fè mal is a general word for 'ache', eg *tet fè mal* means 'headache' and *pye fè mal* means 'sore foot'.

Pronouns – Creole	
I/me	*m/mwen*
you (singular)	*ou/w*
he/she/it	*li*
you (plural)	*nou*
we	*nou*
they	*yo*

GLOSSARY

artisanat – craft workshop

camionette – form of public transportation; large trucks piled with people and sacks of goods

colmado – combination corner store, grocery store and bar

comedor – eatery

compas – traditional Haitian music; fusion of dance band and merengue beats

department – administrative province of Haiti

estasyon – bus station

fôret – forest

galerie – art gallery

gede – pronounced gay-day; family of lwa that includes Baron Samedi and Maman Brigitte

gingerbread – Haitian architectural style of the late 19th and early 20th centuries

houngan – Vodou priest

île – island

Lavalas – pro-Aristide political movement

lwa – Vodou spirits

mambo – Vodou priestess

marché – market

Minustah – UN Stabilization Mission to Haiti

moto-taxi – motorcycle taxi

musée – museum

peristyle – Vodou temple or ceremonial altar

plage – beach

publique – collective taxi

rara – performance ritual during Lent when temple ceremonies are taken to the streets by marching bands of musicians, singers and dancers

rue – street

taptap – local bus; minibus

Tontons Macoutes – notorious guards created under François Duvalier, named for a child-stealing traditional bogeyman character; also known as Volontaires de la Sécurité Nationale

Vodouisant – follower of Vodou

behind the scenes

SEND US YOUR FEEDBACK

We love to hear from travelers – your comments keep us on our toes and help make our books better. Our well-traveled team reads every word on what you loved or loathed about this book. Although we cannot reply individually to postal submissions, we always guarantee that your feedback goes straight to the appropriate authors, in time for the next edition. Each person who sends us information is thanked in the next edition – and the most useful submissions are rewarded with a free book.

Visit **lonelyplanet.com/contact** to submit your updates and suggestions or to ask for help. Our award-winning website also features inspirational travel stories, news and discussions.

Note: We may edit, reproduce and incorporate your comments in Lonely Planet products such as guidebooks, websites and digital products, so let us know if you don't want your comments reproduced or your name acknowledged. For a copy of our privacy policy visit lonelyplanet.com/privacy.

OUR READERS

Many thanks to the travelers who used the last edition and wrote to us with helpful hints, useful advice and interesting anecdotes:

B Mariel Backman **C** Marcus Carlsson **D** Dan Duerr **F** Erica Felker-Kantor **G** Gregorio García Marín, Jardena Guttmann **H** Frans Huber **I** Elizabeth Irwin **K** David Katz, Eelco Keij, Julianne Kenny **L** Marie-France Legault **N** Charlotte Norton **P** Aristea Parissi, Susan Peeters, Phillip Petman, Aspa Plakantonaki, Natanya Pucci **R** Cynthia C Rignanese, Thomas Rosenau **S** Kristen Scislow, Mike Sintetos, Malte Srocke, Beth Stark **T** Mike Thorsten **V** Laura Vaughn

AUTHOR THANKS

Paul Clammer

Travel in Haiti is always an amazing experience, but my trips in 2010 were particularly humbling, seeing the aftermath of the earthquake and the fortitude of the Haitians. Special thanks to Michael, Walnes and the St Joe's family. Thanks also to Jacqualine Labrom, Emily Troutman, Landon Yarrington, Bette Gebrian, Tessa Lewis, Nat Segaren, Leah Page, Gabie Vincent and Thor Burnham.

Michael Grosberg

Rebecca Tessler, my heart, is always with me. Gracias to Isabel Rosario, Oscar Jr and his father and Pinky Rodriguez in Jarabacoa; Mark Fernandez and Tim Hall for their help in Puerto Plata; mountain biker Maximo Martinez; Mariam Matías and her brother David from Constanza; Steve McKenney from Luperon; chef Rafael Vasquez; Martin Pantallon in Santo Domingo. To Carly Neidorf for her support and presence. And of course to my co-author Kevin Raub, coordinating author Paul Clammer, commissioning editor Catherine Craddock-Carillo and managing editor Bruce Evans.

Kevin Raub

Special thanks to my wife, Adriana Schmidt Raub, who put up with me missing yet another Christmas and New Year's Eve to research this book. Along the way, Vanessa Welter, Verena Müller, Arturo Diaz, Leo Salazar, Leslie Silver, Elsi Cruz, Robert Jackson, Kim Beddall, Tess Mclean Cannon, Maura Rendes, Satí Rose, Anita Boucher and Jim Petka, Ecotour Barahona, Marta Bearzotti, Andrea Pogliaghi, Beatrice Orsini, Fabrizio Orsini and Elisa Chiesa – my fellow Italian trekkers!

ACKNOWLEDGMENTS

Climate map data adapted from Peel MC, Finlayson BL & McMahon TA (2007) 'Updated World Map of the Köppen-Geiger Climate Classification', *Hydrology and Earth System Sciences*, 11, 1633–44.

Cover photograph: Dominican Republic, Sosua, two dancers and parrot/Sakis Papadoppoulos, Getty. Many of the images in this guide are available for licensing from Lonely Planet Images: www.lonely planetimages.com.

THIS BOOK

This 5th edition of Lonely Planet's *Dominican Republic & Haiti* guidebook was researched and written by Paul Clammer, Michael Grosberg and Kevin Raub. Previous editions were written by Paul Clammer, Michael Grosberg, Jens Porup, Gary Prado Chandler, Liza Prado Chandler, Scott Doggett, Leah Gordon and Joyce Connolly.

This guidebook was commissioned in Lonely Planet's Oakland office, laid out by Cambridge Publishing Management, UK, and produced by the following:

Commissioning Editors Catherine Craddock-Carrillo, Kathleen Munnelly

Coordinating Editors Tom Lee, Gina Tsarouhas
Coordinating Cartographers Valeska Canas, Mark Griffiths
Coordinating Layout Designer Paul Queripel
Managing Editors Helen Christinis, Bruce Evans, Annelies Mertens
Managing Cartographer Alison Lyall
Managing Layout Designer Jane Hart
Assisting Editors Andrea Dobbin, Bella Li, Matty Soccio
Assisting Cartographers Enes Basic, Ildiko Bogdanovits, Julie Dodkins, Mick Garrett, Maritza Kolega, Joelene Kowalski, Andy Rojas, Andrew Smith, Brendan Streager
Cover Research lonelyplanetimages.com
Internal Image Research Aude Vauconsant
Color Designer Paul Queripel
Indexer Marie Lorimer
Language Content Annelies Mertens, Branislava Vladisavljevic

Thanks to Ryan Evans, Lisa Knights, Susan Paterson, Martine Power, Rebecca Skinner, Gerard Walker

index

OUR STORY

A beat-up old car, a few dollars in the pocket and a sense of adventure. In 1972 that's all Tony and Maureen Wheeler needed for the trip of a lifetime – across Europe and Asia overland to Australia. It took several months, and at the end – broke but inspired – they sat at their kitchen table writing and stapling together their first travel guide, *Across Asia on the Cheap*. Within a week they'd sold 1500 copies. Lonely Planet was born.

Today, Lonely Planet has offices in Melbourne, London and Oakland, with more than 600 staff and writers. We share Tony's belief that 'a great guidebook should do three things: inform, educate and amuse'.

OUR WRITERS

Paul Clammer

Coordinating Author; 25 Top Experiences, Plan (Haiti); Port-au-Prince & Around; Southern Haiti; Northern Haiti; Understand (Haiti); Survive (Haiti) Sometime molecular biologist, tour leader and now travel writer, Paul has a penchant for heading to places many people head away from – Haiti sits alongside Afghanistan, Pakistan and Nigeria as countries he's covered for Lonely Planet. Paul would like to think that Haiti first came to his attention from reading Graham Greene's *The Comedians*, but secretly wonders if childhood viewings of *Live and Let Die* didn't also play their part. In the aftermath of the 2010 earthquake, Paul volunteered clearing rubble in Léogâne, before returning to research the new edition of this guide. His website is www.paulclammer.com.

Read more about Paul at:
lonelyplanet.com/members/paulclammer

Michael Grosberg

Plan (Dominican Republic); Santo Domingo; North Coast; Central Highlands; Understand (Dominican Republic); Survive (Dominican Republic) This is the second edition of the Lonely Planet *Dominican Republic* guidebook Michael has worked on. In addition to his Lonely Planet assignments, he's visited the DR on other occasions going back to his graduate school days when he was focusing on the literature and culture of Latin America. Michael is based in Brooklyn, New York City, and usually writes just down the street from several Dominican restaurants where he gets his lunch. A reformed academic/journalist by trade, Michael has worked on more than 15 Lonely Planet books.

Read more about Michael at:
lonelyplanet.com/members/michaelgrosberg

Kevin Raub

Punta Cana & the Southeast; Peninsula de Samaná; The Southwest & Península de Pedernales Kevin Raub grew up in Atlanta and started his career as a music journalist in New York, working for *Men's Journal* and *Rolling Stone* magazines. The rock 'n' roll lifestyle took its toll, so he needed an extended vacation and took up travel writing while ditching the States for Brazil. In the DR, he found the Southeast all it was cracked up to be, but it was the Southwest that shocked and awed, leaving him gobsmacked that this spectacular coast was so vehemently ignored by travelers. His advice? Go to the Peninsula de Pedernales! This is his 12th Lonely Planet guide. You can find him at www.kevinraub.net.

Read more about Kevin at:
lonelyplanet.com/members/kevinraub

Published by Lonely Planet Publications Pty Ltd
ABN 36 005 607 983
5th edition – October 2011
ISBN 978 1 74179 456 4
© Lonely Planet 2011   Photographs © as indicated 2011
10 9 8 7 6 5 4 3 2 1
Printed in China

how to use this book

These symbols will help you find the listings you want:

- ◉ Sights
- 🏃 Beaches
- 🏃 Activities
- 🍃 Courses

- 👉 Tours
- 🎪 Festivals & Events
- 🛌 Sleeping
- 🍴 Eating

- 🍷 Drinking
- ☆ Entertainment
- 🛍 Shopping
- ❶ Information/ Transport

Look out for these icons:

- **TOP CHOICE** Our author's recommendation
- **FREE** No payment required
- 🍃 A green or sustainable option

Our authors have nominated these places as demonstrating a strong commitment to sustainability – for example by supporting local communities and producers, operating in an environmentally friendly way, or supporting conservation projects.

These symbols give you the vital information for each listing:

- ☑ Telephone Numbers
- ☉ Opening Hours
- P Parking
- ⊝ Nonsmoking
- ✳ Air-Conditioning
- @ Internet Access

- 🛜 Wi-Fi Access
- 🏊 Swimming Pool
- ✒ Vegetarian Selection
- 🍽 English-Language Menu
- 👪 Family-Friendly
- 🐾 Pet-Friendly

- 🚌 Bus
- ⛴ Ferry
- Ⓜ Metro
- Ⓢ Subway
- ⊖ London Tube
- 🚋 Tram
- 🚆 Train

Reviews are organised by author preference.

Map Legend

Sights
- ● Beach
- ● Buddhist
- ● Castle
- ● Christian
- ● Hindu
- ● Islamic
- ● Jewish
- ● Monument
- ● Museum/Gallery
- ● Ruin
- ● Winery/Vineyard
- ● Zoo
- ● Other Sight

Activities, Courses & Tours
- ● Diving/Snorkelling
- ● Canoeing/Kayaking
- ● Skiing
- ● Surfing
- ● Swimming/Pool
- ● Walking
- ● Windsurfing
- ● Other Activity/ Course/Tour

Sleeping
- ● Sleeping
- ● Camping

Eating
- ● Eating

Drinking
- ● Drinking
- ● Cafe

Entertainment
- ● Entertainment

Shopping
- ● Shopping

Information
- ● Bank
- ● Embassy/ Consulate
- ● Hospital/Medical
- ● Internet
- ● Police
- ● Post Office
- ● Telephone
- ● Toilet
- ● Tourist Information
- ● Other Information

Transport
- ● Airport
- ● Border Crossing
- ● Bus
- ● Cable Car/ Funicular
- ● Cycling
- ● Ferry
- ● Metro
- ● Monorail
- ● Parking
- ● Petrol Station
- ● Taxi
- ● Train/Railway
- ● Tram
- ● Other Transport

Routes
- Tollway
- Freeway
- Primary
- Secondary
- Tertiary
- Lane
- Unsealed Road
- Plaza/Mall
- Steps
- Tunnel
- Pedestrian Overpass
- Walking Tour
- Walking Tour Detour
- Path

Geographic
- ● Hut/Shelter
- ● Lighthouse
- ● Lookout
- ▲ Mountain/Volcano
- ● Oasis
- ● Park
-)(Pass
- ● Picnic Area
- ● Waterfall

Population
- ● Capital (National)
- ◉ Capital (State/Province)
- ● City/Large Town
- ● Town/Village

Boundaries
- International
- State/Province
- Disputed
- Regional/Suburb
- Marine Park
- Cliff
- Wall

Hydrography
- River, Creek
- Intermittent River
- Swamp/Mangrove
- Reef
- Canal
- Water
- Dry/Salt/ Intermittent Lake
- Glacier

Areas
- Beach/Desert
- + + + Cemetery (Christian)
- × × × Cemetery (Other)
- Park/Forest
- Sportsground
- Sight (Building)
- Top Sight (Building)